THIS BOOK IS DEDICATED TO FILM BUFF BEN
AND TO THE MEMORY OF
FRANÇOIS TRUFFAUT (1932-1984)

THE MOVIE DIRECTORS STORY

JOEL W. FINLER

OCTOPUS BOOKS

Prelim photography: George Taylor

Golden Panaflex camera
kindly provided by
Samuelsons Film Services.

First published 1985 by
Octopus Books Limited
59 Grosvenor Street
London W1

© 1985 Octopus Books Limited

ISBN 0 7064 2288 0

First impression

Printed in Hong Kong

CONTENTS

PREFACE

This book is devoted to the directors of the popular, mainstream Anglo-American cinema, with special emphasis on Hollywood. All the major American and British directors are included, along with a representative cross-section of secondary figures, and a number of Europeans who have enjoyed substantial American careers.

Beginning with early pioneers like D.W. Griffith and Allan Dwan, and extending to current figures like Martin Scorsese, Steven Spielberg and the Australian Peter Weir, we have split the directors into three main chronological groups. Within each grouping the major creative figures have been balanced by a selection of specialist directors working largely in particular genres – like the musical, Western or thriller – and a group of competent craftsmen who were the backbone of the studio contract system which flourished in the middle years. Though the choice of directors included in this book is necessarily subjective, an attempt has been made to balance artistic with other considerations. Thus, certain directors are included on the basis of remarkably extensive careers, others because they are representative of a particular studio's style. Some are here with a small output but a significant one, and various indicators of popular success, such as box office hits and Oscar nominations, have also influenced our selection. In this way it is hoped that we have succeeded in capturing the flavour of each era, as well as giving some indication of the changing role of the movie director over more than seven decades. Such changes, it will be shown, are related to changes in the film industry in general.

Originally the director was simply one who took charge of, and was responsible for, all the elements that went into the completed movie. In the early silent days he not only instructed the actors in front of the camera – talking to them, encouraging and influencing their performances while filming was in progress – but he organised the props, costumes and settings with the help of a number of assistants. After filming was completed he would supervise the editing to achieve the final result. The assistants soon began to specialise, however, and by about 1920 the director himself was likely to be filming with a crew which might include art director, props man and editor, among others. With the growth of the large studios, these personnel were put under contract and, for a time, especially during the peak studio years of the 30s, the freedom of the individual entrepreneurial director was severely restricted. Despite the limitations imposed on them, however, many of the leading directors – those tough and determined enough to stand up to the studio bosses – were able to maintain a semblance of their own personal style. For the director was the only person who was in a position to control all aspects of the actual filming process.

By the 40s, however, important changes were taking place, for there emerged a new breed of successful writer-directors who were in a position to exercise more control over the final result. Also the decline of the old studios opened the way for many established directors to develop new careers as independent producer-directors. During the 50s and 60s many of the top directors, veterans like John Ford, Howard Hawks, and Alfred Hitchcock, and more recent arrivals – Elia Kazan, John Huston and Billy Wilder, for example – achieved a welcome maturity and directed some of their best movies. More clearly than ever, one could see the contrast between these talented and creative men, involved as they were in every aspect of the production, and the merely competent craftsmen of the studio years who had been content to work on an assignment basis and who generally fell by the wayside once their contracts expired. This was further confirmed in later years, and in the 70s in particular, with the arrival of a new group of young directors. Many of these were actor-directors or, more significantly, writer-directors, and they often served as their own producers as well. These young men, specialists in many aspects of film production, helped to reshape the modern American cinema, and were also instrumental in raising the status of the director once again.

If there is a single thread running right through this book, it is provided by that small but powerful group of American companies which have long dominated the film industry. In the old days the studio provided a real home for the director to function among a permanent group of stars and technicians; during recent years the companies have provided much-needed financial support and continuity for many individual directors. In the 30s the studio could virtually determine the pattern of a director's career. Thus the talented, British-born James Whale became a specialist in sophisticated horror at Universal, while most directors naturally gravitated to the studio where they felt most at home – action directors like Michael Curtiz and William Wellman to Warner Bros., sophisticated continentals like Ernst Lubitsch and Rouben Mamoulian to Paramount. And George Cukor's reputation as a 'women's director' was less to do with the fact that he couldn't direct men than to his long and fruitful stay at MGM where the top female stars generally outnumbered and overshadowed the men. All-important collaborations between director and star often took place within a studio context – Clarence Brown and Greta Garbo at MGM, Josef von Sternberg and Marlene Dietrich at Paramount, John Ford and Henry Fonda at Fox. In later years, too, there are many examples: Alfred Hitchcock and James Stewart teamed up at Paramount in the 50s; the collaboration between Don Siegel and Clint Eastwood developed out of the revival of Siegel's career at Universal in the 60s; and the Woody Allen-Diane Keaton partnership was backed by United Artists in the 70s.

Even the most successful Hollywood whizz kid of them all, Steven Spielberg, owes a debt to a studio, which he has repaid many times over. For Spielberg began as a twenty-one year-old at Universal in the early 70s where he was able to work his way up from TV programmes to TV movies, and then to features.

In examining the careers of so many leading directors and endeavouring to capture the special and unique qualities of each of them, the book simultaneously provides a survey of, and an introduction to, the development of the Anglo-American cinema from the silent days up to the present – part of a fascinating and continuing story . . . . . .

ACKNOWLEDGEMENTS

This book would not have been possible without the dedication and encouragement of my editor Robyn Karney. My thanks also to ever-efficient in-house editor David Burn, art editor Pat Sumner and editorial assistant Tammy Collins. Most of the photographs come from my own collection but I would like to record my special appreciation for the help given by Michelle Snapes and the National Film Archive stills department, Artificial Eye, Jerusalem Cinémathèque, Barrie Pattison and Peter Woodland in supplying additional material.

Joel W. Finler
London, 1985

CHAPTER ONE
1920-1939

*Independent, creative, sometimes geniuses, the directors were
the driving force in the golden silent years, shaping an art.
By 1929 the Hollywood hills were alive with the sound of music
and the studio moguls ruled like despots over a star-spangled
empire. Now the director was held to loyal subjection…*

It was the directors, those men and women who
made the movies, who set the tone of the early
American cinema. As a group they were generally tough and resourceful and came from many
different professions and backgrounds. Many
started out in the theatre – actors, directors,
stage managers; several were writers, journal-
ists, or artists; some were trained engineers, or
had other practical skills which were useful in
solving the many technical problems which
could, and often did, develop during filming.

They came to Hollywood from all over the
world – Herbert Brenon and Rex Ingram were
Irish, Mack Sennett and Allan Dwan came from
Canada, Maurice Tourneur was French and
Chaplin, of course, English, while some of the
most supremely gifted came, later, from Germany and from Austria.

The early years of the cinema were characterised by a ruthless rivalry and freewheeling
competition between a large number of small
companies. New studios sprang up – and/or
disappeared – over night. But while all this was
going on behind the scenes, the directors got on
with turning out their one and two-reelers.
Allan Dwan and his cowboy actors were expert
shots and were continually on the lookout for

Above: On location for the filming of James Cruze's splendidly realistic epic Western, *The Covered Wagon* (1923), which was edited by Dorothy Arzner.

Left: One of the leading pioneer film-makers, Edwin S. Porter (foreground left), who made *The Great Train Robbery* (1903), directs at the Edison Studios, circa 1908.

thugs hired by the monopolistic Patents Co. to
sabotage their filming. He was the leading
director for the American Film Co., while
Edwin S. Porter had directed or supervised all
the Edison pictures beginning with *The Life Of
An American Fireman* and *The Great Train
Robbery* in 1903. D.W. Griffith started at Biograph and was so indispensible that when he left
in 1913 the company simply collapsed. He alone
emerged as the single dominant producer-
director figure prior to World War I, a position
further confirmed by the phenomenal success
of *The Birth Of A Nation* in 1915.

By the middle and late teens the ruthless
competition of the early years, and the
changeover to making more elaborate and expensive feature-length films, had taken its toll.

The trend towards a greater concentration of power in a few large companies became evident, and continued on into the 20s until it began to threaten the independence of the movie directors themselves.

Names like Griffith, Chaplin, DeMille and Von Stroheim became well known all over the world and attested to the premier position of the American film industry. It had emerged from World War I, which had crippled its European rivals, stronger than ever, and lured away many of the most talented stars and, especially, directors – Lubitsch and Murnau from Germany, Curtiz from Austria, Sjöström and Garbo's mentor, Mauritz Stiller from Sweden.

The leading producer-directors were among the most powerful and respected figures in Hollywood during the 20s and had contributed to developing the art of the silent cinema to its fullest possible potential. But by the end of the decade and with the arrival of sound, all of them (with the notable exception of Chaplin) had lost their independence. The remarkable directing careers of Griffith, Von Stroheim, Ingram and others reached a premature end. The industry was now in the control of a small number of giant, vertically integrated companies led by Paramount, the newly formed MGM, and

Above: Warner Bros. boasted a formidable array of contract directors during the 30s. The handful here with studio chief Darryl Zanuck (centre with cigar) are – from left to right – Michael Curtiz, Alan Crosland, John Adolfi, Robert Milton, Roy Del Ruth, Ray Enright, Alfred E. Green, Lloyd Bacon.

Left: Cecil B. DeMille, with his scriptwriter Jeanie Macpherson and Sid Grauman of Grauman's Chinese Theatre, planning the spectacular premiere of *The King Of Kings* in 1927.

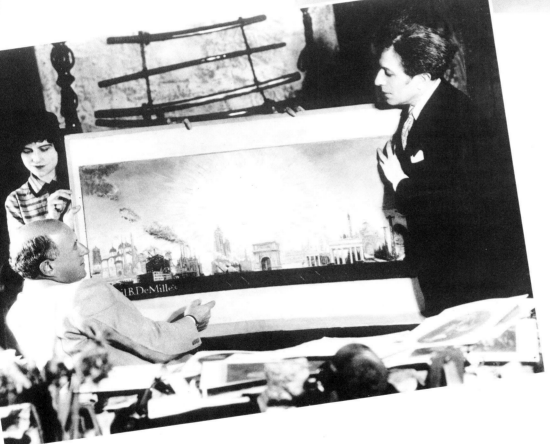

Cedric Gibbons, who was head of the art department; he was the one who set the tone for the whole studio ...'

The arrival of sound which had increased the cost and technical complexity of film-making, also served to restrict the freedom of the directors. They were more tied to studio filming than ever before. It was now less easy to avoid producer interference by taking their film unit off on location as had been done in shooting many of the most remarkable silents from Von Stroheim's *Foolish Wives* and *Greed* to James Cruze's *The Covered Wagon*, John Ford's *The Iron Horse* or William Wellman's *Wings*.

Whereas during the 20s many of the top directors had shared the spotlight with the stars, the 30s clearly belong to the stars and the studios. Success as a director meant finding a suitable home at a sympathetic studio where, if a director had special gifts, he could display them to some extent even within the limitations of the system. Clarence Brown at MGM, Frank Capra at Columbia, Ernst Lubitsch at Paramount all exemplified this.

The 30s was thus not the best decade for the directors, in spite of the quality of the studio resources and technicians put at their disposal. But it is surprising how quickly things can change, even in Hollywood. Already waiting in the wings by the late 30s was a whole new generation of *writers* including Preston Sturges, John Huston and Billy Wilder, who would graduate to directing during the 40s, bolstered by new arrivals like Orson Welles, Alfred Hitchcock and Vincente Minnelli, all men who would help restore much-needed prestige to the role of the movie director during the years which followed.

Warner Bros. which grew rapidly during the late 20s. These studios not only produced and distributed their own pictures but owned many of the theatres as well. A new and more efficient releasing and exhibition pattern meant that production, too, could be organised on a more efficient basis. They were able to turn out a regular number of quality films each year from directors, stars and technicians who were all under contract. There was less room than ever for the brilliant but independent-minded director who refused to fit into the system.

The hard working contract director could expect to be assigned to as many as three or four films per year with little time for pre-production planning or alterations. By the time he was given the script, most of the roles would be already cast with the studio's contract stars and the sets already constructed. Later, during editing, he would already be on to his next production. Not surprisingly the studio's 'house style' – opulent and sophisticated at Paramount; characteristically low-key in the case of Warner Bros., glossy and glamorous at MGM – was more likely to be determined by the leading cameramen and art directors than by the directors. The supervising art directors, in particular, were especially powerful, thus Elia Kazan discovered that 'MGM was not run by Pandro Berman, not even by Louis B. Mayer, but by

DOROTHY ARZNER

Born San Francisco, 3 January 1900. **Died** 1979

After seven years at Paramount, during which time she had worked her way up from a lowly story department typist to the cutting department, and then to editor-in-chief of some of the studio's biggest pictures, Dorothy Arzner was ready to leave: 'I went out to my car in the parking lot, had my hand on the door latch, when I decided after so many years I was going to say 'goodbye' to someone important and not just leave unnoticed and forgotten'. She returned to the office of production head B.P. Schulberg, but he was in conference. She then spotted producer Walter Wanger just passing and called out to him, 'Oh, you'll do'. She said goodbye and told him she was leaving for Columbia to direct her first picture. Schulberg was quickly summoned. He offered to promote her to the scenario department with a possibility of directing, but she stood firm. Recognising that he would lose her, Schulberg finally offered her a French play called 'The Best Dressed Woman In Paris' for her first production as 'writer-director'. Thus began the directing career of the only woman to join the ranks of the major Hollywood directors during the late 20s, a position she maintained for a period of almost twenty years, from 1926 through 1943, working for many of the top studios and directing leading stars such as Clara Bow, William Powell, Claudette Colbert and Joan Crawford.

Dorothy Arzner began her working life as a waitress in her father's Hollywood cafe which was frequented by movie personalities. After driving an ambulance in World War I, she worked on a newspaper before being hired, in 1919, by William De Mille as a stenographer in the script department at Famous Players. From there she worked her way up to become an editor. Miss Arzner first made her name at Paramount as the editor of *Blood And Sand* (1922), in which she adroitly matched close-ups of Valentino with stock bull-fighting footage, thereby saving the studio a lot of money. Producer-director James Cruze was so impressed by her work on this picture that

he asked her to edit his blockbuster Western, *The Covered Wagon* which was a big hit in 1923. An exceptionally talented woman, she developed a second and parallel career as a scenario writer during the mid-20s and was clearly capable of making the transition to directing which had been her goal all along. She remained at Paramount for thirteen years, and directed one of the studio's first talkies, *The Wild Party* (1929), the story of a flapper who organises her college friends into a society called 'the hard-boiled maidens', much to the consternation of the authorities. The movie starred one of Hollywood's hottest properties, the 'It' girl, Clara Bow.

During the 30s Miss Arzner was much in demand. She was hired by RKO to direct Katharine Hepburn in her second

picture (and her first starring vehicle), *Christopher Strong* (1933). Brought in by Sam Goldwyn as replacement director on an ill-fated adaptation of Emile Zola's *Nana* (1934), Arzner was unable to overcome the shortcomings either of the script or of Anna Sten's limited acting talent. *Craig's Wife*, starring Rosalind Russell, followed for Columbia in 1935, and Joan Crawford requested Miss Arzner for the major production, *The Bride Wore Red* (1937), at MGM. But the director was not happy working in the biggest dream factory of them all, and returned to the smaller studios for her last features.

Although most of her pictures were straightforward 30s studio projects, Arzner was noted for her sympathetic handling of her actors. Her professionalism earned the respect of her crews, and her readiness to do battle with the front office and with troublesome producers undoubtedly contributed to the growing acceptance of directors gaining more creative control over their pictures from the 40s onwards. She certainly managed to stamp a personal, feminist approach on the heroines who were most often the focal point of her pictures and, during recent years, she has been 'rediscovered' by a new generation of feminist writers and critics – notably for her last feature, *Dance Girl Dance*.

Miss Arzner retired from directing features in 1943 due to ill health. She continued to make WAC training films and TV commercials, also teaching film for a time at UCLA. As the first woman member of the Director's Guild of America, she was honoured by a special DGA tribute in 1975, four-and-half years before her death.

'In all Arzner's films it is the woman's search for an identity and independent existence beyond and outside the male universe which gives her themes coherence . . . Dorothy Arzner always establishes her female protagonists as the subject of action existing apart from the distorting mirror of male phantasy.'

Claire Johnston, 1975

Left: A woman in very much a man's world. Dorothy Arzner, the first woman to earn a serious place in the Hollywood hierarchy of directors, photographed in the studio at the beginning of her directing career in the 20s.

Above: A very young and beautiful Katharine Hepburn in a moment from *Christopher Strong* (1933), her first starring vehicle, directed by Arzner.

Left: The 'It' girl, Clara Bow (left), who was born and reared in appalling poverty and misery, broke away from her background to become one of early Hollywood's major box-office stars. In 1929 she starred in the early talkie, *The Wild Party*, for director Arzner.

BUSBY BERKELEY

Born Los Angeles, 29 November 1895. **Died** 1976

Often imitated, never equalled, and responsible for a durable and pervasive influence on the Hollywood musical, Busby Berkeley was one of the most celebrated film-makers to emerge from Hollywood during the 30s. His name immediately conjures up images of scantily clad show girls arranged in kaleidoscopic patterns, observed from a variety of angles, or followed by a moving camera as they go through their elaborate routines in time to the music. Berkeley is best remembered for his years at Warner Bros., beginning in 1932 when he was given the opportunity to create the musical numbers for *42nd Street*. The studio kept him busy working on an average of four to five pictures per year, while he, in turn, drew on all the studio's resources, making regular use of the largest sound stages on the lot. Elaborate revolving or multi-level sets – like the vast waterfall set for the 'By A Waterfall' number in *Footlight Parade* (1933), populated by a seemingly endless number of water maidens – were his stock-in-trade. He made use of outsize 'Pop art' props: the giant gold coins which dwarf the chorus girls in the opening number of *Golddiggers Of 1933*, extra-large cut-outs of the Manhattan skyline in *42nd Street*, the giant jigsaw puzzle pieces fitted together to form an immense face of Ruby Keeler in *Dames* (1934).

Less a choreographer in the conventional sense than a creator of special visual effects, there was seemingly no limit to his witty, inventive and sometimes *risqué* images. Elaborate camera movements and unusual camera angles were blended with *trompe l'oeil* and trick effects, abstract patterns and discontinuous, dream-like, almost surrealistic jumps which were breathtakingly original at the time and which have provided audiences with an archetypal vision of 30s Hollywood glamour that has never lost its appeal. Berkeley, more than any other film-maker, demonstrated Orson Welles' comment that the cinema is 'the greatest train set in the world'. Yet Berkeley could be surprisingly inventive in staging intimate moments – a quiet love scene between Dick Powell and Ruby Keeler, for example, played out against a simple backdrop. In fact, his numbers often start out quite simply, like the shot of Joan Blondell as the street singer at night in *Golddiggers Of 1933*, beginning the song 'Remember My Forgotten Man' which then opens out to tell the story of the soldiers of World War I returning home to face the Depression and the soup kitchen handouts.

Berkeley took great pleasure in devising the most astonishing and elaborate routines to be executed with split-second timing, and had the ability to visualise even the most complex sequences in advance. As he recalled in later years, 'I never needed retakes. I would plan it all so carefully in my mind, I knew *exactly* what I wanted hours before I got to the studio ... I had the best talent, the best designers, the best writers ... I asked nothing that wasn't possible ...'.

Left: Thirty-eight year old Busby Berkeley against a montage from *Golddiggers Of 1933*. The number, 'My Forgotten Man', was a moving, inventive and audacious evocation in song and dance of World War I glory and its inglorious aftermath.

Below: *42nd Street* (1933) contained some of Berkeley's most spectacularly vigorous choreography – indeed, the movie as a whole was a watershed in the development of the screen musical in terms of original songs (by Dubin, and Warren), casting (Dick Powell, Ruby Keeler, Ginger Rogers), a sharp satirical and risqué script (Rian James), and superb photography (Sol Polito). Almost fifty years later, Broadway borrowed from Hollywood to pay homage to Berkeley with a spectacularly successful stage version of '42nd Street'.

Known for his singleminded determination to bring his vision alive on the screen, Berkeley could occasionally be found drilling holes in the floor or roof of the sound stage in order to achieve the kind of daring perspective which he required for a particular shot. Inevitably, his unusual methods led to his being branded as a maverick by Hollywood standards, and his growing reputation as a difficult character to control led to problems during the later years of his career. In addition, he was a hard task-master. According to Joan Blondell, it was a bit

easier for the stars, 'but those poor Berkeley girls ... They just worked themselves to a frazzle. Six days a week, including Saturdays ... There were no unions in those days ...'

William Berkeley Enos was born into a theatrical family. His mother was an actress and his father a stage director, and he himself was on the stage at the age of five. Although Berkeley's career was interrupted by a break for war service, he put the time to good use by devising elaborate drill routines which could be performed by hundreds of troops in perfect synchronisation, another image which was to characterise his later choreography. During the 20s Buzz developed into one of the leading choreographers on Broadway, and in 1930 he was invited out to Hollywood by producer Sam Goldwyn to recreate on film the musical routines which he had devised for the successful Ziegfeld show, 'Whoopee', starring Eddie Cantor. Although he had had no previous film experience, Berkeley immediately demonstrated an instinctive grasp of the medium. Throwing aside the familiar proscenium arch stage conventions which shackled so many of the film musicals of the period, he managed to inject some vitality into an otherwise weak and stagey production. He immediately dispensed with the multiple camera crews generally used for such productions and concentrated on the single camera which mattered. He had an eye for spotting attractive showgirls, and introduced the idea of filming them in close-ups, thus assisting in developing The Goldwyn Girls, and so giving a boost to the early careers of Betty Grable, Paulette Goddard and Lucille Ball. (He acquired a reputation as a ladies man in his private life, too, and married six times). Most striking of all in *Whoopee*

were kaleidoscopic shots of Indian maidens wearing colourful feathered head-dresses (this was one of the few movies filmed in the early Technicolor process). At the very beginning of his film career Berkeley had already put his unique stamp on the movie musical.

A vast number of mainly forgettable and unimaginative musicals had been turned out by all the studios during 1929-30 to exploit the novelty of sound. The major box-office hits of 1929 included MGM's *Broadway Melody*, Warner Bros.' *Gold Diggers Of Broadway* and RKO's *Rio Rita*. *Whoopee*, too, was a hit the following

year, but it proved to be the last. The novelty wore off and audiences began to stay away. Berkeley, however, remained much in demand to create the musical numbers for such pictures as Mary Pickford's *Kiki* (United Artists, 1931) and additional Eddie Cantor vehicles for Goldwyn. By the end of 1932 Darryl Zanuck, the production chief at Warner Bros., decided that it was time for a musical revival which would take advantage of the more sophisticated techniques now available. Thus, *42nd Street* was conceived and, with it, a seven-year contract at Warners for Berkeley.

Above: A characteristic array of girls, girls, girls from the aptly-named *Dames* (1934). The movie was the Warner formula as before – golddiggers, sugar daddies, songs by Dubin and Warren and, of course, Ruby Keeler (illustrated here inside the mirror). But it was Berkeley's contribution which, once again, elevated *Dames* to some status in the Hollywood musical.

Left: Again from *Dames*, an archetypal geometric kaleidoscope, formed by intricate arrangements of beautiful girls, and shot from overhead for maximum visual impact.

'Berkeley had pretty much the run of everything he did. If you're a winner, as he was, nobody fights you. The 'powers' were in the business for the money, and all they cared about was that he brought it in. Berkeley got what he wanted.'

Wini Shaw in 'The Real Tinsel'

The Warner musicals generally followed a predictable plot formula: the ups and downs experienced by the leading characters – showgirls, stars, director and financial backers – in their efforts to put on a successful stage musical. Thus, the natural climax of each picture was provided by Berkeley in the form of a series of striking musical numbers, conceived and presented as fully self-contained sequences without any regard for what could in reality fit onto a stage. *42nd Street* ended with 'Shuffle Off To Buffalo', 'I'm Young And Healthy', and the title number finale, and *Golddiggers Of 1933* with 'Remember My Forgotten Man'. Finally, *Footlight Parade*, the last of this remarkable trio of 1933 releases, presented the ultimate expression of the Berkeley creative persona, with Buzz himself making a brief uncredited appearance as a dance director and the lead played by James Cagney as a kind of Berkeley 'alter ego', a character with a special gift for devising lavish stage prologues to precede the main film show at cinemas. This allowed Berkeley to pull out all the stops on three spectacular and contrasting numbers which brought the movie to a stunning conclusion: the pre-Hays Code naughtiness of 'Honeymoon Hotel' with the girls as thinly disguised hookers was followed by the extravagant 'By A Waterfall' and, finally, Cagney demonstrating his remarkable talents as a hoofer in 'Shanghai Lil'.

The extent of Berkeley's phenomenal popular success at this time can be gauged from the fact that, during the space of slightly over one year, from mid-1932 through late 1933, four of his movies – *The Kid From Spain* (Goldwyn/UA, 1932). *42nd Street*, *Roman Scandals* (his last for Goldwyn) and *Footlight Parade* – were among the top grossing hits of the decade. The Warner Bros. pictures in particular helped to ensure the survival of that studio, which was badly hit by the Depression. In gratitude, the studio gave Buzz an opportunity to extend his range and co-direct his first non-musical, *She Had To Say Yes* (1933). And late in 1934 he was given an entire feature on his own, *Golddiggers Of 1935*, which earned him the first two of his four Oscar nominations for dance direction. (This was a new, short-lived Academy Award category which was discontinued after 1937. Amazingly, Berkeley never did win an Oscar), Other pictures followed, including *Honeymoon Hotel* (1937) and *Garden Of The Moon* (1938), but his musicals were running out of steam and his non-musical pictures failed to generate much interest. He closed out his long stint at Warner Bros. in 1938 with an uncharacteristic film, *They Made Me A Criminal*, starring John Garfield.

Signed up by MGM early in 1939, Buzz was one of the first people to be hired by fledgling musical producer Arthur Freed to join his new unit. Here Berkeley found himself in a very different world, that of idealised family entertainment. He was assigned to a series of Judy Garland-Mickey Rooney pictures, and the first, *Babes In Arms*, was such a huge hit that a number of sequels followed. Now Buzz was forced to control his imaginative flights of fancy, and his extravagances. But he was accustomed to being

authoritarian on the set and gave his young stars a difficult time. His methods were not always appreciated at MGM, and producer Freed knew that it was necessary to keep his talented genius under control. Buzz had been demoted solely to dance director on *Lady Be Good* early in 1941, yet had caused the picture to run far over budget on the musical numbers alone. On *For Me And My Gal* the following year, Judy Garland helped newcomer Gene Kelly to cope with the difficult Mr Berkeley, and this picture turned out to be the last directed by Buzz at MGM entirely on his own. Early in 1943 he was taken off *Girl Crazy* after his filming of the 'I Got Rhythm' number led to a dispute with musical arranger Roger Edens who was Freed's right-hand man. In 1948 he received credit for directing *Take Me Out To The Ballgame*, yet he had directed the non-musical sequences only. The new team of Gene Kelly and Stanley Donen staged the musical numbers as a trial run for their first major feature as co-directors, *On The Town*, the following year. And in 1949 Berkeley's much troubled relationship with Garland ended badly when he (and then she) was removed from *Annie Get Your Gun*.

However, Berkeley's most remarkable achievement during the 40s, and perhaps the masterpiece of his entire career, came during 1943 when he was loaned out to 20th Century-Fox for *The Gang's All Here*. Fox production chief Darryl Zanuck had been producing a series of popular Technicolor musicals that made stars of Betty Grable, Alice Faye and Carmen Miranda. Buzz was given the opportunity to apply his imaginative talents in colour for the first time since *Whoopee*, and he came up with two of his most astonishing and eye-boggling numbers: Carmen Miranda was 'The Lady With The Tutti Frutti Hat', wearing an elaborate headdress of fruit and supported by sixty tropical showgirls and sixty unmistakably phallic, giant-size bananas. The finale involved two 50-foot

high and 15-foot wide revolving mirrors which created endless patterns for the dancers placed between them.

Inevitably, the last years of Berkeley's career proved something of a letdown. He continued working at MGM during the early 50s, and choreographed spectacular aquaballets for Esther Williams in *Million Dollar Mermaid* (1952) and *Easy To Love* (1953). His last contribution came in 1962 when he devised the elaborate circus numbers for the ambitious film version of *Billy Rose's Jumbo*, adapted from the stage show by Rodgers and Hart. And in 1971, five years before his death, he helped supervise a revival of the successful stage show, 'No, No Nanette', which brought his 30s star, Ruby Keeler, back to Broadway. The lavish David Merrick musical, '42nd Street', in 1980 appeared as a homage to the great Busby Berkeley musicals of the 30s. A smash hit all over America and in London, it represented perhaps the culmination of the rediscovery of Berkeley by a new generation of moviegoers which has been taking place since the 60s.

Below: The brilliant innovator closed out the early 50s at MGM with some breathtaking inventions for aquabat Esther Williams. The movies themselves, in terms of plot and acting, bordered on the risibly weak, but they are enshrined forever by Berkeley's explosive, vividly multi-coloured set-pieces. The still shows Esther (centre) in a sequence from *Easy To Love* (1953).

FRANK BORZAGE

Born Salt Lake City, Utah, 23 April 1893. **Died** 1962

The great romanticist of the American cinema, known best for the emotional intensity and the quality of his love stories, Frank Borzage had a very up and down career in Hollywood. Although he worked as a director from 1916 to 1961, he was at his best during the middle years, from the Oscar-winning *Seventh Heaven* (1927) to the anti-Nazi drama, *The Mortal Storm* in 1940. Thereafter, the quality of his pictures fell off badly. A stylish director who demonstrated a great technical facility early in his career, he was also known for his work with a wide range of Hollywood actresses from Pauline Starke and Norma Talmadge in the silents to Margaret Sullavan and Joan Crawford during the 30s, and was highly successful in introducing the pairing of Janet Gaynor and Charles Farrell during the late 20s. Unusually for a Hollywood director, he appeared able to preserve a certain thematic and stylistic consistency in his best works throughout his career. Thus, his last memorable picture, *Moonrise* (1948), expresses much of the same passion and dramatic intensity (with 40s *film noir* overtones) which informed his late silents and early sound films during those years when he was reaching full maturity as a director.

Frank first became attracted to acting as a teenager, and served a rigorous apprenticeship as a prop boy and then bit player with a touring theatre company. He landed in Hollywood when he was twenty and began acting in westerns for producer Thomas Ince. By 1916 he had graduated to directing and acting in fea-ture-length Westerns for the Mutual and Triangle companies. He soon developed a mastery of film technique. A relatively early picture like *Until They Get Me* (1917), for example, is more memorable for its location photography and smooth-ly edited continuity, than for its acting, or its plot. Since the Westerns of these early years were often romantic and melo-dramatic in flavour, with the emphasis on drama rather than action, they proved to be a fertile training ground for Borzage the romanticist, who never returned to the genre during the later years of his career. Gloria Swanson recalled doing one picture with him, *Society For Sale*, in 1918. She was unimpressed with his qualities as a director: 'The story was silly and old fashioned, (and) he shot the entire picture in the studio, avoiding lo-cation scenes altogether'. But he was still developing his skills. His close collabora-tion with the distinguished scriptwriter Frances Marion during the early 20s cul-minated in a pair of dramatic pictures starring Norma Talmadge (eldest of the three Talmadge sisters), including the highly successful *Secrets* (1924) which was one of the top hits of the decade. The following year (1925) Borzage was signed by the Fox studio where he joined leading directors John Ford and Raoul Walsh. Between them they were responsible for most of the studio's prestige productions and box-office hits during this period.

Borzage established himself as a lead-ing Hollywood director in 1927 with *Seventh Heaven* followed by *Street Angel* (1928), both starring the screen's newest and most popular romantic pair, Janet Gaynor and Charles Farrell. *The River* (1928) came next, another powerful and lyrical love story starring Charles Farrell, but teamed, this time, with Mary Duncan. All three were visually stun-ning, reflecting the contribution of cameraman Ernest Palmer and art direc-tor Harry Oliver. Although perhaps the most remarkable of the group, *The River* is least well-known, having suffered the same fate as other late 1928 silents in being ousted by the novelty of early sound movies. By contrast, *Seventh Heaven* and *Street Angel* were both smash-hits. At the core of *Seventh Heaven* was the nicely ob-served, bitter-sweet relationship which develops between a Paris sewer cleaner and an unhappy girl of the streets. The stylised settings conveyed a distinctly European flavour, while the sensitive (and sensual) performance of the petite Janet Gaynor, whose 'girl-next-door' ap-pearance was far removed from the typi-cal, glamourised starlet of the period, won her the first ever Oscar as Best Ac-tress. The first Best Director award went to Borzage. (Harry Oliver was nominated for his 'interior decoration', and the pic-ture, too, was nominated, but lost to Wil-liam Wellman's aviation drama, *Wings*).

Borzage easily made the transition to sound with *They Had To See Paris* (1929), the first talkie to star the likeable Will Rogers who remained one of Fox's top stars until his death in 1935. *Bad Girl* (1931) demonstrated Borzage's skill in mixing comedy and heavy drama and earned him a second Oscar. The Fox

Above: Frank Borzage was one of the pioneers of the soft-focus look, an approach which invested his screen lovers with a lyrical romantic aura that set them apart from the less pleasant realities around them.

Left: Janet Gaynor (left), George E. Stone (background centre), Charles Farrell (right) and Albert Gran (far right) in *Seventh Heaven* (1927). This first-class example of Borzage at his best won the first ever Oscars for Best Actress and Best Director.

studio was hard hit by the Depression in 1932, and Borzage left, after seven years, to go independent for a time. He was immediately hired by Paramount to direct *A Farewell To Arms*, but found that his two stars presented something of a problem. The tall, softspoken Gary Cooper was clearly in awe of Helen Hayes' reputation as one of the leading actresses on Broadway who was just beginning to make a name for herself in films. She, in turn, was wary of Coop's reputation as a playboy and lady-killer. In a successful effort to break the ice between the couple, Borzage apparently had the idea of a picture session, in costume, using a couch for a prop. This incident gives a hint of the evocative, intimate style adopted by Borzage for the picture. The World War I background of Hemingway's tragic love story is superbly sketched in at various points, but the film is most notable as an example of controlled studio filming in black-and-white. The low-keyed photography of Charles Lang effectively captured the European atmosphere and preserved the intimacy of the fine performances by Cooper and Miss Hayes, ably supported by Adolphe Menjou's cynical Major. But the real star was the director, who demonstrated that those same qualities which he had developed in his best silent pictures could still work effectively within the sound cinema of the 30s. Although he was not nominated for an Oscar, the picture was; Lang won the cinematography award, while a second award reflected the picture's finely judged use of sound.

Borzage faced a rather different problem with his stars on *A Man's Castle* (1933). A close personal friend of Spencer Tracy and his wife, Louise, the director was embarrassed by the real life romance which developed between Tracy and his co-star, Loretta Young. In any case the picture turned out superbly, easily the best of the four Borzage-Tracy movies of the 30s and gave a boost to the aspirations of the tiny Columbia studio. Set against the background of the American Depression, it was another romantic story in the familiar Borzage vein, bearing an unmistakable resemblance to *Seventh Heaven*. The picture – about a love affair between unmarried unemployeds – was unconventional, even a bit 'amoral', by Hollywood standards, but proved that Tracy could play a romantic lead and brought out the almost ethereal quality of the young Loretta's beauty. In *Little Man What Now?* (Universal, 1934) which followed, the setting was the German post-war Depression of the 20s, again concentrating on a moving depiction of a love relationship. The stars were Douglass Montgomery and Margaret Sullavan, who lit up the screen for the first time in only her second picture.

These two movies were the high point of Borzage's independent period which included additional work at Warner Bros. (two movies each with Dick Powell-Ruby Keeler and Kay Francis-George Brent). Paramount's *Desire* (1936) turned out more Lubitsch (who produced) than Borzage, while *History Is Made At Night* (1937), a likeable off-beat mixture of comedy and drama, starring Charles Boyer and Jean Arthur, was Borzage's last independent production (for

Walter Wanger and UA). Signed to a contract by MGM, he was reunited with Spencer Tracy (*Three Comrades*, 1938) and Joan Crawford (*The Shining Hour*, 1938) – Crawford had played a bit part in Borzage's *The Circle* (MGM, 1925) at the beginning of her career. In fact, the most interesting of his MGM pictures were the two which starred Miss Sullavan. The anti-Nazi theme first hinted at in *Little Man* became more explicit in *The Mortal Storm* (1940) and was made even more so in *Three Comrades*. *Three Comrades* also merits a footnote in the history of the cinema as the one time that F. Scott Fitzgerald's name appeared on the

screen, for his script adaptation of Remarque's novel.

The quality of Borzage's work declined during later years. *The Spanish Main* (RKO, 1945) was no more than an enjoyable swashbuckler spoof (filmed in Technicolor), while the highlight of his period at Republic – a Poverty Row studio attempting to upgrade its image – was *Moonrise* starring Dane Clark and Gail Russell. He made no films between 1948 and 1958, an unlikely victim of 50s 'blacklisting'. His last major production was *The Big Fisherman* (1959) for Disney, which he completed just three years before his death.

Above: Gary Cooper, and the illustrious Broadway actress, Helen Hayes, starred in *A Farewell To Arms* (1932).

Below: Douglass Montgomery and Margaret Sullavan in *Little Man What Now?* (1934). Miss Sullavan, who made her first major screen impact in this movie, was one of Hollywood's most gifted actresses. Unfortunately, she was also one of the most unstable, and made only sixteen films before dying of a barbiturate overdose at the age of forty-nine.

CLARENCE BROWN

Born Clinton, Massachusetts, 10 May 1898.

Clarence Brown enjoyed a long and distinguished career at MGM. Known as a sensitive director of actors, he was also a fine technician with a strong visual sense acquired during his early years as an assistant to director Maurice Tourneur whom he credits with first inspiring his love of the cinema. Brown studied engineering and was employed for a time by an automobile company during the early 'teens. An avid moviegoer, he was impressed by the pictures he saw which were credited to the Peerless Studio in Fort Lee, New Jersey, and finally decided he wanted to try working in the movies himself. Arriving at the studio in hopes of landing a job, it turned out that the leading director, Maurice Tourneur, was just then looking for a new assistant. In spite of his lack of experience, Brown managed to talk himself into the job by pointing out to Tourneur the advantage of hiring a 'fresh brain' whom he could influence in his own way.

Brown soon proved himself a hardworking and willing assistant, and graduated to editing, title writing, and directing many of the exterior sequences which were of less interest to Tourneur. He looked forward to directing his own pictures and got his first opportunity in 1920 when he co-wrote a script called *The Great Redeemer* for Metro with the young actor, John Gilbert, who also starred in it. Brown's later comments in an interview with Kevin Brownlow give one the flavour of what film-making was like during those early years when many of the best directors were constantly improvising with new techniques, and Brown

took advantage of his early training as an engineer, as his following recollection suggests: 'In *The Last Of The Mohicans* (Associated Producers, 1920) we made much use of lighting effects and weather atmosphere. We used smokepots to create the suggestion of sunrays striking through woodland mist. The rainstorm in the forest was simply a fire engine and a hose. When the girls are escaping from the Indian ambush, I put the camera on a perambulator. We built it from a Ford axle, with Ford wheels, a platform, and a handle to pull it down the road . . .'

After co-directing his last pictures with Tourneur, Brown quickly established himself on his own and made his mark at Universal during the years 1923-25. His sensitive handling of *Smouldering Fires* (1924), about the difficulties experienced by a 40-year-old woman when she falls for and marries a young man in his mid-twenties, and *The Goose Woman* (1925), another strong dramatic picture which starred Louise Dresser, immediately thrust Brown into the ranks of the leading Hollywood directors.

In 1925 he was signed up by producer Joseph Schenck at United Artists to direct Valentino in *The Eagle*. Based on a Zorro-type story in the Fairbanks swashbuckling mold, not only did Valentino give one of his best performances, but the movie is superb to look at, with a notable contribution from cameraman George Barnes. Much of the credit for the film's success, however, must be attributed to the witty script of Hans Kraly.

The following year (1926) marked a major turning point for Brown. He was

signed to a contract by the newly flourishing studio, MGM, where he was to work for the remainder of his career. His very first film there, *Flesh And The Devil*, occupies a special place in the history of the cinema. Here the Garbo magic was fully captured on the screen for the first time. Her co-star was John Gilbert, and their performances in the love scenes undoubtedly benefitted from their real-life romance, as well as from the imaginative soft-focus photography of William Daniels. Working with the shy Garbo required the most sensitive and caring attention from both Brown and Daniels. Brown quickly found that a tactful, low-key approach yielded the best results: 'I had a way with Garbo that didn't embarrass her . . . In those days (of silent pictures) directors used to yell from behind the camera. I never, never gave her directions in front of someone else . . . I used to direct her very quietly. I never gave her a direction above a whisper. Nobody on the set ever knew what I said to her; she liked that . . .'. This was the first of Brown's six movies with Garbo, mainly concentrated during the years 1926-31 and spanning the all-important transition to sound. Five of them were photographed by Daniels, who became her favourite cameraman and shot most of her pictures with other directors as well. Yet he insists that he always remained sensitive to the requirements of each different production. 'I'd give each director what he wanted. My lighting of Garbo varied from picture to picture. There wasn't one Garbo face in the sense that there was a Dietrich face.'

Above: The legendary heart-throb of the 20s, Rudolph Valentino, in *The Eagle* (1925). The film was not only an excellent vehicle for its star who acquitted himself admirably, but it consolidated the growing reputation of the still young Clarence Brown.

Left: Brown will always be remembered for his association with Greta Garbo. He had a special gift for dealing with the aloof, sensitive, vulnerable Swedish beauty, and is seen here (left of the camera) setting up a take for *Flesh And The Devil* (1926), his first Garbo vehicle. With Garbo here is Lars Hansen, another Swedish star, who played her husband in this steamy and powerful story of a doomed triangular romance which exploited Garbo's special magic to the full. William Daniels is behind the camera.

'Occasionally I would go and see my own pictures at public theatres – and sometimes I would sneak out before they began. Today I see a picture of mine on television, cut from an hour and ten minutes to forty-five minutes. At the point when you've got to see what happens next, up comes a commercial for an underarm deodorant. Then they go back to the picture. Well, I don't.'

In marked contrast to *Flesh And The Devil*, Brown's next MGM picture he regards as his toughest assignment ever. *The Trail Of '98* (1928), an epic story of the Alaska goldrush, was filmed under the most difficult, wintry conditions imaginable, making use of mountain locations near Denver, Colorado. Back at the studio Brown returned to directing more intimate, personal stories on a smaller scale; in other words, the kind of pictures he did best. Unlike some of the fast-working contract directors, like 'one-take' Woody Van Dyke, Brown was characterised by the care and attention which he devoted to each of his pictures, rarely directing more than two per year. He and Garbo were Oscar-nominated for both of the pictures they made together in 1930, *Anna Christie* and *Romance*, their first talkies, and Brown was nominated a third time for *A Free Soul* (1931) starring Norma Shearer, but neither Garbo nor Brown ever won an Oscar. (She received an 'honorary Oscar' in 1954.)

Such was the director's new prestige that he was much in demand by all the top stars at MGM, and his subsequent career reads like a veritable star chronology. *A Free Soul*, for example, had given a boost to the career of up-and-coming star Clark Gable in a small role; during the 30s Brown went on to direct many more pictures with Gable, and with Joan Crawford, both together and separately. He directed Helen Hayes and Lionel Barrymore during the early 30s, James Stewart and Myrna Loy in the late 30s and, in the 40s, Spencer Tracy who starred in *Edison The Man* (1940) as well as in *Plymouth Adventure* (1952), Brown's last picture.

In Brown's last two movies with Garbo she was cast opposite Fredric March and Basil Rathbone in *Anna Karenina* (1935), and paired with Charles Boyer in *Conquest* (1937). Both were, as usual, solidly crafted and stylish productions with fine performances, but they failed to generate much enthusiasm at the box-office and were passed over by the Academy, except for Boyer's nomination for his portrayal of Napoleon. Costing a little over $1 million, *Anna Karenina* managed to make a reasonable profit, but *Conquest* cost almost twice as much and recorded a loss. Both were clearly overshadowed by *Camille* (1937), directed by George Cukor, and the delightful *Ninotchka* (1939) from Ernst Lubitsch. During the late 30s it became apparent that Brown's position as MGM's most prestigious women's director was being usurped – notably by Cukor.

Making a slight change of direction, Brown renewed his interest in rural 'Americana' during the 40s, beginning with *Edison The Man*, and turned his attention to the studio's most promising juveniles. Mickey Rooney starred in an entertaining adaptation of Saroyan's *The Human Comedy* (1943); Rooney and the young Elizabeth Taylor played in *National Velvet* (1945), and Claude Jarman Jr was the young star of *The Yearling* (1946), both highly popular and successful movies and Brown's first in colour. He was Oscar-nominated for all three.

Clarence Brown had been able to survive so long at MGM because his quality of film-making served as a generally up-market version of studio boss Louis B. Mayer's well-known preference for family entertainment. When Dore Schary took over as the studio's new production chief, however, Brown demonstrated his versatility by embarking on a film version of William Faulkner's *Intruder In The Dust* (1949), the most socially-conscious subject he treated in his long career. Effectively filmed in black-and-white, with excellent performances from all the cast, especially Juano Hernandez, Porter Hall and Claude Jarman Jr, the picture was Brown's most original effort for many years. His career, however, wound down during the early 50s. A major disappointment was the failure of his ambitious Technicolor film about the Pilgrims, *Plymouth Adventure*, and he retired in 1953.

Left: *Conquest* (1937), also known as *Marie Waleska*, starred Garbo, and the polished Frenchman, Charles Boyer as Napoleon. On set here, Garbo looks on while director Brown (in polo neck) positions his emperor. Cinematographer Karl Freund is in the eyeshade, and technical director George Richelevie is on Brown's left.

Below left: Basil Rathbone and Garbo in Brown's version of *Anna Karenina* (1935). The star had previously essayed Tolstoy's ill-fated heroine in a silent adaptation of the novel, titled *Love*, with John Gilbert as Anna's lover, Count Vronsky (Fredric March played the Vronsky part in this one).

Below: Claude Jarman Jr (left), Jane Wyman and Gregory Peck in *The Yearling* (1946). An appealing tear-jerker about the young son of a farmer who becomes attached to a stray deer, it was the director's first venture into colour and very successful. It garnered Oscar nominations for Brown, Peck, Wyman and Best Picture, and won for its colour photography (Charles Rosher, Leonard Smith and Arthur Arling).

FRANK CAPRA

Born Bisquino, near Palermo, Sicily, 18 May 1897

Frank Capra is best remembered today as the leading 'Populist' director of 30s Hollywood. His own rise from penniless immigrant to one of the most celebrated movie directors in the world, was reflected in his films which appeared to convey an unshakeable belief in the 'great American dream' and the essential goodness of the common man. Unusually for a major Hollywood director, he also held strong political and social beliefs which he attempted to express through his movies, particularly during the years after 1934 when he won his first Oscar for *It Happened One Night*. At the peak of his popularity during the mid and late 30s his pictures appealed to film critics and audiences alike, so much so that he won two further Oscars. Conscious of the need to cloak his 'message' within a framework which would please the viewers, he worked with many of the leading stars of the period. Capra's formula, whereby the little man could be seen to triumph over corrupt businessmen or unscrupulous politicians, was developed in close collaboration with his favourite scriptwriter, Robert Riskin, and verged on the simplistic. Yet the dramatic and comic possibilities were often compelling. Audiences were encouraged to identify with his heroes (Gary Cooper or James Stewart, often supported by the delightful Jean Arthur) in such pictures as *Mr Deeds Goes To Town* (1936), *You Can't Take It With You* (1938) or *Mr Smith Goes To Washington* (1939), in which they challenged a corrupt system, frequently personified by the pompous Edward Arnold.

Capra was well served by his actors, particularly during the period 1935-41 when the message was in danger of swallowing up his characters. In spite of his oft stated belief in the *individual*, his pictures tended to deal in generalities and were only saved by his sense of humour, fast pace, and the performances of his stars and supporting cast. After the war he found that the world had changed and audiences were no longer attracted to his particular blend of comedy and social comment. He returned to the kind of uncomplicated comedy characteristic of his early years, even remaking two of his earlier pictures.

Capra was only six when his family emigrated from Italy to the US and settled in California. Used to fending for himself from an early age, he worked his way through the California Institute of Technology, then tried a variety of jobs, travelling all over the States before he ended up back in California and developed an interest in the cinema. He directed his first short film in 1922 but quickly recognised how little he knew about movie making. In typically thorough Capra fashion he determined to learn everything he could about his new profession. He took a poorly paid job as lab assistant and gradually worked his way up to prop man and editor on a series of comedy shorts directed by Bob Eddy. A brief stint as a gag man on Hal Roach's 'Our Gang' comedies followed, and led

him to the Mack Sennett studio. Here he worked as a gag writer on comedy two-reelers starring one of Sennett's newest discoveries, Harry Langdon. Contrary to the claims made by Capra, Langdon had already established his screen persona in his earlier shorts, but Capra was clearly the main creative force at work on Langdon's shorts of this period. The director was instrumental in developing Langdon's potential and in helping him to make the leap from two-reelers to full-length features. He co-wrote and co-directed (uncredited) Langdon's first feature in 1926 for First National, *Tramp, Tramp, Tramp*, in which Harry was teamed with a young Joan Crawford. (He was an unlikely competitor in a marathon cross-country walk). As *Photoplay* noted at the time, 'This picture takes Langdon's doleful face and pathetic figure out of the two-reel class and into the Chaplin and Lloyd screen dimensions'. The two features which followed, with Capra as sole director (and co-writer), *The Strong Man* (1926) and *Long Pants* (1927), stand as Langdon's two masterpieces. A hint of later Capra can be seen in the mixture of comedy with social themes, and even in the character of Harry himself as an archetypal innocent let loose in a corrupt adult world with unexpected, and sometimes devastating, results. In *The Strong Man* the innocent hero thwarts the bad elements in a small town by destroying the saloon, while in *Long Pants* small town values are contrasted with the evils of life in the big city.

Given the boot by Langdon who decided that henceforth he would direct his own pictures, Capra found himself unemployed for a time. He directed a feature, *For The Love Of Mike* (1927), which did not turn out well, and even returned briefly to work with Sennett at a much reduced salary. When he received an offer to direct features for the tiny Columbia studio toward the end of 1927 he readily accepted, although he had no way of knowing just how significant this new job would turn out to be. For, during the next dozen years or so, the fortunes of Frank Capra and the Columbia studio would be inextricably linked. He would soon develop into their top director and, singlehanded, help to lift the studio from the ranks of the also-rans on Poverty Row into one of the Hollywood majors.

Starting out with typical Columbia B features, Capra was assigned by studio boss Harry Cohn to one of the studio's first As, *Submarine*, in 1928. A service drama starring Jack Holt and Ralph Graves, it also turned out to be the studio's first with sound effects, and Capra went on to direct their first talkie, *The Donovan Affair*, the following year. One of those Hollywood directors, like Clarence Brown and Allan Dwan, who were trained as engineers, Capra put his technical expertise to good use. As he said in an interview with Donald McCaffrey, 'I was a graduate chemical engineer, so I knew about sound, knew about the physics of sound. I was able to cope with the sound engineers so that they would not dictate to me ... I freed myself from their autocracy as fast as I could ... I began to use sound in pictures as another fine tool rather than as a handicap ...'.

During the early years of sound Capra alternated Jack Holt-Ralph Graves service pictures like *Flight* (1929) and *Dirigible* (1931) with comedies and dramatic pictures. He gave a big boost to the early career of Jean Harlow by casting her in *Platinum Blonde* (1931), but his big discovery was Barbara Stanwyck, who was promptly signed up by Columbia as one of their leading stars. She and Capra made four films together, including *The Miracle Woman* (1932), a satirical drama in which she played a character loosely based on the well-known evangelist, Aimee Semple Macpherson, and Capra's remarkable (and distinctly atypical) venture to the Far East, *The Bitter Tea Of General Yen* (1932). The latter was a stylish and atmospheric picture, making use of soft focus photography, and was notable for Stanwyck's performance, projecting that mixture of independence and vulnerability which became her trademark in later years. Around the same time he completed *American Madness*, a topical and dramatic movie about bank failure during the Depression and the large number of little people affected. It clearly anticipated his social conscience pictures of the late 30s, while *Lady For A Day* (1933), featuring May Robson, re-established him as a leading comedy director. He brought Damon Runyon to life on the screen with the aid of a fine collection of character actors, here cast as Runyonesque figures, who would reappear in many of his later movies.

In his autobiography, *The Name Above The Title*, Capra has written at length about his difficulties in setting up his next project, originally titled 'Night Bus'. The original script was turned down by a number of leading stars – Myrna Loy, Margaret Sullavan, Miriam Hopkins, Constance Bennett – although, in all fairness to them, there were many improvements by the time the picture reached the screen as *It Happened One Night* (1934). Capra's first break came when MGM contractee Clark Gable was ordered to do the movie by Louis B. Mayer, and Claudette Colbert agreed only because Harry Cohn was paying her twice her usual fee. The picture was a phenomenal success. Gable was excellent as 'fun-loving, boyish, attractive, he-man rogue that was the *real* Gable', while Claudette fitted easily into the role of the beautiful but spoilt runaway heiress. They made an excellent comedy team and enjoyed playing together, even injecting a few spontaneous, improvised moments into the story. *It Happened One Night* swept the board at the Oscar ceremony for 1934, winning the Best Picture, Actor, Actress, Director and Screenplay Awards. It made the name of Columbia studios, and of Capra, who had been disappointed the previous year when he had been nominated, but failed to win the Oscar for directing *Lady For A Day*. He was even elected as the new president of the Academy, a post he held for four years. Blending comedy with social comment in *Mr Deeds Goes To Town* and *You Can't Take It With You*, Frank acquired two more Oscars for his mantelpiece,

Above: Clark and Claudette in perhaps the most famous sequence from *It Happened One Night*, the hitch-hiking scene in which the macho man tries every trick in the book to flag down a driver. When he fails, the supposedly naive girl hitches up her suspender in the middle of the road, and ... wham!

Left: One of the director's characteristic formula classics, *Mr Deeds Goes To Town* (1936), starred Gary Cooper and the enchanting Jean Arthur, an attractive and accomplished actress reminiscent in type of the revered Carole Lombard.

'Capra's is a great talent all right, but I have the uneasy feeling he's on his way out. He's started to make movies about themes instead of about people.'
Alistair Cooke, 1936

while the latter also won for Best Picture. In between he directed *Lost Horizon* (1937), an ambitious fantasy with social overtones adapted from the novel by James Hilton. Capra's last pictures before America's entry into the war – *Mr Smith Goes To Washington* (1939) and *Meet John Doe* (Warner Bros., 1941) – showed unmistakable signs that he was beginning to repeat himself and was perhaps taking himself too seriously. *Arsenic And Old Lace*, completed for his new studio, Warner Bros., early in 1942 (but not released until 1944), suggested a weak attempt at something a bit different, a straightforward adaptation of Joseph Kesselring's well-known black comedy hit from the stage.

Leaving Hollywood behind, Capra welcomed the opportunity to contribute to the war effort by directing a series of government sponsored documentaries entitled *Why We Fight*. Although this was his first venture into the documentary field, he and his excellent group of collaborators succeeded admirably and won a Best Documentary Oscar for the first in

Above: Jane Wyatt (left) and Ronald Colman in the screen version of James Hilton's *Lost Horizon*. The set is 30s Hollywood's notion of a Tibetan paradise.

Left: James Stewart (right) as the idealistic senator berates Claude Rains (in spectacles) in *Mr Smith Goes To Washington*, an archetypal Capra entertainment which garnered seven Oscar nominations and one award – for Lewis R. Foster's story.

Below: Director Capra on set for *A Hole In The Head*, his penultimate film, instructs Frank Sinatra, Keenan Wynn and Joi Lansing.

the series, *Prelude To War* (1942). After the war he returned to sentimental social comedy with James Stewart in the disappointingly old-fashioned *It's A Wonderful Life* (1946), but fared somewhat better with a movie adaptation of the Howard Lindsay-Russel Crouse political play, *State Of The Union* (1948) starring Tracy and Hepburn. But Frank Capra had lost his independence and his career was clearly in decline. A pair of Bing Crosby vehicles – *Riding High* (1950) and *Here Comes The Groom* (1951) – were followed, after a gap of eight years, by his last two features: *A Hole In The Head* (1959) starring Frank Sinatra and Edward G. Robinson, and the Bette Davis-Glenn Ford vehicle, *Pocketful Of Miracles* (1961), an entertaining but unoriginal remake of his own earlier picture, *Lady For A Day*. Thus concluded a remarkably long and successful career.

'Hollywood film-making of today is stooping to cheap salacious pornography in a crazy bastardization of a great art.'
1971

CHARLIE CHAPLIN

Born London 16 April 1889. **Died** 1977

The bowler-hatted figure of the little tramp with baggy trousers, a cane and outsize shoes is one of the most famous and enduring images of the cinema. Charlie Chaplin's rags-ro-riches story began when he first went on the stage at the age of five. The failing health of his mother, a music hall singer who was no longer able to support her two sons, meant that Charlie and his elder half-brother Sydney were forced to fend for themselves. He got his first break at nine, touring with a juvenile act called 'Eight Lancashire Lads', and a mixture of legitimate stage parts and music hall acts followed. In 1907 he joined Sydney in one of the Fred Karno comedy troupes, where he quickly rose to starring roles, and, on his second tour to the US in 1913, was signed to a one-year movie contract by comedy film-maker Mack Sennett.

More prophetic than accurate, a 1914 advert announced his arrival: 'First appearance in Keystone comedies of Chas (sic) Chaplin the famous English pantomimist (in) *Making A Living*. Chaplin proves himself a film player of the first rank by his performance in this film, which is full of farcical and unexpected incident, and which will cause roars of laughter from beginning to end'. For his second short, *Kid Auto Races At Venice*, Chaplin put together an improvised tramp costume that worked so well and became so closely identified with him that he hardly varied it for the next twenty years. Having appeared in only eleven shorts as star or co-star with other Sennett comics like Mabel Normand, Ford Sterling and Fatty Arbuckle, by mid-April Chaplin was already directing and improvising his own scenarios, rarely working from a *written* script.

Chaplin's pictures proved so popular that by the end of his first year he could demand much better terms for the renewal of his contract. When Sennett balked, Chaplin simply signed with Essanay instead. His salary was boosted from $175 to $1250 per week, plus bonus, and he was allowed to shoot his pictures on a more reasonable schedule, by comparison with the frantic pace of filming which was the norm at Keystone. In addition, he found a new and eminently compatible cameraman at the studio, Rollie Totheroh, who was to remain with him for the next thirty eight years, and a new leading lady, Edna Purviance. Her quiet and conventionally feminine style – she had had no previous acting experience – was well-suited to Chaplin's introduction of more sentimental and romantic elements into his pictures. In *The Tramp* (1915), for example, Chaplin foils a gang of crooks, is a comical failure as a farmhand and loses the girl to her fiancé, but is last seen walking jauntily off into the distance, an ending which he was to trademark as his own. Other Essanay two-reelers of note included *Work*, The *Bank* and *A Night In The Show* (all 1915).

Charlie's movie career seemed to be following a natural progression. In 1916 he moved on to the Mutual Film Com-

pany at a salary of $10,000 per week plus $150,000 bonus. Here his two-reel shorts were made with even more care and attention to detail and by 1917 a series of comic masterpieces emerged, including *Easy Street*, *The Cure* and *The Immigrant*. In addition, Mutual's wide foreign distribution meant that Charlie's popularity began to grow at an astonishing rate throughout the world.

A unique opportunity to observe Chaplin in action directing and developing his pictures was provided by a recent three-part television series compiled by Kevin Brownlow, *Unknown Chaplin* (1982). Charlie invariably tried out his ideas without a fully worked out scenario, shooting 'off the cuff' as it were, and seeing in what direction this would lead. And here, for the first time, one was able to see the principle at work. Thus, the series of rushes show an initial idea regarding an artist's cafe being dropped, then restarted, and finally developed into a fully worked out cafe sequence in which Charlie is joined by Edna Purviance. Henry Bergman is replaced by the giant-sized Eric Campbell, turning the head waiter into a more formidable and sinister figure. The artist theme is even recalled by one concluding bit – a modelling advance from an artist provides the couple with the money to get married. Having filmed that series of comical incidents and encounters which Chaplin recognised as providing him with the second (and concluding) reel of his picture, only then does he go back and film the opening which shows Charlie and Edna as immigrants aboard a ship bound for the United States. The picture was, of course, *The Immigrant*.

In 1917 Charlie moved on yet again, taking many of his favourite actors and technicians with him. His new million-dollar contract with First National gave him complete independence and the opportunity to build his own studio. Although the contract was for eight two-reelers at $125,000 each, *A Dog's Life* emerged as his first three-reeler, while his comic but tasteful spoof on war in the trenches, *Shoulder Arms* (also in 1918), was initially conceived as a short feature or five-reeler. (Some of the cut footage can be seen in part three of *Unknown Chaplin*). Although both must be included among the masterpieces of Chaplin's early career, there is a suggestion here that he may have already begun to

Above: Chaplin, in his characteristic little tramp persona, with Edna Purviance in *Work*, which he also wrote and directed at Essanay in 1915.

Below: A scene from the five-reel *Shoulder Arms* (1918), Chaplin's famous satire on trench warfare made for First National.

feel hampered by the restrictive provisions of his new contract. He was apparently unable to convince the short-sighted First National executives that a move into feature-length pictures made good economic sense, and that providing him with more money to make better (and longer) movies could produce far better results at the box-office. In fact, this was the direction in which Chaplin was heading, along with most of the other major film-makers of the period, whether First National concurred or not. The pair of shorts he completed in 1919, for example, were less than his best work, while the project which he first began to develop later that same year aroused his enthusiasm for more. It grew out of his initial idea of making a movie with a remarkable little boy (Jackie Coogan) who is found and adopted by the familiar tramp character. The shooting occupied him throughout most of 1920, and the picture turned out to be his first short feature, *The Kid*. Since to First National it was only a comedy stretched out beyond the normal two reels, Chaplin had to fight with the company to receive a more substantial payment. Ironically, it was advertised as '6 reels of joy – the great picture upon which the famous comedian has worked a whole year'. A phenomenal hit, *The Kid* proved to be the biggest grosser at the box-office since D.W. Griffith's *The Birth Of A Nation*, with First National sharing in profits which they really hardly deserved.

During the following years Chaplin fulfilled the terms of his First National contract with three last shorts of which only one, the four-reel *The Pilgrim* (1923), was at all memorable. At last he was free to direct and produce for his own distribution company, United Artists, which he had helped to form back in 1919 with Mary Pickford, Douglas Fairbanks and D.W. Griffith. But, rather than the expected comedy, UA was presented with a serious social drama, *A Woman Of Paris*, toward the end of 1923. Designed as a vehicle for his former star and companion, Edna Purviance the acting honours went to dapper Adolphe Menjou, while, uniquely, director Chaplin made only a cameo appearance. A remarkably mature and accomplished film, it was well received by the critics but, significantly, was only moderately successful with film audiences.

At this time Charlie's position as Hollywood's leading comedian was being challenged by both the highly successful Harold Lloyd and the remarkable Buster Keaton. Returning to the comedy vein, Charlie embarked on an ambitious feature which turned out to be his masterpiece, *The Gold Rush* (1925). Blending studio filming with a few spectacular location shots, Charlie transplanted his tramp into an alien and snowbound setting. Here he was forced to cope with blizzards, frostbite, starvation and a hunger-crazed Mack Swain who keeps imagining him as a giant edible chicken. The picture's box-office success matched that of *The Kid*. A minor, if enjoyable feature, *The Circus*, followed. Filmed in 1927 it earned Chaplin his first Oscar nominations, for best actor and comedy director and, at the first ever

Oscar ceremony, he received a special honorary award.

Demonstrating the truly ageless and seemingly indestructible qualities of his tramp, Charlie surprised everyone by continuing to feature him in two last 'silent' pictures – *City Lights* (1931) and *Modern Times* (1935). Both had a musical sound track composed by Chaplin, and he even broke the silence toward the end of *Modern Times* with an improvised gibberish song, the first time his voice had been heard in one of his films. His ambitious attempt at an anti-Hitler satire, *The Great Dictator* (1940), saw him performing adroitly in a pair of contrasting roles, as a Jewish barber (a close relation of the tramp) and a Hitler caricature called Adenoid Hynkel. Chaplin's last popular success, it gained Oscar nominations for best picture, actor and screenplay, while Chaplin won the New

York Film Critics Award for best actor. *M. Verdoux* (1947) which followed after a gap of almost seven years represented yet another new departure, a black comedy with the director-star in the Landru-like title role. *Verdoux*, with its attack on the morality of war, provoked boycotts, and the beginning of the anti-Chaplin political smear campaign which finally drove him from America. *Limelight* (1952) was a sentimental drama set in London which recalled Chaplin's own music hall origins. Although he had a fine and expressive voice and proved himself an excellent screen actor, his shortcomings as a director were sometimes embarrassingly evident, in spite of the efforts of associate directors Robert Florey (on *Verdoux*) and Robert Aldrich (on *Limelight*) as well as leading Hollywood cameraman, Karl Struss (*Dictator* and *Limelight*). Chaplin's

'I remain one thing and one thing only, and that is a clown. It places me on a far higher plane than any politician.'
1960

Above left: In the background, Tom Wilson, in the foreground Jackie Coogan, immortalised as *The Kid*, Chaplin's first feature-length film made for First National in 1921. Coogan became an immensely famous child star, being paid half-a-million dollars bonus by MGM to leave First National and join them.

Left: Mack Swain (left) with the star in *The Gold Rush* (1925), another huge box-office success for Charlie.

Below: On location in Truckee, northern California, Charlie the actor gets behind the camera to become Chaplin the director and set up a shot for *The Gold Rush*.

Left: What the poster doesn't mention is that *Modern Times* (1935) was the film in which Charlie Chaplin's voice was heard for the first time – albeit only with a song in gibberish towards the end. Otherwise silent, the film marked the end of Chaplin's efforts to avoid sound movies.

last two pictures, *A King In New York* (1957) and *A Countess From Hong Kong* (1966), held attraction only for those especially interested in his career. He had severed his connections with United Artists during the 50s, so they were his first films for over thirty years which were not distributed by UA.

Chaplin's private life had featured in the headlines ever since his early days as a star. He apparently led an active love life, while in later years his political interests were in the spotlight. In the words of Adela Rogers St Johns, '... the lovers' lane Charlie Chaplin has trod ... is strewn thick with every kind of romance.

No man in modern history has loved and been loved by so many beautiful, brilliant and famous women'. His four marriages worked out at one teenage bride for each decade: film extras Mildred Harris in the 'teens and Lita Grey in the 20s, followed by the young Paulette Goddard (later to star in two of his pictures) in the 30s and, finally, Oona O'Neill, daughter of the famous playwright, Eugene O'Neill. His last, and most satisfactory, marriage (which produced eight children, including actress Geraldine) lasted until his death and sustained him during the difficult 40s when he had to fight a nasty paternity suit which dragged on for years, and when the Red Scare paranoia led him to be unfairly vilified in the press for his alleged left-wing sympathies. In 1952 he settled permanently with his family in Switzerland, vowing never to return to America. His bitterness was expressed in his film *A King In New York*. All was forgiven twenty years later, however, when he returned to the States for the first time to receive an honorary Oscar. He was knighted by the Queen of England in 1975, two years before his death.

Left: *The Great Dictator* remains a telling and masterly satire on Fascism in general and Hitler in particular. It was released – audaciously, it seems now – in 1940 when World War II was already under way.

Below: Chaplin, in his late seventies, pictured on set with the luscious Sophia Loren during filming of *A Countess From Hong Kong* (1966), which co-starred Marlon Brando. The last work from an acknowledged genius, the film, alas, was a very lacklustre swan song.

JOHN CROMWELL

Born Toledo, Ohio, 23 December 1888. **Died** 1979

A contract director for most of his career, John Cromwell's output was extremely variable in quality. A talented and intelligent director, he was certainly capable of better things and, as an actor himself, he developed a reputation in the 30s as one of Hollywood's finest and most sympathetic women's directors. Yet he brought off some tougher assignments when given the opportunity. *The The Prisoner Of Zenda* (1937) for Selznick/UA was one of the best swashbucklers ever; later he directed Bogart in *Dead Reckoning* (1947) for Columbia, a memorable 40s *film noir*, and closed out his main Hollywood stay with a remake of the classic 20s gangster story, *The Racket* (RKO, 1951).

Cromwell served an apprenticeship on the stage as an actor, then stage manager from his late teens. Thus, he had many years of theatre experience behind him by the time he was summoned to Hollywood in 1929, already aged forty, to take up a new career as a movie director. He was signed by Paramount, the most enterprising of the major studios, in its search for new talent from the theatre once the talkies had arrived. Although he developed a good working relationship with a young producer named David Selznick, Cromwell was generally dissatisfied with his treatment by the studio. The break came in 1932 when he found out that he was *not* going to be offered *A Farewell To Arms*, a project which particularly interested him. By now, however, Selznick was production boss at RKO, and Cromwell quickly found a new home there. He began to experience greater artistic freedom, but his material continued to be uneven in quality. The best of his three pictures with Irene Dunne was *Ann Vickers* (1933), based on a Sinclair Lewis novel about a social worker interested in prison reform. *The Silver Cord* (1933), by contrast, was an extremely dated adaptation of a play about a young man's efforts to free himself from a domineering mother. Cromwell had first directed the piece on stage during the early 20s.

Late in 1933 he offered the female lead (opposite Leslie Howard) in *Of Human Bondage* to Bette Davis. She immediately saw this as the big opportunity of her early

career, but 'Warners absolutely refused to lend me out (to RKO),' she recalled in her autobiography. 'The part of Mildred was something I had to have. I spent six months in supplication and drove Mr Warner to the point of desperation – desperate enough to say yes – anything to get rid of me.' In the event Miss Davis' powerful performance in the role established her as a major star.

When Selznick set himself up as an independent producer in 1936, he hired Cromwell to direct his first picture, *Little Lord Fauntleroy*, and their next together, *The Prisoner Of Zenda*, proved to be the highlight of Cromwell's career. The film benefitted from a first class group of technicians and a star-studded cast headed by Ronald Colman, Madeleine Carroll, Douglas Fairbanks Jr, Raymond Massey, and a young David Niven in his first important role. A witty script, lively performances, and charisteristically stunning camerawork by the brilliant James Wong Howe all contributed to a vastly entertaining movie.

Cromwell closed out the 30s at RKO in fine form with a pair of pics starring Carole Lombard (*Made For Each Other* and *In Name Only*), and an excellent adaptation of Robert Sherwood's *Abe Lincoln In Illinois* (1940). Raymond

Massey was rewarded with an Oscar nomination for perhaps his best ever film performance in the title role in the latter, while Cromwell himself appeared in the small part of John Brown. *Since You Went Away* (1944), a superior example of wartime propaganda told from the feminine point of view, was produced and scripted by Selznick. It was a big box-office hit and the only Cromwell movie to be nominated for the Best Picture Oscar, with further nominations going to Claudette Colbert, Jennifer Jones and Monty Woolley. A powerful women's prison drama for Warner Bros., *Caged* (1950), once again earned Oscar nominations for its two stars, Eleanor Parker and Hope Emerson. Finally, *The Racket* (1951) brought Cromwell's career full circle for he had both acted in and directed the stage version in 1928. In his early 60s, Cromwell returned to his first love, the theatre, and only directed one last film of note, a powerful 'exposé' of Hollywood stardom, loosely based on the career of Marilyn Monroe and scripted by Paddy Chayevsky – *The Goddess* (1958). Shortly before his death the director reappeared on the screen, playing small roles in two Robert Altman pictures, *Three Women* (1977) and *A Wedding* (1978).

Top: Douglas Fairbanks Jr (left) and Ronald Colman (right) engage in some good-natured rehearsal for a duel in *The Prisoner Of Zenda* (1937). Seated next to the camera, wearing a hat, is the great cinematographer James Wong Howe; standing on the other side of the camera, foreground, is director Cromwell.

Above: Leslie Howard and Bette Davis making *Of Human Bondage*. Miss Davis' portrayal of Somerset Maugham's amoral waitress established her as a star.

Left: Cromwell closed out his career as an actor once again for the distinguished director, Robert Altman. Here he offers spiritual ministrations to Lillian Gish in *A Wedding* (1978).

GEORGE CUKOR

Born New York City, 7 July 1899. **Died** 1983

Known primarily for his sensitive direction of his casts, especially of his actresses, George Cukor came to Hollywood via Broadway. His pictures presented a sophisticated blend of comedy and drama, were frequently adapted from plays or novels, and reflected his stage origins in the best sense. An intelligent interpretive director rather than an innovator, and devoted to his actors, he was nonetheless careful not to neglect the visual side of his pictures. A man of impeccable taste, he worked closely with many of the leading Hollywood technicians to ensure that his movies wore a suitably stylish look.

Cukor acquired the label of a 'woman's director' during the 30s – the peak decade for many of Hollywood's most glamorous and talented female stars, including Greta Garbo, Joan Crawford, Norma Shearer, Katharine Hepburn and Jean Harlow. Cukor directed them all and, although he disliked the label, it stuck to him even in later years when he went on to make a wider variety of pictures. Meanwhile, he moved from Paramount to RKO, then on to MGM which boasted the lion's share of top female stars. Late in his career he worked with Marilyn Monroe, Audrey Hepburn, Anouk Aimée and Maggie Smith, while Jacqueline Bisset and Candice Bergen starred in his last picture, *Rich And Famous* (1981) back at MGM. During his middle years, he, like many of the other 30s directors, was faced with the decline of the studio system. During the late 40s and early 50s, at a time when other directors were thinking of retirement, he met the challenge head-on, demonstrating his capacity to mature and develop. He turned to new scriptwriters (Garson Kanin and Ruth Gordon), new stars (Judy Holliday, Jack Lemmon, Aldo Ray), rediscovered an 'old' star (Judy Garland), a new genre – the musical – and new techniques, directing movies in colour and CinemaScope during the 50s with the help of a new, hand-picked team of collaborators.

Born in New York City, Cukor was attracted to the stage at an early age. He gained his first experience as a stage manager in Chicago and Rochester and did a little acting, too, before he emerged as one of the leading Broadway directors during the mid and late 20s. Hired as 'dialogue director' with the coming of sound, one of his first pictures was *All Quiet On The Western Front* (Universal, 1930) directed by Lewis Milestone. He then graduated to co-directing a number of film adaptations of stage plays for Paramount, of which the most interesting was a spoof of the Barrymore family, *The Royal Family Of Broadway* (1930) starring Fredric March. For his first solo effort, *Tarnished Lady* (1931), he was assigned to try and turn the studio's newest theatrical arrival, the flamboyant Tallulah Bankhead, into a movie star. But as he later pointed out, Miss Bankhead was 'a most exciting, brilliant actress on the stage whose quality of excitement never quite

worked on the screen'. Then a dispute with producer and co-director Ernst Lubitsch over *One Hour With You* (1931) led to Cukor's departure from Paramount. The movie itself – nominated for an Oscar as Best Picture – is a delight, and whatever the extent of Cukor's contribution, is very much to his credit. He was immediately hired by RKO, rejoining producer David Selznick who had encouraged him early in his film career. Cukor's first at RKO, with Selznick as executive producer, was a gem. *What Price Hollywood?* (1932 – similar to the later *A Star Is Born*) stands as one of the best pictures ever made about the movie colony, benefitting from a witty, intelligent (and Oscar-nominated) script by Adela Rogers St Johns. Here Cukor demonstrated his ability to make the most of his material, combining comedy with drama and location shooting with studio work, while eliciting wonderful performances from Lowell Sherman and

Constance Bennett (sister of Joan).

The following year, 1933, was a turning point for Cukor. *Dinner At Eight*, based on the play by George S. Kaufman, was a highly successful superstar production and Cukor's first at MGM, while *Little Women* marked the high point of his RKO years and his early collaboration with Katharine Hepburn (he had given Kate her first film role opposite John Barrymore in *A Bill Of Divorcement*, 1932). It was also the first of a new series of classic costume picture adaptations. With this screen version of Louisa May Alcott's perennial best-seller, Cukor demonstrated his characteristically tasteful approach to a classic piece of Americana. New England in the mid-19th century was effectively brought to life on the screen, while Miss Hepburn's tomboyish qualities were perfectly suited to the lead role of the independent-minded sister Jo. *Little Women* proved to be RKO's biggest box-office hit of the decade and was

Above: *Dinner At Eight* was George Cukor's first film for MGM. Glossy, witty and mordant, the film was serviced by a cast of superstars who responded superbly to their director. Among them, Billie Burke (left), as the society hostess who is giving the 'dinner at eight', greets Jean Harlow, the floozie wife of rough-diamond industrialist Wallace Beery (centre).

Below: On set during the filming of *Little Women* in 1933, Cukor talks to his star, Katharine Hepburn. Kate was ideally cast as the hoydenish – later loving wife – Jo, in this immensely successful adaptation of Louisa May Alcott's classic. The other three girls, Beth, Amy and Meg, were played by Jean Parker, Joan Bennett and Frances Dee.

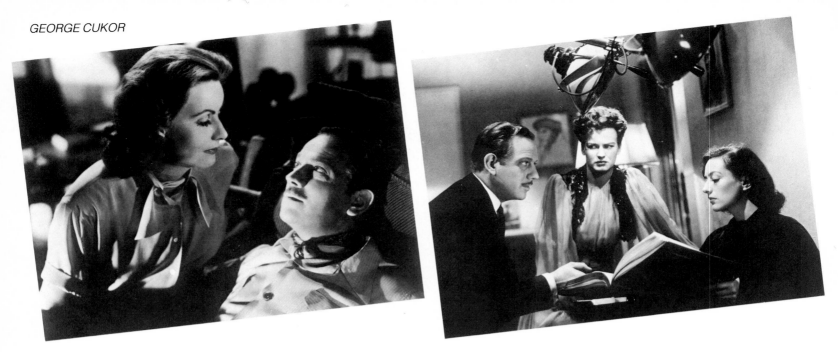

nominated for Best Picture, while Cukor received the first of his five Oscar nominations for his direction.

Continuing his collaboration with Selznick at MGM, Cukor next directed a likeable version of Charles Dickens' *David Copperfield* with a partly English cast, headed by young Freddie Bartholomew and Basil Rathbone, and with W.C. Fields as an unforgettable Micawber. A reasonably faithful (if sentimental) adaptation of the novel, the picture was a success and was nominated for a Best Picture Oscar (it lost out to MGM's *Mutiny On The Bounty*). The same, alas, could not be said for *Sylvia Scarlett* (1935), a decidedly off-beat (some would say risible) project for RKO starring Cary Grant and Edmund Gwenn as a pair of British con-men, with Katharine Hepburn in short hair and rather fetching masculine attire posing as Gwenn's son for much of the time.

Selznick left MGM to go independent in 1936, but Cukor was immediately taken up by producer Irving Thalberg who was just then embarking on two of his pet projects, for Norma Shearer (Mrs Thalberg) and Garbo, both prestigious costume adaptations which were among his last to reach the screen before his premature death later that year. These films marked the beginning of a remarkable cycle of women's pictures from Cukor at MGM during the years 1936 through 1942 when the studio was at its peak – a cycle which reflected the strengths and weaknesses of the studio and of Cukor as a director. Although MGM spared no expense in its $2 million production of *Romeo And Juliet*, the result was a tasteful and lavishly designed, but ultimately unsuccessful attempt to adapt Shakespeare to the screen. Norma Shearer and Leslie Howard played the leads with John Barrymore as Mercutio. *Camille*, on the other hand, proved the perfect vehicle for Garbo, who dominated the picture from beginning to end and gave perhaps her most sensitive and moving performance. (She won the New York Film Critics Award but, incredibly, lost the Oscar to Luise Rainer).

An all-star, all-female cast was assembled for MGM's *The Women* (1939) based on the Clare Booth Luce play. Offered as a consolation to Cukor after he

had been dismissed from Selznick's *Gone With The Wind*, the cast included four actresses who were among the original contenders for the role of Scarlett O'Hara – Paulette Goddard, Joan Crawford, Norma Shearer and Joan Fontaine. The ultimate 30s women's picture, it was also clearly bringing the end of an era. Cukor directed two movies with Joan Crawford as she was nearing the end of her long stay at MGM, and had the dubious distinction of directing the last, and least memorable, pictures of both Garbo and Shearer during 1941-42.

During this same period the director continued his long standing collaboration with Katharine Hepburn. She was teamed with Cary Grant in a delightful screwball comedy, *Holiday* (Columbia,

1938), and they came together again, joined by James Stewart, to star in the film version of another Philip Barry play, *The Philadelphia Story* (MGM, 1940). The model of a well-made movie in which all the pieces fall perhaps a bit too neatly into place, Miss Hepburn gave a delightful performance in a role which was specially written for her. Having played Tracy Lord on the stage to much acclaim, the part served as a perfect vehicle for her return to the screen. Stewart won an Oscar for his engaging performance as a reporter who becomes briefly involved with Hepburn. Although she and Cukor and the picture all received nominations, they failed to win. (Kate did win the New York Film Critics Award, however.)

The movies that Cukor subsequently

nominated for Best Picture, while Cukor

Above left: It fell to Cukor to direct Garbo's last film, *Two-Faced Woman* (1941). Here, she is pictured, as beautiful as ever, with co-star Melvyn Douglas but, alas, the film was extremely badly received and, some say, was the major factor in Garbo's decision to retire.

Above: Melvyn Douglas, Osa Massen (centre) and Joan Crawford in a scene from *A Woman's Face*. An out-and-out melodrama, the movie featured the glamorous Crawford as a scarred and embittered woman who turns to a life of crime.

Left: In 1938, Cukor directed the magic combination of Cary Grant and Katharine Hepburn in *Holiday* for Columbia. A highly successful screen version of a hit Broadway comedy by Philip Barry, it had been filmed in 1930 as an early and undistinguished talkie, with Robert Ames and Ann Harding, directed by Edward Griffith.

'I once said, my chief claim to fame will be that I once lost 72lbs and I fired Bette Davis.'

made during the 40s were less than his best. At a time when many leading directors were becoming independent producer-directors, and a new generation of writer-directors (Welles, Wilder, Huston) were first making their mark, Cukor was in danger of becoming a has-been. Thus, it was fortunate that when he returned, after a short wartime break, he was immediately able to develop a close working relationship with the script-writing husband-and-wife team of Garson Kanin and Ruth Gordon which extended over seven pictures during the years 1947-53. *A Double Life* (Universal, 1947) was a strong dramatic picture which featured an Oscar-winning performance from Ronald Colman as a mentally unbalanced actor, gave Shelley Winters her break, and earned Cukor his third Oscar nomination. But the high point of his collaboration with the Kanins came a couple of years later with a pair of

Left: At the age of 61, Cukor directed Marilyn Monroe and French star Yves Montand in *Let's Make Love*, a musical for 20th Century-Fox. He is seen here welcoming his stars to the sound stage. Although the director's magic touch with glamorous leading ladies was unimpaired, the film remains memorable only for Marilyn's rendition of 'My Heart Belongs To Daddy', and for the gossip that surrounded her and Montand, leading to ill-feeling from Mrs Montand, better known as Simone Signoret, and Arthur Miller, then married to Monroe.

The cost rose to a formidable $5 million, and in order to make sure of a profitable return, half-an-hour was cut from the three-hour running time. The picture was a success with critics and at the box-office, but Cukor was extremely bitter about the cuts, although he did return to work for Jack Warner ten years later on *My Fair Lady* (1964). Another extremely expensive production, filmed on elaborate studio sets, the picture was little more than a carefully recreated film version of the highly successful stage original, but with a miscast Audrey Hepburn subbing for Julie Andrews' 'Liza Doolittle. The picture actually lost money at the box-office in spite of winning the Best Picture Oscar, and Cukor, too, was finally awarded an Oscar for one of his least interesting productions. Ironically, Cukor's death in 1983 came a few days before he was due to attend a première of a newly reconstructed, full-length version of *A Star Is Born*.

Left: Cukor rehearsing the glorious but miscast Audrey Hepburn for the ballroom scene in *My Fair Lady*, an expensive but not madly successful screen version of the Lerner-Loewe musical. Although very flawed, it won the director an overdue Oscar.

Below: Still with an eye for feminine beauty and talent, a very old man of eighty-two is photographed with his last leading ladies. The remarkable Cukor directed Candice Bergen (left) and Jacqueline Bisset in *Rich And Famous* (1981), his final film for MGM and his own swan song.

classic comedies: *Adam's Rib* (MGM, 1949), in which Spencer Tracy and Katharine Hepburn played husband-and-wife lawyers who find themselves in court on opposing sides on a difficult case, was the best of the Tracy-Hepburn collaborations; while *Born Yesterday* (Columbia, 1950) about the educating of a 'dumb' blonde ex-chorus girl, brought the sublimely gifted Judy Holliday to screen stardom. Judy triumphed on the screen as she had on the stage, winning an Oscar, while Cukor gained yet another nomination, his fourth. Not only was Cukor dealing with contemporary American themes and characters in these pictures but, stylistically, he had broken away from the enclosed studio set-ups of

the 30s, and was increasingly to be found filming on location.

Late in 1953 Cukor was signed by Warner Bros. to direct Judy Garland in an expensive musical remake of the 1937 picture, *A Star Is Born*. For Miss Garland it was the biggest challenge of her career and drew on her qualities as both dramatic actress and singer, mixing light moments and comedy with the serious and even tragic. Cukor's patience and his well-known talent for handling difficult actresses was tested to the full by Judy's insecurities and unpredictability. The problems in filming were multiplied by the technical difficulties in shooting in the new CinemaScope process, and the picture was also Cukor's first in colour.

MICHAEL CURTIZ

Born Budapest, 24 December 1888. **Died** 1962

One of the best known of Hollywood 'characters', an obsessive film-maker and ruthless dictator on the set in the Cecil B. De Mille mold, Michael Curtiz's excesses and eccentricities have been well documented over the years. 'He strode about wearing breeches and riding boots and brandishing a fly whisk,' according to David Niven, and spoke broken English with a thick Hungarian accent. On location for filming *The Charge Of The Light Brigade* (1936) he yelled into a megaphone, 'Okay, bring on the empty horses', providing Niven with the title for his second volume of Hollywood reminiscences. Best known as a director of action and spectacle, he strove to make the scenes as realistic as possible. 'Nothing delighted him more than real bloodshed,' recalled Errol Flynn in his autobiography, while to Joan Blondell he was 'a cruel man with actors and animals'. And babies. Cameraman Hal Mohr caught him pinching a baby (on *A Million Bid*, 1927) to make it cry on cue, and parted company with Curtiz midway through filming *Noah's Ark* in 1928 for he objected to Curtiz needlessly risking the lives of hundreds of extras in the flood sequences. Yet he couldn't help but be impressed, for 'He had a great artistic instinct'. Curtiz proved to be the ideal contract director for the Warner Bros. studio where he remained for almost thirty years. He was a meticulous and efficient craftsman who brought a touch of 'class' to the typical studio product, yet managed to work, more or less, within the constraints of the tight Warner budgets. One of the studio's prestige productions of the late 30s, *Angels With Dirty Faces* (1938) cost only about $600,000 and was quite a success, earning both Curtiz and James Cagney their first Oscar nominations. Cagney won four years later for his performance in another Curtiz movie, *Yankee Doodle Dandy* (1942), while Curtiz himself won the following year for directing *Casablanca*.

These titles alone give some idea of the director's range. During the course of his long career he made every type of picture, and averaged a phenomenal four movies per year during his peak period at Warner Bros. (1929-44). Born Mihaly Kertész, he was active as an actor and director from 1912-18 in the early days of the Hungarian film industry, and went on to direct movies in Austria and other Western European countries during the 20s. His 1924 Austrian film, *Die Slavenkönigen (Moon Of Israel)*, impressed Jack Warner who brought him to the US in 1926. He soon became a staple fixture at the Warner studio. Dolores Costello starred in many of his movies during the late 20s including his first 'part-talkie', the epic *Noah's Ark*. Assigned to a variety of projects during the early 30s, and working with many different stars, including William Powell, Kay Francis, Joan Blondell and Bette Davis, Curtiz took it all in his stride. His pictures of note ranged from the musical, *Mammy* (1930), starring Al Jolson, to gangster movies (*20,000 Years In Sing Sing*, 1933, starring Spencer Tracy) to horror (*The Mystery Of The Wax Museum*, 1933, with Fay Wray and Lionel Atwill). His first with Cagney was the fast-paced *Jimmy The Gent* (1934), while Paul Muni starred in a typically tough Warner Bros. social drama, *Black Fury* (1935). Curtiz thrived on these projects, attacking each new one with ferocious skill and an apparently instinctive understanding of film technique, lighting, camera movement and editing.

The fortunes of Curtiz were closely tied to those of the studio. Warner Bros.' recovery from the Depression from 1935 led to a general upgrading of the studio's product and of Curtiz's assignments, beginning with *Captain Blood*. It was Jack Warner who decided to take a chance on a new young actor, Errol Flynn, in the lead role, with a 19-year-old Olivia de Havilland as his co-star. The Tasmanian-born Flynn fitted perfectly into the part of the English doctor who, through force of circumstances, becomes a pirate captain. The picture turned out well, Curtiz's first to be nominated for a Best Picture Oscar, while Flynn – to be typecast as the dashing and romantic hero of costume adventure pictures – became a star virtually over night. They were to make a dozen movies together in all, mostly prestige productions which fitted in with the 'new look' Warners. *Captain Blood* was followed by *The Charge Of The Light Brigade* (1936), which featured an astonishing action climax that fulfilled the promise of the picture's title. Although Flynn was nominally the co-star of *The Private Lives Of Elizabeth And Essex* (1939), Bette Davis effectively dominated throughout, while *The Sea Hawk* in 1940 brought the Flynn-Curtiz-Warner Bros. cycle of British historical pictures to a fittingly action-packed conclusion. But the undoubted high point of the cycle was *The Adventures Of Robin Hood* (1938), one of the studio's first and most accomplished ventures into Technicolor. Curtiz di-

Below left: The swashbuckling pirate-hero *Captain Blood* (Errol Flynn), takes time off for some suitably smouldering romance with a beautiful woman (Olivia de Havilland). The movie, made in 1936, was the first of an astonishingly successful and popular cycle of Curtiz-Flynn action romances which shot the dashing Errol to stardom and did no harm to his leading lady either. Certainly, the film secured Curtiz's position as one of Warner's leading contract directors.

Below: *The Private Lives Of Elizabeth And Essex* in 1939 continued Errol Flynn's run of costume dramas. However, as the ill-fated consort of Queen Elizabeth I of England, he was less at ease than usual and, not surprisingly, was acted off the screen by the formidable Bette Davis. For Curtiz, however, it was another creditable enterprise.

rected with great flair, having replaced co-director William Keighley, and was ably supported by a top production team who garnered three Oscars for their efforts. A witty script, and fine performances from a stellar cast, including Basil Rathbone, Claude Rains and Eugene Pallette, supported Flynn who was at his best and ensured that *Robin Hood* would be remembered as one of the great swashbucklers of all time.

1938 was a good year for Curtiz. *Robin Hood* was nominated for Best Picture, while Curtiz received two nominations – for directing *Angels With Dirty Faces* and *Four Daughters*, a sensitive and entertaining picture centring on the life of a New England family, starring Claude Rains, and, in one of his earliest roles, John Garfield. It was so successful that it spawned three sequels, two of them directed by Curtiz who, now in his 50s, showed no signs of slowing down. He directed Flynn in a number of Westerns and moved on to war-related themes during the early 40s. *Dive Bomber* (1941) was his last with Flynn, *Captain Of The Clouds* (1942) starred Cagney in a tribute to the RAF, followed by a pair of patriotic musicals – *Yankee Doodle Dandy* (1942) and Irving Berlin's *This Is The Army* (1943). But the surprise wartime success began life as a run-of-the-mill studio project, intended to star contract players

Ronald Reagan, Dennis Morgan and Ann Sheridan, working in an exotic overseas setting created on the back-lot by Carl Jules Weyl. The project took on a new life when, instead of Reagan, Humphrey Bogart was cast as a world-weary expatriate American who runs a bar in North Africa, and a genuine European flavour was injected into the film with the casting of Ingrid Bergman as the heroine torn between love and duty, and Paul Henreid as her husband. A perfect matching of actors and characters down to the smallest parts, a well constructed script which fused wartime propaganda with idealism and sentiment, atmospheric photography from Arthur Edeson and an evocative Max Steiner score were all married superbly by director Michael Curtiz to create *Casablanca*, a smash-hit at the box-office. This still popular and durable movie won the Best Picture

Oscar, while Curtiz was awarded the only director's Oscar of his career.

In 1945 Curtiz directed Joan Crawford in her Oscar-winning performance as *Mildred Pierce* (1945), was hired away from Warners for the first time to direct 20th Century-Fox's lavish production of *The Egyptian* (1954) in colour and CinemaScope, and ended his career in 1962 with a John Wayne Western, *The Comancheros*. But the main thread running through his later years was a musical one. From the sub-standard Cole Porter biopic, *Night And Day* (1946), starring Cary Grant, to a series of Doris Day musicals for Warners, he moved over to Paramount to direct the first ever VistaVision production, the highly popular *White Christmas* (1954), and even one of Elvis Presley's early vehicles, *King Creole* (1958). Although these were far from memorable, he remained active up to the very end.

Above: The Curtiz/Flynn period adventures came to a grand climax with *The Adventures Of Robin Hood* (1938). The script was crisp and entertaining, the cast was first-rate, and Errol himself had never been more appealingly heroic. But it was the expert use of Technicolor that really set the movie apart – viewed today, it still ravishes the eye.

Left: A famous scene from a famous film: Dooley Wilson (at piano), Humphrey Bogart and Ingrid Bergman in *Casablanca* (1943), the film which, more than deservedly, won director Curtiz his only Oscar. Viewed annually on TV by millions of people who weren't even born when the movie was made, the durability of *Casablanca* is arguably unsurpassed.

Below: Curtiz (right), looking every inch the European autocrat he was, photographed during filming of *Night And Day* (1946). His commanding presence couldn't save the movie, although the music was great. On the left, looking understandably pensive, is producer Arthur Schwartz.

'Curtiz turned out over a hundred films for Warner Bros. over the years. His English was notoriously bad, and obviously he couldn't say "No".'
Ronald Bergan in 'A to Z of Movie Directors'

ROY DEL RUTH

Born Philadelphia, 18 October 1895. **Died** 1961

One of the many directors who got their early start in the rough and tumble of two-reel silent comedy, Roy Del Ruth had an interesting if uneven, career in Hollywood. After some early experience as a journalist he entered the movies in 1915 as a gagman, then director, for Mack Sennett. Among the stars he directed were Ben Turpin (*Bright Eyes*, 1922) and Harry Langdon (*His New Mama*, 1924). Del Ruth was one of the first directors signed up by the newly expanding Warner Bros. studio in 1925. Here he continued to specialise in comedies starring the likes of Monte Blue and Louise Fazenda, and also directed Myrna Loy in a number of her early exotic roles, heavily made up to play half-castes or Orientals. Of special interest was his collaboration with an enterprising young scriptwriter named Darryl Zanuck, who was so prolific that he regularly adopted at least two different *noms de plumes*, Gregory Rogers and Mark Canfield.

The studio flourished during the late 20s with the introduction of sound. Young Zanuck rose to production manager, then production chief, and Del Ruth, too, was assigned to a number of major productions. During 1929 he first became identified with the movie musical when he directed the original sound version of *The Desert Song* – the screen's first all-talking, all-singing operetta starring John Boles – followed by a lavish two-colour Technicolor production, *Gold Diggers Of Broadway*, which proved a big success at the box-office. However, Del Ruth only clearly broke away from the stagebound conventions of the early talkies, and demonstrated his abilities as a director of sophisticated sound films for the first time, with *Three Faces East* (1930), in which Erich von Stroheim gave a compelling performance as a German spy. One of Warner Bros.' most professional and hard-working directors, he averaged five pictures per year from 1930 through 1933. An excellent adaptation of Dashiell Hammett's *The Maltese Falcon* in 1933 starred Ricardo Cortez. It was a memorable film for excellence in all departments, but has been somewhat un-

fairly eclipsed by the later, more famous John Huston version. James Cagney firmly established his now familiar fast-talking, wise-cracking screen persona in the group of pictures he made with Del Ruth shortly after the release of *Public Enemy* (1931), most notably in *Blonde Crazy* (1931), paired with Joan Blondell, and *Taxi* (1932). And Del Ruth directed the even faster-talking Lee Tracy as a gossip columnist in Tracy's best early movie, *Blessed Event* (1932).

Del Ruth left Warners in 1934 to direct Ronald Colman in *Bulldog Drummond Strikes Back* (1934) and a lively Chevalier musical, *Folies Bergère* (1935), for Zanuck's new 20th Century company, and an Eddie Cantor vehicle, *Kid Millions* (1934), for Sam Goldwyn (all three were distributed by United Artists). The latter was most notable for its musical fantasy final reel which featured the new, three-strip Technicolor.

Outsized props were the order of the day at MGM where Del Ruth established himself as a director of lavish musicals. Most spectacular of his creations there was the famous battleship finale of *Born To Dance* (1936), the best of his three films with dancer Eleanor Powell. During the following years he divided his

time between movies for ice-skating star Sonia Henie (at Zanuck's 20th Century-Fox) and Technicolored musicals like *Dubarry Was A Lady* (1943) and *Broadway Rhythm* (1944) at MGM, with the odd comedy thrown in. An attempt to set himself up as an independent producer-director after the war fizzled out, and he returned once again to Warner Bros. Unfortunately the mixture of Doris Day musicals and remakes were less than earthshaking, and he wound up his second Warners stint late in 1953 with a colour and 3-D horror remake, *Phantom Of The Rue Morgue*. By the late 50s he had sunk to directing B pictures. A horror flick, *The Alligator People* (20th Century-Fox, 1959) and a B thriller, *Why Must I Die?* (1960) starring Mrs Howard Hughes (Terry Moore), brought his once solid career to an undistinguished end.

Top: A scene from Warner's *The Gold Diggers Of Broadway*, one of Roy Del Ruth's early (1928) musical successes. Ann Pennington is dancing on the table, Nick Conway strums the guitar, Lilyan Tashman is seated with a glass of champagne, and Conrad Tearle is in the doorway, far left.

Above: Director Del Ruth discusses a point concerning the 'Rap Tap On Wood' number for *Born To Dance* (1936) with his star, Eleanor Powell (right). Looking on is Eleanor's mother.

Left: James Cagney with Noel Francis in *Blonde Crazy* (1931). The multi-talented Cagney belied his established psychopathic criminal screen persona with a sparkling comedy performance.

CECIL B. DeMILLE

Born Ashfield, Massachusetts, 12 August 1881. **Died** 1959

Cecil B. DeMille (the 'B' is for Blount) is known to audiences all over the world as the great showman of Hollywood, who directed spectacular Biblical epics like *Samson And Delilah* (1949) and *The Ten Commandments* (1923 and 1956). But perhaps less well understood is the very real contribution he made to the early American cinema.

The son of a playwrighting clergyman father, and a mother who ran a theatre company, the young Cecil studied at New York's Academy of Dramatic Arts, and made an acting debut on Broadway when he was nineteen years old. He spent several years acting for and managing his mother's company, as well as collaborating with his successful elder brother William in writing a number of plays, before turning to directing and producing. During these years, DeMille had worked with Jesse Lasky on a number of musical shows. When Lasky suggested that De Mille join him and former glove salesman Samuel Goldfish in starting a new motion picture company in 1913, he readily agreed, especially as he was broke, had a wife and young daughter to support, and the others were putting up the money. Thus, the Jesse L. Lasky Feature Play Company was born.

The partners immediately committed themselves to making feature-length pictures, and, in order to evade the Trust which controlled the motion picture industry, they sent Cecil West to shoot their first movie, a screen adaptation of the Western stage play, *The Squaw Man* (1913), starring Dustin Farnum and co-directed by Oscar Apfel who had had some previous film experience. Everything depended on the success of this first production – not only the money which they had scraped together to start the movie, but all the additional money owed to exhibitors which Goldfish, later known as Sam Goldwyn, had managed to raise to complete it. What had started out as an extremely risky and uncertain venture ended triumphantly, for *The Squaw Man* was a big success. Not only did it launch the careers of three men who were to become fixtures of the American film industry, but it had a wider significance, too, for it accelerated the trend toward feature-length productions and toward establishing California as the new home of American moviemaking. New buildings and roadways were added to the converted barn in Los Angeles which had served as their first, improvised studio and which now became the fully fledged 'Lasky Studio'. As DeMille himself recalled in his autobiography, 'Before the end of 1914 we had five directors and five cameramen at work and a stock company of eighty players. The barn was kept, though ... In December 1956 the old barn itself was officially dedicated as a 'registered landmark' by the California State Parks Commission and the Historical Landmarks Committee of Los Angeles County'. The barn had come to symbolize the beginnings of that crazy, magical place known as Hollywood.

Although other directors were employed by the company, DeMille was determined to maintain his position as the leading director, while also doubling as a supervising producer of movies which he did not direct. For his own pictures he lost no time assembling an outstanding group of collaborators. His brother William arrived, and soon developed into an excellent scriptwriter and director. Cecil's interest in the visual side of his pictures was reflected in the quality camerawork of Alvin Wyckoff, the costumes of Claire West and the production designs of Wilfred Buckland, whom De Mille had first known many years before as a leading designer in the theatre. Among the many innovations pioneered by DeMille in collaboration with Wyckoff and Buckland was the use of controlled interior lighting, so-called 'Lasky Lighting', combined with imaginatively designed sets and props. Lasky rightly referred to Buckland as 'the first bona fide art director in the industry'. The best early example of Buckland's artistic qualities is provided by *The Cheat* (1915), an atmospheric melodrama in which the lighting, sets and Oriental artefacts were used to heighten the story, which remains powerful and effective even when viewed today. (It was remade in 1923 and in 1931). A society woman (Fannie Ward) who borrows $10,000 from a rich Oriental (Sessue Hayakawa) is unable to pay him back, is branded by him, but shoots him in revenge. As this fast-paced social drama built to its courtroom climax, it demonstrated DeMille's new assurance.

That same year (1915) he embarked on a series of costume pictures starring Geraldine Farrar, the famous opera

singer, beginning with *Maria Rosa* and *Carmen* and culminating two years later with *Joan The Woman* (1916) and *The Woman God Forgot* (1919), both written by Jeanie Macpherson. *Joan* is remembered as DeMille's first big historical picture, and provided Buckland with the opportunity to design some of the most remarkable and elaborate sets yet seen in Hollywood. Less well known is *The Woman God Forgot*, a historical epic which featured sex, romance and religion – not necessarily in that order – exotic settings, scantily clad women, and a dramatic battle climax between the Spanish conquistadores and the native Aztec warriors. In short, this was the classic DeMille recipe, revealed on screen for the first time. The strong romantic

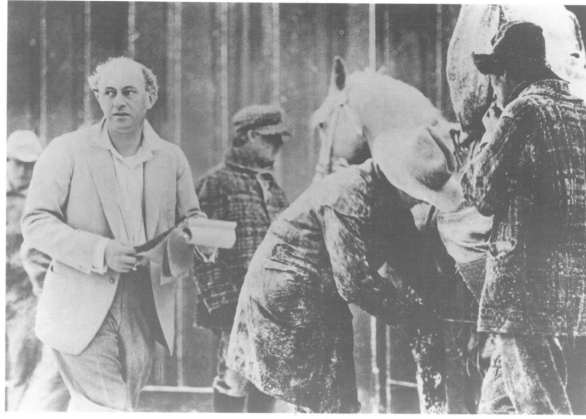

and sexual attraction between the princess and the soldier combined the sensual with the religious: 'I will become a Christian,' read the title, 'if I can be *your* Christian!'. The Aztec palace and temple settings were strikingly designed, again by Buckland, while the sarongs worn by the slave girls and handmaidens represented a first for Paramount eighteen years before the arrival of Dorothy Lamour, for the Lasky Company had by now merged with Zukor's Famous Players to form Paramount Pictures.

DeMille became more selective in his material during the post-World War I period, and averaged only two or three productions per year. Anticipating the flapper era and the freer moral climate of the 20s, he embarked on a new series of lightweight social comedies that satirised the pretensions of the *nouveau riche* and the upper classes generally. This allowed him to indulge the use of glossy settings,

'The result of all these stupendous efforts? Something roughly comparable to an eight-foot chorus girl, pretty well put together but much too big and much too flashy... What he has done is throw sex and sand into the moviegoers eyes for almost twice as long as anybody else has ever dared to.'

Review of *The Ten Commandments* in 'Time Magazine', 1956

and to dress the women in fabulous clothes, while at the same time making the moral points which appealed to him, as in *Male And Female* (1919), adapted from J.M. Barrie's play, 'The Admirable Crichton', and the best known of the series. His leading star of the period was the petite but legendarily glamorous Gloria Swanson, who had a distinct talent for comedy, while Elliott Dexter and Thomas Meighan alternated as her male co-stars. Costume episodes in flashback of 'historical visions' were often featured. According to Miss Swanson, 'He believed in reincarnation and tried to demonstrate it in these pageants... He actually believed that people had to come back to earth and suffer for the sins of their past lives'. For the Babylonian 'vision' in *Male And Female*, Gloria was required to appear on screen with a real lion, while two trainers armed with whips stood by. DeMille's filming of *The Ten Commandments* in 1923 represented a logical extension of this pattern. The Biblical prologue served to introduce the main story set in modern times. The cost of the picture escalated to a massive $1.5 million, making it one of the most expensive ever filmed up to that date and caused a dispute with Paramount boss

Adolph Zukor. A major portion of the budget was spent on the ancient story which required thousands of extras, and elaborate special effects, such as the parting of the Red Sea and the pursuit of Israelites by the Pharoah's chariots.

The picture proved to be a spectacular and profitable hit, but DeMille made his break with Paramount early in 1925 after another dispute with Zukor. He purchased the old Ince Studios and planned to release his films through the newly reorganised PDC (Producers' Distributing Corp.), serving as production head of the studio as well as continuing to direct his own projects. The enterprise soon ran into financial trouble for, although his initial productions were not successful, in 1926 he nonetheless embarked on his long cherished ambition to film *King Of Kings*. He had the unusual idea of opening the story with an orgy in progress at the palatial home of Mary Magdalene. But aside from this piece of sensationalism, the picture was painfully slow, dull and conventional in its treatment of the life of Christ. The cost soared to $2 million and, though the movie was moderately successful at the box-office, the losses were substantial. DeMille's independence was further threatened by the

studio's other financial difficulties, and by the industry upheaval created by the arrival of sound in 1928.

That same year he signed to direct three pictures for MGM. His first talkie, *Dynamite* (1929), was followed by his first (and last) attempt at a musical, *Madame Satan* (1930), which featured an extraordinary masked ball finale on board a Zeppelin. The bizarre costumes were credited to Adrian, while the imaginative sets were designed by future director Mitchell Leisen, DeMille's regular art director. DeMille finished off his MGM contract with yet another (his third) film version of *The Squaw Man* (1931). The failure of all three of his MGM movies meant that he was faced with the problem of establishing himself as a leading director of sound films. Given a fresh opportunity at Paramount in 1932, he immediately launched into the production of another cherished project, *The Sign Of The Cross*, hoping to demonstrate that he could work effectively within a relatively

Above: King of the epic Biblical spectacular, Cecil B. first attempted *The Ten Commandments* as a silent in 1923.

Left: Charles Laughton (left) as Nero, Claudette Colbert as Poppaea, and Fredric March as Marcus Superbus in *Sign Of The Cross* (1932).

Below: In 1934 DeMille (centre) brought his imagination to bear on *Cleopatra* with Warren William (left) as Caesar, and the lovely Parisian-born Claudette Colbert (right) in the title role. After her spate of *femme fatales*, Colbert went on to win an Oscar for Capra's *It Happened One Night*, and became one of Hollywood's most glamorous and sophisticated comediennes.

Right: DeMille bestrides his characteristic world like the colossus among showmen that he undoubtedly was.

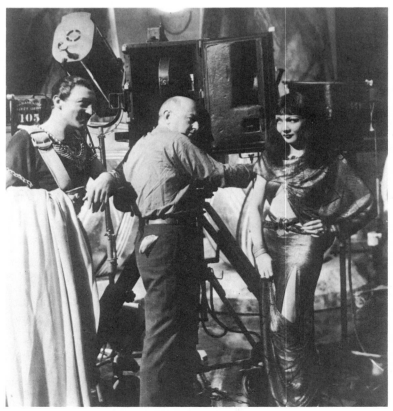

tight budget and with a new generation of stage-trained stars like Claudette Colbert, Fredric March and Charles Laughton. The picture's success meant that De Mille was able to resume his position at Paramount as a relatively independent producer-director, and he remained there for the rest of his career.

During the following years his costume epics gave way to a series of large-scale Westerns, most often starring Gary Cooper. The best of the cycle was the lively and colourful *Unconquered* (1947), in which Coop was paired with Paulette Goddard, DeMille's favourite 40s actress. Set during the pre-Revolutionary War period, the plot was full of unexpected twists and featured a classic pair of villains played by Howard da Silva and Boris Karloff. Unfortunately, in his late 30s Westerns, DeMille appeared overawed by the conventions of the genre, and by the myth of the West. His conventional treatment of his heroines meant that the decidedly *un*conventional Jean Arthur was wasted as Calamity Jane in *The Plainsman* (1936), ditto Barbara Stanwyck in *Union Pacific* (1939). The predictable plot lines further suggest that DeMille has been overrated as a storyteller.

ding DeMille and DeMille the showman is pointed up most clearly in his first film to be nominated for a Best Picture Oscar, *Cleopatra* (1934). Here the respectful, literary treatment of Caesar's story in the opening reels, not aided by Warren William's performance, is weak and unimaginative. But the picture comes to life in the second half with Claudette Colbert and Henry Wilcoxon (Antony) on Cleopatra's spectacular barge. Also nominated for a Best Picture Oscar was DeMille's last movie, *The Ten Commandments*. In spite of the pointed Cold War introduction narrated by DeMille himself and reflecting his own staunchly right-wing political views, the picture itself is extremely colourful and entertaining. The director who began his career in a converted barn was here able to avail himself of all the resources of the modern cinema – elaborate special effects, location filming in Egypt, Technicolor, and Paramount's superb widescreen VistaVision process. DeMille never won an Oscar for directing but was awarded a special honorary Oscar in 1949 and the Irving Thalberg Award in 1952.

Above: Two of Hollywood's possibly least talented but certainly most well-endowed stars, Victor Mature and Hedy Lamarr, portrayed *Samson And Delilah* (1949). Overblown hokum, but the destruction of the temple at the end was spectacular in the best Cecil B. tradition and the movie was a box-office success, although today it is hard to understand why.

Left: In 1956, DeMille returned to *The Ten Commandments*. Nominated for several Oscars, including that for Best Picture, the remake starred Charlton Heston (illustrated) and availed itself of all the advances Paramount had made by the mid-50s. It was a big hit, and the enormous supporting cast included stars (and non-stars) as disparate as Judith Anderson and Debra Paget, Yul Brynner and Cedric Hardwicke!

Below: Wheels turn full circle: a scene from Billy Wilder's cruel dissection of Hollywood, *Sunset Boulevard* (1950), in which aging movie queen Gloria Swanson (left) played Norma Desmond, an aging movie queen, and Cecil B. DeMille (right) appeared as himself.

Similarly, *The Greatest Show On Earth* (1952), the only DeMille production to win the Best Picture Oscar and earn him his sole directing nomination, was extremely unoriginal, and, dare one say, boring, in its overly respectful and clichéd treatment of the circus theme. De Mille's contribution to the war effort, *The Story Of Dr Wassell* (1944), starring Gary Cooper, suffers from similar short-comings and is only redeemed by a few notable action sequences.

The director was rather more successful as the master of sheer spectacle. His treatment of ancient times on the screen, from the flashback sequences in his 20s movies up to *Samson And Delilah* (1949) and *The Ten Commandments* (1956), both big box-office hits, demonstrate an instinctive flair which was not dimmed by age. The contrast between the dull, plod-

'He could always fool the public and he always knew it. He was one hundred per cent cynical. There wasn't a moment when he wasn't acting. He was so good a ham that he could sell anything.'

Adela Rogers St Johns in 'The Parade's Gone By' (Kevin Brownlow)

WILLIAM DIETERLE

Born Ludwigshafen, Germany, 15 July 1893 **Died** 1972

William Dieterle is best remembered for his work at Warner Bros. during the late 30s when Paul Muni won his Oscar for *The Story Of Louis Pasteur* (1936), the studio won its first Oscar for *The Life Of Emile Zola* (1937), and Dieterle himself received his only Oscar nomination. But he directed a wide variety of movies during his twenty five years in Hollywood and the best ones, like *The Last Flight* (1931), *The Hunchback Of Notre Dame* (1939), and *The Devil And Daniel Webster* (1941), were *not* biopics.

First attracted to the stage as a teenager, young Wilhelm (as he then was) served as a prop boy and played bit parts with a travelling theatre company in Germany. He joined the Max Reinhardt theatre in Berlin after World War I, but was increasingly in demand as a film actor. He appeared in such classic silent

pictures as Paul Leni's *Waxworks* (1924) and F.W. Murnau's *Faust* (1926). During the late 20s he both acted in and directed a dozen films, including an extraordinary drama about homosexual relationships in prison, *Geschlecht In Fesseln* (*Sex In Chains*, 1928), and his first historical biopic, *Ludwig II King Of Bavaria* (1929).

Invited to Hollywood to act in German language versions of American pictures like *Moby Dick* (1930), in which he played the John Barrymore role of Ahab, he soon acquired an anglicised first name, William, and a new status as a director. His first picture, *The Last Flight* (1931), was a remarkably assured and memorable tribute to the 'lost generation' of the postwar years. A Warner Bros. follow-up to the successful Howard Hawks film, *The Dawn Patrol* (1930), with the same star (Richard Barthelmess) and writer (John Monk Saunders), the superbly scripted story concerns four young American fliers who stay on in Paris after the war, together with a the scatty girl who tags along with them.

Dieterle was less fortunate in his following assignments which included the usual mixture of action movies (*The Devil's In Love*, 1933), domestic triangle drama (*Man Wanted* and *Jewel Robbery*, both 1932), and the occasional typical Warner social conscience picture like *Lawyer Man* (1932). Two Bette Davis vehicles, the musical, *Fashions Of 1934* and *Fog Over Frisco*, a thriller with a cult reputation for its incredibly fast-paced action, were followed by a first, forgettable, biopic, *Madame Du Barry*, starring Dolores Del Rio. In 1935, however, the studio began upgrading its product and he had the opportunity to work as co-director with his old mentor, Max Reinhardt, on a lavish and surprisingly successful adaptation of *A Midsummer Night's Dream*. The remarkable sets were designed by Anton Grot, while the Oscar-winning photography of Hal Mohr brought the fantasy forest alive on the screen, and a lively cast included James Cagney and Mickey Rooney.

Dieterle began his collaboration with Paul Muni on *Dr Socrates* (1935) and con-

tinued with one biopic per year up to *Juarez* (1938); he carried on with Edward G. Robinson in *Dr Ehrlich's Magic Bullet* and *A Despatch From Reuters* (both 1940), and finally concluded over at MGM with Van Heflin as *Tennessee Johnson* (1942), the vice-president who became President when Lincoln was shot. Far better than the biopics, however, were his two RKO productions, *The Hunchback Of Notre Dame* (1939) and *The Devil And Daniel Webster* (1941), both of which tapped Dieterle's talent for handling imaginative subjects with an element of the fantastic or even grotesque. It was this imaginative vein which Selznick recognised when he hired Dieterle to direct his wife, Jennifer Jones, in *Portrait Of Jennie* (1948), the kind of fantasy-romance so popular during the 40s.

As well as returning to film in Europe in later years, Dieterle made *Salome* (Columbia, 1953) with Rita Hayworth, while his last big budget effort for Paramount that same year was the distinctly unmemorable *Elephant Walk*. His career came full circle when he returned to shoot his Wagnerian biopic, *Magic Fire* (1956), on location in King Ludwig's castles in Bavaria. He retired in 1960.

Above: Director William Dieterle (centre left) lines up a shot of Dolores Del Rio (right) for *Madame Du Barry* (1934). Under the camera arc light is top cinematographer Sol Polito.

Left: Donald Woods (left) and Paul Muni (right) in *The Story Of Louis Pasteur* for which Muni won an Oscar. He and Dieterle are both forever remembered for their work on a better class of biopic.

Below: *Portrait Of Jennie* (1948) starred the beautiful Jennifer Jones (right) and Joseph Cotten (left). A bizarre fantasy about a girl who is really dead, it called out all Dieterle's expertise and earned much acclaim for its polished achievement, despite the absurd plot.

ALLAN DWAN

Born Toronto, 3 April 1885. **Died** 1981

The Canadian-born Allan Dwan was one of the most remarkable and durable figures associated with the early development of the American cinema. He made an astounding 400-plus movies, having first become involved in pictures by chance in 1909, after training as an electrical engineer. He was still at it half-a-century later, directing in CinemaScope and colour, and even turning his hand to television. During the very earliest years his methods of filming and choice of location were influenced by the need to keep one step ahead of the men from the Patents Trust and their hired thugs who took pot shots at the camera. 'We were forced to go into remote spots to work,' he recalled in a long interview with Peter Bogdanovich, 'and also to arm our cowboys and ourselves – we all wore sidearms. Our cowboys had loaded rifles and they stood sentry duty and watched for snipers while we worked.' Dwan's extraordinary early experiences directing Western one-reelers served as the basis for Bogdanovich's own feature, *Nickelodeon* (1976) starring Ryan O'Neal and Burt Reynolds.

When Dwan started out in pictures he was very much on his own. 'I'd pile everyone into two buckboards and off we went out into the country to make a picture. On the way out, I'd try to contrive something to do. I'd see a cliff . . . or a flume. It carried water from one ranch to another in the air like a great bridge . . . And I wrote something called *The Poisoned Flume* (1911).' Having filmed a struggle between the hero and villain on the cliff, the last scene of the picture, Dwan then worked backwards in the story to explain that the villain had been poisoning the flume. 'That was the typical way of making pictures in those days. All off the cuff.'

Characterised by his practical qualities, mechanical skills and sense of humour, he was able to turn out two one-reelers each week. Shooting Monday to Wednesday, he developed and edited the negatives on Thursday and Friday, then took the weekend off and began again on Monday. He went to see other people's pictures whenever he could and learned new techniques from the screen, particularly from D.W. Griffith, who impressed him the most with his use of back lighting, restrained acting and judicious close-ups. Moving on to the direction of short features during 1914-1915, Dwan joined Griffith's Triangle company for a time. He directed the Gish sisters and Norma Talmadge, and was responsible for devising the remarkable camera elevator on tracks for filming the giant Babylon set in *Intolerance* (1916). Most fruitful of all was his close collaboration with Douglas Fairbanks on a number of short features. *Robin Hood* (United Artists 1922) represented the culmination of their collaboration, the most remarkable Fairbanks costume feature of the 20s and one of the undoubted masterpieces of the silent era. Here Dwan proved equally adept at organising a costly and elaborate production, drawing on the talents of a remarkable team both in front of and behind the camera.

During the 20s Dwan worked for a time at Paramount's Astoria Studios on Long Island, glad to get away from the pressures of Hollywood. Here he gave a welcome boost to the career of Gloria Swanson whom he developed into a fine comedienne in such movies as *Zaza* (1923) and *Manhandled* (1924). After one last silent swashbuckler with Fairbanks, *The Iron Mask* (1929), Dwan easily made the transition to sound films, working

mainly at Fox where he directed Claire Trevor pictures, Shirley Temple vehicles and the Ritz Brothers. (A Comedy version of *The Three Musketeers*, 1939, with Don Ameche was a delight). He was even given a big budget for the Tyrone Power historical epic, *Suez* (1938), but mostly turned out superior comedies and Westerns on tiny budgets through the 40s and 50s. He continued directing until 1958, but his last big success was *Sands Of Iwo Jima* (1949) which was nominated for four Oscars, including the first for star John Wayne, and was the biggest box-office hit ever for the tiny Republic Studios.

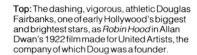

Top: The dashing, vigorous, athletic Douglas Fairbanks, one of early Hollywood's biggest and brightest stars, as *Robin Hood* in Allan Dwan's 1922 film made for United Artists, the company of which Doug was a founder.

Above: A portrait of Allan Dwan taken in the mid-20s.

Left: A scene from *Tennessee's Partner* (1955), starring future president, Ronald Reagan (centre left), here with Leo Gordon (centre) and Rhonda Fleming.

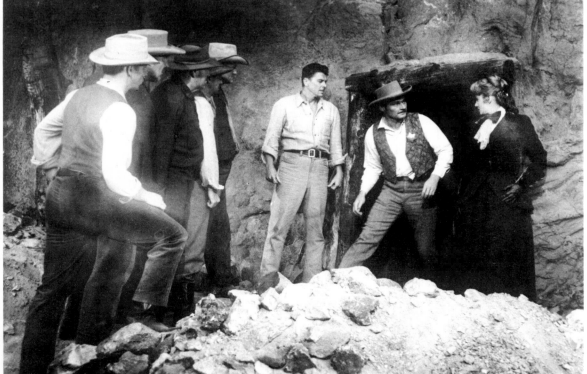

'I am a businessman. I have a commercial mind. A man can make the most artistic picture ever filmed, but if it plays to empty houses it hasn't achieved a thing for Art or for Humanity. The great problem of the pictures is the welding of art and business.'

1920

ROBERT FLAHERTY

Born Iron Mountain, Michigan, 16 February 1884. **Died** 1951

An almost legendary figure in the history of the cinema, Robert Flaherty is often referred to as the 'father of the documentary', mainly due to the astonishing success and impact of his remarkable first production, *Nanook Of The North* (1922). A charismatic figure in real life and by all accounts a spell-binding storyteller and raconteur, he was an instinctive film-maker and a true poet of the cinema, who both photographed and directed most of his pictures. He had a remarkable visual sense and sensitivity, and was characterised by his creative interpretation of the reality which he wished to present on the screen. He liked to concentrate on the experiences of a single family or one or two local people whom he virtually turned into actors, rather than attempting to present a scrupulously faithful record of the people and their customs as he found them. For this highly personal approach he has been criticised by documentary purists on the one hand, while on the other, his lack of discipline and inability to work from a pre-planned script meant that he was never able to adjust to the organisational demands of commercial film-making. His career is littered with projects which never got started or which he didn't complete.

Flaherty got his first taste of adventure as a youth travelling with his mining prospector father in the Hudson's Bay area of Canada. His interest in ethnic culture and life as an explorer led to his first attempts to record Eskimo life with a motion picture camera in 1913. Although this initial attempt was destroyed in a fire, he returned in 1920 with better equipment and the result was *Nanook*, a primitive, yet immensely moving work. The world-wide success of the picture led to an offer from Paramount to finance a similar venture in the South Seas. After months of immersing himself in the life of the Samoans, aided by Frances, his faithful wife and assistant, and his younger brother, David, he returned in 1925 with *Moana*. Filmed on the new panchromatic film stock which was sensitive to the subtleties and textures of the setting, it presented a lyrical record of the life of a Samoan boy and his family. The picture was more assured than *Nanook* technically, but lacked the latter's drama in reflecting an easier way of life. Paramount was disappointed, and this superb picture was ineptly marketed, failing at the box-office through no fault of the director.

During the following years he suffered many setbacks in his efforts to set up suitable projects, and he managed to complete only two more features and one long short of note during the following twenty five years. *Man Of Aran* (1934), filmed in the Aran Islands off the coast of Ireland, dramatised the struggle of the island's fishermen to wrest a livelihood from the sea. In *The Land* (1942), filmed in the US, Flaherty came closest to an undramatised observation – of the poverty-stricken migrant farm labourers in the American South and West. Finally, in *Louisiana Story* (1948) he followed the adventures

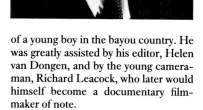

of a young boy in the bayou country. He was greatly assisted by his editor, Helen van Dongen, and by the young cameraman, Richard Leacock, who later would himself become a documentary film-maker of note.

It is ironical that the three major features on which Flaherty collaborated unsatisfactorily as co-director turned out successfully. *White Shadows In The South Seas*, co-directed by Woody Van Dyke, was quite an imaginative venture for MGM. With sound effects and music added, it was the studio's first sound film. Premiered in July 1928, audiences could hear the MGM lion roar for the first time ever, while the superb photography won an Oscar for Clyde de Vinna. *Tabu* (1932), co-directed by F.W. Murnau was a last, stunning masterpiece from the great German silent film director. More Murnau than Flaherty, the picture also won an Oscar for the atmospheric cinematography of Floyd Crosby. Finally,

Left: Robert Flaherty's most celebrated achievement will always be *Nanook Of The North*, made in 1922. In this rare still, Nanook is entertained (and bemused) by his first encounter with a gramophone.

Korda's *Elephant Boy* retained much of Flaherty's original footage shot in India and represented a more equal division between his work and that of co-director Zoltan Korda. A great popular success, the picture also introduced the world to Flaherty's discovery, the remarkable boy actor from India, Sabu.

Left: A portrait of Flaherty taken in the 30s.

Below: A scene from *Elephant Boy* (1937) featuring Sabu, the Indian boy actor whom Flaherty discovered, and who went on to achieve movie stardom.

VICTOR FLEMING

Born Pasadena, California, 23 February 1883. **Died** 1949

The way Allan Dwan tells it, he was looking for an expert mechanic to repair his car and was introduced to a young man who turned out to have some photographic equipment in his garage. 'How'd you like to go into the moving picture business and be a photographer?' Dwan asked. 'He joined us and became a very good friend of mine. He learned the camera very quickly and became an excellent cameraman. And then a fine director later.' The young man was Victor Fleming. He first made his name as part of the close-knit unit working on the early Fairbanks pictures during 1916-17 which included directors Dwan and John Emerson, and Anita ('Gentlemen Prefer Blondes') Loos who wrote many of the inventive and entertaining scripts.

After serving as a cameraman in the US Army Signal Corps and as President Wilson's personal cinematographer at the Versailles peace conference, Fleming returned to Hollywood after the war to find that his old friend, Douglas Fairbanks, was one of the founder partners of the new United Artists. Fleming photographed Doug's first for the new company, *His Majesty, The American* (1919), then graduated to directing the next two.

In 1922 Fleming was signed to a directing contract by Paramount where he remained for the rest of the decade, specialising mainly in outdoor action-adventure pictures and Westerns. *Mantrap* (1926) provides a good example of Fleming's strengths as a director. Clara Bow (with whom Fleming had an intense love affair), just emerging as one of the studio's leading stars, gave a lively and spirited performance in her characteristic role of a city-girl flapper; the plot led her to the wilds of Canada with predictable results, and the opportunity for effective location photography. This reflected the contribution of ace cinematographer James Wong Howe who particularly enjoyed working with Fleming. The director really made his name the following year with *The Way Of All Flesh*, the first American film of the celebrated German actor, Emil Jannings. Depicting the tragic events which befall an elderly bank clerk, the film was rather too obviously designed to capitalise on the success of the star's best-known German picture *The Last Laugh*, but was effective enough to win a Best Picture Oscar nomination, while Jannings received the first ever Best Actor award. Finally, Fleming closed out his Paramount years in style with his, and Gary Cooper's, first all-talkie, *The Virginian* (1929), which established the drawling Coop as a sound star.

Fleming arrived at MGM early in 1932. He enjoyed a big success with his second MGM picture, *Red Dust*, and was quickly accepted as one of the studio's leading contract directors. He remained with MGM for thirteen years, virtually the rest of his career, but was selective in his choice of titles. Working mainly with his few favourite stars – Gable, Tracy, Harlow – he averaged only one picture

per year. *Red Dust* matched Harlow's wise-cracking floozie with Gable's virile, yet romantic, tough guy for the very first time. The MGM backlot was converted into a reasonable facsimile of an Indo-Chinese rubber plantation, and Hal Rosson contributed some atmospheric photography. He became Fleming's favourite 30s cameraman (and was briefly married to Harlow). The picture,

based on an undistinguished play, displayed obvious weaknesses, but it came along at just the right time to boost the status of both its stars and of Fleming, who directed them both again, but separately. Harlow appeared in two comedies, *Bombshell* (1933), a bitingly satirical look at Hollywood stardom, and *Reckless* (1935), her only musical which suddenly turns serious in the second half. He made

'Don't be a damn fool, David. This picture is going to be one of the biggest white elephants of all time.'

To Selznick when offered a percentage instead of a salary for *Gone With The Wind*

four more movies with Gable who became a close personal friend.

Treasure Island (1934) was an MGM project appropriate to Fleming's talent for bringing adventure stories alive on the screen while drawing the best from his actors, and the genial but two-faced character of Long John Silver perfectly suited the talents of Wallace Beery. Then, in a rare loan-out to 20th Century-Fox, Fleming guided a young Henry Fonda through his first film role in *The Farmer Takes A Wife* (1935). In his autobiography, *Fonda, My Life*, the actor acknowledges his gratitude to Fleming for forcing him to tone down his performance and recognise the difference between stage and film acting (Fonda had previously played the same role in the theatre). The following year saw the first of Fleming's five movies with Spencer Tracy. *Captains Courageous* was another successful MGM-style adaptation of a classic adventure story (by Kipling), and Fleming managed to preserve some of the tougher and harsher qualities of the original while avoiding much of the sentimentality. Tracy won his first Oscar for his performance as Manuel, the Portuguese fisherman, while the picture was Fleming's second to be nominated for Best Picture, although he himself had never received a nomination.

In 1938 Fleming took to the air with his two actor friends, Gable and Tracy, who enjoyed working together, and Myrna Loy providing the love interest. A superior MGM star vehicle, *Test Pilot* occasionally slowed down to a crawl but was very well served by the aerial sequences and pieces of screwball comedy. The picture was Fleming's third to receive a Best Picture nomination.

Then, late in October, the director was confronted with the biggest challenge of his career when the studio selected him as a rather surprising choice to take over from the previous directors, Richard Thorpe and George Cukor, on the extremely expensive and troubled production of *The Wizard Of Oz*. The technical problems were immense, complicated by the fact that this was only MGM's second feature in Technicolor, requiring special cameras, additional lighting and particular care with the design and filming of sets and costumes. From Fleming's previous output it was not clear whether he possessed the qualities required by such a fantasy subject. But he met the challenge head on. He scrapped all existing footage, collaborated closely with the large production team to integrate music, dialogue and visuals, and dispensed the necessary lightness of touch. He worked closely with cameraman Hal Rosson to make the picture *move*, making liberal use of crane shots and a mobile camera in presenting the colourful Munchkinland setting, for example, yet was equally adept at developing the dramatic moments.

Above: Fleming moved into the really major league in 1938 when he took over as director on *The Wizard Of Oz*, the enchanting Technicolored screen version of Frank L. Baum's classic story. Judy Garland (above) became a major star with her performance as Dorothy and her immortal rendering of 'Over The Rainbow'. Dorothy's companions, The Cowardly Lion, The Tin Man and The Scarecrow, with whom she followed 'The Yellow Brick Road' to Oz, were played respectively by Bert Lahr, Jack Haley and Ray Bolger.

Left: After *The Wizard Of Oz*, Fleming's status was acknowledged by the studio assigning him to *Gone With The Wind*, the epic screen adaptation of Margaret Mitchell's epic Civil War romance novel. Once again, as with *Oz*, the director took over from George Cukor. Here, Fleming (right) and Clark Gable talk to Vivien Leigh on set.

If the success of *The Wizard Of Oz*, which made Judy Garland into a major star, suggested that Fleming at his best was more than simply a competent craftsman, director of action movies and of male stars, convincing proof was provided by his next assignment. In mid-February 1939 he was pulled off *The Wizard Of Oz*, shortly before the completion of principal photography, and placed in charge of David Selznick's lavish production of *Gone With The Wind*. Ironically, he again replaced Cukor but was, in fact, probably better equipped than Cukor to balance the intimate and spectacular elements of the film, while working more speedily and benefitting from his most recent experience with Technicolor filming. (He unwittingly continued to receive behind-the-scenes assistance from Cukor whom star Vivien Leigh secretly visited to work on the interpretation of her role). *Gone With The Wind* was a triumph for all concerned, earning Oscars for Fleming, Vivien Leigh and Best Picture, among others, although Gable had to be content with only a nomination for his fine performance as Rhett Butler.

Unfortunately, Fleming's subsequent career proved to be anti-climactic. He made three more films with Spencer Tracy, of which *Tortilla Flat* (1942) was the most interesting. *Dr Jekyll And Mr Hyde* (1941) has generally been compared unfavourably with the earlier Fredric March version, but it was not the fault of either Fleming or Tracy, since the scriptwriters substantially reduced the Jekyll side of the story, thus rendering the central struggle between good and evil far less convincing. Fleming directed one last MGM movie with Gable, *Adventure* (1945), and ended his career with an overblown and misconceived Technicolor epic for producer Walter Wanger, *Joan Of Arc* (RKO, 1949) starring Ingrid Bergman.

Above: *Gone With The Wind* was, and remains, one of the biggest box-office grossers in the history of the cinema. The role of Scarlett O'Hara, the wilful and wayward Southern belle, was certainly the most sought after role ever. Paulette Goddard and Bette Davis were among the eager stars considered and rejected before producer David Selznick – with filming already under way – cast an English actress named Vivien Leigh and made her an international name. It was a magic pairing with Gable's Rhett Butler. The pictures show Gable (top left); Leigh (below left); Leigh with Harry Davenport (the doctor) helping to tend a wounded soldier (top right) after the spectacular burning of Atlanta (bottom right).

Left: John Garfield (right), Hedy Lamarr and Spencer Tracy in *Tortilla Flat* (1942), from John Steinbeck's novel about Mexican half-breeds grappling with poverty in California.

ROBERT FLOREY

Born Paris, 14 September 1900. **Died** 1979

Frenchman Robert Florey fell in love with the movies as a child after watching the great pioneer George Méliès making his early fantasy films. Almost sixty years later Florey finished off his own, long, movie career directing episodes of *The Twilight Zone* and *The Outer Limits* for TV. During the intervening years he worked as a journalist, actor, writer and experimental film-maker, as well as assistant to many of the leading American directors before establishing himself as a director in Hollywood. A compulsive film-maker, he directed screen tests, second units and, especially, B-features during his peak years. When the movie offers dried up with the decline of the Bs, he turned to television and was one of the first directors to establish himself in this new medium.

Although he directed every type of pic-

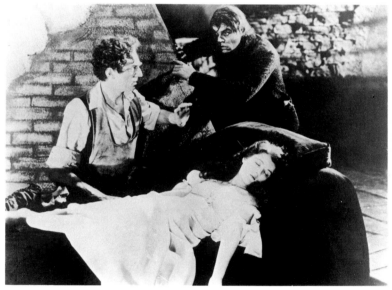

ture from comedies and musicals to gangster flicks and fantasy, Florey's name is most often associated with the classic black-and-white thriller and horror movies of the 30s and 40s. He gained his initial experience working on one-reelers in Switzerland, then became an assistant to the French director, Louis Feuillade. His activities as a journalist took him to Hollywood, where he combined writing about movies with work as a gagman on comedy two-reelers and as an assistant to Henry King, King Vidor and Frank Borzage among others. During 1927-28 he collaborated with Slavko Vorkapich on a number of experimental shorts including *The Life And Death Of 9413 – A Hollywood Extra*, which presented a wry comic variation on the theme of the downtrodden but hopeful employee, popularised at the time by the performances of Emil Jannings, and making use of an imaginative blend of trick effects and stylised photography and acting. Around this same time Florey established himself at Paramount's Astoria Studios on Long Island. Here he directed the first tests and sound movies of a distinguished group of stage stars including Fanny Brice (*Night Club*, 1928), and Edward G. Robinson and

Claudette Colbert (*The Hole In The Wall*, 1929). The most memorable of this group was the first Marx Bros movie, *The Cocoanuts* (1929, from their Broadway success). Florey succeeded admirably in overcoming the technical restrictions of early sound filming and provided some much-needed visual interest, even filming dance patterns from a high angle in a style later identified with Busby Berkeley. He even managed to keep up with the freewheeling Marxes. 'Luckily I had five cameras going at all times. If one or even two of the brothers went out of range I could always cut to a close-up. ...'.

Arriving at Universal in 1931, Florey played an important role in the studio's horror cycle. He did much of the preparation work on *Frankenstein* (1931) and was set to direct, but was replaced by James Whale and given *Murders In The Rue Morgue* (starring Bela Lugosi) instead. Although nominally based on the Edgar Allan Poe story, the film was strongly Expressionistic in style and derived its inspiration more from *The Cabinet Of Dr Caligari* (1919). Florey divided his time between Warner Bros. and Paramount during the rest of the 30s, working with many of the top stars (eg

Bette Davis, Barbara Stanwyck, Errol Flynn) in some of their least memorable pictures. The 40s found him directing a couple of As at Warner Bros. – a relatively lavish Technicolor remake of *The Desert Song* (1943) starring Dennis Morgan, and an unusual World War II drama, *God Is My Co-Pilot* (1945). He made an effective return to the horror genre with the film of a chilling story, *The Beast With Five Fingers* (1946), his most famous movie, lifted out of the B rut by a fine performance from Peter Lorre.

On a somewhat different tack, the director suffered some unfortunate studio interference at 20th Century-Fox in filming *Roger Touhy, Gangster* (1944) – a forerunner of the post-war trend toward a semi-documentary style of filming on authentic locations. A pair of thrillers in 1950 brought Florey's movie career to a close, but he soon made his mark in TV where he remained active for another dozen years, winning the first ever Directors Guild award for Television Direction in 1953 with his Four Star Playhouse production, *The Last Voyage*, starring Charles Boyer and Regis Toomey.

Above: Posing for the stills camera between takes of *The Cocoanuts* (1929) are, left to right: Ray Cozine (assistant director), co-director Joseph Santley, Zeppo Marx, Groucho, cameraman George Folsey, Chico, Harpo, and co-director Robert Florey.

Left: Bela Lugosi, Sidney Fox (foreground) and Noble Johnson in *Murders In The Rue Morgue* (1932), adapted from Edgar Allan Poe – but barely retaining any of its source material. Warner Bros. remade it as *Phantom Of The Rue Morgue* (1954).

Below: Florey was one of the first established Hollywood directors to move to television when his big screen career was in decline. He distinguished himself in the new medium, winning the first Directors Guild Award for *The Last Voyage* (1953). Here, assistant Robert Houser, and director Florey (in overcoat) line up a take featuring the two stars of the piece, Charles Boyer (left) and Regis Toomey.

JOHN FORD

Born Cape Elizabeth, Maine, 1 February 1895. **Died** 1973

Widely regarded as one of America's greatest directors, it is appropriate that John Ford got his start in that most American of genres, the Western. His career spanned over fifty years, from the mid-teens through the mid-60s, and encompassed a variety of pictures, although he will always be best known for his Westerns – classics such as *Stagecoach* (1939), *She Wore A Yellow Ribbon* (1949) and *The Searchers* (1956), and other American subjects, both historical (*Young Mr Lincoln*, 1939) and contemporary (*The Grapes Of Wrath*, 1940), and for a special interest in war pictures like *They Were Expendable* (1945).

Ford was only nineteen when he arrived in Hollywood to join his older brother Francis, who was already established as a writer-director-star of Western shorts and serials at Universal Studios. After serving a brief apprenticeship as a stuntman, bit part player, prop man and then assistant director to his brother, John graduated to directing early in 1917. On even his earliest Westerns at Universal, Ford and his star, Harry Carey, were left to their own devices, and wrote their own scripts, and the director developed a taste for making his pictures without any outside interference, which remained with him throughout his career. In later years, even on relatively large budget productions, he would not tolerate producers appearing on his set or interfering in any way. When Sam Goldwyn arrived on the set of *The Hurricane*, (1938), and requested Ford to shoot more close-ups of Dorothy Lamour, he was told off by Ford and ejected from the sound stage.

Quite early on Ford demonstrated his ingenuity at beating the system. When he and Carey wished to develop one of their pictures into a feature-length five-reeler, they simply ignored the objections of the studio executives and completed the film by scrounging extra film stock on the sly. The success of the picture, *Straight Shooting* (1917), meant that from then on they were allowed to turn out one five-reeler each month. An extremely accomplished work for a young director who had only been making pictures for about six months, *Straight Shooting* tells a *Shane*-like story about a gunman who joins up with the homesteaders in their range war against the cattlemen. Ford's off-beat sense of humour is evident from the first appearance of the star (Carey) who sticks his head out of a tree on which a reward notice for his capture has just been posted. The picture demonstrates Ford's ability to tell a story simply and directly, along with a sure visual sense reflecting a special talent for composition and the framing of shots. These early Westerns served as a good training ground for Ford since, as he himself stressed, 'they weren't shoot-'em-ups, they were character stories' which gave him the opportunity to work closely with his actors. Here, too, he acquired a taste for spontaneity of performance which later developed into a mastery of getting

the best from his actors in the very first take of a scene.

Ford's interest in the Western was related to a fascination with American history and tradition. During the course of his career he moved back in time to the Civil War era in *Young Mr Lincoln* (1939) and the Revolutionary War (*Drums Along The Mohawk*, 1939), and forward to contemporary America in the late 30s (*The Grapes Of Wrath*, 1940) and to World War II. Ford's *oeuvre* provides a remarkable panorama of almost 200 years of American history on the screen. Yet, born into an Irish immigrant family, his interest in Irish and British themes provides a second important thread running through his pictures from *The Prince Of Avenue A* (1920) and *The Shamrock Handicap* (1926) to *The Informer* (1935), and *The Quiet Man* (1952).

The director easily made the transition to non-Westerns. On loan-out to Fox in 1920 to direct *Just Pals*, he demonstrated a real feeling for the characters, and the small town setting which is viewed with great warmth and humour. The studio's executives were so impressed that they offered him an extremely favourable contract. This began an association which lasted for twenty years. For the first ten years Ford remained exclusively at Fox, combining Westerns (most often starring Tom Mix) with other types of pictures including an early John Gilbert movie, *Cameo Kirby* (1923), about a Mississippi riverboat gambler. Late in 1923 he was given the opportunity to direct *The Iron Horse*, Fox's answer to Paramount's extremely successful Western epic, *The Covered Wagon* (1923). In telling the story of the race to complete the transcontinental railroad, Ford naturally

shot the picture on location, though the hardships experienced by the cast and crew filming in Nevada in the winter of 1923-24 were similar to the actual events being depicted on screen. Ford introduced numerous classic Western themes and situations into the film, all kept well under control, and preserved a nice balance between the more personal story, following the experiences of the young hero (George O'Brien) and the larger historical events. In spite of the film's success, Ford was back directing more or less routine movies during the following years, although he was given one more opportunity of note in 1926 with *Three Bad Men*. Again the personal story was set against a broader landscape, climaxing in a spectacular land rush sequence. But the picture was not a hit and Ford turned his back on the Western, returning to smaller scale pictures like the extremely success-

Above: Four Sons was one of Ford's biggest early box-office successes, although it was a minor and sentimental film. The tale of a Bavarian mother who loses three of her four sons in World War I, it was cast entirely with unknown people, none of whom ever became any better known – Margaret Mann, Francis X. Bushman Jr, James Hall, Charles Morton and George Meeker.

Above: A formal portrait of John Ford taken during the 30s.

Left: English actress Margot Grahame (her American screen debut) and Victor McLaglen in Ford's renowned film version of Liam O'Flaherty's *The Informer* (1935). Bleak, powerful and dramatic, the picture won Oscars for Ford, McLaglen, Dudley Nichols (screenplay) and Max Steiner (music), and was nominated for Best Picture.

ful *Four Sons* (1928) set in Germany during World War I.

Ford's early sound career at Fox was relatively undistinguished, but in 1931 he was loaned to Sam Goldwyn for a prestigious production of *Arrowsmith*, based on the Sinclair Lewis novel and starring Ronald Colman. The picture restored Ford to the front rank of Hollywood directors and was his first to be nominated for a Best Picture Oscar. Although he was always most at home in a man's world, he was able to inject qualities of earthy good humour and tough resourcefulness into *Pilgrimage* (1933), which featured a convincingly gutsy performance from Henrietta Crosman as the mother whose son is killed in World War I, reprising the main theme of *Four Sons*. In three films starring the irrepressible Will Rogers, who was the top male star at Fox, Ford recognised, and took advantage of, his remarkable talent for ad-libbing. The results were remarkably fresh and frequently hilarious. *Judge Priest* (1934) is perhaps the best of the bunch.

The most famous of his 30s Irish movies, *The Informer* (RKO, 1935), based on the novel by Liam O'Flaherty, was not really one of the director's favourites although it won him his first directing Oscar along with the first ever New York Film Critics Awards for Best Picture and Director. A follow-up picture, *The Plough And The Stars* from Sean O'Casey's play, was less successful; ditto a prestige production of *Mary Of Scotland* starring Katharine Hepburn, both produced at RKO in 1936. But these proved merely temporary setbacks. Kipling's *Wee Willie Winkie* (1937), with the main character's sex suitably changed, was really a Western transplanted to India – an entertaining and popular vehicle for Shirley Temple and rather different from her usual pictures. Its success, along with *The Hurricane* (1938), firmly re-established Ford's commercial standing just as he was reaching his peak as a director. The films he completed during the three years from late 1938 through 1941 were unmatched by any other American director of the period.

Stagecoach, Ford's first Western for twelve years, had a strong literary slant, with the emphasis on character archetypes rather than action as a means of

appealing to a wider audience. The picture was a hit and the most honoured of his Westerns – the only one to be nominated for Best Picture and directing Oscars and winning Ford the New York Film Critics Award for the second time. Just as *The Iron Horse* had given added prestige to the silent Western, *Stagecoach*, and Ford's first Technicolor production, *Drums Along The Mohawk*, contributed immensely to the late 30s revival of the genre. *Stagecoach* marked the first of many occasions when Ford filmed in Monument Valley, a location which has become particularly identified with him, and was the first with John Wayne as the star. The highly entertaining *Drums Along The Mohawk*, starring Henry Fonda, has been unjustly neglected over the years, perhaps overshadowed by the director's better known films of this period and sandwiched between two outstanding works also starring Fonda – *Young Mr Lincoln*, one of Ford's best historical pictures, and *The Grapes Of Wrath* from Steinbeck's novel. This latter represented the outstanding culmination of his development during the 30s, combining his new assurance with his actors and his attraction to prestigious literary subjects, with a superb use of natural landscapes and settings atmospherically

brought to life on the screen by ace cinematographer Gregg Toland. A fine cast was headed by Fonda (Oscar-nominated for the first time), Jane Darwell (supporting actress Oscar) and John Carradine, while Ford won his second directing Oscar, a Best Picture nomination and his third New York Film Critics Award. The picture rather over-shadowed his second outstanding 1940 release, The *Long Voyage Home* (Wanger/UA), which earned him yet another Best Picture Oscar nomination. Here a group of

'I have never thought about what I was doing in terms of art, or "this is great", or "world-shaking", or anything like that. To me it was always a job of work – which I enjoyed immensely – and that's it.'

Left: Henry Fonda, John Carradine (centre) and John Qualen survey the devastation of farmland in Oklahoma which will lead the Joad family to join the gruelling trek to California in *The Grapes Of Wrath* (1940). Ford's screen version of Steinbeck's novel remains an undisputed masterpiece of the American cinema and, not surprisingly, gave the director one of his four Oscars.

Below Left: John Wayne (left), Donna Reed and Robert Montgomery in *They Were Expendable* (1945), a modest but effective film about life in the PT boats during the war in the Pacific.

Below: John Wayne with Claire Trevor in Ford's most famous – if not necessarily best – Western, *Stagecoach* (1939). Wayne's appearance as the Ringo Kid in this movie marked the turning point in his career and set him on the road to mythic stardom.

Left: Ten years on from *Stagecoach*, John Wayne played a cavalry officer in another memorable Ford Western, the Technicolored *She Wore A Yellow Ribbon* (1949). Here, on location are the star, the director (centre) and Ben Johnson (right).

Eugene O'Neill's one-act plays were effectively adapted for the screen by Dudley Nichols, Ford's favourite 30s scriptwriter, Finally, *How Green Was My Valley* (1941), Ford's last production before he left Hollywood for war service, won him Oscars for Best Picture and director. A solidly crafted and faithful adaptation of the novel by Richard Llewellyn, whose depiction of life in a Welsh coal mining village struck a sympathetic note with Ford – his warm and intimate treatment of family life was never more deeply felt.

Ford's contribution to the war effort included a pair of notable, Oscar-winning documentaries as well as *They Were Expendable* – a superior action picture for MGM, about the PT boats fighting in the Pacific, and starring Robert Montgomery and John Wayne. Once again Ford contributed to the upgrading of the western during the post-war years. *My Darling Clementine* (20th Century-Fox, 1946) starred an older and wiser Henry Fonda as sheriff Wyatt Earp; John Wayne demonstrated his new maturity as an actor in a series of four Ford Westerns during 1948-50. Most memorable was the Technicolored *She Wore A Yellow Ribbon* (1949), produced for his own new production company, Argosy Pictures. *Wagonmaster* (1950) represented Ford's definitive, personal tribute to the pioneers, an ensemble piece in which he deliberately avoided using big star names. Accepting the trend toward colour filming, he made effective use of Technicolor and locations in Ireland for *The Quiet Man* (1952, which brought his fourth Oscar), and in Africa for *Mogambo* (MGM, 1953). Then, in 1956, he took advantage of the superb new VistaVision process to film his last Western masterpiece, *The Searchers* (Warner Bros.). An

Left: *Wagonmaster* (1950) followed the adventures of a pioneers' wagon train journeying to Utah. Eschewing big star names, Ford's cast included Ward Bond (left), Ben Johnson (centre left), Joanne Dru (centre), Alan Mowbray (centre right), Ruth Clifford (right) and Francis Ford (far right).

Below: Another Best Director Oscar came John Ford's way for *The Quiet Man* (1952), a vigorous comedy set in rural Ireland and redolent of the Irish spirit. The stars were John Wayne in a guise very different from his Western heroes and Maureen O'Hara, both seen here with Barry Fitzgerald (left).

evocative picture, full of rich resonances which drew on Ford's great familiarity with and love for the genre and all it represents, it brought together many of his favourite themes – his mixed feelings about the hero (as personified by Wayne), his attitude to the pioneer family and way of life, and his respect for, yet revulsion towards the Indians. Stunning to look at, Ford's placement of his characters within the vast western landscapes was never more expressive.

Although he continued directing for another ten years, Ford had little more to offer. Such 60s efforts as the 'talky' and studio-bound *The Man Who Shot Liberty Valance* (1962) or the rather more elaborately mounted *Cheyenne Autumn* (1964), appear merely anti-climactic. Ford retired from feature films after one last, disappointing production, *Seven Women* (MGM, 1966).

SIDNEY FRANKLIN

Born San Francisco, 21 March 1893. **Died** 1972

Sidney Franklin spent most of his career as a director (and producer) at MGM. He was one of a group of directors recruited by the studio shortly after its first big successes in the mid-20s. Franklin, along with Clarence Brown, Robert Z. Leonard and Jack Conway, remained with MGM throughout the peak studio years of the 30s and 40s, each of them having accommodated himself to the fact that the stars came first at MGM and that the contract directors were virtually interchangeable. Yet Franklin's most famous and successful picture was not a typically glossy MGM star vehicle at all, but a harsh depiction of the life of Chinese peasants in *The Good Earth* (1937).

Franklin arrived in Los Angeles in 1913 and managed to land a few bit parts as an actor. He worked for a time as an assistant cameraman, then, in 1914, joined his older brother, Chester Franklin, to co-direct a series of one-reel children's comedies for D.W. Griffith. The brothers soon graduated to feature-length pictures and, when Chester was drafted into the army late in 1917, Sidney began directing on his own. His ability was recognised by producer Joseph Schenck who hired him to direct his actress wife, Norma Talmadge, and Thomas Meighan in a series of dramatic pictures in 1918. Franklin also directed producer-star Mary Pickford in the last of her pictures in 1919 just before she became a founder member of United Artists. One of the Pickford films, *Heart O' The Hills*, provided rising star John Gilbert with one of his first good roles. Continuing to develop and expand his range, Franklin directed Norma Talmadge in one last production in 1921, *Smilin' Through*. The dual lead in this romantic drama provided Miss Talmadge with one of the best opportunities of her career, and the picture was a box-office hit. It made Franklin's name, and he moved on

to direct Miss Talmadge's sister, Constance, in a number of romantic comedies including *Her Sister From Paris* (1925) in which she played twin sisters.

Franklin began his long association with MGM during 1926-27 with a pair of pictures starring Marion Davies. The second, *Quality Street* (1927), from the play by J.M. Barrie, co-starred Conrad Nagel. Miss Davies gave one of her most endearing performances as the spinster teacher who attempts to win back her long-lost officer suitor, who turns up ten years later, by pretending to be her own niece. It was scripted by Hans Kraly who worked on virtually all of Franklin's movies from 1925 through 1931. Formerly a writer for Ernst Lubitsch, he was succeeded by another European-born Lubitsch scripter, Ernest Vajda, during 1932-34. With his preference for adaptations of lightweight plays, often English or Continental in origin, Franklin clearly benefitted from this Lubitsch inheritance, while the 'English touch' was provided by his regular dialogue writer, the English-born Claudine West.

A clear stylistic and thematic continuity was provided by Franklin's writers and by those actresses who starred in his pictures. Thus, in the 30s the sophisticated Norma Shearer inherited the mantle of Norma Talmadge, even starring in the remake of *Smilin' Through*, while Greer Garson took over in the Franklin-produced, English-flavoured films of the 40s. Franklin's long and fruitful collaboration with Shearer and her producer husband, Irving Thalberg, at MGM included four other play adaptations of note beginning with *The Actress* (1928) from Pinero, continuing with *The Last Of Mrs Cheyney* (1929) from Lonsdale and *Private Lives* (1931) from Noel Coward, and concluding with *The Barretts Of Wimpole Street* (1934).

The director's intelligent and sensitive

film version of the Pearl Buck novel, *The Good Earth*, represented something of a departure for him. One of the most expensive MGM productions up to that date, it earned Franklin his only Oscar nomination. The picture itself was also nominated, while Oscars were awarded to star Luise Rainer and cinematographer Karl Freund. Unfortunately, the death of Thalberg in 1936 left Franklin without the back-up support which he felt he needed as a director, and he turned to producing instead. He enjoyed his greatest success as producer in 1942 when *Random Harvest* was nominated for Best Picture and the second of his Greer Garson productions, *Mrs Miniver*, won the top award and a number of other Oscars. Franklin, appropriately, received the Irving Thalberg producer's award that year. He continued producing throughout the 40s and early 50s and brought his career to an end when he directed one last picture, a weak remake of *The Barretts Of Wimpole Street*, in 1956.

Top: Marion Davies, the young director Sidney Franklin (centre), and assistant director Hugh Boswell – helping to keep Sidney upright on his roller-skates – during the making of *Quality Street* (1927). Miss Davies was the mistress of newspaper tycoon William Randolph Hearst who poured millions of dollars into promoting her career.

Above: Leslie Howard, looking rather odd in silver hair and moustache, with Norma Shearer (Mrs Irving Thalberg) in *Smilin' Through* (1932). An archetypal drama of mayhem and passion, this Franklin film was so well-made that it won a Best Picture nomination.

Left: Franklin received his only personal Oscar nomination for his screen version of *The Good Earth* (1937). Paul Muni (left) added an impressive Chinaman to his portfolio of international impersonations.

'Sidney Franklin was a good director – good producer, too. Too good; he over-emphasized goodness. He was beyond perfection in his work. He was a wonderful talent, and the closest friend I have in the picture business.'

Clarence Brown, 1965

TAY GARNETT

Born Los Angeles, 13 June 1894. **Died** 1977

In marked contrast to Sidney Franklin who enjoyed a safe and secure home at MGM, turning out glossy but tasteful entertainments for most of his career, Tay Garnett's film-making was characterised by unevenness and unpredictability. One of the few independent directors in Hollywood during the 30s and 40s, he bounced from one studio to another and made pictures for every one of the eight major companies. But his most sustained and productive period was at Franklin's studio, MGM, during the mid-40s. The link between them was Greer Garson: Franklin produced her films during 1942-43 and Garnett carried on directing her during 1944-45, but the high point of his MGM years was undoubtedly his stylish version of James M. Cain's study of lust and violence, *The Postman Always Rings Twice* (1945).

Another director who came to films from an engineering background, Garnett studied at MIT and became a flier during World War I. He got his start in the rough and tumble of the Sennett studio during the early 20s as a gagwriter then comedy scriptwriter. In the late 20s he moved on to the DeMille studio where he continued as a writer, then graduated to directing. His first picture of note was *Bad Company* for RKO Pathé. Garnett's personal and unusual entry in the early 30s gangster cycle, *Bad Company* concentrated on characters and relationships, presented with psychological insight rather than action or violence, while introducing some offbeat humour and expressionistic touches.

With *One Way Passage* (Warner Bros., 1932) Garnett was well-served by a cast headed by William Powell and Kay Francis. The stylish visuals and a flexible use of the camera helped to make this the first of the director's memorable cycle of 30s seagoing films. At Universal in 1932 he developed an extraordinary international project called *S.O.S. Iceberg*, starring Rod La Rocque and German actress-director Leni Riefenstahl, and filmed on the west coast of Greenland. When Garnett was hired by producer Irving Thalberg to direct *China Seas* (1935), with an all-star MGM cast (Wallace Beery, Clark Gable, Jean Harlow, Rosalind Russell) and a budget of over a million dollars, it was clear that he had made it to the front rank. Beery again headed an all-star cast in Garnett's *Slave Ship* (20th Century-Fox, 1937), another rousing sea adventure; for producer Walter Wanger in 1938, Garnett scripted – from his own experiences as a sailing enthusiast – *Trade Winds*. His sea cycle ended on a high note in 1940 at Universal with *Seven Sinners*, featuring a delightful performance from Marlene Dietrich at her most glamorous, as a South Seas siren who is enough to make any man (in this case, John Wayne) forget about the Navy.

Garnett arrived back at MGM in 1943 and made his contribution to the war effort with a pair of films both featuring an all-male cast. *Bataan* (1943) dealt with the war in the Philippines, starred Robert

Left: Tay Garnett's special expertise with seafaring adventure drama was acknowledged by Thalberg giving him a budget in excess of a million dollars to make *China Seas* (1935). The director was also given a prestige cast headed by Clark Gable (centre) and Wallace Beery (right). They are rehearsing a scene with little Carol Ann Beery, watched intently by Garnett (seated) and cameraman Ray June (standing left).

Taylor and offered plenty of battle action. Gene Kelly had his first dramatic role in *The Cross Of Lorraine* (1944), a well-crafted POW movie depicting the efforts of the French to carry on fighting the Germans even after defeat. Following two Greer Garson vehicles, both family dynasty sagas of the type popular during the 40s, Garnett got his big break with *The Postman Always Rings Twice*. The unlikely pairing of John Garfield with Lana Turner, the latter given one of her rare opportunities to prove that she could act, really struck sparks. The picture proved to be one of the most successful *films noirs* and Garnett's last memorable picture, although he continued directing for another twenty five years. His later work included a weak Technicolored musical version of *A Connecticut Yankee In King Arthur's Court* (Paramount, 1949) starring Bing Crosby, and a major contribution to the 1956 Cinerama production, *Seven Wonders Of The World*. Demonstrating his ability to roll with the

punches, when the film offers dried up he turned to TV, directing episodes for *Wagon Train*, *Naked City* and *Bonanza* until the 60s.

Above: Gregory Peck (seated), with Arthur Shields (left), Reginald Owen (standing centre) and Preston Foster (right) in *The Valley Of Decision* (1945), a dynastic romance in which an Irish housemaid marries the master's son. Not typical Garnett fare, and certainly a departure for Greer Garson who played the maid!

Left: Lana Turner and John Garfield in *The Postman Always Rings Twice* (1945), Garnett's best-known film and one of the finest of all the *films noirs* of the period.

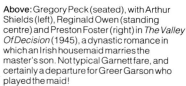

'It was a real chore to do Postman *under the Breen office, but I think I managed to get the sex across. I think I like doing it better that way. I'm not a voyeur, and I don't like all the body display you get in pictures nowadays. I think that's just a crutch for untalented directors and writers.'*
1964

EDMUND GOULDING

Born London, 20 March 1891. **Died** 1959

Cultivated and sensitive, and homosexual in an era when it was especially difficult to be so, Edmund Goulding was both highly and fondly regarded by most of those who worked with him and knew him well. He is best remembered for the four pictures he made with Bette Davis, who considered him 'one of the few all-time great directors of Hollywood', while Louise Brooks referred to him as 'this incomparable director who was also a successful actor, singer, songwriter, novelist, playwright and screenwriter'. In his book, 'Bring On The Empty Horses', David Niven recalled Eddie as 'eccentric but also a first-class director. Performers, male and female, loved to work with him because, an actor once himself, he understood their problems, tiptoed over their egos and above all, never made light of their built-in insecurities'. Although he directed Errol Flynn, David Niven and an all-male cast in an excellent remake of *The Dawn Patrol* (1938), and a pair of Tyrone Power pictures in the 40s, Goulding was best known as a director of women's pictures. The top stars who appeared for him over the course of thirty years ranged from Joan Crawford, Greta Garbo and Gloria Swanson, through Ginger Rogers, to Marilyn Monroe in one of her early roles.

Goulding began acting on the London stage as a teenager, then emigrated to the US after World War I. He established himself as an actor and writer in New York, then broke into films and was extremely active as a scriptwriter during the early 20s. Quickly adapting himself to American subjects, he scored a notable early success scripting the superb *Tol-'able David* (1921), a story of rural life in the South, and launched his career as a writer-director at MGM in 1925 with another film set in rural America, *Sun-Up*. In his next pictures Goulding established himself as an outstanding director of actresses, giving a big boost to the early career of Joan Crawford with *Sally, Irene And Mary* (1925) and *Paris* (1926), and directing Garbo (with John Gilbert) in one of the best of her early pictures, *Love*

(1927), a silent version of Tolstoy's 'Anna Karenina'.

With his strong theatre background, Goulding was well placed to take advantage of the arrival of sound. He was even regarded as something of an expert, having written an article on 'The Talkers In Close-Up' for the *National Board Of Review Magazine* in July 1928. That year he wrote the script for *Broadway Melody*, MGM's first big all-talking musical success; he was hired by Gloria Swanson to write and direct her first talkie, The *Trespasser* (UA, 1929), and was one of the directors who contributed to *Paramount On Parade* (1930). In 1932 he was brought back to MGM where he directed Marion Davies in the delightful *Blondie Of The Follies* and was given an all-star cast for *Grand Hotel*. In the eyes of David Niven this movie represented 'his greatest triumph in the realm of personality

Above: Stylish, elegant, English, Edmund Goulding in the 30s was reminiscent of Noel Coward in appearance. Here, he is photographed on set for *Grand Hotel*, directing a scene between Wallace Beery (centre) as the lecherous industrialist who has dishonorable designs on a luxury-loving stenographer (Joan Crawford, right). The film was doctored and remade as *Weekend At The Waldorf* in 1945, directed by Robert Z. Leonard with an enormous cast that included Ginger Rogers, Walter Pidgeon, Lana Turner and bandleader Xavier Cugat. Despite all that it is quite forgotten.

JESSICA'S GIRL

handling ... Goulding flattered, badgered, bullied or cajoled this spiky troupe (including Garbo, Beery, Crawford and John Barrymore) until it was individually and collectively eating out of his hand'. The movie was a big box-office hit and winner of the the Best Picture Oscar. The director's next, *Riptide* (1934) with Norma Shearer was not a success and he found himself at Warner Bros. during the late 30s. Here he directed *The Dawn Patrol* and the best of his Bette Davis movies, *Dark Victory* (1939).

Moving on to 20th Century-Fox during the 40s, Goulding directed Tyrone Power in an ambitious but not very successful adaptation of Maugham's *The Razor's Edge* (1946). An uncharacteristic and distinctly offbeat *noir* drama followed – *Nightmare Alley* (1947). Depicting the rise and fall of a small-time carnival operator and con-man, effectively portrayed by Power, the picture was also memorable for the atmospheric, low-keyed photography of Lee Garmes. Goulding then turned to comedy subjects during the early 50s and finished his career with a pair of weak CinemaScope productions – *Teenage Rebel* (1956) starring Ginger Rogers and *Mardi Gras* (1958) with Pat Boone.

Left: Bette Davis and Humphrey Bogart in *Dark Victory*, the best of four films that Goulding made with Davis. A melodramatic tearjerker about a society girl bravely facing premature death through illness, Davis' performance and the overall polish of the film lent it all an improbable conviction that works even today. A worn retread, *Stolen Hours*, made in 1963 with Susan Hayward, doesn't measure up and never did.

Below left: Basil Rathbone, David Niven (centre) and Errol Flynn (right) in *The Dawn Patrol* (1938). This remake of Howard Hawks' version of only eight years earlier, demonstrates the resilience of the uncompromising story of World War I flyers doomed to die. Goulding brought in a first-class film in all departments, and one that is still affecting to watch.

'The infant industry has taken the ribbons from her hair. She has put away some of her bright toys – she is growing up. She may have a child one day, and the child's name may be Television, but that's another story.'
1929

D.W. GRIFFITH

Born Crestwood, Kentucky, 22 January 1875. **Died** 1948

The tall, imposing figure of D.W. (David Wark) Griffith stands alone, dominating the landscape of the early American cinema. During the years from 1908 when he arrived at the Biograph Studios through 1920 when he had his last big hit with *Way Down East*, no single individual had so marked an effect on the development of the cinema both in the US and abroad as did Griffith. He directed over 400 shorts and 20 features during this period, pictures which were widely seen and imitated, and which influenced a whole generation of American directors. As an independent producer with his own company, he supervised the early productions of directors like Allan Dwan, Jack Conway, Sidney Franklin and Raoul Walsh. He gave a start in movies to many future directors including Erich von Stroheim, Tod Browning, W.S. 'Woody' Van Dyke and George Hill, among others, all of whom served as assistant directors on his epic production, *Intolerance* (1916). And John Ford's first movie experience was as one of the Klansmen riding to the rescue on horseback in the climax to *The Birth Of A Nation* (1914).

Although he tended to be aloof and formal in manner, Griffith had a good sense of humour and inspired great loyalty in his actors and associates, many of whom remained with him for many years, and he always encouraged his assistants to make suggestions. According to a young actor named Joseph Henabery, 'When anybody did something on their own initiative he would really enjoy it'. From his earliest days as a director Griffith benefitted from his talented collaborators, men like cameraman Billy Bitzer who was an essential part of his production team for sixteen years. Along the way they acquired an excellent young camera assistant, Karl Brown, who later developed into a cameraman and director himself, and a young script and titles writer named Anita Loos, while Walter Hall designed, and Frank Wortman constructed the amazing sets for *Intolerance*. During his peak years Griffith assembled an outstanding production team, from Bitzer at the top down to the lowliest of

assistants. And then there were the stars, especially that group of promising young actresses who all got their start in movies with him at the Biograph Studios – an impressive list headed by Mary Pickford and Lillian Gish, and including Dorothy Gish, Mabel Normand, Mae Marsh and Blanche Sweet. When Griffith left Biograph in 1913 he took all the members of his stock company with him and Biograph was finished.

There are interesting parallels between the careers of Griffith and De-Mille. Both were aspiring actor-playwrights attempting to break into the theatre during the early 1900s. DeMille was the more successful of the two and only turned to films late in 1913 around the very time that Griffith was going independent. Yet in the space of those five years, since Griffith had begun directing, he had completed well over 400 shorts (mainly one-reelers) and a short feature – surely one of the most sustained and amazing creative feats in the history of the cinema. When Griffith had first arrived at Biograph as an actor and writer who had failed to make much impression in the

legitimate theatre, he was a real neophyte who, as an actor, had wrestled with a stuffed eagle in Edwin S. Porter's *Rescued From An Eagle's Nest* (1907). Still hoping to establish himself in the theatre, he regarded the movies as an inferior medium and was only reluctantly persuaded to try his hand at directing. He immediately demonstrated a remarkable visual sense and a natural gift for film-making.

His pictures were so successful that he soon found himself directing or supervising the entire output of Biograph. By 1908 many of the basic techniques of the cinema – close-ups, cross-cutting, camera movement etc – had been discovered, but were still used in crude or unimaginative ways. Griffith's great contribution was his ability to draw on these techniques (and a few new ones, like back-lighting, first developed by Bitzer) and use them sparingly, for the fullest expressive and dramatic effect. In addition, he encouraged his actors to develop a new and subtler style of 'filmic' acting, different from that used on the stage, and found that he got the best results with young and relatively inexperienced players who had less to 'unlearn'. (Griffith never did manage to break away entirely from the theatre influence; for most of his career he continued to adhere to the 'frontal' view of characters and action and was never able to adapt his working methods to the modern technique of angle followed by reverse angle, cutting between two actors in a sequence.)

Griffith's Biograph shorts attracted larger audiences than ever before and, to many viewers, were a true revelation in demonstrating the artistic medium. 'D.W. Griffith influenced all of us', noted John Ford, 'He started it all ... Griffith was the one who made it an art.' Of special interest, too, was the remarkable diversity of the Biograph material. The shorts ranged from dramas, comedies, and adaptations from a wide variety of literary sources, to the occasional 'gangster picture', and many Westerns.

Above: The long, lean frame of David Wark Griffith poses for the camera. There can be no doubt that this picture was taken during location filming, although it is impossible to pinpoint the exact time and place. The postage stamps – legitimate US government issue – are both a tribute and a testimony to this great pioneer of cinema art.

Left: 'The leader of the whole business' as director Allan Dwan said of him, Griffith is seen here directing Henry Walthall in 1913. (The film is not identifiable.) On the left, operating his still primitive but effective camera, is Billy Bitzer, the pioneering cinematographer who was the first to develop back-lighting.

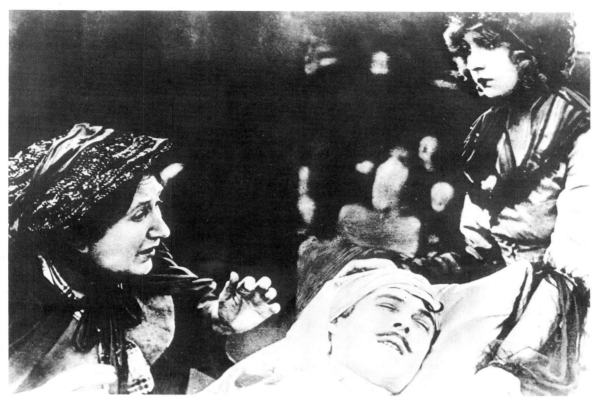

'At times his films may seem démodé, *out of fashion, but a hundred years from now, if they are still shown, people will realise that feeling transcends fashion, they'll see how strong and clear they are.'*

George Cukor

Left: Josephine Crowell, Henry B. Walthall and the young Lillian Gish in a scene from *The Birth Of A Nation* (1914), one of the director's most famous and ambitious films which made an immense, and sometimes inflammatory, impact on audiences. It topped the box-office records for a quarter-of-a-century until it was outstripped by *Gone With The Wind*.

Griffith appears to have had a special affection for this last genre, casting Mary Pickford as an Indian maiden in a number of shorts. *Song Of The Wild Wood Flute* (1910) is memorable for its striking landscape photography and a terrific cigarette-smoking Indian villain, while *Iola's Promise* (1912) features a superbly staged Indian attack on a wagon train. Griffith made excellent use of a wide variety of settings and from 1911 onwards spent part of each year filming in California, thus playing an important role in the establishment of Southern California as the new centre of American movie-making. By 1913 it was apparent that Griffith had gone about as far as he could within the one-reel format. He had directed his first two-reeler, *Enoch Arden*, in 1911 and a few others had followed including *The Battle Of Elderbush Gulch* (1913), another Western and one of the last of his Biograph productions. His fine staging of the action sequences, imaginative location photography and ingeniously complex plot gave some indication of what he could accomplish within the length of a feature. That year (1913) a number of European-made features, including the eight-reel Italian epic, *Quo Vadis?*, were screened in the US for the first time. Griffith was more determined than ever to work within the longer format and shot his first four-reeler, *Judith Of Bethulia*, in spite of the opposition of Biograph and shortly before his departure from the company. Although a Biblical epic which makes use of some impressive sets and large-scale crowd and battle scenes, the main emphasis is on the intimate moments, especially the love-hate relationship which develops between Judith (Blanche Sweet) and Holofernes (Henry B. Walthall).

When Griffith joined Reliance-Majestic late in 1913 as head of production, he immediately embarked on a series of feature-length productions to launch the new company. The most interesting of the group was an unusual fantasy-horror subject, *The Avenging Conscience*, based on Edgar Allan Poe's 'The Tell-Tale Heart'. A masterful and atmospheric psychological study, it represented yet another landmark in his early career, a notable forerunner of *The Cabinet Of Dr Caligari* (1919) and other psychological horror films. While directing or supervising other projects in 1914, Griffith was preparing to film by far his most ambitious production to date, a 12-reel (three-hour) adaptation of Thomas Dixon's novel, 'The Clansman'. Dealing with the American Civil War, and its aftermath as experienced by the South, the picture combined war and action sequences with historical reconstructions of such events as the burning of Atlanta, Lee's surrender to Grant and Lincoln's assassination by John Wilkes Booth (played by Raoul Walsh). It provided important roles for many of the leading members of Griffith's stock company including Lillian Gish, Mae Marsh and Henry Walthall. And it demonstrated once again the director's talent for blending intimate, personal stories and romance – the war as seen through the eyes of one family, the Camerons of Piedmont, South Carolina – with a broad, epic view of events on a scale never before attempted by any American director. At a cost of $110,000, a considerable sum at the time, the result was truly astonishing,

Below: This is designer Walter Hall's drawing of his set for the Babylonian sequences in *Intolerance* (1916). There has been little in the history of the movies – up to and including the present day with its modern technological resources – which has equalled these constructions for sheer scale and spectacle. The Babylonian episode was released in the US in 1919 as a separate feature called *The Fall Of Babylon*. The cast of *Intolerance* included Elmo Lincoln, who went on to become the screen's very first Tarzan in 1918.

both on the screen and at the box-office. Attempting a new style of publicity and promotion, and charging $2 per ticket, the film, newly retitled *The Birth Of A Nation*, shattered all box-office records at the time and for years to come. Twenty-five years later another Civil War subject, *Gone With The Wind*, matched it at the box-office, but the true extent of *The Birth Of A Nation*'s worldwide success can only be estimated, with a gross in the range of $15-60 million. The impact of the picture all over the world was immense and unprecedented and confirmed Griffith's position as the leading figure in the American cinema. But, at the same time, the film's strongly pro-Southern and anti-Negro bias, reflecting Griffith's own background (his father had distinguished himself fighting for the South) aroused a strong backlash from blacks and civil rights groups. President Wilson even referred to the film as 'writing history with lightning'.

This controversy may have played a part in determining the subject of his next production, *Intolerance*. Far exceeding *The Birth* in scope, it intercut different stories set in four separate eras of history as a means of lending the film a universal appeal. In fact, work began on the film even before the première of *The Birth Of A Nation* early in 1915. The first section to be filmed was a modern dramatic story about a young husband wrongfully accused of murder, and touching on a variety of contemporary social themes, with moving performances from two of Griffith's favourite actors, Robert Harron and Mae Marsh. It was followed by a costume drama set in 16th-century France, a Biblical story, and, finally, a story set in ancient Babylon. For this latter Walter Hall designed an amazing 140-foot high set decorated with a row of giant trumpeting elephants. For sheer spectacle, the Babylonian sequences of *Intolerance* have rarely been equalled on the screen. But for whatever reasons (one of which might have been Griffith's tendency to preach to his audiences) the film – amazingly – was not a success.

Intolerance is D.W. Griffith's undoubted masterpiece and marks the peak

of his career. Deeply in debt, never again was he able to work with a budget even approaching the $2 million mark. He enjoyed a moderate success with the war film, *Hearts Of The World* (1918), and with two excellent pictures starring Lillian Gish in 1919: *True Heart Susie*, a delightful and unpretentious story of country life, beautifully photographed on location, and *Broken Blossoms*, a more dramatic and tragic tale set in the Limehouse district of London, with the subtle and effective playing of the luminous Miss Gish ably supported by Richard Barthelmess. Early in 1919, Griffith had joined Chaplin, Pickford and Fairbanks as one of the founders of United Artists,

and later that year he built his own studio at Mamaroneck, New York. But his attempt to preserve his independence proved to be a losing battle. *Way Down East* in 1920 was a big hit, but from that point on his films failed to attract the necessary audiences. He made one talkie of note, *Abraham Lincoln* (1930) featuring a fine performance from Walter Huston, but *The Struggle* (1931) flopped badly and Griffith's directing career was at an end. Sadly, there was no place for him in a Hollywood dominated by the big studios. All but forgotten for the last eighteen years of his life, he was at least awarded an honorary Oscar in 1935, and is now widely recognised for his special genius.

Above left: The director, in suit, tie, waistcoat and hat as ever was, directing *Intolerance*. He holds a vast megaphone through which to communicate with his cast. The little boy on the left is Ben Alexander who went on to appear in *Hearts Of The World* (1918).

Above right: Robert Harron (left) and Walter Long in a dramatic moment from the 'modern' sequences in *Intolerance*.

Left: Lillian Gish and Robert Harron, co-starred in *True Heart Susie* (1919). The popular Bobby Harron was tragically killed, aged twenty-six, by an accidentally discharged firearm. The luminous Miss Gish continued to appear in films until the age of eighty-eight – a formidable and surely unique record. Although loved and revered to the present day for her quite extraordinary screen presence and acting ability, the major stardom which should have been hers proved elusive. Griffith once said of her: 'She is not only the best actress in her profession, but she has the best mind of any woman I have ever met'.

'He was a hypnotist with his girls. He had them so wrapped up and they believed so devoutly in him that whatever he asked them for, they'd do. And he himself was quite a ham, he had that big southern voice. He was a delightful guy, but very lonely, I think.'

Alan Dwan to Peter Bogdanovich in 'The Last Pioneer'

REX INGRAM

Born Dublin, 15 January 1893. **Died** 1950

Rex Ingram was the third of the Irish-born directors who rose to prominence during the early years of the American cinema (Sidney Olcott and Herbert Brenon were the others). A talented sketch artist and sculptor, Ingram's pictures demonstrated a fine pictorial sense and a marked ability with actors. Unfortunately, due to ill health, a running dispute with MGM, and the coming of sound, his career declined during the late 20s, ending when he was only thirty five years old. During his peak years, however, from 1920 to 1925, the quality of his productions stood comparison with those of any of the leading directors of the period.

Ingram was just over eighteen when he emigrated to the US. He studied sculpture at Yale before developing a special interest in the cinema. Then, in 1913, he landed a job at the Edison studios in New York as a scriptwriter, actor and designer, moving over to Vitagraph in mid-1914 and on to Fox in 1915. Although tall and handsome, he was not a very good actor and soon abandoned his efforts in favour of writing and directing. After almost three years of active apprenticeship, he got his first big break as a writer-director at Universal where he turned out a series of five-reel features during 1916-17, working with minor stars of the period such as Violet Mersereau, Cleo Madison and Wedgewood Nowell.

During 1918-19 Ingram experienced some personal problems. His first marriage was breaking up, he enlisted in the Royal Canadian Flying Corps but didn't see any war service, fell ill for a time, and returned to Universal to find that his services were no longer in demand, although he managed to complete two last pictures for the studio late in 1919 before moving to Metro. With a reputation as a 'crazy Irishman' and a hard taskmaster, Ingram had problems with the cameraman on his first Metro production which brought him close to disaster. With his sculptor's eye on the possibilities of using lighting for enhancement, Ingram now aspired to a new and stylish visual quality in his pictures. He persuaded production chief Maxwell Karger to let him make some tests with a new young cameraman, John Seitz. Seitz became Ingram's regular cameraman for the next six years and, together, they established the high visual standard which characterised all of Ingram's pictures during his peak years,

Ingram's directorial qualities as demonstrated in his first Metro productions had so impressed June Mathis, the head of the studio's script department, that she chose him to handle the prestige production of *The Four Horsemen Of The Apocalypse* in 1920. The cost of the picture escalated to $1 million as Ingram devoted all possible care, attention and new-found expertise to this project which represented the biggest opportunity of his career. Not only was the picture visually impressive, but Ingram also extracted fine performances from his relatively inexperienced lead couple,

Rudolph Valentino and Alice Terry. The movie was a phenomenal success and both Valentino and Terry became stars overnight. Ingram's name was made and, in 1922, he married Alice Terry.

Building on this success, the director turned out a number of stylish costume productions for Metro during the following years, including *The Prisoner Of Zenda* (1922) and *Scaramouche* (1923), both starring Ramon Novarro, another Ingram discovery who confirmed the director's reputation as a 'star maker'. When Metro merged into MGM in 1924, Ingram was bitterly disappointed at not being given *Ben-Hur* (1925) to direct, and attempted to preserve his independence by transferring his production unit

to Europe. He supervised the construction of his own Victorine Studios in Nice, and directed a masterful adaptation of the Ibañez novel, *Mare Nostrum* (1925) with yet another new star discovery, Antonio Moreno. The second of his Nice-based productions, *The Magician* (1926) from Somerset Maugham, reflected his attraction to the fantastic and bizarre and was a key work in the development of the horror film genre. *The Garden Of Allah* in 1927 was his last for MGM. One last silent followed before he prematurely retired from directing after his only talkie, *Baroud* (1932).

Left: Rex Ingram, himself a talented artist, demonstrates the correct use of the palette to Rudolph Valentino. The film in the making was *The Four Horsemen Of The Apocalypse* (1921), which turned out a huge success, bringing stardom to Valentino and fully establishing the director's credentials.

Left: Ramon Novarro, another star in the then fashionable 'Latin lover' mold, was also an Ingram discovery. Here, he is with the lovely Alice Terry in a 1923 Ingram film for Metro, *Where The Pavement Ends*. The previous year, Miss Terry had become Mrs Ingram in private life.

Below: Novarro in Ingram's version of Rafael Sabatini's swashbuckling novel, *Scaramouche* (1923). The film was very successfully remade with Stewart Granger, a bevy of beauties, and Technicolor, by MGM in 1952.

BUSTER KEATON

Born Piqua, Kansas, 4 October 1895. **Died** 1966

With his sad, expressive eyes peering out of a typically deadpan face, placed on an extraordinarily acrobatic body, Buster Keaton's comic persona, in contrast to the other well-known silent comics, was built on his unique genius for underplaying. Keaton was ahead of his time. During the 20s he was overshadowed by Chaplin and Harold Lloyd, yet it is Keaton's work that has best stood the test of time, and today he is widely regarded as the greatest comic film-maker of them all. Like Chaplin, Keaton began on the vaudeville stage at a young age, and was a highly skilled star performer by his early twenties when he first turned to films. Unlike Chaplin, however, who capitalized on his Tramp character for so long, Keaton opted for a somewhat more flexible and totally unsentimental approach – while preserving the same basic characteristics of his resourceful, unsmiling little man from film to film, he changed his inner character in accordance with the demands of each different picture. These ranged from the naive young hero of *Our Hospitality* (Metro, 1923) to the timid little projectionist of *Sherlock Jr* (Metro, 1924) and the dedicated Confederate engine driver of *The General* (UA, 1926). A performer whose versatility and acrobatic skills matched those of Chaplin, Keaton got his start in pictures as a supporting actor and then co-star with his friend, Fatty Arbuckle, who also wrote and directed their shorts during 1917-19. Immediately attracted to this new medium, Keaton endeavoured to learn everything he could about the film-making process. He only began directing and starring in his own shorts during the early 20s and by this time had gained an exceptional understanding of the medium.

From the very first, Keaton's pictures were characterised by a special attention to visual qualities and settings, and an interest in the kind of detail which could

only be captured on the screen. He was fascinated by all manner of things mechanical, as reflected in the ingenious and unconventional mechanized houses in *The Scarecrow* (1920) and *The Electric House* (1922). He had a special affection for trains, both ancient (*Our Hospitality*, Metro, 1923), and 1860s style (*The General*), and had great fun with boats in The *Boat* (1921). *The Love Nest* (1923) and his feature-length masterpiece, *The Navigator* (MGM, 1924). And although most of his pictures were set in contemporary times, he was equally at home in period dress and settings. Most important of all, in his many outstanding films

Keaton demonstrated his genius for integrating his performance within a fully realized cinematic milieu. Early on in his career Keaton assembled a fine creative team, including writer Clyde Bruckman, technical effects man Fred Gabourie and cameraman Elgin Lessley, who all worked closely with him for many years.

Late in 1919 Joseph Schenck, the producer of the Arbuckle shorts, gave Keaton the opportunity to begin directing his own two-reelers for release through Metro. When Keaton married Natalie Talmadge in 1921, he became Schenck's brother-in-law, for Schenck's movie star wife, Norma, was Natalie's

older sister. Schenck, in fact, continued to function as Keaton's producer for nine years, covering virtually his entire directorial career. Aside from one feature, *The Saphead* (1920), adapted from a popular play, Keaton spent the period from 1920 though 1923 directing and starring in an excellent series of two-reelers. Nicely varied in style and theme, these pictures provided him with an ideal opportunity to develop further as a film-maker. The best of these shorts are fully realized gems which stand up on their own, while often exploring themes to which he would later return and develop in his features. For example, in *Neighbors* (1920), young Buster's efforts to woo and win his girl in spite of the spirited opposition of their feuding parents, anticipates a similar situation in *Our Hospitality*. The picture also demonstrates Keaton's excellent visual sense, making ingenious use of a large, composite back yard set, linking the tenements where the characters live, in a manner similar to his use of the giant ocean liner 'set' in *The Navigator*. The

Top: Unusually, a straight portrait of the great Buster Keaton.

Above: *The Three Ages* (1923), parodying Griffith's *Intolerance* (1916), was the film which marked Keaton's transition from shorts to features. Here, he is seen in the caveman sequence with an appropriately agonised Margaret Leahy over his shoulder.

Left: Keaton's affinity with boats as a setting in which his resourceful heroes could function, was evident in his last two-reeler, *The Love Nest* (1923). In this scene he adopts a characteristically perilous stance in looking out to sea.

the final reels. If the 'solution' appears worse than the problem, he does in fact manage to win out in the end.

But undoubtedly the fullest and most satisfying use of this plot structure occurs in Keaton's masterpiece, *The General*. In the first half the courageous little Confederate engineer refuses to admit defeat and follows his stolen train north. The turning point comes when he overhears the Yankee battle plans and thus is able to ensure a Confederate victory as well as recapture his train and rescue the girl. Superb stunt work, location photography and the full scale staging of a battle make this the most elaborate and remarkable of all his features. Here Keaton succeeds in blending an intimate story with large scale, historical events in a manner which matches the very best of 'serious' pictures. Yet it is extremely funny as well.

'What a raw deal they gave poor Buster. When his wife divorced him, Joe Schenck made sure that he didn't own his films, so he could never resell them. He didn't have a cent... Poor little Buster with his three thousand dollars-a-week, trying to live like a millionaire. It was impossible. So they broke him.'

Louise Brooks in 'The Parade's Gone By' (Kevin Brownlow)

destruction of the house in *One Week* (1920), his first short masterpiece, represents a miniature version of the cyclone's destruction of the town in *Steamboat Bill Jr* (UA, 1927). Keaton also welcomed the opportunity to introduce dream or fantasy sequences into shorts like *The Playhouse* (1921) and *Daydreams* (1922), a theme which is given its ultimate expression in the later *Sherlock Jr*.

He made the transition from shorts to features in 1923 with *The Three Ages*, inter-cutting three parallel stories set in three different eras of history, a comic send-up of Griffith's *Intolerance*. This was followed by *Our Hospitality*, a true piece of Americana which featured a delightful journey on an 1830's railway and succeeded admirably in capturing the period atmosphere. A real 'family' picture for Keaton, it included a supporting role for his vaudevillian father, while the heroine, whom Buster rescues from a dangerous waterfall in one of his most spectacular stunts, was played by his wife, Natalie. This was the first of that remarkable and varied group of features which he directed during the mid-20s (from 1923 through 1927). Even the weakest of them have much to offer. Thus, *Go West* (MGM, 1925) is redeemed by an almost surrealistic chase climax in which Buster, dressed in a devil's costume, complete with tail, is pursued through the streets of downtown Los Angeles by a herd of longhorn cattle; while *College* (UA, 1927) gave him an opportunity to demonstrate his graceful athleticism. *Sherlock Jr* is justly celebrated for its film-within-a-film, dreamlike jump-cutting, and for its inter-weaving of reality and fantasy.

In many of his features, Keaton developed a linear plot structure with each event leading on logically to the next one. The turning point which occurs about midway gives the picture a nicely symmetrical shape and reflects the progress of his dedicated hero: in the first half he has been carried ever deeper into a situation over which he has lost control, while in the second half he gradually wins out over adversity and generally gets the girl as well. In *Our Hospitality* the turning point comes when the unwitting hero realizes for the first time that he is caught in the middle of a family feud and is then forced to work out a solution. In The *Navigator* Buster's singleminded pursuit of his girl has landed them both helplessly

adrift on the ocean in a giant liner, the little man confronted by a hostile environment – a typically Keatonesque theme. He proves his versatility and ingenuity when he manages to bring the ship under control, and even foil some bloodthirsty savages. In order to gain his inheritance in *Seven Chances* (MGM, 1925), Buster has to get married immediately. He proposes to a variety of women, including his own girl, all of whom turn him down. But everything changes (in the second half) after he places an advert in the paper: 'Wanted a Bride. Prominent Young Broker Falls Heir to $7 Million if he Marries by 7 Today.' The response is phenomenal. When hundreds of women wearing bridal veils begin arriving at the church, he is forced to flee for his life. The picture then develops into one of the most extended and inventive chase sequences of all time, occupying much of

Above left: In *Sherlock Jr* (1924), one of his most celebrated exercises in interweaving fantasy and reality.

Left: Catastrophically marooned in mid-ocean on a deserted liner in *The Navigator* (1924). The object of his affections is Kathryn McGuire. Never was Buster's talent for physically adroit sight-gags put to richer use.

Below: Watched by a bunch of sceptical onlookers, Buster proposes to one of a number of women in a desperate attempt to marry in time to inherit a fortune. The film was *Seven Chances* (1925), one of the director-comedian's best.

was also accounted for by the movement toward a greater concentration of power in a small number of giant studios. He was only one of a number of film-makers who lost their independence or retired around this time.

Ironically, although Keaton was allowed less creative freedom at MGM during 1928-32 and the costs of his pictures were more strictly controlled, they were more successful at the box-office than any of his silent masterpieces. Although his first two MGM pictures, *The Cameraman* (1928) and *Spite Marriage* (1929) could compare reasonably with his silents, his subsequent artistic decline was rapid, and by 1932 his career as a major star was reaching its end. His marriage, too, had deteriorated badly, ending in divorce in 1932, and a by now severe drinking problem led him to a spell in a

'You see, I'm the guy that made a picture called The Playhouse. *I played all the parts. With double exposures, I'm the whole orchestra. I'm the people in the boxes, in the audience, on the stage. . . . So on the credit titles we put the cast of characters. They're all Keaton. I was deliberately kidding most of the guys in motion pictures, especially a guy by the name of Ince.'*

His comic gags were never more smoothly and inventively worked into a feature length story, based on a true incident which took place during the American Civil War. The first of Keaton's films for United Artists, *The General* was, alas, only moderately successful at the box office and, ironically, marked the beginning of the end for Keaton the film-maker.

Having started at Metro, Keaton had become an MGM star when Metro was absorbed into the new studio in 1924. Then when his producer, Joseph Schenck, joined UA in 1925, Keaton followed and his UA pictures during 1926-27 included two of his best, *The General* and *Steamboat Bill Jr.* Schenck has been blamed for convincing Keaton to rejoin MGM in 1928, a decision which Keaton himself has called, 'the biggest mistake of my life', for it forced him to relinquish total control over his pictures. His departure from UA, however, was merely part of a complete reorganisation of the tiny and unprofitable, though prestigious company, which then recorded the first solid profit in its history in 1928. Keaton's UA pictures had *not* been profitable. Throughout his career, the box-office success of his films was determined more by the distributor handling them than by the quality of the films themselves. UA was particularly weak in this respect, and Keaton has claimed that they badly bungled the release of *Steamboat Bill Jr*, the first of his features to actually lose money. The UA situation was

further complicated by the fact that this film and *The General* had been his most expensive to produce. His most successful had been those handled by MGM during 1924-26, headed by *Battling Butler* (1926) and *The Navigator*. In fact, 1925 was clearly the peak year for silent comedy and included the top hits ever for both Chaplin (*The Gold Rush*) and Harold Lloyd (*The Freshman*). The fact that Keaton's masterpiece, *The General*, did only moderate business (released in December, 1926), while Lloyd's superb feature, *The Kid Brother*, released early in 1927 fell far short of *The Freshman* and even failed to match the success of many of his earlier features, suggests that the popularity of the silent film comedy had begun to wane even before the arrival of sound. Keaton's loss of independence

psychiatric clinic. After a short break during the mid-30s, ill and short of money, he returned to starring in a series of comedy shorts and then found regular employment as a bit part player in Hollywood pictures up to the end of his life. It was a sad decline for a man who was one of the greatest comedy talents in the history of the cinema. (A weak biopic, *The Buster Keaton Story*, was filmed by Paramount in 1957). Fortunately, he lived long enough to see his early pictures rediscovered and hailed as masterpieces during the 60s – he was awarded an honorary Oscar in April 1960 and, for a personal appearance at the Venice Film Festival in 1965, received the biggest and most prolonged ovation of any artist there before or since. Some months later, Buster Keaton died of cancer.

Above: If any proof were needed of Keaton's world-wide appeal, it is amply demonstrated by the Russian poster advertising *The General*. The film, released in 1926, was the comedian's first feature for United Artists and, although since regarded as one of his finest works, it failed to set the box-office alight at the time and was instrumental in his decline.

Left: A scene from Charlie Chaplin's *Limelight* (1952). Chaplin (right) wrote and directed the film, composed the well-known theme music – for which he won an Academy Award – and starred as a broken-down music hall comedian. The movie is widely felt to be highly sentimental and egotistically self-indulgent, demonstrating some of Chaplin's worst excesses. Keaton, however, was superb. So much so, that Chaplin attempted to eliminate unfavourable comparison by keeping Buster's cameo as tiny as possible. However, *Limelight* saw the beginning of Buster's resurrection as a revered figure. This resulted in the making of the rather feeble biopic of his life, the fee for which finally brought him financial stability.

HENRY KING

Born Christiansburg, Virginia, 24 June 1888. **Died** 1982

One of the most solid and dependable of American directors, Henry King first broke into films in 1912 and enjoyed a rich and varied career spanning fifty years, over thirty of them spent at one studio, Fox (later 20th Century-Fox). Having begun as an actor, then director during the teens, he functioned as an independent producer-director through much of the 20s, then moved on to Fox in the 30s where he was one of the first to work extensively in colour, then CinemaScope, the wide-screen process promoted by Fox during the 50s. Like all the best contract directors, he was extremely versatile and dealt with a wide variety of subjects, but he harboured a special affection for American rural subjects and small town settings which he returned to periodically throughout his career. Inevitably, his fortunes were tied to those of his studio, Fox, and its stars. A fine and sympathetic director of actors, he worked with Janet Gaynor and Will Rogers, the studio's two leading stars during the early 30s, Alice Faye and Jennifer Jones a few years later, Gregory Peck and Susan Hayward in the 50s. But his longest and closest working relationship was with Tyrone Power. They made eleven films together over twenty or so years, beginning with *Lloyds Of London* (1936) which provided Power with his first starring role and concluding with one of the handsome and popular star's last, *The Sun Also Rises*, in 1957.

First attracted to the theatre as a young man, King spent three-and-a-half years gaining valuable experience in touring stock companies before turning to the movies in 1912. A director from 1915, he had his first big success in 1919 with *23½ Hours Leave* starring Douglas Maclean, but continued to average five films per year with H.B. Warner and then Pauline Frederick as stars. Then, late in 1921, he formed his own production company, Inspiration Pictures with Richard Barthelmess. *Tol'able David*, the first of their five movies together, was the best. Based on a story originally purchased for Barthelmess by D.W. Griffith, the subject held an immediate appeal for King. 'With part of the picture I relived the days of my boyhood,' he noted in an interview with Kevin Brownlow. 'I was born over the mountains, less than eight miles from where we photographed it.' Barthelmess gave an excellent performance as the simple farm boy who grows to manhood and vindicates his family's honour in a climactic, David-and-Goliath like fight with the tall local bully played by Ernest Torrence. Effectively filmed on location from a script by Edmund Goulding, with important contributions from King, the film captures the feel of small town life and is rich in nicely observed details and authentic characterisations, from the mother suckling her baby in a rocking chair to the general store loungers.

Consolidating his new position as a leading producer-director, King next teamed up with another ex-Griffith star, Lillian Gish. This time King's interest in

location filming took him to Italy in search of authentic settings and atmosphere. *The White Sister* (1923) represented one of the first attempts to film a modern religious story of a type later made popular by King with *The Song Of Bernadette* exactly twenty years later, and it was the first time an American production company had travelled to Italy. The results were fully justified. Not only was the picture visually striking, but Miss Gish gave an excellent performance along with a handsome English discovery named Ronald Colman who emerged as a new star. The couple were reteamed the following year in *Romola*, a somewhat less successful costumer set in 15th-century Italy, with William Powell a memorable villain in one of his early roles.

In 1925 King directed *Stella Dallas*, scripted by Frances Marion for producer Sam Goldwyn. The kind of prestige literary adaptation identified with Goldwyn, particularly during the 30s, it was more modest in its aims than the sound remake (also produced by Goldwyn and starring Barbara Stanwyck). The picture concentrated on the character of the mother, convincingly portrayed by Belle Bennett, while Ronald Colman was rather wasted, but it turned out to be the first smash hit for both King and Goldwyn, and they stayed together for three more pictures including a successful Western, *The Winning Of Barbara Worth* (1926), best remembered as providing Gary Cooper with his first good role.

Although King easily made the transition to sound and refused to be intimidated by the 'sound experts' who were brought in to help out, he surrendered his independence in 1930 to sign with Fox. One of a number of leading independent producer-directors faced with a Hollywood newly dominated by the giant studios, King appears to have adjusted quite easily to the new set-up. He directed Will Rogers in *Lightnin'* (1930), had a hit with Janet Gaynor in *Merely Mary Ann* (1931), and achieved his big-

gest 30s hit when both stars appeared together in *State Fair* (1933). Here the director's affection for small town, mid-West America is palpable, while the film itself provided the perfect vehicle for one of Rogers' familiar, lovable and folksy characterisations.

After Fox's merger with 20th Century in 1935, King's position was unaffected. He got on well with new production chief, Darryl Zanuck, and obviously benefitted from the revitalization and financial recovery which took place under Zanuck's leadership. King was immediately assigned to the studio's first Technicolor production, *Ramona* (1936), featuring two new Fox stars, Loretta Young and Don Ameche. *Lloyds Of London* (1936) launched the young Tyrone Power and he went on to star in three of Fox's top box office successes during 1937-38, all American historical subjects of a type which appealed to both Zanuck and King. In both *In Old Chicago* (1937) and *Alexander's Ragtime Band*, Power was teamed with Alice Faye and Don Ameche. *Chicago* was Fox's answer to the

Top: Ronald Colman, Lois Moran and Alice Joyce (right) in *Stella Dallas* (1925), a three-handkerchief weepie and a box-office smash for King, and producer Sam Goldwyn.

Above: Will Rogers and Janet Gaynor as father and daughter in the folksy family film *State Fair* (1933). The formula worked again in a Technicolor musical version in 1945 with Charles Winninger and Jeanne Crain in Will and Janet's roles, but was a dismal failure in 1963 (Tom Ewell, Pamela Tiffin).

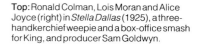

Left: *Alexander's Ragtime Band* (1938) was an archetypal Fox musical of the period, and starred King's handsome protegée, Tyrone Power (illustrated centre, playing the fiddle). The ample and good-natured trio in the foreground are merely bit players adding to the general fun of a cast that included Alice Faye, Wally Vernon and Helen Westley.

MGM hit *San Francisco* (1936), with a spectacular fire climax to match the latter's earthquake, while *Alexander's Ragtime Band* was an enjoyable and evocative musical of a type recalled by Scorsese's *New York, New York* exactly forty years later. Here Alice Faye played the successful nightclub singer with Power as the struggling jazz musician, but the picture is most memorable for the music of Irving Berlin. In the Technicolored Western, *Jesse James*, filmed late in 1938, Power was co-starred with Henry Fonda.

Zanuck's major move into colour ahead of the other studios meant that King was encouraged to shoot in Technicolor. By the time of the delightful and colourful Ty Power swashbuckler, *The Black Swan* (1942), Henry King had more colour films to his credit than any other Hollywood director, and his prestige had never been higher. He was Oscar-nominated for two of Zanuck's favourite projects, the religious drama, *The Song Of Bernadette*, starring the beautiful Jennifer Jones, and *Wilson* (1944), a superbly mounted biopic of the President, which unfortunately failed to appeal to 40s wartime audiences. The nostalgic, saccharine *Margie* (1946) was a hit, however, while the expensive Power costumer, *Captain From Castile* (1947) was a major disappointment. King's collaboration with a new Fox star, Gregory Peck, got off to a fine start in 1949 with a powerful war drama, *Twelve O'Clock High*, followed by a serious, adult Western of note, *The Gunfighter* (1950). These proved to be

'Having been an actor myself, I rehearse in a different way from most directors. I may have doubts that a scene can be done. So, without you knowing, I walk through the scene and try all the bits of business, just to see the difficulties. I don't want anyone to imitate me, but if I walk through it and it works out well, why I know an actor can do it.'

1967

Above: The almost ridiculously 'tall, dark and handsome' Tyrone Power was the *Captain From Castile* (1947). A lavish period adventure film, it looked wonderful but was extremely dull and a disappointment to all concerned. Power himself, one of Hollywood's most well-liked stars, died tragically of a heart attack at the age of forty-five while on location in Madrid for *Solomon And Sheba*.

King's last black-and-white movies. He returned to a stylish use of colour with a memorable piece of Americana, *I'd Climb The Highest Mountain* (1951) starring Susan Hayward; *David and Bathsheba* (1951), an early entry in the 50s Biblical cycle, teamed Miss Hayward with Peck, and they co-starred again the following year in King's creditable attempt to bring Hemingway's *The Snows Of Kilimanjaro* to the screen. From 1953 on, all King's pictures were in CinemaScope *and* colour. Solidly crafted and entertaining movies like *Carousel* (1956) and *The Sun Also Rises*, again from Hemingway, failed to match the best of the director's earlier work, and he retired after completing an adaptation of Scott Fitzgerald's *Tender Is The Night* in 1961.

Left: Gregory Peck and Susan Hayward made an attractive – if not exactly authentic – biblical pair as *David And Bathsheba* (1951), the versatile director's early contribution to the 50s cycle of the genre.

Below: Director King (standing centre) demonstrates a point during the making of *The Snows Of Kilimanjaro* (1952), another Peck-Hayward starrer. The prone figure is that of Gregory Peck.

ALEXANDER KORDA

Born Pusztaturpaszto near Turkeve, Hungary, 16 September 1893. **Died** 1956

Although Alexander Korda is best known as an ambitious, enterprising and flamboyant producer, who had a major influence on the development of the British cinema for a period of about twenty years from his first arrival in England in the early 30s to the early 50s, he was also a very competent director. He started directing movies while a young man in Hungary, and returned to the director's chair periodically throughout his career. He worked initially as a writer and journalist with a special interest in the cinema, but the outbreak of war in 1914 affected the availability of films from abroad and gave him the opportunity to establish himself as a director. Although still only in his early twenties, Korda soon developed into one of the leading writer-directors of the fledgeling Hungarian film industry, and by 1917 he was producing his films as well. With his own production company and studio, he also supervised films from other directors. In 1919, a series of post-war political upheavals led to Korda being appointed 'comissioner of film production' in the Karolyi government, but he was forced to flee for his life when the regime fell, and he was rescued by his wife, the actress Maria Corda (sic).

For the next dozen years Korda became a well-travelled director on the international scene, making films in five different countries. The first stop was Vienna, where he and Maria collaborated with a pair of Hungarian refugee writers, Lajos Biro and Ernest Vajda, both later to earn distinction in Hollywood. Of special interest was his effort to emulate Americans Griffith and DeMille by mixing a modern story with Biblical spectacle in *Samson And Delila*, (1922) starring Maria. The couple moved on to Berlin in 1923-26 where Maria starred in all her husband's pictures. Arriving in Hollywood in 1927, he found it difficult to adapt to the American studio system. Here he was regarded as just another contract director, while the arrival of sound virtually finished Maria's career in spite of her performance in his most successful Hollywood production, *The Private Life Of Helen Of Troy* (1927).

Returning to Europe in 1931, Korda collaborated with French playwright Marcel Pagnol on the film version of *Marius*, the first of a trilogy and the first time that Korda's painter brother, Vincent, served as his art director. In 1932, the director moved to London where he found the backing to set up his own production company, London Films. His first productions for the new company were *The Wedding Rehearsal* (1932), and *The Private Life Of Henry VIII* (1933) which proved to be a spectacular world-wide success. Characterised by its witty, 'humanising', even disrespectful approach to historical figures, it was the first British movie to be nominated for a Best Picture Oscar, while Charles Laughton won the Oscar for his extraordinary performance in the title role. Although filmed quickly and cheaply, the quality of

the picture reflected the contributions of a talented team which Korda had assembled, including writers Arthur Wimperis and Lajos Biro, French cameraman Georges Périnal and a new group of contract stars – Robert Donat, Laughton, Elsa Lanchester and the dark-haired beauty, Merle Oberon, Korda's one real discovery, whom he married in 1939.

An energetic showman in the American mold, Korda attempted to inject a new vitality into the depressed British film scene of the mid-30s. In 1935 he built the Denham Studios, and his generally solidly crafted and tasteful productions gave a major boost to the early film careers of a long list of distinguished British stars including Laurence Olivier, Vivien Leigh, Ralph Richardson, Rex Harrison, James Mason and Flora Robson. His activities as a producer left him little time to direct, but *Rembrandt* (1936) was a memorable and worthy vehicle for Laughton and Lanchester. His British studio empire collapsed in 1938-39 and, in 1941, he returned to Hollywood to direct Olivier and Vivien Leigh in *That Hamilton Woman*. Here he was joined by Vincent and his other brother Zoltan, who had directed a number of his British productions, most notably *The Drum* (1938) and *The Four Feathers*

(1939). During the post-war years Alex served as executive producer on a number of outstanding British productions including *The Third Man* (1949), *Hobson's Choice* (1953) and, finally, Olivier's *Richard III* (1956).

Top: Alexander Korda (left), photographed in the grounds of Denham Studios with his designer brother, Vincent.

Above: Anne of Cleves (Elsa Lanchester) entertains Henry VIII (Charles Laughton) with a late-night card game in her boudoir. *The Private Life Of Henry VIII* (1933), was Korda's first truly major international success, and won Laughton a merited Oscar which put this distinguished actor firmly on the movie map.

Left: The breathtakingly beautiful Vivien Leigh (centre) was *Lady Hamilton* (1941), mistress to Lord Nelson, who was played by Leigh's real-life husband, Laurence Olivier. The movie, rather more informally, was distributed in the US where it was made, as *That Hamilton Woman*. With Miss Leigh in the still are Sara Allgood and Henry Wilcoxon.

FRITZ LANG

Born Vienna, 5 December 1890. **Died** 1976

Fritz Lang was a leading figure of the German cinema which flourished during the pre-Hitler era of the 20s and early 30s. Arriving in the US in 1934, he quickly adapted to his new country and new language, and continued active in the American cinema for the next twenty years. Although he made a number of excellent pictures there, they were few and far between and he was never able to fulfil his true potential within the restrictions of the American studio system. Best known for his thrillers, he was one of the first directors to recognise the possibilities of using this popular genre for making pointed political and social comments – on the state of postwar German society with *Dr Mabuse Der Spieler* (1922), and for a thinly disguised attack on the evils of Nazism in *The Testament Of Dr Mabuse* (1933). A similar social consciousness can be found in many of his best American films, like *You Only Live Once* (Wanger/UA, 1937), about the difficulties experienced by an ex-con trying to go straight and *The Big Heat* (Columbia, 1953), in which an honest cop attempts to expose the organised crime and political corruption in an American town. Thus, there is a continuity which runs through much of Lang's *oeuvre*, underlined on his return to Germany in 1960 when he resuscitated the character of Mabuse in his last film, *The Thousand Eyes Of Dr Mabuse* (1960), thus bringing his career full circle. One of the most distinctively modern of directors, Lang's pictures hold up well through their sophisticated treatment of 20th century themes: the alienation of the individual from modern society and man's continuing struggle versus hostile, and frequently corrupt, social and political forces over which he has no control. 'The fight of the individual against destiny is probably the basis of all my films,' Lang has suggested.

Yet during the course of his forty plus years as a director Lang made a variety of pictures. During the silent period, in particular, his films ranged from action adventure and historical epic, to fantasy and science fiction. The son of an architect, he had, himself, trained briefly in that profession before turning to painting and then the cinema. All of his early pictures are characterised by his finely developed pictorial sense, imaginative use of lighting, composition and photography, while *Die Nibelungen* (1924) and *Metropolis* (1927) featured some of the most impressive sets and studio-designed landscapes of the 20s. Lang also developed a reputation as a perfectionist who paid meticulous attention to the smallest details. On his first major production, *Die Spinnen* (*The Spiders*, 1919), he enlisted the services of an expert on Inca culture to help with the authentic studio reconstruction of sculptures, buildings and costumes. This immensely lively and entertaining action-adventure serial in two feature-length parts was his first popular success and an early forerunner of the kind of movie recently made popular by Steven Spielberg with his *Indiana Jones*

epics. Impressive in scope, this, Lang's first 'American'-flavoured movie combined the qualities of a Western with those of an adventure film and thriller, anticipating a number of his later productions. An ambitious but fully realised work, *Die Spinnen* clearly marked the arrival of a major new talent on the German film scene.

His next film of note was *Der Müde Tod* (*The Weary Death*, also known as *Destiny*, 1921) which he co-wrote with his future wife, Thea von Harbou. (She was his regular script collaborator from 1919 until his hasty departure from Germany in 1933 when she joined the Nazi party!) A movie in three parts, it represented a major advance over *Die Spinnen*, demonstrating Lang's qualities as a fine director of actors. Here his careful attention to characterisation balanced the fantasy qualities and dream-like special effects (some of which were directly imitated by Douglas Fairbanks in his *Thief Of Bagdad* a few years later). More romantic than expressionistic in tone, the film demonstrated Lang's characteristic use of light-

Above: *Metropolis* (1927), now firmly entrenched as a classic in spite of its flaws, was a landmark in cinema history. Inspired by Lang's first visit to New York, the movie starred Rudolph Klein-Rogge (illustrated centre) as a mad scientist and Brigitte Helm as a robot woman. The extraordinary skyscraper landscape for this futuristic fantasy was, incredibly, studio-built.

Left: Lang's durable masterpiece and his first talkie, *M* (1931) starred Peter Lorre as a psychopathic child murderer. The film is brilliant in both conception and execution and brought international recognition to the previously unknown Lorre. The actor continued to work in Germany for a couple of years but, like Lang, exiled himself when the Nazis took power in 1933. He went to Paris, then London and, in 1935, to Hollywood.

hero in *You Only Live Once*, and in *The Return Of Frank James* (1940), a superb and underrated 'adult' Western. Lang made a pair of interesting thrillers with Edward G. Robinson during the 40s, and Dana Andrews was the hero of his last pair of American films in the 50s. But his later American career is best remembered for *The Big Heat* (starring Glenn Ford), and for the roles he provided for two of the great female stars of the American cinema – Marlene Dietrich in *Rancho Notorious* (1951) and Barbara Stanwyck in *Clash By Night* (1952). Lang retired from directing in 1961, but was invited back to give a memorable, final performance as himself, sort of, in Jean-Luc Godard's *Le Mépris* (1963).

Left: Sylvia Sidney and Henry Fonda starred in *You Only Live Once* (1937), one of the director's first Hollywood films. The run-of-the-mill story – petty crook framed for murder escapes from jail and tries to make it to Canada with his wife – was elevated by Lang's gift for images and for drawing first-rate performances from his actors.

Below: Gloria Grahame and Glenn Ford in *The Big Heat* (1953). Realistic and very, very violent, the film is forever enshrined in cinematic memory for the scene where Lee Marvin disfigures Miss Grahame by throwing boiling coffee in her face.

ing for dramatic effect for the first time. The two-part feature, *Dr Mabuse Der Spieler* presented a chilling portrait of a fictitious master-criminal, reflecting Lang's fascination with the psychopathic mind.

Then, in a surprise change of direction, Lang ventured into Germany's mythic past with *Die Nibelungen*, yet another lengthy, two-part feature. Here the director's carefully controlled and stylised treatment of his legendary characters placed them within remarkable artificial landscapes and symmetrical, spacious sets, but one is impressed rather than involved. This is also the case with *Metropolis*. A landmark in the development of science fiction on the screen, it was inspired by Lang's first visit to New York City in 1924. The suitably spectacular sets, representing an imaginary underground city of the future, memorable special effects and an unforgettable robot woman played by Brigitte Helm, were not matched by the naive plot and serious weaknesses in characterisation and acting.

Lang was back on safer, more familiar ground with *Spione* (*The Spy*, 1928), an adventure thriller in the Mabuse mold. The master spy was played by Lang's favourite 20s actor and Mabuse figure, Rudolph Klein-Rogge, who had also appeared as the megalomaniac scientist in *Metropolis*. Again the film is notable for striking imagery and effects, including a terrific night chase sequence along abandoned country roads, and a spectacular train crash. Space travel was the subject of Lang's last silent, *Frau Im Mond* (*Woman In The Moon*, 1928), which included his famous invention, the countdown, while his scientific advisors on the film graduated to building *real* rockets not many years later.

If there was a question as to how well this most visual of directors would cope with sound, he gave a definitive answer with his first talkie and his masterpiece, *M* (1931). Originally titled *Mörder Unter Uns* (*The Murderer Amongst Us*), Lang initially ran up against unexpected opposition to the project from members of the Nazi party who did not realise that the film was merely about a child murderer. Avoiding the wilder extravagances of his earlier, silent thrillers, here Lang made use of a tightly constructed plot balancing the activities of the police with the efficiently organised criminals and gangsters who unite to catch the fugitive in a manner reminiscent of *The Threepenny*

Opera. Not only was the film superbly photographed, with an imaginative use of sound, but the many characters were deftly brought to life with great economy, perception and wit. Most impressive of all was Peter Lorre's portrayal of the psychotic murderer, a sensitive, revealing, and still durable performance.

Lang's stature in the German film industry was such that he was invited to take charge of making Nazi films by Goebbels, who was doubtless unaware that Lang was half Jewish. The filmmaker fled: first to France, then to the US where he had secured a contract with MGM. Here he spent a year and only managed to complete one film (produced by Joseph Mankiewicz), an effective anti-lynching drama entitled *Fury* (1936). With Spencer Tracy cast as the innocent victim of mob violence, the film reflected Lang's recognition of the need to present his hero as a John Doe, man-of-the-people type to appeal to American audiences. Henry Fonda portrayed the Lang

Above: Fritz Lang, aged seventy-three, as he appeared on screen in Jean-Luc Godard's *Le Mépris* (1963).

Left: In 1957, Lang returned to Germany for a while where, in 1960, he resuscitated his famous criminal, Dr Mabuse. *The Thousand Eyes Of Dr Mabuse* was, in fact, his last film. The still shows Werner Peters (left), and Gert Frobe who became a well-known heavy in English and American movies from the mid-60s on, most notably in the title role of the James Bond, *Goldfinger* (1964).

MERVYN LEROY

Born San Francisco, 15 October 1900.

Mervyn LeRoy spent virtually all of his long career with two of the leading Hollywood studios, Warner Bros. and MGM. He went about as far as it was possible for a contract director to go during the peak studio years of the 30s and 40s and, when the 50s decline set in, he attempted to continue as an independent producer-director for a time, albeit with only varying degrees of success.

A small, lively young man who had appeared on the stage from the age of twelve, LeRoy first broke into films as a bit part player during the early 20s. He soon graduated to script and gag writing on a series of both comedies and serious pictures starring Colleen Moore, and then began directing comedies for the same company, First National. His favourite actress on these early pictures during 1928-30 was Alice White, and together they made the jump to sound with, appropriately enough, a pair of musicals featuring a gangster theme – *Broadway Babies* and *Playing Around* – both filmed in 1929. Musicals and gangsters occupy an important niche in LeRoy's later career. The classic gangster movie, *Little Caesar*, first shot his name to prominence along with that of star Edward G. Robinson late in 1930. Robinson has provided a capsule description of LeRoy as 'that cheery, bubbling, joking director assigned to guide me through this film. Mervyn was so likeable that I distrusted him instantly... But I soon learned something about Mervyn that makes him special... More than any director I know, Mervyn is the

audience... Add to this his technical proficiency and you have a knowledgeable director – knowledgeable, too, of his own shortcomings.'

Punchy and hard-hitting, *Little Caesar* was over-talkative like many early sound films (many of the best lines came from the original novel by W.R. Burnett) and it was crudely put together. But it had a gritty topicality, reflecting the new realities of the 30s, and was sustained by an archetypal performance from Edward G. It effectively set the tone for many of the gangster movies that followed, and established a style which came to be associated with Warner Bros. LeRoy and Robinson followed up with a similarly hardhitting attack on scandal sheet journalism in *Five Star Final* (1931). An extremely over-rated film, based on a melodramatic play, it was the first LeRoy production to be nominated for a Best Picture Oscar. Only Robinson's performance as a tough New York editor is at all memorable. He was excellent, too, as the condemned murderer in their last, downbeat movie together, *Two Seconds* (1932). But the undoubted masterpiece of LeRoy's early career was *I Am A Fugitive From A Chain Gang* (1932). Rightly known as the most uncompromising of all the Warner Bros. social conscience pictures, it also marked an advance in LeRoy's techniques. Breaking away from the studio-bound qualities of his early sound movies, he made effective use of location filming which lent the necessary authenticity to the subject. The replica of a Southern prison farm was constructed on the Warner ranch, while the dramatic rock breaking sequence was filmed in a real rock quarry nearby. Paul Muni gave an extremely modern and convincing performance in the title role which, taken together with *Scarface* the previous year, elevated him to the ranks of the top Hollywood stars.

Both Muni and the picture were nominated for Oscars, and Muni was offered a new, favourable Warners contract.

In contrast to all the heavy drama of 1932, 1933 proved to be a lighter but no less memorable year for LeRoy. His first with Cagney as a likeable, fast-talking conman, *Hard To Handle*, effectively set against a nicely observed Depression background, was one of the earliest examples of a new genre, the 30s screwball comedy. On loan to MGM, LeRoy directed the comedy team of Marie Dressler and Wallace Beery in *Tugboat Annie*, an entertaining sequel to their smash-hit *Min And Bill* (MGM, 1930). Then he made his most successful contribution to the Busby Berkeley/Warner Bros. musical cycle of the early 30s with *Golddiggers Of 1933*. Conceived as a quick follow-up to the highly successful *42nd Street*, it, too, starred Dick Powell, Ruby Keeler and Ginger Rogers, but with the addition of two of LeRoy's favourite actresses,

Above: One of LeRoy's lesser known Warner dramas was *Big City Blues* (1932). Here the director (right) and an assistant (far right) rehearse a scene with, from left to right, Eric Linden, Inez Courtney, a very young Humphrey Bogart, Joan Blondell, Ned Sparks, Gloria Shea, Lyle Talbot.

Below left: Edward G. Robinson in *Little Caesar* (1930), the tough gangster film which brought the names of both star and director into the limelight.

Below: Paul Muni is brutally flogged in *I Am A Fugitive From A Chain Gang* (1932), one of Warner's earliest, toughest and very best social conscience films.

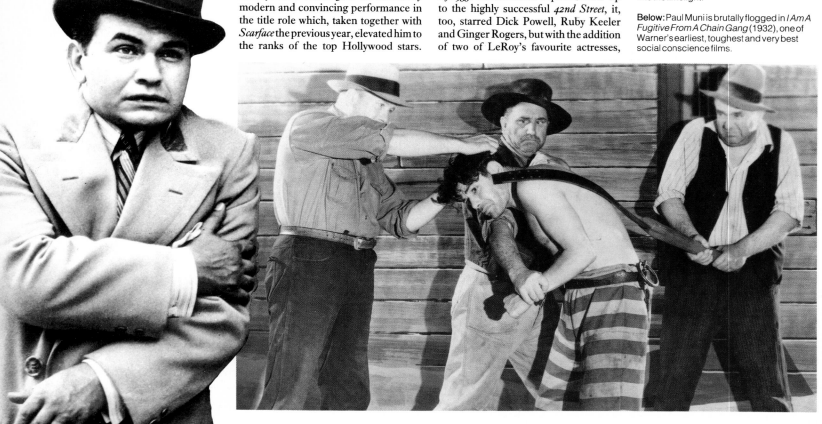

red Ronald Colman as an amnesia victim and was enormously entertaining and successful. His Technicolored version of *Little Women* (1949) was extremely disappointing, while his last three MGM movies during the early 50s, including *Latin Lovers* (1953), the last of four movies with his star discovery Lana Turner, merely highlighted the decline in the once glorious MGM musical. In between, his Italian-based production of *Quo Vadis?* (1951) presented his most impressive achievement as a director of large-scale spectacle.

Operating as an independent producer-director releasing his pictures through Warner Bros., LeRoy served as co-director on *Mr Roberts* (1955), and enjoyed hits with the service comedy *No Time For Sergeants* (1957) and with the superior musical *Gypsy* (1962). He retired from directing in 1965 and received the Irving Thalberg Award in 1975.

> 'Less cold a thinker than Curtiz, not so competent a technician but probably, on balance, more deserving of praise as an artist of ideas. If, however, the poorer Curtiz films are disappointing, LeRoy's failures are impossible to watch . . . Given a silly plot, he had no concept of changing it as Curtiz did. He merely gave up and let it control his film.'
>
> John Baxter in 'Hollywood in the 30s'

Aline MacMahon and Joan Blondell.

Extremely active during the 1930-33 period when he averaged five or six films per year, LeRoy's output matched that of other prolific Warner Bros. contract directors like Curtiz, Del Ruth and Lloyd Bacon. But there were already signs, toward the end of 1933, that the studio was beginning to make room in its busy production schedule for a limited number of prestige products. Thus, for *The World Changes* (1933) LeRoy was reunited with Paul Muni who was attracted to the film by the challenge of portraying the development of the leading character who ages from twenty to ninety. A moderately successful mini-epic, the film spanned seventy years of American history in a manner similar to that of King Vidor's *An American Romance* (for MGM) just ten years later. A similarly ambitious production in 1934 was LeRoy's *Oil For The Lamps Of China*, starring Pat O'Brien, which drew attention to the unscrupulous behaviour of the giant multinational corporations. Then, late in 1935, for his first large scale costumer, *Anthony Adverse*, LeRoy was given a $1 million budget and a 60-day shooting schedule – about double that for a normal A feature, but far less than a similar picture would have cost at MGM. If the result was distinctly unmemorable (even the presence of Fredric March in the title role failed to bring it to life), the film did demonstrate the director's ability to control the large resources of an epic production.

They Won't Forget (1937), an over-dramatised but effective attack on Southern bigotry and mob rule starring Claude Rains, was easily the equal of Fritz Lang's *Fury* for MGM the previous year. Also remembered for introducing Lana Turner to the screen (in the small role of a college-girl murder victim), it was LeRoy's last Warners film of note, for he signed with MGM in 1938. Employed solely as a producer on a number of films during 1938-39, most notably *The Wizard Of Oz*, LeRoy returned to directing with *Waterloo Bridge* (1940). The first of his glossy prestige productions at MGM, it was competently directed and acted (by Vivien Leigh and Robert Taylor as the star-crossed lovers). But it was too modern in style and failed to capture the

feel of the World War I period, reflecting, too, a softening in LeRoy's approach more in keeping with the MGM 'house style'. He was reunited with Edward G. Robinson on a Warners-style newspaper story, *Unholy Partners* (1941) and directed Robert Taylor as gangster *Johnny Eager* (1941), with Lana Turner co-starring. One war picture of note, *Thirty Seconds Over Tokyo* (1944), followed, then a pair of Gable vehicles, but the best indication of the new 'MGM style' LeRoy was provided by the three pictures he made with Louis B. Mayer's favourite new female star, Greer Garson – *Blossoms In The Dust* (1941, the director's first in Technicolor), *Random Harvest* (1942), and *Madame Curie* (1943). All three were nominated for Best Picture, while LeRoy earned his only Oscar nomination ever as director for *Random Harvest*, which star-

Above left: Lana Turner and Clark Gable in *Homecoming* (1948), an undistinguished romantic melodrama set during World War II, with Gable as a society doctor who is called up and Turner as an army nurse with whom he has an affair.

Left: In 1951, LeRoy undertook the historical, biblical epic with a vengeance in making the three-hour long *Quo Vadis*. A publicity blurb at the time claimed that 'Ancient Rome is going to the dogs, Robert Taylor is going to the lions and Peter Ustinov is going crazy!'. The movie picked up five Academy nominations (of which direction was *not* one). The still shows Deborah Kerr as the ill-fated Christian heroine, Finlay Currie, and Roman commander hero Robert Taylor.

Below: Director LeRoy (left) discusses a point with Natalie Wood during the filming of *Gypsy* (1962). This was a splendidly realised screen version of the Arthur Laurents-Jule Styne-Stephen Sondheim smash-hit Broadway musical, itself based on the life of the famous Gypsy Rose Lee, who elevated striptease to an (almost respectable) art.

ERNST LUBITSCH

Born Berlin, 28 January 1892. **Died** 1947

Known as the master of light and sophisticated, Continental-style comedy, Ernst Lubitsch was the most famous European director to arrive in Hollywood during the early 20s, and his success paved the way for that large number of expatriate directors who flocked to California during the late 20s and 30s. Lubitsch began his career as an actor, and was strongly influenced by the great German stage director, Max Reinhardt, who employed him for a time during 1911-12. The theatre influence was present throughout much of Lubitsch's career, and many of his films were adapted, if rather loosely, from plays or operettas. His pictures drew on the traditions of the Viennese operetta, French farce, and historical romantic fiction yet, from quite early on, he demonstrated a remarkable visual flair and an instinctive understanding of filmic language. The rich inventiveness of his pictures was coupled with careful and detailed preparation, working closely with his script collaborators and actors. According to Maurice Chevalier, his favourite 30s star, 'Lubitsch ... always rehearsed with his leading players before beginning the film. For at least a week beforehand you worked hard so as to be entirely inside a part by the time you were in front of the camera ... all you had to do was relax and let him guide you'.

Having first begun directing and starring in comedy shorts in 1915, by 1917-18 he had already assembled a regular team of collaborators. The first Lubitsch stock company was headed by actresses Pola Negri (who first made her name in his 1918 production of *Carmen*) and Ossi Oswalda who starred in his first big comedy hit, *The Oyster Princess* (1919). His favourite actors, Emil Jannings and Harry Liedtke, co-starred with Negri in his smash-hit of the early 20s, *Madame Dubarry* (1919). Retitled *Passion*, it became the biggest box-office success of any foreign silent film ever released in the US. Behind the camera was Theodor Sparkuhl, with an outstanding group of set and costume designers reflecting the great care that Lubitsch took with the *look* of his pictures. But perhaps the most important of all were his scriptwriters. When he went to Hollywood in 1923 he took his favourite writer, Hans Kraly, with him. During the 30s his regular script collaborators were Ernest Vajda and Samson Raphaelson, while Charles Brackett and Billy Wilder joined him on a pair of movies during the late 30s.

Lubitsch was justly famous for the manner in which he and his writers could retouch and embellish a scene. In his silent adaptation of Oscar Wilde's *Lady Windermere's Fan* (Warner Bros., 1925) the director captured all the nuances of the play with the addition of a few touches of his own. The attitude of London high society to the leading female character, a 'fallen woman', was easily expressed through the lift of an eyebrow, a brief but meaningful glance; the story lent itself to subtle visual touches so that, at Ascot she,

rather than the race, is the main focus of attention. In *One Hour With You* (Paramount, 1931, co-directed by George Cukor) Maurice Chevalier speaks his thoughts directly to the camera (and the audience) in a kind of filmic aside at various points, a very modern example of the famous 'Lubitsch touch'.

First invited to Hollywood by Mary Pickford to direct her in *Rosita* (UA, 1923), Lubitsch was put under contract by the then tiny Warner Bros. studio which was attempting to boost its prestige. *The Marriage Circle* (1924) was immediately followed by *Three Women*, billed as an 'Ernst Lubitsch Master Production'. The studio publicity of the time was already describing him as the 'master of refined comedy and intimate detail' and referring to 'his uncanny ability in

Above: Ernst Lubitsch, Hollywood's prime early purveyor of screen sophistication, began his career as an actor in his native Germany. He directed and starred in a series of comedies about Moritz, a young Jewish shop assistant. The films are forgotten and their copies lost, but this rare still shows Lubitsch as Moritz in about 1915.

Left: Pola Negri as the Czarina Catherine in *Forbidden Paradise* (1924), rehearsing on set with director Lubitsch. The fiery and exotic Negri's Hollywood career was killed by the coming of sound but, until then, she was one of the reigning queens of Paramount along with Gloria Swanson. The pair of them were built up as enemy rivals by the publicity department.

Below: Jeanette MacDonald and Maurice Chevalier were paired by Lubitsch for the last time in *The Merry Widow* (1934). An incredibly lavish and joyful treatment of Lehar's operetta, the film was made for MGM, although the magic partnership of Jeanette and Maurice had commenced at Paramount with *The Love Parade* (1929) which marked the director's talkie debut.

handling sets and players so that they appear to be actual, living reproductions and not merely actors and scenery' (sic).

Lubitsch went to the larger Paramount studio to direct Pola Negri as Catharine the Great in his first big costume production in the US, *Forbidden Paradise* (1924). Then, after completing his stint at Warner Bros., he was hired by MGM to direct a stylish silent version of the operetta, *The Student Prince* (1927) starring Ramon Novarro and Norma Shearer. It was a lightly likeable movie, but did little to add to Lubitsch's already solid reputation. *The Patriot* (1928), however, reunited him with Emil Jannings, earned him his first Oscar nomination, and brought him back to the studio where he made his home for most of the next ten

to pass the Hays Office censorship code.

Lubitsch served as Paramount's production chief during 1935-36, but in 1937 returned to directing with the Marlene Dietrich-Gary Cooper vehicle, *Angel* (1937). It was well below standard, but he was back on form with *Ninotchka* (MGM, 1939), starring Greta Garbo in her best-ever comedy role as a strait-laced Russian official who gradually warms to the delights of Paris and love, under Melvyn Douglas' guidance. Lubitsch directed one last masterpiece, *To Be Or Not To Be* (1942), an extremely inventive and witty black comedy about a troupe of actors, led by Carole Lombard and Jack Benny, thwarting the Nazi occupiers in Poland. The technicolored *Heaven Can Wait* (20th Century-Fox, 1943) earned Lubitsch his last of three Oscar nominations for directing. He never won, but was awarded a special honorary Oscar in 1946. His last picture, *That Lady In Ermine* (20th Century-Fox, 1948), was completed after his death by Otto Preminger.

'In no part of any Lubitsch picture did he have an actor who was not just right. You rehearsed a whole week on the picture without shooting anything at all . . . He knew his actors very well, and he wanted something from them that even they didn't know they had.'

Edward Everett Horton in 'The Real Tinsel'

years – Paramount. In 1929, after one last silent, *Eternal Love* for UA, Lubitsch made the transition to sound, choosing an operetta-style musical, *The Love Parade* (Paramount, 1929) for his talkie debut. Maurice Chevalier and Jeanette MacDonald were teamed for the first time in this slightly risqué, sophisticated, charming and European-flavoured entertainment set in a mythical Ruritanian kingdom, and rich in examples of the 'Lubitsch touch'. It not only earned the director his second consecutive Oscar nomination, but set him on course as a major director of Hollywood musicals. By the time of *The Smiling Lieutenant* (1931) and *One Hour With You* (1932), he had brought the genre to an early peak. Music and story were integrated in the latter, and the witty dialogue was delivered with characteristic Gallic charm by Chevalier. He made a splendid partner for Jeanette MacDonald (better than Nelson Eddy who succeeded him over at MGM), his strong personality constantly playing against her with charm and humour, and avoiding sentimentality. Their last picture with Lubitsch was a remake of *The Merry Widow* (1934), its stunning and elaborate sets and costumes and a lavish budget of $1.6 million making it one of the most expensive MGM movies up to that date. Anita Loos mentions in her autobiography that she was assigned to the picture by producer Irving Thalberg with instructions to keep the director focussed on the human element. 'No matter who wrote Ernst's scenarios, he himself put in the 'Lubitsch touches' that made his films unique . . . Any love scene Ernst directed might just be warming up when his camera would zoom away from the sweethearts to focus

on a pair of fancy bedroom slippers, the hero's pearl-buttoned spats, or an ornate piece of *bric-à-brac*.'

In a non-musical vein Lubitsch directed two of his most lively and sophisticated comedies around this time – *Trouble In Paradise* (1932) and *Design For Living* (1933). Both are set in Paris and demonstrate the amount of mileage which Lubitsch could wring from a triangle relationship. In *Trouble In Paradise* the urbane Herbert Marshall played a gentlemanly thief torn between his crooked associate, Miriam Hopkins, and his rich, attractive employer, Kay Francis. *Design For Living* – a classic *ménage à trois* situation with Miriam Hopkins joining a pair of carefree bohemian friends, painter Gary Cooper and playwright Fredric March – was adroitly adapted from the Noel Coward play by Ben Hecht

Above left: On set between takes of *Trouble In Paradise* (1932) are the honey-toned English actor Herbert Marshall, director Lubitsch and – looking a little like Grace Kelly – Kay Francis. The movie, a highly sophisticated triangle comedy, was set in Paramount's (and Lubitsch's) favourite city, Paris, which the studio designers were adept at recreating on the back-lot.

Left: The gorgeous Garbo, seen here with co-star Melvyn Douglas, delivered a sparkling comedy performance in *Ninotchka* (1939).

Below: *To Be Or Not To Be* (1942) was serviced by a gifted cast topped by Jack Benny (centre), the sublime Carole Lombard (centre right) and Robert Stack (right of Lombard). A comic masterpiece which still delights, the plot concerned a company of actors in Poland who outwit the Nazi occupiers. Brilliantly satirical and inventive, the film – given its date – was also extraordinarily audacious.

ROUBEN MAMOULIAN

Born Tiflis, Georgia, Russia, 8 October 1898

First attracted to the stage as a young man, Rouben Mamoulian had his early training at the Moscow Arts Theatre, then came to England with a touring theatre company in 1920. It was not long before he moved to America and established himself as a director of opera (at Rochester, NY), and then of plays with the prestigious Theatre Guild in New York City. An unknown quantity as far as films were concerned he, like many other leading stage directors, got his big break with the coming of sound in 1929 when he was hired by Paramount to direct *Applause*. The studio was just in the process of bolstering its already formidable array of top European talent but, unlike those Continental directors who were happy to go on directing European subjects, Mamoulian refused to be type-cast. He began by directing four very different pictures during 1929-32, when his versatility stood him in good stead. He started out with a downbeat American backstage musical (*Applause*), then contributed a noteworthy entry to the early 30s gangster cycle, *City Streets* (1931). His *Dr Jekyll And Mr Hyde* (1931) represented Paramount's answer to Universal's successful horror flicks, while the romantic, French-flavoured *Love Me Tonight* (1932) contributed to the musical revival of that year.

Applause featured a fine performance from Helen Morgan in her first film role, and some adroit camerawork by George Folsey. A tracking and panning camera was used to introduce the burlesque

house show and the girls on stage early in the picture. The real New York City, rather than the artificial Hollywood version, was captured on the screen as Mamoulian made use of actual locations and street noises, one of the benefits of filming in nearby Long Island. Mamoulian's imaginative treatment of sound effects, dialogue and music reflected his years of stage experience, and his experimental use of sound in a number of his best-known productions like that of 'Porgy' in 1927. If he appeared to be striving too hard (and a little self-consciously) for 'artistic' effects in *Applause*, his approach had become more assured and less obtrusive by the time of *City Streets* (1931). During the intervening year the director had returned briefly to the theatre, but for *City Streets* he finally made a break with New York and trav-

elled out to Paramount's West-coast studios – a move which also marked his new commitment to the cinema. Given a larger budget, a pair of top stars and a Dashiell Hammett story to work with, Mamoulian came up with a likeable and offbeat gangster movie. Sylvia Sidney played the innocent-looking but tough-talking girl who convinces young Gary Cooper that he is a sucker to stick to his straight, low-paying job. (A variation of this theme reappears in Mamoulian's 1939 film version of Clifford Odets' *Golden Boy* for Columbia, where the stars were Barbara Stanwyck and William Holden.) A film of character rather than action, Mamoulian had both Miss Sidney and Guy Kibbee playing against type, while he once again capitalised on location filming and the use of naturalistic and subjective sound.

Left: Gary Cooper (left) starred in *City Streets* (1931), a first-class gangster movie and only Mamoulian's second excursion into film.

Below: Garbo and Gilbert in *Queen Christina* (1933). This period romance, in which the star was dressed in masculine attire for the most part, remains one of her most renowned vehicles for which, perhaps, Mamoulian's contribution as director is not always sufficiently remembered.

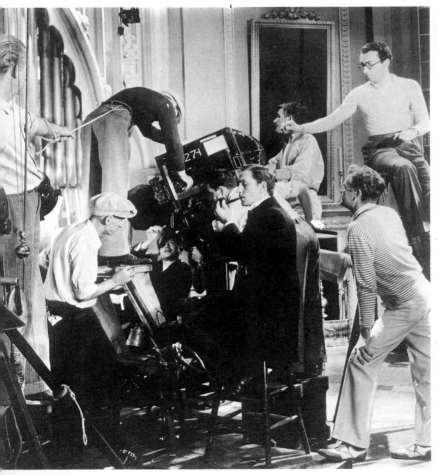

With *Dr Jekyll And Mr Hyde*, Mamoulian 'ventured abroad' so to speak, for his subject matter – to Victorian England. In fact, he did not return to an American subject for six years and, during this period, he developed a reputation as an intelligent and sensitive director of costume pictures, working with a number of Hollywood's top female stars and collaborating with first-rate art directors, most notably, Paramount's Hans Dreier. *Dr Jekyll* is justly famous for Fredric March's Oscar-winning performance, for Dreier's atmospheric studio reconstruction of Victorian London, and for its transformation sequence: colour filters

Left: The elegant Dr Jekyll, who will transform into the monstrous Mr Hyde, lights his pipe. He is, of course, Fredric March. Director Rouben Mamoulian sits on the ladder (right) lining up the shots for what is often considered the best screen version of Stevenson's classic. The others starred John Barrymore (silent, in 1920) and Spencer Tracy (1941).

were removed one at a time to gradually reveal more and more of the actor's make-up so that Jekyll becomes Hyde in front of our eyes without a cut. Both Jekyll and Hyde are fully developed characters, giving added force to the struggle which goes on between them.

According to Mamoulian his next picture, *Love Me Tonight*, was hurriedly put together at the request of Adolph Zukor, the head of Paramount, who had two expensive stars, Chevalier and MacDonald, under contract, but no film to put them in. The stylish, skilful result gives no indication of any lack of preparation. While reflecting the influence of Lubitsch and René Clair, *Love Me Tonight* emerged as one of the most original and delightful of 30s musicals. A polished script was bolstered by some inspired songs from Rodgers and Hart, as well as fine performances from a cast which, aside from Chevalier at his most beguiling and MacDonald at her most winsome, included C. Aubrey Smith, Myrna Loy, Charles Butterworth and Charlie Ruggles. By pre-recording the entire score before shooting, Mamoulian was able to achieve a flowing counterpoint between sound and image which brought his fantasy marvellously alive on the screen.

Suddenly Mamoulian found himself in demand as a director of stylish vehicles for a number of Hollywood's leading actresses. Best of the bunch was *Queen Christina* (MGM, 1933), in which Garbo was reunited for the final time with her 20s flame, John Gilbert. It was his last performance of note – he died in 1936 – but Garbo totally dominated the picture which was perfectly designed to match star and subject. Her range as an actress was never better captured on film, with her special blend of romantic, independent and aristocratic qualities – even her athleticism and seldom utilised sense of humour – balanced by her introspective qualities and vulnerability. Paramount also chose Mamoulian to direct Dietrich in the first of her films away from her mentor and regular director, Josef von Sternberg, *Song Of Songs* (1933), a romantic costumer set in 19th-century Germany. For Sam Goldwyn he directed the Russian-born Anna Sten in an adaptation of Tolstoy's 'Resurrection', retitled *We Live Again* (UA, 1934), and Pioneer Pictures hired him to direct Miriam Hopkins as *Becky Sharp* (RKO, 1935), based on a stage version of Thackeray's 'Vanity Fair'. Famous as the first Technicolor feature, it was not one of the director's best achievements – cheap looking and studio-bound, it was little more than a filmed play, and the use of colour was surprisingly unimaginative. Then, in 1935, Mamoulian returned to the theatre after a long absence to direct the celebrated first production of Gershwin's 'Porgy And Bess'.

For his last intensive period of film activity, Mamoulian was hired by Darryl Zanuck at 20th Century-Fox. The result was a pair of outstanding pictures starring Tyrone Power. *The Mark Of Zorro* (1940) demonstrated the director's talent for handling an action picture with real verve and vitality, and it remains one of the classic Hollywood swashbucklers. In *Blood And Sand* (1941) he was given the

opportunity to work in colour once again, and under more favourable circumstances. Notable for its toned-down use of colour and chiaroscuro in the many dimly lit and night sequences, the bright, over-exposed bull-fighting arena presented a striking and dramatic contrast, and the picture won an Oscar for colour cinematography.

Back in New York again, Mamoulian directed that huge landmark of the American musical theatre, 'Oklahoma!', for Broadway in 1943. For the next dozen years he remained active in the theatre and was only invited back to Hollywood by MGM to direct two last musicals. *Summer Holiday* (1947) was a delightful piece of musical Americana in the tradition of *Meet Me In St Louis* (1944), while *Silk Stockings* (1957), a captivating musical remake of *Ninotchka*, gave him his first opportunity to work in CinemaScope. The dance and musical numbers were first rate, with Fred Astaire at the top of his form. In the Garbo role, Cyd Charisse's short-comings as an actress were evident, but less so than usual, and as a dance partner to Astaire, she was sublime. Sadly, this proved to be Mamoulian's last movie, for he was replaced on both *Porgy And Bess* (Goldwyn, 1959) and *Cleopatra* (20th Century-Fox, 1963) due to artistic disagreements.

Above: Adolphe Menjou (left) and a very, very young William Holden in *Golden Boy* (1939), the film adaptation of Clifford Odets' powerful play about an underprivileged youth who is torn between twin ambitions to be a prizefighter and violinist.

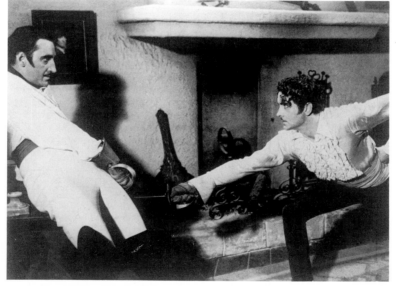

Left: Basil Rathbone (left) and Tyrone Power duel in *The Mark Of Zorro* (1940), a classic swashbuckler which demonstrated the director's ability to turn his stylish hand to any subject matter.

Below: Fred Astaire dances 'The Ritz Roll And Rock', a contemporary satirical nod in the direction of youth in *Silk Stockings* (1957). Often compared to Lubitsch, it was perhaps appropriate that Mamoulian should have directed this delightful musical version of *Ninotchka* (1939). In this one, Cyd Charisse danced her way through the Garbo role.

LEO McCAREY

Born Los Angeles, 3 October 1898. **Died** 1969

First attracted to the cinema after he had been studying law at the University of Southern California, Leo McCarey served his apprenticeship as a 'scriptgirl', then assistant director to Tod Browning during the early 20s. Signed up by comedy producer Hal Roach in 1923, he spent the following six years as a gag writer, director and supervisor at the Roach studio. McCarey worked closely with comedian Charley Chase on many of his best shorts like *Bad Boy* and *His Wooden Wedding* (both 1925). Then, in an inspired moment in 1926 he brought Laurel and Hardy together as a comedy team for the first time and worked mainly on their movies during the following years, directing and writing some and supervising most of the others. It was here that he developed his taste for improvisation and visual comedy.

After leaving Roach he tried his hand directing features – for Pathé and for Fox, and first made his name as the director of one of the most successful Eddie Cantor vehicles for producer Sam Goldwyn, *The Kid From Spain* (UA, 1932). He then signed a contract with Paramount, the home of many of Hollywood's top comedy stars, and immediately found himself attempting to cope with the Marx Brothers who had specially requested him for *Duck Soup* (1933). Their previous movies had been little more than undisciplined versions of shows they had developed on stage, full of bits of inspired lunacy, but never satisfactorily fitted together. In *Duck Soup* the anti-war, anti-establishment satire and loosely controlled anarchy was familiar Marx material. But McCarey's guiding hand made all the difference. Without attempting to impose himself on their comedy routines, he did at least manage to keep them under control long enough to get the shots in the can. 'They were completely mad,' he commented later. 'I couldn't get them all together at one time – one was always missing.' He brought in his old friend Edgar Kennedy from the Roach studio to do a comedy scene with Harpo and introduced a few favourite silent comedy routines like the mirror without a glass gag which has never been done better. (Caught trying to steal the plans of war from Margaret Dumont's safe at night, Harpo and Chico, dressed identically to Groucho, try to convince him that what he's seeing is his own mirror image). The last, and unquestionably the best, of the early Marx comedies at Paramount, *Duck Soup* did not do well at the box-office, and was, incredibly, dismissed by many of the critics as just another Marx Bros picture. Not a personal favourite of McCarey's either, his final comment was, 'the most surprising thing about this film is that I succeeded in not going crazy.'

Six Of A Kind (1934) which followed was more Burns and Allen than W.C. Fields, while McCarey enjoyed directing the Mae West movie *Belle Of The Nineties* (1934) because it gave him an opportunity to work with Duke Ellington and

his band. Moving away from comedy 'star vehicles' to a vein of Populist and sentimental human interest comedy similar to that favoured by Frank Capra, McCarey emerged during 1935-36 as Paramount's answer to the successful Capra (at Columbia) with *Ruggles Of Red Gap* (1935) and *Make Way For Tomorrow* (1936), and then was hired by Columbia when the studio found itself in a contractual dispute with Capra!

Charles Laughton gave perhaps his best ever comedy performance as Ruggles, the English butler whose master loses him in a card game to a visiting American nouveau riche couple who take him back with them to the Western town of Red Gap, Washington. The rest of the picture represents the natural and logical working out of this initial situation. Ruggles gradually becomes more indepen-

Top: It is to Leo McCarey that credit goes for creating a landmark in film comedy history by his inspirational pairing of Laurel and Hardy. He supervised many of their films, directed a few and wrote others. The still shows fat Ollie (left) and thin Stan in *Leave 'Em Laughing* (1928), supervised by Leo, and photographed by another future illustrious director, George Stevens.

Above: *The Kid From Spain* (1932), an Eddie Cantor (illustrated) vehicle for Sam Goldwyn was a huge success for the star and made McCarey's name.

Left: In 1934, McCarey directed the fabled Mae West in *Belle Of The Nineties*, in which she played a saloon entertainer. It was not one of her – or his – best efforts.

dent, democratised and Americanised, as suggested in his famous recitation of Lincoln's Gettysburg Address. An excellent collection of down-to-earth, middle-aged character actors led by Charlie Ruggles, ZaSu Pitts and Maude Eburne kept keep the picture from lapsing into sentimentality, and led McCarey into his next movie, *Make Way For Tomorrow*, about the plight of an elderly couple (Victor Moore and Beulah Bondi) who are mistreated by their grown-up children and forced to separate. This sensitive and unusual drama did so badly at the box-office that it led to McCarey's departure from Paramount after four years with the studio.

Quickly snapped up by the tyrannical Harry Cohn at Columbia, he began work on *The Awful Truth* (1937), the kind of inventive domestic comedy he did best. Cohn was baffled and annoyed by McCarey's casual and improvisational methods of working: 'I hired you to make a great comedy so I could show up Frank Capra,' he complained to the director. 'The only one who's going to laugh at this picture is Capra.' How wrong he was. Cary Grant, cast opposite Irene Dunne, responded well to McCarey's unusual approach with the first of those debonair and witty performances with which he became identified. A great success, *The Awful Truth* was Oscar-nominated for Best Picture and screenplay, while the director won his first award, following hot on the heels of Capra who had won for Columbia's *Mr Deeds Goes To Town* the previous year.

In 1938 McCarey directed Charles Boyer and Irene Dunne in *Love Affair*, a romantic movie which mixed comedy and drama. Highly successful, it earned Leo another Oscar nomination (for the original scenario) and marked the beginning of his association with RKO as an independent producer-director-writer. In *Once Upon A Honeymoon* (RKO, 1942) he tried unsuccessfully to mix comedy and romance with anti-Nazi propaganda, but bounced back the following year (1943), returning to Paramount for *Going My Way*. The movie was a mix of comedy and social message, although it was so lacking in any specifically 40s feel, or even references to the war, that it could easily have been filmed in the 30s. The picture opened with the arrival of Bing Crosby as a new style, modern priest whose luggage includes golf clubs, tennis racquet and fishing rod. Changing out of his wet clothes into very un-priest-like casual dress – slacks, tennis shoes and St Louis Browns sweat-shirt – he is confronted by the cantankerous, conservative elderly priest, played by Barry Fitzgerald giving one of his most memorable character performances. Unfortunately, the delightful comedy byplay of the opening is left behind as the film becomes progressively more sentimental and 'uplifting' and develops into a familiar clichéd, Capra-style conflict between the nasty bankers and businessmen versus the nice priests and their parish church which is in financial difficulties. Phenomenally successful, the winner of seven Oscars including Best Picture, actor (Crosby), supporting actor (Fitzgerald) and a pair for McCarey, the formula worked so well that the director immediately directed a

sequel, co-starring Crosby, with Ingrid Bergman cast as a suitably practical, down-to-earth Sister Superior. Another charming and sentimental movie, *The Bells Of St Mary's* (1945) proved to be an even bigger hit and the most profitable in the entire history of RKO.

By 1948 Capra's *Mr Deeds* – Gary Cooper – had become McCarey's *Good Sam* (RKO, 1948), a small town good Sam-aritan whose generosity to others is exploited to the point where he is turned into a pauper and is forced to change his ways. The last, and least, of McCarey's human interest morality tales of the 40s, it was followed, after a three year gap, by *My Son John* (Paramount, 1951), a nasty piece of anti-Communist propaganda only memorable for the sad fact that

McCarey succeeded in completing it in spite of the death of star Robert Walker during filming. (For Walker's important death scene he ingeniously used outtakes from Hitchcock's 1951 *Strangers On A Train*.) For his last group of movies he joined 20th Century-Fox in 1956. He had a modest success with a glossy CinemaScope remake of his own *Love Affair*, retitled *An Affair To Remember* (1957) and starring Cary Grant and Deborah Kerr; *Rally Round The Flag, Boys!* (1958) was a weak attempt to revive the screwball comedy, with Paul Newman looking distinctly uneasy in the lead. A sentimentalised drama of a pair of priests defying the Communists in 40s China, *Satan Never Sleeps* (1961), brought McCarey's long career to an undistinguished end.

Top: Barry Fitzgerald (left) and Bing Crosby in *Going My Way* (1943). This somewhat sentimentalised tale of priests young and old, and the Good Church warding off the Bad World, was phenomenally successful and won seven Oscars.

Above: Leo McCarey was undoubtedly a livelier character than this formal posed portrait would indicate.

Left: Cary Grant and Deborah Kerr starred in a lush, tug-at-the-heartstrings romance with witty, sophisticated overtones. The film was *An Affair To Remember* (1959), and was a remake of McCarey's own 1938 hit, *Love Affair*, which had starred Charles Boyer and Irene Dunne. This one was also highly professional and very enjoyable.

LEWIS MILESTONE

Born Chisinau near Odessa, Russia, 30 September 1895. **Died** 1980

Lewis Milestone knocked around Hollywood for over forty years trying his hand at virtually every type of picture. He began in silent comedy and in the 60s was filming in colour and Ultra Panavision 70, and even tried working in television '...to find out what it was all about... The experience was horrible.' Along the way he worked for every major studio, many of the minor ones and leading independent producers such as Hal Roach, Howard Hughes and Sam Goldwyn. His career reads like a veritable chronology of Hollywood movie-making: He first made his name as a top director during 1929-31 with an Oscar winning World War I comedy, *Two Arabian Knights* (Hughes/UA, 1927), early entries in the gangster cycle, the outstanding serious war picture *All Quiet On The Western Front* (Universal, 1930), and tackled the newspaper theme in the hard-hitting *The Front Page* (Hughes/UA, 1931). During the 30s he mixed musicals with star vehicles, but his career was given a much needed lift in the 40s when he returned to his first love, the war picture. Milestone followed the trend into colour during the late 40s and, with the decline in the studios, found himself working mainly abroad. He returned to the war genre periodically

throughout his career – the conflict in the Pacific in the Technicolored *Halls Of Montezuma* (20th Century-Fox, 1951), British and Greek commando raids in *They Who Dare* (1953) and the Korean war in *Pork Chop Hill* (UA, 1959). His last picture was the much-troubled remake of *Mutiny On The Bounty* (MGM, 1962) starring Marlon Brando, on which he was brought in to replace British director Carol Reed. An accomplished and craftsman-like director, Milestone suffered from the fact that ever since his phenomenal success with *All Quiet* his name carried an aura of prestige, but little clout. Thus studios were tempted to hire him to beef up projects which were unworthy of him and he accepted, staying in motion pictures, as he put it, '..in the expectation that the next film might give you a chance to redeem yourself. Everyone in the film industry has to compromise – you're faced with the alternative of staying out and telling everybody what a big hero you are.'

Milestone's career presents an interesting contrast with that of the similarly Russian-born Rouben Mamoulian who always had a second career in the theatre to fall back on. Milestone emigrated to the US at the age of seventeen and, ap-

propriately enough for the future specialist in war movies, got his start in pictures during the war as a cutter and assistant director of training films in the US Army Signal Corps. After the war he made his way to Hollywood where he worked as a cutter, then assistant director and script writer for director William Seiter. He was given an opportunity to direct by Jack Warner, who provided him with a young scriptwriter named Darryl Zanuck for his first two features starring Marie Prevost. Milestone had his first big success in 1927 with *Two Arabian Knights*, a follow-up to the 1926 hit movie, *What Price Glory?* (Fox) directed by Raoul Walsh. The movie starred William Boyd, and Louis Wolheim whom Milestone had brought out to Hollywood after seeing him in the stage version of *What Price Glory?* The love interest was provided by Mary Astor who recalled the picture as 'a real goodie' about 'a couple of American soldiers escaping from (German) army imprisonment in the uniforms of Arabian prisoners.' Most vivid in Miss Astor's memory, however, were the nights spent in the cold and murky water of San Pedro harbour, an unpleasant way to get a comedy sequence on film.

The Racket (Hughes/Paramount, 1928) was a successful film adaptation of the hit play set in Chicago gangsterland with Wolheim in the role of the gangster Nick Scarsi (played by Edward G. Robinson on stage). It was Milestone's third film for the young millionaire and aspiring movie mogul, Howard Hughes, and added to the director's growing prestige by demonstrating his expertise in dealing with a serious and topical dramatic subject. Paramount demonstrated remarkable prescience by teaming Milestone with star Emil Jannings in *Betrayal*, then releasing the picture in May 1929 to coincide with the first ever Oscar awards ceremony when both men emerged as winners – Jannings as Best Actor and Milestone as Best Comedy Director for *Two Arabian Knights*. Milestone's standing had never been higher, and he was hired by Universal to direct the studio's ambitious production of *All Quiet On The Western Front*, from the novel by Erich Maria Remarque. This was the first time the director was given an opportunity to work on such a large scale, and one of the strengths of the picture was the manner in which it succeeded in blending the personal, intimate story with a more comprehensive view of war and the battlefields. Although an early talkie, Milestone refused to be intimidated by the demands of the sound technicians. He insisted on working with one camera, as before, and carefully preplanned all the shooting with drawings of each camera set-up, a kind of storyboard treatment which he adopted here for the first time and continued to use in his later pictures. The battles were filmed on a *mesa* in California which came closest to matching the European terrain. For his superb staging of the battle sequences he made use of a mobile camera and even Universal's giant camera crane, first designed for use in Paul Fejos' *Broadway* (1929). 'All the long tracking shots were done with a silent camera unless the scene involved dialogue. We used dubbing and post-synching not for dialogue but for sound-effects... Utilising something I'd learned from watching war footage, I reproduced the smoke of battle by burning a lot of second-hand tyres... Any time we didn't like the background we obscured it with smoke.' The battle scenes were so convincing that shots have since turned up in compilation documentaries about the war.

For the picture Milestone assembled a talented team of collaborators including ace cameraman Arthur Edeson, and art director Charles D. Hall who made a remarkable job of creating a little German town covering four acres. Lew Ayres was outstanding as the young German soldier caught up in the horrors of war, but Louis Wolheim almost stole the picture in the third of his Milestone roles as the grizzled veteran soldier, Katczinsky. One of the most highly acclaimed American films of the 30s, *All Quiet* won Oscars for Best Picture and Best Director, and boosted the prestige of Universal. (The studio had to wait 43 years for its second winner, *The Sting* in 1973). It was a box-office hit as well, but was not profitable due to its high cost of $1.25 million.

Milestone immediately consolidated his position as a top director with a lively and fast moving adaptation of the classic newspaper play by Hecht and MacArthur, *The Front Page*. He was somewhat less successful, however, with his film version of Somerset Maugham's *Rain* (UA, 1932) starring Joan Crawford. His first musical, *Hallelujah, I'm A Bum* (UA, 1933), starring Al Jolson, was charming and original, and the only musical of the period to be placed uncompromisingly in the context of the Depression. Although the films which followed were distinctly variable in quality, Milestone managed to direct two outstanding productions during the late 30s: *The General Died At Dawn* (Paramount, 1936) was a superior action drama starring Gary Cooper and Akim Tamiroff, while *Of Mice And Men* (Roach/UA, 1939) from John Steinbeck's poignant novel, demonstrated Milestone's ability to handle an intimate dramatic subject. Most memorable of his many later war movies was *A Walk In The Sun* (20th Century-Fox, 1945), which followed the experiences of a single American patrol after the landing on the beach at Salerno. *The Strange Love Of Martha Ivers* (Paramount, 1946) was Milestone's sole venture into 40s *film noir*. It chalked up a dominating performance from Barbara Stanwyck, and marked the screen debut of Kirk Douglas. For his first colour subject, Milestone turned again to Steinbeck and came up with *The Red Pony* (Republic, 1949), a likeable late entry in that 40s animal pet cycle which had included *Lassie Come Home* (1943), *National Velvet* (1944) and *The Yearling* (1946), all from MGM. Milestone directed little of note during the 50s, and retired in the mid-60s after the ill-fated *Mutiny On The Bounty* and some TV work.

'Although his initial reputation rested on a monument against war, his Second World War projects settled for the glamour of battle and the standard group of unambiguous soldiers.'

David Thomson in 'A Biographical Dictionary of the Cinema'

Top: Joan Crawford and Walter Huston (father of John) rehearse on set for *Rain* (1932). Milestone is seated behind the camera. Somerset Maugham's steamy story of a missionary in the tropics lusting after a prostitute, has seen several screen versions including a silent, *Sadie Thompson* (1928) starring Gloria Swanson, and *Miss Sadie Thompson* (1953) with lush Rita Hayworth in Technicolor *and* 3-D.

Above: Milestone made *A Walk In The Sun* in 1945. It was a powerful, perceptive and well-made war film, although whether it quite lived up to the poster's hype is another matter!

Left: Another of the director's later war films was *The Purple Heart* (1944). The cast were Charles Russell (seated), Sam Levene (standing left), Farley Granger (foreground centre) and Dana Andrews (right).

VICTOR SJÖSTRÖM

Born Silbodal, Sweden, 20 September 1879. **Died** 1960

The father of the early Swedish cinema, Victor Sjöström had his early education in the USA where his father, a failed businessman, had brought the family in the hope of regaining his fortune. It was an unhappy experience, and when his mother, a former actress, died, the boy returned to Sweden. At sixteen he decided to become an actor, and after only four years was an established theatre actor and director. He appeared in his first picture, *De Svarta Maskerna* (1912), directed by that master of early Swedish film-making, Mauritz Stiller, who provided the scenario for Sjöström's own first film as director (and actor) later that year, *Trädgardsmästaren*. During the following years Sjöström occasionally appeared for Stiller, and was extremely active as a director. He completed forty features between 1912-20, also acting in and writing the scripts for many of them.

Sjöström, like Stiller, worked for Charles Magnusson's pioneering Svensk Biografteatern company where he had a stock company of actors and a regular group of collaborators behind the camera. Sjöström's films were notable for their striking location photography, yet he most often drew his inspiration from literary sources and was characterised by his talent for relating his characters to their often natural and primitive settings. Thus, his first important film, *Ingebörg Holm* (1913) – successful throughout Europe – and his Swedish masterpiece, *The Outlaw And His Wife* (1917), were based on contemporary plays. During the years when European film-making was badly disrupted by the war, the Swedish cinema, led by Sjöström and Stiller, flourished as never before or since. It set a standard of maturity in the treatment of characters and relationships, in photography and in imaginative power, which even the Americans found hard to match. Unfortunately, this quality proved impossible to sustain during the 20s and, in 1923, spurred no doubt by the commerical failure of several of his own films, Sjöström went to Hollywood, where he accepted an offer from the Goldwyn company.

When the company merged into the newly formed MGM, Sjöström – his name changed to Seastrom – directed the very first MGM production, *He Who Gets Slapped* (1924). An atmospheric and inventive circus drama with expressionistic overtones, it provided interesting roles for three new MGM stars, Lon Chaney, Norma Shearer and John Gilbert, and was both a critical and box-office success. Assessing Sjöström's overall career is difficult because nearly all of his earliest silent films have been lost, as well as most of his MGM productions including the Garbo vehicle, *The Divine Woman* (1927). Her co-star was the Swedish actor, Lars Hansen, who had been brought over specially to play opposite Lillian Gish in another Sjöström film of note, *The Scarlet Letter* (1926). Yet even if the lost movies were to be rediscovered, it is unlikely that any of them would match *The Wind* (1928). An extraordinary drama of the American West, it was filmed in the Mojave desert where Sjöström's use of the American landscape went beyond any demands of 'naturalism'. In the climactic final reels when the heroine (Lillian Gish) is going out of her mind, menaced by the villain and isolated by a seemingly endless sand storm,

'. . . fresh from Sweden, my wife and all the associations of a lifetime left behind, I felt lost among the big sets and great technical facilities of which I understood next to nothing and wondered if the day would come when I'd be on my way back to Sweden, a failure.'

Sjöström achieves an almost surrealistic intensity and power. Exquisitely lit and photographed, and boasting a charismatic central performance by Gish (supported by Hansen and Montagu Love), the film endures as a masterpiece, yet it was not a box-offfice success, and marked the decline of Miss Gish's position as a major Hollywood star. For Victor Sjöström, the coming of sound brought his directing career to a virtual close. After one MGM talkie, *A Lady To Love* (1930), starring Edward G. Robinson, and a sound film back in Sweden, he returned to direct one last time, in England, with *Under The Red Robe* in 1937. However, he appropriately rounded out his career during the 40s and 50s by acting in a number of movies, most notably as the old professor in Ingmar Bergman's *Wild Strawberries* (1957).

Top: Victor Sjöstrom (left) directs Greta Garbo and Lowell Sherman in *The Divine Woman* (1927). Sadly for the army of Garbo lovers, the film is lost.

Above: The apprehensive young bride (Lillian Gish) is served undrinkable coffee by her clumsy but loving husband (Lars Hansen) on their wedding night in his primitive log cabin which is to be her home, and her only flimsy protection against *The Wind* (1928).

Left: Sjöstrom the actor as the dying professor in Ingmar Bergman's *Wild Strawberries* (1957). With him here is Bibi Andersson.

JOHN M. STAHL

Born New York City, 21 January 1886. **Died** 1950

A complete assessment of John M. Stahl's career is made difficult by the fact that relatively few of his many silent pictures have survived. However, it is clear that he developed a special interest in domestic drama and 'woman's pictures' quite early on, and remained remarkably consistent in this throughout his forty-plus years as a director. Having acted on the stage as a young man, Stahl soon turned to the cinema and was directing regularly from 1914. The quality and type of his pictures appealed to fledgling producer Louis B. Mayer who was attempting to expand his small production company (releasing through First National) in 1920. Stahl signed with Mayer and remained with him for eight years, including the early years of MGM. Throughout this period the young director continued to specialise in marital drama and the occasional comedy-drama. His movies most often concerned an unfaithful husband or wife, the break-up of their marriage due to jealousy or misunderstandings, then a change of heart leading to a reconciliation in time for the final fade out. Lewis Stone most often played the husband – he would become a staple figure at MGM a few years later – paired with a variety of silent actresses: Barbara Castleton in *The Child Thou Givest Me* (1921), Helene Chadwick in *Why Men Leave Home*, and Florence Vidor in *Husbands And Lovers* (both 1924). The titles say it all. Stahl acquired a mastery of the most advanced techniques of filming and editing, and leading Hollywood editor Margaret Booth, who got her start with him, remembers the director as a 'hard task-master. He was a perfectionist; he kept doing things over and over again. He shot every sequence so it could be cut in many different ways'.

At MGM under Mayer, Stahl directed only three pictures during 1926-27, of which the most interesting was *Lovers?* (1927) starring Alice Terry and Ramon Novarro. Like many of the leading directors he disliked the new, large studio set-up, and gave up directing to turn independent producer. He went into partnership with the small Tiffany Company, which was duly renamed Tiffany-Stahl, but the venture only lasted for three years and, by late 1930, he was back directing once again, this time at Universal where he spent most of the 30s. Here he made his name as a stylish master of the 'woman's picture', a genre which enjoyed great popularity during these years. His films were characterised by their fluid style and expressive use of close-ups. In 1932 Irene Dunne starred in his film adaptation of the Fannie Hurst weepie, *Back Street*, the first of three versions of the story to be filmed. Rather better, with its blend of fully developed characters and racial/social overtones was *Imitation Of Life* (1934), starring Claudette Colbert and Louise Beavers, the only Stahl film to be nominated for a Best Picture Oscar. Finally, *Magnificent Obsession* (1935), again with Irene Dunne, completed Stahl's trilogy of famous 30s

weepies, all of which were remade, the latter two in glossy colour versions by producer Ross Hunter (for Universal).

Along the way Stahl also directed Margaret Sullavan in her first, remarkable screen performance as the unhappy heroine of *Only Yesterday* (1933). Then, in 1937, he returned to MGM to direct *Parnell*, a typical example of the studio's stylish productions of the late 30s, but with Clark Gable miscast in the title role.

During the 40s Stahl found himself at

20th Century-Fox where he directed an enjoyable Gracie Fields-Monty Woolley comedy, *Holy Matrimony* (1943), but is best remembered there for a pair of rather more serious efforts. *The Keys Of The Kingdom* (1944) provided Gregory Peck with his first major screen success as a Scottish missionary in 19th-century China, while Stahl pulled out all the stops in one last remarkable production, *Leave Her To Heaven* (1945), a larger than life woman's drama starring Gene Tierney. Given the opportunity to work in colour for the first time, the result was stunning and earned an Oscar for Leon Shamroy's

lighting. Stahl's prestige was at its peak in 1945 when these two movies earned more than half a dozen nominations between them, including one each for Peck and Tierney. (Although he was one of the founder members of the Academy, Stahl was never personally nominated for an Oscar). He was replaced on *Forever Amber* (1947) by Otto Preminger, but made four more films before his death, concluding with *Oh, You Beautiful Doll* (1949), a run-of-the-mill musical biopic.

Left: Little Richard Hendrick (centre), known at the time as 'The Wonder Child Of The Screen', was *The Child Thou Gavest Me* (1921). The movie was one of a string of early marital dramas which young John Stahl (right) directed for mogul-to-be, Louis B. Mayer (left).

Left: Claudette Colbert (right), Ned Sparks and Louise Beavers in *Imitation Of Life* (1934). Nominated for Best Picture, this sturdy melodrama was remade by Douglas Sirk with Lana Turner in 1959.

Below: Irene Dunne and John Boles in the classic weepie, *Back Street* (1932), remade twice more.

JOSEF VON STERNBERG

Born Vienna, 29 May 1894. **Died** 1969

Generally regarded as Hollywood's outstanding visual stylist, Josef von Sternberg is best known for the series of movies he made with Marlene Dietrich during the early 30s, although he first made his mark in the silents, and continued active until the early 50s.

Relatively early in his career, Von Sternberg developed a reputation as an uncompromising perfectionist on the set, following that other famous Hollywood 'von' – Stroheim. But in contrast to Stroheim's striving for authenticity of detail in his recreation of mainly European settings on the screen, Sternberg was more concerned with the overall 'effect'. His imagined exotic settings, all created on the Paramount backlot, ranged from China, Spain and the Chicago underworld, to Morocco, and Russia under Catherine the Great. As he pointed out, 'When I made *Underworld* (1927) I was not a gangster, nor did I know anything about gangsters. I knew nothing about China when I made *Shanghai Express* (1932). These are not authentic. I don't value the fetish for authenticity. On the contrary, the illusion of reality is what I look for, not reality itself'.

A true 'auteur', who strove to realise his personal vision on the screen, Sternberg not only collaborated closely on all aspects of his pictures but took an active part in the design, did his own editing and even photographed some of his films himself – an unheard of activity for a Hollywood director. Most important of all stylistically was the photography, with the play of light and shadow always carefully controlled. As he wrote in his autobiography, 'Fun In A Chinese Laundry', 'The extensive range of black-and-white with its numberless variations is capable of producing all the visual drama that may be required. But above all, the greatest art in motion picture photography is to be able to give life to the dead space that exists between the lens and the subject before it. Smoke, rain, fog, dust, and steam can emotionalize empty space, and so can the movement of the camera'. He carried this notion to its fullest expression in his last and most baroque picture with Dietrich, *The Devil Is A Woman* (1935), which appears as a remarkable exercise in filmic textures. The light filters through the slatted windows, through the lattice-work or the leaves of overhanging trees, the smoke of cigarettes is ever present, and key scenes take place in the pouring rain and a misty dawn. Dietrich appears in a seemingly endless variety of striking costumes decorated with ruffles, lace or sequins, with flowers or combs in her hair, while the stylised sets conjure up a fantasy vision of Spain. Every element in the picture contributes to the overall effect. Sternberg at his best could achieve the most astonishing blend of atmospheric photography, imaginative sets and costume designs, and remarkable performances from his actors, all integrated into a unified whole. This is not only true of his best silents like *Underworld* and *The Docks Of New York* (1928), when all the different elements could more easily be controlled, but of his best early sound films as well. Even his

actors were required to 'fit into the scheme of things' as he so succinctly put it. 'When I direct, endless pains are taken to make the purpose clear, and I do my best to conduct the procedure on an impersonal level. The actor has to fit into the scheme of things, and if he understands he does so gladly; if he fails to understand he must be told exactly what to do and think... The making of a film provides time for little else than outright manipulation of an actor's body and mind...'

Inevitably, certain actors rebelled. After two pictures with Sternberg, William Powell insisted that he never would work with him again (he had it written into his contract); stars such as the young Gary Cooper in *Morocco* (1930) or Victor McLaglen in *Dishonored* (1931), were apt to feel left out as Sternberg concentrated his efforts on his Dietrich heroines who were the main centre of his interest. The

Above: Betty Compson and George Bancroft in *The Docks Of New York* (1928), one of a pair of high quality silent gangster films made by Von Sternberg.

Below left: Cooper and Dietrich in *Morocco* (1930), the first of six films which Marlene made in Hollywood with the director who immortalised her.

Below: Marlene as *Blonde Venus* (1932), a movie of which documentary film-maker Pare Lorentz said, 'The story has all the dramatic integrity of a sashweight murderer's tabloid autobiography'. Indeed, the script caused dissension between the star and her mentor, and a temporary parting of the ways.

working relationship between them was instinctive and intimately close. He succeeded in turning her into one of the most glamorous and alluring of stars, a Continental woman of mystery and a mythic figure of 30s Hollywood whose popularity easily rivalled that of Garbo. Their collaboration continued off the set as well and led to much gossip at the time, resulting in a threatened lawsuit from Sternberg's wife. Dietrich's husband was more understanding. For they merely enjoyed each other's company, and Sternberg valued her advice on all aspects of their pictures together. An intelligent woman who learned quickly, under Sternberg's guidance she developed a fine understanding of the principles of motion picture photography and an exceptional rapport with the camera, which she put to good use in later work.

The remarkable surface appearance of Sternberg's films has led some critics to attack him for superficiality. He has himself contributed to such criticism by his oft expressed lack of interest in storyline or plot. ('I care nothing about the story, only how it is photographed and presented.'). He may not deal with the larger political and social issues of the period, but this hardly means that his films lack content or can be dismissed as trivial. Typically, the director's main emphasis is on characters and relationships and he most often, as in the masterful *Shanghai Express* (1932), concentrates his interest on a central love relationship. Extremely mature and sophisticated in his treatment of his characters, they are sketched in with a few deftly observed touches and subtly revealing details. The film has been referred to as a *Grand Hotel* on wheels, but this is misleading. For, in contrast to *Grand Hotel*'s intercutting of a number of different stories of equivalent

importance, here there is but one main story, revolving around Shanghai Lily (Dietrich) and her love for an English officer (Clive Brook). Making use of the trappings of an exotic adventure, the picture is really about love, about the need for the Brook character to ignore convention and accept Lily unconditionally for the remarkable lady she is; and he hardly deserves her. Full of plot twists and witty dialogue, it is significant that Sternberg's scriptwriter here, and on a number of other pictures, was the accomplished Jules Furthman. Other leading Sternberg collaborators of the highest quality at Paramount during the early 30s included costume designer Travis Banton, art director Hans Dreier who created the impressive, stylised Chinese settings for *Shanghai Express* and was Oscar-nominated for his work on *Morocco*, and cameramen Bert Glennon, Lucien Ballard, and Lee Garmes who was nominated for *Morocco* and who won an Oscar

for *Shanghai Express*. This latter was Sternberg's most successful picture of the 30s and the only one of his to be nominated as Best Picture and for Best Director. (Marlene, however, received her only nomination for *Morocco*.)

During these years (1930-32) Sternberg's prestige was at its height. The studio bosses were initially willing to allow him a degree of freedom in making his pictures since they were not expensive, were sufficiently glamorous and popular, and fitted in with the star sytem. He had earned the studio's gratitude by providing it with one of the very top stars, and the fact that Marlene was initially unwilling to work with any other director further strengthened his position. However, such a situation could hardly be expected to last. A dispute developed over the script of *Blonde Venus* (1932), one of Sternberg's most personal but not too successful productions, and Marlene finally agreed to do a picture – *Song Of Songs* (1933) – with another Paramount director, Rouben Mamoulian.

Back with Sternberg again late in 1933, they began work on *The Scarlet Empress*, one of the director's most entertaining and visually striking pictures. It provides a fascinating example of how he could bend the studio system to his own will, taking a popular genre and making it distinctively his own. Ostensibly pre-

Above: Josef von Sternberg directs a scene in the sleazy nightclub in *The Blue Angel* (1930). The plump, somewhat nondescript girl standing with legs astride is, believe it or not, the young Dietrich. Her performance as Lola Lola, the nightclub slut who humiliates and destroys an elderly schoolmaster (Emil Jannings), remains legendary and swept her to international stardom.

Below left: With the English actor, Clive Brook, in *Shanghai Express* (1932). They are former lovers, reunited by fate after several years, during which she has become a woman of dubious character who gives utterance to the memorable line, 'It took more than one man to change my name to Shanghai Lily'!

Below: Dietrich, looking devastating in the uniform of a Russian army officer is held ceremonially aloft in *The Scarlet Empress* (1933), a pictorially brilliant fantasy about the love life of Catherine the Great.

which introduced her to American audiences, and launched them both on a new career.

After his departure from Paramount in 1935 Sternberg was involved in a number of productions. Many of them – like *Sergeant Madden* (MGM, 1939) or *Jet Pilot* (RKO, 1951) – were not really suitable subjects for him, while others like Alexander Korda's ambitious vehicle for Charles Laughton, *I, Claudius* (1937) ran into production difficulties and was – sadly on the basis of existing footage – never completed. Sternberg generally managed best in the exotic Far East. *Macao* (RKO, 1950) shows a few flashes of his genius, while *The Shanghai Gesture* (UA, 1942) was his last Hollywood production of any real distinction. It was appropriate that he should travel to Japan to film his last and outstanding movie, *Anatahan* (aka *The Saga Of Anatahan*) in a studio-created jungle set in Kyoto.

sented as another star vehicle for Dietrich, Sternberg in fact proceeded to turn the true story of young Catherine the Great of Russia into a witty, inventive, tongue-in-cheek treatment of history which appears to have baffled and alienated both audiences and critics at the time. In Sternberg's hands, the theme of Catherine's rise to power became an audacious and sensual stylistic exercise. One can only marvel here at perhaps the most remarkable achievement of Sternberg's career, demonstrating his ability to produce a lavish looking picture at minimal cost through an ingenious use of camera angles, extraordinary gargoyles and statues, montage effects, and even the re-use of crowd scenes from Lubitsch's *The Patriot*. But the box-office failure and the departure of producer B.P. Schulberg meant that Sternberg's days at the studio were numbered. *The Devil Is A Woman* early in 1935 marked the end of his productive eight-year stay at Paramount.

Sternberg had first arrived at the studio in 1927 after experiencing some difficulties as a director. He completed his first feature, *The Salvation Hunters* (1925), after having served a ten-year apprenticeship in the cutting rooms and as an assistant director. Although cheaply made and somewhat pretentious, it was an extremely promising film, demonstrating Sternberg's undoubted talents. But he had been taken off a pair of MGM productions, and his picture for Chaplin, *The Woman Of The Sea*, (aka *The Sea Gull*, 1926) was withdrawn by Chaplin and never released. Hired by B.P. Schulberg to do a salvage job on *Children Of Divorce*, Sternberg finally got his big break with *Underworld*. The first major gangster picture success which initiated the popular cycle of the late 20s, it was a clearly individualistic production, with the gangster elements subordinated to the director's primary interest in the visual possibilities

of the genre and in the emotional development of the main characters. Here, as in his other silent masterpiece, *The Docks Of New York* (1928), the gruff but likeable hero was played by George Bancroft, while his idealised heroine was realised by the stylish Evelyn Brent.

Having completed his first, not-too-successful talkie, *Thunderbolt* (1929), Sternberg sailed for Germany. Requested by star Emil Jannings for his first sound film, the UFA/Paramount production of *The Blue Angel* (1930), Sternberg's search for an actress to play the leading female role led him to the discovery of Dietrich, then a relatively minor German stage and screen actress. Her suitably earthy performance as Lola Lola dominated the picture, and Sternberg invited her to Hollywood to co-star with Gary Cooper in *Morocco*, the picture

Top left: *The Devil Is A Woman* (1935), and the woman is, of course, Dietrich. It was her last film with Von Sternberg, and perhaps the most ornate, baroque and stylised to date. Set in late 19th-century Madrid, it cast the star as a *femme fatale* on a grand scale, and decked her out in an extraordinary number and variety of outfits.

Left: Von Sternberg in 1950, with Janet Leigh, during the making of *Jet Pilot*, a poor spy film unsuited to its director's particular gifts, and to which he brought nothing of distinction. The film's release was delayed until 1957.

Below: *The Saga Of Anatahan* (1953), filmed on location in Japan, was Von Sternberg's last work, and a worthy tribute to his talents. The film recreated the true story of a group of Japanese marines on an island, who continued to man their positions for seven years after World War II because they did not believe Japan had been defeated.

ERICH VON STROHEIM

Born Vienna, 22 September 1885. **Died** 1957

On that day in 1929 when Erich von Stroheim was removed as director from the Joseph Kennedy/Gloria Swanson production of *Queen Kelly* it virtually brought an end to the career of one of the most extraordinary, gifted and influential directors in the history of the American cinema. He went on to work as an occasional scriptwriter and screen actor in America and France during the next twenty-five years, and had only one opportunity to direct a sound film that, alas, was never released. Throughout his directorial period, Stroheim's extravagance, both real and alleged, and his recurring problems with producers and censors meant that few of his pictures were released in the form he intended. This makes it difficult, if not impossible, to assess the full extent of his originality and talent. It also means that he came to symbolise the plight of the creative and independent-minded director in a Hollywood which was increasingly coming to be dominated by a small number of giant studios where the producers held sway. As the director, writer and, often, star of his pictures, Stroheim was one of the best-known director personalities of the post-war decade, 1919-29. Yet his reputation rests on nine pictures in all, of which only his first two were released in the form he had intended, and one of these has subsequently been lost. The complex catalogue of Stroheim productions reads as follows:

Queen Kelly (UA, 1929)
– uncompleted, limited release only
Merry-Go-Round (Universal, 1923)
– Stroheim removed midway through production
Walking Down Broadway (Fox, 1932)
– film never released, partly re-shot by other directors
Foolish Wives (Universal, 1922), *Greed* (Goldwyn Co./MGM, 1924) and *The Wedding March* (Paramount, 1928)
– all extra-long features. Stroheim hoped to screen them in two parts, but all were severely cut for release after Stroheim removed
The Merry Widow (MGM, 1925)
– about one reel cut for release and some additional censor cuts made
Blind Husbands (Universal, 1919)
– filmed and released as planned
The Devil's Pass Key (Universal, 1920)
– filmed and released as planned, but is now lost

For many years Stroheim's personal life was also shrouded in mystery and, to a certain extent, one can see him as the victim of his own myth as well as of the exaggerated publicity and overblown stories of his extravagant behaviour. Born into a middle-class Jewish family in Vienna, he emigrated in 1909 at the age of twenty-four. Once in America, he created an almost entirely fictitious version of his own background. 'Erich Oswald' became an aristocratic 'Erich von' (with a long string of additional names tacked on) and a practising Catholic, and maintained the veracity of his fabricated biog-

raphy up to the very end of his life. Playing the role of the European aristocrat brought low by circumstances, he tried his hand at a number of different jobs in and around New York, travelled to San Francisco in 1912, and then on to Hollywood in 1914. Hoping to break into films, he tried to sell some scenarios he had written, but was initially forced to eke out a meagre existence as an extra and bit player in such pictures as *The Birth Of A Nation* (1914) and *Old Heidelberg* (1915).

Employed by the Griffith organisation, Stroheim acquired further experience as an assistant director and technical advisor on European subjects and continued to play small roles. During 1917-18 when America entered the war, he specialised in playing nasty German officers and became famous as 'the man you love to hate'. The last and most notorious of this series of roles came in *The Heart Of Humanity* (1918), featuring a powerful rape sequence during which he tossed a baby out of an upstairs window. The picture brought him to Universal studios for the first time, and marked a turning point in his life and career. The end of the war meant that he was no longer in demand as a screen 'Hun', and he was forced to return to the scenarios which he had been writing from time to time, in an effort to establish himself as a writer-director. He was supported in this endeavour by the new woman in his life, Valerie Germonprez, who had been a bit player in *The Heart Of Humanity* and was to become his third wife for the next twenty years. (He was just reaching the end of the second of his two disastrous marriages, both of which had taken place during the six years since he went West.)

Universal Pictures had been established by Carl Laemmle in 1912. As an enterprising producer he had discovered, or helped to develop, many leading silent stars and directors, but his highly idiosyncratic methods of running the studio, combined with his unwillingness to pay the inflated salaries which the top stars demanded, meant that he kept losing actors and qualified personnel to other companies. The rapid turnover at the studio made it easier for Stroheim to get his initial break as a writer-director-star early in 1919, with one of his projects called 'The Pinnacle'. Retitled *Blind Husbands*, Stroheim's first feature was a remarkably assured and accomplished work for one who had had virtually no

Left: Sam de Grasse (right) and Erich von Stroheim fight it out on an Austrian mountain top in *Blind Husbands* (1919). The film gave Von Stroheim his big break as writer, director and star, but he ran well over budget – a habit which stuck and got worse.

Above: Attired in sharp clothes and sporting a shooting stick, Von Stroheim talks to Norman Kerry during the filming of *Merry-Go-Round* (1923). When the budget began to run riot, Irving Thalberg replaced the director.

Below: Gibson Gowland and ZaSu Pitts in a brutal and powerful scene from *Greed* (1924), which ran nine hours in its original form. Robert E. Sherwood said of the film, 'Von Stroheim is a genius – *Greed* established that beyond all doubt – but he is badly in need of a stopwatch'.

previous experience directing actors. The story was a fairly conventional triangle drama revolving around an Austrian officer's pursuit of a young American wife while she is on holiday and neglected by her husband. Avoiding the stock characters of stage melodrama, Stroheim gave the situation a modern depth and sophistication lacking in most films of the period. Although the lieutenant (played by Stroheim) thinks of himself as a smooth ladykiller, there is a strong suggestion that the husband is aware of his attentions to the wife, but couldn't care less. Stroheim rightly objected to the change of title, for the husband in the film is the least 'blind' of the three main characters. In the climax the husband is revealed as an expert mountain climber, while the lieutenant is a coward and a weakling, appearing even comical (one of the film's feebler touches) when left alone on a mountain top, yelling and praying, with the shadows of vultures above him. Most remarkable of all is the director's attention to details of behaviour, as well as of props and settings. A Tyrolean world is brought convincingly to life on the screen, although the film was shot in California. For the first time, but not the last, Stroheim ran far over budget, but this time with the support of the studio, which recognised the exceptional quality of the project. Originally allocated the most stingy of programmer budgets – $25,000 – the final cost was about five times that, and thus equivalent to that of a typical prestige production of the period. It ended up earning a substantial profit and was an unqualified success with both critics and audiences.

Stroheim added further to his reputation with *The Devil's Pass Key*, another triangle drama concerning an American couple abroad. Set in a studio-created Paris, the picture included some advanced experiments with tinting and toning (colour) effects and cost some 50% more than *Blind Husbands*. But its success made it possible for the director to embark on his first really ambitious production, *Foolish Wives*, in mid-1920, assembling a team which was to remain with him for a number of years. Added to the cameramen of his first pictures, was art director Richard Day, while his favoured stock company of actors included Maude George, Dale Fuller and Cesare Gravina. As the designer of the picture's impressive Monte Carlo sets, Day's contribution was the first of note from a man who was to have a long and distinguished Hollywood career. The film marked the natural culmination of Stroheim's early development at Universal as a director and star with his most sustained and memorable performance. As the central character who links the many subplots and is rarely off the screen, his bogus Russian officer represented a blend of the lieutenant in *Blind Husbands* with the seducer of *Pass Key*. Stroheim's typically uncompromising and satirical look at the filthy rich and the hangers-on in Monte Carlo brought him more notoriety when the picture was released. He was, in fact, the director who first brought a new, European sophistication to the American screen, a few years before the arrival of Lubitsch, Von Sternberg and

Top: Mae Murray and Tully Marshall in *The Merry Widow* (1925), a silent version of the operetta (sic!) in which a bankrupt monarch orders a nobleman (played by John Gilbert) to woo a rich American widow. Full of strange surprises, the film was a hit.

Above: A poster advertises *Walking Down Broadway*, Von Stroheim's first – and last – opportunity to direct a sound film. He made it in 1932 but, alas, owing to studio politics in which he was not involved, the movie was never released. Boots Mallory, it must be said, was not destined for stardom, but she made some interesting marriages – her second husband was James Cagney's producer brother, William, and her third, the attractive Herbert Marshall.

Left: Von Stroheim's last major project as both director and star was *The Wedding March* (1928). The film, a farrago of sex and violence, had the director/star, seen here with Maude George, as a doomed Hapsburg prince.

'The difference between me and Lubitsch is that he shows you the king on the throne and then he shows you the king in his bedroom. I show you the king in his bedroom first. That way when you see him on the throne you have no illusions about him.'

others. But he was accused of alienating American film audiences, and there were censor cuts in addition to the severe cuts inflicted by the releasing studio on his six-hour original version. Nonetheless, it was another prestige success for Universal, and did well at the box-office, although it lost money due to the excessive costs. At $1 million it was Universal's most expensive production to date. The filming had been brought to a premature halt by the young production manager, Irving Thalberg, who also prevented Stroheim from starring in his next film so that he could be removed from the director's chair if necessary. And that is exactly what happened when he began to run over budget on *Merry-Go-Round*. Yet much of Stroheim survives in the picture, completed by Rupert Julian but retaining Stroheim's cast, crew and sets, and adhering closely to his shooting script.

Immediately signed by the Goldwyn Company, Stroheim saw the opportunity at last to film his pet project, *Greed*, based on the novel 'McTeague' by Frank Norris, and using many of his favourite cast and crew who had come with him from Universal. (The stars were Gibson Gowland, the guide from *Blind Husbands*, and ZaSu Pitts in her most remarkable non-comedy role.) With its realistic American setting the film is often regarded as the exception among Stroheim's other 'Continental' projects, yet it had much in common with them in its original nine-hour version. It represented the ultimate example of his obsessive interest in details of character and setting, and his fondness for counterpointing and enriching the main plot with one or more subplots. Filmed in 1923, by the time *Greed* was ready for release late in 1924, Goldwyn had merged with Metro and Mayer to form MGM with Stroheim's old nemesis, Irving Thalberg, as production chief, and the release version was severely cut. The director nonetheless agreed to make one film for the new company, a bizarre and very personal reworking of *The Merry Widow*, starring Mae Murray and John Gilbert. A tremendous box-office hit, it made back all the money the studio claimed it had lost on *Greed*, but Stroheim had already moved on to what was to prove his last major project as director and star, *The Wedding March*. Set in the Vienna of the declining Hapsburg empire, it returned

to themes which he had originally hoped to develop in the ill-fated *Merry-Go-Round*. Once again, mounting costs caused a rift with the producer (Pat Powers), and the project was passed on to

Paramount, who released the film in a truncated form. After Stroheim's last silent project, the ill-fated *Queen Kelly*, his directorial career was virtually over, but Fox gave him an opportunity in 1932 to prove that he could direct on a smaller scale and stay within a normal budget. Unfortunately he appears to have been the victim of a producer battle behind the scenes which meant that his film, *Walking Down Broadway*, was never even released. Employed for a time as a scriptwriter back at MGM, he got his best offers as an actor – opposite Garbo in *As You Desire Me* (1932) and then in France, where his best remembered part was as the prison commandant in Jean Renoir's *La Grande Illusion* (1937). In the US during the 40s he appeared in two Billy Wilder pictures of note: as Rommel in *Five Graves To Cairo* (Paramount, 1943) and, memorably, as Gloria Swanson's enigmatic butler in *Sunset Boulevard* (Paramount, 1950). During the 50s he appeared in a few last movies in France, where he preferred to live with the companion of his later years, the actress Denise Vernac.

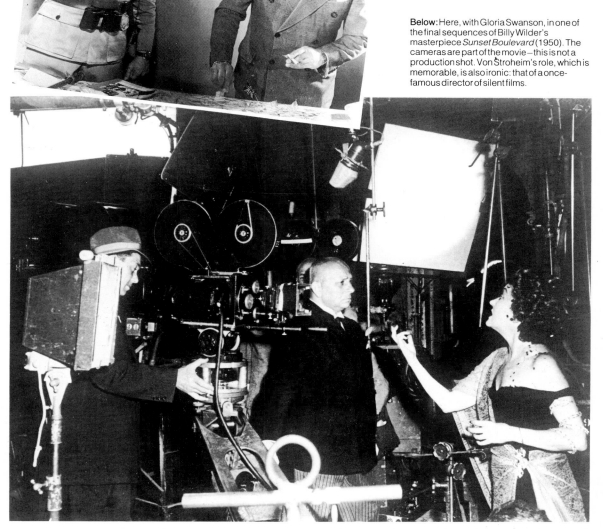

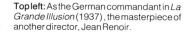

Top left: As the German commandant in *La Grande Illusion* (1937), the masterpiece of another director, Jean Renoir.

Left: Field Marshal Erwin Rommel in conference with Erich von Stroheim! This is a Paramount publicity still for Billy Wilder's *Five Graves To Cairo* (1943), in which Von Stroheim gave a fine performance as the renowned soldier. He did *not* play a dual role.

Below: Here, with Gloria Swanson, in one of the final sequences of Billy Wilder's masterpiece *Sunset Boulevard* (1950). The cameras are part of the movie – this is not a production shot. Von Stroheim's role, which is memorable, is also ironic: that of a once-famous director of silent films.

KING VIDOR

Born Galveston, Texas, 8 February 1894. **Died** 1982

One of the most dependable and consistent of American directors, King Vidor was both flexible and eclectic in his tastes, but selective in his choice of projects, and directed many outstanding pictures during the course of more than forty years behind the camera. Accommodating himself to the studio system, he alternated between commercial assignments and projects of personal significance throughout much of his career. But whatever the enterprises, his qualities as a director, and his ability with actors, meant that few of his pictures could ever be termed routine.

Born in 1894 – the period of the cinema's beginnings, Vidor was one of the first young directors to grow up with the movies. As a teenager he worked in the local nickelodeon taking tickets and as a projectionist. He tried his hand at shooting items for the newsreels and some comedy shorts before he decided to head for California – in a partly paid for Model T-Ford – with his young wife, actress Florence Vidor. The year was 1915, and the Vidors arrived penniless. Florence was initially the more successful of the two, and King was forced to work his way up from clerk to scenario writer to director of shorts before finally getting to direct short features. He even managed to set up his own little studio for a time, and Florence starred in a number of the pictures he made during 1919-22 as an independent producer-director. Then the money ran out. The young director was employed by Metro, and then by Goldwyn where he met and worked with the actress who was to become his second wife, Eleanor Boardman. Their contracts were transferred to the newly merged MGM in 1924 where she starred in his films. Although Vidor was recognised as a competent, even exceptional, director, and his movies were generally well received, he was unhappy churning out what he regarded as 'ephemeral films'. Taking his complaint to the young production chief, Irving Thalberg, they decided on a World War I subject as the most promising solution, and Laurence Stallings, the author of the current hit play, 'What Price Glory?', was hired to write an original script. Unfortunately, all he had provided was a short scenario when he decided to head back to New York; Vidor accompanied Stallings on the train and chased him all over New York, taking copious notes as the writer reminisced about his war experiences. Vidor and scriptwriter Harry Behn finally gathered enough material for the picture to go ahead, and so *The Big Parade* (1925) was born.

Vidor's original idea was to present the war from the viewpoint of the 'average man'; to stress the personal, intimate story rather than the large-scale or epic qualities. For the lead role he selected John Gilbert whom he had directed in two of his previous MGM movies. Gilbert's slight awkwardness in the unfamiliar role of a typical doughboy was ideally suited to the theme of the civilian sud-

denly thrust into the middle of a war taking place in a foreign country where he couldn't even speak the language. Impressed by the quality of the footage he had seen, Thalberg urged Vidor to shoot additional battle scenes, including an impressive shot of a seemingly endless convoy of trucks, troops and planes, 'the big parade', moving up to the front. The picture still ended up costing less than $400,000 and was released in the autumn of 1925, a few months after the box-office success of Von Stroheim's *The Merry Widow*. It was phenomenally successful, and the most profitable film in the first fifteen years of MGM's history (prior to *Gone With The Wind*, 1939), turning Gilbert into a top star, making the names of Vidor and Thalberg, and giving a great financial boost to the studio. Vidor's contract with the Goldwyn Company, like those of Sjöström and Von Stroheim, had guaranteed a percentage of the profits of their pictures. But the shrewd Thalberg managed to persuade them to change this. Considering that Vidor would have earned a small fortune from *The Big Parade*, he took it quite philosophically: 'I thus spared myself from becoming a

Above: Renee Adorée, a favourite star of the early 20s, King Vidor and John Gilbert during filming of *The Big Parade* (1925). Both an impressive visual spectacle and an affecting anti-war film, this production fully established Vidor's reputation.

Left: Vidor relaxes with Marion Davies during a break in shooting *Not So Dumb* (1929), an early sound movie and the third of three they made together.

Below: Director (centre with script under arm) and crew survey a Tennessee location during *Hallelujah* (1929).

millionaire instead of a struggling young director trying to do something interesting and better with a camera'.

At least he was treated relatively well by the studio during the next six years. He was requested by MGM's newest superstar, Lillian Gish, for *La Bohème* (1926), his first major costume picture, with John Gilbert as co-star. In typical Gish fashion she insisted on rehearsals before filming began and threw herself so convincingly into the role of the tubercular, tragic Mimi that Vidor and Gilbert feared for her life during her final death scene, the last sequence to be filmed, just in case... Her remarkable performance dominated the film, but Gilbert was more the centre of interest as *Bardelys The Magnificent* (1926), an entertaining swashbuckler which co-starred Eleanor Boardman. But Vidor was at his best with contemporary American subjects like *The Crowd* which he shot in 1927, one of the last outstanding productions of the silent era.

'Someone once asked me if I would rather direct a battle scene with 6000 soldiers or a love scene with two important stars. Without hesitation I answer, "the battle scene".'
1974

With its moving depiction of the plight of the ordinary office worker in a big city, 'one of the crowd', the picture emerged as one of the director's most personal, and an unusually downbeat subject for MGM. Eleanor Boardman was cast as the wife, but the lead part was played by a completely unknown young actor named James Murray whom Vidor had spotted among the extras on the studio backlot.

Vidor's last silents were a pair of delightful comedies starring Marion Davies, the lively and attractive mistress of publisher William Randolph Hearst whose production company financed her movies through MGM. But with the coming of sound Vidor was quick to seize the opportunity to demonstrate his ability to cope with the new technology. Instead of waiting for a studio assignment, he saw a chance to develop one of his own pet projects – a film with an all-black cast which he now envisaged as a part musical. Demonstrating his commitment by offering to invest his own salary, he got the studio's approval and headed South to Memphis, Tennessee. In order to avoid the technical restrictiveness of early sound filming in the studio, he had the idea of shooting on location and adding the sound later. *Hallelujah* (1929) turned out to be one of the most imaginative of the early talkies, was a great critical success, and earned Vidor the second of his five Oscar nominations. He had gained his first for *The Crowd*, while the third came in 1931 for directing *The Champ*, one of his commercial ventures and his biggest popular success of the 30s.

During the early 30s Vidor had branched out in yet another area. His combined interest in Americana and in location filming led him to try his hand at a Western. *Billy The Kid* (1930), starring Johnny Mack Brown, was filmed in the innovative 70mm widescreen process known as 'Grandeur' and was one of a group of prestigious early sound Westerns. Vidor was to return to the Western genre at various stages in his career for it allowed him to explore the more violent, dramatic and very American qualities of character which interested him but did not fit into his contemporary subjects. Thus, his concern with contemporary social problems was expressed in such films as *Street Scene* (UA, 1931) and the

Depression drama, *Our Daily Bread* (UA, 1934), while his interest in Americana was reflected in his stylish adaptation of *H.M. Pulman, Esq.* (1941) and his underrated Technicolor epic of the steel industry, *American Romance* (1944). But it was in the larger-than-life drama of the Western that Vidor found his fullest expression during his later years. His Western epic, *Duel In The Sun* (1946), for producer David Selznick and starring Jennifer Jones, was his best-known 40s production, but he returned to the same themes of passion and violence, with Jones again starring, in the smaller scale *Ruby Gentry* (20th Century-Fox, 1952). He brought Ayn Rand's dramatic novel, *The Fountainhead* (Warner Bros.) to the screen in 1949, while *Man Without A Star* (Universal, 1955) was a powerful modern Western starring Kirk Douglas. Vidor's last outstanding production before retiring in the late 50s, was a creditable attempt to adapt Tolstoy's *War And Peace* (Paramount, 1956) with Henry Fonda's Pierre as the last of the true Vidor screen heroes. It also brought him his final Oscar nomination. Surprisingly, he never actually won the coveted statuette, but his distinguished career was acknowledged with a special honorary award from the Academy in 1978.

Above: Spencer Tracy (centre) in *Northwest Passage* (1940), an authentically flavoured adventure that was intended to have two parts. Only the first, however, was made but was well received. Co-star Robert Young is on the left.

Left: *Duel In The Sun* (1946), a large-scale Western, starred Jennifer Jones (right) as a half-breed girl who arouses two brothers to violent rivalry. The screenplay was co-written by the film's producer, David Selznick, who married the strikingly beautiful Miss Jones in 1949, having built her into a star.

Below: Audrey Hepburn (foreground) was a winning Natasha in Vidor's version of *War And Peace* (1956). The movie was a praiseworthy attempt to bring Tolstoy's epic masterpiece to the screen but, though visually powerful, it was somewhat cold and plodding.

RAOUL WALSH

Born New York City, 11 March 1887. **Died** 1980

Raoul Walsh is best remembered today for his years at Warner Bros. as a tough action director, of such stars as James Cagney, Errol Flynn and Humphrey Bogart, and for his later Westerns and war pictures during the 50s. He managed to beat the studio system by his willingness to be typecast as a director of outdoor adventure movies. Allowed a large measure of freedom within the genre (and despite his often modest budgets) he succeeded in turning out a high proportion of unpretentious, enjoyable, even memorable, black-and-white pictures. During the 50s he was given larger budgets, colour and CinemaScope, and continued active throughout the decade, filming with established stars like Clark Gable as well as a newer generation of younger stars including Aldo Ray and Rock Hudson. He had one last smash-hit in 1955 with the war movie, *Battle Cry*, for Warner Bros., thirty years after his first big war film hit, *What Price Glory?* (Fox, 1926). In fact, it is often forgotten that Walsh first flourished during the 20s – perhaps due to the fact that he experienced a lean patch during the 30s with a gap of almost ten years between his early films of note and his arrival at Warner Bros. in 1939. Yet, the middle and late 20s stand out as his most varied and successful period.

Walsh's early life reads like one of his own adventure films. Raised in New York City, he left his family and went off for several years to seek his fortune in the wide open spaces. He worked for a time as a cowpuncher in Texas and Mexico, as a gravedigger and a doctor's assistant in Montana, did some bronco busting for the US Cavalry, and got his very first taste of showbusiness as a klansman riding a horse across the stage on a treadmill and

carrying a burning cross in a play version of 'The Clansman' seven years before the same subject was to inspire D.W. Griffith's *The Birth Of A Nation* in 1914. Young and handsome, an exceptional horseman and able to perform amazing rope tricks, he later headed back to New York and had no trouble finding regular employment in pictures, first with Pathé and then with Biograph. He was aware of the superior quality of the Biograph shorts and of Griffith's contribution in particular and was very happy to join the company when it headed out to California about 1911.

Walsh worked hard as a Griffith assistant and actor for a few years and was soon given an opportunity to direct. For *The Life Of General Villa* (1914), one of the first movies he directed, he made an extraordinary and dangerous trip to Mexico where he rode with, and shot footage of, the real Pancho Villa for inclusion in the movie. Walsh himself played the young Villa, as well as co-directing, and later that same year (1914) appeared as John Wilkes Booth in *The Birth Of A Nation*. But he was more interested in directing than acting, and accepted a lucrative offer to join the newly expanding Fox company in 1915.

He began at Fox with one of the first ever feature-length gangster films, *Regeneration*, shot on location in New York City and on the Bowery. He followed this by directing Theda Bara in *Carmen*, rushed out in 1915 to beat the DeMille/Geraldine Farrar version into the theatres. During the following years Walsh turned out a variety of features including drama, comedies and Westerns, mainly for Fox and most often starring Miriam Cooper or his younger actor brother George Walsh. By 1924 he had

GLORIA SWANSON in "Sadie Thompson"

Based on the Story by W. SOMERSET MAUGHAM
Directed by RAOUL WALSH
- UNITED ARTISTS PICTURE -

a substantial body of work behind him, but the picture which suddenly thrust him into the limelight was *The Thief Of Bagdad* (UA, 1924), produced by and starring Douglas Fairbanks. One look at the elaborate Bagdad sets, designed by William Cameron Menzies, convinced Walsh that this would be the best picture he had ever made. The film was indeed a tremendous critical and box-office success, and a landmark in the development of screen fantasy.

Changing tack yet again, the director found himself at Paramount. Remembering his success with Theda Bara years before, producer Jesse Lasky hired him to direct Pola Negri, Jetta Goudal and Greta Nissen. With his status as a top director assured, Fox was happy to get him back in 1926, signing him to a new seven-year contract and immediately offering him the prestigious war film *What Price Glory?* from the hit play. Walsh was faced with the problem of adapting the play: 'To me the story's earthy dialogue and army and Marine profanity were every bit as important as the action', he wrote in his autobiography. In fact, he succeeded admirably in capturing the spirit of the original, concentrating on the

Above: Raoul Walsh not only directed Gloria Swanson in *Sadie Thompson* (1927), a version of Somerset Maugham's 'Rain', but was persuaded by the star to appear in it as well. Here, they are seen together on the advertising poster. Walsh lost an eye while shooting *In Old Arizona* (1929), and wore an eyepatch for the rest of his life.

Left: *What Price Glory?* (1926) made the director's name and remains a celebrated war film. The still taken during filming shows Barry Norton (foreground left), Leslie Fenton, Dolores Del Rio, Victor McLaglen, Edmund Lowe and, in eyeshade, Raoul Walsh.

'I'll tell you what constitutes a tender and gentle love scene for Raoul Walsh: it is a scene where he can burn down a whorehouse.'

Jack Warner in 'The Hollywood Professionals' (Kingsley Canham)

rivalry between Captain Flagg and Sergeant Quirk (Victor McLaglen and Edmund Lowe) with Dolores Del Rio as the girl. They even mouthed the vulgar dialogue, providing a field day for lip readers and giving the film a little spice of notoriety. Having created one of the cinema's most famous male love-hate relationships, Walsh enjoyed an even bigger hit with the 1929 talkie sequel, *The Cock-Eyed World*. (The same characters appeared in two further Walsh movies, while *What Price Glory?* was remade by John Ford in 1952).

Gloria Swanson was so impressed by *What Price Glory?* that she hired Walsh to direct her in *Sadie Thompson* (for UA) in 1927 and convinced him that he was just right for the role of O'Hara. Some elaborate juggling was involved to gain the approval of the Hays Office. They had to change the original title from 'Rain'; Reverend Davidson, the fanatical and hypocritical missionary (played by Lionel Barrymore), became plain 'Mister' Atkinson, and the language was toned down. On-screen kisses had to be confined to three seconds but, off-screen, Walsh had fallen for his married co-star in a big way. (Inevitably, filming ended, and so did romance).

best opportunity of his early career. However, Walsh's Warner years are best remembered for his collaboration with Flynn and Cagney. After Flynn's bust-up with Curtiz, Walsh became his favourite director beginning with *They Died With Their Boots On* (1941); others included *Gentleman Jim* (1942) and the outstanding war picture, *Objective Burma* (1945). Having arrived at Warners to direct Cagney in *The Roaring Twenties* (1939), it was appropriate that Walsh should direct him in his last great gangster role as Cody Jarrett in *White Heat* (1949).

During the 50s Walsh mixed seafaring with war and Westerns. *The Tall Men* (1955) was the best of his three films with Gable. It was made for 20th Century-Fox where he did most of his directing during 1955-61, including an uncharacteristic venture into the Biblical epic with Joan Collins in *Esther And The King* (1960). In 1963 he returned to Warners to direct his last picture, a disappointing but still stylish Western, *A Distant Trumpet*, starring Troy Donahue.

Above: Walsh directed James Cagney (left) in one of his most celebrated gangster roles, the psychopathic, mother-fixated Cody Jarrett in *White Heat* (1949). Here, the killer and a henchman threaten lawman Edmond O'Brien. The film's ending, where Cagney plunges into a rooftop drum, screaming 'Look Ma, top of the world', is one of the most famous final fades in film history.

Left: Teresa Wright and Robert Mitchum in the psychological Western, *Pursued* (1947). The marriage depicted was a dark, violent, vengeful coupling in what remains a very powerful film.

Below: Robert Ryan (right) looking remarkably like Gary Cooper, with Clark Gable in *The Tall Men* (1955).

A great success for all concerned, Miss Swanson's performance earned her a much deserved Oscar nomination, while for Walsh the film preserves his one notable screen role of the 20s. Sadly, he lost his right eye while out on location filming *In Old Arizona* (Fox, 1929), his first talkie as actor-director. Fox's *The Big Trail* (1930), an epic Western filmed in the 70mm 'Grandeur' process, flopped at the box-office and is remembered as the film which did *not* turn its young lead, John Wayne, into a star. The decline of Fox's fortunes meant that Walsh was confined

to minor projects before he left to freelance, being reduced to a diet of comedies and musicals before he arrived at Warner Bros. in 1939. Here his qualities as a fine director of actors were more evident than ever before. His work with Bogart and Ida Lupino on *They Drive By Night* and *High Sierra* in 1940 contributed greatly to turning them into stars, while *Strawberry Blonde* (1941) gave a large boost to the career of the young Rita Hayworth. *Pursued* (1947) stands as the most outstanding psychological Western of the 40s, and gave Robert Mitchum the

WILLIAM A. WELLMAN

Born Brookline, Massachusetts, 29 February 1896. **Died** 1975

Known as a bit of a hell-raiser when young, and affectionately nicknamed 'Wild Bill' Wellman, he was tall and handsome and was originally invited out to Hollywood by Douglas Fairbanks to become a movie actor, but the war intervened. As a youth William Wellman tried his hand at a variety of jobs, even played professional hockey, and had learned to fly a plane. Relatively early in the war he was one of the few Americans who joined up with the French forces, and made it into the Lafayette Flying Corps. Something of a war hero, he finally arrived in Hollywood in 1919 and appeared in a couple of pictures – *Knickerbocker Buckeroo* and *Evangeline* (directed by Raoul Walsh), but quickly realised that he was more interested in working behind the camera. Starting as a prop boy then graduating to assistant director, he was given his first chance to direct with a series of Dustin Farnum and Buck Jones Westerns at Fox during 1923-24. Producer B.P. Schulberg signed him for Paramount in 1926, where he just had time to establish himself with a pair of features, when the opportunity arose for him to direct the studio's World War I flying picture, *Wings* (1927). A project which had been initiated by Jesse Lasky, it was taken over by West Coast studio boss Schulberg who fought with the front office in New York to get approval for a generous $1 million budget. As Paramount's prestige entry in the war cycle, the studio considered a number of directors, including the possibility of borrowing King Vidor from MGM. But Wellman rightly saw the project as his big chance and endeavoured to convince Schulberg that he was uniquely qualified due to his own war experience, and that he would have no difficulty handling the large resources involved.

Following in the steps of Vidor, who had made his name in 1925 with *The Big Parade* for MGM, and Walsh's 1926 success with *What Price Glory?* for Fox, Wellman got his big break with *Wings*. Drawing on his military background, he took charge of the production in the manner of a general mustering his troops for battle. On location in Texas, he assembled an outstanding team of stunt fliers for the aerial sequences which were planned, and indeed turned out to be, the most spectacular and convincing ever filmed up to that date. He even delayed filming to capture the exact cloud formations necessary to give background and perspective to the dogfights. The battle sequences on the ground, filmed with the co-operation of the US Army, were also impressive, Wellman having striven for authenticity and a sense of conviction. Although Buddy Rogers and Richard Arlen played the leads, Clara Bow was the real star, and gave a suitably lively and sexy performance as the girl-next-door who later turns up as an ambulance driver in France, while Gary Cooper made a brief but memorable appearance in one of his earliest film roles. In spite of the weaknesses in plot and characterisation,

Above: Only Wellman's third feature, *Wings* (1927), with its authentic aerial battle sequences, was the recipient of the first ever Best Picture Oscar.

Left: The stars of *Wings* were Charles 'Buddy' Rogers and the ebullient Clara Bow (in a somewhat unexpected guise as a field ambulance driver!).

Below: *The Public Enemy* (1931) gave James Cagney (left) the first of his legendary vicious gangster roles and made him a star. With him here, 'The Blonde Bombshell', Jean Harlow who, tragically, died only six years later aged twenty-six.

Wings won the first ever Oscar for Best Picture and initiated a new vogue for aerial combat movies – resulting in *Hell's Angels* (UA, 1930) and *The Dawn Patrol* (Warner Bros., 1930) among others – and including Wellman's own follow-up production, *Legion Of The Condemned* (1928), with Gary Cooper starring.

Beggars Of Life (1928), Wellman's first part-talkie, cast Wallace Beery, as a likeable tramp, opposite Louise Brooks as a young fugitive who dresses as a man to evade the police. Miss Brooks' own memories of working with William Wellman were less than complimentary: 'So intrigued was I by the quiet sadism practised by Billy behind the camera, especially in his direction of women, that I began to investigate his past life ... More than a director, he resembled an actor who was uncertain in his part'. In fact, Wellman himself has claimed that, after a succession of unhappy marriages, he was 'saved' by his fifth wife, Dorothy Coonan, whom he met at Warner Bros. around 1932. (A former Busby Berkeley girl, she gave a convincing performance as a teenage girl dressed as a boy – a curious echo here of Louise Brooks – in Wellman's *Wild Boys Of The Road* (Warner Bros., 1933), one of the best of the studio's socially conscious pictures of the 30s, about runaway teenagers living rough during the Depression).

Wellman had easily made the transition to sound filming while at Paramount, but joined Warner Bros. soon afterwards and secured his reputation with *The Public Enemy* in 1931, the third film for his new studio. Although Warner Bros. had already filmed *Little Caesar*, Wellman convinced production chief Darryl Zanuck that his picture would be tougher and more violent, and when he transferred James Cagney from a supporting role to the lead, the picture's success was assured. A far more accomplished production than *Little Caesar*, the film offered a number of memorable, still

famous moments like gangster Cagney pushing a grapefruit in Mae Clarke's face, or the chilling moment near the end when Cagney's dead body, trussed up from head to toe, is delivered to his mother's door. Wellman next directed *Night Nurse* (1931), the first of three films which helped boost the young Barbara Stanwyck to stardom. After leaving Warner Bros. in 1933 he never again signed up with any one studio. During the rest of the 30s he alternated between 20th Century, MGM, Selznick and Paramount, and by the end of his career he had worked for every one of the major studios excluding only Universal. For Zanuck's 20th Century Pictures the director made an entertaining version of Jack London's *The Call Of The Wild* (1935) starring Clark Gable.

But 1937 was Wellman's best year. Independent producer David Selznick, whom he had first known at Paramount ten years before, gave him the opportunity to work in Technicolor for the first time. *A Star Is Born* and *Nothing Sacred* were notable examples of a restrained and naturalistic use of colour within contemporary settings. One of Wellman's most honoured pictures, *A Star Is Born* won a special Oscar for cinematography with nominations for both stars (Fredric March and Janet Gaynor), for Best Picture, and for Wellman both as director

(his first) and co-writer of the original story, for which he won his only Oscar. The story was partly based on his own observations of Hollywood life over two decades, and partly on the 1932 classic, *What Price Hollywood?*; while *Nothing Sacred* boasted a witty and inventive screenplay from Ben Hecht, reflecting Wellman's own preference for the well-written script.

Returning to Paramount, and to the air, Wellman used Technicolor to obtain

some stunning aerial effects in *Men With Wings* (1938), and was reunited with Gary Cooper on the adventure movie *Beau Geste* (1939). 'A rugged picture', as Wellman recalled, it was filmed on location in the middle of the desert near Yuma, Arizona. At his peak as a director and much in demand, Wellman enjoyed alternating between various genres. *The Oxbow Incident* (20th Century-Fox, 1943) was one of the first of a new breed of adult Westerns, while *The Story Of G.I. Joe* (UA, 1945) was a superior war movie which elevated Robert Mitchum to real stardom. With *Gallant Journey* (Columbia, 1946) Wellman took to the air once again; then he tried his hand at small town Americana with the Capraesque *Magic Town* (RKO, 1947) starring James Stewart and *The Happy Years* (MGM, 1950). He had his last two big box-office hits (and won his last two Oscar nominations) for directing *Battleground* (MGM, 1949) and *The High And The Mighty* (Warner Bros., 1954). But it was clear that the decline of the studios during the 50s signalled the end of his directing career, for he was not happy functioning as a 'producer-director'. His last pictures were on the whole rather poor, and he retired in 1958 after a favourite project, *Lafayette Escadrille* (Warner Bros., 1958) was badly cut by the releasing studio.

Above left: Fredric March and Janet Gaynor in *A Star Is Born* (1937), filmed in colour and garlanded with praise, nominations and Oscars. A hard-hitting drama about Hollywood and considered a classic, the story was given a superb musical treatment in 1954, starring Judy Garland and James Mason, and was made yet again – transferred to the pop music world – with Barbra Streisand and Kris Kristofferson in 1976. It did little justice to its predecessors.

Above: Director Wellman chats to Janet Blair on location for *Gallant Journey* (1946), a movie about flying pioneer John Montgomery (played by Glenn Ford) who first took to the air in 1883.

Far left: The sadistic officer (Brian Donlevy, foreground right) confronts his men in *Beau Geste* (1939), Wellman's version (there were others in 1926 and 1966) of P.C. Wren's Foreign Legion classic. Others here: Robert Preston (2nd left), J. Carrol Naish (in front of him), Gary Cooper, Broderick Crawford and Ray Milland.

Below Left: Van Johnson (far left), a fellow soldier, and John Hodiak (right) confront the enemy in *Battleground* (1949).

'A great hit to me is a picture that has lived for years. It's unfair, I guess. Guys say to me, "Gee, you made *Wings!*". Well, they're too goddam young ever to have seen it, but they tell you it must have been a great picture. Well it was great, but it wasn't anywhere near as great as they think it was.'
1964

JAMES WHALE

Born Dudley, England, 22 July 1896. **Died** 1957

One of the most enigmatic of Hollywood figures, James Whale's relatively brief directing career was concentrated into the 30s decade. As an English director in the US he specialised in British and Continental subjects, but was most closely identified with the classic horror film cycle at Universal during 1931-35. He preferred working with English actors, often collaborated with English scriptwriters, and even had English art director Charles D. Hall, Universal's leading 30s designer, on several pictures. A sophisticated and stylish director with a strong visual instinct and a wicked sense of humour, Whale often succeeded in turning an otherwise routine subject into a memorable film experience. At his best, although working within the constraints of relatively small budgets, a few of his films stand among the finest achievements of 30s Hollywood.

Whale worked for a time in a boring manual job before the war, while pursuing his interest in drawing and painting in his spare time. Captured by the Germans, he got his first taste of the theatre in a POW camp. He continued a stage career after the war, acting in the British provinces and then in London, where he soon began designing and directing. His biggest success in both latter capacities came in 1929 with 'Journey's End', the R.C. Sherriff play about life in the trenches during World War I. The play ran first in London and then in New York, and made Whale the logical choice to direct the movie. First he gained some filming experience as dialogue director on *The Love Doctor* (Paramount, 1929), then directed most of the interior dialogue scenes for the Howard Hughes flying epic *Hell's Angels* (UA, 1930).

Journey's End (1930) was set up as a mainly British production (producers George Pearson and Michael Balcon), but was filmed at the small Tiffany studios in the States due to the superior sound facilities there. Little more than a solidly crafted filmed play, the picture served as a useful apprentice work for Whale, who quickly moved on to Universal where he directed a somewhat more cinematic adaptation of another play, *Waterloo Bridge* (1931). He apparently got on well with the Laemmles who ran the studio, and who offered him *Frankenstein* (1931). He immediately made the project his own, casting his friend Colin Clive from *Journey's End* in the title role and selecting another British actor, Boris Karloff, to play the monster. The director worked closely with production designer Danny Hall and make-up expert Jack Pierce in designing the appearance of the monster, and thus helped to originate one of the most famous archetypal images of the cinema. The picture cost less than $300,000 and its fabulous success immediately established Whale as one of the studio's two top contract directors (the other was John Stahl).

If *Frankenstein* was somewhat crude and primitive-looking and rather lacking in humour, Whale more than made up for

it in the increasingly sophisticated horror productions which followed – *The Old Dark House* (1932), *The Invisible Man* (1933), and his masterpiece, *The Bride Of Frankenstein* (1935). For this latter he assembled a remarkable collection of characters. Colin Clive reprised his tortured scientist; Karloff was again the monster, but more humanised and sympathetic; the wicked and eccentric old Ernest Thesiger echoed his role in *The Old Dark House*; and Elsa Lanchester in a dual role portrayed authoress Mary Shelley and the monster's extraordinary-looking mate. The bride's unique and memorable make-up was once again Whale's conception.

Whale only directed two more pictures within the congenial Universal set-up – the delightfully crazy black comedy, *Remember Last Night?* and the relatively large budget musical, *Show Boat* (1936) starring Irene Dunne and Helen Morgan. He left Universal after *The Road*

Back (1937) was taken away from him and its ending changed. His later pictures of note included a stylish pair of costumers, *The Great Garrick* (Warner Bros., 1937) and *The Man In The Iron Mask* (UA, 1939), but his career was virtually ended

in 1939. He retired to his painting and occasionally directed in the theatre. Depressed by the severe illness which suddenly struck him in 1956, he committed suicide in his swimming pool the following year.

Left: Director James Whale in 'civvies' in the World War I dug-out for *Journey's End* (1930) with, left to right, Ian Maclaren, Charles Gerrard, producer George Pearson, David Manners, an unidentified small-part player and, seated, Colin Clive and Billy Bevan.

Below: Elsa Lanchester and Boris Karloff in Whale's masterpiece of horror, *The Bride Of Frankenstein* (1935).

Below left: Gloria Stuart and Ernest Thesiger in *The Old Dark House* (1932), a stylish horror comedy based on a novel by J.B. Priestley. Connoisseurs of the genre today rate the film very highly indeed, and the amount of generous critical praise in print is a tribute to James Whale's unique approach to, and mastery of, his material.

'To all I love. Do not grieve for me. My nerves are all shot and for the last year I have been in agony day and night . . . except when I sleep with sleeping pills – and any peace I have by day is when I am drugged by pills. I have had a wonderful life but it is over and my nerves get worse and I'm afraid they will have to take me away . . . so please forgive me all those I love, and may God forgive me too . . . The future is just old age and pain . . . Goodbye all and thank you for all your love. I must have peace and this is the only way.'

James Whale's suicide note

SAM WOOD

Born Philadelphia, 18 July 1883. **Died** 1949

One of the big surprises of the 40s was the sudden emergence of Sam Wood as a director of some consequence. Well past middle-age and with twenty years behind him as a conscientious, hard working, dull director, he was nominated for an Oscar for directing *Goodbye Mr Chips* (MGM, 1939), which was also nominated for Best Picture, while star Robert Donat won the Best Actor award. Wood was clearly at this peak during these years. *Chips* was but the first of five pictures nominated for Best Picture, and he was himself nominated again for directing *Kitty Foyle* (RKO, 1940) which won Ginger Rogers her only Oscar, and *Kings Row* (Warner Bros., 1942).

Wood had first arrived in California as an enterprising young businessman dealing in real estate. Attracted to the movie business around 1908, he tried a little acting before moving behind the camera as a production assistant then assistant director. A couple of years as principal assistant to Cecil B. DeMille prepared him for the chance to direct on his own with former DeMille stars like Wallace Reid (in 1920) and Gloria Swanson. Miss Swanson, however, was not impressed by his talent. After grinding out nine pictures with him during 1921-23, she recalled, 'Each one was worse than the last ... the only things that changed were the number and length of dresses I wore and the face of the leading man!'.

Wood himself finally rebelled at the routine assignments he received from Paramount and broke with the studio in 1924. However, he was picked up by MGM three years later and spent the next thirteen years as one of the studio's most dependable contract directors. He handled top stars on the way down: John Gilbert in his second unsuccessful talkie, *Way For A Sailor* (1930), and a pair with Ramon Novarro; and stars on the way up: Joan Crawford in *Paid* (1930), Spencer Tracy and Myrna Loy in *Whipsaw* in 1935. He and cameraman Hal Rosson were sympathetic and supportive in their treatment of Jean Harlow on the set of *Hold Your Man* (1933), her first picture after the suicide of her husband, MGM producer Paul Bern. (Rosson became her next husband soon after.) Assigned to the first MGM Marx Brothers movie, *A Night At The Opera* (1935), Wood succeeded in fine style, delivering a major box-office hit, although Groucho complained that 'This jerk we have for a director doesn't know what he wants, so he shoots everything twenty times and hopes there's something good in it'.

Sent to England to direct Robert Donat as Mr Chips, he also started a new MGM star, Greer Garson, on her highly successful movie career. Wood was much in demand after leaving MGM. The combined talents of Jean Arthur and Charles Coburn made *The Devil And Miss Jones* (RKO, 1941) a highly enjoyable comedy, while *Kings Row* was notable for drawing quality from young Ronald Reagan. *The Pride Of The Yankees* (Goldwyn/RKO, 1942), Wood's first

with Gary Cooper and based on the true life of baseballer Lou Gehrig, was more of a sentimental drama than a sports biopic. Having had his first taste of Technicolor as one of the directors brought in to help out on *Gone With The Wind* (MGM, 1939), Wood got Cooper and Technicolor for Hemingway's *For Whom The Bell Tolls* (1943). The acting honours were stolen by Katina Paxinou as the formidable guerilla leader, Pilar, and Ingrid Bergman looking ravishing in close-cropped hair in her first colour film, but the movie, running almost three hours, emerged as one of the major hits of the 40s. It was also the director's biggest ever success, and demonstrated his ability to handle an epic-scale production. However, it was, alas, largely downhill for Wood from this point on. The reteaming

Above: Sam Wood (seated left) directs The Marx Brothers in *A Night At The Opera* (1935). The movie was a huge hit but Wood was still considered no more than a run-of-the-mill MGM contract director.

Left: Ronald Reagan and Ernest Cossart in *King's Row* (1941), a five-star melodrama remembered not only for Reagan's truly excellent performance, but for the compelling hold it exerts on audiences. The great English critic, James Agate, called it 'half masterpiece and half junk', which is a not unreasonable assessment. The film garnered nominations for Wood, for James Wong Howe (whose moody photography certainly helped), and for Best Picture.

Below: *For Whom The Bell Tolls* (1943), a three-hour epic version of Hemingway's epic novel about an American fighting in the Spanish Civil War, revealed Ingrid Bergman (centre) in colour for the first time. Here, she looks on apprehensively, clutching Gary Cooper's arm, while a guerrilla fighter gives Akim Tamiroff (right) a problem. The film, though somewhat ponderous, was a big success for Wood.

of Bergman and Cooper in *Saratoga Trunk* for Warners in 1943 was far less successful; ditto Cooper and Teresa Wright in *Casanova Brown* (RKO, 1944). Joan Fontaine starred as *Ivy* (Universal, 1947) in the director's only post-war movie of note, but he continued active up to the end, returning to MGM for three

last movies completed in 1949 – a Clark Gable war drama, *Command Decision*, a James Stewart baseball biopic (*The Stratton Story*), and *Ambush*, a Robert Taylor Western. Finally – and sadly – it must be mentioned that, during the 40s, Wood supported the Red Scare witch hunts conducted by the HUAC in Hollywood.

'Sam Wood was selfish; he wasn't interested in my job, and he never gave me enough time. He didn't want to devote time to photography – unlike Sidney Franklin, who was so tasteful, so highly sensitive.'

Charles Rosher (cameraman) in 'The Parade's Gone By' (Kevin Brownlow)

CHAPTER TWO
1940-1959

A period heralded by war in which the writer-director emerged, exerting a new influence and signalling the return of independence. By the late 50s the damaging effects of McCarthyism on the industry were wearing off but a new rival, television, had come to stay. Under its threat the studios were floundering and the contract system was on its way out...

There were many changes taking place in American society during the 40s, both internally and in its relations with the rest of the world, and these were naturally reflected in the movies coming out of Hollywood. In contrast to the predominantly escapist entertainment of the 30s, the impact of the Second World War, the dawn of the Atomic Age and the Cold War which followed meant that the US rapidly 'came of age' during the 40s. A larger proportion of the pictures attempted to deal with contemporary life and problems, to reflect, directly or indirectly, the mood of the times.

It was the writers, directors and writer-directors who were in the vanguard of the move to introduce more noticeably adult themes and subjects into the movies, and, in fact, the status of the director received a major boost during the decade, in contrast to the 30s which had been dominated more by the stars and producers working within the studio system. There was, in fact, a virtual explosion of directorial talent. Established directors like Ford, Hawks and Wyler flourished during the 40s joined by a large contingent of veteran English and Continental directors, many of them exiled by the war in Europe (Renoir,

Above: Director Tay Garnett (left) takes a break with his two stars, John Garfield and Lana Turner, while shooting *The Postman Always Rings Twice* (1946), one of the classic *films noirs* of the period.

Left: Orson Welles (right) directs *Citizen Kane* (1941), from a temporary wheelchair while an injured ankle heals. Cameraman Gregg Toland is behind the camera (peaked cap) and the young actress on the left is Dorothy Comingore.

Hitchcock, Clair, Siodmak and Sirk, among others). Of special interest – and, indeed, artistic significance – was the number of leading 30s scriptwriters who made a successful leap to writer-director: Preston Sturges led the way in 1940, followed by John Huston, Billy Wilder, Joseph Mankiewicz and others. Finally, there was an impressive selection of gifted newcomers,

some of them true innovators, who came mainly from the New York theatre, and were spearheaded by Orson Welles, Elia Kazan and Vincente Minnelli.

Some indication of the extent of the explosion which got the 40s decade off to such an impressive start can be gained from the fact that Hitchcock, Sturges, Welles, Huston, Renoir and René Clair all made their Hollywood directorial debuts during 1940–41, while John Ford's releases in-

cluded *The Grapes Of Wrath* and *How Green Was My Valley* (both from 20th Century-Fox) and Howard Hawks had the biggest hit of his career with *Sergeant York* (Warner Bros). Gregg Toland, the most influential of Hollywood cameramen, took advantage of the latest technical advances in film stocks and lenses to extend the creative possibilities of black-and-white film-making, working in close collaboration with Orson Welles, John Ford and William Wyler. His ability to handle complex, deep focus compositions and long takes with a technique which was equally effective for both high and low-keyed photography helped to set the tone for the 40s, a decade remembered today as the last great era of black-and-white studio film-making in the US. The faster film stock, lighter cameras and improved recording equipment made it easier to film on location, too. During the postwar years there was a major trend toward using more authentic settings and locations, both in the US and, increasingly, abroad. In fact, many of the leading directors like Ford, Stevens, Huston and Wyler were absent from Hollywood during most of the war when they were thrust into the unfamiliar role of documentary film-makers. In making their contribution to the war effort they developed new skills and were strongly influenced by what they saw. When they returned to Hollywood, they no longer wanted to operate according to the old pre-war ways. The most dramatic example here is that of Wyler, whose film about the problems of returning veterans, *The Best Years Of Our Lives* (Goldwyn/RKO, 1946) made a huge impact.

This was one of many successful pictures which dealt with current social problems during the mid and late 40s, coinciding with the emergence of the *film noir* cycle. The *noir* films, too, were often used to comment on the contemporary American scene – most favoured themes dealt with the corruption of police, politicians or greedy businessmen. Unfortunately, many of the most socially conscious directors and writers were the target of HUAC (House Un-American Activities Committee) when it set out to investigate the

Above: Eva Marie Saint and James Mason examine the widescreen VistaVision camera used to photograph them in Hitchcock's *North By Northwest* (1959).

Left: John Huston (left), producer Darryl Zanuck and actor (in this case) Orson Welles talk to former movie actress-turned-famous gossip columnist, Hedda Hopper, during filming of *The Roots Of Heaven* (1958).

alleged Communist infiltration of Hollywood in 1947. This 'Red' scare could not not have come at a worse time. It caused a major setback in Hollywood's attempts to deal with adult subjects on the screen and, with box-office receipts in any event falling, the studios needed all the help they could get to stem the decline. Thus, the 40s ended on a distinctly downbeat note, with the studios cutting back on production and decreasing their lists of contract stars and technical personnel. Directors who had been with the same studio for twenty years or more suddenly found themselves out of work during the early 50s. And further HUAC hearings in 1951, with the figure of Senator McCarthy lurking in the background, led to an unofficial political blacklist which destroyed or severely damaged the careers of many leading talents. Directors like Robert Rossen, Joseph Losey and Jules Dassin left to find work abroad, as did John Huston, who was not a victim, but was simply appalled at the turn of events and felt unable to carry on working in Hollywood. Edward

Dmytryk and Elia Kazan, sadly perhaps, 'recanted' and were restored to favour.

On a more positive note in their efforts to attract the public back into the cinemas and compete with black-and-white TV, the studios concentrated their efforts on 'A' pictures in colour, utilizing both Technicolor and the newly introduced (and cheaper) Eastmancolor, and turned to such technical innovations as 3-D, CinemaScope, VistaVision and other large (and wide) screen processes. Colour filming had been largely shunned by the leading directors and cameramen during the 40s when it was used mainly for musicals and the occasional costume picture. Musicals director Vincente Minnelli stood virtually alone as an original colour stylist in the US, while the accomplished and innovative colour filming of Michael Powell in Britain was unique and unmatched by any American director. Now strong pressures were exerted on directors to make use of the new techniques during the early 50s. Many of the top directors, now turned producer-directors, were working in colour for the first time including Huston, Renoir, Stevens, Sternberg and

Sirk, while for Cukor, Fuller and Kazan their first in colour was in CinemaScope, too. There was a major emphasis on glossy blockbusters, costume pictures and historical epics, many of them filmed abroad to take advantage of picturesque foreign or exotic locations and cheaper labour costs. There was a major revival of the Western, a genre which flourished as never before (or since), that brought to the fore a number of less well-known directors like Anthony Mann, Budd Boetticher and Delmer Daves, and provided a new lease of life for such veterans as Ford and Hawks. Of special note was the unexpected new boom in science fiction and fantasy, reflecting the fears and paranoia of the period as seen in Don Siegel's *The Invasion Of The Body Snatchers* (1957) or *The Incredible Shrinking Man* (Universal, 1956).

In fact, black-and-white was far from dead. Columbia had a pair of major Oscar-winning successes with *From Here To Eternity* (1953) directed by Fred Zinnemann and *On The Waterfront* (1954) from Kazan, and during the late 50s there was a major move back to the more intimate black-and-white filming of earlier years. Clearly the 50s was a more diverse and interesting period than it is often given credit for. In spite of the fact that relatively few new directors got their start during these years, the most interesting by far were those who broke into films from TV during the late 50s and early 60s, proving that TV could be of some benefit to the film industry as a training ground for new talent. Initially demonstrating a clear preference – and talent – for small scale black-and-white filming, such directors as Penn, Lumet, Frankenheimer, Peckinpah, Mulligan and Ritt in the US, Richard Lester, John Schlesinger, Ken Russell and John Boorman in Britain, would play an important role in helping to reshape the Anglo-American cinema during the 60s and 70s – and easily adapting to the wider screen, and to colour, in later years.

ANTHONY ASQUITH

Born London, 9 November 1902. **Died** 1968

A solid and dependable, if generally un-imaginative, director, Anthony Asquith made a variety of entertaining and successful pictures and worked with many top British and international stars. However, his particular and noteworthy contribution to the cinema is to be found in the screen versions of classic British plays in which he specialised during the middle years of his career.

The son of Lord Asquith, Britain's famous Liberal Prime Minister from 1908-16, Asquith's background was appropriately cultivated. He was educated at Winchester, and Balliol College, and became actively involved in film-making during the last years of the silent era (1927-29), directing one silent film of note, *Cottage On Dartmoor* (1929). He followed this with his first talkie, *Tell England* (1931), a war movie which featured some effectively staged battle sequences, but his career failed to take off during the 30s when his pictures – including an undistinguished Alexander Korda production, *Moscow Nights* (1935) starring Laurence Olivier – were largely routine.

The big turning point came in 1938 when Asquith was given the opportunity to co-direct Shaw's *Pygmalion*, starring Leslie Howard as Professor Higgins and Wendy Hiller as Eliza Doolittle. Their marvellous performances, both Oscar-nominated, and the film's international success – it was nominated for the Best Picture Oscar and won Oscars for adaptation and screenplay – established Asquith as one of Britain's leading directors. Terence Rattigan's *French Without Tears* (1939), adapted by the playwright with producer and scriptwriter Anatole De Grunewald, was the first of several collaborations with Asquith, the two writers remaining the director's favourite choice for such ventures.

The revival of Asquith's career during the late 30s paralleled that of the British film industry generally, which experienced an unprecedented boom during the war and immediate post-war years. Asquith contributed a notable pair of war

pictures: *We Dive At Dawn* (1943) memorably captured the details and atmosphere of life within the confines of a submarine, while *The Way To The Stars* (1945) acutely observed the quiet heroism of the men and women operating an RAF bomber station and gave Asquith his first opportunity to work with actor Michael Redgrave. In between, Asquith directed a Gainsborough costumer, *Fanny By Gaslight* (1943), with James Mason as the dissolute Lord and Phyllis Calvert as the sweet and much put upon Victorian heroine, rescued by the dashing young hero (Stewart Granger) who kills Mason in a duel. *The Demi-Paradise* (also 1943) is best remembered for Laurence Olivier's remarkable character performance as a Soviet engineer visiting England in 1939.

By the late 40s Asquith was at his peak as a director, and had earned a reputation for his sympathetic handling of his actors. He brought three quality play adaptations to the screen between 1948-52. The gifted (and tragically ill) Robert Donat was never more effective than as

the compassionate defence barrister in Rattigan's *The Winslow Boy* (1948), while Michael Redgrave delivered two remarkable and contrasting performances in the same playwright's *The Browning Version* (1950) – as the failed and disillusioned classics master – and Wilde's *The Importance Of Being Earnest* (1952), where he demonstrated his stylish talent for high comedy opposite Joan Greenwood and the formidable Edith Evans. During later years Asquith returned to Shaw with *The Doctor's Dilemma* (1958) and *The Millionairess* (1960), the latter best remembered for its unlikely but successful pairing of Peter Sellers and Sophia Loren. Asquith also enjoyed working with stars of the new generation, including Dirk Bogarde and Leslie Caron, and gave young Paul Massie his best ever role in the effective war thriller, *Orders To Kill* (1958). The director rounded off his career in the 60s with a pair of star-studded but sadly weak international co-productions – *The V.I.P.'s* (1962), a feeble farrago which boasted the presence of Burton and Taylor, and *The Yellow Rolls Royce* (1964), starring Rex Harrison and Ingrid Bergman.

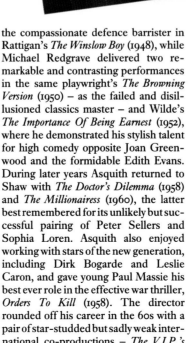

Top: Leslie Howard as Professor Higgins and Wendy Hiller as the Cockney flower-seller, Eliza Doolittle, whom he transforms into a 'lady', in the superb screen version of *Pygmalion* (1938). Asquith co-directed the film with Howard.

Above: *The Millionairess* (1960) teamed brilliant British comedian Peter Sellers with voluptuous Italian beauty Sophia Loren, and is always remembered for the actor's inimitable impression of an Indian.

Left: Director Asquith (left) on location in Malaga, Spain, with Leslie Caron and David Niven, for *Guns Of Darkness* (1962). The plot dealt with a plantation owner and his wife in Latin America who get caught up in a violent rebellion – not typical Asquith territory.

BUDD BOETTICHER

Born Chicago, Illinois, 29 July 1916

As Hollywood's resident expert on bull-fighting, Budd Boetticher specialised in Westerns and bullfight movies. He brought an original and personal style to his Westerns during the late 50s which have earned him a small, but essential, niche in American movie history. Budd began in films as, appropriately enough, a technical advisor on Mamoulian's remake of *Blood And Sand* in 1940, after having spent some time in Mexico training as a matador. He spent a year or two as an assistant director before graduating to full directorial status on a number of B features for Columbia, and the tiny Monogram studio. Averaging an economical 65 minutes in length, these included *A Guy, A Gal And A Pal* (Columbia, 1945) starring future producer Ross Hunter, and *Behind Locked Doors* (1948), Lucille Bremer's last movie. His big break came late in 1950 when he managed to interest Republic Pictures in backing a favourite project of his, then called 'Torero'. The movie, retitled *The Bullfighter And The Lady* (a change opposed by the director), starred Robert Stack as an American who learns about bullfighting in Mexico. The quality of the script earned Boetticher an Oscar nomination in 1951 (his only one), and brought him a contract to make Westerns and actioners for Universal.

In the mid-50s, he moved on to work for other major studios. At 20th Century-Fox in 1955, Anthony Quinn played *The Magnificent Matador* for Budd, and later that year the director demonstrated a mastery of the thriller with *The Killer Is Loose*, starring Joseph Cotten and Rhonda Fleming for United Artists. He then directed the seven Randolph Scott Westerns which represent his best-remembered contribution to the genre. The cycle began with *Seven Men From Now* (Warner Bros., 1956), produced through John Wayne's Batjac company, and the first of four scripted by Burt Kennedy who went on to become a Westerns director himself during the 60s. Boetticher has called attention to the fact that most of his Scott Westerns represent variations on the same general storyline: 'A man whose wife has been killed is

searching out her murderer. In this way I can show quite subtle relations between a hero, wrongly bent on vengeance, and outlaws who, in contrast, want to break with their past'.

Of special interest is Boetticher's treatment of the lead villain in these pictures. Rather than the typical cliché baddie, the villains tend to appear as fully developed characters and worthy adversaries for Scott's hero. Richard Boone in *The Tall T* (Colombia, 1957) and Claude Akins in *Comanche Station* (Columbia, 1960), exemplified this approach, as did the 'heavy' in *Seven Men From Now*, which provided Lee Marvin with one of the best roles of his early career. *The Tall T* serves as an excellent example of Boetticher and Scott's partnership at its best. An economical and intimate Western about stagecoach passengers held captive by outlaws at an isolated relay station, the film presents a sophisticated and off-beat study in group psychology, exploring what happens when a bunch of desperate characters are suddenly thrown together. Richard Boone as the likeable villain displayed a nice line in black humour, while Maureen O'Sullivan made one of her rare, late movie appearances as the mature, but still attractive, heroine. But it

Above: Joseph Cotten and Rhonda Fleming starred in one of Boetticher's early thrillers, *The Killer Is Loose* (1956), about a bank robber seeking revenge for the death of his wife at the hands of a policeman.

Left: The appropriately titled *Seven Men From Now* (1956), produced through John Wayne's company, Batjac, was the first of seven Westerns made by Boetticher with Randolph Scott starring. Here, during a break in filming, Wayne (left) visits director (right) and star.

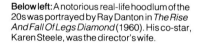
Below left: A notorious real-life hoodlum of the 20s was portrayed by Ray Danton in *The Rise And Fall Of Legs Diamond* (1960). His co-star, Karen Steele, was the director's wife.

was Boetticher's blonde wife, Karen Steele, who took the leading female roles in most of his later Westerns, as well as playing Legs Diamond's girlfriend (later wife). An exceptional gangster flick made with great style and spirit, *The Rise And Fall Of Legs Diamond* (Warner Bros., 1960) derived its vitality from the crazed, intense energy of Ray Danton's performance in the lead role, although it has to be said that he bore little resemblance to the real-life gangster.

Having had his fill of Hollywood, Budd Boetticher returned to Mexico to make *Arruza* (1969), a documentary feature about the Mexican bullfighter, Carlos Arruza. In 1969 he directed one last feature, *A Time For Dying*, and provided the original scenario for *Two Mules For Sister Sara* (Universal).

'One wonders where directors like Boetticher find the energy and the inspiration to do such fine work, when native critics are so fantastically indifferent that they probably couldn't tell a Boetticher film apart from a Selander or worse'

Andrew Sarris in 'The American Cinema'

RICHARD BROOKS

Born Philadephia, 18 May 1912

One of the last of the contract directors employed by MGM during the 50s, Richard Brooks went on to develop an independent career as producer-director-writer in later years. Attracted to hard-hitting subjects with a strong social theme, he had his biggest successes with *The Blackboard Jungle* (MGM, 1955), *Elmer Gantry* (UA, 1960), *In Cold Blood* (Columbia, 1967) and *Looking For Mr Goodbar* (Paramount, 1977). During his relatively long career, he worked with many top stars ranging from Cary Grant, Elizabeth Taylor and Paul Newman, to the new generation like Diane Keaton, Richard Gere, Warren Beatty and Goldie Hawn.

A former journalist and novelist who had also worked in radio and directed in the theatre, Brooks was employed as a scriptwriter, first at Universal (interrupted by war service) and then at Warner Bros. There he worked on *Brute Force* (1947) for Jules Dassin and *Key Largo* (1948) with John Huston, around the same time that his novel, 'The Brick Foxhole', was being adapted into the highly successful *Crossfire* (RKO, 1947).

As a measure of Brooks' growing prestige, he was hired by MGM in 1949 with the understanding that he would be allowed to try his hand at direction. The studio's new production chief, Dore Schary, was himself a former script-writer-turned-producer who had been responsible for the production of *Crossfire* at RKO, a socially conscious film typical of the kind which appealed to him. He had been hired by MGM to help balance the studio's glossy Louis B. Mayer image with some more serious projects, and he regarded Brooks as a promising prospect who could handle mature, adult subjects. But the studio was in financial trouble, and the insecure bosses didn't know what they wanted. Thus, the story of Brooks' MGM years is mainly a tale of compromises and missed opportunities, although, in retrospect, he valued the chance to gain directing experience and even to make mistakes. ('The trouble today is that you don't make mistakes any more, they're too expensive').

Since Cary Grant was the star of *Crisis* (1950), his first film as writer-director, Brooks was forced to drop the idea of the surgeon hero as a widower with a nine-year-old daughter and provide a young wife and love interest instead (although the film was meant to be a political drama set in a South American country under a Peron-type dictator). Similarly, Brooks was forced to compromise in his treatment of the tough sergeant in *Take The High Ground* (1953), while *The Last Time I Saw Paris* (1954), adapted from an F. Scott Fitzgerald story, was overly sentimentalised. The two latter were Brooks' first movies in colour, which suggests some softening of approach.

The most interesting of Brooks' early films was his one non-MGM production, *Deadline USA* (20th Century-Fox, 1952), a tough newspaper picture starring Humphrey Bogart, Kim Hunter and Ethel Barrymore (in black-and-white). Brooks finally got stubborn and refused to compromise on the *The Blackboard Jungle* which he directed in 1954, and had the satisfaction of proving the studio bosses wrong. But, according to him, 'MGM's front office didn't even want to release the picture!'. An inexpensive but effective black-and-white production, it starred Glenn Ford as a high school teacher in New York coping with a violent and rebellious bunch of students led by Vic Morrow, Sidney Poitier and future movie director Paul Mazursky. A big success, both with the critics and at the box-office, it started a new cycle of juvenile delinquent movies and earned Brooks his first Oscar nomination.

The situation at MGM did not improve after the departure of Schary, and the bosses were more insecure than ever. As late as 1957 Brooks describes a preview of his latest film, *Something Of Value*: 'They had fourteen guys sitting around a table, and one guy would say . . . 'I didn't like the music in the sixth reel'. And another would say. . . . 'My dentist hates it . . .'! At least Brooks' own standing had been upgraded by this time, so he was able to close out his MGM years with a pair of prestige productions which marked the beginning of a new phase in his career – as an adaptor of major literary works, both novels and plays, to the

Above: *The Blackboard Jungle* (1955), was very much a social drama of its time, and the first notable film in a juvenile delinquency cycle. Here, Glenn Ford (standing) does battle with his defiant class of rebellious slum kids led by Vic Morrow (centre left) and Sidney Poitier (centre right).

screen. From late 1957 when he shot Dostoievsky's *The Brothers Karamazov*, through 1964 when his large-scale version of Conrad's *Lord Jim* was filmed in Super Panavision 70, these were peak years for Brooks. He was most at home, however, with American subjects and had his biggest successes with Tennessee Williams' steamy marital drama *Cat On A Hot Tin Roof*, and *Elmer Gantry*, from the Sinclair Lewis novel about a

Above: Elizabeth Taylor as Maggie the Cat, in Brooks' excellent screen adaptation of *Cat On A Hot Tin Roof* (1958).

Left: A powerful exposé of commercial Bible-punching, *Elmer Gantry* (1960) starred Burt Lancaster as the preacher. He, Brooks (as writer) and Shirley Jones won Academy Awards, and the picture and its music (Andre Previn) garnered nominations.

powerful Bible-punching preacher. Both pictures reflected Brooks' taste for larger-than-life characters and situations, but remain solidly respectable and lack the kind of flair which a more imaginative director like Kazan brought to similar subjects. Yet both had just the kind of qualities which appeal to Academy members and were nominated for the Best Picture Oscar, while Brooks himself was nominated for directing and scripting *Cat* and won his only Oscar for the *Elmer Gantry* screenplay. *Cat* provided memorable roles for Elizabeth Taylor and Paul Newman (both nominated for Oscars), although Brooks was forced to tone down the original play's homosexual theme, and the film also suffered from a rather too neatly upbeat ending. *Gantry* was the better of the two, benefitting from Burt Lancaster's charismatic and Oscar-winning performance, and from the twists and turns, ups and downs, of Lewis' ingenious plot. Shirley Jones won a supporting actress Oscar, too, while Brooks ended up marrying Lancaster's co-star, Jean Simmons (they divorced some years later).

Returning to MGM and to Tennessee Williams, with Paul Newman again starring, Brooks directed *Sweet Bird Of Youth* in 1961. Another downbeat subject, only some strong performances from a fine cast, including Geraldine Page, Shirley Knight (both Oscar-nominated) and Ed Begley (winner of the best supporting actor Oscar), saved the picture. And, once gain, Brooks was forced to tack on an unconvincing happy ending. Some fine acting and stunning location photography in Super Panavision couldn't save *Lord Jim*, either. Flushed with the success of *Lawrence Of Arabia* (1962), Columbia expected a repeat of David Lean's success: after all, Peter O'Toole was starring and Freddie Young was behind the camera, but it flopped badly. '*Lord Jim* should have been a small picture,' Brooks readily admitted years later. 'The problem was that it grew too big.' Its failure led Brooks to transfer his areas of interest and, from 1966 up to the present date, he has concentrated almost entirely on Westerns and thrillers. He was encouraged in these genres by his initial success with *The Professionals* (Columbia, 1966), followed by *In Cold Blood*. *The Professionals* transferred Homer's *Iliad* to a Western setting with Claudia Cardinale, the wife of an American millionaire, as the Helen figure, held captive by a Mexican bandit (Jack Palance), equating to Paris. A group of American mercenaries representing the Greeks, and led by Burt Lancaster, attempt to fetch her back. *In Cold Blood* was an uncompromisingly harsh black-and-white film, true to the letter and spirit of Truman Capote's best-selling documentary novel about a real-life, unmotivated and brutal killing of a Kansas family.

After one disastrous attempt at writing and directing an original dramatic picture starring his wife, Jean Simmons – *The Happy Ending* (UA, 1969) – Brooks returned to thrillers and Westerns during the 70s. He had his last big hit with the dramatic thriller, *Looking For Mr Goodbar*, starring Diane Keaton. Still active during the 80s, his most recent effort is the gambling movie, *The Fever* (1985).

Left: In 1961, Brooks returned to Tennessee Williams for subject matter and filmed *Sweet Bird Of Youth*. One of Broadway's finest actresses, Geraldine Page, recreated her original role as an aging actress. Paul Newman was her young, feckless lover.

Below: The glamour of Peter O'Toole in Technicolor and Super Panavision could not save *Lord Jim* (1964), Brooks' unwieldy version of Joseph Conrad's novel.

Bottom left: Director Brooks (right) rehearses with English actor Ian Bannen (left) and Gene Hackman for *Bite The Bullet* (1975). The movie, about endurance horse racing marathons in the West around the turn of the century, was shot on locations in Nevada, New Mexico and Colorado.

'Already perceptible in his first movie, Crisis (1950), were the writer-director's liberal views expressed in a heavy, literal style, overstating the obvious'

Ronald Bergan in 'A-Z of Movie Directors'

JULES DASSIN

Born Middletown, Connecticut, 18 December 1911

Jules Dassin was first invited out to Hollywood by RKO in 1940 on the basis of his acting, and his work in the New York theatre. He was given an opportunity to direct at MGM where he made a successful one reeler adaptation of Poe's *The Tell-Tale Heart* (1941) and was immediately upgraded to features. He directed one of Joan Crawford's last, forgettable MGM movies, *Reunion In France* (1942), shortly before her departure to Warner Bros., and *The Canterville Ghost* (1944), an enjoyable wartime comedy starring Charles Laughton. Rebelling at the steady diet of lightweight fare to which he was assigned, he left MGM in 1946. At the smaller Universal studio he teamed up with producer Mark Hellinger on a pair of black-and-white thrillers. Dassin was clearly more attracted to strong dramatic subjects with a social theme, not unlike Richard Brooks who scripted *Brute Force*, the first of Dassin's *films noirs* in 1947. One of the most violent of 40s movies, it was set in a prison and starred Burt Lancaster, Charles Bickford, and Hume Cronyn as a sadistic head guard who likes to listen to Wagner in his spare time. The prisoners, too, are brutal in their behaviour: a suspected informer is forced to his death by three men armed with blow-torches. The running conflict between guards and prisoners builds to an extremely violent climax when an attempted mass prison break is foiled – with the death of all concerned.

Dassin's love of high drama was kept in check for *The Naked City*, a low-key, documentary-style treatment of a police murder investigation in New York City. It was shot on location in 1947, with an appropriately gritty style, by William Daniels. Previously Garbo's favourite cameraman, Daniels had made a drastic break from MGM's glossy studio filming, and was rewarded with an Oscar for his efforts. The picture's remarkable climax featured an extended chase through the Lower East Side ending up

at the Williamsburg Bridge. Barry Fitzgerald played a diminutive but shrewd detective, while hefty Ted de Corsia made a formidable villain and was already well on his way to becoming one of Hollywood's leading heavies. Some years later, the title and semi-documentary style of the picture was adopted for one of the best of television's cop series, *Naked City*.

Dassin's next two pictures were made for Fox, where he continued in the same mould. *Thieves' Highway*, filmed in 1948, starred Richard Conte as a California trucker who stands up to, and ultimately defeats, a corrupt wholesaler (Lee J. Cobb) and his thugs. In style and subject the film clearly anticipated *On The Waterfront* (Columbia, 1954), and reflected Dassin's characteristic sympathy for the little man in conflict with a large, and frequently corrupt, organisation.

In 1949 Dassin's location filming took him to London with Richard Widmark for *Night And The City*, the last and least memorable of his cycle of US-based thrillers. While his stylised use of London as a background was quite effective, and the chase and action sequences

efficient, the dialogue and characterisation left much to be desired. Named in the testimony of his fellow director, Edward Dmytryk, as a member of the 'Communist faction' in Hollywood, Dassin was immediately blacklisted. Forced to seek work in Europe, he was fortunate in his first French feature, *Rififi* (1954), now a minor classic and particularly remembered for its ingenious and effective 25-minute burglary sequence played without dialogue.

Dassin first directed Greek actress Melina Mercouri in the French/Greek production *Celui Qui Doit Mourir* in 1956. Four years later, the pair enjoyed a huge hit with *Never On Sunday* (1960). The star won an Oscar nomination for her delightfully extrovert performance as a fun-loving prostitute, while the director was nominated for both script and direction. Twenty-two years later, the Greek Minister of Culture, as Miss Mercouri had become, paid a return visit to the waterfront of Piraeus, the film's main setting, to announce an official clean-up of the picturesque but seedy area. She and Dassin had married in 1966 and made a number of movies together during the 60s and 70s, but the director retired after making the disappointing *Circle Of Two* in Canada in 1980.

'Everything that is violent interests me. Everything that is brutal makes me sick. Sometimes I admire violence. Sometimes I respect violence. And sometimes I fear it'

DELMER DAVES

Born San Francisco, 24 July 1904. **Died** 1977

Recognised for his versatility, Delmer Daves served a twenty-year apprenticeship as prop boy, scenarist and scriptwriter before becoming a director. He started out as an assistant to James Cruze during the 20s and played a few bit parts, moved to MGM during the early 30s, then on to Warner Bros. in 1934 for four years. A useful period as a freelance writer followed until, in 1943, he returned to Warner Bros. and was given the opportunity to write and direct *Destination Tokyo*. A solidly crafted but rather 'talky' war movie, it starred Cary Grant in a rare unromantic role. Taking place mainly within the confines of an American submarine, the film represented the first of Daves' many contributions to the war effort. *The Very Thought Of You* (1944) depicted the stresses and strains in a wartime marriage, while the all-star cast of *Hollywood Canteen* the same year had some fun with a series of sketches designed to draw attention to the activities of the real Hollywood canteen which was set up to entertain servicemen. *Pride Of The Marines* (1945) was based on the real-life story of war hero Private Al Schmid who had been blinded by a Jap grenade at Guadalcanal, but it was less of a war movie than an intimate and powerful drama of a type which appealed to Daves. With its emphasis on Schmid's problems in adjusting to his blindness and to civilian life, and with John Garfield giving one of his strongest screen performances, the picture was an obvious forerunner to *The Best Years Of Our Lives* (Goldwyn/RKO, 1946) and *The Men* (Kramer/UA, 1950).

Whether working with other script-writers like Albert Maltz (*Pride Of The Marines*) or Richard Brooks (*To The Victor*, 1948), or working from his own scripts, as in *The Red House* (UA, 1946) and *Dark Passage* (Warner Bros., 1947), Daves was a solid and dependable director. But he rarely rose above the quality of his original material. His heavy-handed treatment of the David Goodis thriller, *Dark Passage*, for example, while faithful to the original, fails to lift the movie above the run-of-the-mill 40s *films noirs*, in spite of a first-rate cast headed by Humphrey Bogart and Lauren Bacall and some striking San Francisco settings. More promising for Daves was his first picture for his new studio, 20th Century-Fox, and his first Western – *Broken Arrow* (1950). A native Westerner whose grandfather was a pioneer and Pony Express rider, Daves had always been interested in the history of the West and the plight of the Indians. With its story of a white scout who marries an Indian girl and tries to make peace, *Broken Arrow* was one of the first major productions to treat the Indian with respect. It initiated a new cycle of pro-Indian Westerns and helped establish James Stewart, and, to a lesser extent, Jeff Chandler (who played the Indian chief Cochise), as leading Western stars of the 50s.

Unfortunately, the promise of *Broken Arrow* was not fulfilled. As a contract director at Fox, Daves was landed with rather too many routine assignments, repeating the pattern of his situation at Warner Bros. During an era when leading directors were experiencing a new freedom as independent producer-directors, he carried on with such projects

as *Treasure Of The Golden Condor* (1952) and *Demetrius And The Gladiators* (1953), one of the first CinemaScope movies, and only returned to Westerns in 1954 after his departure from Fox. Of special interest was his collaboration with star Glenn Ford and ace cameraman Charles Lawton Jr at Columbia, which resulted in *Jubal* (1955), and the memorable *3:10 To Yuma* (1957). *Cowboy* (1958) took a hard (and sometimes amusing) look at the real life of a trail hand as seen and experienced by writer Frank Harris (Jack Lemmon). Having made his contribution to the development of the adult Western, Daves turned mainly to romance and comedy during the 60s, and retired after directing *The Battle Of The Villa Fiorita* for Warner Bros. in 1964.

Above: Van Heflin (left) and Glenn Ford in *3:10 To Yuma* (1957) an unusual, tense, and effectively intimate Western.

Below left: James Stewart and Debra Paget in *Broken Arrow* (1950), the first Western made by Daves, and a significant contribution to the genre in its pro-Indian sentiments.

Below: Delmer Daves working on a storyboard – drawing visual sequences – for *Kings Go Forth* (UA, 1958), a not very distinguished war melodrama that starred Frank Sinatra, Tony Curtis and Natalie Wood.

'The movies of Delmer Daves are fun of a very special kind. Call it Camp or call it Corn. The director does not so much transcend his material as mingle with it'

Andrew Sarris in 'The American Cinema'

EDWARD DMYTRYK

Born Grand Forks, Canada, 4 September 1908

Edward Dmytryk was at his best in the mid-40s when he displayed a crisp, efficient style which perfectly suited his small-budget, *noir* subjects, and reflected his training as an editor. He was the first of three leading RKO directors – Robert Wise and Mark Robson were the others – who had been top editors.

First attracted to the movies as a youth, Dmytryk worked his way up from messenger boy and lowly assistant during the 20s to assistant editor, then full editor status, at Paramount during the 30s. He edited *Ruggles Of Red Gap* (1935) for Leo McCarey and *Zaza* (1939) for George Cukor, and benefitted from Paramount's special system whereby editors were allowed to work closely with the directors during filming, rather than being confined to the cutting room. Dmytryk was first given some B pictures to direct at Paramount (1939-40) and then at Columbia (1940-42), including an above-average horror thriller, *The Devil Commands* (1941), starring Boris Karloff. But his career really took off with his first low-budget movie at RKO in 1942, *Hitler's Children*. Little more than a strongly dramatised and violent exercise in anti-Nazi propaganda, it cost only $205,000 to make and earned a profit of over $1½ million, making it one of the two or three most successful movies in the studio's history. During the following years Dmytryk emerged as RKO's blue-eyed boy, providing the studio with an unbroken series of small-budget hits. The director had turned his attention, with equal success, to Japan in *Behind The Rising Sun* (1943), while *Back To Bataan* starred John Wayne in an up-to-date movie about the war in the Philippines which was one of

RKO's top hits in 1945. *Murder My Sweet* (aka *Farewell My Lovely*) came out in 1944, the year which marked the real beginnings of 40s *film noir*. It was the first of a number of outstanding screen adaptations of Raymond Chandler's novels, and it provided Dick Powell with a tough movie persona far removed from his 30s juvenile crooner roles. The new-look Powell burst onto the screen as hard-boiled private eye Philip Marlowe trying to unravel the mystery behind cool blonde Claire Trevor and a missing jade necklace. With an effective mixture of muted photography, pacy editing, and stacatto, Chandleresque dialogue, the picture couldn't – and didn't – miss.

Dmytryk, writer John Paxton and producer Adrian Scott followed up with *Cornered* (1945), another thriller starring Powell, then moved on to the excellent *Crossfire* (1947), based on a novel by Richard Brooks. A fine cast was headed by Robert Young, with both Robert Mitchum and Robert Ryan (as the sleazy villain) making the most of early starring roles. *Crossfire* provides one of the best examples of how important social themes (in this case anti-semitism) could be effectively treated within a low-key, thriller format. It was Dmytryk's first to be nominated for a Best Picture Oscar, and gave him his only directing nomination. By now, however, Dmytryk, along with Adrian Scott and a number of others, was under investigation by the House Un-American Activities Committee for alleged left-wing activities. He continued directing in England, but returned to the US and was sentenced to a six-month prison term in 1950, the only director among the group of Hollywood Ten.

After his release and subsequent 'recanting', he was removed from the industry's blacklist. Hired by producer Stanley Kramer for three pictures during 1952-54, he had a big hit with the last of these, *The Caine Mutiny* (Colombia, 1954) which was also nominated for a Best Picture Oscar. Much in demand during the 50s, Dymtryk handled many large-scale pictures, working mainly in colour and CinemaScope at 20th Century-Fox, and found himself in charge of MGM's lavish Civil War epic, *Raintree County* (1956). Unfortunately, the director's work for the large screen never seemed to match the quality of his early small-scale black-and-white successes; nonetheless he continued directing, mainly in Europe, throughout the 60s and up to the mid-70s when he retired.

Above: Agnes Moorehead and Humphrey Bogart in *The Left Hand Of God* (20th-Century-Fox, 1955), not one of Dmytryk's (or Bogart's) most memorable films. The dog-collar turns out to be concealing a fugitive American flier rather than a priest.

Below left: American Marine colonel John Wayne organises his band of guerrilla fighters in the Philippines in *Back To Bataan* (1945).

Below: Director Dmytryk (seated) discusses a plot point with English actor Robert Newton during the making of *Obsession* (1948), a British murder thriller.

'Nelson Algren's trashy novel at least contained some serious writing, but director Edward Dmytryk is strictly a hack'

Steven H. Scheuer on *Walk On The Wild Side* in 'Movies on TV'

STANLEY DONEN

Born Columbia, South Carolina, 13 April 1924

At the age of ten Stanley Donen was dancing in the theatre and, at sixteen, was on Broadway in the chorus of 'Pal Joey', which starred Gene Kelly. The following year (1941), he assisted Kelly with choreography for 'Best Foot Forward', thus commencing a partnership which took him to Hollywood and defined the first stage of his film career as a vital contributor to the Hollywood musical.

Following Kelly to the West coast, Donen assisted Charles Walters in choreographing the film version of *Best Foot Forward* (MGM, 1943), then resumed his partnership with Kelly on the Rita Hayworth starrer, *Cover Girl* (Columbia, 1944). The two men returned to MGM as integral members of producer Arthur Freed's famed 'Freed Unit' – and, in 1945, they worked on *Anchors Aweigh* which successfully paired Gene and Frank Sinatra, beginning a vogue in 'sailors-on-leave' musicals. Donen did a handful of pictures without Kelly then, in 1948, they co-choreographed and directed the musical numbers for what had long been a pet project, *Take Me Out To The Ball Game*. Always intent on becoming fully-fledged directors, the pair were given their big opportunity with *On The Town* (1949). Notable for the integration of song and dance into the storyline, the movie gained a fresh vibrancy from the innovative use of actual New York locations. Another 'sailors-on-leave' tale, it starred a sparkling sextet headed by Kelly, Sinatra, and Ann Miller, and was a resounding box-office success. Freed immediately gave Donen his first solo assignment with *Royal Wedding* (1950), starring Fred Astaire.

By 1951 Stanley Donen, who had started out as Gene Kelly's 'eye behind the camera', had reached full directorial status. Nonetheless, it was as co-director and choreographer with Kelly that he achieved his greatest success with the now classic *Singin' In The Rain* (1951). A funny and original satire on the problems caused to the silent cinema by the arrival of sound, the film was ebulliently inventive and gave full rein to the on-screen talents of Kelly, Donald O'Connor and Debbie Reynolds. Donen continued as an MGM contract director for a few years, where his most notable success was *Seven Brides For Seven Brothers* in 1954 – the same year in which he made a respectable biopic about composer Sigmund Romberg, *Deep In My Heart*, which starred Jose Ferrer, and in which Gene, with his brother Fred, danced a guest spot. Gene and Stanley were reunited as co-director/choreographers for *It's Always Fair Weather* (1955), but the film was a major disappointment. Taking a number of key MGM personnel with him, as well as the inimitable Fred Astaire, Donen departed his *alma mater* in 1956 to make the delightful *Funny Face*, co-starring Audrey Hepburn, at Paramount. Two more musicals followed for Warner Bros., both adaptations of stage shows: *The Pajama Game* (1957) with Doris Day, and *Damn Yankees* (1959).

But the great musical cycle had passed its peak and Donen, now a producer as well as a director, and dedicated to the sophisticated, soufflé-style of entertainment, turned to comedy – working largely in England and Europe.

Once More With Feeling, Kay Kendall's last film before her tragic death, was a feeble vehicle, unworthy of both its star and its director. The latter's expertise crystallised, however, in the success of *Charade* (Universal, 1963), a witty, romantic thriller set in Paris and starring an urbane Cary Grant and an edible Audrey Hepburn. (He repeated the formula with Gregory Peck and Sophia Loren in *Arabesque*, 1966, to lesser but still appealing effect.) *Two For The Road* (1967), again with Hepburn, and co-starring the no less attractive Albert Finney, was an uneven attempt to chart the fashionable marital morés of swing-ing 60s Britain. *Staircase* (1969), about two aging homosexual hairdressers, represented something of a departure in subject, and the presence of Richard Burton and Rex Harrison did little to redeem the general mishandling of this adaptation of Charles Dyer's play. *The Little Prince* (Paramount, 1974), a musical version of St-Exupéry's whimsical fantasy, returned its director to more familiar ground but, although lovely to look at, it was not a success. By 1978, Donen was looking to vintage Hollywood for inspiration and came up with *Movie, Movie*, a double-bill pastiche offering some memorable moments for addicts of the genre but it was not box-office. In 1979, Donen lent his presence to Sci-Fi with *Saturn 3* and, by 1984, he had returned to comedy with *Blame It On Rio*, starring Michael Caine, but with little else to recommend it.

'Anybody who says that every picture is not a collaboration is an idot! It's a question of how much you collaborate and who you collaborate with'

1958

Above: Stanley Donen (centre right) discusses a costume design for *Deep In My Heart* (1954), with Gene Kelly (left), Jose Ferrer, and an MGM design assistant.

Below left: Kay Thompson (left), Fred Astaire and Audrey Hepburn on the Eiffel Tower in *Funny Face* (1956).

Below: Audrey Hepburn reading to Thomas Chelimsky who, she hopes, can lead her to a cache of stolen money in Donen's glossy thriller, *Charade* (1963).

SAMUEL FULLER

Born Worcester, Massachusetts, 12 August 1911

A strong and uncompromising individualist, Samuel Fuller worked his way up within the Hollywood system from B-movie scriptwriter to B-movie writer-director and, eventually, to some As. He is at his best in black-and-white, adopting a clean, crisp and economical style. Used to working quickly and cheaply, he likes to move the camera about and make use of longish takes alternating with strong close-ups. A preference for unusual camera angles helps to disguise the smallness of the sets and provides a greater visual variety at minimal cost, and he is most at home within an urban setting, as in *Pickup On South Street* (20th Century-Fox, 1953), framing his shots through doorways and down corridors or empty streets. The shots are edited together with a real flair for directness and simplicity which marks Fuller as a genuine primitive, recalling the early films of D.W. Griffith or the fast-moving style of 30s Warner Bros. gangster flicks.

The visual imagery and vitality of his black-and-white movies during the 50s and early 60s was much appreciated by the younger generation of European *cinéastes* like Jean-Luc Godard and Wim Wenders who expressed their admiration for his work in print or cast him in their pictures. Playing a small role in Godard's *Pierrot Le Fou* in 1965, for example, Fuller delivers a memorable line which neatly encapsulates his attitude to the cinema: 'A film is like a battleground – love . . . hate . . . action . . . violence . . . death . . . in a word – emotion!' This is the stuff of tabloid headlines or comic strip balloons, the true expressions of an ex-crime reporter and pulp journalist which, indeed, Fuller was during his formative years. Working on such papers as the 'New York Journal' and the 'New York Graphic' during the 20s, he served a tough apprenticeship as a copy boy and assistant before working his way up to rewrite man and ace reporter. By the mid-30s he had developed a new career as a pulp novelist (*Burn, Baby, Burn*, 1935), and scriptwriter – *Gangs Of New York* and *Federal Manhunt*, both filmed by Republic in 1938. He served with distinction in the US First Infantry Division during World War II, then returned to B's after the war, first as scriptwriter – on Douglas Sirk's *Shockproof* (Columbia, 1948) – then as a writer-director, beginning in 1948 with *I Shot Jesse James*, the first of three cheapies he made for the tiny Lippert company. It starred Preston Foster and John Ireland, and already Fuller's originality of approach was demonstrated in his powerful use of close-ups and fast-paced editing.

After *The Baron Of Arizona* (1950), an unusual Western drama starring Vincent Price, Fuller scripted and directed a pair of tough war movies about American troops in Korea fighting the 'Reds'. A topical subject for Fuller the ex-newspaperman, the fight against the Red menace was a theme which would recur in later pictures. Still working within the constraint of tiny budgets he was able to take advantage of the new management at United Artists in 1952 to film *Park Row*, one of his pet projects about American newspaper publishing in New York City during the 1880's. Playing the irascible but enterprising new owner-editor of the paper was chunky, cigar-chomping Gene Evans, making his third Fuller film in a row; his physical resemblance to the director suggests that he represents the latter's alter ego.

Finally, in 1952, 20th Century-Fox gave Fuller his first opportunity to show what he could do with an A-budget and leading stars. *Pickup On South Street* was the first of a group of movies which he made for the studio during the mid-50s, the only period in his career when he was contracted to a Hollywood major. The picture was originally intended to star Marilyn Monroe, but Fuller found Jean Peters a more than adequate replacement in the role of the hooker and gangster's moll who joins with pickpocket Richard Widmark to foil a communist spy ring. Fuller's best known 50s movie, this gripping thriller was photographed in typically high-contrast black-and-white, and shot in no more than twenty days on location in downtown Los Angeles, using 'a lot of tricks' to make it look like New York. The alternately tender and brutal love scenes between the pair of tough, street-wise characters played by Widmark and Peters certainly struck sparks off the screen, but the movie was effectively stolen by the remarkable Thelma Ritter, Oscar-nominated for her memorable performance as a layabout and police informer.

The success of the newly introduced CinemaScope in 1953 caused plenty of headaches at Fox, not least for Sam Fuller who was persuaded by studio boss Darryl Zanuck to make a submarine picture, *Hell And High Water* (1954) in the new process. He did rather better with *House Of Bamboo* (1955). As photographed by Joe Macdonald, it is Fuller's most effective colour film, with Robert Stack starring as a US undercover agent investigating the activities of a ruthless gang of American ex-servicemen led by Robert Ryan. Ryan's performance as a tough but sympathetic villain dominates

Above: Gene Evans (2nd right with cigar) played the lead in *Park Row* (1952), written, produced and directed by Fuller, and dealing with a subject close to his heart – newspapers.

Below: Richard Widmark in a moment of action from *Pickup On South Street* (1953).

1959) was a detective thriller set in Los Angeles' Little Tokyo, while *Underworld USA* (Columbia, 1960) dealt with the evils of organized crime. *Shock Corridor* (1963) took place mainly in an insane asylum , while the heroine of *The Naked Kiss* (1965) was a reformed prostitute. This gives an idea of the range of Fuller's pictures, all filmed cheaply and avoiding big name stars. The sole exception during these years was the relatively large scale war movie *Merrill's Marauders* (Warner Bros., 1961) which provides an interesting link with *The Big Red One* (UA, 1980). Both films follow the exploits of a particular American infantry unit during World War II with Jeff Chandler and Lee Marvin as the stars. Making something of a comeback during recent years Fuller returned to the US in 1981 to direct his first film there in sixteen years, the anti-racist *White Dog*. So controversial was this movie that the studio, Paramount, was afraid to distribute it – a perverse tribute, perhaps, to the grand old man of American B-movies.

'Politics doesn't interest me . . . I'm not interested in who's a Red or an anti-Commie. If I feel that the hero should be a Fascist, I'll make him a Fascist. if he should be a Leftist I'll make him one. I'm just interested in character'
1969

the film. As in *Pickup* and in other, later *films noirs*, Fuller concentrates on the central relationship – set against a perceptively observed social background, and here complicated by the fact that Stack is finally forced to betray Ryan and kill him. There are some superbly staged action sequences, but Fuller, as always, is more interested in characters and relationships than action *per se*, although he is sometimes incorrectly labelled an 'action director'.

Fuller had three films released in 1957, the beginning of his last productive period in the US. After an offbeat Western, *Run Of The Arrow* for RKO, starring Rod Steiger, he returned to Fox and his preferred black-and-white for *China Gate*, the first American movie about the guerrilla war in Vietnam, and *Forty Guns*. This was his last and best Western and demonstrates Fuller's ability to bring fresh vitality to a familiar subject – the frontier town terrorised by a local cattle baron (or, in this case, baroness) played by Barbara Stanwyck, and her forty gunmen. 'Each scene, each shot of this savage and brutal Western . . . is so rich in invention – despite an incomprehensible plot – and so bursting with daring conceptions,' wrote Jean-Luc Godard, 'that it reminds one of the extravagances of Abel Gance and Stroheim . . .' It moves along at a remarkable pace with little time wasted on plot or sub-plots, although there is a typically intense love-hate relationship between gunman hero Barry Sullivan and Miss Stanwyck. Fuller's audacious use of the wide screen, blending long takes and moving camera shots with giant close-ups, unusual angles and shock cuts, all integrated into a powerful and original whole anticipates the arrival of Peckinpah and Leone in the 60s.

The director was equally daring in his treatment of postwar Germany in *Verboten!* (RKO Columbia, 1958), which included documentary footage and a visit to the war crimes trials in Nuremburg. This unfairly neglected work was followed by a series of black-and-white crime movies set in contemporary America and presenting a distinctly downbeat view of society. *The Crimson Kimono* (Columbia,

Above left: Barbara Stanwyck in *Forty Guns* (1957). This tough and excellent Western varied the formula of frontier town terrorised by cattle baron, by casting Miss Stanwyck as the cattle baron.

Left: Jeff Chandler starred in *Merrill's Marauders* (1961), a large-budget (by Fuller's standards) war adventure movie, set in Burma. Lots of blood-and-guts action.

Below: Fuller (left) is revered by several European film-makers and has acted for them on a couple of occasions. In German director Wim Wenders' movie, *The State Of Things* (1982), the veteran played an American film director. Here he is with Wenders.

HENRY HATHAWAY

Born Sacramento, 13 March 1898

Born into a show business family, young Henry Hathaway used to join his actress mother on location when she was playing in early Allan Dwan one-reelers. He too became a bit actor: 'Whenever there was a kid stolen by the Indians and he turns out to be Jack Kerrigan (the star) in later life, that was me.' Young Henry continued to play small roles, also working as a prop boy during the teens. Feeling more at home behind the camera, he gave up acting and, after a break for war service, established himself as one of the leading assistant directors in Hollywood during the 20s. In this capacity he began his long association with Paramount in 1923, working notably under Josef von Sternberg and Victor Fleming. In contrast to the practice in Europe where the assistant director works closely with the director on all aspects of the film, in the US and Britain he serves as a kind of 'foreman' on the set, and generally has little to do with the creative side of film-making. Hence, relatively few American directors have risen from the ranks of assistant. One of the most durable and dependable of Hollywood directors, with a winningly unpretentious quality about him, Hathaway represents the ideal version of assistant director-turned-director although, according to scriptwriter Wendell Hayes he was 'not the most articulate man in the world ... He maintains control of his set and of his crew and actors by being cantankerous and rather cruel sometimes ... Easy for a writer to work with, but dreadful for actors, he's probably the toughest son-of-a-bitch in Hollywood'.

The flavour of Hathaway's quick, efficient and strictly functional approach comes across in his own description of his methods: 'I always cut in the camera,' he asserts. 'I don't shoot a whole master shot (general shot of a sequence) all the way through. I start it and then I get into the two-shots and then the close-up and then I get out of it ... There's a reason for each scene, and as soon as you hit it, get out as fast as you can ... It's a problem of timing and making your point and getting the hell out of the extraneous things.'

If Hathaway never directed any real masterpieces, he was virtually unique among Hollywood directors in his ability to maintain the same high standard of filming for almost forty years. Directing at Paramount during the 30s, he left after a dispute and soon found a new home at 20th Century-Fox where he spent most of the next twenty years. He continued to thrive on into the 60s, after the decline of the old studios and, at a time when many other directors of his generation were retiring, he had three of the biggest hits of his career: *How The West Was Won* (MGM, 1962), *The Sons Of Katie Elder* (1965) and *True Grit* (1969), the two latter produced by Hal Wallis for Paramount. A solid, craftsmanlike director, Hathaway never attempted to build on his early successes with Gary Cooper during the 30s and apparently had no desire to break out of his mould. He was content with the mixture of action pic-

tures, dramatic thrillers and Westerns assigned to him, and claims he never turned down a script in all his years at Fox (though he did substantially rework some of them): 'I've never had an unhappy moment in my life that I can remember as far as working is concerned'.

On promotion to full director, he first handled half-a-dozen Zane Grey B-Westerns starring Randolph Scott during 1932-34. But he was soon directing As, and never looked back. Leaving the Western behind, he established himself as a leading director with a nicely varied group of movies starring Gary Cooper. Most important was *The Lives Of A Bengal Lancer* (1935), nominated for a Best Picture Oscar and earning Hathaway his only directing nomination. Cooper's most popular movie up to that date, it initiated a new cycle of British Imperial subjects and was most memorable for its action sequences. These were filmed at Lone Pine, California, the same setting used to recreate Imperial India in such films as *The Charge Of The Light Brigade* (Warner Bros., 1936) and *Gunga Din* (RKO, 1939). Hathaway then tackled the dream-like fantasy of *Peter Ibbetson* (1936), a quite uncharacteristic romantic drama, with the same professionalism he brought to his other, more down-to-earth action subjects. He made a fine job of it, but never again tried anything in the same vein. He and Coop next took to the sea, still for Paramount, with *Souls At Sea* (1937), then went off to the Philippines to fight for Sam Goldwyn in *The Real Glory* (UA, 1939).

Hathaway added considerably to his reputation in 1936 when he directed *The Trail Of The Lonesome Pine*, the first Technicolor movie to be filmed substantially on location. An old-fashioned story of feuding mountain folk which has been filmed twice before, a fine cast (headed by Henry Fonda and Sylvia Sidney) and the

novelty of the attractive colour helped to make this the first Technicolor hit of the 30s. Hathaway's now solid reputation as a director of action adventure pictures landed him a new contract with 20th Century-Fox in 1940. He occasionally returned to film in colour as in *The Shepherd Of The Hills* (Paramount, 1941), his first with John Wayne, and *Home In Indiana* (20th Century-Fox, 1944), an entertaining, if sentimental, slice of Americana. But he maintained his repu-

tation with a series of tough war pictures and thrillers in black-and-white during the 40s and early 50s.

Hathaway's straightforward method lent itself perfectly to the new style of location thriller which occupied him during the years 1945-48. *The House On 92nd Street* (1945), initiated by former documentary producer Louis de Rochemont, was the very first of this new breed of *film noir*. 'This story is adapted from the espionage files of the FBI' announced the opening title. The approach may have been suitably low-key, and the cast was liberally sprinkled with new and unfamiliar faces but, as usual in these ventures, the true facts were given a suitably fictionalised treatment. A follow-up picture, *Thirteen Rue Madeleine* (1946), starred James Cagney in a tribute to the wartime activities of the OSS, partly filmed in Canada as a stand-in for occupied France. Far more effective, however, was *Kiss Of Death* (1947), starring Victor Mature and Richard Widmark (his debut) in the kind of tough and violent crime thriller which Hathaway (and Hollywood) did best. The director brought his personal *noir* cycle to a close with the memorable *Call Northside 777* (1948), aided by a finely judged performance from James Stewart whose easygoing style fitted in well with the demands of location filming.

An effective small-scale drama with a strong suspense element, *Fourteen Hours* (1951) was also based on a true story. The film was lifted by fine performances from Richard Basehart as the man on the ledge who threatens to jump, and Paul Douglas as the simple, nice-guy cop who attempts to rescue him. To this day Hathaway bitterly regrets being forced by the studio to provide a happy ending. Reflecting a strong Hitchcockian influence, *Niagara* (1952) was a superior Technicolored thriller designed as a starring vehicle for Marilyn Monroe.

A much travelled man, Hathaway went to Europe to film *The Black Rose* (1950), *Seven Thieves* (1960) and *Circus World* (1964), and to Africa for *White Witch Doctor* (1953). From 1957 on he developed a close working relationship with John Wayne, and was most successful with his Westerns during the 60s. According to James Stewart, Hathaway took on much of the responsibility for solving the serious script and directing problems on *How The West Was Won* and really 'saved the film'. But he is probably best remembered for directing Wayne in his Oscar-winning performance in *True Grit* (1969), his last movie of note, although he continued directing during the early 70s and only retired in 1974, having spent about sixty-five years in the film industry.

'To be a good director you've got to be a bastard. I'm a bastard and I know it'

Above left: Director Hathaway (right) setting up a sequence for *Fourteen Hours* (1951), with Paul Douglas (centre) and Richard Basehart.

Below: Marilyn Monroe in *Niagara* (1952), a suspense thriller in which she played a faithless wife who is plotting to murder her husband. It was Monroe's first major role.

Bottom: James Stewart in *How The West Was Won* (1962), Hathaway's best-known Western and one of the biggest hits of his career.

HOWARD HAWKS

Born Goshen, Indiana, 30 May 1896. **Died** 1977

An all-round sportsman, flier and racing car driver who studied engineering, Howard Hawks was first attracted to the movies in his youth. He started in the property department of Famous Players-Lasky (later Paramount) and did a variety of jobs ranging from cutter and assistant director, to casting director, script supervisor and producer during the early 20s. After writing and directing a number of one-reel comedies starring Monty Banks, Hawks made his name as a scriptwriter of feature films before finally establishing himself as a feature director at Fox in 1926. A genuine independent throughout most of his fifty-year career, Hawks made pictures for every one of the eight major studios as well as for Goldwyn. In Hollywood, directors – no less than stars – tend to be typecast, but Hawks successfully resisted this and demonstrated a remarkable versatility. Drawing on his own wide experience and interests, he directed outstanding examples of many different genres ranging from gangster movies (*Scarface*, UA, 1932), thrillers (*The Big Sleep*, Warner Bros., 1946), and war (*Sergeant York*, Warner Bros., 1941) to action drama (*Only Angels Have Wings*, Columbia, 1939, and *Hatari!*, Paramount, 1962), Westerns (*Red River*, UA, 1948, and *Rio Bravo*, Warner Bros., 1959) and comedies (*20th Century*, 1934, and *His Girl Friday*, 1940, both for Columbia), with even the odd musical (*Gentlemen Prefer Blondes*, 20th Century-Fox, 1953) thrown in. Such diversity was at least partly responsible for the fact that he failed to receive adequate recognition for the outstanding quality of much of his work until relatively late in his career – in contrast to Hitchcock, for example, who was closely identified with one type of film. Yet, like Hitch, he combined a highly personal approach with a popular and entertaining style which appealed to audiences. His four big hits during the 40s, for example, were a typically varied bunch – *Sergeant York*, *The Big Sleep*, *Red River* and 20th Century-Fox's *I Was A Male War Bride* (1949) – and assured his continued independence.

Refreshingly unpretentious and straightforward in his attitude to filmmaking, Hawks regarded himself as a craftsman and storyteller. He appreciated the importance of starting with a good script – 'I'm such a coward that unless I get a great writer, I don't want to make a picture'. Thus, he regularly employed the best writing talents available – Ben Hecht, William Faulkner, Charles Lederer, Leigh Brackett and Jules Furthman each worked on four or more of his movies. He always collaborated closely, though uncredited, with his writers, and continued to make alterations and adjustments up to, and even during, the on-set filming in order to preserve freshness and spontaneity.

Having spent the late 20s at Fox, his only extended stay at a single studio, Hawks went on to demonstrate his qualities as a fine director of actors and dialo-

gue in his first talkies, *The Dawn Patrol* (Warner Bros.) and *The Criminal Code* (Columbia), both filmed in 1930. These two movies reflect his ability to fit in with general Hollywood trends while simultaneously preserving his own special viewpoint. Thus, *The Dawn Patrol* gives the most authentically downbeat view of all the World War I flying pictures, while *The Criminal Code*, little Columbia's prison flick, was competition to MGM's more prestigious *The Big House* (1930) and Warner Bros.' *20,000 Years In Sing Sing* (1932) directed by Curtiz. What the Hawks films lacked in star power and budget, they gained from the quality of photography, acting and (Oscar-nominated) scripts.

Hawks' first masterpiece, and the very best of the early 30s gangster cycle – *Scar-*

face – was filmed in 1931. It was characterised by its offbeat and underplayed black humour, fast pace and editing, and the oblique, even abstract manner in which the frequent and violent killings were presented. The film's style is established in the opening sequence. The camera tracks past the debris of a party (streamers, confetti, empty bottles) – recalling a famous sequence in Von Sternberg's *Underworld* (Paramount, 1927) also scripted by Ben Hecht – to the back room of a nightclub. A shadowy figure with a gun is seen only indistinctly, two shots ring out and a body slumps in the corner. Much of the film takes place at night; a chase through deserted city streets; sudden bursts of gunfire shattering the silence as Tony Camonte (Paul Muni) gets rid of a gangster rival.

'I've seen so many pictures
where the hero gets in the
moonlight and says silly
things to a girl. I'd reverse
it and let the girl do the
chasing around'
1972

Another gangster leader (Boris Karloff) is seen relaxing at a bowling alley. The camera pans to follow the progress of his ball. All the pins go down but one which spins about, then falls, as the sound of gunfire rings out. The scene then fades and we know that Karloff is dead. In typical Hawks style, the women (Ann Dvorak and Karen Morley) appear as tough as the men, while comic relief is provided by Camonte's bumbling secretary (Vince Barnett).

Clearly, Hawks' close collaboration with Hecht during the early and mid-30s, when he was first establishing his directorial style, was of crucial importance, as was his pattern of alternating between different genres and different studios. During 1931-35 Hawks moved easily from *Scarface* (for producer Howard Hughes and United Artists) to a pair of action dramas at Warner Bros., *The Crowd Roars* (1932) starring James Cagney, and *Tiger Shark* (1932) with Edward G. Robinson. A brief and unsatisfactory stint at MGM followed, but was useful in beginning his long and close friendship with William Faulkner who worked with him on the script of the war movie, *Today We Live* (1933), starring Gary Cooper. Then back to Columbia to direct one of the first and best of the screwball comedies, *20th Century*, and on to *Barbary Coast* (1935) a Western drama for Sam Goldwyn. These last two were scripted by Hecht, drawing attention to the kind of 'cross-fertilisation' typical of Hawks. For not only did he enjoy making different types of films, but he also liked to intermingle them: 'A comedy is virtually the same as an adventure story', according to Hawks. 'The difference is in the situation – dangerous in an adventure story, embarrassing in a comedy. But in both we observe our fellow beings in unusual situations. You merely emphasize the dramatic or the comical aspects of the hero's reactions. Sometimes you mix them up a bit. My serious pictures usually have their comic side ... It's possible to do comedy scenes even at very tragic moments...' Like the hilarious sequence of Kirk Douglas having his finger amputated in *The Big Sky* (RKO, 1952), or the attempts to sober up and rehabilitate

Robert Mitchum in *El Dorado* (Paramount, 1967), while the comedy, *His Girl Friday*, concerns an escaped murderer and the suicide of his girlfriend.

The most professional of directors, with a mastery of pacing, technique, dialogue and atmosphere, Hawks valued professionalism in others. One of the central themes of his films is his interest in professionals – racing drivers, fliers, lawmen, private eyes, all getting on with the job in hand – and the camaraderie which develops between men working together. Yet, unlike so many other male-orientated directors, he was ahead of his time in his treatment of his female characters, outspoken and independent-minded ladies like the ace reporter played by Rosalind Russell in *His Girl Friday* or the wise-cracking other Russell, Jane, in *Gentlemen Prefer Blondes*. The theme that attracted Hawks to *20th*

Century, early in his career, was that of a mature, older man (John Barrymore) trying to cope with an attractive but tough-minded and temperamental girl (Carole Lombard). He went on to rework and enrich the same pattern in his 40s thrillers scripted by William Faulkner and starring Bogart and Bacall (who fell in love and married during their Hawks assignments). The theme resurfaced in the delightful *I Was A Male War Bride*, starring Cary Grant and Ann Sheridan, in which Hawks proved that he could still get mileage out of the screwball comedy; then reached its fullest expression in *Rio Bravo* (most notably), *Hatari!* and *El Dorado* – all three scripted by Miss Leigh Brackett who had co-scripted *The Big Sleep* many years earlier. Here, the middle-aged John Wayne, who starred in all three, attempted to cope with young Angie Dickinson, Elsa Martinelli and

Top: The debonair and handsome Cary Grant (left), whose Hollywood career spanned over thirty years, made several of his best comedies for Howard Hawks. Here he is with co-star Rosalind Russell, a worthy adversary, in *His Girl Friday* (1940).

Above: Yet another military honour is pinned to the heroic chest of *Sergeant York* (1941), the role that won Gary Cooper his first Best Actor Oscar, as well as the New York Film Critics' Award. The story of a blundering backwoods yokel who becomes a war hero, the film made a big impact at the time and received seven Academy nominations (excluding Cooper's).

entry in the shortlived animal experiment/eccentric hero cycle of early 50s comedies, reunited with Cary Grant who was admirably supported by Ginger Rogers and Marilyn Monroe in *Monkey Business*; this was 20th Century-Fox's answer to *Harvey* (1950), the Ronald Reagan starrer *Bedtime For Bonzo* (1951) and *Francis* (the talking mule) – all made by Universal.

During his last active years Hawks returned repeatedly to the Western with the masterful *Rio Bravo* (essentially the last of the 50s cycle of classics), the Western-transposed-to-Africa – *Hatari!*, and the highly amusing *El Dorado*, which matched Wayne and Robert Mitchum as a pair of aging lawmen. *Rio Lobo* was his last, and definitely less than his best. Hawks was awarded a very deserved and long overdue special honorary Oscar in 1974, three years before his death.

Charlene Holt respectively, with appropriately comical results. Of special note is the fact that by this time the aging Hawks could identify closely with the plight of his hero, similarly advanced in years.

For those actors and actresses who were receptive to Hawks' informal methods of working, the benefits were immeasurable. No other Hollywood director was responsible for boosting the careers of so many major stars. He turned Paul Muni into a movie star in *Scarface* and first demonstrated Carole Lombard's qualities as a comedienne in *20th Century*. Ditto Katharine Hepburn and Cary Grant in their first screwball comedy, *Bringing Up Baby* (RKO, 1938). He provided Frances Farmer with the best role of her short, unhappy career in *Come And Get It* (Goldwyn/UA, 1936), and discovered Lauren Bacall as a New York model and brought her out to Hollywood for her first two pictures (with Bogart). *Red River* not only provided young Montgomery Clift with his first movie role but proved for the first time – even to John Ford – that 'the big son of a bitch (John Wayne) could act'. During the 50s Hawks took a major hand in turning Marilyn Monroe into a star, proving that she could both act and sing in *Monkey Business* (20th Century-Fox, 1952) and *Gentlemen Prefer Blondes*, while *Rio Bravo* gave a big lift to Angie Dickinson. Hawks had a few failures, too, like Sherry Lansing who gave up acting after appearing in his last film, *Rio Lobo* (1971) and turned to producing instead; a Hawksian career woman in real life, she became the first woman to head a major Hollywood studio (20th Century-Fox) a few years later.

Hawks used the Warner Bros. studio as a kind of 'home base' through much of the 30s and 40s. He appreciated the professionalism of the studio's personnel both in front of and behind the camera, utilising the services of a number of outstanding cameramen like Polito, Hickox and Wong Howe, as well as a fine selection of tough male stars. As he moved from studio to studio, Hawks was happy to take advantage of the talent available on the spot, bringing only his own writers with him. His work with Cary Grant, perhaps his favourite and most flexible star, during 1938-40 was the only time in his career that Hawks used the same star three times running. Subsequently,

Sergeant York marked a turning point for Hawks, launching him spectacularly into the 40s with the biggest hit of his career and earning Gary Cooper his first Oscar. It also earned the director his only Oscar nomination.

Attuned to the current trends in Hollywood, he directed another superior war movie, *Air Force* (Warner Bros., 1943) starring John Garfield, and the best of the 40s private-eye flicks, *The Big Sleep*, then made a major contribution to the postwar revival of the Western with *Red River*. A truly epic piece of pioneering Americana, very long, and exquisite to look at, the film must rank, along with the Ford masterpieces, as one of the great classic Westerns. Then, serving as producer only, he put his stamp firmly on *The Thing (From Another World)* for RKO in 1951, a Hawks movie in all but name and one of the very best of the 50s Sci-Fi movies. Hawks also directed the sole outstanding

ALFRED HITCHCOCK

Born London, 13 August 1899. **Died** 1980

One of the most truly famous names among Hollywood directors, Alfred Hitchcock remained essentially British in his attitudes, sense of humour and low-keyed style of directing throughout his career. Known as the 'master of suspense', he was a great popular entertainer who made fifty-three features during a career which spanned more than half-a-century. The universal, timeless quality of his best work, his themes and preoccupations, is reflected in the work of many followers who imitated him throughout the 60s and 70s, including Polanski, De Palma and François Truffaut.

As a director of psychological thrillers, Hitchcock used the popular thriller format as a means of probing deep into the fears, foibles and neuroses of modern man. His pictures work on many levels. Technically polished, with inventive plots and often witty dialogue, they have an immediate audience appeal. He capitalised on the gifts and personalities of top stars like Ingrid Bergman, Cary Grant, Grace Kelly and James Stewart, and, in spite of his reputation for having a low opinion of actors, provided them with splendid opportunities, and gave several breaks to unknowns – usually cool blondes – such as Tippi Hedren. Hitchcock's pictures are full of surprises. He enjoys using his stars in different and unexpected ways. He made Cary Grant a murderer in *Suspicion* (RKO, 1941; although finally forced to change the ending), while the heroine in *Psycho* (Paramount, 1960), played by Janet Leigh, was a thief who is killed off half-way through the picture. Acquiring the services of Sean Connery fresh from his initial macho successes as James Bond, Hitch cast him in the role of a sensitive, caring and complex hero in *Marnie* (Universal, 1964); similarly, he provided Robert Walker, the handsome young MGM star, with the best role of his career as a homicidal psychopath in *Strangers On A Train* (Warner Bros., 1951). Hitchcock often presents us with attractive heroes or heroines who turn

out to be suffering from serious psychological problems – Gregory Peck in *Spellbound* (UA, 1945), James Stewart in *Vertigo* (Paramount, 1958), Tippi Hedren in *Marnie* – which naturally leads to unexpected complications. Thus, many of his best films emerge almost as cautionary morality tales – about the dangers of falling in love with and attempting to sort out the psychological problems of a wanted murderer (*Spellbound*) or a compulsive lady thief (*Marnie*); or the risks involved in spying on one's neighbours (*Rear Window*, Paramount, 1954) or in spending the night alone in an isolated motel (*Psycho*). With his characteristically wicked sense of humour, Hitch was fond of placing his characters under stress and observing their insecurities. Handsome middle-class heroes played by Robert Donat in *The 39 Steps* (1935) and Cary Grant in *North By Northwest* (MGM, 1959), suddenly find themselves wanted for murder and on the run from the real murderers as well as the police, and are thus forced to develop new and surprising resources in order to survive. Similarly, the attractive tennis-playing hero of *Strangers On A Train* (Farley Granger) finds it difficult to carry on with his normal life after an encounter with a psychopath who wants to engage in an exchange of murders, while the wealthy, bored heroine of *The Birds* (Universal, 1963) suddenly finds herself and her family under attack for no apparent reason. For Hitchcock didn't spare his heroines either. His favourite cool blonde actresses as represented by Grace Kelly, Janet Leigh, Eva Marie Saint and Kim Novak during the 50s were often made to suffer, although the ugly physical torture inflicted on Tippi Hedren in *The Birds* was somewhat exceptional even by his standards.

Hitch is uninterested in professional criminals or gangsters. He is, however, fascinated by psychologically disturbed people and unconventional villains. He is fond of presenting the latter as attractive, even charismatic, figures, and takes spe-

cial care to make them fully developed and interesting characters. This is evident in many of his best films: Joseph Cotten (*Shadow Of A Doubt*, Universal, 1942), Claude Rains (*Notorious*, RKO, 1946), James Mason (*North By Northwest*), Anthony Perkins (*Psycho*), are prime examples. Hitchcock's movies are further individualised by their telling use of details – the knife in *Blackmail* (1929), the glass of milk in *Suspicion*, the dropped cigarette lighter in *Strangers On A Train* – all elevated to significance by an artful camera. He obviously enjoys treating national monuments with the proper disrespect, using them as giant props for staging the final climax of such movies as *Blackmail* (on the roof of the British Museum), *Saboteur* (Universal, 1942 – on the torch of the Statue of Liberty), *North By Northwest* (across the giant sculptured heads of Mount Rushmore).

Concerning himself with every aspect of his films, Hitch served as producer-director on most of his productions from the mid-40s. He was known for the care and attention which he put into his scripts and for his meticulous pre-production

Above: Hitchcock discusses a script point with his leading lady, Margaret Lockwood, while filming *The Lady Vanishes* (1938), his classic British thriller which won him the New York Film Critics' Award.

Below left: Joan Fontaine as the awkward, shy and nameless heroine of *Rebecca* (1940), and Laurence Olivier as Maxim de Winter, the dashing and mysterious hero.

Below: Patricia Collinge (left), Teresa Wright and Joseph Cotten in *Shadow Of A Doubt* (1943), Hitchcock's first true excursion into the authentic American way of life, and an effective suspense drama which demonstrated his ability to terrorise through sinister characterisation.

'When I came to America 25 years ago to direct *Rebecca*, David Selznick sent me a memo. I've just finished reading it. I think I may turn it into a motion picture. I plan to call it The Longest Story Ever Told'

1965

Above left: Farley Granger (left) meets a persuasive stranger (Robert Walker) in *Strangers On A Train* (1951), with dire consequences. Granger mismanaged his career which became sporadic and undistinguished; the gifted Walker, who had a history of depression, drunkenness and breakdown, died, aged thirty-three, in the middle of filming *My Son John* (1951).

Left: Grace Kelly, later Princess Grace of Monaco, was perhaps the most beautiful of all Hitchcock's beautiful, icy blondes. Here, she fights to ward off Anthony Dawson in *Dial M For Murder* (1954), a moderately gripping adaptation of a very successful stage thriller by Frederick Knott.

Below: Thelma Ritter, Grace Kelly and James Stewart in *Rear Window* (1954), one of the director's best and most durable films, and one of four which Stewart made for Hitchcock.

planning. (Major projects were abandoned by him after much hard work when he felt that the script was not quite right.) His pictures demonstrate his instinctive feel for the all-important, correct pace, mixing long takes with short shots in order to gain the most effective balance between revealing, intimate details, and creating and sustaining the overall mood. He was concerned with involving the spectator, and was famous for his ability to manipulate audiences. One of the outstanding craftsmen-directors, Hitchcock was often attracted to technical challenges –as in *Rear Window* in which the camera never leaves the apartment of the injured photographer hero confined to his wheelchair; or *Rope* (Warner Bros., 1948) with its unbroken ten-minute takes, or the extraordinary special effects problems which had to be solved in filming *The Birds*. He devised many bold and original camera effects, like the elaborate crane shot across the dance hall in *Young And Innocent* (1937), the crash of the plane into the sea in *Foreign Correspondent* (UA, 1940), and a simultaneous use of the zoom forwards and dolly backwards to express the feeling of *Vertigo* experienced by the hero (James Stewart).

Having gained his early experience in the silents as a sketch artist and art director, Hitchcock retained his remarkable visual sense throughout his long career. He began directing for Gainsborough Pictures and British producer Michael Balcon during the mid-20s and first made his mark, appropriately enough, with a gripping silent thriller, *The Lodger*, starring matinée idol Ivor Novello in 1926. That same year he married his script girl and assistant, Alma Reville, who continued to collaborate on the scripts of many of his later films. During the late 20s he managed to establish himself as a leading British director and confirmed his position with an imaginative first talkie, *Blackmail* (1929). The film is an entertaining thriller and serves as an early example of Hitchcock's preoccupation with the complex relationship between attacker and victim,

innocent and guilty, police and suspect.

He made a wide variety of movies during these early years, but they were variable in quality and he appeared to have no particular vision. It was only in 1934 when he rejoined Balcon at Gaumont-British that he embarked on that series of films which definitively put his stamp on the British cinema of the 30s. *The Man Who Knew Too Much* (1934) – which he remade twenty-two years later in colour and VistaVision – was followed

Kelly with Cary Grant; *The Trouble With Harry* (1955); *The Man Who Knew Too Much* remake, and *The Wrong Man* (Warner Bros.) with Henry Fonda in the title role – a downbeat film based on a true story (both 1956); *Vertigo*, the last of his four with James Stewart and co-starring Kim Novak, and *North By Northwest*, his last with Cary Grant. Finally, he rounded out the decade with *Psycho*. Meanwhile he had become a more familiar public figure than ever, hosting his own, extremely successful TV series, *Alfred Hitchcock Presents*, a natural extension of the cameo appearances in his pictures which had come to be regarded as one of his trademarks. He was, in fact, the first major film-maker to recognise the possibilities of television and directed a number of the best episodes himself.

Inevitably his career began to wind down during the 60s. After two last exceptional pictures, *The Birds* and *Marnie*, he completed only four more, none of them up to the high standards which he had set himself. But both *Frenzy*, filmed back in England in 1972, and *Family Plot* (Universal, 1976), his final film, while disappointing, displayed a few last flashes of his genius.

'In a good movie, the sound could go off and the audience would still have a perfectly clear idea of what was going on'
1968

Above left: On location at La Salle Street station in Chicago, Eva Marie Saint walks towards the camera, the microphone boom above her head. The porter with her bags is Cary Grant, Hitchcock (pointing, back to camera) directs operations, and the movie is *North By Northwest* (1959).

by *The 39 Steps* (1935) starring Robert Donat and Madeleine Carroll. *Young And Innocent* (1937) is an undeservedly neglected little masterpiece, while *The Lady Vanishes*, starring Margaret Lockwood, earned Hitchcock the New York Film Critics directing award for 1938. That same year he reached agreement with independent Hollywood producer David Selznick; Hitch was attracted to the US by the generally superior quality of American studio film-making and by a lucrative four-picture contract. Ironically, his first Hollywood project, *Rebecca*, filmed in 1939, was more British than American, adapted from the novel by Daphne du Maurier with a mainly British cast. A tremendous success, it was the only Hitchcock film which won a Best Picture Oscar, with the director himself, Joan Fontaine, Laurence Olivier and Judith Anderson all nominated. While fulfilling the terms of his Selznick contract during the 40s, Hitch alternated between Wanger, RKO, Universal and 20th Century-Fox. By late 1942 he felt ready to attempt a small but ambitious American subject, *Shadow Of A Doubt*. Presenting a penetrating view of small town America, it was one of the first 40s thrillers to be filmed on location. Hitch could anticipate trends, yet generally remained a law unto himself. He was never really a part of the 40s *film noir* movement, for example, although his two Ingrid Bergman movies, *Spellbound* and *Notorious*, could be so classified. *Notorious* was by far the better of the two and Hitch's best ever spy thriller, though the story was characteristically encased in psychological drama. It boasted a superb cast, with Cary Grant and Claude Rains teamed with Miss Bergman. Hitchcock was Oscar-nominated three more times during the 40s and once in the 50s, but rarely for his best pictures. Extraordinarily – indeed, shamingly for Hollywood – he never won an Oscar, but did receive the Irving Thalberg Award in 1967 in recognition of his achievements.

Left: Anthony Perkins as the mad Norman Bates in *Psycho* (1960), perhaps the most famous of all psychological murder thrillers.

Below: Hitchcock directing Australian actor Rod Taylor and Suzanne Pleshette in his horror film *The Birds* (1963), in which Nature turns the attack on Man.

The Bergman films were big hits, but a lean period ensued. A disappointing last film for Selznick (*The Paradine Case*, 1947) was followed by his first venture into independent production and his first two colour movies. But both *Rope* (1948) and *Under Capricorn* (1949) were less than his best; ditto *Stage Fright* (1950). However, *Strangers On A Train* (1951), an effective adaptation of the novel by Patricia Highsmith, marked an important comeback for him, and was his first picture with Robert Burks who remained his regular cameraman for the next thirteen years. Then finally, in 1954, fifteen years after he had arrived in Hollywood, Hitch managed to put it all together, assembling a congenial group of technicians and favourite stars at Paramount, where he had been offered an extremely favourable contract as an independent producer-director. Already in his mid-fifties, he nevertheless embarked on the most exceptional period of his career beginning with *Rear Window* and followed by *To Catch A Thief* (1955) pairing Grace

Above: For *Frenzy* (1972), a particularly nasty story about a psychopathic sex murderer, Hitchcock returned to London and an all-English cast headed by Jon Finch. Here, he is on location in London's West End.

Right: Barbara Leigh-Hunt as one of the unfortunate victims strangled with a necktie in *Frenzy*. The film, an attempt by Hitchcock to come up to date, was unsavoury but not very distinguished.

JOHN HUSTON

Born Nevada, Missouri, 5 August 1906

A man of many talents and interests – expert rider, horse breeder and boxer, painter, writer, actor and raconteur, with a special love for animals – John Huston has never been a dedicated film-maker and never became a part of the Hollywood scene. Active as a director over forty years, he averaged a steady one film per year throughout most of this period. A professional and craftsmanlike director who also writes most of his own scripts, he is best known as a fine adaptor of novels (and, occasionally, plays) to the screen. 'The directing of a film, to me, is simply an extension of the process of writing,' Huston has stated. 'It's the process of rendering the thing you have written.' The unevenness of his films is due in part to the variable quality of his original sources and the commercial pressures which have led him to work on some unsuitable projects. He has often succeeded better with unpretentious, off-beat subjects like the W.R. Burnett thriller, *The Asphalt Jungle* (MGM, 1950), or the eccentric black comedy of *Beat The Devil* (UA, 1954) not to mention his excellent wartime documentaries. More recently such projects as *Fat City* (Columbia, 1972), *The Life And Times Of Judge Roy Bean* (1972), *The Man Who Would Be King* (1975) and *Wise Blood* (1979) helped to revive his career during the 70s.

youngster (while his father was attempting to achieve his first stage success), that John developed his many interests. He earned a small income from boxing, did some acting, spent a brief period in the Mexican cavalry, and became intensely interested in painting. But faced with the need to support himself and his young wife during the late 20s, he turned to writing short stories and plays, and worked for a time as a journalist.

Huston had his first taste of Hollywood during 1930-31 when he was hired as a scriptwriter. At Universal he worked on *A House Divided* (1931) directed by his friend, William Wyler, and *Law And Order* (1932) – both starring his father – and *Murders In The Rue Morgue* (1932) directed by Robert Florey. Unable to cope with his now alcoholic wife and with no further offers of work, he left for England where a promised scriptwriting job failed to materialise and he was virtually destitute for a time. He only began to recover from these lean years in 1937 when he did some acting on the stage, married again, and was given a second crack at Hollywood. Hired by Warner Bros., he was soon working on prestige projects like *Jezebel* (1938) with Wyler, and *Juarez* (1938), which benefitted from his experiences in Mexico, although he claims that his script was ruined by the changes insisted on by the star, Paul Muni. In 1940 he received his first Oscar nomination for co-scripting *Dr Ehrlich's Magic Bullet*

Above: A scene from Huston's remarkably assured and atmospheric debut film, Dashiell Hammett's *The Maltese Falcon* (1941). It was also the debut of Sydney Greenstreet (seated). His henchman, played by Peter Lorre, looks on as Greenstreet is questioned by Humphrey Bogart's private eye.

Left: Humphrey Bogart (left) and Walter Huston in *The Treasure Of The Sierra Madre* (1948). Huston, the director's father, won an Oscar for his performance.

Huston has led a colourful life, has travelled widely and married five times, yet is dedicated and close to his family. Never at home in Hollywood, the anti-Communist hysteria which surfaced during the late 40s (and the death of his father in 1950) contributed to his decision to settle in Ireland where he remained for twenty years, enjoying the life of a country squire when he wasn't filming, before moving to Mexico with his family in more recent years. He had a close relationship with both his parents, in spite of the fact that they had separated when he was quite young, and was particularly close to his famous actor father, Walter Huston, who won an Oscar for his performance in his son's *The Treasure Of The Sierra Madre*. It was while travelling with his mother as a

'I completely story-boarded The Maltese Falcon because I didn't want to lose face with the crew. I wanted to give the impression I knew what I was doing'

and, the same year, *High Sierra* linked him with Bogart for the first time. He was again Oscar-nominated for co-scripting *Sergeant York* (1941) for director Howard Hawks, who claims that he recommended *The Maltese Falcon* (1941) to Huston for his first attempt at directing and pointed out the advantages of a project which was ready-made for filming: 'It's hard enough to direct your first picture ... You go and make *The Maltese Falcon* exactly the way Hammett wrote it, use the dialogue, don't change a goddam thing and you'll have a hell of a picture'.

Huston was incredibly fortunate with the picture. George Raft who was originally selected by the studio to play private eye Sam Spade turned it down, and Bogart got the role. The cast was filled out by Sydney Greenstreet (his debut) as the mysterious and cultured villain, a bulky giant appropriately paired with the tiny, whining, scheming Peter Lorre for their first of many films together. Mary Astor was the attractive but lying and lethal heroine, and Elisha Cook Jr the intense, tough little gunsel. All were perfectly cast and remain best remembered for this movie. Walter Huston was even persuaded to make a brief cameo appearance for his son. A solidly crafted and extremely entertaining work in the tough Warner Bros. tradition, and now a cult classic, it didn't seem to matter that the characters were two-dimensional and too 'talky'. Huston made a fine job of fitting all the pieces together, and demonstrated his qualities in handling actors. He was nominated for an Oscar for his faithful script adaptation, which remained more Hammett than Huston. The first of the 40s private eye the beginning of 40s *film noir* and opened up a whole new career for Humphrey Bogart who finally made the breakthrough to superstar status.

The director, however, had little time to enjoy *his* new status. He directed Bette Davis in an enjoyably larger-than-life drama, *In This Our Life* (1942), then joined the US Army Signal Corps, leaving Bogart tied up and held hostage by Japanese soldiers in *Across The Pacific* (1942). Writer-director Vincent Sherman was assigned by Jack Warner to devise and film an ending after Huston had left. For his first wartime assignment, Huston headed north where he supervised the filming of *Report From The Aleutians* (1943). In 1944 he found himself in Italy following the exploits of a particularly hard-pressed American infantry regiment, filmed as *The Battle Of San Pietro*. 'No war film I have seen has been quite so attentive to the heaviness of casualties,' wrote critic James Agee at the time. 'None has so levelly watched and implied what it meant in such full and complex terms.' Huston had directed, scripted, and spoken the narration. Finally, in 1945, he made his most remarkable documentary of the war, *Let There Be Light*. Banned from showing by the US War Department due to the sensitivity of its subject – the treatment and rehabilitation of shell-shocked soldiers in an army hospital – it was, remarkably, not released until 1980.

Returning to Warner Bros. in 1947, Huston picked up where he left off, immediately getting to work on a favourite

Above: Katharine Hepburn and Humphrey Bogart paired as a spinster missionary and a gin-sozzled river boat captain in *The African Queen* (1951). It was an inspired idea which showed both stars at their glittering best.

Left: Playwright Arthur Miller (right) and his wife Marilyn Monroe confer with Huston during production of *The Misfits* (1961).

Below: Richard Burton and Ava Gardner in *The Night Of The Iguana* (1964).

project which he had been planning for a number of years – a screen adaptation of B. Traven's *The Treasure Of The Sierra Madre*. Although highly acclaimed at the time and winning Huston his only Oscars for directing and script, it has not worn well. A three-character film about an unlikely group of American prospectors in Mexico, it starred Bogart in an unusual, nasty and paranoid, but fascinating character role. Unfortunately, the character came across as shallow and two-dimensional when juxtaposed with the remarkable performance from the grizzled old veteran, Walter Huston, who stole the picture (and a well deserved Oscar). Bogart fared rather better for Huston with his more likeable character role as Charlie Allnutt, the skipper of *The African Queen*, four years later. Both pictures suffered, however, from Huston's essentially 'literary' approach to characters and relationships.

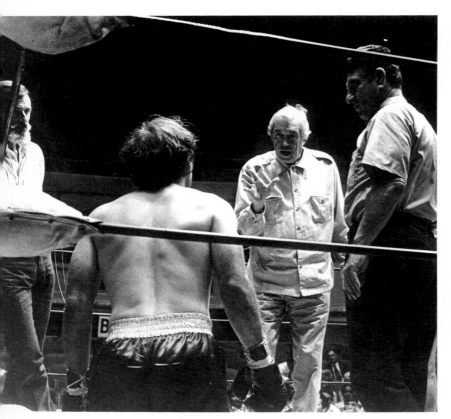

turn out well, Huston had better success on a smaller scale, reverting to black-and-white during the early 60s. *The Misfits* (UA, 1961) occupies a special place in the history of Hollywood as the last film of both Gable and Marilyn Monroe and the only film written by Arthur Miller. *Freud* (Universal, 1963) provided Montgomery Clift with his last good role, while Richard Burton had one of the best movie parts in his career in *The Night Of The Iguana* (MGM, 1964) and made the most of it. Huston was less fortunate with *The Bible* (20th Century-Fox, 1965). The best thing in it was his own engaging performance as Noah and his great rapport with the animals on the ark. *Reflections In A Golden Eye* (Warner Bros., 1967) represents one more of the director's failed attempts to adapt a complex and 'adult' work of fiction (by Carson McCullers) to the screen. Huston survived a bad patch during the late 60s and emerged more strongly during the 70s with a fine boxing picture (*Fat City*), his best Western (*The Life And Times Of Judge Roy Bean*), from a John Milius script, and his best adventure picture (*The Man Who Would Be King*), the last benefitting from the inspired casting of Sean Connery and Michael Caine. Giving no sign of slowing down in the 80s, Huston tackled his first large-scale musical, *Annie*, for Columbia in 1981, and another favourite literary project, Lowry's *Under The Volcano* (20th Century-Fox, 1984) distinguished only, it must be said, by an impressive performance from Albert Finney.

'Maybe it's what Hemingway says about writing. "You must write it as if you were there." Maybe, I just try to do it as if I were there'

Above left: Director Huston (2nd right) in the boxing ring directing a sequence for *Fat City* (1972), a bleak study of a has-been champion which starred Stacy Keach.

Below left: The cigar-smoking, grizzled giant is Huston. Here, he talks to Sean Connery, on location in Morocco for *The Man Who Would Be King* (1973).

Below: Paul Newman, as the legendary 'hanging judge' of the West, in *The Life And Times Of Judge Roy Bean* (1972).

In between, Huston and Bogart closed out their Warner years with one last hit, *Key Largo* (1948), co-scripted by Richard Brooks from the Maxwell Anderson play. Huston spent a few years at MGM where he worked on the *Quo Vadis?* (1951) project which he did not direct. *The Asphalt Jungle* was not only a superbly atmospheric thriller with fine performances from a non-starry cast headed by Sterling Hayden, Jean Hagen and Huston's friend, Sam Jaffe, but was the first of a new breed of 'caper' movies of a type which was done to death in later years. *The Red Badge Of Courage* (1951) was another one of Huston's literary projects which came unstuck and was badly cut by MGM after the director had departed for Africa to begin shooting *The African Queen*. This latter marked Huston's definitive break with Hollywood and the first of a series of films made abroad. It also serves as a prime example of the trend toward shooting more pictures in colour and was, in fact, the first colour movie for Huston, Bogart and Katharine Hepburn. A big hit, it gave a welcome boost to the newly reorganised United Artists and earned Huston Oscar nominations for script and direction for the second year running (following on from *The Asphalt Jungle*). The delightfully quirky pairing of Hepburn and Bogart lit up the screen and earned them both Oscar nominations, with Bogie emerging a winner for the only time in his career. The formula worked so well that Huston re-used it a few years later with Robert Mitchum and Deborah Kerr as a US Marine and a nun stranded on a desert island in the Pacific during World War II in *Heaven Knows Mr Allison* (20th Century-Fox, 1958).

The twenty-minute opening of *Moulin Rouge* (UA, 1952) is stunning, with its lively dancing, colourful costumes and setting, all observed during a particular evening which draws to a close with the solitary dwarf figure of the painter Toulouse-Lautrec wending his way home through the dark Paris streets. Unfortunately, nothing which followed matched this. Huston got much-needed help from Truman Capote on the script of *Beat The Devil*, a vastly entertaining spoof adventure thriller which reunited Huston and Bogie (in Italy) for the last time. Huston himself has written in his autobiography that '*Moby Dick* (Warner Bros., 1956) was the most difficult picture I ever made'. He was faced with the problems of filming on the open sea with a rebuilt 19th-century, three-masted sailing ship while trying to control a giant, 90-foot long model of the Great White Whale. A creditable attempt to adapt Melville to the screen, the film was passed over for Oscars, but won Huston the New York Critics' directing award. After a run of relatively large-scale and expensive colour pictures which did not

Above: The director instructs Japanese actress Eiko Ando for a scene in *The Barbarian And The Geisha* (1958).

Right: Huston and musical star Ann Reinking on set for the filming of *Annie* (1982). Huston came unstuck with this sumptuously expensive (approximately $35 million) film version of the hit Broadway musical. It was not a success, and it was not good.

ELIA KAZAN

Born Kadi-Keu, a suburb of Istanbul, 7 September 1909.

Arriving in the US as an immigrant, aged four, with his Greek parents, young Elia Kazan was made painfully aware of being an outsider in his adopted country. Strictly brought up, he was not allowed to mix with other boys. His family was hit hard by the Depression, but he managed to work his way through college, and then briefly attended Yale Drama School when he developed a special interest in the theatre. An aggressive and angry young man, he joined the Communist Party for a time and gained his first stage experience with the politically committed, 'leftish' Group Theatre during the 30s. Aware of his limitations as an actor, Kazan also worked as a stage manager and apprentice director, tried his hand at radio acting and play writing, but was interested, most of all, in films. He acted in and co-directed a number of shorts and appeared in a couple of features directed by Anatole Litvak in 1940-41.

Kazan's first breakthrough as a theatre director came in 1942 with Thornton Wilder's 'The Skin Of Our Teeth' starring Fredric March, the success of which soon led to more offers than he could handle. But his ambition was to make movies, and in 1944 he accepted an offer from 20th Century-Fox to direct *A Tree Grows In Brooklyn* as the first of a non-exclusive, five-picture deal. Extremely

limited in his technical knowledge of film-making, he had at least selected a subject he felt at home with, set in the New York of his youth, and was given much technical assistance by cameraman Leon Shamroy. A faithful, if sentimental, adaptation of the popular novel by Betty Smith, it already suggested some of the qualities associated with the later, mature Kazan – a special sensitivity to characters, and to relationships – often dramatic or violent – within the American family, as well as a remarkable talent for directing actors (James Dunn won the support-

ing actor Oscar and Peggy Ann Garner a special juvenile award). The picture served as a good apprentice piece, but by the time it was released the young director was back on Broadway, and only returned to Hollywood in 1946 when he was given two films in quick succession. The filming of *Sea Of Grass* turned out to be his most disappointing Hollywood experience. Attracted to the original novel, a Western drama set in turn-of-the-century New Mexico, he arrived at MGM to find that the entire movie was to be filmed on the backlot. Added to that, he did not

get on well with Spencer Tracy whom he felt was miscast. Quickly returning to Fox he was on more familiar ground with *Boomerang*, a crime drama revolving around an unsolved killing in a small New England town. The movie, based on a true incident, was partly filmed on location, and again, Kazan concentrated on characters and dialogue rather than milieu and made so little use of the settings that he could have just as easily been shooting at the studio.

1947 was another memorable year in Kazan's now prolific and extremely successful dual film and theatre career. He directed Arthur Miller's first big stage success, 'All My Sons', early in the year then, with Lee Strasberg, started the famous Actors Studio in New York as a training ground for young actors. He directed one film, *Gentleman's Agreement*, then rounded out his year in the theatre with the phenomenally successful 'A Streetcar Named Desire', starring Marlon Brando and marking the beginning of Kazan's long and fruitful collaboration with playwright Tennessee Williams. The play received the Pulitzer Prize, while *Gentleman's Agreement* was a big critical and box-office success, winning the Best Picture Oscar and giving Kazan his first directing statuette. In this picture, as in *Pinky* which followed in 1949, he made a worthy attempt to treat serious social issues on the screen – anti-semitism in the former, anti-black pre-

Above: The charismatic, animal power of Marlon Brando was fully unleashed on cinema audiences when his portrayal of Stanley Kowalski in *A Streetcar Named Desire* (1951), was filmed. Here, he is seen with Vivien Leigh as the haunting and haunted Blanche Dubois.

Left: Julie Harris and James Dean starred in *East Of Eden* (1954). The role of an adolescent in rebellion was tailor-made for Dean's special brand of moodiness, and he was Oscar-nominated for this, his first lead performance. *Rebel Without A Cause* came next, then *Giant*, and then his death in a car smash.

'Most actors want to be heroic, sexy and noble. They won't allow you to make them look silly. The gang I have around me are more like people and less like actors'

(on the set of *Baby Doll*, 1956)

judice in the latter – thus reflecting the interests of Fox production chief Darryl Zanuck as well as his own left-wing political background. Solidly crafted and well acted (aside from the serious miscasting of Jeanne Crain as Pinky over which Kazan had no control), they brought to a close the first phase of his movie career. He had established himself as one of the most favoured directors with critics and audiences alike. Kazan's unbroken run of 40s hits, followed by the success of *A Streetcar Named Desire* (Warner Bros., 1951), *On The Waterfront* (Columbia, 1954) and *East Of Eden* (Warner Bros., 1955), made him one of the two or three most consistently commercially successful of Hollywood directors during this period. After *Pinky* in 1949, he began to rethink his movie career, feeling dissatisfied at not having been more of a cinematic innovator.

Things changed, however, in 1950

of his original Broadway cast to Hollywood, but the studio, seeking a movie 'name', forced him to drop Jessica Tandy in favour of Vivien Leigh. Brando, in particular, was closely identified with the new, naturalistic style of acting developed at the Actors Studio and popularly referred to as 'the Method', and proved that it was even more powerful on the screen than in the theatre. *Streetcar*, the actor's second picture, was the first to unleash his great charisma and vitality on the screen. With the pairing of Brando and Vivien Leigh, the picture presented a fascinating juxtaposition of the new and the more traditional styles of acting. Miss Leigh gave the most remarkable performance of her post-war movie career as the sad, deranged Blanche Dubois, and won her second Oscar, while Brando was nominated for his suitably earthy Stanley Kowalski, and both Kim Hunter and Karl Malden won supporting Oscars.

Above: Director Kazan (right), very much an extrovert on the set, demonstrates a Greek-style dance step to a bit player for the party scene in *Splendor In The Grass* (1961).

Left: Carroll Baker as the child bride and Karl Malden as her husband in *Baby Doll* (1956). 'Time' magazine called it 'just possibly the dirtiest American-made motion picture that has been legally exhibited . . .', while the usually abrasive Pauline Kael said it was 'A droll and engrossing carnal comedy'!

Below: Lee Remick and Andy Griffith were paired in *A Face In The Crowd* (1957), Kazan's savage exposé of the corrupting qualities of show business fame.

with his next picture *Panic In The Streets*. A thriller revolving around a manhunt theme, it was reminiscent of *Boomerang* but a far superior work, and reflected Kazan's attempt to break out of the conventional Hollywood mold – to which end he was determined to shoot on location in New Orleans. 'We shot on the whorehouse streets, in the low bars, in the wharfs. I kept the whole process of picture-making creative,' Kazan asserts, 'instead of rigid devotion to a script'. Concentrating on film-making through most of the 50s (aside from a select few stage productions), Kazan now began to draw on his theatre experience as part of his effort to inject a new, original, and personal quality into his films. With *Panic In The Streets* he was still forced to use studio contract stars like Richard Widmark and Paul Douglas, but cast a pair of his own extremely effective actors, Jack Palance and Zero Mostel, in supporting roles. For the film version of *A Streetcar Named Desire*, however, he brought most

Joining with Brando, Kazan then attempted to marry his new cinematic fluency with the new acting in *Viva Zapata* (20th Century-Fox, 1952) about a Mexican revolutionary, but achieved it most successfully of all in *On The Waterfront* two years later. Here Brando was starred opposite Method-trained Rod Steiger in his first important screen role, and Lee J. Cobb who had appeared in *Boomerang* and had starred in Kazan's celebrated 1949 stage production of Arthur Miller's 'Death Of A Salesman'. An entirely New York-based movie, *Waterfront* clearly symbolised Kazan's break with Hollywood and manifested his desire to relate his films more closely to real contemporary life and social issues. He was greatly assisted in bringing the picture's gritty milieu to life by the outstanding East Coast cameraman, Boris Kaufman, who won an Oscar for

his contribution along with Kazan (his second), Brando, scriptwriter Budd Schulberg and supporting actress Eva Marie Saint, all capped by the Best Picture award. Unfortunately, the picture's naturalistic qualities were marred by an unconvincingly upbeat ending and the film itself became caught up in the controversy surrounding Kazan's 'friendly' testimony to the House Un-American Activities Committee regarding his (and others) membership of the Communist Party. This political stance seriously affected attitudes to Kazan and cast an unfortunate shadow over his later career.

The director next cast another young Method-trained actor, James Dean, in his highly successful adaptation of John Steinbeck's *East Of Eden*. The exception among Kazan's 50s pictures, it was the only one to be filmed in CinemaScope, in colour, and with a historical subject. Set in California during the World War I era, it proved that the director's methods were well suited to dealing with America's past, to which he became increasingly attracted during the 60s. The central theme, of the strongly felt relationships and conflicts between parents and children, links *East Of Eden* with *Splendor In The Grass* (Warner Bros., 1961) six years later. Kazan attacked both subjects with characteristic intensity and a lyricism far removed from the bland naturalism of his earliest films. Both pictures, in fact, took him back to the time of his own youth, and he himself has suggested that, to a large extent, he personally identified with the rebellious young hero of *East Of Eden*. How far Kazan could make a subject his own can be appreciated in the case of *Splendor*, filmed from an original screenplay by William Inge, yet given the texture and richness of a novel by the director's style.

Still sporadically active in the theatre, Kazan had directed Inge's hit play, 'The Dark At The Top Of The Stairs' in 1957, but remained faithful to Tennessee Williams with productions of 'Camino Real' (1953), 'Cat On A Hot Tin Roof' (1955), and 'Sweet Bird Of Youth' (1959). They also worked together on *Baby Doll* (Warner Bros., 1956). Marking a nice change in pace from his many heavy and serious pictures, this one was lightweight and slightly offbeat, alternating between the serious and the comic, and perfectly capturing a particularly seedy aspect of the Old South. Carroll Baker never again matched her performance here. Kazan then introduced two more of his discoveries, Lee Remick and Andy Griffith, in *A Face In The Crowd* (Warner Bros., 1957), and remained in the South for his third film in a row, *Wild River* (20th Century-Fox, 1960). Advertised as 'Elia Kazan's smouldering story of the South! The Rushing, Frightening Flood of Their Passions . . . Like the Wild River', the picture was, in fact, a superbly photographed and deeply felt attempt by Kazan to treat the social and economic situation of the South during the 30s. *Wild River*, like *Splendor*, and *America, America* (Warner Bros., 1963), about the struggles of Kazan's own uncle to reach America as an immigrant, presents yet another facet of Kazan's continuing fascination with America in the 20th century. He returned to the contemporary scene with *The Arrangement* (Warner Bros., 1969), adapted from his own novel, and attempted to deal with the impact of Vietnam on American society in *The Assassins* (1971), filmed in 16mm in collaboration with his son, Chris Kazan.

His last picture to date was a star-studded attempt to being Scott Fitzgerald's *The Last Tycoon* (Paramount, 1976) to life on the screen with the help of a Harold Pinter script. Like all his late films, it failed to recapture the qualities of his best 50s works.

Kazan's great contribution to both the theatre and the cinema in America has been unique, and he influenced a whole generation of actors with 'the Method'. While best remembered in this regard for his close collaboration with Marlon Brando, he had amazing success with a large number of actors and actresses, mostly young discoveries like James Dean, Carroll Baker, Warren Beatty, Zohra Lampert and Stathis Giallelis, as well as not-so-young performers like Karl Malden, Rod Steiger and Jo Van Fleet. But the nature of his contribution was necessarily intense and very special and, not surprisingly, was concentrated into a relatively brief period from the late 40s through the mid-50s. Now retired from directing, Elia Kazan has occupied himself during recent years as a novelist, and in 1982 completed the trilogy which he had begun with 'America, America' in the early 60s.

Left: The young, unknown and wonderful looking Greek actor, Stathis Giallelis, played the lead in *America, America* (aka *The Anatolian Smile*, 1963), Kazan's autobiographical odyssey about the struggle of a poor Greek immigrant to reach America.

Below: Kazan directs Kirk Douglas and Faye Dunaway in *The Arrangement* (1969), a screen version of his own novel which dealt with the emotional and marital crises of a successful advertising man who attempts to opt out. The book was better than the film.

Bottom: A good-humoured moment during a break in the filming of *The Last Tycoon* (1976). Sharing the joke are French star Jeanne Moreau, Robert De Niro and the director. The film was a critical failure.

'Kazan is a great director. He is probably as much a manifestation of the auteur theory as you could find. He's a magnificent machine in film-making, regardless of what your feeling might be about him politically'

Warren Beatty, 1974

GENE KELLY

Born Pittsburgh, 23 August 1912

Gene Kelly first burst on the Hollywood scene, via Broadway, with a brash, virile and new style of dancing during the early 40s. It wasn't long before he developed into a leading, innovative screen choreographer as well as an actor and dancer, and by the end of the decade he was directing his pictures. As a youth, however, Gene had been more interested in sports than in dancing, and it was only the influence of his elder brother, Fred, and his mother which pushed him to a dancing career. He had some success in a dancing act with Fred in and around Pittsburgh, and he became popular as a dance teacher. But he was already in his late twenties, relatively old for a dancer, when he made it to Broadway. His first big stage hit came when he created the title role in Rodgers and Hart's 'Pal Joey' in 1940, and he choreographed 'Best Foot Forward' the following year. Signed up by producer David Selznick Kelly found himself starring opposite Judy Garland in *For Me And My Gal* (MGM, 1942). For a year or so he alternated between straight dramatic roles and musicals at MGM, but it was not until he was loaned to Columbia to star with Rita Hayworth in *Cover Girl* (1943) that he got his first chance to choreograph for the screen. The 'alter ego' number in *Cover Girl* had him dancing down the street in tandem with his double-exposed other self, a delightful and inventive solo which he created with the assistance of Stanley Donen.

The year 1943 also saw a landmark in the American musical, with the arrival of Rodgers and Hammerstein's 'Oklahoma!', directed for the stage by Rouben Mamoulian with innovative choreography by Agnes de Mille. The new dance idiom which Kelly was attempting to develop for the screen represented a movie counterpart to the stylistic advances being made in the theatre by Miss de Mille, Martha Graham and others. Back at MGM Kelly and the young Donen went to work on *Anchors Aweigh* (1945), which provided Gene with a further opportunity to develop his exuberant, all-American dancing style, teamed with Frank Sinatra – and with Jerry mouse in a trick number which mixed live action and animation. Kelly was nominated for an Oscar for his performance.

After a break for war service, he was back at MGM with Donen and producer Arthur Freed, planning a musical with a baseball theme, and adopting a suitably tongue-in-cheek swashbuckling persona which he carried off with great style in *The Pirate* (1947), which he also choreographed, and *The Three Musketeers* (1948). In late 1948 he was able to go ahead with his baseball musical, *Take Me Out To The Ball Game*. Here Gene combined his love of sport and dance with the 40s vogue for musical Americana (the movie was set during the early years of the century). He and Donen directed all the musical numbers and collaborated with their favourite scriptwriters, Betty Comden and Adolph Green, for the first time. The cast was headed by Kelly,

Sinatra, Jules Munshin and Betty Garrett, all back together by the spring of 1949 to begin shooting *On The Town*.

These were the peak years for Gene Kelly as dancer, choreographer and director. His partnership with Donen in directing *On The Town* and the superlative *Singin' In The Rain* in 1951 represented the culmination of his efforts to develop a new style of choreography, using the dance expressively as an extension of his screen character. He also upgraded the dance with a remarkable extended ballet sequence in Vincente Minnelli's *An American In Paris* (1951), and with his own feature-length dance picture, *Invitation To The Dance* filmed in 1952. Kelly was awarded a special Oscar in 1951 at the same time that *An American In Paris* won the Best Picture award.

During later years he turned to directing for television, beginning with *Dancing – A Man's Game* in 1958, and directed comedy films like *Gigot* (1960) and *A Guide For The Married Man* (1967), both for 20th Century-Fox. His one major contribution to the late 60s musical is represented by *Hello Dolly!* (1969), again for Fox, a mega-budget flop which starred a vibrant but miscast Barbra Streisand and Walter Matthau. On a more up-beat note, he co-hosted both parts of MGM's *That's Entertainment* in the 70s, proving that he could still turn a step with the best of them.

'We shot a lot of it [On The Town] in New York and showed sailors . . . singing and dancing through the streets of New York. You can't imagine how crazy everybody thought this was at the time, but it changed the face of musicals and also influenced the New Wave in France'

Top: Frank Sinatra (foreground), Gene Kelly (centre), and Jules Munshin, three gobs on riotous leave in *On The Town* (1949).

Above: Debbie Reynolds, Kelly (centre) and Donald O'Connor in the sparkling *Singin' In The Rain* (1951), the peak achievement in Kelly's collaboration with Stanley Donen.

Left: Walter Matthau and Inger Stevens, husband and wife in *A Guide For The Married Man* (1967), rehearse with Kelly (right). This was the versatile Gene's successful excursion into directing a non-musical comedy.

HENRY KOSTER

Born Berlin, 1 May 1905

Henry Koster gave the movies Deanna Durbin in the 30s and CinemaScope in the 50s. His name is closely identified with lightweight family entertainment, and his thirty years in Hollywood are neatly enclosed between the Deanna Durbin musical, *Three Smart Girls* (Universal, 1936) and *The Singing Nun* (MGM, 1966), a late musical vehicle for Debbie Reynolds. Highly successful in turning out enjoyable and popular movies – mainly musicals, and comedies, and a few costume pictures, with more serious matters rarely allowed to intrude – he too was a refugee from Nazi Germany, along with a group of tougher and more serious directors like Fritz Lang, Robert Siodmak and Billy Wilder.

A sophisticated and cultured man of many talents, Koster was educated at the Berlin Academy of Fine Arts and worked as a journalist, cartoonist and film critic. He was in his early twenties when he left newspaper work to join the innovative and flourishing German film industry in the mid-20s. A prolific scenario and script writer, Koster turned to directing in 1932 shortly before Hitler's rise to power. He left Germany, but was able to continue working for a time in Austria where he teamed up with Hungarian musical producer Joe Pasternak, and thus had some reasonable directing experience behind him by the time he arrived in Hollywood (together with Pasternak) in 1935.

Koster, Pasternak and fifteen-year-old Deanna Durbin all made their Hollywood feature film debut with *Three Smart Girls* in 1936, followed immediately by *One Hundred Men And A Girl* (1937). Both were extremely successful at the box-office, were nominated for Best Picture Oscars and gave a desperately needed boost to the badly sagging fortunes of Universal studios. *One Hundred Men And A Girl* cast Deanna as the daughter of an out-of-work trombone player (Adolphe Menjou). She sets out to get the help of Leopold Stokowski in launching a new orchestra to provide work for one hundred unemployed musicians. An unabashedly sentimental but entertaining star vehicle, the Depression theme was kept discreetly in the background and all ended deliriously with Deanna marching the orchestra into Stokowski's house, where he gives in and conducts them in Liszt's 'Hungarian Rhapsody No 2' from the top of his staircase. Koster went on to direct the young soprano in four more Universal musicals before rejoining Pasternak at MGM. Highly regarded as a comedy director, he was hired by Sam Goldwyn to direct Cary Grant and Loretta Young in a sentimental comedy, *The Bishop's Wife* (RKO, 1947), and earned his only Oscar nomination. He had another big success with *Harvey* (Universal, 1950) starring James Stewart in one of his most likeable roles as Elwood P. Dowd whose favourite companion is an invisible, six-foot-high rabbit. Koster and Stewart got on so well that they collaborated on a serious flying

drama, *No Highway* (20th Century-Fox, 1951), and were back together for three more comedies during the early 60s.

In between Koster established himself as one of the most reliable contract directors at Fox, graduating from Betty Grable musicals and Clifton Webb comedies to prestige costumers in the studio's newly introduced CinemaScope process. The larger and wider screen appealed since, as he wrote, 'With CinemaScope a director is at last free of the camera and has an unparalleled chance to demonstrate his ability to move actors logically and dramatically . . . He is free to concentrate on the chief task of drawing superb performances from his players . . .'. Koster delivered a smash hit with the very first CinemaScope production, *The Robe*, in 1953, but was less successful with those that followed, including the fictionalised biopic *Desiree* (1954) starring Jean Simmons, with Marlon Brando as Napoleon. Richard Todd was *A Man Called Peter*, while Bette Davis returned to the role of Queen Elizabeth I (she had played it sixteen years earlier) in *The Virgin Queen*,

both in 1955. Koster directed one last musical of note, Rodgers and Hammerstein's Broadway show *Flower Drum Song*, for producer Ross Hunter back at his old studio, Universal, in 1961. He retired from directing in 1966.

Top: Deanna Durbin, aged fifteen and accompanied by Leonid Kinskey on the piano, delivers an aria in *One Hundred Men And A Girl* (1937). One of Durbin's very best films, it marked the Hollywood feature film debut of both star and director.

Above: *The Robe* (1953), the biblical epic from Lloyd C. Douglas' best-selling novel, was the first CinemaScope film and a hit for Koster. The still shows Michael Rennie (centre) as Simon called Peter.

Left: Henry Koster (centre) rehearses with Jean Simmons and Marlon Brando (as Napoleon) in *Desiree* (1954), a blatant fiction about a supposed romance between the Emperor and a shopgirl.

DAVID LEAN

Born Croydon, Surrey, 25 March 1908

When David Lean emerged from semi-retirement in 1983 to begin directing *A Passage To India* (Columbia), it marked the return of one of the most respected figures of the British cinema after a thirteen-year absence from film-making. Lean's early rise from tea boy to editor, and then to one of the most successful of all British directors, ran parallel to the development of movie making in England – the transformation from the bleak years of the 30s to the 40s revival and the international co-productions of later years. One of the last active links with the British silent cinema, Lean got his start on *Quinneys*, directed by Maurice Elvey in 1927, having been attracted to the cinema at an early age – in spite of a strict Quaker upbringing, in which he was forbidden to go to the pictures as a boy. During the following years he rose from clapper boy to cutting room assistant and then assistant director. By 1930 he had achieved full editor status and worked on newsreels and 'quota' quickies (the cheap features turned out by British studios during the 30s). He refused the offer to direct such movies, but concentrated instead on becoming more proficient as an editor. In the mid-30s he worked on important features like Paul Czinner's *Escape Me Never* (1935), Asquith's *French Without Tears* (1939) and Michael Powell's *49th Parallel* (1941). By the early 40s he was recognised as one of the top editors in England. His skill contributed some much needed pace to *Pygmalion* (MGM, 1938), for example, and producer Gabriel Pascal gave him the opportunity to direct some sequences (uncredited) on *Major Barbara* (1941).

Finally, in 1942, Lean was chosen by Noel Coward to serve as his co-director on his wartime tribute to the British navy, *In Which We Serve* (UA, 1942). Here Coward's fine script (nominated for an Oscar) used a flashback form to tell the stories of the sailors on a British warship torpedoed in the Mediterranean. Coward himself starred as the captain of a destroyer on which much of the action took place, composed the music, and produced the film. *In Which We Serve* was nominated for a Best Picture Oscar, while Coward received an appropriate special honorary award. A big hit both in Britain and the US, it was the ideal vehicle to launch David Lean on his directing career. The combination of Lean as director, Coward as writer-producer, Anthony Havelock-Allan as associate producer and future director Ronald Neame as lighting cameraman worked so well that they went on to do three more films together through their own company, Cineguild, financed by J. Arthur Rank. *In Which We Serve* had among its cast young Richard Attenborough in his first, small film role and Celia Johnson in *her* screen debut. She starred again with John Mills and Kay Walsh (David Lean's first wife) in Lean's first solo outing, *This Happy Breed* (1944). Another pro-British, wartime effort, adapted by Coward from his own play, this was propaganda of the very

highest quality, a loving tribute to the British way of life filmed in suitably restrained Technicolor. Episodic in structure, it told the story of a South London family during the years between the two world wars. While slightly condescending in its treatment of the lower-middle classes, the film succeeded admirably in bringing a particular milieu to life on the screen, aided by fine performances from a cast headed by Robert Newton, Stanley Holloway, Celia Johnson, John Mills and Kay Walsh. In place of the usual talky, stagebound feel of plays adapted to the cinema, *This Happy Breed* looked as if it was filmed in a real house rather than a studio, moving freely between interiors and exteriors and making use of depth of field through through windows, back

gardens etc, while the dialogue, too, was suitably economical.

The picture amply demonstrated Lean's solidly professional craftsmanship and his special ability with actors. These same qualities were evident in the Technicolored *Blithe Spirit* (1945) which followed. Again based on a Coward play, the film emerged as a delightful British version of the kind of screwball domestic comedy with a fantasy theme which was currently popular in the US. But whereas, for example, *I Married A Witch* (UA, 1942) and *Here Comes Mr Jordan* (Colombia, 1941) were filmed in black-and-white, *Blithe Spirit* was greatly enhanced by its use of colour. When the ghostly apparition of Rex Harrison's first wife appears, she is clothed in wispy, flowing

Top: Celia Johnson and Trevor Howard in *Brief Encounter* (1945), Lean's accurate and moving film of an unlooked for and, finally, unconsummated, love affair between two respectably married people. How things have changed forty years on!

Above: Future director Richard Attenborough made his screen debut acting in the David Lean-Noel Coward collaboration, *In Which We Serve* (1942).

Left: Alec Guinness as Fagin and John Howard Davies as young Oliver in Lean's splendid screen version of Charles Dickens' *Oliver Twist* (1948).

allowed him within the Rank production umbrella. As Lean wrote, 'J. Arthur Rank is often spoken of as an all-embracing monopolist who must be watched lest he crush the creative talents of the British film industry. Let the facts speak for themselves, and I doubt if any other group of film-makers anywhere in the world can claim as much freedom'. On the Dickens films, *Great Expectations* (1946) and *Oliver Twist* (1948), the high standards of British film technicians behind the camera, and actors of the calibre of John Mills, Alec Guinness, Robert Newton and Jean Simmons in front, made Lean's job that much easier. Both art director John Bryan and the cameraman Guy Green (a future director himself) won Oscars for bringing a superbly stylised Victorian England to life on the screen in *Great Expectations* (and

'I always keep at a slight distance from the actors in every film, because if I get too chummy it's difficult to instruct them on the set and expect to be obeyed'

green in contrast to the severe reds and wine-coloured dresses favoured by his second wife. Margaret Rutherford stole the movie, however, with her delightful performance as the tweedy, eccentric, spiritualist, Madam Arcati. *Brief Encounter* (1945), in contrast, was a serious marital drama filmed in black-and-white which earned Oscar nominations for Celia Johnson, for Noel Coward's script (again based on one of his plays) and for Lean (his first). A restrained and slightly mannered treatment of the illicit love affair between a suburban housewife and a married doctor (Trevor Howard) its value today is that of a nostalgic period piece, but it added immeasurably to Lean's prestige, and remains popular.

Moving on from Coward to Charles Dickens, Lean demonstrated a special flair for adapting literary classics to the screen, and was more involved than ever before in co-writing his own scripts and taking advantage of the creative freedom

rejoined Lean for *Oliver Twist*). These films also marked the beginning of Lean's long and rewarding collaboration with Alec Guinness. Unfortunately, Guinness' performance as Fagin, meant to be seen as a broad, comic caricature of a Jewish villain, was regarded as anti-semitic in the US and led to Lean's worst ever experience with censorship. The irony was apparent to him when 'they cut the character down to the bare plot bones, and in so doing had removed all the comedy... In my opinion this version *was* anti-semitic...'.

Making another change in subject matter, Lean was less successful with a pair of pictures starring his second wife, Ann Todd. *The Passionate Friends* (1948) was a more complex variation on the *Brief Encounter* theme of the unfaithful wife, making use of multiple flashbacks, and was followed by *Madeleine* (1949), based on a true story of a Victorian lady accused of murdering her lover. In 1950, Lean left Rank to join Alexander Korda's

Top left: David Lean (left) has a word with one of the most magically gifted of all screen actors, Charles Laughton, during the filming of *Hobson's Choice* (1954).

Above: At the heart of *The Bridge On The River Kwai* (1957), Lean's Oscar-studded epic of the war against the Japanese in Burma, was the conflict between enemy officers Alec Guinness (left) and Sessue Hayakawa. Hayakawa's Hollywood career commenced as far back as 1914, and he gained a place in the hall of fame for his performance in DeMille's *The Cheat* (1915), a restrained study in brutality which would no doubt have won an Oscar had they yet been invented.

Left: Katharine Hepburn and Rossano Brazzi shared a bitter-sweet love affair in *Summer Madness* (1955).

London Films. Demonstrating the kind of meticulous preparation which would characterise all his late projects, Lean completed two films for Korda in four years. He was attracted to the true story of the breaking of *The Sound Barrier* (UA, 1952), and did extensive pre-production work on the project before hiring Terence Rattigan to write a strong dramatic script with good parts for Ann Todd and Ralph Richardson. The complex central character of Ridgefield, the aircraft builder determined to succeed where others had failed, provided Richardson with the opportunity to surprise us once again with a slightly off-beat yet deeply felt performance, and one which earned him the New York Film Critics' acting award. Similarly, *Hobson's Choice* (UA, 1954) proved to be a delightful comedy vehicle for another favourite Korda actor, Charles Laughton. For his last black-and-white film Lean succeeded in capturing the authentic 1890s Lancashire atmosphere by shooting on location in Salford. During the following years his striving for cinematic authenticity would take him all over the world.

Lean was immediately off to Venice to shoot *Summertime* (aka *Summer Madness*, UA, 1955). Beautifully photographed in colour, the picture marked a return to a romantic theme, revolving around the brief affair between a middle-aged American tourist (Katharine Hepburn) and a handsome Italian (Rossano Brazzi). A superior 50s example of the 'woman's picture', it was especially well received in the US, earning Oscar nominations for Miss Hepburn, and for Lean who also picked up the New York Film Critics' award for his direction. It was his first international production and marked a major turning point in his career. The decline of British production during the 50s had coincided with a rapid growth in US film investment abroad, particularly in England and Europe. As one of the first British directors to take up this challenge, Lean chose to devote himself entirely to historical subjects, best suited for the new large (and wide) screen. He began auspiciously with *The Bridge On The River Kwai* (Columbia, 1957). Teaming up with American producer Sam Spiegel, Lean found the picturesque locations he was looking for in Ceylon. In spite of the fact that he had a $3 million budget to work with, he concentrated on the psychological conflict between Alec Guinness, giving an Oscar-winning performance as the tough, obsessive C.O. of the British POWs, and Sessue Hayakawa, Oscar-nominated for his equally unbending Japanese POW camp commandant. Here, for the first time, Lean demonstrated that special talent for blending character conflicts on a small scale with larger events. The film was phenomenally successful at the box-office and at the 1957 Oscar ceremony, winning seven awards including Best Picture and Best Director, while the true writers of the Oscar-winning screenplay, Michael Wilson and Carl Forman, both on the industry blacklist, were kept secret.

The hardships of filming in Ceylon were magnified many times as Lean embarked on the most ambitious picture of his career with the desert location shooting of *Lawrence Of Arabia* (Columbia, 1962) during the early 60s. Another large-scale treatment of a historical subject, it introduced a new pair of young actors to the screen, Peter O'Toole and Omar Sharif, and featured Alec Guinness again in one of his most remarkable character roles as Prince Feisal. Scripted by Robert Bolt and photographed by Freddie Young, two of Lean's favourite collaborators of the 60s, the three-and-a-half hour epic deteriorated badly in the second half, but was still impressive enough to win the Best Picture Oscar and to give Lean his second statuette. From the most remarkable World War I desert battles ever seen on film, to the snowy wastes of Russia in the throes of revolution. Here, Lean and Bolt took on rather more than they could handle in attempting to bring Boris Pasternak's weighty novel, *Dr Zhivago* (MGM, 1965) to the screen. An impressive achievement, nevertheless, with location filming in Finland and an entire Moscow street constructed in Spain. This time, however, Lean's special gift for casting let him down badly, in that his assortment of actors, ranging from Sharif and Julie Christie to Rod Steiger and Tom Courtenay, failed to convince as Russians. Still looking for challenges, Lean and Bolt next chose *Ryan's Daughter* (MGM, 1970), an intimate love story set in an obscure Irish village during World War I. It was a well acted, but old-fashioned movie which flopped at the box-office and brought a temporary end to Lean's career. Undaunted by the collapse of his plans to film *The Bounty* during the late 70s, he was back in action once again in 1983 with the kind of English literary subject with an exotic setting which best suits him, adapting E.M. Forster's 'A Passage To India' to the screen, filming on location, and upsetting the Indians with his uncompromising man-made alterations to their landscape. In 1984, he was, most appropriately, knighted for his services to the cinema.

'When I was a tea boy, I never intentionally thought of becoming a director, because I thought it was over some vast distant horizon. Now I am a director, I think only of becoming a better director with each film'

Top: Very much inclined towards epic subjects from the late 50s onwards, Lean enjoyed a big success with *Lawrence Of Arabia* (1962), which introduced Peter O'Toole (illustrated) to the screen and brought him instant stardom—as it did for Omar Sharif.

Above: Director Lean, reunited with Alec Guinness on location in India for the filming of *A Passage To India*. Guinness (left) played Professor Godbole in this adaptation of E.M. Forster's novel. The film collected eleven Oscar nominations, including three for Lean—as director, writer and editor, but only Peggy Ashcroft (best supporting actress) and Maurice Jarre (best original score) took trophies home with them.

MITCHELL LEISEN

Born Menominee, Michigan, 6 October 1898. **Died** 1972

The name of Mitchell Leisen is closely associated with Hollywood at its most sophisticated and glamorous. As a leading costume designer and art director, later turned movie director, he worked with many of the top female stars and spent twenty years at Paramount, the zenith in sophistication among the American studios, and the home of many of Hollywood's most stylish ladies. Leisen had a special talent for comedy and was fortunate in working with some of the top comedy writers during the 30s. His highly developed visual sense served him well when he turned to costume pictures and colour during the 40s. But the trend away from glamorous studio filming, and the decline of the studios, hit him particularly hard and, by the early 50s, his best years were behind him.

First attracted to Hollywood as a young man, Leisen's movie career got off to a terrific start when he was hired by De-Mille to provide Gloria Swanson's lavish costumes for the flashback sequences in *Male And Female* (Paramount, 1919). Leisen continued to design costumes for other DeMille pictures, and for Douglas Fairbanks, during the following years. In 1923 he graduated to joint art director on *The Ten Commandments* (Paramount) and served as DeMille's regular production designer and assistant during 1925-33, earning an Oscar nomination for his work on Cecil B's first talkie, *Dynamite* (MGM, 1929).

Paramount gave him his first opportunity to direct in 1933, and already in his second assignment – *Death Takes A Holiday* (1934), a costume fantasy starring Fredric March – Leisen had established himself as a director of note. The following year (1935) he made the first of nine movies with Fred MacMurray, here given his first major role in *Hands Across The Table*, while for co-star Carole Lombard the film marked a further stage in

her development into a delightful and exceptional comedienne. Miss Lombard was again in peak form opposite Mac-Murray's worthless trumpet player (he played the sax in real life) in *Swing High, Swing Low*, filmed in 1936. During the following years Leisen continued to cast the genial but bland Fred opposite some of Hollywood's most sparkling women, including Barbara Stanwyck, Rosalind Russell and Marlene Dietrich; the ladies were obviously meant to steal the show and generally did so.

'I was getting a little bored with the polite comedies I was doing,' Leisen recalled years later, 'and I decided to cut loose and do a lot of slapstick.' The result

was *Easy Living* (1937), a delightful Jean Arthur-Ray Milland vehicle which marked Leisen's first collaboration with the brilliant scriptwriter Preston Sturges, and the beginning of his most productive period at Paramount (1937-41). From the scriptwriting team of Charles Brackett and Billy Wilder came *Midnight* (1939), one of the most memorable of 30s screwball comedies – here Leisen was at his peak as a comedy stylist, Claudette Colbert was enchanting, and John Barrymore had his last good comedy role, while *Hold Back The Dawn* (1941) showed the more cynical and serious side of Wilder and was the only Leisen picture ever nominated for a Best Picture Oscar.

When both Sturges and Wilder turned to directing, Leisen was forced to look to other sources. The Broadway musical, *Lady In The Dark*, in Leisen's hands became an extraordinary and lavish piece of 40s Technicolor kitsch starring Ginger Rogers and Ray Milland. He succeeded better with adaptations of romantic novels like Daphne du Maurier's *Frenchman's Creek* (also filmed in 1943) which provided Joan Fontaine with her best swashbuckling role, and *Kitty* filmed in 1944 with Paulette Goddard as the girl of the streets who is transformed into an 18th-century English lady. Another adaptation, *Golden Earrings* in 1946, provided Marlene Dietrich with a suitably exotic comeback role as a gypsy secret agent. But it was becoming clear that Leisen had little future in an increasingly deglamorized Hollywood. He continued to direct features for another ten years, concluding with *The Girl Most Likely* (1957) which rates a footnote in the film histories as the last movie produced at the old RKO studio. Leisen retired in the 60s after trying his hand at directing some episodes for TV.

Top: French heart-throb Charles Boyer starred with Paulette Goddard in *Hold Back The Dawn* (1941), a romantic melodrama with a serious theme (a man wanting to emigrate to the US marries a schoolteacher he doesn't love) scripted by Charles Brackett and Billy Wilder.

Above: Director Leisen, formerly a leading designer and clearly a snappy dresser himself, checks costume sketches with star Betty Hutton for *Dream Girl* (1947), a misguided screen adaptation of the hit play by Elmer Rice.

Left: Looking like a vengeful parody of Bizet's Carmen, Marlene Dietrich berates a bashful Ray Milland in *Golden Earrings* (1947).

'I remember how considerate Mitch was of the extras. He always made a point of directing each and every one of them himself . . . giving them some kind of business even if they were way in the back'

Fred MacMurray in 'Hollywood Director' (David Chierichetti)

ANATOLE LITVAK

Born Kiev, Russia, 10 May 1902. **Died** 1974

Anatole Litvak arrived in Hollywood in 1937 and launched himself at RKO with a remake of one of his recent French successes, *L'Equipage*. Now titled *The Woman I Love*, it starred Miriam Hopkins (whom the director briefly married). The movie displayed Litvak's solid virtues – efficiency, a sense of production values, an ability to draw excellent performances from his cast. He immediately moved on to Warner Bros., establishing himself there until 1941. He made nine films, each of which was a reflection more of the studio's range and house style than of any individualistic gift on the part of the director, who nonetheless skilfully handled a variety of subjects.

After working as a stagehand in his teens, he had taken a philosophy degree and then attended a state drama school. A spell as actor and assistant director with a theatre company followed until, in 1923, he joined the Nordkino studios as a set decorator and assistant director. He directed his first film, *Tatiana*, in 1924, then left Russia for Germany, where work as an assistant director followed until 1930, when he began making films for UFA. But this was Hitler's Germany and Litvak was a Jew. He left for England where he made *Sleeping Car* (1933), a comedy with Madeleine Carroll and Ivor Novello, then moved to Paris, joining the Pathé company for three films. The last of these, *Mayerling* (1936), a historical drama starring Charles Boyer and Danielle Darrieux, achieved international success, and brought Litvak an invitation to Hollywood.

At Warner Bros. the director got off to an excellent start with *Tovarich* (1937), a Paris-based comedy about emigré Russian nobility. It teamed Boyer and Claudette Colbert and was a sparkling success. *The Amazing Dr Clitterhouse* (1938), a suspense comedy with Edward G. Robinson followed and, the same year, Litvak turned out the obligatory Bette Davis potboiler – a minor vehicle called *The Sisters*. Again, the film was well made and well acted and Litvak was rewarded with *Confessions Of A Nazi Spy* (1939). Filmed late in 1938, it was Hollywood's very first anti-Nazi movie, and remarkably topical and accurate in depicting the Nazi menace. The director adopted a semi-documentary approach which worked very well, and drew a notable performance from Edward G. Robinson. In 1940 he directed John Garfield in *Castle On The Hudson*, a remake of *20,000 Years In Sing Sing*; then, the same year, he produced his biggest success so far, *All This And Heaven Too*. An out-and-out period melodrama redolent with passion, intrigue and drama, it was set in 19th-century France and starred Charles Boyer and Bette Davis. Eyewash it might have been, but it garnered three Academy nominations, including Best Picture. Three more well-made but routine films followed: *City For Conquest* (1940), *Out Of The Fog* (1941), and *Blues In The Night* (1941).

Now an American citizen, Litvak

joined the army and collaborated with Frank Capra on the 'Why We Fight' series. He was in charge of combat photography and filming of the Normandy invasion and received the Legion of Honour and the Croix de Guerre. On his return to Hollywood he made his two best films: *Sorry Wrong Number* (Paramount, 1948) won an Oscar nomination for Barbara Stanwyck as a bed-ridden invalid who overhears (on the telephone) a plot to kill her. First grade in all departments, it was followed by what was perhaps Litvak's most deeply felt film and the only one to earn him a Best Director nomination – *The Snake Pit* (20th Century-Fox, 1949). Set in a female insane asylum, the movie was hard-hitting and harrowing, and conveyed a plea for better treatment of the mentally ill. It collected five nominations, including Best Picture and Best Actress (Olivia de Havilland).

From the 50s, Litvak returned to working in Europe. His craftsmanship remained undiminished but, increasingly, he seemed ill at ease with his material. Apart from the success of *Anastasia* (20th Century-Fox, 1956), which brought Ingrid Bergman back from exile and won her an Oscar, Litvak's output was intermittent and largely undistinguished (although the spy story, *Decision Before Dawn*, 20th Century-Fox, 1951, received a best picture nomination) and concluded with a hopelessly incoherent attempt at 'fashionable' suspense drama, *The Lady In The Car With Glasses And A Gun* (Columbia, 1970).

Top: Litvak's first big Hollywood hit, the Oscar-nominated *All This And Heaven Too* (1940) starred Bette Davis (left), Charles Boyer and Barbara O'Neil (centre).

Above: Mark Stevens and Olivia de Havilland in *The Snake Pit* (1949). The title refers to the female insane asylum where the film was set.

Left: A candid shot of Litvak with Samantha Eggar, the English star of his last (and least) film, *The Lady In The Car With Glasses And A Gun* (1970).

JOSHUA LOGAN

Born Texarkana, Texas, 5 October 1908

Joshua Logan ranks as one of the most gifted and successful of American theatre directors, with a special interest in musicals. In a long career, his string of Broadway hits included 'Mister Roberts', which he co-wrote, 'Annie Get Your Gun', the musical 'Fanny' which he co-adapted from Pagnol's celebrated 'Marseilles Trilogy', and William Inge's Pulitzer Prize-winning 'Picnic'. He developed his interest in the theatre while studying at Princeton, where he organised the University Players during the late 20s. A summer stock group, the Players had the distinction of launching the careers of numerous future stars including Henry Fonda, James Stewart and Margaret Sullavan. After college, Logan won a scholarship to study under Stanislavski at the renowned Moscow Arts Theatre. He returned to the US in 1932 and commenced his Broadway career, directing, and also acting in, numerous plays, and made his first excursion to Hollywood in the mid-30s where he was dialogue director on a couple of movies including the Dietrich-Boyer vehicle *The Garden Of Allah* (Selznick/UA, 1936). He co-directed *I Met My Love Again* (Wanger/UA), a romantic drama starring Henry Fonda and Joan Bennett in 1937.

Back on Broadway he had a big hit with 'On Borrowed Time' in 1938 and was much in demand. In 1940 he placed himself in a psychiatric hospital having suffered a severe bout of the mental illness which would plague him throughout his life. After war service with Air Force Combat Intelligence, his return to Broadway brought him continued success and, in 1956, led him back to Hollywood to direct the screen version of *Picnic* (Columbia). He was dropped in at the deep end with location filming and CinemaScope (James Wong Howe photographed the picture), but he also had an excellent cast topped by William Holden. The story concerned the arrival of a stranger in a sleepy Midwestern town whose temporary presence has a marked effect on the lives of the townsfolk. Already there were signs of Logan's tendency to overload the screen with top-heavy imagery, but the movie was very successful and earned four nominations, including Best Picture and Director. Later the same year he made *Bus Stop* (20th Century-Fox), another folksy piece from another Inge play and enormously successful. It starred Marilyn Monroe who delivered a memorable portrayal, both hilarious and vulnerable, of a backwoods floozie, and it won a nomination for newcomer Don Murray as her cowboy beau. *Sayonara* followed in 1957. Beautiful to look at, it boasted a splendid performance from Marlon Brando as an air force major in love with a Japanese actress – ''Madame Butterfly' with a happy ending' as one critic remarked. It garnered Oscar nominations for Logan and Best Picture, with supporting awards going to Red Buttons and Miyoshi Umeki. For the film version of *Fanny*

(Warner Bros., 1961) the songs were omitted, but the charm was preserved, particularly in the enchanting performances of Charles Boyer, Maurice Chevalier and Leslie Caron, and it, too, was nominated for Best Picture.

A sensitive and brilliant director of actors, Logan's name is, unfortunately, most closely connected with three distinctly unwieldy large-budget musicals – all originally stage shows which suffered from the common weakness of failure to rethink them cinematically. Thus, the natural settings combined with the giant wide screen, merely drew attention to the stage conventions, plot weaknesses, and certain inadequacies of casting. *South Pacific* (20th Century-Fox, 1958), was not only overlong, but the director employed a series of ill-judged colour filters which gave the movie a literally jaundiced look. *Camelot* (Warner Bros., 1967), the Lerner and Loewe Broadway hit, starred Richard Harris, Vanessa Redgrave and Franco Nero. Jack Warner lavished $15

million on it and it showed. It was nominated for cinematography and won for art direction and costumes, but was overlong, heavy-handed and irredeemably stagebound. Then came *Paint Your Wagon* for Paramount in 1969. Another Lerner-Loewe show, it was not up to much in the original and the film was

worse. It cost $17 million, was dull and interminable, and will be remembered only for Lee Marvin's flat but endearing delivery of 'Wandrin' Star'. That was Logan's last film but, in 1977 aged 69, he produced, directed, acted and sang in his first nightclub show at The Rainbow Grill, New York.

Left: Looking very different from the debonair lover of his musical comedy hey-day, Maurice Chevalier gave a charming and affecting performance in *Fanny* (1961), a big hit which starred Leslie Caron in the title role.

Above: The splendid Broadway actress, Eileen Heckart (left), with Marilyn Monroe in William Inge's *Bus Stop* (1956). The latter played a simple backwoods girl earning a living as a café singer.

Left: Vanessa Redgrave relaxes with an anachronistic cigarette while Joshua Logan casts an eye over one of the stupendously lavish sets for *Camelot* (1967). The film, unlike the original stage show, was not a success.

'*Picnic* and *Bus Stop showed that Logan, a man of the theatre, was keenly aware of the more intimate nature of films. It is ironic that Sayonara, which is not derived from a play, should turn out so artificial*'

Gordon Gow in 'Films and Filming', 1958

ALEXANDER MACKENDRICK

Born Boston, 1912

Characterised by his offbeat, Scottish sense of humour, Alexander Mackendrick liked to mix the ordinary with the extraordinary, the plausible with the fantastic. He first made his name as one of the most talented of Ealing comedy directors, but was attracted to unusual, serious subjects as well, like *Mandy* (1952) about the problems of a remarkable deaf girl, and had a special gift for working with children. His reputation is based on nine features, five of them made for the Ealing Studio during 1948-55. A sadly wasted talent, he flourished within the friendly give and take and artistic freedom provided by Ealing, but had few opportunities to direct following the sale of the studio in 1955, after which he worked mainly in the US and abroad.

Born to Scottish parents while they were visiting America, Mackendrick grew up in Scotland and was educated at Glasgow Art School. He worked briefly in advertising, then broke into films as a scriptwriter in 1937 and was employed variously as a writer and director of shorts, cartoons and documentaries during the following years, and during the war when he was attached to the Ministry of Information's Psychological Warfare Unit. Hired as a writer by Ealing Studios after the war, he worked on the scripts of *Saraband For Dead Lovers* in 1947 and *The Blue Lamp* (released in 1949) and was given his first opportunity to direct a feature – *Whisky Galore* – in 1948. The film (one of the first of the famous Ealing comedies) was based on a novel which was itself derived from a true wartime incident when a ship loaded with whisky ran aground on an isolated island of the Outer Hebrides, and the islanders naturally regarded the cargo as God-given booty. Shot on location in the Hebrides, the film demonstrated Mackendrick's talent for bringing a milieu to life on the screen. Rich in authentic atmosphere and detail and visually striking, the story itself was so extraordinary and amusing that it needed little in the way of embellishment to make a delightful and entertaining movie. Mackendrick followed with *The Man In The White Suit*

(1951) with the studio's top star, Alec Guinness, in the title role. It presented a pointedly satirical attack on the establishment, and the narrow-minded attitudes of big business and unions alike who combine to try and suppress Guinness' amazing invention – an indestructible suit. The extraordinarily clever script earned Mackendrick his only Oscar nomination – as co-writer.

These were the most productive years of his career. Another unusual – and serious – subject, *Mandy*, followed in 1952. About the education and treatment of deaf children, it was treated by Mackendrick with great sensitivity. The kids were terrific as was the star, young Mandy Miller who had appeared briefly in *The Man In The White Suit*. But a weak subplot concerning her unsympathetic father (Terence Morgan) was clearly overdramatized and unnecessary and suggests that Mackendrick was unsure of himself in this, his first dramatic film. But he was back on more familiar territory with *The Maggie* (1954) about a rich American (Paul Douglas) who is continually outwitted by the crew of an old Scottish 'puffer' boat. American writer William Rose joined Mackendrick on *The Ladykillers* (1955), the last of the classic Ealing comedies. A black farce, it was much darker in tone than the usual

Ealing product, with Alec Guinness looking more sinister on the screen than he had since his Fagin seven years before.

Invited to direct the hard-hitting *Sweet Smell Of Success* (UA, 1957), an exposé of the seedier side of New York's night life and the gossip columnists, Mackendrick demonstrated his adaptability, and drew memorable performances from Burt Lancaster and Tony Curtis. Unfortunately, he was taken off *The Devil's Disciple* (UA, 1959) for working too slowly and had to wait a number of years before he was given *Sammy Going South* (Paramount, 1963) by ex-Ealing boss, producer Michael Balcon. Mackendrick's one last outstanding picture of the 60s, however, was *A High Wind In Jamaica* (20th Century-Fox, 1965). An extremely effective adaptation of Richard Hughes' novel of adventure, terror and bizarre behaviour experienced by a group of children aboard a 19th-century pirate ship, it was Mackendrick's blackest movie. A weak attempt at satirising the trendy life in sunny California, *Don't Make Waves* (MGM, 1967), brought Mackendrick's directing career to an end, aside from a little television work. He remained in California, however, as the Dean of the film department of the California Institute of the Arts up until 1978.

Top: Gordon Jackson (left) and a bit player surrounded by cases of serendipitous booty in Mackendrick's hit comedy – and his first feature – *Whisky Galore* (1948).

Above: On location for *The Man In The White Suit* (1951), director Mackendrick, surrounded by his crew, confers with his stars, Joan Greenwood and Alec Guinness (foreground centre).

Left: Edith Atwater, Tony Curtis and Burt Lancaster in *Sweet Smell Of Success* (1957). Curtis' performance as a corrupt, seedy and ambitious press agent put paid to any notions that he was just a pretty face.

JOSEPH L. MANKIEWICZ

Born Wilkes-Barre, Pennsylvania, 11 February 1909

Joseph Mankiewicz spent over twenty years in Hollywood as an accomplished writer, producer and director. A charming, intelligent, witty and handsome young man, he was romantically involved with many glamorous stars ranging from Joan Crawford and Frances Dee to Judy Garland and Linda Darnell, among others, and was three times married. As a director, his softspoken and sensitive approach got fine results from established stars (Bette Davis, Marlon Brando) and less confident performers (Gene Tierney, Linda Darnell) alike – although he was unable to turn Elizabeth Taylor into a convincing Cleopatra. He is perhaps best remembered as the writer-director of *All About Eve* (20th Century-Fox, 1950).

Educated at Columbia University, Joe

'I am never quite sure whether I am one of cinema's elder statesmen or just the oldest whore on the beat'
1972

Left: Joseph Mankiewicz did not direct his first picture until 1945, after more than fifteen years as a writer and producer in Hollywood. The film, *Dragonwyck*, a brooding period mystery romance, starred Gene Tierney, seen here (right) with Anne Revere and Walter Huston.

scripted a pair of moderately successful Joan Crawford vehicles during 1934-35 which marked the beginning of a close professional and personal relationship lasting for nine years. He became Crawford's most trusted MGM producer when he was promoted in 1935, while also accounting for more than his fair share of the studio's most prestigious productions ranging from Fritz Lang's *Fury* (1936) to *The Philadelphia Story* (1940) and *Woman Of The Year* (1941), the first film to team Hepburn and Tracy. Busy in his private life, too, Joe divorced his first wife in 1937 and married Viennese actress Rosa Stradner two years later. Temporarily separated from his

Left: *A Letter To Three Wives* (1949) marked Mankiewicz's elevation to the first rank of Hollywood writer-directors. One of the wives was Ann Sothern, here with Kirk Douglas.

Below: The director's most fondly remembered achievement is the cruel, witty, acidic *All About Eve* (1950). Here Bette Davis (left) as Broadway star Margo Channing greets Marilyn Monroe (in a bit part) and George Sanders as critic Addison de Witt. It was during this party scene that Miss Davis uttered the now legendary line, 'Fasten your seat belts, it's going to be a bumpy night'.

spent a number of months as a journalist in Berlin in 1928. Back in the States the following year, he was offered a writing job at Paramount where his older brother, scriptwriter Herman, headed the scenario department. Joe started out in the lowly job of writing intertitles for the silent versions of movies distributed to film theatres which had not yet converted to sound. Only twenty, the youngest writer at the studio, and overshadowed by his famous brother, he was determined to succeed. He soon established himself as a specialist in comedy dialogue which he wrote for a number of Jack Oakie movies beginning with *Fast Company* (1929). The young Mankiewicz had his first big success, nominated for an Oscar, as co-writer of *Skippy* (1931) starring the ten-year-old Jackie Cooper. But the high point of his early career as a writer was a hilarious and topical satire on the 1932 Olympics, *Million Dollar Legs* starring Oakie and W.C. Fields.

In 1934 Joe married Universal contract starlet Elizabeth Young and began work at MGM where he scripted *Manhattan Melodrama*, famous as the movie which Dillinger had been watching when he was caught and shot by the FBI. He

second wife in 1943, Joe's close relationship with rising MGM star Judy Garland led to a row with studio boss Louis B. Mayer and a break with the studio.

Although a well-paid, successful producer, Mankiewicz has always insisted that he never wanted to be a producer, that his only goal had been to become a director. The abrupt break with MGM suddenly landed him at the more congenial 20th Century-Fox studio where directors were more highly valued and better treated than at MGM. He produced and co-scripted *The Keys Of The Kingdom* (1944) directed by John Stahl, then, aged thirty-six, was given his first opportunity to direct with *Dragonwyck* (1945), due to the illness of Ernst Lubitsch who served as producer instead. Recognising his need to learn the craft of directing, Joe served an 'apprenticeship' for a few years working on a diverse group of pictures, mainly from scripts provided by other writers. *Dragonwyck* was an atmospheric, American-Gothic romance starring Gene Tierney, with Vincent Price in the first of his tortured hero-with-a-guilty-secret roles. It was a big hit. *Somewhere In The Night* was an effective 40s *film noir* immediately followed by a solidly crafted slice of Americana – Ronald Colman starring as *The Late George Apley* (1946) adapted from John P. Marquand. *The Ghost And Mrs Muir* (1947) was a lighthearted fantasy which wore a bit thin in the final reels. Rex Harrison starred (with Gene Tierney), and also played the convict on the run in *Escape*, filmed in Britain in 1947.

Finally, in 1948 Mankiewicz felt ready to combine his talents as writer and director on *A Letter To Three Wives*. A witty and satirical look at small town married life among the country club set, the film demonstrated that he had a genuine gift for bringing a milieu alive on the screen and for getting the best from his cast. The dark family drama, *House Of Strangers* (1949) was followed by *No Way Out* (1950), Mankiewicz's contribution to the late 40s cycle of films of social comment (here racial bigotry and violence) and providing Sidney Poitier with his first movie role. Joe had completed shooting on this latter by March 1950 when he won Oscars for both scripting and directing *A Letter To Three Wives* and was just about to start filming a favourite project, *All About Eve*. 'I'd had the general idea in mind for a

long time,' he later recalled, 'but I never had a middle – a second act.' He found it in a story by Mary Orr, but adroitly transformed it to fit his purposes. The picture expresses Mankiewicz's lifelong fascination with and attraction to the theatre. Although he was never able to write a successful play, *Eve* gives full expression to his mastery of movie dialogue which was never better employed, before or since. The acerbic lines were delivered at a cracking pace by a steller cast headed by Bette Davis, Anne Baxter (as Eve), Celeste Holm and Thelma Ritter, all of whom were nominated for Oscars, while George Sanders won for his portrayal of the appropriately named critic, Addison de Witt. Joe's only movie to win the Best Picture Oscar, he naturally walked off with the screenplay award, and, a little surprisingly, repeated as Best Director, in spite of stiff competition from Billy Wilder for *Sunset Boulevard*.

Elected president of the Screen Directors Guild in May 1950, Mankiewicz won a famous victory over Cecil B. De-Mille and his Right-wing cronies who had resorted to McCarthyite smear tactics in an attempt to impose their views on the Guild membership and remove Mankiewicz from office. Determined to get away from Hollywood, Joe brought his prolific Fox years to an end in 1951 with the wordy but enjoyable play adaptation *People Will Talk*, followed by the stylish spy thriller *Five Fingers* scripted by Michael Wilson from a true story, with suitably witty dialogue supplied by the director. Now resident in New York, he returned to his old studio, MGM, in 1952 to put together an intelligent and successful adaptation of Shakespeare's *Julius Caesar*. In a mixed British and American cast, Brando tried hard as Antony, James Mason was miscast as Brutus and John Gielgud gave everyone a lesson in the art of Shakespearian acting.

After one venture into opera, staging 'La Boheme' at the Met, Joe embarked on a new, international phase in his career which took him to Europe for *The Barefoot Contessa* (UA, 1954) – his first as an independent with his own company – to Viet Nam for a poor adaptation of Graham Greene's *The Quiet American* (UA, 1957), to England to make Tennessee Williams' *Suddenly Last Summer* (Columbia, 1959), and to Italy for his attempts to salvage 20th Century-Fox's much troubled production of *Cleopatra*

during 1961-62 – an assignment which had a disastrous effect on his career. He returned to the US and Warners in 1969 to direct his first Western, *There Was A Crooked Man* ... best summed up by Henry Fonda as '... a very good script. It just didn't work as a movie.' It was Joe's first American film for fourteen years, since his sole stab at musical comedy with *Guys And Dolls* (Goldwyn/MGM, 1955) which, although highly enjoyable, had failed to capture the vitality of the stage original. In 1972 he directed his last movie, *Sleuth* (20th Century-Fox). Although starring Laurence Olivier and Michael Caine, it was little more than a competently filmed play, and a disappointing end to a remarkable career.

Above: Elizabeth Taylor in *Suddenly Last Summer* (1959).

Below: Mankiewicz, suitably stripped to withstand the Roman heat, talks to Elizabeth Taylor on the set of *Cleopatra* (1963). Judging from his good-humoured demeanour, he couldn't have foreseen the extent of the catastrophe in the making ...

Below left: One of Britain's finest classical actors, John Gielgud (left) was Cassius in *Julius Caesar* (1953). James Mason (right) was Brutus, Marlon Brando an amazing 'Method' Mark Antony.

ANTHONY MANN

Born San Diego, 30 June 1906. **Died** 1967

Spanning three decades as a director, Anthony Mann first made his name during the 40s with cheap B features and *films noirs* and, by the 60s, he was filming big budget international productions in Europe. But he is best remembered for the years inbetween, the 50s, when he established himself as one of the leading directors of Westerns and developed a close working relationship with James Stewart, in particular. Mann arrived in California around 1939 and was already directing his first feature, *Dr Broadway*, for Paramount, by the end of 1941. Having previously worked as an actor and director in the New York theatre, he was briefly employed by Selznick, then served as an assistant to Preston Sturges on *Sullivan's Travels* (Paramount, 1941), and heeded Sturges' advice to him that 'it's better to have done something bad than to have done nothing.' 'So, the first picture, good or bad, that came along, I decided to do,' Mann later recalled, 'and this was *Dr Broadway*.'

Carrying on with a selection of B-features – drama, thrillers, and musicals – he moved from Republic to RKO and then on to Eagle Lion, averaging better than two movies per year. Of special interest was his last for Republic, *The Great Flamarion*, filmed in 1944. Erich von Stroheim in the title role carried the picture in a part which was obviously meant for him and was closely related to his real life character, a gruff exterior concealing the sensitive person underneath. Here Mann, at a relatively early stage in his career, demonstrated a strong visual sense and grasp of film techniques, and made effective use of a mobile camera at various points. During the late 40s the director specialised in *film noir*. *T-Men* in 1947 provided him with his first chance to work on a B-movie with a larger budget and at a less frenetic pace. He also collaborated on the screenplay with his

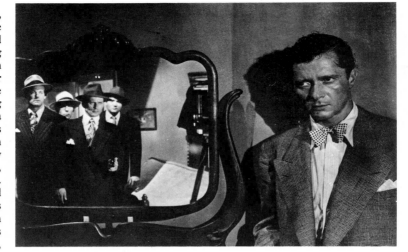

favourite scriptwriter of this period, John C. Higgins, and cameraman John Alton. The result was a superior example of the type of 40s thriller filmed on location and loosely based on a true story (in this one, about how a pair of Treasury agents, Dennis O'Keefe and Alfred Ryder, operate undercover to expose a gang of counterfeiters). Mann probed beneath the surface of his male heroes with real psychological insight, going beyond the more superficial semi-documentary style of Hathaway or Dassin, for example, resulting in powerful and occasionally violent work, whose low-keyed photography made the name of Alton, too. The success of *T-Men*, followed by *Raw Deal* in 1948, led to a new contract with MGM early in 1949. Again Mann and Alton went on location, to the San Joaquin Valley, to film another story concerning a pair of government undercover agents, *Border Incident*. Here, Mann's dramatic use of natural landscapes clearly anticipated the style of the Westerns which he would soon begin filming.

Mann immediately put his stamp on

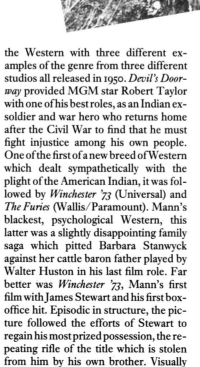

the Western with three different examples of the genre from three different studios all released in 1950. *Devil's Doorway* provided MGM star Robert Taylor with one of his best roles, as an Indian ex-soldier and war hero who returns home after the Civil War to find that he must fight injustice among his own people. One of the first of a new breed of Western which dealt sympathetically with the plight of the American Indian, it was followed by *Winchester '73* (Universal) and *The Furies* (Wallis/Paramount). Mann's blackest, psychological Western, this latter was a slightly disappointing family saga which pitted Barbara Stanwyck against her cattle baron father played by Walter Huston in his last film role. Far better was *Winchester '73*, Mann's first film with James Stewart and his first box-office hit. Episodic in structure, the picture followed the efforts of Stewart to regain his most prized possession, the repeating rifle of the title which is stolen from him by his own brother. Visually impressive, the film was photographed by veteran cameraman William Daniels and

Top: Dennis O'Keefe (far left) is forced to watch his friend and fellow undercover agent, Alfred Ryder, cornered (and subsequently killed) while he remains powerless to help in *T-Men* (1947).

Above: James Stewart in *Bend Of The River*, the first of seven colour films which star and director made together about a pioneer trek into Oregon, it co-starred Arthur Kennedy, Julie Adams and Rock Hudson.

Left: Director Anthony Mann and star Barbara Stanwyck examine a reel of takes from *The Furies* (1950), a Western with interesting but somewhat laboured Freudian overtones.

embodied several Mann themes – sibling rivalry, family conflict and violence, with a typically complex and unconventional hero, and a characteristically effective use of Western landscapes.

There was a two-year gap before he and Stewart made a follow-up, *Bend Of The River* (Universal, 1952), which demonstrated that he could work just as effectively in colour. It was the first of seven (all in colour) which director and star made together during 1952-55, mixing Westerns with straight drama, adventure and even a musical biopic, of Glenn Miller. *Bend Of The River* and *The Far Country* (Universal, 1954) took them to the far Northwestern area of the US, to Oregon and Alaska with the pioneering

Julia Adams, Janet Leigh, Ruth Roman, and in *The Man From Laramie*, Cathy O'Donnell, and veteran actress Aline MacMahon in a fine supporting role as a stubborn lady rancher.

The Mann-Stewart Westerns were quite successful at the box-office, but it was a pair of non-Western movies which emerged as their smash hits. *The Glenn Miller Story* (Universal, 1954) succeeded admirably in recreating the big band era of the 30s and early 40s. The opening forty minutes were particularly good, full of subtle, underplayed humour, with Stewart's musician a lovable eccentric, and some nice interplay between him and June Allyson as his wife. If the second half became too sentimental, at least Mann

families and gold miners. The action is effectively set against vast expanses of virgin forest, roaring rivers and, occasionally, snowy landscapes and snow-capped mountains. As in the best Westerns of Boetticher, the hero (Stewart) is generally matched against a strong, interesting and believable villain – played by Arthur Kennedy in *Bend Of The River* and by Robert Ryan in *The Naked Spur* (MGM, 1953). This latter was filmed on location in the mountainous region of Colorado and concerned the efforts of bounty hunter Stewart to bring in his outlaw prey. The last of the Stewart Westerns, *The Man From Laramie* (Columbia, 1955), pitted him against Arthur Kennedy once again in a powerful drama of ambition, revenge and family conflict. In spite of the fact that this was his first film (impressively photographed) in CinemaScope, Mann was not overwhelmed by the large screen. He continued to be equally attentive to the kind of quiet and intimate moments which can be found in all his films and are generally associated with his heroines played by actresses like

had some terrific music to fall back on. Stewart and Allyson were reteamed later that year (1954) at Paramount for another (less memorable) VistaVision hit, *Strategic Air Command*, about a baseball player called for Air Force duty.

Aside from the offbeat comedy of *God's Little Acre* (UA, 1957), Mann rounded out the 50s with a last useful group of Westerns. In *The Tin Star* (Paramount, 1957) Henry Fonda played another one of Mann's mature but morally ambiguous heroes, an experienced gunman who passes on his knowledge to the green young sheriff (Anthony Perkins). *Man Of The West* (UA, 1958) stands as Mann's most expressive and powerful, but not entirely successful, attempt to raise Western drama to the level of Greek tragedy, impressively acted by Gary Cooper and Lee J. Cobb. The epic qualities of this film led him to adapt a classic Western to the large screen, Edna Ferber's *Cimarron* (MGM, 1960), but he was unable to shoot on location as he wished and the mutilated result is disowned by him. Further developing his interest in

the epic form, he came to Europe for the final stage of his career. Having been replaced as director of *Spartacus* (Universal, 1960), he proceeded to direct two of the most intelligent of the early 60s epics for producer Samuel Bronston, both scripted by Philip Yordan who had worked on some of his previous films. Charlton Heston starred as the legendary Spanish hero *El Cid* in 1961; a smash hit, it was followed by *The Fall Of The Roman Empire* in 1963, which was an expensive flop in spite of an impressive cast headed by Sophia Loren, James Mason, Alec Guinness and Stephen Boyd. Mann rounded off his career with an exciting actioner based on a true story of Norwegian underground heroics during World War II – *The Heroes Of Telemark* (Columbia, 1965). He died during the filming of *A Dandy In Aspic* (Columbia) in 1967, and the film was completed by its star, Laurence Harvey.

Above: Gary Cooper (right) and Arthur O'Connell in *Man Of The West* (1958), one of Mann's most ambitious Westerns, about a reformed gunman who is talked into rejoining his former cohorts to rob a bank.

Left: Janet Leigh and James Stewart in *The Naked Spur* (1953). The script, by Sam Rolfe and Harold Jack Bloom, received an Academy Award nomination.

Below: Kirk Douglas (left) and Richard Harris in *The Heroes Of Telemark* (1965), a large-scale World War II action adventure, based on a factual incident.

VINCENTE MINNELLI

Born Chicago, 28 February 1910.

Vincente Minnelli once claimed in an interview: 'I like realism, in all pictures'. Seldom can any artist in the cinema have been quite so obtuse about the precise qualities of his own work; for, whatever were Minnelli's gifts, a tendency to gritty realism could not be counted among them. Beginning his career in the Broadway theatre, and principally associated in the cinema with the musical, that most euphoric and least realistic of all Hollywood genres, he was a master of decorative stylisation; and if a governing theme can be discerned in his oeuvre, equally in his musicals, comedies and melodramas, it is that of the interplay between truth and fantasy, reality and artifice. In consequence, one of the emblematic props of a Minnelli film was, not unexpectedly, the mirror. Speaking of his 1949 version of Flaubert's *Madame Bovary* (with Jennifer Jones, Van Heflin and James Mason as the novelist himself), he explained: 'Throughout the picture I kept using mirrors, the mirror in the farm showing her always trying to glamorise herself, dreaming of something she wasn't; in the seminary, where she read the French romantic novels of the time; and then in the ballroom, when she glances into the glass and sees herself surrounded by men in the one perfect image that fulfils her romantic hopes'.

Minnelli was virtually 'born in a trunk'. At the age of three he was already a full-fledged member of the Minnelli Brothers Dramatic Tent Show, which toured the US in the ebbing years of vaudeville. Even when a student, he happily moonlighted as a painter of billboards and, following a brief stint as a photographer's aide, worked as assistant stage manager on the kind of live movie theatre shows immortalised by Busby Berkeley in *Footlight Parade* (1933). Subsequently, he was hired as a costume designer in New York, being assigned to create sets and costumes for an operetta, *Du Barry*, at the request of the soprano Grace Moore. And in 1933, still in his early twenties, he

was appointed art director of Radio City Music Hall. If ever a film-maker were properly trained for the kind of work in which his reputation would be founded, it was Vincente Minnelli.

Having staged a number of prestigious Broadway shows, he was invited to Hollywood by MGM producer Arthur Freed to become one of the leading figures in the studio's efforts to reinvigorate – indeed, revolutionise – film musical. As a Broadway director, Minnelli had not merely been conerned to nurture his performers, but had frequently designed their costumes and supervised their lighting. What he studied at MGM, thanks to Freed's careful and intensive grooming, were specifically filmic skills; and he was only gradually eased into direction by being permitted to stage isolated musical numbers in such films as *Strike Up The Band* (1940), *Babes On Broadway* (1941), both starring his future wife, Judy Garland, and *Panama Hattie* (1942) starring Ann Sothern. In at least the latter work, Minnelli's contribution

proved far more stylish and imaginative than the film as a whole.

In 1942 he directed his first solo feature *Cabin In The Sky*, a charming all-black musical fantasy featuring the formidable talents of Ethel Waters, Lena Horne, Louis Armstrong, Duke Ellington and Cab Calloway. Minnelli did a remarkable job and, if the film sometimes seems cramped and impersonal, this is almost certainly due to its relatively small budget and the fact that he was denied the expressive possibilities of colour, a crucial dimension in almost all of his mature work. *I Dood It* (1943), a limp Red Skelton farce which he had been assigned to 'save' after its original director had been dismissed, was a totally unsatisfactory experience but, in 1944, he completed his first truly 'Minnellian' work: *Meet Me In St Louis* was an enchanting slice of turn-of-the-century Americana starring Judy Garland (whom he married the following year and divorced in 1951: Liza Minnelli

Above: Judy Garland aboard the trolley in *Meet Me In St Louis* (1944). She was at her most enchanting in this beautifully realised work and, the following year, the director became the second of her five husbands.

Left: Minnelli gives his wife, Judy Garland, a couple of pointers for her 'Look For The Silver Lining' number in *Till The Clouds Roll By* (1946), a lavish biopic of composer Jerome Kern. Judy played Broadway star Marilyn Miller. Her husband directed her numbers – Richard Whorf directed the movie.

Below left: Fred Astaire and Lucille Bremer in the romantic 'This Heart Of Mine' number from *Ziegfeld Follies* (1944.

'Lust For Life remains my favourite film, simply because it contains more of my favourite moments than any other film I've directed'

is, of course, their daughter) and based on the 'New Yorker' stories of Sally Benson. *Meet Me In St Louis* is perhaps most notable in film history for the subtle way in which the musical numbers evolve with total conviction out of the unshow-bizzy narrative. As Minnelli put it: 'I liked to feel that numbers should be given as much importance as dramatic sequences, that they should be woven into the story completely in a way they hadn't been hitherto.' The youthful and nostalgically light-hearted nature of the material (one of its highlights was a celebrated Halloween sequence with the delightful Margaret O'Brien) should not deceive one regarding the genuine riches to be found here, for the picture repays reviewing many times. It established Minnelli as the outstanding colour stylist of the 40s musical with a flowing camera technique to match. A tremendous box-office hit, the film made Garland's name, and paved the way for the cycle of outstanding MGM musicals in Technicolor which followed.

His succeeding film was a new departure. *The Clock*, a magical if sentimental comedy-drama of a young soldier (Robert Walker) with a 48-hour pass in New York, during which he meets, courts and marries a secretary (Judy Garland), was filmed almost entirely on the MGM lot in 1944; it was delicately handled by Minnelli, who drew near-miraculous performances from the two principals and a cluster of eccentric supporting actors. In the next year, however, the director returned to his more outlandishly garish style with the musical extravaganza *Yolanda And The Thief*, whose stars – Fred Astaire and, especially, the somewhat inadequate Lucille Bremer – were all but swamped by the outrageous cod-Latin American decors. In a sense, its problem – an intermittently chronic one for the director – was that of reconciling purely narrative exigencies with his own often overripe flair for visual elaboration. This did not arise with *Ziegfeld Follies*, a plotless spectacle which opened in Heaven, with the great showman (played

by William Powell, not for the first time in the American cinema) imagining an ideal cast for one of his shows, and whose highlight, one of Minnelli's finest achievements, was the 'Limehouse Blues' ballet with Astaire. For some critics and spectators, over-elaboration seriously cramps the charm of such musical entertainments as *The Pirate* (1948), starring Gene Kelly and Judy Garland, scored by Cole Porter and set in an extremely airless and

stagey Caribbean; *Brigadoon* (1954), Lerner and Loewe's whimsical fantasy about a Scottish village which materialises only once in a century; and *Kismet* (1955), a leaden Arabian Nights fairy tale with Howard Keel, Ann Blyth and Dolores Gray which borrowed its score from Borodin and its style straight from Broadway. Even such a splendid example of the genre as *An American In Paris*, winner of an Oscar for the best film

Top: Howard Keel (centre) in *Kismet* (1955), from the Broadway musical to a score by Borodin, and not one of Minnelli's memorable achievements. There were two previous, non-musical versions, in 1930 and 1944.

Above: The devastating Cyd Charisse in the Michael Kidd-choreographed 'Girl Hunt' ballet from *The Band Wagon* (1953), a superbly integrated Minnelli musical.

of 1951, could be criticised for its rather pretentious climactic ballet based on the creations of some of the greatest artists of the École de Paris. Yet it remains one of its director's most achieved works, thanks to a wonderful cast (Kelly, Leslie Caron, Oscar Levant), a brilliant Gershwin score and the incomparable zest and elegance with which Minnelli directed the musical numbers.

His natural (if, at the same time, highly artificial) brio was still more strongly in evidence in *The Band Wagon* (1953), in part because it constituted a departure from the 'integrated musical' which he had helped to pioneer and a glorious return to, and celebration of, the kind of dizzy, unrepentant backstage show which he had once sought to displace. Of the remaining musicals, the best is without question *Gigi*, a 1958 adaptation of Colette's novella with a superb score by Lerner and Loewe, unforgettable designs by Cecil Beaton and uniformly enchanting performances from Leslie Caron (in the title role), Maurice Chevalier, Louis Jourdan and Hermione

Gingold. As well as earning a Best Film Academy Award, *Gigi* also won Minnelli himself an Oscar for direction and was his last big hit. In spite of incidental felicities, both *Bells Are Ringing* (1960) and *On A Clear Day You Can See Forever* (1970), the first with Judy Holliday (and Dean Martin), the second with Barbra Streisand, were too uneven to be ranked with his major work.

Though Minnelli is best remembered for his musicals, these actually form less than half of his complete output. He was responsible, for instance, for a few richly textured melodramas, from the dark and velvety *Undercurrent* (1946), with Katharine Hepburn, Robert Taylor and Robert Mitchum, to *The Bad And The Beautiful* (1952), a marvellously racy and entertaining exposé of Hollywood starring Kirk Douglas, Lana Turner, Dick Powell; from *The Cobweb* (1955), an adaptation of William Gibson's novel about the staff and inmates of a mental institution, to *Two Weeks In Another Town*

(1962), a flashy but diverting account of American moviemakers at Cinecittà in the 'dolce vita' 60s which, like *The Bad And The Beautiful*, featured Kirk Douglas in a study of charismatic megalomania. Many of these melodramas went 'over the top' in the first reel and stayed perched up there during their entire running time; but it was one of Minnelli's most striking (and often refreshing) qualities that he was innately incapable of half-measures, as was evident from his overheated but effective and moving biopic of Vincent Van Gogh, *Lust For Life* (1956), with Douglas, again, as the half-demented Dutch artist. When the director attempted to handle more fragile material, such as *Tea And Sympathy* (1956), with John Kerr as a young college student uncertain of his sexuality and his namesake, Deborah, as the understanding professor's wife who initiates him into manhood, the result was fey and unconvincing; and it is possible to prefer the sheer energy and vulgarity of such gaudy spectacles as *Some Came Running* (1959), with Frank Sinatra,

Dean Martin and Shirley MacLaine, and *Home From The Hill* (1960), with Robert Mitchum and Eleanor Parker.

With his cycle of comedies Minnelli, though never forfeiting his flair for the visually fetching, managed to loosen up and, as he himself admitted, 'use a simple style to match the simplicity of the subject'. Thus *Father Of The Bride* (1950), with Spencer Tracy and Joan Bennett, was a charming satire, both relaxed and pointed, of middle-class domesticity; *The Long Long Trailer* (1954) was a droll Technicolor farce with the adulated TV couple of Lucille Ball and Desi Arnaz (these were his biggest hits of the early 50s, along with *An American In Paris*); *Designing Woman* (1957) paired Gregory Peck with Lauren Bacall to striking effect in a plot that one would have considered more Cukorian than Minnellian; and, even as late as 1963, *The Courtship Of Eddie's Father* possessed all the 'warmth and charmth', as Goldwyn might have phrased it, of *Father Of The Bride*.

A sensitive and intelligent man, Minnelli lacked the kind of toughness which would have better enabled him to survive in the Hollywood jungle. Although he remained at MGM for over twenty years, he was forced to make many compromises. He was not given the opportunity to do a dramatic picture in colour, for example, until *The Cobweb* in 1955; then was forced to use CinemaScope, too. In order to film a favourite project, *Lust For Life*, he had to agree to direct *Kismet* against his better judgement. He stayed on at MGM in spite of the fact that some of the most remarkable Paris sequences in *Gigi* were chopped out by the studio bosses and reshot in Hollywood at the behest of Lerner and Loewe. ('I Remember It Well', for example, was shot against a dreadful looking studio backdrop). Finally, *Two Weeks In Another Town* was also badly cut by the studio. Minnelli recalls, 'It's painful to talk about the ruin of that film even now'.

But Minnelli was not well equipped to survive outside MGM either, and by the time he left the studio, in 1963, he was really too old and set in his ways to make a successful fresh start. A ghastly reincarnation farce at Fox, *Goodbye Charlie* (1964), was followed by a risible Burton-Taylor vehicle, *The Sandpiper* (1965) and a curiously unfocused melodrama set in Italy with Ingrid Bergman and his daughter Liza, *A Matter Of Time* (1976). All were commercial flops, and a sad end to a distinguished career.

Above: Spencer Tracy and Joan Bennett as the parents of Elizabeth Taylor in *Father Of The Bride* (1950), a delightful, non-musical comedy, directed with easy flair and gaining Oscar nominations for Tracy and Best Picture.

Left: Louis Jourdan, Leslie Caron and Maurice Chevalier in *Gigi* (1958), the frothy, elegant musical from Colette's novel which won the Best Picture and Best Director awards.

Below: Director Minnelli with stars Kirk Douglas and Cyd Charisse during *Two Weeks In Another Town* (1962), a somewhat melodramatic subject (ex-alcoholic film director attempts comeback) from a best-selling novel by Irwin Shaw. Cut by the studio (MGM), it was not a success for Minnelli.

'I was working for a big commercial studio and I had to accept everything I was given; but there are ways of achieving a certain quality in a film in spite of its lack of promise as a subject; and I hope I managed to raise the level fairly often'

JEAN NEGULESCO

Born Craiova, Rumania, 26 February 1900. **Died** 1984

Jean Negulesco started out directing tough black-and-white thrillers and drama at Warner Bros. during the 40s, but some softening became evident soon after he joined 20th Century-Fox where he remained throughout the 50s. From 1953 onwards, he specialised in glossy and colourful, albeit utterly superficial entertainments filmed in the studio's new CinemaScope process, but he will be most fondly remembered for his earlier and grittier movies.

Negulesco's original aspiration to become a painter drew him to Paris where, as a pupil of the sculptor Brancusi and a friend of Modigliani, he practised his art with a degree of success before emigrating to the US in 1929. His earliest employment in the cinema was as technical advisor on a rape scene in Paramount's *The Story Of Temple Drake* (1933), based on Faulkner's 'Sanctuary'. He progressed as assistant producer, second unit director (notably, on Borzage's *A Farewell To Arms*) and associate director, an unusual credit; he was also responsible for an experimental short, *Three And A Day*, which starred Mischa Auer. When his first assignment at Warner Bros., a version of Dashiell Hammett's 'The Maltese Falcon', fell through because of John Huston's interest in the same project for *his* debut, and he was removed from another film, *Singapore Woman*, before shooting was complete, Negulesco began to despair of ever making it as a feature director. A chance meeting with Anatole Litvak, however, brought another novel to his attention and his career finally got under way with an adaptation of Eric Ambler's *The Mask Of Dimitrios* (1944). Featuring Peter Lorre, Sydney Greenstreet and Zachary Scott as the eponymous adventurer, it was a well-paced, atmospheric thriller with an intriguing flashback structure. He followed this with two further Lorre and Greenstreet collaborations, *The Conspirators* (also 1944) and *Three Strangers* (1946); and, in a different key, made his delirious melodrama with Joan Crawford and John Garfield, *Humoresque* (1947). Crawford's suicide in the latter film, wading into the ocean to the overwrought strains of Wagner's 'Liebestod' from *Tristan And Isolde*, is a choice specimen of Hollywood kitsch.

The triumph of his career came with another melodrama, *Johnny Belinda* (1948), whose heroine – a young deaf mute played by Jane Wyman – was a considerable source of concern to Warner's executives, perhaps, as Negulesco once suggested, because it was the studio which had originated the talkies! Nevertheless, it had the perhaps unique distinction of receiving Oscar nominations in every category (excluding costume design), twelve in all and including Negulesco's only nomination for directing. The only winner was Jane Wyman. The director followed it with another of his best works, *Road House* (1948), the first at his new studio, Fox, and starring Ida Lupino and Cornel Wilde with

Richard Widmark in one of his juiciest characteristically sadistic roles. According to Negulesco, what Zanuck hoped to achieve was the kind of film 'we used to make at Warner Bros., with Pat O'Brien and Jimmy Cagney, in which every time the action flagged we staged a fight and every time a man passed a girl she'd adjust her stocking or something, trying to be sexy'. A pretty fair comment on the pleasures of *Road House*.

His subsequent work under Zanuck, however, proved consistently inferior, from *The Mudlark* (1950), a sentimental period drama with Irene Dunne as Queen Victoria and Alec Guinness as Disraeli, to the soft-focus avalanche of 'women's pictures' with which he was latterly associated. He had smash hits with two of the first CinemaScope films, *How To Marry A Millionaire* (1953) starring Marilyn Monroe, Lauren Bacall and Betty Grable, and *Three Coins In The Fountain* (1954), nominated for a Best Picture Oscar. Of less interest was *Woman's World* (1954), followed by the musical *Daddy Long Legs* with Fred Astaire and Leslie Caron (1955), *Boy On A Dolphin* (1957), *A Certain Smile* (1958) and the none too appropriately titled *The Best Of Everything* (1959).

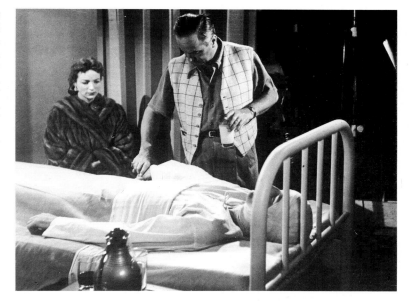

Left: Director Negulesco directs actress Beatrice Straight in a flashback sequence from *Phone Call From A Stranger* (1952), a somewhat forced and unmemorable 'compendium' drama.

Above: *Johnny Belinda* (1948), starred Jane Wyman as a deaf mute in an isolated fishing community who is raped, and Lew Ayres as the sympathetic local doctor who gets involved. A powerful melodrama in its day, it remains Negulesco's most prestigious Hollywood film.

Left: The one and only Marilyn in *How To Marry A Millionaire* (1953), an inoffensive but pale echo of *Gentlemen Prefer Blondes* and the first CinemasScope comedy. It was a smash hit for the director.

MICHAEL POWELL

Born Canterbury, England, 30 September 1905.

The most original, imaginative and distinctively modern of British directors and, for many years, one of the most underrated, Michael Powell, enjoyed his biggest successes during the 40s, in close partnership with the Hungarian-born scriptwriter Emeric Pressburger. Together they forged a uniquely flavoured creative collaboration, bringing many unusual, and original, subjects to the screen, and working in Technicolor at a time when most other 'serious' directors were filming in black-and-white.

It was fortuitous that young Michael's father owned a hotel at Cap Ferrat in Southern France, not far from Rex Ingram's Victorine Studios. First attracted to the cinema as a teenager, he got some valuable early experience as an assistant and bit player on a number of Rex Ingram productions, and has recalled Ingram's influence, beginning with *Mare Nostrum* (MGM) in 1925. 'It was a great film to come in on . . . a spectacular film, full of enormous tricks with a great theme and an international cast. It was the kind of film that gives you ideas that stay with you all your life.'

Back in England Powell found occasional work as a scriptwriter and second unit director, and directed a pair of short B-features in 1931. These were moderately successful, and demonstrated his talent for getting good results in spite of tight schedules and miniscule budgets. For example, with *Star Reporter* (1932), when he needed some shots of an ocean liner docking, he simply went off to Southampton with a hand camera and shot the footage himself. Powell treated these 'quota quickies' as a challenge and had turned out over twenty of them – comedies, thrillers and adventures – by 1936 when he got his first real break with *The Edge Of The World*, shot on the remote Shetland island of Foula and dramatising the plight of its aging and dwindling population. (The director returned to a similar theme and setting, but with a more assured treatment, in *I Know Where I'm Going* in 1945.)

Taken up by producer Alexander Korda, Powell was assigned to direct Conrad Veidt in *The Spy In Black* (1939) from a weak script about Skapa Flow and German attempts at naval sabotage during World War I. But it all came right with the appearance of a new writer, Emeric Pressburger, who did a fine job of reworking the original. Powell went on to co-direct an additional pair of films for Korda: *The Lion Has Wings* (1939), a morale-boosting propaganda feature, was rushed out at the beginning of the war, while *The Thief Of Bagdad* (1940) provided a welcome taste of screen fantasy and a first chance to work in Technicolor. He directed the ship and harbour sequences and most of the scenes with Sabu. Meanwhile, his budding partnership with Pressburger forged ahead with the wartime thriller *Contraband* (1940), filmed in a blacked out London, followed by *49th Parallel* (1941), a propaganda adventure movie

about the experiences of the crew of a German submarine stranded in Canada. Nominated for a Best Picture Oscar under its American title, *The Invaders*, Pressburger picked up an Oscar for his original story, and was jointly nominated with Powell for the original screenplay of their next together, *One Of Our Aircraft Is Missing* (1942). Neatly reversing the situation of *49th Parallel*, the main characters were members of a British bomber crew forced to bail out over occupied Holland.

Demonstrating an authentically creative approach to wartime subjects which encompassed off-beat humour and a sense of the absurd, Powell's unconventional but British viewpoint was balanced by Pressburger's Continental sophistication and ensured that their movies were full of surprises. By 1943 they had firmly established their production company, The Archers, within the Independent Producers group backed by J. Arthur Rank, and were ready to really stretch themselves. This they did magnificently with *The Life And Death Of Colonel Blimp*, photographed in Technicolor by Georges Périnal and designed by Alfred Junge. A sophisticated, original and complex work, almost three hours long, it used a flashback structure in covering approximately forty years in the life of its leading character. Counterpointing the experiences of a young British officer (Roger Livesey) with his German counterpart (Anton Walbrook), the film is both intimate and witty in treating their personal stories, yet broad in scope, ranging from the Boer War and 1902 Berlin, to 1918 Flanders and London at war in 1942. Along the way it touches on those changes in the military mentality

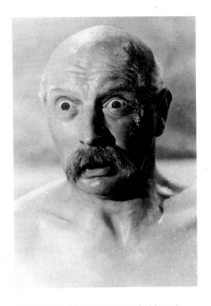

Above: Roger Livesey – a remarkable make-up job – as the elderly Blimp in *The Life And Death Of Colonel Blimp* (1943), an imaginative treatment of the hero, spanning three wars.

Left: Novelist Rumer Godden (seated centre) visits the set at Pinewood Studios during filming of her novel, *Black Narcissus* (1946). She was photographed with star Deborah Kerr and, standing left to right, Emeric Pressburger, director Powell, and art director Alfred Junge.

Below: One of the best ballet films ever made, and Powell's colour masterpiece, *The Red Shoes* (1948) starred Moira Shearer, here dancing with Robert Helpmann (left) and Leonid Massine (right).

wartime drama (in black-and-white), *The Small Back Room* (1949). Jennifer Jones as a wild country girl and the picturesque Shropshire landscapes made *Gone To Earth* (aka *The Wild Heart*, 1950) a memorable experience, while David Niven was charming and witty as *The Elusive Pimpernel* (1950). For *The Tales Of Hoffmann* (1951) and *Oh Rosalinda!* (1955), P & P found their inspiration in Jacques Offenbach and Johann Strauss respectively. *Hoffmann* reunited many of the dancers and collaborators from *The Red Shoes*, but except for a few brilliant sequences, fell far short of the earlier work. Still looking back to the 40s, P & P brought their long and fruitful partnership to a close with a pair of war pictures, *The Battle Of The River Plate* and *Ill Met By Moonlight* in 1956.

Working on his own Powell directed one last memorable movie, a genuinely chilling psychological horror, *Peeping Tom* (1959), which rivals Hitchcock's *Psycho* (Paramount, 1960) as the scariest movie to come from a major director and which, to Powell's surprise, was attacked by censors and critics alike. He directed a few last features and some TV episodes during the 60s, and most recently served as technical advisor on a Russian production, *Anna Pavlova*.

'Powell can easily be written off as an eccentric decorator of fantasies. Against persistent British attempts to dignify realism, Powell must have seemed gaudy, distasteful and effete'

David Thomson in 'A Biographical Dictionary of the Cinema'

Left: The sultry and beautiful Jennifer Jones starred in *Gone To Earth*, aka *The Wild Heart* (1950), from the romantic novel by Mary Webb.

Below left: Director Powell at work with Robert Rounseville and ballerina Ludmilla Tcherina, making the 'Venice' sequences for *The Tales Of Hoffman* (1951).

Below: Ballerina and actress Moira Shearer appeared in *Peeping Tom* (1959). Here, she is with Carl Boehm who played the lead role of the young murderer.

which take place, from the anachronistic German officer code of duelling, to the rise of Nazism and the 'total warfare' of World War II. The project was so disliked by Churchill that he considered trying to stop it, on the grounds that it was 'detrimental to the morale of the army'; he wanted to ban the completed version, or at least keep it from going abroad, but was convinced by Minister of Information Brendan Bracken that, 'as the film is so boring, I cannot believe that it will do any harm . . .'.

A bizarre, but atmospheric and likeable wartime morality tale, *A Canterbury Tale* (1944), was filmed in and around the director's home town and was followed by *I Know Where I'm Going*. Then Powell and Pressburger embarked on a series of ambitious Technicolor productions beginning with *A Matter Of Life And Death* (1946) starring David Niven, which presented a new variation on the theme of heavenly visitors to earth which was popular during the 40s. The stunningly photographed and designed *Black Narcissus* (1947), adapted from Rumer God-

den's novel, demonstrated Powell's great technical facility with colour, wedded to his love of exotic subjects. The main setting, a monastery in the Himalayas, was effectively brought to life in a British studio. Deborah Kerr starred and the film won Oscars for art direction and cinematography. But Powell's legitimate claim to be regarded as the *leading* director working in colour during the 40s was triumphantly confirmed by his masterpiece, *The Red Shoes* (1948). Here colour was seen by him as an 'essential element of the film's theatrical, fantasy and non-naturalistic conception'. The best film ever made about the ballet and the nature of the creative process, it starred Moira Shearer, Leonid Massine and Robert Helpmann along with Anton Walbrook. A smash hit in the US and one of the most successful British films of all time, it was nominated for Best Picture and Screenplay Oscars, and won for its evocative score (by Brian Easdale) and the superb colour art direction.

Having reached their creative peak, Powell and Pressburger made one last

OTTO PREMINGER

Born Vienna, 5 December 1906

One of a select group of Jewish-Viennese directors who brought a special European sensibility to Hollywood, Otto Preminger's early years were far from typical of the Jewish middle class, for his father was the Prosecutor General to the Hapsburg Empire. The young man also studied law, but was more interested in the theatre, and did a little acting for Max Reinhardt. He preferred directing, however, was active in the Austrian theatre during the early 30s, and was engaged to direct a play in New York late in 1935. He continued on to Hollywood with his first wife, actress Marion Mill, where he was contracted by 20th Century-Fox and directed a pair of B pictures – a Lawrence Tibbett musical and a comedy starring Ann Sothern and Jack Haley – but a dispute with studio chief Darryl Zanuck over the production of *Kidnapped* (1938) ended his Fox contract and caused him to be blackballed by the other studios. His Hollywood directing career appeared to be over before it had begun.

Unable to find work in Tinseltown, he returned to the New York theatre and directed a number of plays during 1938–41, including 'Margin For Error' by Clare Booth Luce. When an actor cast in the role of a Nazi agent dropped out, Otto was persuaded to take his place and, along with the play, was a big hit. The screen rights were acquired by 20th Century-Fox, and Otto found himself back at the same studio he had left under a cloud four years before, adamant that he would only act in the film version of the play if he was also allowed to direct it.

The success of *Margin For Error* (1942) gained Preminger a new contract as producer and director. He was assigned to produce *Laura* (1944) with Rouben Mamoulian directing but, when problems developed and Mamoulian left, Otto was ready to take over. This was just the opportunity he needed to demonstrate his qualities as a director handling a first rate script and cast, the latter headed by Gene Tierney, Dana Andrews, and Clifton Webb who had been specially selected for the movie (his first sound film) by Preminger and became a leading Fox star for the next fifteen years. *Laura* presented an original and inventive reworking of a situation familiar in psychological murder mysteries – a detective (Andrews) attempting to uncover the true murderer from a group of suspects, each with a possible motive. The film established the now familiar Preminger style – a love of long takes and a fluid camera, following the movements of his characters and observing them in a particularly impersonal and objective manner. A great success for all concerned, *Laura* picked up four Oscar nominations including one for Webb (as supporting actor) and for Preminger (his first), while Joseph LaShelle won the award for his fine camerawork. Preminger thus joined the ranks of the many outstanding 'new' directors of the early 40s (Kazan and Mankiewicz among them) whose arrival both reflected and rein-

forced a new upgrading of the status of the director in Hollywood. As a contract director, however, Otto was given few opportunities to display his talent, but he did demonstrate versatility with his varied assignments. He replaced the ailing Lubitsch on a lightweight costume piece, *Royal Scandal*, late in 1944, then was reunited with Dana Andrews on the thriller *Fallen Angel* (1945), which also starred Alice Faye in one of her rare dramatic roles. Some of her best scenes ended up on the cutting room floor, contributing to her decision to retire, for the studio was building up co-star Linda Darnell at Faye's expense. Consequently, Preminger found himself reluctantly directing Miss Darnell in a pair of Technicolor costumers – *Centennial Summer* (1946) and *Forever Amber* (1947) – both moderate hits.

Preminger was back on form (in black-and-white) with *Daisy Kenyon* (1947), a perceptive triangle drama in which he successfully avoided the clichés of the 'woman's picture', demonstrating a lucid and sensible approach to his characters and some nice humorous touches. (Joan Crawford was the career woman torn between two men – Dana Andrews and Henry Fonda.) Then Otto completed the Lubitsch-Betty Grable musical, *That Lady In Ermine* (1948) after the death of Lubitsch, remade an earlier Lubitsch movie, *Lady Windermere's Fan* (Warner Bros., 1925) now simply retitled *The Fan* (1949), then made a welcome return to

film noir during 1949–52. Jose Ferrer was an effective villain in *Whirlpool* (1949), exerting his hypnotic control over Gene Tierney, while *Where The Sidewalk Ends* (1950) reunited the *Laura* team of Tierney, Andrews and top cameraman Joseph LaShelle. A sophisticated *policier* scripted by Ben Hecht, the old master of the genre, it had a gritty, naturalist feel reflecting Preminger's development away from the studio filming of earlier years. Extensive location filming featured too in *Angel Face* (1952), the last and best of Preminger's *noir* cycle, made on loanout to RKO, about the destructive relationship between chauffeur Robert

Left: Six years after the success of the superior *film noir, Laura*, its stars, Dana Andrews and Gene Tierney, were reunited for *Where The Sidewalk Ends* (1950). About a policeman who accidentally kills a suspect and tries to implicate a gang leader, the film was unusual in its moral slant.

Above: As an actor, Preminger specialised in the arrogant Nazi officer image. This is how he appeared as the POW camp commandant in Billy Wilder's successful *Stalag 17* (1953).

Below: Frank Sinatra, whose career has proved him to be a very gifted dramatic actor, wrestled with heroin addiction in *The Man With The Golden Arm* (1955). Kim Novak, with him here, was one of his co-stars.

Mitchum and the sweetly lovely Jean Simmons, cast against type as a spoilt, rich and murderous girl.

The years 1952–53 marked a turning point for Preminger in both his private and professional life. Known as a ladies' man who escorted some of the most attractive women in Hollywood during the 40s – a then secret affair with Gypsy Rose Lee produced a son – his playboy years were over when he married for the second time. His contract with Fox was coming to an end, and he was eager to strike out on his own as an independent producer-director. For his director friend Billy Wilder he agreed to play a Nazi officer on the screen one last time, appearing in his best remembered role as the arrogant prison camp commandant of *Stalag 17* (Paramount, 1953) just before directing his first independent production, *The Moon Is Blue* (UA, 1953).

the all-black musical *Carmen Jones* allowed Dorothy Dandridge to give a stunning and sexy performance.

During later years, Otto Preminger's movies became bigger, but not necessarily better, as he travelled all over the world. A disastrous version of Shaw's *Saint Joan* (UA, 1957) starring his much publicised discovery, Jean Seberg, was shot in England; he went to France for *Bonjour Tristesse* (Columbia, 1957); to Israel for *Exodus* (UA, 1960). These were all adapted from novels, as were the excellent *Advise And Consent* (Columbia, 1962) dealing with the political scene in Washington, and the international production, *The Cardinal* (Columbia, 1963), which earned Otto his first Oscar nomination for direction since *Laura*. But the best film of these years was, in fact, a relatively small scale black-and-white adaptation of the Robert Traver novel, *Anat-*

Above: Marilyn Monroe starred as a saloon singer in *River Of No Return* (1954), a CinemaScope and Technicolor Western set during the California Gold Rush.

Far left: Harry Belafonte strangles the faithless Dorothy Dandridge in the all-black musical, *Carmen Jones* (1954). Only the most rigid purists among opera lovers could object to this clever reworking of Bizet's *Carmen*, with its glorious music intact but given appropriate new lyrics by Oscar Hammerstein II.

Left: *Anatomy Of A Murder* (1959) starred James Stewart (left) as a small-town defence lawyer, here with eminent jazz musician Duke Ellington. A powerful drama from a best-selling novel, it gave George C. Scott his first notable part, as the prosecuting counsel.

During the following years he emerged as a leading director personality in the tradition of other tough, uncompromising men like Stroheim and De Mille. Known as a hard taskmaster, his reputation as one of Hollywood's most autocratic and temperamental directors was naturally connected with his Nazi screen roles and was further reinforced by the controversy surrounding a number of his productions. *The Moon Is Blue*, for example, was little more than a filmed play, shot quickly and cheaply in simultaneous English and German language versions. But because it used such banned words as 'seduce' and 'virgin' the film was refused a Production Code Seal. United Artists agreed to release the film anyway; the ensuing controversy gained much free publicity and turned it into an unexpected smash hit. Otto again challenged the Code in making a film about drug addiction, *The Man With The Golden Arm* (UA, 1955) starring Frank Sinatra, and had an even bigger hit. In between (in 1954) he returned to Fox where he made his first movies in the studio's new widescreen CinemaScope process, demonstrating a real fluency and inventiveness in adapting to this new format. *River Of No Return* was a romantic and entertaining Western (with songs) starring Marilyn Monroe and Robert Mitchum, while

omy Of A Murder (Columbia, 1959), in which James Stewart gave one of his best ever performances as the easygoing but shrewd small town lawyer defending Ben Gazzara against a murder charge. A big hit, it was nominated for seven Oscars including Best Picture.

Preminger continued active as a director throughout the 60s and early 70s with a series of generally disappointing productions of which the most interesting was the New York-based black comedy, *Such Good Friends* (Paramount, 1971) starring Dyan Cannon.

'Preminger is a great showman who has never bothered to learn anything about making a movie... no one is more skilled at giving the appearance of dealing with large controversial themes in a bold way, without making the tactical error of doing so'

Dwight MacDonald in 'The New Yorker', 1964

NICHOLAS RAY

Born La Crosse, Wisconsin, 7 August 1911. **Died** 1979

One of the most perceptive, sensitive and talented of American directors Nicholas Ray, alas, never really fulfilled his great promise. Having spent a dozen years working in Hollywood, followed by a brief period in Europe during the early 60s, Ray virtually gave up directing during the last seventeen years of his life. He worked as a lecturer in film studies and collaborated on a few non-commercial projects with his students and with the German director, Wim Wenders who specially admired him. He was the subject of a documentary, *I'm A Stranger Here Myself* (1974), the title quoting an appropriate line from his own feature, *Johnny Guitar* (1953). During his final year Ray starred in and co-directed *Lightning Over Water* with Wenders, a powerful final *hommage* and testament. The diversity of Ray's early training and work experience provided a useful background for him as a movie director whose early films were all concerned with aspects of contemporary American society. He had studied architecture at the University of Chicago (under Frank Lloyd Wright), acted on stage (directed by Elia Kazan), wrote and directed for the radio, and travelled widely around the US writing and directing community theatre and developing his interest in American folk culture.

Reunited with Kazan in Hollywood in 1944, he served as 'creative assistant' on *A Tree Grows In Brooklyn* (20th Century-Fox), then made his own name as a director soon after, collaborating with producer John Houseman on one of the first television dramas of note, *Sorry Wrong Number*, followed by *They Live By Night* filmed for RKO in mid-1947. Already in this, his first feature, Ray demonstrated a full command of filmic language, a special talent for working with new, young, and relatively inexperienced stars (Farley Granger and Cathy O'Donnell), and a strong emotional involvement with his characters. The picture was fresh and original in its treatment of the familiar theme of a pair of doomed lovers on the run who, as an opening title states, were 'never properly introduced to the world we live in'. There was more than a hint of the kind of social consciousness (and social conscience) which would feature in many of Ray's subsequent movies. Similarly, the parallel between the older and younger generations was taken up in his follow-up picture, *Knock On Any Door*, filmed in 1948 and the first of two he made for Humphrey Bogart's company, Santana (releasing through Columbia), with Bogart starring. More conventional than *They Live By Night* in its treatment of juvenile delinquency (seen as the result of a broken home and poverty), the film provided John Derek with his first major role and Ray with his first hit. Under RKO's eccentric new owner, Howard Hughes, *They Live By Night* was not widely released until late in 1949, after *Knock On Any Door*, and around the time that Ray was completing his second (and better) Bogart movie, *In A Lonely Place*. Bogie's performance as a hard-boiled and occasionally violent screenwriter presents a fully developed example of the type of alienated modern hero who appeared in many Ray films, here well-matched by Gloria Grahame (Ray's second wife), as the sympathetic and intelligent girl who is initially attracted but wisely leaves him in the end.

Another intense relationship at the core of *On Dangerous Ground* (1950) was made convincing by fine performances from Robert Ryan and Ida Lupino. For some reason Ray himself has referred to this film as an 'absolute failure' – possibly because of the upbeat ending – yet it stands out as an excellent example of how the director at his best could use the thriller format as the basis for an extremely moving and effective human drama. It was filmed back at RKO, the studio where Ray would spend the next few years developing an unusual working relationship with Howard Hughes, who wanted him to take over as production chief. Ray refused, but he did agree to re-shoot parts of a number of movies which Hughes considered unreleasable in their present form including John Cromwell's *The Racket* (1951) and Von Sternberg's *Macao* (1952), as well as directing a weak John Wayne vehicle, *Flying Leathernecks* (1951) in Technicolor. He closed out his RKO years with *The Lusty Men*, a well-acted action-drama about rodeo riders which made superb use of yet another well-matched couple, Robert Mitchum and Susan Hayward. The film was one of a number of memorable releases in RKO's last good year, 1952.

In many respects Ray's next movie marked a departure for him. He was hired, along with a first-rate cast and crew, by the tiny Republic studio in an effort to upgrade its B-picture image. The result was *Johnny Guitar*, his first Western, and his first venture into 19th-century America, which provided him with his first opportunity to work creatively in colour. (He would only once return to black-and-white – for *Bitter Victory*, Columbia, 1957.) A marvellously over-the-top entertainment, it was the best picture ever filmed in Republic's own Trucolor process. The film presented a highly original and witty reworking of a classic Western situation; and the limited tonal range was used by Ray in an appropriately stylised, symbolic manner which suited the larger-than-life Freudian drama, pitting gun-toting saloon owner Joan Crawford against Mercedes McCambridge and her vengeful cronies.

It was a moderate hit and Ray followed with another Western, *Run For Cover* (Paramount, 1954) starring James Cagney and filmed in the new VistaVision widescreen format. But the director was soon back to his preoccupation with contemporary American society in *Rebel Without A Cause* (Warner Bros., 1955), his best known picture and biggest 50s hit. One of his most personal and carefully prepared projects, it presented the fullest expression of his earlier interest in the theme of youthful rebellion and the 'generation gap' – here seen through the eyes of the teenagers themselves. Ray worked closely with his young cast, particularly his charismatic star, James Dean. More of a stylised and deeply felt view of 50s youthful alienation, than a strictly naturalistic one, *Rebel*'s reputation over the years as a cult classic has been given greater poignancy by Ray's painful death from cancer, matched by the violent and horrible deaths of all three of its young stars – Dean, Sal Mineo and, most recently, Natalie Wood. (Both Mineo and Wood were nominated for Oscars, while Ray received his only nomination for writing the original story.)

Inevitably, the star aura of *Rebel* overshadowed the director's next film – and sadly undervalued masterpiece – *Bigger Than Life* (20th Century-Fox, 1956), produced by and starring James Mason

as a school teacher hooked on drugs. Again Ray demonstrated his mastery of CinemaScope and proved that an intimate family picture and serious character study could be handled effectively within the new format (and in colour). The film presents Ray's most penetrating critique of American middle-class values. It was not commercially successful and proved to be his last dealing with contemporary American society. During the following years he moved ever farther away from his current interests, with flawed ventures into the outlaw Western – *The True Story Of Jesse James* (20th Century-Fox, 1957), 19th-century ecology – *Wind Across The Everglades* (Warner Bros., 1958), and 30s gangsters – *Party Girl* (MGM, 1958). It is perhaps significant

'Nicholas Ray is not the greatest director who ever lived, nor is he a Hollywood hack. The truth lies somewhere in between'

Andrew Sarris in 'The American Cinema'

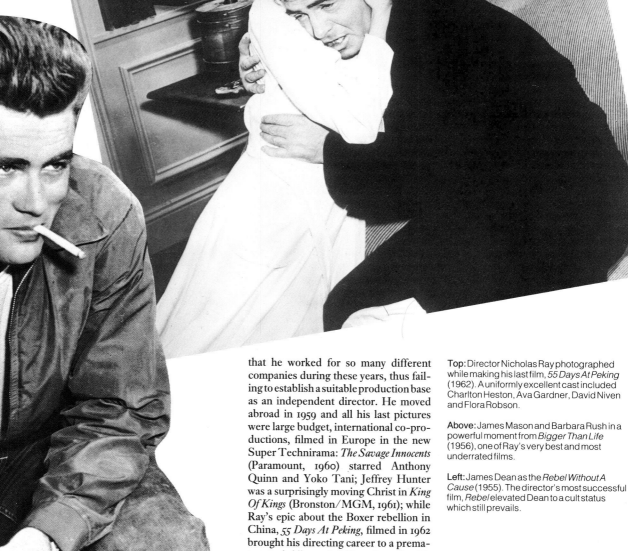

that he worked for so many different companies during these years, thus failing to establish a suitable production base as an independent director. He moved abroad in 1959 and all his last pictures were large budget, international co-productions, filmed in Europe in the new Super Technirama: *The Savage Innocents* (Paramount, 1960) starred Anthony Quinn and Yoko Tani; Jeffrey Hunter was a surprisingly moving Christ in *King Of Kings* (Bronston/MGM, 1961); while Ray's epic about the Boxer rebellion in China, *55 Days At Peking*, filmed in 1962 brought his directing career to a premature end. All were intelligently made with some fine performances, but they failed to live up to expectations at the box-office, and Nicholas Ray was through.

Top: Director Nicholas Ray photographed while making his last film, *55 Days At Peking* (1962). A uniformly excellent cast included Charlton Heston, Ava Gardner, David Niven and Flora Robson.

Above: James Mason and Barbara Rush in a powerful moment from *Bigger Than Life* (1956), one of Ray's very best and most underrated films.

Left: James Dean as the *Rebel Without A Cause* (1955). The director's most successful film, *Rebel* elevated Dean to a cult status which still prevails.

137

CAROL REED

Born London, 30 December 1906. **Died** 1976

Widely respected as one of the most solid and craftsmanlike of British directors, Carol Reed's career ran parallel to David Lean's for many years. Reed got a good head start as a director during the 30s when Lean was still an editor; both were employed for a time by J. Arthur Rank during the 40s, when Reed was clearly at his peak with a series of memorable movies which led to his being knighted in 1952 (his films won the top British Film Academy award for three consecutive years from 1947–49); by chance both directors came unstuck on a similar project late in their careers: Reed was replaced as director of MGM's *Mutiny On The Bounty* by Lewis Milestone in 1961, while Lean did extensive pre-production work on his *Bounty* project in the late 70s, but never got to direct it.

First attracted to the stage as a young man, Reed was employed by mystery writer Edgar Wallace from 1927 on as an occasional actor, then director of stage versions of his novels, and finally as a collaborator on movie adaptations. He worked briefly as a dialogue director and assistant director before co-directing a romantic comedy, *It Happened In Paris*. This was followed by his first solo effort, an entertaining adventure movie, *Midshipman Easy* (1935).

In spite of the diversity of his films, which ranged from adventure and thrillers to comedy and drama, with the odd musical thrown in, there is a central theme which runs through much of Reed's work. He prefers to observe his characters *displaced* from their normal surroundings. They are faced with the problems of coping with a strange, alien or even hostile environment, or just simply feel out of place – like Margaret Lockwood, the young nurse in *Bank Holiday* (1938), who is haunted by memories of a recent, tragic maternity case. In this picture, which first established Reed as a director of note, he mixed comedy and drama in observing the variety of ways in which a cross section of British characters experience a holiday weekend by the sea. Miss Lockwood was similarly far from home as one of the gold-digging showgirls trying to make it on their own in the light and entertaining comedy *A Girl Must Live* (1939), scripted by Frank Launder, and makes her definitive appearance as Reed's favourite 'damsel in distress' in the Launder-Gilliat scripted *Night Train To Munich* (1940). Here she played a Czech refugee trying to rescue her scientist father from the Nazis with the assistance of Rex Harrison, who effectively stole the film in one of his best early roles. He represented the Reed ideal of the resourceful British hero abroad, brave and witty in foiling the nasty Nazi agents, and the prototype for Reed's later war movies. In a brief diversion, the theme of the hero alienated from his lower-class background by virtue of his education (*The Stars Look Down*, 1939), and through inherited wealth (*Kipps*, 1942) – provided the opportunity for Michael Redgrave to demonstrate his versatility relatively early in his film career: intelligent and sensitive in the former, slow, bumbling and simpleminded in the latter.

Meanwhile, back at the home front, the familiar war situation of a group of men uprooted and flung together in the British conscript army in *The Way Ahead* (1944) fitted well into the Reed *oeuvre*. One of the very best of the many British war movies, it starred David Niven as the typically resourceful British officer type and was notable for the authentic treatment of basic training. (Reed had previously directed a training documentary, *The New Lot* in 1942, and served as co-director of the Oscar-winning feature-length documentary compilation film, *The True Glory*, 1945.)

Reed's first postwar production, *Odd Man Out* (1947), starred James Mason as

Above: Nancy Price and Michael Redgrave in *The Stars Look Down* (1939). The young Redgrave became one of England's most famous and distinguished theatrical knights. Married to actress Rachel Kempson, he fathered three gifted children, Vanessa, Corin and Lynn.

Left: Reed's collaboration with Graham Greene led to *The Fallen Idol* (1948), starring young Bobby Henrey. The boy is pictured here with Geoffrey Keene (left), Jack Hawkins, and Bernard Lee – later well-known as James Bond's 'M' (right).

Below: Carol Reed (centre) on set during filming of *The Third Man* (1950) with Orson Welles (left) and Joseph Cotten.

a wounded IRA man on the run, one of the most moving screen evocations of Reed's displaced, and in this case, doomed, hero. Packed a little too full of incident and atmospheric imagery to be entirely satisfactory, its stylised 'effects' were blended with a naturalistic use of locations, tellingly photographed in black-and-white by Robert Krasker. Although the film was well received, Reed left Rank to join Korda's London Films. In keeping with the pattern of successful British director-writer partnerships during the 40s (for example, Powell-Pressburger, Lean-Coward, Asquith-Rattigan), Carol Reed had worked closely with Frank Launder and Sidney Gilliat during 1938–42, but now embarked on his most successful collaboration, with distinguished novelist Graham Greene, on a pair of his best films.

The friendship between a butler and a young boy was the subject of the sensitively directed *The Fallen Idol* (1948). Apparently Reed was responsible (with Greene's approval) for some changes in the original story which made it an altogether lighter affair. As Greene himself explained, 'the subject no longer concerned a small boy who unwittingly betrayed his best friend to the police, but dealt instead with a boy who nearly procured his arrest by telling lies in his defence'. Outstanding performances from Ralph Richardson and young Bobby Henrey helped to lift the picture above the level of a simple thriller, with Jack Hawkins in one of his best early roles as a sympathetic police detective. But again, as with *Odd Man Out*, Reed was not entirely successful in integrating the extreme camera angles and stylised effects with the more naturalistic filming of London streets and settings.

No such problem existed with *The Third Man* (1950), Reed's most fully achieved work. Filmed in the deserted night-time streets, cafes and sewers of occupied, postwar Vienna, here the bare and unfriendly settings contributed palpably to the creation of mood. For Reed and writer Greene who collaborated closely on the script, everything came together. The fine international cast was headed by Joseph Cotten, Trevor Howard and Orson Welles who contributed some of his own best dialogue, including the famous 'cuckoo clock' speech; and the superbly appropriate and justly celebrated zither music of Anton Karas was matched by the low-keyed, Oscar-winning black-and-white photography of Robert Krasker. The most British of directors, Reed was always reluctant to take on non-British subjects, yet was one of the first British directors to start filming regularly abroad, beginning with *The Third Man*. Although the leading stars were American, the central theme of the film reflects the attitudes of the British, their civilising influence on Vienna and, through Major Calloway (Howard), on the Joseph Cotten character, an American thriller writer, who is forced to repudiate his unscrupulous friend, Harry Lime. (The English are even lightly parodied in the person of the elderly Wilfrid Hyde-White.)

Reed's continuing fascination with the Englishman (or woman) abroad is the central theme in many of the pictures

which followed. It was most fully developed in his fine adaptation of Joseph Conrad's adventure-drama, *An Outcast Of The Islands* (1951), starring Trevor Howard with Ralph Richardson, Wendy Hiller and Robert Morley, and filmed on locations in Borneo and Ceylon. Reed returned to Graham Greene for an offbeat and moderately successful spy thriller, *Our Man In Havana* (1960) starring Alec Guinness. But *The Man Between* (1935) was little more than a rehash of *The Third Man*, set in occupied Berlin and with Claire Bloom as the newly arrived Englishwoman and James Mason in the title role. A variation on the same theme was used by Reed once again with Laurence Harvey as the Englishman on the run in Spain in *The Running Man*

(1963). Clearly the director's career was on the wane after 1951. *A Kid For Two Farthings* (1955), with Diana Dors, was an enjoyable but sentimental fable set in London's East End and his first venture into colour. He had CinemaScope, too, for *Trapeze* (1956) and Todd-AO (70mm) for *The Agony And The Ecstasy* (1965), glossy international co-productions which are not recognisable as Carol Reed projects. But, in 1968, in the autumn of his career, he made a surprising and uncharacteristic comeback with his first musical, *Oliver!*, which gave him his first Oscar (he had been nominated twice, for *The Fallen Idol* and *The Third Man*). A pair of last and, it must be confessed, forgettable, movies in the early 70s were followed by retirement.

Top: The multi-talented Alec Guinness starred in another Reed-Greene collaboration, *Our Man In Havana* (1960). He played a salesman who misguidedly allows himself to be recruited as a spy in this wry espionage thriller. With him, Maureen O'Hara.

Above: It fell to David Lean to translate Dickens' *Oliver Twist* to the screen in 1948, with Alec Guinness as Fagin, head of a den of boy thieves. Twenty years later, Carol Reed had a stab at the musical version, *Oliver!*, written and composed by Lionel Bart. Ron Moody (centre) recreated his stage success as Fagin, Mark Lester (right) was Oliver, and Jack Wild (2nd left) The Artful Dodger.

JEAN RENOIR

Born Paris, 15 September 1894. **Died** 1979

The outstanding French director of the 30s, a Hollywood director of note in the 40s, and one of the truly great figures of the cinema in the last fifty years, Jean Renoir was born in 1894 just as the Lumière brothers were perfecting their Cinématographe and was first attracted to the movies by the early films of Chaplin and Stroheim. The son of the renowned Impressionist painter, Auguste Renoir, he often modelled for his father and matured within an artistic environment which profoundly influenced his attitude to the creative process.

Renoir first established himself as a leading director early in the 30s, but never really became part of the French film industry. He arrived in the US late in 1940, a refugee from occupied France, and settled permanently in California. When he began filming abroad in the 50s he was following the pattern of many American directors, working in colour for the first time and directing international co-productions which made use of top international stars. In endeavouring to preserve his independent and individual approach to film-making, Renoir's career was littered with marvellous projects which never got made. His reputation grew during the 50s and 60s when his best, earlier films were rediscovered and re-released. He came to be regarded as the greatest living French director and served as an inspiration for the new young directors (and former film critics) of the *Nouvelle Vague* like Truffaut and Godard, yet he had great difficulty finding financial backing for his projects during these years and was only able to complete four pictures during 1957–69, two of them made for French television.

Jean Renoir had worked in ceramics for a time during the early 20s before he first began making films with a close group of friends and with his wife, Catherine Hessling, a former model of his father's, as the star. *La Fille De L'Eau* (1924), filmed on picturesque locations, was followed by an ambitious and expensive production of *Nana* (1926), loosely adapted from Zola's famous novel. It was a resounding commercial flop and forced him to work on a cheaper and more intimate scale in the pictures which followed. *The Little Match Girl* (1928), for example, was a delightful and imaginative fantasy shot in a tiny, improvised studio with the close co-operation of a number of his favourite collaborators including the cameraman Jean Bachelet. This film marked a fitting conclusion to the director's first period of cinematic experimentation.

The next film, *Tire Au Flanc* (1928), was an amusing tale of army barracks life among a group of new recruits. It reflected Renoir's special talent for comedy, and treated the sexual intrigues and class conflicts in a light vein while satirising middle-class behaviour, and provided Renoir with his first opportunity to work with the remarkable young Swiss-born actor, Michel Simon. Forced to fall back on commercial pro-

jects for a time, the director made the big breakthrough to sound with three very different productions – all edited by his second 'wife', Marguerite Renoir – during 1931–32, which immediately established him in the front rank of French directors. Unlike many silent directors, he welcomed sound and rightly recognised that it could enrich the cinema's means of expression: 'It was as if someone had opened a secret door of communication between the film-maker and his audience'. His early sound films not only demonstrated the same visual qualities as his silents, partly filmed on location in and around Paris, but encouraged him to collaborate more closely with his actors than ever before. Renoir was fortunate in having Michel Simon as his star on *La Chienne*, filmed in Monmartre in 1931, and *Boudu Sauve Des Eaux*, set in a bookshop by the Seine, in the Bois de Boulogne, and along the banks of the Marne in 1932. They worked closely together in solving problems of filmic characterisation at a time when most 'talkies' were little more than filmed plays. A former boxer and acrobat, Simon brought a special physicality and sensitivity of gesture and movement to his roles, most clearly demonstrated in the *clochard*, Boudu. The film was in fact partly based on a play, a conventional 'boulevard comedy' which Renoir totally transformed into a remarkable film.

Similarly, he drew a fine performance from his older brother, the actor Pierre Renoir, as the screen's first Maigret in *La Nuit Du Carrefour* (1932), a remarkable early sound thriller adapted from Simenon. Pierre's restrained portrayal of the shrewd police inspector was exactly right, the force of Maigret's presence was felt rather than dramatised, and fitted in with the naturalistic but low-keyed approach, blending professional and non-professional actors and filmed on location using direct sound. This least known and sadly underrated of Renoir's early sound films, along with *La Chienne* and *Boudu*, marks an important stage in his develop-

ment as a perceptive and committed observer of contemporary French society, Thus, in *Toni* (1934) he examines the plight of immigrant workers in the south of France, while *Le Crime De M Lange* (1935) deals with a successful worker's co-op in Paris coinciding with the rise of the Popular Front. Already with *Lange* there is clear evidenc of Renoir's maturing. He succeeds remarkably in bringing the film's central courtyard milieu to life and achieves a terrific interaction among the large and varied cast. The fresh, lively and improvised feel can be attributed to the director's close collaboration with scriptwriter (and poet) Jacques Prévert, who was invited to join the director and

Top: Catherine Hessling (centre), Renoir's wife at the time, played the title role in *Nana* (1926), an ambitious but unsuccessful adaptation from Zola's famous novel of an amoral actress who comes to an early and tragic end.

Above: Michel Simon in *La Chienne* (1931).

Left: Pierre Renoir (centre), the director's brother, was the first screen incarnation of Simenon's famous Inspector Maigret. The film was *La Nuit Du Carrefour* (1932).

'My French friends all ask me the same question: "Why have you chosen to live in America? You're French and you need a French environment". My answer to this is that the environment which has made me what I am is the cinema. I am a citizen of the world of films'

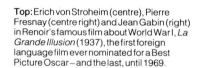

actors on the set during the shooting. According to Renoir, the best lines were discovered in this way. Most of all, the film demonstrated Renoir's ability to achieve a complex and original mixture of comedy, drama and social comment.

La Grande Illusion (1937) was Renoir's greatest international success of the 30s (and the only foreign language film to be nominated for a Best Picture Oscar until Costa Gavras' *Z* in 1969). Again he collaborated with a leading scriptwriter (Charles Spaak) in a personal venture into the past for him, drawing on his own memories as a reconnaisance pilot in World War I and on the experiences of fellow pilots who had been taken prisoner. Again, the performances were uniformly excellent from a cast which included Erich von Stroheim as the commandant of the German POW camp, Jean Gabin and Marcel Dalio. But the true fulfilment of Renoir's development during the 30s came with *La Règle Du Jeu* (*The Rules Of The Game*) in 1939. Here he drew on the long French theatre tradition and comedy of manners to present his most pointed critique of French bourgeois society only a few months before the outbreak of war. Renoir's undoubted masterpiece, the film presents his most ambitious efforts as producer-director, scriptwriter and actor within a single work. (He had previously played small roles in the delightful bitter-sweet comedy *Une Partie De Campagne*, 1936, and in *La Bête Humaine*, 1938.) Shot largely in sequence, the film truly *evolved* during its making, as Renoir worked on writing and rewriting the script, balancing and rebalancing the many and varied characters and relationships, plot and subplots. A complex work which operates on many levels, mixing farce with drama and tragedy, *La Règle Du Jeu* baffled and enraged French audiences at the time, was attacked by the right-wing press – Renoir was regarded as a leading representative of the 'left' – and fared no better when he tried cutting it. The film was even banned by the government as 'demoralising' shortly after the outbreak

of war. Revived after the war in a truncated form, the complete version was only rediscovered and re-released – to wide acclaim – in 1959.

Arriving in the US with his Brazilian scriptgirl, Dido, who was to become his (official) second wife in 1944, Renoir was soon signed to a contract by 20th Century-Fox. He was unhappy with most of the scripts which were offered to him, but finally found something American which he liked, a Dudley Nichols script based on the novel *Swamp Water* (1941). A very Ford-like subject, following in the line of recent Fox productions like *The Grapes Of Wrath* (1940) and *Tobacco Road* (1941), the cast included a number of Ford regulars such as John Carradine, Ward Bond and Russell Simpson, as well as top character actors Walter Brennan and Walter Huston, along with a pair of new, young stars, Anne Baxter and Dana Andrews. Convincing studio boss Darryl Zanuck to let him shoot extensive location footage in Georgia, the results were excellent, and a gripping and well acted drama emerged.

Unhappy with Fox, Renoir left in 1942. The balance of his American films were made for the two companies which allowed the largest degree of freedom to independent producers and directors – RKO and UA. For RKO he made *This Land Is Mine*, an unusual but not entirely successful pro-French propaganda feature designed to open the eyes of the American public to the difficulties currently being experienced by the French under German occupation. Charles Laughton played the timid 'anti-hero' schoolteacher, again from a Nichols script. Renoir then returned to the American, rural South for the movie which is widely regarded as his finest 40s achievement, *The Southerner* (UA, 1945),

Top: Erich von Stroheim (centre), Pierre Fresnay (centre right) and Jean Gabin (right) in Renoir's famous film about World War I, *La Grande Illusion* (1937), the first foreign language film ever nominated for a Best Picture Oscar – and the last, until 1969.

Above: Jean Renoir and Nora Gregor in *La Règle Du Jeu* (*The Rules Of The Game*, 1939). Acknowledged as a masterpiece, this ambitious film was produced, written and acted in by its director.

Left: Zachary Scott in *The Southerner* (1945), the only film to earn Renoir a Best Director Oscar nomination.

which earned him his only Oscar nomination for directing. Making extensive use of locations, the film was beautifully photographed by Lucien Andriot, but the central plight of a poor farming family was overdramatised, and the cast, led by Zachary Scott and Betty Field, was not up to Renoir's usual standard. Once again, however, Renoir the great humanist shone through, although he was still not fully at ease working in English. With *The Diary Of A Chambermaid* (UA, 1946), he achieved his most successful 'back-lot' production with the help of his favourite art director, Eugene Lourie. The subject itself presented a kind of extension of *The Rules Of The Game* in which the servants' view of the goings-on above stairs was one of the main themes. The cast was headed by the husband-and-wife team of Paulette Goddard and Burgess Meredith, the latter also serving as producer. Potentially the most interesting and unusual of Renoir's films was *The Woman On The Beach* (RKO, 1947), a bleak and downbeat *film noir* drama which, unfortunately, did not appeal to American audiences and was badly cut.

In marked contrast was *The River* (UA, 1951), filmed in India from the novel by Rumer Godden. With its three young heroines, and its soft colour photography, the picture marked a new stage in Renoir's development in which his feminine characters came to hold the limelight. Anna Magnani gave an incredible performance as the member of a *commedia dell'arte* theatre troupe in 18th-century Peru in *The Golden Coach*, filmed in Italy in 1952; Ingrid Bergman was delightful in the disappointing *Elena Et Les Hommes* (1956). Of special note was the fact that Renoir was reunited on all three of these films with his cameraman nephew, Claude Renoir, who had first

worked with him as long ago as *Toni* (1934) and who developed into one of the leading French cameramen specialising in colour. In between came the marvellous *French Cancan* (1954), the second of his trilogy of colourful costumers and a kind of homage to his painter father which reunited him with French star Jean Gabin. If these films suggested that Renoir was mellowing in old age, the suggestion proved misleading. In 1959 he produced one of his blackest movies

for French TV, an updated version of 'Dr Jekyll And Mr Hyde' retitled *Le Testament Du Dr Cordelier*, starring the extraordinary Jean-Louis Barrault. Finally, with *The Vanishing Corporal* (1962), Renoir directed one last masterpiece, making use of a number of young French actors in a black comedy about French prisoners in World War II, a kind of blend of *La Grande Illusion* with the knockabout comedy of *Tire Au Flanc*. Renoir was awarded an honorary Oscar in 1974.

'Although I don't regret my first American films, I know for a fact they don't come close to any ideal I have for my work . . . They represent seven years of unrealized works and unrealized hopes, and seven years of deceptions too . . .'
1952

Left: Renoir demonstrates how he wants it done! The actress is Paulette Goddard, the film *Diary Of A Chambermaid* (1946). Another version was made eighteen years later, in French, by Luis Buñuel with Jeanne Moreau.

Below left: The young English actress, Adrienne Corri, whose career never quite achieved what it promised, was featured in *The River* (1951), from the novel by Rumer Godden, filmed on location in India.

Below: The unlikely figure of Jean Gabin attempts the dance, with Françoise Arnoul, in *French Can-Can* (1954). Photographed by Claude Renoir, the film was ravishing in its evocation of the Paris of yesteryear. Guest artists included Edith Piaf and Patachou.

MARK ROBSON

Born Montreal, 4 December 1913. **Died** 1978

The decline of the Hollywood studios during the 50s meant that former contract directors faced new problems in a world of independent productions and 'deal making'. Not Mark Robson. A former editor and B-movie director, he flourished during an era when producers were attempting to bring more mature, adult subjects to the screen, filmed in colour and the new widescreen processes. Popular, best selling novels – suitably toned down for mass consumption, and with their characters adjusted to fit the demands of this or that top Hollywood star – proved the best source of material. James Michener, Budd Schulberg, Grace Metalious, John O'Hara, Irving Wallace, Jacqueline Susann, Kurt Vonnegut and J.D. Salinger were thus all grist to the Robson mill.

A student of political science, economics and law, Robson was attracted to the movies as a young man and was fortunate to find work first at Fox and then, in 1935, at RKO, where he remained for a dozen years. Working his way up from prop boy to assistant editor, by the late 30s he had become assistant to leading editor (and future director) Robert Wise, who was, in fact, a year younger than Robson. The pair handled films from the studio's top directors – William Dieterle, Garson Kanin, Dorothy Arzner – but the arrival of Orson Welles represented an important turning point for both men, who were confronted with their greatest creative challenge in editing the three Mercury productions – *Citizen Kane* (1941), *The Magnificent Ambersons* (1942) and *Journey Into Fear* (1943).

According to Robson, when Welles was 'evicted' from RKO 'most of the people who had been associated with him were punished', and he himself was demoted to the B-pictures department. This turned out to be extremely fortunate, for he was able to join the new unit just being set up by producer Val Lewton to make a series of low cost horror movies. During the years 1942 through 1945 Lewton produced eleven innovative and distinctive pictures and, aside from Lewton himself, it was Robson who made the most important contribution to the cycle, editing the first three and directing five others. These, his first movies as a director, began with an excellent pair of atmospheric thrillers, *The Seventh Victim* and *The Ghost Ship* both filmed in 1943. They demonstrated his talent for working quickly and effectively with only minimal resources, learning to use lighting for 'dramatic purposes'. A later pair of chillers starred Boris Karloff. *Bedlam* (1946) combined thriller elements with social concern, the latter a theme which had attracted Robson to *Youth Runs Wild* (1944), about young people facing family dislocation during World War II.

Contemporary social themes were also treated in the pair of films he directed for producer Stanley Kramer in 1949. Both scripted by Carl Foreman, *Champion*, about the fight racket, was the better of the two, earning well-deserved Oscar nominations for its stars, Kirk Douglas and Arthur Kennedy; *Home Of The Brave*, from a successful stage play, dealt with racial prejudice. After a brief, unsatisfactory stint with Goldwyn and a rare venture into comedy with *Phffft* (Columbia, 1954), Robson had his first big, glossy hit with *The Bridges At Toko-Ri* (Paramount, 1954) adapted from James Michener. Another downbeat treatment of the fight game, *The Harder They Fall* (Columbia, 1956) from a Schulberg novel is best remembered as Bogart's last movie. Robson earned his only Oscar nominations in consecutive years for directing the classy soap opera, *Peyton Place* (1957) starring Lana Turner, and the rather better adventure melodrama, *The Inn Of The Sixth Happiness* (1958) with Ingrid Bergman. Both were filmed for 20th Century-Fox, the home of the glossy CinemaScope movie of the 50s and Robson's new home for a number of years. Here, too, he made his trashy but entertaining, *Valley Of The Dolls* (1967), another smash hit. Maintaining an impressive record of at least one big box office success in each decade, Robson hit pay dirt one last time with the disaster movie, *Earthquake* (Universal, 1974). Thinking big up to the very end, he died while directing *Avalanche Express* in 1978.

Top: Oscar-nominated Arthur Kennedy (left) and Kirk Douglas in *Champion* (1949), an effectively downbeat movie about an over-ambitious prizefighter who dies as a result of boxing injuries.

Above: Director Mark Robson (right) with Paul Newman during filming of *The Prize* (1963). It was an excellent treatment of Irving Wallace's best-selling espionage novel.

Left: Ingrid Bergman starred as Gladys Aylward, a former English servant who became a missionary in China, in Robson's romantic biopic, *The Inn Of The Sixth Happiness* (1958).

'Fantastic. North Wales looks far more like China than China'

Robson explaining why he was filming *The Inn Of The Sixth Happiness* in Wales

143

ROBERT ROSSEN

Born New York City, 16 March 1908. **Died** 1966

Robert Rossen was one of the directors worst hit by the political blacklist during the early 50s. Ironically, this came shortly after he had achieved a remarkable critical and box-office success with his third feature film, *All The King's Men* (Columbia, 1949). Rossen first developed an interest in writing and theatre while a student at New York University in the late 20s. He was associated with a number of politically leftish theatre groups like the Washington Square Players in the 30s, but achieved some success on Broadway, too, as both playwright and director. This led to a contract as a scriptwriter at Warner Bros. in 1936, where he immediately established himself as a master of the studio's characteristically hard-hitting style of contemporary thrillers and social drama, beginning with *Marked Woman* and *They Won't Forget* (both 1937). These were followed by *The Roaring Twenties* and *Dust Be My Destiny* (both 1939), the latter being the first of three pictures to star Rossen's fellow New Yorker, John Garfield, before Rossen left the studio to freelance for a time during the mid-40s. He wrote the script for the excellent war picture, *A Walk In The Sun* (20th Century-Fox, 1945), and the *noir* thriller, *The Strange Love Of Martha Ivers* (Paramount, 1946), both directed by Lewis Milestone. Taking advantage of the current popularity of *film noir* and following in the footsteps of other new writers-turned-directors like Huston and Wilder, Rossen began directing in 1946. He started by scripting and directing *Johnny O'Clock* (for Columbia), a useful apprentice work which starred Dick Powell in his new 40s tough-guy image. Then Rossen teamed up with writer (later director) Abraham Polonsky on *Body And Soul* (1947) starring John Garfield in the kind of gutsy role he did so well, as the boy from the slums determined to succeed as a boxer. According to editor Bob Parrish, Rossen was uncertain how to shoot the climactic final fight until ace cameraman James Wong Howe suggested filming it like a real fight, supplementing the main camera crew with a number of ex-combat cameramen, each equipped with an Eyemo hand-held camera. The result, edited by Parrish, was a knockout, and earned him an Oscar, with nominations for Garfield and for Polonsky's punchy, street-wise dialogue. Unfortunately, *Body And Soul* was one of the pictures targeted by the HUAC investigations. The attacks on Rossen, Polonsky and Garfield for their past left-wing associations virtually destroyed their careers in the early 50s. (Polonsky made a comeback in the 60s, but Garfield died tragically of a heart attack in 1952.)

Rossen and Parrish collaborated again on *All The King's Men*. Taking advantage of his new status as producer-director, Rossen determined to shoot virtually all the film on location and to avoid star names in the cast. Result: Broderick Crawford, then a little-known B-movie actor, won an Oscar, as did Mercedes

McCambridge in her first film role. Parrish was nominated for editing, Rossen for both direction and script, and the movie won the Best Picture Oscar.

Rossen directed a bullfight drama, *The Brave Bulls*, for Columbia in Mexico in 1951. It was on his return from there, the same year, that he had to cope with HUAC and the blacklist, and so based himself for a time in Italy. There he directed *Mambo* (1954), followed by one of the more intelligent 50s costume epics, *Alexander The Great* (UA, 1956), but had his biggest hit with the controversial, British-based *Island In The Sun* (20th Century-Fox, 1957). He was truly back in form with his most personal and deeply felt project, returning to the pool halls of his youth for *The Hustler* (20th Century-Fox, 1961), starring Paul Newman, which earned three Oscar nominations – for Best Picture, directing and writing – along with the New York Critics' directing award. Before his death, Rossen then completed one last, interesting psychological drama, *Lilith* (Columbia, 1964) starring Jean Seberg and Warren Beatty.

Left: Broderick Crawford (centre), up till then a B-picture actor, was thrust into the upper ranks through his Oscar-winning, starring role in *All The King's Men* (1949). The movie – voted Best Picture – was a hard-hitting study of politics and power corruption.

Above: Robert Rossen rehearses one of the more junior members of his cast for *The Brave Bulls* (1951), a somewhat unmemorable drama about a Mexican matador, played by Mel Ferrer (right).

Left: Paul Newman and Myron McCormick in *The Hustler* (1961), a superb drama about a pool player. Memorable, Oscar-nominated, supporting performances came from Jackie Gleason, Piper Laurie and George C. Scott, and the film remains a testament to Rossen's abilities at their best.

GEORGE SIDNEY

Born Long Island City, New York, 4 October 1916

Most movie books refer to George Sidney's parents as 'show people'. His father, Louis K. Sidney, may indeed have started out as an actor, but soon switched to stage manager, then to managing movie theatres for Loew's and gradually worked his way up to a leading executive position with Loew's/MGM by the 40s. Young George was a music student and briefly a performing musician before he too joined MGM in 1932. Still a teen-ager, he was the studio's youngest ever assistant director, test director and second unit director, working in the shorts department which served as a useful training ground for many promising young directors including Jacques Tourneur and Fred Zinnemann. Still only in his early twenties when he was assigned to direct a number of 'Our Gang' shorts in 1938–39, Sidney recalled, 'I was only seven years older than the oldest kid'. (For obvious professional reasons, he had added five years to his age – many reference books still list his birth date as 1911.)

At the same time that his father was doing a short stint as a producer at Culver City, George directed a pair of Oscar-winning shorts. Late in 1940, just turning twenty-five, he was given his first B-feature to direct, a comedy called *Free And Easy* and starring Robert Cummings. After two more 'B's' he was entrusted with a pair of the studio's very first Technicolor musicals, *Thousands Cheer* (1943) and *Bathing Beauty* (1944), vehicles designed to help launch a number of new young stars including Gene Kelly, Kathryn Grayson and Esther Williams. Kelly and Grayson were reunited, along with Dean Stockwell and Frank Sinatra, in the colourful *Anchors Aweigh* (1945). Little more than an entertaining showcase for the stars, like the Jane Powell vehicle, *Holiday In Mexico* (1946), which followed, these pictures (excluding *Bathing Beauty*) all bore the stamp of producer Joe Pasternak who was 'recycling' the plot of his Deanna Durbin success *One Hundred Men And A Girl* (Universal, 1937).

Sidney was also the original director assigned to *Ziegfeld Follies* by producer Arthur Freed early in 1944 but, after one month of filming, he felt that the picture was not going well and asked to be removed. He was replaced by Vincente Minnelli, but a number of Sidney sequences remain in the film, most notably the opulent opening number, 'Here's To The Ladies' with Fred Astaire and Lucille Ball. Back with Freed again the following year Sidney redeemed himself with *The Harvey Girls*, an entertaining musical Western starring Judy Garland, and the young director's best picture to date. It was a smash hit when it was released early in 1946, and his next three movies also went over big at the box-office. Thus Sidney established a unique record among Hollywood directors of the 40s with five big hits in a row. Last of the group was *The Three Musketeers* (1948), which reunited the director and Gene Kelly. It was an enjoyable Technicolored

swashbuckler which demonstrated Sidney's special flair for blending tongue-in-cheek comedy with lively action sequences within a convincing period setting. Better yet was *Scaramouche* (1952) with its elaborately choreographed duels and fluid camerawork.

In between he had directed two more major musicals of note – *Annie Get Your Gun* (1950), on which (with a little help from his father) he replaced Charles Walters, and a lavish Technicolor remake of *Showboat* (1951). He rounded out his MGM years with a 3-D version of *Kiss Me Kate* (1953), best remembered for its musical numbers, and an Esther Williams vehicle, *Jupiter's Darling*, in 1954. Having spent over twenty years at the studio, Sidney left (around the same time that his father retired) and went on to Columbia. The highlight of his years there was, undoubtedly, the musical *Pal Joey* (1957) starring Frank Sinatra and Rita Hayworth. Still best known as a director of movie musicals, in spite of his moderately successful ventures into straight drama like *Jeanne Eagels* (1957), or comedy (*Who Was That Lady?*, 1959), Sidney made a good try at adapting *Bye, Bye, Birdie* to the screen in 1962 and retired after making *Half-A-Sixpence* for Paramount in 1967.

Top: Concert pianist Jose Iturbi, who specialised in playing himself in a string of popular musicals in the 40s, here with MGM's soprano ingenue, Jane Powell, in *Holiday In Mexico* (1946).

Above: On set for the successful swashbuckler, *Scaramouche* (1952) are – left to right – director George Sidney, camera operator John Nickolaus, Stewart Granger in costume, and cinematographer Charles Rosher. Granger, who starred in the title role, is shooting his own 16mm version of the Eleanor Parker scenes they are watching.

Left: Sidney and Rita Hayworth discuss an up-coming scene for *Pal Joey* (1957).

145

ROBERT SIODMAK

Born Memphis, Tennessee, 8 August 1900. **Died** 1973

'I like making gangster pictures,' Robert Siodmak wrote in 1959. 'Not that I had much choice when I went to Hollywood eighteen years ago because at that time the crime picture was very much in vogue ... As is usual in the film city, if you are successful at making a certain type of picture then you are given more of them to make. You have to be one of the boys!'

In fact, Siodmak was prolific during his Hollywood years, directing twenty-one features in slightly over ten years (1941–51), most of them crime movies of superior quality. These years occupy the middle ground in a career stretching over a forty-year period. Born in Tennessee to German-Jewish parents, young Robert grew up and was educated in Germany. After completing university and trying a banking job, he began working, more happily, in films. Graduating from title writer, he then made a remarkable directing debut with *Menschen Am Sonntag* in 1929. Edgar Ulmer was co-director from a script by Siodmak's younger brother Curt, aided by Billy Wilder, while cameraman Eugen Schufftan was assisted by Fred Zinnemann. Filmed entirely on location in a 'neo-realist' style, it was a nicely observed small budget feature, following the experiences of a handful of characters on a typical sunny Sunday in and around Berlin. The movie was generally well received, and gained Siodmak a contract with the giant UFA studio where he directed a variety of movies during the following years. Of special interest was the ingenious black comedy, *The Man Who Seeks His Own Murderer* (1931) with Wilder and Curt again collaborating on the script. After directing *The Burning Secret* (1932), a sensitive marital drama and his seventh feature, the director (and his brother) fled the Nazi regime to join Wilder and Schufftan in Paris. Siodmak was one of the few German directors, along with Ophuls and Pabst, who developed a second career of note in France during the 30s. For the seventh (and last) of his

French films, the 1939 thriller *Pièges* (*Snares*), with its offbeat characters, he assembled a cast of some quality headed by Chevalier, von Stroheim and Pierre Renoir. Its low-keyed style clearly anticipated Siodmak's *noir* period of the 40s.

Joining Curt and other German expatriates in Hollywood, Siodmak directed a collection of B-pictures before he was offered *Son Of Dracula* at Universal, from an original scenario by his brother. He succeeded in turning it into an extremely entertaining and stylish horror with the help of some excellent special effects. Signed to a seven-year contract by Universal, he was next given Maria Montez and Technicolor for *Cobra Woman* and again demonstrated his flair for handling intractable material. (The script was one of the first credited to writer and future director Richard Brooks.) Toward the end of that same year (1943), Siodmak directed *Phantom Lady*, the first of those

'Something was bound to happen when a former Alfred Hitchcock protegée (Joan Harrison, producer) and a former director of German films were teamed on the Universal lot – something severe and unrelenting, drenched in creeping morbidity and gloom'

Bosley Crowther on *Phantom Lady* in the 'New York Times', 1947

Left: Hardly representative of the material Siodmak would have chosen for himself, *Cobra Woman* (1943), a lot of nonsense about a South Seas girl abducted by snake worshippers, starred the fiery Maria Montez.

Above: Ella Raines, the young heroine of *Phantom Lady* (1944), discomforts a bartender out of whom she is trying to elicit information which would help Alan Baxter, wrongly accused of murder.

excellent psychological suspensers with which he made his name during the following years. Siodmak's special talent for directing this type of picture and his characteristically dark view of human nature is often credited to his Germanic origins. He was not the only one: Hollywood's *film noir* cycle had gotten well under way early in 1944 with a notable group of European-born directors at the forefront of the movement: Billy Wilder had just completed *Double Indemnity* at Paramount, immediately followed by Negulesco's *The Mask Of Dimitrios* for Warner Bros., while Preminger made his name at Fox with *Laura* at about the same time that Lang was completing *The Woman In The Window* for RKO.

Siodmak, in particular, demonstrated his mastery of atmospheric and controlled studio filming during these years, leavened by an appropriately black sense of humour. In addition, he was brilliant at matching actors and actresses to their

Left: Thomas Mitchell, Lew Ayres (centre) and Olivia de Havilland in *The Dark Mirror* (1946), in which the actress played identical twins, as did Bette Davis the same year in *A Stolen Life* (Warner Bros.). In spite of such powerful rivalry, Miss de Havilland did rather well!

roles. Ella Raines had her best ever role as the dedicated and resourceful heroine searching for the missing *Phantom Lady* among the dimly lit streets and seedy bars of the Universal backlot at night in an effort to clear her boyfriend of a murder charge. Charles Laughton was superb as the sympathetic, intelligent husband in Victorian London who disposes of his shrewish wife in *The Suspect* (1944), while George Sanders was never better on the screen than as *Uncle Harry* (aka *The Strange Affair Of Uncle Harry*, 1945), Siodmak's effective study of repressed passions in a New England family. Similarly, the director made good use of Dorothy McGuire's blandly innocent quality, casting her as the menaced, mute heroine of the scary, if old-fashioned, chiller, *The Spiral Staircase* (1945). Finally, he directed *The Dark Mirror* early in 1946 with Olivia de Havilland giving a chillingly effective performance in a dual role as identical twins, one of whom is a mentally deranged killer. Siodmak's only dud during these years was *Christmas Holiday* (1944), a drama adapted from Somerset Maugham with both Gene Kelly and Deanna Durbin wildly miscast.

A prestigious year for Siodmak, 1946 also marked a slight turning point in his development. Leaving the studio-based psychological thriller behind him, he readily adapted to the new postwar trend toward more location shooting. He gained his only Oscar nomination for directing *The Killers* (1946), the first of his more naturalistic thrillers and a box-office hit. The classic short story by Hemingway provided the film with an effective opening reel, and scriptwriter John Huston (uncredited) added most of the rest. Making use of a complex flashback structure, Siodmak sustained the atmosphere well, aided by a fine, non-starry cast (including Ava Gardner in an early role and Burt Lancaster in his first picture), and by the suitably low-keyed, flexible camerawork of Woody Bredell. As recalled by Siodmak, filming on location did not always go according to plan. 'The robbery scene in one long crane shot was done in a single take: everything was very confused, with people not knowing where they ought to be, a car backed up wrong and left in the middle of the road, and so on, but curiously enough the result turned out to give just the right effect . . .?.

Siodmak was responsible for two more outstanding examples of the new type of thriller in 1948: on loan to up-market 20th Century-Fox, the director made a rare trip East for *Cry Of The City*. Telling the familiar story of childhood pals now on different sides of the law, Siodmak's intelligent treatment of the two leading characters was matched by the performances of Victor Mature and Richard Conte. The sexual theme which had simmered beneath the surface of earlier Siodmak movies was more clearly in evidence in *Criss Cross*, filmed back in the warmer climes of Los Angeles. Here Yvonne De Carlo played the *femme fatale* to Burt Lancaster, with Dan Duryea as the third in the triangle. But in both these films Siodmak demonstrated the continuing importance of firm stylistic control in achieving good results on location (as in the studio). He developed the

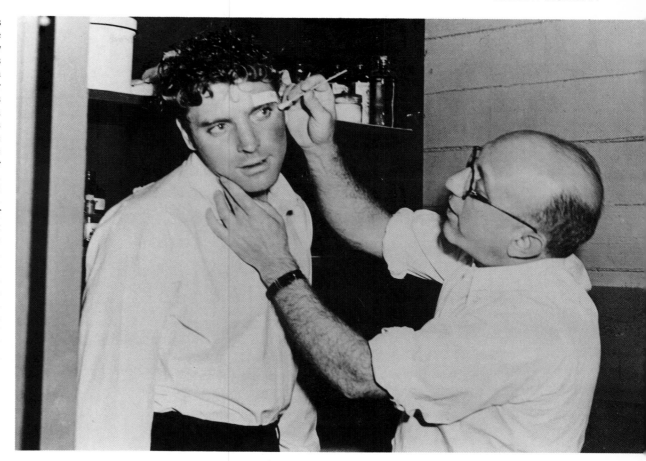

theme of sexual obsession further, but less satisfactorily, in *The File On Thelma Jordon* (Paramount, 1949) starring Barbara Stanwyck; and a different form of obsession – gambling – was the subject of the Dostoevskian *The Great Sinner* (MGM, 1949). After this last burst of productivity, Siodmak appears to have had little further use for Hollywood. He made a triumphant return to filming in Europe and in Technicolor with the British based *The Crimson Pirate* (Warner Bros., 1952). This delightful and lively tongue-in-cheek swashbuckler reunited him with Burt Lancaster in a fantasy world far removed from 40s *film noir* and allowed his sense of fun to take over.

Siodmak continued to direct, mainly in Germany, for another seventeen years, but few of his films were widely seen and none matched up to the best of his earlier work. Best known of the later group is his one attempt at a Western (filmed in Spain), the disappointing *Custer Of The West* (1966) starring Robert Shaw.

Top: Director Siodmak personally puts the finishing touches to Burt Lancaster's 'injury' make-up for *The Killers* (1946), Lancaster's debut film.

Above: *Criss-Cross* (1948), a tense *film noir* whose plot combined crime and sexual intrigue, starred Burt Lancaster (right), Yvonne de Carlo and Dan Duryea (seated centre). With them are Alan Napier (left) and John Miller.

Left: *The Crimson Pirate* (1952), one of the livelier 50s swashbucklers, marked a change of pace for Siodmak, although his star was once again Burt Lancaster (centre), here with Nick Cravat and Eva Bartok.

DOUGLAS SIRK

Born Hamburg, 26 April 1900

A profoundly cultured man with a distinguished theatrical record, Douglas Sirk turned to directing films during the late 30s and arrived in Hollywood in 1939, a refugee from Nazi Germany. His fragmented and uneven career during the 40s and early 50s lacked any clear sense of direction, and he was in danger of becoming yet another European casualty of the Hollywood studio system until things began to fall into place for him at Universal in the early 50s.

Born in Germany to Danish parents, Sirk grew up in Denmark, but returned to Germany to complete his studies. Concurrently, he had begun painting and writing and landed a minor post in the Deutsches Schauspielhaus in Hamburg, one of the city's most prestigious theatres. Called upon to replace a resident director at short notice, his surprise success launched him on a theatrical career which was to span fifteen years. During this period, he was responsible for productions of works by Molière, Strindberg, Büchner, Ibsen, Shakespeare, Wedekind, Shaw – and others as celebrated as they were numerous. Because of increasing harassment from the Nazi authorities, Sirk finally decided to transfer his allegiance to film, in which medium – at least, in the early 30s – an artist's political orientation was judged of less significance. Thus he made a number of striking films at UFA, most memorably *Stützen Der Gesellschaft* (1935), an adaptation of Ibsen's 'Pillars Of Society', *Schlussakkord* (1936), and two splendid Zarah Leander vehicles, *Zu Neuen Ufern (Life Begins Anew*, 1937) and *La Habanera* (also 1937), filmed for the most part in Tenerife. In December of that same year, Sirk left Germany for Rome, ostensibly to scout locations for a new film: he never returned.

A confused interim period ensued, with Sirk working on various abortive projects (including the opportunity, which he wisely declined, to complete Renoir's *Une Partie De Campagne*) in France and Holland. In 1939 he was invited to Hollywood by Warners to direct an American version of *Zu Neuen Ufern*; the film was never made and his contract was terminated, as was a subsequent one with Columbia. It was at MGM that he completed his first American production, *Hitler's Madman* (1942), an account of the assassination of Heydrich (played by John Carradine) and the destruction of the village of Lidice (Sirk had actually met Heydrich in Germany). He followed this with a quartet of films for UA: *Summer Storm* (1944), an unconvincing adaptation of Chekhov's only novel; *A Scandal In Paris* (1945), a witty and deliriously bizarre thriller in which George Sanders played the celebrated criminal-turned-detective, Vidocq; *Lured* (1946), a thriller, again with Sanders, which ought to have been entitled 'Lurid'; and *Sleep, My Love* (1947), a visually elaborate but psychologically simplistic is-she-mad-or-is-she-being-driven-mad story which starred Claudette Colbert,

Don Ameche and Robert Cummings.

Before moving definitively to the studio which would become his second home, Universal, he made a trio of minor oddities, the best of which was a tough *film noir* co-scripted by Samuel Fuller, *Shockproof* (1948), and the strangest, *The First Legion* (1950), set almost entirely in a Jesuit seminary with such improbable priests as Charles Boyer, William Demarest and Leo G. Carroll. A quirky, elusive personality could already be detected in the ragbag of films which comprised his *oeuvre* to date, but it was at Universal that Sirk was to develop into an authentic *auteur*, possessed of his own preoccupations, both visual and thematic. The process was a slow one, to be sure: such titles as *Mystery Submarine* (1950), *Thunder On The Hill*, *The Lady Pays Off* and *Weekend With Father* (all 1951) are not destined to ring down the ages. But, again in 1951, he made *Has Anybody Seen My Gal?*. A charmingly

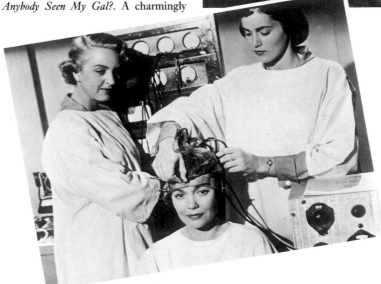

Above: Don Ameche (left), rather better remembered as one of 20th Century-Fox's leading men in Alice Faye or Betty Grable musicals, ventured into the realms of psychological melodrama with Claudette Colbert (right) in *Sleep My Love* (1947), one of Sirk's early Hollywood ventures.

Left: Jane Wyman (centre) in *Magnificent Obsession* (1954), the first of Douglas Sirk's major melodramas of the 50s.

Below: Agnes Moorehead (left) with Jane Wyman, once again the tormented heroine, this time in *All That Heaven Allows* (1955), in which she co-starred for the second time with Sirk's protégé, Rock Hudson.

fresh and exuberant musical as American (and tasty) as apple pie, it boasted a witty and entertaining script, and fine performances from a cast headed by irascible old Charles Coburn as a rather unlikely cupid to the younger generation. Most important of all, it was Sirk's first in colour, his first with Rock Hudson whom he helped to develop into a major Universal star, and the first of a self-styled 'trilogy of little American stories' followed by *Meet Me At The Fair* and *Take Me To Town*, both filmed in 1952. This latter brought him together with ace colour cinematographer Russell Metty and producer Ross Hunter for the first time. (Sirk himself has stressed that 'I wanted to do all these pictures in colour, which I considered very essential to this type of picture to give it the necessary warmth and glow and, commercially, to add box-office power to their rather second-rate star value'.) Together they were to forge a creative team which would give a major boost to the fortunes of the studio, developing a glossy approach to the American middle-class milieu that was suitable for both drama and (Doris Day) comedies, and

'Sirk's latest films have all the ludicrous extravagances of plot used time and again in TV soap opera, but when he was making his bold and lush movies, TV had yet to discover sexual and social themes'

Ronald Bergan in 'A-Z of Movie Directors'

Left: Rock Hudson and Dorothy Malone in *Written On The Wind* (1957), now widely regarded as the finest of Sirk's Technicolor melodramas. Certainly, the roots of 'Dallas' and 'Dynasty' are clearly detectable, but the movie remains far superior to either.

which Hunter alone would carry on successfully into the early 60s.

Their first smash hit was *Magnificent Obsession* in 1954, a remake of John Stahl's 30s melodrama which had starred Irene Dunne and Robert Taylor. Here the stars were Rock Hudson and Jane Wyman, the latter Oscar-nominated for her moving performance as the wife and mother who is blinded in an accident but comes to love and forgive the young man responsible. They were reunited on the far superior and better structured follow-up picture, *All That Heaven Allows* (1955). Miss Wyman stole the acting honours once again as a young widow torn between her attraction to a simpler life, as represented by Hudson, and the superficial, country club world she knows only too well. Thus coldly stated the plot sounds ingenuous, but Sirk's great strength was his talent for transforming the material through a simple and direct approach that captures a particular American world on film with great perceptiveness and insight. He was good with the minor characters, too, like Agnes Moorehead's well-meaning but superficial friend, and a very American type of selfishness and insensitivity found in Miss Wyman's children. (German director Rainer Werner Fassbinder, an unabashed Sirk fan, proved that the same formula could still work effectively eighteen years later with his highly successful *Fear Eats The Soul*, 1973.)

But, undoubtedly, the best of Sirk's glossy, larger-than-life, domestic American dramas was *Written On The Wind* (1956), filmed in colour and CinemaScope, and set appropriately in the South of William Faulkner, Tennessee Williams and Edna Ferber's *Giant*. The stars were Rock Hudson and Lauren Bacall, but the most interesting roles fell to Robert Stack and Dorothy Malone as the troubled brother and sister of a Texas oil dynasty. (Both were nominated for supporting Oscars, with Miss Malone emerging a winner.) Sirk's qualities as a visual stylist were never more in evidence, and his use of colour – 'For dramaturgical reasons I felt it needed

violent (primary) colours', he recalled – matched the strong dramatic qualities of the subject.

A black-and-white companion piece followed, with some of the same cast – *Tarnished Angels* (1957) set in New Orleans and adapted from Faulkner's 'Pylon'. But the natural culmination of his 50s development came with his last film, *Imitation Of Life* (1959), affectionately described by Fassbinder as 'a great, crazy movie about life and about death; and about America'. Another Universal remake of a John Stahl-directed picture adapted from a Fannie Hurst weepie, it starred Lana Turner as a typically resourceful but unhappy Sirkian heroine, and it was his biggest hit. Aside from the domestic dramas, during the 50s Sirk also directed a Western, *Taza, Son Of Cochise* (1953), *Captain Lightfoot* (1954), an amiable adventure movie set in 19th-century Ireland, and a war drama, *Battle Hymn* (1956), all starring Rock Hudson. Then, too, there was a moving adaptation of Erich Maria Remarque's *A Time To*

Love And A Time To Die (1957) with the novelist himself playing a small role. But it is for the melodramas that he will be best remembered and for which he has earned his own special niche.

Above: Director Sirk (right) in rehearsal with his two young stars, John Gavin and Lilo Pulver, during *A Time To Love And A Time To Die* (1958), the screen version of Erich Maria Remarque's moving World War II novel.

Left: The director's biggest hit remains a lot of people's favourite Sirk: *Imitation Of Life* (1959), starring Lana Turner (left) and Sandra Dee (right), is an ace 18-carat weepie, familiar to contemporary TV audiences.

GEORGE STEVENS

Born Oakland, California, 18 December 1904. **Died** 1975

Known as a meticulous craftsman and an outstanding director of actors and actresses, George Stevens emerged as one of the most prestigious and successful of American directors and a two-time Oscar winner during the 50s. Working as an independent producer-director during these years, he spent so much time in preparation, shooting and post-production that his films became ever fewer and farther between – he only directed eight features during the postwar period from 1947 up to his retirement in 1969. As he got older he was attracted to ever more serious and weighty themes, far removed from the relatively modest two-reel comedy shorts and comedy B-features on which he had worked during the 20s and early 30s, initially as a cameraman, then as a prolific director.

The son of actor parents, George had himself appeared a little on the stage, but was more attracted to working in films. Having pursued photography as a hobby, he found it relatively easy to break into the film industry as an assistant cameraman during the early 20s. In 1927 he established himself as an essential member of the small and close-knit team behind the early Laurel and Hardy shorts, spearheaded by producer Hal Roach and director/supervisor Leo McCarey. 'Laurel and Hardy were very important to me', Stevens reminisced, 'because as I was coming into the film world, so were they – and we learned together. I was twenty-one when I started with them . . .'.

By late 1930 Roach considered Stevens ready to start directing and gave him the opportunity to develop his own series of two-reel comedies, 'The Boy Friends', a kind of grown-up version of 'Our Gang'. Stevens moved on to Universal in 1932 where he continued to direct comedy shorts and his first B-feature, *The Cohens And Kellys In Trouble*. But it was at RKO that he settled, and remained for the rest of the decade. There, a lively group of Edgar Kennedy shorts led to a further run of comedy B-features during 1934–35 and finally earned the young director his big break and first opportunity to work with a major star, Katharine Hepburn, in an adaptation of the Booth Tarkington novel, *Alice Adams*. A modestly likeable little movie, it turned out to be a surprise hit and nominated for a Best Picture Oscar, with Miss Hepburn, too, nominated for her performance. Stevens followed with another slice of feminine Americana, *Annie Oakley* (1935), a Western starring Barbara Stanwyck, with the accent more on romance than action. Then Stevens was handed Astaire and Rogers at their peak for *Swing Time* (1936), which had some of their best ever dance routines, choreographed by Hermes Pan who recalls, 'I was on the rehearsal stage one morning and there were top lights which were casting shadows on the floor from different angles. So when Fred came in I told him this was an interesting effect for a dance. And from that evolved the 'Bo Jangles' number in which he danced with three

shadows.' The plot was weak, but at least Ginger Rogers was given more of her own life and character in the film and was less overshadowed by Astaire than in their earlier pictures together.

Stevens succeeded less well with a solo Astaire in *A Damsel In Distress* (1937), but had rather more fun with the Ginger Rogers comedy, *Vivacious Lady* (1938), pairing her with James Stewart. And if this contributed further to his reputation as a 'woman's director', he followed it with a marked change of tack, rounding out the 30s in fine style with his most male-dominated picture yet and his first large scale actioner, *Gunga Din* (1939). At slightly under $2 million it was RKO's most expensive film of the decade, but was successful enough to more or less break even. One of the most entertaining of tongue-in-cheek adventure movies, it freely mixed action and drama with humour, and an ideal cast was led by Cary Grant, Victor McLaglen and Douglas Fairbanks Jr, with Joan Fontaine in a supporting role.

Offered a new contract by Harry Cohn in 1940, Stevens was reluctant to accept, having heard that 'unpleasant things happen to directors at Columbia'. Finally Cohn agreed that Stevens could work as a producer-director, entirely free of any interference. Stevens starred Cary Grant with Irene Dunne in *Penny Serenade*

Above: Fred Astaire and Ginger Rogers were at the pinnacle of their success when George Stevens directed them in *Swing Time* (1936). It must be admitted that the assignment was probably more advantageous to the director than to his stars.

Left: The helmeted back belongs to Douglas Fairbanks Jr. Joan Fontaine – spurred on by director Stevens – is embracing him in this rehearsal for a scene in *Gunga Din* (1939), one of the decade's outstanding action romances.

(1941), a bitter-sweet and sentimental marital tale, and with Jean Arthur and Ronald Colman in the slick comedy drama *The Talk Of The Town* (1942). Both were moderately successful (the latter was nominated for a Best Picture Oscar), but the biggest test of Stevens' stint at Columbia came with *The More The Merrier* in 1942. The highly topical idea was provided (for Jean Arthur) by writer-director Garson Kanin and dealt with the comic impications of the wartime housing shortage in Washington and the unlikely threesome who end up sharing an apartment (Joel McCrea, Charles Coburn and Miss Arthur). Proceeding at his characteristically deliberate pace on what would prove to be his last comedy, George tortured Cohn, who could complain to others (but not to Stevens) that he

'exposes more film and shoots more angles than any director I've ever had on the lot.' The result proved to be one of the studio's biggest hits of the early 40s, nominated for a Best Picture Oscar and earning nominations, too, for Jean Arthur, the scriptwriters and Stevens (his first), with a supporting Oscar going to Charles Coburn. A further boost to Stevens' new prestige had come late in 1941 when he had been specially requested by Katharine Hepburn to direct *Woman Of The Year* (for MGM). Once again Garson Kanin had provided the script idea – a fresh reworking of the familiar theme of the super successful career woman and the man who tames her – which led to the inspired, first ever teaming of Kate with Spencer Tracy.

Stevens had little opportunity to enjoy

'George Stevens was a minor director with major virtues before A Place In The Sun, *and a major director with minor virtues after'*

Andrew Sarris in 'The American Cinema'

his new standing, for the war intervened. He was invited to head an Army Signal Corps film unit and was put in charge of the combat photography in Europe from D-Day on to the end of the war and the liberation of the Nazi concentration camps. (Some of the unique colour footage he shot himself has been included in the documentary, *George Stevens: A Film-maker's Journey*, recently completed by his director son, George Stevens Jr).

Stevens returned to his old studio, RKO, for one film after the war, specially requested by one of his favourite actresses, Irene Dunne. *I Remember Mama* (1948) was a sentimental and nostalgic look at a Norwegian immigrant family living in San Francisco just after the turn of the century. Then, during the early 50s, Stevens turned his attention to adapting a trio of well-known American novels to the screen, resulting in the three movies for which he is best remembered. He managed to surmount the problems of updating Dreiser's 'An American Tragedy' – retitled *A Place In The Sun* (Paramount, 1951) – with the help of a fine young cast headed by Montgomery Clift, Elizabeth Taylor and Shelley Winters. Discarding most of the book's social themes, he concentrated more on

characterisation and on developing a highly effective and original visual style.

The general upgrading of the Western attracted Stevens' interest, and in *Shane* (Paramount, 1953), he succeeded in creating the archetypal Hollywood interpretation of the old West. Adapted from the novel by Jack Schaefer, it was Stevens' first in Technicolor, and starred Alan Ladd as the gunfighter hero, a loner idolized by young Brandon de Wilde, and Jean Arthur (brought out of retirement to play the homesteader wife). But it was the star-studded *Giant* (Warner Bros., 1956), adapted from Edna Ferber's novel, which represented the natural culmination of Stevens' long-standing interest in Americana. All a bit overblown and lasting for over three hours on the screen, it is remembered for James Dean's last (and Oscar-nominated) performance. Stevens worked closely with the young star in developing his role, but Dean found his method of 'shooting every scene from every possible angle' overly tedious.

All three productions were successful at the box-office and earned Best Picture nominations, with Stevens receiving Oscars, for directing both *A Place In The Sun* and *Giant* and the Irving Thalberg

award in 1953. He rounded out his career with a characteristically well-crafted, if sentimental adaptation of *The Diary Of Anne Frank* filmed in sombre black-and-white, then had a major personal setback when *The Greatest Story Ever Told* flopped. He retired after one last undistinguished effort, *The Only Game In Town* (20th Century-Fox), starring Elizabeth Taylor and Warren Beatty.

Above: Shane (1953) has become a classic among Technicolor Westerns. Left is young Brandon de Wilde with star Alan Ladd; Jack Palance is the rancher on the right.

Above: Elizabeth Taylor and Montgomery Clift were at the peak of their glamour in 1951 when they starred in *A Place In The Sun*, Stevens' version of 'An American Tragedy' – a sombre story of the corrupting influences both of wealth and of poverty.

Left: James Dean and Elizabeth Taylor in *Giant* (1956), a somewhat sprawling adaptation of Edna Ferber's novel, in which Dean made the last appearance of his brief career (and life).

ROBERT STEVENSON

Born London, 1905.

Robert Stevenson was active as a director for over forty years from 1932 through 1976. In fact, he really had four different and varied careers, one for each decade. During the 30s he first emerged as a British writer and director of note, while the 40s brought him to Hollywood where he was put under contract by David Selznick, then by RKO. He worked for TV during the 50s, and in the 60s was the leading director of live action features for the Disney Studio where he achieved his biggest success.

Educated at Cambridge University, Stevenson first broke into films by working for a newsreel agency, then was employed by producer Michael Balcon at Gaumont-British and Gainsborough studios as a scriptwriter during the early 30s. He collaborated on the scripts of four Victor Saville pictures during 1931-32, two of them starring comedian Jack Hulbert, then worked on a number of British-German co-productions before he began directing himself. He easily made this transition with a pair of movies co-starring Jack Hulbert and his comedienne wife Cicely Courtneidge, but first achieved a reputation as a director a few years later with the costume picture, *Tudor Rose* (1936), a kind of follow-up to Korda's *The Private Life Of Henry VIII* (1933) which starred Nova Pilbeam, a young John Mills, and Cedric Hardwicke as the scheming Earl of Warwick. In 1934 Stevenson married actress Anna Lee who starred in many of his films during the late 30s including an ambitious adaptation of *King Solomon's Mines* (1937) which also starred Paul Robeson and Hardwicke. After the departures of Victor Saville and Alfred Hitchcock from Gaumont, Stevenson stood next in line as that studio's leading director. But he too had his eye on Hollywood and, was signed to a contract by Selznick in 1939.

Once in Hollywood, Stevenson quickly established himself as a director of note during the early 40s, with a variety of films that included a stylish remake of *Back Street* (Universal, 1940) starring Charles Boyer and Margaret Sullavan. *Joan Of Paris* (RKO, 1942) paired Paul Henreid and Michèle Morgan (in their first American picture) as lovers thwarting the Nazi occupying forces; and there was a pair of British literary adaptations of note, *Tom Brown's Schooldays* (RKO, 1940), and *Jane Eyre* (20th Century-Fox) with Joan Fontaine and Orson Welles in his first starring-without-producing role. Stevenson completed this latter film in 1943 shortly before leaving for war service. His postwar career, however, was rather less distinguished. The best of his thrillers was a Dick Powell actioner, *To The Ends Of The Earth* (Columbia, 1948). The worst were *I Married A Communist* (aka *The Woman On Pier 13*, 1949), Howard Hughes own pet anti-Red project which had already been turned down by a slew of directors, including John Cromwell, and *The Las Vegas Story* (1952), set in typical Hughes territory. Both were among RKO's biggest box

office disasters with losses on each estimated at over $600,000.

This seemed like a good time for Stevenson to embark on a new career as a television director on such shows as *Alfred Hitchcock Presents*, *Playhouse Of Stars*, *General Electric Theatre* and *20th Century Fox Hour*. However, no one was more surprised than Stevenson himself by the next development in his career, in 1956. 'I was hired for six weeks (by Walt Disney) but stayed for twenty years.' He had a big hit with his second Disney film, *Old Yeller*, late in 1957 and never looked back. During the following years, in marked contrast to his RKO experience, he had no less than ten more major hits, concluding with *The Shaggy D.A.*, his last feature, in 1976. These children's comedies, best known for their eccentric characters, wacky situations and elaborate special effects were not all that different in flavour from Disney's animated movies. And in some of the best, like the delightful *Mary Poppins* (1964), cartoon characters were freely mixed with live action. *Mary Poppins* won Oscars for best song, score, editing and special effects. The best actress award went to Julie Andrews for her enchanting realisation of P.L. Travers' super-magical Edwardian nanny, and Stevenson's own achievement was acknowledged with an Academy nomination.

Left: Joan Fontaine starred as Charlotte Brontë's bleak and put-upon heroine, *Jane Eyre* (1943). On the right is Henry Daniell as Mr Brocklehurst.

Above: The high success point of Stevenson's extraordinarily varied career was *Mary Poppins* (1964), which brought him his only Oscar nomination. Julie Andrews, here dancing with the chimney sweeps, was enchanting in the title role.

Left: Director Stevenson (right) on location for *One Of Our Dinosaurs Is Missing* (Walt Disney, 1975). The actor in hat and moustache is Clive Revill, one of a cast that was all-British but for the distinguished American actress, Helen Hayes.

PRESTON STURGES

Born Chicago, 29 August 1898. **Died** 1959

'I think the pictures made by directors who have become producer-directors are better than they were when they worked solely as directors. I know it's a more satisfactory way of working. I like to consider myself a picture-maker . . . I like doing it by myself. If I'm wrong then I'd like to be totally responsible for being wrong.' Sadly appropriate words indeed from Preston Sturges, one of the most brilliant and witty of Hollywood 'hyphen-ates' (writer-directors) of the early 40s. For when he tried to add '-producer', it proved to be his undoing. The meteoric rise and fall of Sturges can only be ex-plained thus – that he needed his studio (Paramount) as much as it needed him. His most remarkable and productive period was concentrated into only four years, 1940–43. Virtually all writers on Sturges get their dates wrong and thus miss out on a sad irony of his career. His problems with studio interference and delays in releasing meant that three of his eight Paramount pictures as writer-di-rector, and two of the best – *The Miracle Of Morgan's Creek* and *Hail The Conquer-ing Hero*, both Oscar-nominated for their witty scripts – were not released until 1944 *after* he had left. Paramount prob-ably didn't realise how much they missed him until he was gone, although the gap he left was already being filled by a new and talented writer-director, Billy Wilder. Sturges had jumped out of the frying pan into the fire, as it were, when he teamed up with eccentric multi-millionaire and would-be film producer, Howard Hughes, in a disastrous partner-ship from which Sturges never fully re-covered. The Hughes years resulted in just one feature, an inventive come-back movie for Harold Lloyd, *The Sin Of Harold Diddlebock* (aka *Mad Wednesday*), which was never given a proper release. After this period, Sturges went on to direct only two more American features (at 20th Century-Fox) during 1948–49, both less than his best, and one last movie in France, where he had spent many years as a youth, and where he settled for a while in the mid-50s.

Preston's parents were separated soon after he was born, and his mother took him to live in Paris. When she married a successful Chicago broker named Sol-omon Sturges, young Preston acquired both a stepfather, whom he much ad-mired, and a new name. (He had been born Edmond P. Biden Jr). His unsettled youth was spent commuting with his mother between Paris and Chicago and studying at private schools in France, Germany and Switzerland. Wishing to emulate his successful stepfather, he managed his mother's cosmetics firm in New York for a time and invented a 'kiss-proof' lipstick. But, as yet, Sturges lacked any real focus or ambition. During the 20s he occupied himself with his inven-tions as well as marrying an heiress (the first of his four wives), then he turned to playwriting in 1928 while recovering from a serious appendectomy.

Sturges continued writing and briefly worked as a stage manager, then had his first big success with his play, 'Strictly Dishonorable'. He moved to Hollywood in the early 30s and worked on a wide range of projects, mainly adaptations of plays or stories with little opportunity for him to express his own personal qualities. *The Power And The Glory* (Lasky/Fox, 1933) is of special interest as it was based on Sturges' own original screenplay and told a strong dramatic story, making use of a complex flashback form many years before *Citizen Kane* (RKO, 1941). In ad-dition, Sturges' treatment of 'the great American success story', to which he re-turned with *Diamond Jim* (Universal, 1935), was a favourite theme which he would soon attack satirically in his string of comedies.

After a brief stay at Universal (1934–35), Sturges moved on to Paramount where he found the most congenial pro-duction set-up and made the transition to writer-director. The comedy tone of the delightful *Easy Living* (which he wrote) was most recognisably the voice of Sturges for the first time. Some of the rough edges were smoothed out in keep-ing with the style of director Mitchell Leisen, but a few wacky moments re-mained – like the slapstick free-for-all (literally) in the automat when all the food windows are accidentally flung open. There was plenty of characteristic Stur-gian dialogue to relish, of course, deli-vered by favourite character actors like the prim and proper Franklin Pangborn, the gravel-voiced William Demarest and the dignified, unflappable butler, Robert Greig, all of whom would reappear in Sturges' own later pictures. He was often a visitor on the set while these early movies were being shot, learning about studio methods of film-making, pho-tography and set design, and already painfully aware that only by directing himself could he ensure that his scripts would be treated as he wished. In fact, he only managed to persuade the studio to give him the opportunity to direct by of-fering them the script of *The Great McGinty* (1940) for free. When the film proved to be a success, and won Sturges an Oscar for the script, it was clear that he had established a precedent and was soon followed into the directing chair by a number of other leading 30s scriptwri-ters, including John Huston and Billy Wilder, who well appreciated what Sturges had accomplished.

Above: Brian Donlevy (right), profitably cast against type, was *The Great McGinty* (1940), Sturges' first feature as director and a big Oscar-winning (script) success.

Below: Continuing a penchant for casting against type, the director used Dick Powell – known till then as a sweet-voiced, sweet-tempered crooner – as a go-getter driven by the need to be a success. With him here is Ellen Drew.

Sturges was able to make this breakthrough because he was one of a kind. No other director has ever matched the inspired lunacy of his eight pictures in four years at Paramount, all scripted by him. His witty and sophisticated dialogue has rarely been matched, and he was the master of the one-liner. (Rudy Vallee to Claudette Colbert in *The Palm Beach Story*, 1942: 'Chivalry is not only dead, it's decomposed.'). Immersed for many years in the post-Hays Code, sanitised Hollywood of the 30s, when the screen's Andy Hardy represented small town America and the calculated, populist optimism of Frank Capra served as the yardstick of political commitment, Sturges' reaction was witty and cynical. Hollywood in the 40s was trying hard to grow up and Sturges made very effort to help. He took careful aim at a wide range of American institutions – war heroes, motherhood, the advertising world, politics and so-called 'reform movements' were a few of his many targets. Similarly, he inclined to off-beat role reversals in his leading characters: his men were often clumsy, softspoken, shy and bland, as represented by Joel McCrea, Rudy Vallee, Henry Fonda (in *The Lady Eve*), and Eddie Bracken, the director's favourite, self-deprecating hero. The men often served as foils to aggressive and outspoken women as portrayed by Betty Hutton, Barbara Stanwyck (continually getting the better of Henry Fonda); Veronica Lake sarcastically deflating Joel McCrea's pretensions in *Sullivan's Travels* (1941); or Mary Astor taking aim at McCrea in *Palm Beach Story*: 'How wonderful to meet a silent American again! All my husbands were foreigners – and such chatterboxes!'

Best known for his ingenious plots and witty dialogues delivered at a cracking pace, Sturges was also a master at casting (necessarily so in view of the smallness of some of his budgets), and in directing his actors in their new, and sometimes unfamiliar, roles. He made good use of Brian Donlevy's aggressive qualities to turn him into the outwardly cynical and upwardly mobile McGinty. The comedy was played straight, while the tender side of Donlevy/McGinty was brought home through a beautifully executed cut to our first glimpse of him, newly domesticated late in the film. The initial impact was achieved by the sound of his abrasive voice '... but they had to get up to be earlier than Willie the Rabbit', before one's eyes could register the image of him with one sleepy stepchild on each knee as he reads from a large children's picture book. The director gave ex-crooner Dick Powell his first meaty role as the go-getter hero of *Christmas In July* (1940), whose oddball dedication to the success ethic means that he enters every type of contest or competition in search of an elusive jackpot. Having made his first features on small budgets (of about $350,000) without major stars, he was given Henry Fonda and Barbara Stanwyck for *The Lady Eve*. Miss Stanwyck had previously appeared in the Sturges-scripted *Remember The Night* in 1939, while for Fonda, his role as an absent-minded young millionaire with a passion for snakes provided one of his rare and entertaining ventures into comedy. Sturges' Joel McCrea period immediately followed – three movies in a row with the actor whom he considered sadly underrated, while Joel recalls Sturges as 'the most charming, humorous, talented, gifted man I ever met.'

Sullivan's Travels (1941) was more of a social satire than a comedy, with its barbs pointed at Hollywood and the socially significant aspirations of some movie directors. Echoing 'Gulliver's Travels', the film depicted the chance encounters and experiences of a movie director as he travels around the country looking for the kind of material which can be turned into a 'meaningful' movie. It boasted some of Sturges' wittiest dialogue, but veered a little uneasily between comedy, satire and seriousness. The relationship between McCrea and the Girl, played by Veronica Lake, is handled with affection and wit: 'Don't you think that while Europe is devastated by war a film director can be better employed than in making comedies?' he asks. To which she replies, 'No'.

Continuing the pattern of alternating between social satire and comedy-romance, Sturges and McCrea had their

pair of Eddie Bracken movies in 1943. Here, for the first time, he created an entire crazy world of his own on the studio back lot, his personal view of small town America, peopled by his oddly assorted types. Full of topical references to the war, they represent his suitably backhanded contribution to the war effort and his views on such topics as mother-son and father-daughter relations, on the Marines and heroes and, especially, on local politics. 'Politics is a very peculiar thing, Woodrow,' Harry Hayden explains to Eddie Bracken in *Hail The Conquering Hero*. 'If they want you, they want you. They don't need reasons anymore. They find their own reasons. It's just like when a girl wants a man.' Here Sturges' limited mastery of film technique and tendency to let scenes run on too long is more than balanced by the efforts of his expert lighting cameraman (John Seitz), by the use of long and suitably mobile shots, by Sturges' characteristically superb sense of comedy

'In 22 years, I managed to alienate every one of the seven major studios and soon found myself out of work'

Left: Joel McCrea again, with Claudette Colbert, in probably the funniest of his collaborations with Sturges, *The Palm Beach Story* (1942).

Below: *Hail The Conquering Hero* (1944), starring Eddie Bracken (foreground centre left) and Ella Raines (right of Bracken), was a highly skilful and imaginative satire on heroism, politics and small-town values. There were a couple of remarkably large and intricate crowd scenes – here, the railway station finale is being filmed. Sturges, script to hand, is kneeling below the camera.

biggest hit together with the hilarious *Palm Beach Story*. Here Joel, playing superbly against type, is married to Claudette Colbert. Fleeing south to Palm Beach by train she encounters the Ale and Quail Club, Sturges' most concentrated collection of his favourite, oddball character actors, and Rudy Vallee. Through the various complications which ensued, Sturges' most entertaining satire of the idle rich emerged.

The situation of a dissatisfied wife married to an impractical inventor is taken up in a more serious vein in *The Great Moment* (filmed in 1942). Ever eager to explore new themes and subjects, Sturges here turned to the biopic and to the true story of the invention of anaesthesia, making use of a complex flashback form which recalled his script or *The Power And The Glory* nine years earlier. He adroitly mixed slapstick – William Demarest going berserk after an overdose of laughing gas – with serious drama, but the studio bosses refused to release it. (A severely cut and restructured version appeared early in 1944 and flopped badly).

Meanwhile, Sturges had returned to his favoured vein, comedy-satire, with a

timing, and, most of all, by the astonishing inventiveness of plot and dialogue.

After investing much time and energy in a number of projects in partnership with Howard Hughes, Sturges ended up at 20th Century-Fox where he directed the disappointing *Unfaithfully Yours* (1948) starring Rex Harrison and Linda Darnell, followed by the Technicolored musical Western, *The Beautiful Blonde From Bashful Bend* (1949). Finally, *Les Carnets Du Major Thompson* (1956), an absolute failure filmed in France and starring an ill Jack Buchanan, marked the sad end of Sturges' career. He died three years later.

Left: Rudy Vallee (left) and Rex Harrison in *Unfaithfully Yours* (1948), Sturges' last major film but, unfortunately, not one of the director's most memorable.

FRANK TASHLIN

Born Weehawken, New Jersey, 19 February 1913. **Died** 1972

Frank Tashlin is the only Hollowood cartoonist who became a scriptwriter and director of live action features. Most film buffs know that he began in cartoons where he originated the crazy style of comedy and surreal visual gags for which he is best remembered. But few realise just how important a role he played as a young man in helping to establish the freewheeling stylistic qualities associated with the best Hollywood cartoons during the golden era from the late 30s through the 40s. Tashlin's importance as an innovative cartoonist matched that of his better known later career as a leading director of comedy features starring Jayne Mansfield and the Dean Martin and Jerry Lewis duo during the 50s.

A high school drop-out, young Frank was first attracted to movie cartoons as a teenager. He was still quite young when he landed his first job and rapidly worked his way up from gag writer at the Van Beuren studio (in 1933), to employment with brilliant animator Ub Iwerks (mid-30s), and established himself as an animation director at Warner Bros. during 1936–38. A man of many talents, he had originated his own syndicated comic strip which was carried by a number of newspapers and served as a gag writer for comedy producer Hal Roach. At Warners he joined with other cartoonists, including Tex Avery, Chuck Jones and Bob Clampett, who were busy developing a new style of imaginative and original work. Tashlin played an important role in helping to free the cartoon from naturalistic conventions; he made full use of cinematic methods, introducing a variety of surreal gags, fast editing techniques and in-joke references to current events, well-known personalities, and feature movies in his cartoons.

Tashlin moved on to Columbia (Screen Gems) during the early 40s where he served as production supervisor, hired a new group of young animators, and was instrumental in giving that studio's cartoons a new, improved look. He even had time to write and direct his own cartoons, like the highly inventive *The Fox And The Grapes* (1941). He returned to Warner Bros. for one last outstanding burst of creative activity which included the masterful *Porky Pig's Feast* (1943) and the Oscar-nominated *Swooner Crooner* (1944). But already he was set on breaking into features and signed as a gagman for Paramount. Active as a scriptwriter during the late 40s, he got his first chance to direct when hired to re-shoot half of the Bob Hope vehicle, *The Lemon Drop Kid* (uncredited) in 1950. Other comedies as writer-director followed at Columbia, Paramount and RKO, but his career really took off when he directed the most successful Dean Martin and Jerry Lewis comedy, *Artists And Models* (Paramount, 1955). For the next six years Tashlin had an unbroken string of hits alternating between Jerry Lewis movies at Paramount and glossy CinemaScope comedies for 20th Century-Fox. Demonstrating a remarkable consistency, his films uniquely exploited those very same qualities which he had first demonstrated in his cartoons – a love of outrageous gags and slapstick comedy while satirising a wide range of contemporary (50s) subjects – TV, the advertising industry, rock 'n' roll and Hollywood film-making. His pictures were littered with cultural references and in-jokes, both aural and visual, and while they were often uneven in quality, Tashlin's fine visual sense ensured that they were always colourful and exciting to

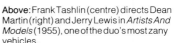

Above: Frank Tashlin (centre) directs Dean Martin (right) and Jerry Lewis in *Artists And Models* (1955), one of the duo's most zany vehicles.

watch. He made particularly good use of the new larger and wider screen and the glossy 50s colour, and French critics like Truffaut and Godard regarded him as the most audaciously modern of 50s comedy directors. Tashlin's undoubted masterpiece was *The Girl Can't Help It* (20th Century-Fox, 1956). About a girl singer dominated by her gangster boy friend, but in love with another guy, there was plenty of room for a classic 50s line-up of rock performers including Gene Vincent, Little Richard, Eddie Cochran and Fats Domino. Most remarkable of all was Tashlin's unselfconscious use of strong, vulgar colours, while Jayne Mansfield made an ideal comic strip heroine.

Tashlin rounded off his career with a pair of Doris Day comedies during 1965–66 and one last, uninspired Bob Hope vehicle, *The Private Navy Of Sgt O'Farrell* (UA, 1968).

Above: Jerry Lewis as *Cinderfella* (1960), an updated reworking of the Cinderella idea with Jerry as the put-upon lacky. It cannot be counted as a success for either star or director.

Left: *The Girl Can't Help It* (1956), Tashlin's best feature comedy, capitalised heavily on Jayne Mansfield's much-publicised (and glaringly obvious) natural assets for its laughs. With her here are Tom Ewell (left), Edmond O'Brien (in bed) and Henry Jones.

'Tashlin sees life in terms of cartoon films in which he treated Jerry Lewis and others as animated drawings, which accounts for much of the cruel and mechanical humour, but also for the crazy flights of fantasy'

Ronald Bergan in 'A-Z of Movie Directors'

RICHARD THORPE

Born Hutchinson, Kansas, 24 February 1896

'He was the most efficient director I ever knew in terms of things technical ... He was not an actor's director by any means, but he made up for it in other ways. The beauty of Thorpe was that, if you had a script you liked, he just shot it.' These comments came from MGM producer Pandro S. Berman who worked with Richard Thorpe on a number of lavish costume movies during the 50s when the director was at his peak. One of the most prolific of Hollywood directors, Thorpe's career spanned a period of forty-five years (1923–67), most of them spent at MGM. He had started out as an actor in vaudeville and musical comedy prior to World War I. Arriving in Hollywood after war service, he continued to act, but soon became more interested in working behind the camera and quickly worked his way up from gagman and propman to editor and assistant director. He began directing in 1923 and during the following years turned out a continual stream of cheap action pictures, B-Westerns, comedies and serials, working for many of the smaller Hollywood companies like Hodgkinson, Tiffany, Mascot and Chesterfield.

His big break came in 1935 when he was hired by MGM, where he remained for almost thirty years. Working at a remarkable pace and averaging three features per year for twenty of those years, he was soon rivalling (and later replaced), the studio's legendary speediest director, 'One-take' Woody Van Dyke, who died in 1943. Thorpe firmly established himself at MGM during 1936–37, reviving the studio's Tarzan cycle (with Johnny Weissmuller and Maureen O'Sullivan as the stars) first begun by Woody in 1931. *Tarzan Escapes* (1936) was followed by Ann Sothern's first MGM comedy, *Dangerous Number* (1936). Then came *Night Must Fall* (1937), from Emlyn Williams' stage play, an uncharacteristic MGM thriller but extremely effective as handled by Thorpe. Robert Montgomery had insisted on doing it in spite of the opposition of the studio bosses. He was charming and likeable one moment, devious and frightening the next, as Danny, the murderous psychopath. The role won him an Oscar nomination, along with Dame May Whitty in her sound film debut as the frightened old lady, and the film made the director's name. He continued to direct a wide variety of movies and gradually moved up from B-features to A's during the early 40s. His peak years which followed reflected the general trends in the MGM output, especially musicals and family entertainment during the 40s, lavish costume pictures and actioners mixed with the occasional musical during the 50s.

Thorpe was, surprisingly, the first of three directors assigned to *The Wizard Of Oz* in 1938, but was replaced after one week of filming and had to wait another five years for his musical debut, a fairly competent and certainly entertaining effort, aided by an all-star cast, called *Two Girls And A Sailor*. Working with producer Joe Pasternak, he went on to direct no less than five Technicolored smash hit musicals during 1945–48, three of them starring Esther Williams. Thorpe guided the unpredictable Mario Lanza though his most successful role as *The Great Caruso* (1951), but the best of the director's musicals was undoubtedly *Three Little Words* (1950), a lively biopic which starred Fred Astaire and Red Skelton as the songwriting team of Bert Kalmar and Harry Ruby. *Ivanhoe*, filmed in England in 1951 with a mainly English cast and production crew, marked a new phase in Thorpe's career as MGM's leading director of costume actioners. A visually stylish production, it was his only film to be nominated for a Best Picture

'His reputation for only needing one take is why we don't remember his films'

James Mason

Above: Johnny Weissmuller, the most famous of the Tarzans, with Maureen O'Sullivan (Mia Farrow's mother) as Jane in *Tarzan Finds A Son* (1939).

Left: A slightly aging, somwehat paunchy but still dashing Robert Taylor was *Quentin Durward* (1955), one of Thorpe's trio of 'Knights and Ladies' movies, instigated by the success of *Ivanhoe* (1951).

Below: Director Thorpe (left) with Angie Dickinson and Glenn Ford during the filming of *The Last Challenge* (1957).

Oscar and was his biggest box-office hit. Co-starring Elizabeth Taylor, it was so successful that it sparked a whole new Hollywood cycle of knighthood movies. Thorpe, star Robert Taylor and producer Pandro Berman did a follow-up pair for MGM, *Knights Of The Round Table* (1953), MGM's first in CinemaScope, and *Quentin Durward* (1955), as well as making a number of other films together. But Richard Thorpe's last film of note was the Elvis Presley cult classic, *Jailhouse Rock* (1957). He retired in 1967 after directing a last Western, *The Last Challenge*, for MGM. His son, Jerry Thorpe, is a chip off the old block, a leading director of action series and movies for American television.

157

JACQUES TOURNEUR

Born Paris, 12 November 1904. **Died** 1977

The Tourneurs are probably the most famous father and son directors in movie history. The outstanding silent film-maker, Maurice, is best known for his work during 1914–25, while son Jacques was most active during the 40s and 50s. They are of about equal importance, unlike other examples such as Richard and Jerry Thorpe, Max and Marcel Ophuls, Jacques and Jean Becker where the sons failed to equal the achievement of their famous fathers.

Known as one of the outstanding visual stylists of the silent cinema, Maurice had originally studied painting and first began directing in France in 1912. He is best remembered, however, for those films he made from 1914 in the US, where he was joined by his young son. His best movies were characterised by a very modern style of lighting and composition as seen, for example, in his excellent adaptation of Conrad's *Victory* (Paramount, 1919). He also worked with a number of the top stars of the period, most notably Mary Pickford.

By the time that Jacques had become involved in film-making as a career, his father had returned to France. Jacques followed him home and was given his first important work as an editor and assistant director during the early 30s, before directing a few minor features of his own. However, by 1934 the younger Tourneur was back in California where he had grown up – and where the pay was better. He was employed by MGM as a second unit director and director of shorts, one of which, *Romance Of Radium* (1937), was nominated for an Oscar. The all-powerful studio chief Louis B. Mayer especially liked one of his two-reel short subjects – a semi-documentary in the *Crime Doesn't Pay* series – on Federal penitentiaries. According to Tourneur, Mayer decided to upgrade it to a four-reel 'featurette' and then to a six-reeler; thus, 'we finished with a full length feature called *They All Come Out* (1939) . . . and that's how I did my first feature at MGM'.

Not surprisingly, the independent-minded director soon left the giant, impersonal MGM and was offered a job by his old friend, producer Val Lewton. They had worked together briefly filming the second unit footage for *A Tale Of Two Cities* at MGM in 1935, and now Tourneur joined him and then editor Mark Robson in the small production unit they were setting up at RKO. Given a large measure of freedom within the relatively small budgets, Tourneur was assigned to direct the first three titles – *Cat People* (1942), *I Walked With A Zombie* (1943) and *The Leopard Man* (1943). In spite of the fact that they were all ostensibly 'lowly' horror films, they were so well scripted, and directed with such exceptional attention to atmosphere and detail, that they are today quite rightly regarded as classics of the genre.

Tourneur was immediately promoted to A-features, specialising in thrillers and actioners. He was given Technicolor for the first time for his first 'outdoor' pic-

ture, *Canyon Passage* (Wanger/Universal, 1946), an action-filled and entertaining Western starring Dana Andrews and Susan Hayward. His most notable entry in the 40s *noir* cycle, *Out Of The Past* (RKO, 1947), had an incredibly complex plot line and an appropriately downbeat ending, with effective low-keyed lighting supplied by Nicholas Musuraca (who had shot *Cat People*). It was perhaps conceived as RKO's answer to *The Big Sleep* (1946) from Warner Bros., just as his first A-feature, *Days Of Glory* (1944), had represented RKO's response to Paramount's *For Whom The Bell Tolls* (1943). Tourneur was rarely given the opportunity to stretch himself as a director. In addition, he generally worked less effectively in colour, as suggested by his many undistinguished efforts during the 50s. But he returned to black-and-white and horror for his last outstanding work, a chilling and powerful screen adaptation of M.R. James' 'Casting the Runes', retitled *Night Of The Demon* (1957), and filmed in Britain with Dana Andrews as

the star. From 1956 on Tourneur divided his time between working in TV and making feature films, and retired in 1966 after directing *City Under The Sea* (aka *War Gods Of The Deep*) in Britain.

Left: Christine Gordon (left), Frances Dee (Mrs Joel McCrea in private life) and the imposing and sinister Darby Jones in *I Walked With A Zombie* (1943).

Above: Director Jacques Tourneur (left) and star Ray Milland take a coffee break during the filming of *Circle Of Danger* (1951) at Shepperton, England.

Left: Dana Andrews (right), the star of Tourneur's first Technicolor movie, *Canyon Passage* (1946), here with Brian Donlevy. Visually immensely pleasing, this Western portrayed pioneering life, and featured the Oscar-nominated song, 'Ole Buttermilk Sky', composed by the great Hoagy Carmichael, with lyrics by Jack Brooks.

CHARLES VIDOR

Born Budapest, 27 July 1900. **Died** 1959

A leading contract director at Columbia during the 40s, Charles Vidor – no relation to his illustrious namesake, King – is best remembered for his three Rita Hayworth pictures and for a famous dispute with studio boss Harry Cohn. Specialising in comedies, musicals and romantic drama, the tall, handsome and charming director had a few romances of his own too, and participated in the Hollywood marriage-go-round. His first wife was Karen Morley, the star of his first Hollywood feature, *The Mask Of Fu Manchu* (MGM, 1932), and his second, actress Evelyn Keyes (1943–45). When they divorced she went on to marry director John Huston, while Vidor's third marriage was to Doris Warner LeRoy, daughter of Warner Bros. boss Harry, and ex-wife of director Mervyn LeRoy.

Vidor first developed an interest in the cinema after World War I – he had served in the infantry – and was employed for a time at the UFA studios in Berlin during the early 20s. Arriving in the US in 1924 he did a brief stint as an opera singer, then moved on to Hollywood where he worked his way up from assistant director and editor to full director status by the mid-30s. He demonstrated his directorial qualities in a wide variety of B-features: a Richard Dix Western, *The Arizonian*, and a tongue-in-cheek crime drama, *Muss 'Em Up*, were both filmed for RKO in 1935, while Akim Tamiroff starred as *The Great Gambini*, the best of Vidor's Paramount pictures in 1937. A long term contract from Columbia boss Harry Cohn marked the beginning of an unpredictable working relationship. *Blind Alley* (1939) was another superior B-thriller, while a couple of up-and-coming young Columbia stars, Glenn Ford and Rita Hayworth, were paired for the first time in *The Lady In Question* (1940), along with the young Evelyn Keyes. By now Vidor had left the B-movies behind. *Ladies In Retirement* (1941) was an extremely effective black drama starring Ida Lupino, Louis Hayward, Evelyn Keyes and Elsa Lanchester. He was then loaned out to RKO to direct Elsa's husband, Charles Laughton in a lively comedy, *The Tuttles Of Tahiti* (1942). Back at Columbia in 1943, a good year for him, he was given the studio's first two Technicolor movies – *The Desperadoes* (1943) was a lightweight Western which paired Glenn Ford and Randolph Scott. Then came *Cover Girl*, Columbia's initial entry in the Technicolor musical stakes. A mainly small-scale, intimate film, it had some terrific dance numbers created by newcomer Gene Kelly (assisted by Stanley Donen), but was designed as a showcase for the studio's top star, Rita Hayworth. The same team of writer Virginia Van Upp, cameraman Rudolph Maté and director Vidor were re-assembled late in 1945 for *Gilda*. With its outrageous eroticism, especially the 'Put The Blame On Mame' striptease number which was only included in the picture as an afterthought, the movie remains the best remembered of the glamorous Hayworth's

40s vehicles. The last (and least) of Vidor's Rita pictures, *The Loves Of Carmen* (1948), also marked the end of his association with Columbia after an absurd court case in which he attempted to get out of his contract by accusing Harry Cohn of verbal abuse.

From 1945 – when Vidor's Chopin biopic, *A Song To Remember* with Cornel Wilde starring, emerged as a surprise hit – up to his death in Vienna of a heart attack in 1959, while directing Dirk Bogarde as Franz Liszt in *Song Without End* (it was completed by George Cukor), Vidor was most closely identified with the ever popular musical biopic genre. He enjoyed his biggest 50s hit with Danny Kaye as a lively *Hans Christian Andersen* (Goldwyn/RKO, 1952), while *Love Me Or Leave Me* (MGM, 1955) emerged as the best film of the director's career. A surprisingly tough and downbeat musical based on the true story of 20s singer Ruth Etting (Doris Day), it featured an electrifying (and Oscar-nominated) performance from James Cagney as the gangster who discovers her. Vidor made Grace Kelly's farewell movie, *The Swan*, for MGM in 1956, then returned once more to the biopic with Frank Sinatra starred as nightclub performer Joe E. Lewis in *The Joker Is Wild* (1957) for Paramount. The same year came the ambitious but misconceived remake of *A Farewell To Arms* for Selznick, the director's last completed picture.

Left: Photographed during the filming of *Cover Girl* (1944) are, left to right, Phil Silvers who was in it, eminent songwriter Sammy Cahn who was visiting the set, stars Rita Hayworth and Gene Kelly, and director Charles Vidor.

Below: Doris Day is generally associated with fluffy comedies, musical and otherwise. However, she turned in an accomplished dramatic performance as famous torch singer, Ruth Etting, whose life was fraught with personal drama, in the biopic, *Love Me Or Leave Me* (1955).

Bottom: Grace Kelly and co-star Louis Jourdan – one of Hollywood's glamorous French imports – in *The Swan* (1956). After this one, the beautiful Miss Kelly went off to preside over the principality of Monaco as Princess Grace.

'I don't believe I ever used such terms with you as idiotic. I may have thought your excessive takes and angles were idiotic, but the most I've said was that they were a waste of my personal money'

Memo from David O. Selznick to Charles Vidor

ORSON WELLES

Born Kenosha, Wisconsin, 6 May 1915

Orson Welles is widely regarded as an unfulfilled genius – a director (and actor) of great talent and originality who astonished the film world with his brilliant first feature, *Citizen Kane* in 1941, but has never been able to equal the achievement. He has been criticised for squandering his talent and for self-indulgence, labelled (absurdly so) as a one-shot wonder, and accused of attempting to steal the scriptwriting credit for *Kane* from Herman Mankiewicz, its 'true' creator. In fact, the picture was a truly unique and unrepeatable phenomenon. A full understanding of how *Kane* came about and the ingredients which made it work is essential in any attempt to appreciate the special strengths and weakness of Welles the director.

The story of *Kane* begins with young Orson, the child prodigy who demonstrated precocious talent as a painter, writer, actor and amateur magician. He first made his name as a teenage actor in Dublin when he took himself to Ireland to sketch, in preference to attending college. An engaging and good-looking young man, he had returned to New York and had established himself as a leading actor and director on the Broadway stage and on radio by the age of twenty-two. In 1937 he founded his own Mercury Theatre in partnership with producer John Houseman. Among those productions for which Welles is best remembered are an all-black version of 'Macbeth' and a modern dress 'Julius Caesar' in which he played Brutus.

By the time he was signed to a Hollywood contract, Welles had already proved his ability to function in the multi-

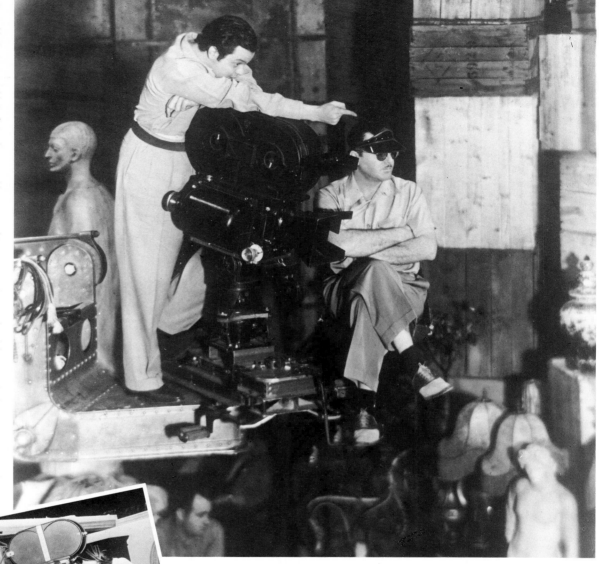

ple capacities of actor, writer, director and producer. His work in radio was as important as that in the theatre. He had demonstrated a remarkable grasp of the then new medium and an ability to use sound and dialogue creatively. His famous 1938 radio production of H.G. Wells' 'The War Of The Worlds' convinced many Americans that the Mar-

tians had indeed landed, causing confusion and panic. When Welles arrived in Hollywood in 1939 he immediately began to educate himself regarding all aspects of the film-making process, determined to make his movie debut with a highly personal and individual first feature. He worked on a number of possible projects including an adaptation of Con-

rad's 'Heart Of Darkness'. But he finally found what he was looking for in a story idea by scriptwriter Herman J. Mankiewicz and they collaborated on the script of *Citizen Kane*, with uncredited contributions from John Houseman and actor Joseph Cotten.

The film was conceived as a satirical treatment of the rise to fame and empty power of a fictitious American newspaper tycoon during the late 19th and early 20th century, loosely related to the true life stories of William Randolph Hearst and Howard Hughes, among others. The highly original script, with its use of a complex flashback form linking and ingeniously overlapping the memories of five different characters while covering fifty years of Kane's life, provided a marvellous opportunity for Welles to employ a vast array of cinematic techniques. Opening with the grotesquely stylised death of Kane (played in unforgettable bravura style by Welles himself), immediately followed by an astonishingly authentic looking 'March of Time'-type newsreel, the pace never slackened. The young director drew on all the resources of the RKO studio and many of its top

Above: The still young Welles hit the peak of his genius early with *Citizen Kane* (1941). Here, he sets up the extraordinary opening scene in the attic of Kane's mansion – a location based on newspaper tycoon William Randolph Hearst's baronial castle-style home. With him is the brilliantly innovative cinematographer Gregg Toland (seated).

Left: Toland (right) and his crew shoot a scene with Orson Welles and British actor George Coulouris who played the conservative, lawyer guardian of the young Kane.

'I dare predict that *Citizen Kane* will endure in the same way certain films of Griffith or Pudovkin endure: no one denies their historical value but no one sees them again. It suffers from grossness, pedantry, dullness. It is not intelligent. . '

Jorge Luis Borges in the Argentinian magazine 'Sur', 1941

technicians, and brought in ace camera-man Gregg Toland to help devise an ex-pressionistic visual style for the film, making use of unusual camera angles, ceilinged sets and a remarkable depth of field which kept foregrounds and back-grounds in focus simultaneously. As Toland recalled, 'In spite of the fact that Welles' previous experience had been in directing for the stage and for radio, he had a full realisation of the great power of the camera in conveying dramatic ideas without recourse to words... The photo-graphic approach to *Kane* was planned long before the first camera turned. That is unconventional in Hollywood where most cinematographers learn of their next assignments only a few days before the scheduled shooting starts.' In all, Toland was on the picture for six months, challenged as he never had been before. Many of the special effects techniques are so sophisticated that viewers are unaware of the extensive use of models and mattes, while a large number of the most complex shots were optically printed. The introduction to the Thatcher Library at one point, for ex-ample, which starts with a tilt down from a towering statue to the actors below was made from two separate stationary shots joined by a travelling split screen with the tilting movement achieved on the optical printer. The eerie echo effects of sound and voices lost in the vast expanses of the library represent but one example of the imaginative use of sound throughout.

Many sequences in the film are recog-nised as classics of their kind, like the breakfast scene between Kane and his first wife with its series of dissolves, flash pans and wipes, used to show the decline of their marriage over a number of years. Here editor (later director) Robert Wise contributed his expertise. Composer Bernard Herrmann was another of the many Welles associates who came with him to Hollywood, and who much ap-preciated the fact that he was regarded as an integral part of the creative team from the beginning of filming. But perhaps most extraordinary of all was the fact that Welles provided virtually the entire cast from his own Mercury Theatre players, none of whom had appeared in a feature film before. Here, that imposingly fine actress, Agnes Moorehead makes the point that 'Orson believed in good acting and realised that rehearsals were needed to get the most from his actors. That was something new in Hollywood: nobody seemed interested in bringing in a group to rehearse. But Orson knew it was necessary, and we rehearsed every se-quence before it was shot.'

From this discussion one gains some idea of the extent of Welles' innovations, stretching many of his collaborators as never before. Clearly, there is no way that any subsequent Welles film could match the originality of *Kane*. As he himself reflected twenty years later, 'Nobody else will make that sort of picture, under those ideal circumstances until another man will give a studio and its facilities to an artist to make the film he wants to make. It sounds terribly simple, but it literally never happens.'

Very much a film of its time, *Kane* rep-resented an ingenious variation on the biopic genre which was currently popu-lar, while Toland was able to take advan-tage of some of the most recent technical advances – faster film stock, improved lighting equipment, specially coated wide-angle lenses and a new, lighter weight camera. Together he and Welles had rejuvenated Hollywood studio film-making, sparking off a new interest in the potential for using stylised lighting and camera effects which would become an integral part of the 40s *film noir* cycle, for example. *Kane* could be said to have launched Hollywood into its last great era of black-and-white film-making during the 40s. In fact, the initial release of the picture was delayed by a threatened law suit from press baron William Randolph Hearst whose papers boycotted the film, and RKO, and it didn't get the wide re-lease it deserved. Nevertheless, it re-ceived the New York Film Critics award for the best picture of the year and nine Oscar nominations that included virtual-ly every technical category. Welles him-self was nominated for Best Picture, actor and director, but had to be content with a shared Oscar as co-author of the winning original script.

Always open to new challenges, Welles had immediately moved on to demons-trate how effectively his methods could be applied to a more conventional period subject. For *The Magnificent Ambersons*, filmed in 1941 with the Mercury players, much of the action takes place in a single, elaborate turn-of-the-century mansion. Here the remarkable set designs of Mark Lee Kirk match those of Perry Ferguson for *Kane*, while cameraman Stanley Cortez recalled his initial introduction to the film, paying a visit to the sound stage and finding Welles rehearsing on eight sets, upstairs and downstairs. He soon

found himself devising some of the most complex movements of lights and camera ever for tracking through the rooms of the mansion. For the ball evening, with danc-ing going on on every floor of the house, the camera performs its own elaborate and balletic dance. The film represented Welles at his most reflective and nostal-gic. A meticulously crafted slice of Americana, it could be seen as a tribute to his own father who was an early auto-mobile manufacturer (like the Joseph Cotten character) and a friend of the author, Booth Tarkington, who wrote the novel on which the picture was based.

Welles here welcomed the opportunity to direct a film without acting in it, but he was back in front of the camera once again giving a typically Wellesian per-formance as the mysterious Colonel Haki, the head of the Turkish secret police, in yet another Mercury pro-duction, *Journey Into Fear*, before *Amber-sons* had finished shooting. Welles' first venture into *film noir*, this strange and

Top: A scene from *The Magnificent Ambersons* (1942) showing the elaborate hallway of the ornate mansion designed by Mark Lee Kirk. In the centre foreground, Joseph Cotten embraces Dolores Costello; on the stairs sit Tim Holt, as the scion of the Amberson dynasty, and Anne Baxter.

Above: A melodramatic thriller about a Nazi criminal who marries an American girl and sets up house in a small Connecticut town, *The Stranger* (1946) was a commercial success for director Welles. He was in it, too, (left) with Edward G. Robinson.

atmospheric spy thriller was produced and supervised by him, but mainly directed by Norman Foster. By late 1941 he was in danger of stretching himself very thin. According to Robert Wise, 'Orson was directing *Ambersons* in the daytime, working all night on *Journey*, and taping 'Lady Esther' radio shows on weekends. He was all over the place...' When he left for Brazil early in 1942 as a goodwill ambassador, and with plans to direct part of a new multi-episode feature there, *It's All True*, *Ambersons* had not yet been edited in final form. While he was filming in Rio, there was a change of management at RKO, ousting George Schaefer who had previously supported him. Suddenly Welles was through at RKO. *Ambersons* was released in a badly mutilated form with forty minutes cut and a new ending tacked on, and *It's All True* was shelved. (According to those few who saw some of it, the Technicolor footage which Welles

Many problems were encountered in filming this baroque, often confusing but always inventive morality tale. The budget soared, retakes were necessary, but it finally emerged as Welles' most fascinating and accomplished post-RKO work. By the time it was released in 1948, however, he and Rita were divorced. For his last 40s production in the US, he persuaded the lowly Republic Studios to let him star in and direct a film version of *Macbeth* (1947). Setting the pattern for all his later productions, it was shot quickly and cheaply under less than ideal conditions, resulting in a flawed but highly original effort.

Taking up residence in Europe where he made most of his later films, Welles generally used his starring roles in other people's movies as the means of financing his own pictures like *Othello* (1951), filmed in Morocco, an adaptation of Kafka's *The Trial* (1961) filmed in Yugo-

'No one can pretend to be a film director unless he also does his own editing... They let the studio janitor cut *The Magnificent Ambersons* in my absence'

Above: Welles with his then wife, Rita Hayworth in *The Lady From Shanghai* (1948). A somewhat confused and fantastical piece, the film was always gripping, and marvellous to look at, culminating in a famous and brilliant set-piece in which Hayworth is gunned down by Welles in a vast hall of distorting mirrors.

Left: Marlene Dietrich and Welles in *Touch Of Evil* (1957), a highly atmospheric, somewhat unpleasant thriller that concerned itself with narcotics and murder.

Below: As Falstaff in *Chimes at Midnight* (1966), adapted from Shakespeare.

had shot was remarkable. It was stored in the RKO vaults and later destroyed).

In an effort to restore his reputation Welles starred as Rochester opposite Joan Fontaine in *Jane Eyre* for 20th Century-Fox in 1943. *The Stranger* was a well-made thriller which Welles directed for producer S.P. Eagle (Sam Spiegel) in 1945 proving that he could complete a commercial assignment keeping to the assigned script and budget. He also co-starred, with Edward G. Robinson and Loretta Young, and the movie proved to be his most successful at the box office. In 1943 he had married Hollywood's most glamorous star, Rita Hayworth, in spite of the opposition of Columbia boss Harry Cohn. She gave a surprisingly good performance in an uncharacteristically downbeat dramatic role and with a new short-cut, blonde head of hair as *The Lady From Shanghai* in 1946, directed by and co-starring Orson (for Columbia).

slavia and France and his two Spanish-based productions, *Mr Arkadin* (aka *Confidential Report*, 1955) and *Chimes At Midnight* (1966), the best of his Shakespeare productions with Welles himself as a memorable Falstaff. He completed one American feature during the 50s, a powerful thriller notable for Welles' most unsympathetic character role as the loathsome local police chief in *Touch Of Evil* (Universal, 1957). In addition there were a number of uncompleted productions, the best known being an intriguing 50s film of *Don Quixote*. A French TV movie version of Isak Dinesen's *The Immortal Story* (1968) and an entertaining feature-length documentary about art forgery, *F For Fake* (1973), were both Welles in a minor key, characteristic of his later years. He was awarded a special Oscar in 1970 and was honoured by the AFI for his lifetime of achievement in films in 1975.

BILLY WILDER

Born Sucha, Austro-Hungary (now Poland), 22 June 1906

A Jewish refugee from Hitler's Europe, the tough, cynical and witty Billy Wilder arrived in the movie capital in the 30s, and emerged as the most modern of 40s writer-directors. He was an acute observer and satirist of aspects of life in his adopted country, gifts which reflected his early training as a journalist and crime reporter. Wilder's American career neatly divides into two main periods – the years as a writer, then director, at Paramount (up to the early 50s) collaborating with scriptwriter, then producer, Charles Brackett, and the later period, beginning in the late 50s, when his co-writer was I.A.L. Diamond and his pictures were financed by the Mirisch Bros and released through United Artists.

The mainstream development of Billy Wilder can be traced through half a dozen movies which he made over a period of twenty-four years, all filmed in stark black-and-white and beginning with one of the first and best of 40s *films noirs*, *Double Indemnity*, in 1943. Casting an often jaundiced eye on American life, Wilder played a major role in forcing Hollywood to handle more mature, adult subjects. He dealt with the problems of alcoholism in *The Lost Weekend* (1944), Hollywood and stardom in *Sunset Boulevard* (1950), exploitative journalism in *Ace In The Hole* (1951) – all for Paramount. Office politics and the pressures of life in the big city were under scrutiny in *The Apartment* (UA, 1960) and shyster lawyers in *The Fortune Cookie* (UA, 1966), although his output did include a number of lighter movies.

As a transplanted European, Wilder was fascinated by the cultural love-hate relationship between Europe and the US. A recurring theme in many of his films concerns the clash of cultures which results when Americans arrive in Europe – first treated in a light and entertaining manner in *The Emperor Waltz* (1947), a musical fantasy starring Bing Crosby, and Wilder's only early excursion into Technicolor. The theme is given a more characteristically downbeat treatment in *A Foreign Affair* (1948) dealing with the harsh realities of life in postwar, black market Berlin, while in *One, Two, Three* (UA, 1961) he returned to the same city thirteen years later to comment on Cold War politics and East-West relations, his witty dialogue delivered at a cracking pace by Hollywood veteran James Cagney. *Avanti* (UA, 1972) found Wilder in a more mellow mood following the experiences of American businessman Jack Lemmon in Italy to reclaim the body of his dead father, while *Fedora* (1977) starred another of his favourite actors, William Holden, as a writer trying to make contact with a reclusive ex-Hollywood star – *Sunset Boulevard* revisited. Wilder's European movies have never been as original or successful as the American ones. These two latter along with the Parisian comedy of pimps and prostitutes, *Irma La Douce* (UA, 1963), and *The Private Life Of Sherlock Holmes* (UA, 1970) set in Victorian London, sug-

gest that he has been distancing himself from the contemporary American scene. 'They say Wilder is out of touch with his times – frankly I regard it as a compliment,' Wilder stated in 1976. 'Who the hell wants to be in touch with these times?' Yet, ironically, Wilder's perceptive treatment of contemporary themes has been one of his special strengths since he first began directing, and it is, alas, not difficult to perceive the nature of his later decline.

Billy grew up in Vienna where he briefly attended university but left to become a reporter. Moving to Berlin during the late 20s, he supplemented occasional newspaper work by giving Charleston lessons – he was especially fond of American jazz – and by working as a male 'taxi dancer'. Attracted to the cinema, he soon became adept at writing silent film scenarios and turned out vast numbers of them, generally uncredited. His first credit of note was for his contribution to the script of *Menschen Am Sonntag* (1929) directed by Robert Siodmak. With the arrival of sound he was more in demand than ever and wrote scripts for major stars, but with Hitler's rise to power he left for Paris. He already had his eye on Hollywood, however, and stayed in France just long enough to co-script and co-direct *Mauvaise Graine* (1933), starring a young Danielle Darrieux.

Arriving in New York early in 1934, Wilder was soon on his way to Hollywood, but his lack of fluency in English meant that he experienced a couple of extremely difficult years before he was able to make a breakthrough as a scriptwriter. By early 1936 he had acquired a contract with Paramount. After working on a number of movies on his own, Wilder was teamed with Charles Brackett on the Lubitsch comedy *Bluebeard's*

Above: Ray Milland as Don Birnam, the tormented alcoholic, in Wilder's fine (and harrowing) study of alcoholism, *The Lost Weekend* (1944).

Left: Billy Wilder, fondly regarded as a frustrated actor by his stars, gives John Lund (centre) a demonstration in how he wants him to embrace Marlene Dietrich in *A Foreign Affair* (1948).

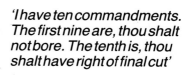

'I have ten commandments. The first nine are, thou shalt not bore. The tenth is, thou shalt have right of final cut'

Eighth Wife (filmed for Paramount in 1937). During the following years the partnership flourished as they turned out half a dozen memorable scripts, three of them for director Mitchell Leisen. They worked on the delightful screwball comedy *Midnight* which starred Claudette Colbert and John Barrymore in 1938, and Wilder earned his first of many Oscar nominations in 1939 for scripting the Garbo comedy *Ninotchka*, again for Lubitsch, but at MGM. He was nominated twice more in 1941, for the Howard Hawks comedy *Ball Of Fire* (Goldwyn/RKO, starring Cooper and Stanwyck), and *Hold Back The Dawn* (Paramount) about the efforts of Charles Boyer to gain American citizenship by taking advantage of a naive American schoolteacher (Olivia de Havilland).

More dynamic and aggressive than Brackett, Wilder was frequently and demonstrably unhappy about the way that their scripts had been treated, by director Leisen in particular, and was eager to turn to directing with Brackett serving as producer. As Wilder himself pointed out, 'I became a director because of my scripts. I wanted to protect them . . . I got the job after making myself rather unpopular as a writer.'

Following on the heels of other writers turned director like Preston Sturges and John Huston, Wilder got his first opportunity to direct in 1942 with *The Major And The Minor*. He purposely chose a lightweight comedy in the Sturges mold for his first film, the plot of which required Paramount's big romantic star, Ray Milland, to fall in love with Ginger Rogers masquerading as a twelve-year-old girl. Wilder thought that the studio expected him to make a mess of the film

and return to scriptwriting, but it was a big hit and he quickly moved on to another commercial project, making his contribution to the war effort with *Five Graves To Cairo* (1943), starring Erich von Stroheim as Rommel.

By this time the restless Wilder, ever in search of new challenges, felt it was time to try something more ambitious. A temporary rift with Brackett led to Wilder

offering writer Raymond Chandler a first taste of scriptwriting as they collaborated in bringing James M. Cain's novel, *Double Indemnity*, to the screen. Having succeeded in knocking the screenplay into shape, Wilder was faced with the problem of convincing a leading male star to take the role of Cain's crooked hero who comes to a bad end. Fred MacMurray (co-starred with Barbara Stanwyck) finally agreed to do it and the casting was perfect. By revealing the sleazy, darker underside to his ambitious, 'nice guy' character, Wilder not only destroyed Fred's All-American screen image for ever, but also cast doubt on the American materialist dream which went with it. The film was firmly grounded in a particularly Californian style of luxurious living – filmed extensively on location – but, most important of all, Wilder in-

Above: The cast of *Sunset Boulevard* (1950), poses for a publicity still. Wilder's durable masterpiece was hardly the good-natured romp indicated here. Only Erich von Stroheim (right) is in character as he, Nancy Olson and William Holden gaze at silent movie star Norma Desmond – otherwise Gloria Swanson, making a stunning comeback.

Below left: William Holden won an Oscar for his role in the POW film, *Stalag 17* (1953).

Below: Marilyn Monroe and Tom Ewell in *The Seven Year Itch* (1955) – a seemingly risqué but actually rather innocent comedy about a married man's fling with the girl upstairs.

jected a new cynical and bitter tone while aiming for a lowkeyed, underplayed style which marked the picture as an early and influential example of 40s *film noir*.

Wilder's role as a perceptive social critic was more in evidence in *The Lost Weekend*, filmed the following year (1944). He was attempting to break new ground with a serious and realistic depiction of alcoholism, but once again had trouble casting the hero, an alcoholic writer. He wanted the unknown José Ferrer, but when the studio insisted on a more attractive star, he ended up casting Ray Milland interestingly against type. Reunited with Brackett as producer and co-writer, Wilder again opted for extensive location shooting, this time in New York City, in an effort to bring the authentic milieu of seedy bars and pawn shops alive on the screen. The Paramount bosses didn't like the film and didn't know what to do with it. It was shelved for a time, then released a number of months later. Much to everyone's surprise it turned out to be Wilder's biggest box office hit of the 40s and won the Oscar as Best Picture of the Year (1945), with an additional statuette going to Milland and a pair to Wilder as director and co-writer.

In the meantime Wilder had travelled to Europe as head of the Film Section of the US Army's Psychological Warfare Division in 1945, then went off to the Canadian Rockies to shoot *The Emperor Waltz* and returned to Berlin for *A Foreign Affair*. Finally, to round off the decade, he set his sights on a target closer to home, namely Hollywood. Wary of adverse reaction from the movie colony, Wilder kept the new project firmly under wraps while it evolved from a lightweight treatment about an aging ex-movie queen, with Mae West or Mary Pickford as the possible star, into a pointed satire on Hollywood. Gloria Swanson was better suited to this new concept and gave an astonishing performance, while Paramount contract star, William Holden, a last minute replacement for Montgomery Clift, was perfectly matched to the role of the failed screenwriter turned gigolo. When preview audiences laughed at the prologue set in the morgue, Wilder replaced it with one of the most stunning yet economical of opening sequences, narrated by Holden as his dead body is dragged from a swank swimming pool off *Sunset Boulevard*. The presence of Erich von Stroheim in the cast conjured up memories of the Hollywood of a bygone age, while a clip from *Queen Kelly* (UA, 1929) appropriately connected him with silent star Swanson; Buster Keaton, Cecil B. DeMille and others made brief appearances as themselves. This audacious and inventive picture is marred only by an ineffective romantic subplot between Holden and Nancy Olson. Wilder the cynic is much more telling, but the abrasive tone of the film was a source of irritation to Brackett and, in spite of winning a screenplay Oscar, this marked the end of their collaboration. (Nominated for eleven Oscars, *Sunset Boulevard* only won in the minor categories, ousted by *All About Eve*.)

As if to prove the point, Wilder's first post-Brackett movie, *Ace In The Hole* (aka *The Big Carnival*, 1951), emerged as his

Left: Daphne, and Sugar Kane skip merrily along the passage of a Palm Beach hotel. They are actually Jack Lemmon and Marilyn Monroe in the superlative *Some Like It Hot* (1958), one of the director's undisputed masterpieces.

Below: Jack Lemmon, Shirley MacLaine (centre) and Edie Adams at the office party in *The Apartment* (1959), a trenchant satire on big city businessmen's morals – as well as a touching and funny romance.

most nasty and virulent work. The movie starred Kirk Douglas as a hard-boiled reporter determined to exploit the tragic situation of a young man trapped by a mountain cave-in for all it is worth. Though undeniably powerful, it was the least successful of all his early pictures at the box-office, and during the following years he directed a number of play adaptations which were entertaining and successful, but failed to match the originality of his 40s productions. Wilder was nominated for Oscars for directing *Stalag 17* (1953; William Holden won an Oscar) and for *Sabrina* (1954). Both were hits for Paramount, but he left after eighteen years with the studio. *The Seven Year Itch* (20th Century-Fox, 1955), adapted from the play by George Axelrod and starring Marilyn Monroe, was Wilder's first in CinemaScope, a comedy, and an even bigger hit.

Love In The Afternoon (1957) starring Audrey Hepburn and Gary Cooper was another enjoyable adaptation, scripted in collaboration with I.A.L. Diamond who became Wilder's new partner and sparked off a remarkable return to form. Together they worked on two quite different original scripts (for Mirisch/UA)

which represented Wilder at his mature peak: *Some Like It Hot* in 1958 was his comedy masterpiece – a hilarious and inventive script, it had marvellous performances from a cast headed by Marilyn Monroe, Jack Lemmon and Tony Curtis, and all contained within the framework of a superbly realised homage to the black-and-white gangster movies of the 30s (with George Raft and Pat O'Brien present to add that extra bit of authenticity). *The Apartment* (starring Shirley MacLaine and Jack Lemmon) which followed in 1959, although a 'happy ending' comedy romance, marked a return – in its main themes – to the black and bitter contemporary situations of Wilder's earlier pictures. At his peak as both writer and director, Wilder picked up two more Oscars along with the Best Picture award. He and Jack Lemmon went on to make many more movies together. The director teamed him with Walter Matthau for the first time in *The Fortune Cookie*, brought them back together for a remake of *The Front Page* (Universal, 1974) and again for *Buddy Buddy* (MGM, 1981), but the old magic was clearly missing and the brilliant Billy Wilder has not made another picture since.

Above: Wilder (right) rehearses James Cagney for a scene in *One, Two, Three* (1961), a wild farce with political East-West undertones.

ROBERT WISE

Born Winchester, Indiana, 10 September 1914

A solid, dependable, craftsman-like director who has made every kind of picture and worked for virtually all the major studios during almost forty years of directing, Robert Wise had a fairly humble beginning to his career. Forced to quit college and go to work at the age of nineteen, his elder brother helped him to land a first job in 1933 at the RKO studio, where he was employed as a shipping room clerk, then assistant sound effects cutter and assistant editor. By 1939 he had worked his way up to co-editor on a number of the studio's major productions such as *The Hunchback Of Notre Dame*. He finally achieved full editor status during the early 40s, when he gained widespread recognition for his collaboration with Orson Welles on *Citizen Kane* (1940), earning his first Oscar nomination, then on the much troubled production of *The Magnificent Ambersons* (1942). He was also forced to re-edit that film and was involved in some re-shooting after Welles was sacked.

Wise and his assistant, Mark Robson, were demoted to B-pictures along with other remnants of the Welles unit, but were fortunate to be assigned to producer Val Lewton who gave them both their first opportunity to direct in 1943. Working as editor on *The Curse Of The Cat People*, Wise was asked to take over from Gunther von Fritsch who had fallen far behind schedule on what was *his* first feature. This was a happy accident for Wise, the consummate professional, who had been eager to break into directing for some time and had previously done some second unit work. During the following years he made eight more movies for RKO, of variable quality, starting with a costume picture, *Mademoiselle Fifi*, adapted from De Maupassant and starring Simone Simon. Set during the Franco-Prussian war and shot on a tiny budget, its comment on the theme of collaboration with the enemy was given a newly topical meaning in 1944. The third and best of his Lewton productions was an extremely effective and scary horror film, *The Body Snatcher* (1945), from a Robert Louis Stevenson story. It had a strong cast headed by Boris Karloff and Henry Daniell, a fine script (co-written by Lewton himself) and was set in a superbly atmospheric studio re-creation of Edinburgh in the 1830s.

Unfortunately, Wise had to wait another three years (and four more pictures) before he was given the opportunity to direct his first A feature, *Blood On The Moon* (1948), a dramatic and solidly crafted Western starring Robert Mitchum. This was immediately followed by *The Set-Up*, the last and best of Wise's RKO years, a downbeat and distinctly 40s boxing picture which took an uncompromising look at the seedy side of the fight game. Suitably subdued photography was provided by Milton Krasner and Wise was fortunate to get Robert Ryan, who had had some experience as a boxer, for the leading role of the fighter reaching the end of the line. He

was not only convincing in the ring but had a tragic, even heroic stature.

Recognising the difficulties involved in working under the studio's eccentric new boss, Howard Hughes, the director was glad to get *The Set-Up* completed and move on to 20th Century-Fox in the early 50s. The best of Wise's Fox films was *The Day The Earth Stood Still* (1951), his first venture into sci-fi. The picture was characterised by a solid and sensible approach and benefitted from an extremely intelligent script about an alien visitor to earth, a kind of superior human being, who comes to deliver an anti-war warning to the human race. A quality studio production in every respect, with excellent photography, special effects, art direction and score, and fine performances from Patricia Neal and Michael Rennie,

Above: Shelley Winters (left) and Nina Foch in *Executive Suite* (1954), a gripping big business boardroom drama which showed how the goings on affected the lives of the people involved.

Left: Susan Hayward gave a memorable performance as Barbara Graham, the true-life victim of the electric chair, in Wise's graphically anti-capital punishment drama, *I Want To Live!* (1958).

Below: *West Side Story* (1961), a modern Romeo and Juliet tale, set to electrifying music by Leonard Bernstein (lyrics by Stephen Sondheim), and with vibrant and innovative choreography by Jerome Robbins, was given a naturalistic screen treatment, on location in New York, by Robert Wise. The still shows The Jets, one of the rival street gangs whose warfare ends in tragedy.

it was a moderate hit and helped to spark off a 50s sci-fi cycle. In his only non-Fox movie of the early 50s, *The Captive City* (UA, 1952), Wise effectively blended 40s *film noir* technique with a topical 50s theme – that of the need to expose the activities of organised crime. The movie referred to the current investigations of the Kefauver Committee, with Senator Kefauver himself making a brief appearance. Initiating another 50s cycle – this time the executive boardroom drama – Wise made *Executive Suite* for MGM late in 1953. The film reunited him with producer John Houseman with whom he had worked on *Citizen Kane*, and was memorable for the fine performances from an all-star cast headed by Fredric March, William Holden, Barbara Stanwyck, Shelley Winters and June Allyson. Wise spent the mid-50s at MGM where he directed a young Paul Newman in the

role that made his name in *Somebody Up There Likes Me* (1956), based on the early life of boxer Rocky Graziano.

Moving on to UA late in 1957 Wise directed Clark Gable and Burt Lancaster in *Run Silent, Run Deep*, a submarine drama, followed by the powerful and harrowing anti-capital punishment picture, *I Want To Live!* (1958). Based on the true story of vice girl Barbara Graham, allegedly framed for committing murder and subsequently executed, it featured an Oscar-winning performance from Susan Hayward and earned Wise his first directing nomination.

All the pictures discussed thus far were filmed in black-and-white, the preferred format for serious dramatic subjects of the type most favoured by Wise. But he had occasionally worked in colour, and in CinemaScope, on a few of his less memorable productions such as his sole venture into ancient costume spectacle, *Helen Of Troy* (Warner Bros., 1955) and the James Cagney Western *Tribute To A Badman* (MGM, 1956). No other major director could match Wise for the extraordinary diversity and general quality of his pictures during the 50s. Most obviously lacking was a musical – which is just the genre in which he proceeded to make his name in the 60s. In fact, the years 1959–61 marked something of a turning point for him. While continuing his association with UA, he assumed the role of producer-director for the first time and cut back on the number of his productions. Having directed eighteen features during the 50s, he made only six pictures in the 60s, three of them large budget musicals in colour, filmed in the new wide screen 70mm processes.

First of the three was *West Side Story* (UA, 1961) on which Wise was meant to serve as producer and co-director with the show's original stage director-choreographer, Jerome Robbins. It was the Robbins contribution, the remarkable

and innovative dance sequences, some of them filmed on the streets of New York which made *West Side Story* an exceptional musical both on stage and in the cinema. But unfortunately Robbins fell badly behind schedule and was removed from the film, leaving Wise to carry on alone. Wise could afford to be generous in sharing the directing credit and an Oscar with Robbins, for he was back four years later winning the Best Director Oscar for the phenomenally successful *The Sound Of Music* (20th Century-Fox, 1965). Both pictures also won the top Oscar along with a number of other awards, and for a short period Wise was one of the hottest properties in Hollywood. But in between the large budget filming, the director returned to his favoured black-and-white for a last pair of more intimate movies: *Two For The Seesaw* (UA, 1962) and *The Haunting* (1963). The former was adapted from

William Gibson's Broadway success and reunited him with Robert Mitchum, cast against type opposite Shirley MacLaine; the latter, an undistinguished horror film, was made in Britain.

After the failure of his lavish musical biopic of Gertrude Lawrence, *Star!* (20th Century-Fox, 1968) with Julie Andrews, Wise returned to more familiar territory during the 70s with the intelligent and gripping sci-fi drama, *The Andromeda Strain* (Universal, 1971). The reincarnation fantasies of the young girl in *Audrey Rose* (UA, 1977), related to his very first feature (*The Curse Of The Cat People*), and brought his career full circle. Ever willing to take on new challenges, Wise directed one big 70s disaster movie, *The Hindenburg* (Universal, 1975), and one last spectacular (and uncharacteristic) sci-fi, *Star Trek – The Motion Picture* (Paramount, 1979), less memorable for its characters than for its special effects.

Above left: Julie Andrews (left), Christopher Plummer and Eleanor Parker in *The Sound Of Music* (1965). Long, lush and wildly sentimental, this Rodgers and Hammerstein musical about the Von Trapp family (children here in the background) and their governess (Andrews) who outwit the Nazis, was based on a true story and was one of the biggest box-office successes in history.

Above: Robert Wise directs Julie Andrews for a scene in *Star!*, the unsuccessful though lavish attempt at a biopic of the enchanting Gertrude Lawrence.

Below: James Olson (left), Paula Kelly and George Mitchell in *The Andromeda Strain* (1971), an intelligent and successful excursion into sci-fi for Wise.

WILLIAM WYLER

Born Mulhouse, Alsace-Lorraine, 1 July 1902. **Died** 1981

The second son of Swiss-German-Jewish parents, William Wyler grew up in Alsace and Switzerland and studied in Paris, but his big opportunity came when a meeting with his mother's cousin, Carl Laemmle, led to the offer of a job in Universal's New York office in 1920. A year later he was transferred to Universal City in California. A lowly assistant and bit player at first, Wyler had become an experienced assistant director by 1925. He was one of many assistants who worked briefly on the large crowd scenes on *Ben-Hur* for MGM that year, and got his chance to direct his first two-reel Western, *Crook Buster*, back at Universal soon after. As he recalled, 'At the time I first came to Universal it was like a school for film-makers. If you wanted to direct, they gave you the cheapest, smallest pictures that they made to cut your teeth on: two-reel Westerns . . .'.

By late 1927 Wyler was directing five-reel Westerns, and in 1928 had a moderate success with his first silent comedy, *Anybody Here Seen Kelly?* starring Bessie Love. He welcomed the arrival of sound and the opportunity to move entirely away from the Western and work with top actors. He directed John Barrymore who gave a bravura performance in *Counsellor At Law* (1933), adapted from the Elmer Rice play, and demonstrated a special talent for directing the ladies, too. In 1934 Constance Cummings starred in *Glamour*, and Universal's newest young star, Margaret Sullavan, played the lead in *The Good Fairy*. Wyler married her later that same year. (She had divorced Henry Fonda in 1933, but for Wyler it was his first. They divorced in 1936 then, in 1938, Wyler married bit part actress Margaret Tallichet, a union which lasted up till his death). Benefitting from a witty, if slightly sentimental, script by Preston Sturges, *The Good Fairy* was a light comedy-romance which emerged as the most assured of Wyler's early movies. But it was his last for Universal. The director had already outgrown the then struggling and unadventurous studio and was looking for more prestigious opportunities. What he found was Sam Goldwyn, the leading independent producer in Hollywood, who hired him to direct a film adaptation by Lillian Hellman's of her own hit play, 'The Children's Hour', retitled *These Three*, in 1935. This marked the beginning of a tempestuous but productive seven-year relationship during which time Wyler emerged as her producer's leading director. Miss Hellman reworked the play in accordance with Goldwyn's understanding with censor Will Hays that he would eliminate the play's well-known lesbian theme. The main point of the original, however, to expose small town intolerance and bigotry, sparked off by the malicious and unfounded accusations of a child, was retained. A quality production of the kind which came to be associated with all Wyler-Goldwyn productions, the director drew outstanding performances from his cast (headed by Miriam Hopkins, Joel McCrea and Merle Oberon), and was aided by the topnotch Goldwyn technicians led by cameraman Gregg Toland, art director Richard Day and editor Daniel Mandell.

Attracted to quality properties, most often plays like *Dodsworth* (1936), which earned him his first Oscar nomination, and *Dead End* (1937), Wyler soon established himself as one of Hollywood's classiest directors, known as a perfectionist and hard taskmaster who demanded much of his cast, but achieved results which justified the hard work and multiple takes for every scene. He developed a close working (and personal) relationship with Bette Davis, in particular, who regarded him as her favourite director. They made three films together

during 1938–41, all adapted from popular plays which provided Davis with some of the meatiest roles of her early career and three Oscar nominations. She won for *Jezebel* (1938) which, along with *The Letter* (1940), was made for Warner Bros. – Wyler's only 'loanouts' during his Goldwyn period. The third (and best) for Goldwyn, *The Little Foxes* (1941) was scripted by Lillian Hellman from her own play and was notable, too, for the deep focus photography of Gregg Toland. Wyler had also directed a memorable version of Emily Brontë's *Wuthering Heights* (1939). Laurence Olivier, whose Heathcliff earned him his first Oscar nomination, credits Wyler with opening his eyes to the possibilities of the cinema, while Toland received his only Oscar for the atmospheric photography. Then Wyler made a rare return to the Western, with the emphasis on characterisation and underplayed humour (rather than

Above: William Wyler's first important feature was *Counsellor-At-Law* (1933). Here, he enjoys an informal chat on the set with his star, John Barrymore (right).

Below left: Herbert Marshall as the invalid husband and Bette Davis as his almost supernaturally ruthless wife, Regina, in Wyler's version of Lillian Hellman's *The Little Foxes* (1941). Tallulah Bankhead originally created the role on Broadway, and Elizabeth Taylor attempted it on Broadway and in London in 1983 with disastrous results.

Below: Wyler (left) and cameraman Gregg Toland rehearse with Dana Andrews and Virginia Mayo for *The Best Years Of Our Lives* (1946), the director's Academy award-winning study of returning war veterans.

action) from stars Gary Cooper and Walter Brennan in *The Westerner* (1940). The latter stole the film with his Oscar-winning portrayal of the likeable villain, Judge Roy Bean.

Finally, after being nominated three years running, Wyler won a Best Director Oscar and had a really big hit with *Mrs Miniver* (MGM, 1942), starring Greer Garson. A tasteful piece of pro-British propaganda showing how a 'typical' middle-class family coped with the Blitz and wartime privations, it was Wyler's last feature before he left for war service. By early 1943 he was himself stationed in England and in charge of an air force combat camera crew. He completed a pair of documentaries, flying a number of dangerous missions to get the footage he needed. Strongly influenced by his wartime experiences, Wyler returned to direct his last for Goldwyn, determined to make a picture which spoke to audi-

biggest successes with his actresses, getting Oscar-winning performances from Olivia de Havilland in *The Heiress* (1949), adapted from Henry James, and Audrey Hepburn whom he specially selected to star in her first American picture, *Roman Holiday* (1953). Wyler continued to mix contemporary pictures and dramatic thrillers like *Detective Story* (1951) and *The Desperate Hours* (1955) with costumers (*Carrie*, 1952) and Western drama – *Friendly Persuasion* (1956) and *The Big Country* (UA, 1958), his first two features in colour. As ever he turned for his sources to plays and novels, and was assisted by his older brother, Robert Wyler, who often served as his associate producer and co-scriptwriter.

In 1958, thirty-three years after he had been employed as an assistant on MGM's silent epic, *Ben-Hur*, Wyler accepted the studio's offer to direct the lavish remake. In typical Wyler fashion he

'I could please the highbrow critics by not showing it (the chariot race in Ben Hur) at all. I could just show two men standing by a window taking bets who'd win'

Above: Director Wyler at work on a scene for *Roman Holiday* (1953), with his protégée Audrey Hepburn while Mario de Lanni looks on. This, her first American picture, catapulted the enchanting Miss Hepburn from relative obscurity to major stardom.

Left: Jack Hawkins (left) and Charlton Heston cast adrift in *Ben-Hur* (1958), a long and lavish Technicolor remake of the famous silent epic.

Below: Wyler (seated foreground) instructs technicians during the making of *The Collector* (1965), while Samantha Eggar (left) looks on. This adaptation of John Fowles' claustrophobic study in psychosis co-starred Miss Eggar and Terence Stamp, and earned Wyler his ninth Oscar nomination.

ences about real contemporary issues. He found what he was looking for in MacKinlay Kantor's 'Glory For Us', about the difficulties faced by three veterans returning to civilian life after the war. It became *The Best Years Of Our Lives* (1946), a sensitively directed film, which was most memorable for those episodes concerning (and played by) a veteran, Harold Russell, who had lost both hands in a wartime explosion. The film won Oscars for Wyler, for scriptwriter Robert Sherwood and actors Fredric March and Harold Russell, and set box-office records as the biggest hit of the 40s.

Having completed his Goldwyn contract, Wyler joined fellow directors Frank Capra and George Stevens in setting up their own, independent production company, Liberty Films. Due to financial problems it was taken over by Paramount where Wyler directed his next group of films during 1949–55. Again he had his

put special emphasis on characterisation, aided by a large number of scriptwriters. (Karl Tunberg alone received official credit, but much essential dialogue was provided by Christopher Fry). In spite of Wyler's efforts the movie is best remembered for its spectacle, and the thrilling chariot race staged by Andrew Marton and Yakima Canutt. A smash hit and the winner of a record total of eleven Oscars including Best Picture, it provided the director with his last great moment and his third Oscar. He continued directing during the 60s, and in 1965 received his ninth Oscar nomination (a record) for *The Collector* (Columbia), as well as the Irving Thalberg Award. He displayed his finesse directing Barbra Streisand in her first, and Oscar-winning movie role (and *his* only musical), *Funny Girl*, for Columbia in 1968, and retired after one last disappointing movie, *The Liberation Of L.B. Jones* (Columbia, 1970).

FRED ZINNEMANN

Born Vienna, 29 April 1907

A dedicated and strong-minded director who has chosen his projects carefully, Fred Zinnemann has only made seven pictures in the last twenty-six years, all of them filmed outside the US. One of that distinguished group of American directors who originally came from Vienna, Fred left there when he became interested in the cinema (having completed studies in law). Since the Austrian film industry was tiny and offered few opportunities, he chose Paris as the best place to learn the technique of a cameraman and worked there briefly before moving on to Berlin. There he served as assistant cameraman on a few films including *Menschen Am Sonntag* (1929), directed by Robert Siodmak.

With the arrival of sound, Zinnemann immediately recognised the technical dominance of Hollywood and travelled to the US where he hoped to find work as a cameraman but, due to union restrictions, he was reduced to working as an extra in *All Quiet On The Western Front* (Universal, 1930) and then as an assistant to fellow Austrian, director Berthold Viertel during 1930–32. In 1934 he accepted an offer to direct a semi-documentary about the life of a group of fishermen living in a remote region of Vera Cruz in Mexico. Filmed in difficult conditions over a period of ten months as a Mexican-American co-production, produced and photographed by Paul Strand, the resulting picture, *The Wave*, impressed MGM sufficiently for that studio to offer Zinnemann a contract to direct shorts. 'The MGM shorts department was an excellent preparatory school for directors,' Zinnemann noted, 'because we had all the time in the world to prepare a film, but were obliged to shoot it very fast . . . This was meant to teach us that time was money . . .'

Joining such budding young directors as George Sidney and Jacques Tourneur, Fred turned out a large number of shorts on a variety of subjects during the following years. One of his earliest, the one-reeler *That Mothers Might Live*, won a short film Oscar in 1938, while *Forbidden Passage*, a dramatised two-reeler in the 'Crime Does Not Pay' series (about the successful activities of the US Immigration Service), was nominated in 1941. Later that year he directed his first short feature, *Kid Glove Killer*, in which the new MGM contract star, Van Heflin, played a forensic scientist who tracks down a murderer with the help of his trusty assistant (Marsha Hunt).

Zinnemann went on to direct a number of features for MGM. For his first A, *The Seventh Cross* (1944), adapted from a popular novel by the German writer Anna Seghers, the director was offered a major star, Spencer Tracy. Tracy played the lone survivor of a group of escapees from a German concentration camp, and was so impressed by the young director that he took every opportunity to praise Zinnemann's work. The picture did indeed succeed in giving a reasonably convincing feel of Germany under Nazi rule, with notable contributions from the veteran German-born cameraman Karl Freund, and a good collection of character actors. *The Search*, concerned with the plight of young war refugees, starred Montgomery Clift, was filmed on locations in Europe in 1947, and won the director an Oscar nomination; while *Act Of Violence* (1948) was an effective thriller which featured a terrific, offbeat cameo from Mary Astor, almost unrecognisable as a 'two-bit tart'.

Breaking away from MGM in 1949, Zinnemann teamed up with producer Stanley Kramer on three pictures, and directed three other films as well during 1950–53, the most productive and prestigious period of his career. During these years he developed a reputation as an outstanding director of actors and was known especially for his success with young and untried screen talent, not unlike Kazan who worked with many of the same stars. *The Men* (Kramer/UA, 1950), for example, is best remembered for the powerful performance of Marlon Brando – in his first movie role – as a paraplegic war veteran, with a cast which

included a number of real paraplegics. 'Marlon, as part of his preparation, spent three weeks in the ward, living with these men,' Zinnemann recalled, 'so that not only could he imitate their movements but he understood them very deeply.'

In 1951 Zinnemann won his second

Above: Van Heflin (left) and Robert Ryan in *Act Of Violence* (1948), a tense drama about a former soldier who sets out to track down a prison camp informer. Well-characterised and absorbing.

Below: Gary Cooper and Grace Kelly in Zinnemann's famous Western, *High Noon* (1952). Extremely well-made though it was, its familiar theme tune stands up better than the movie nowadays.

Oscar for *Benjy*, a documentary short which he made for the Orthopaedic Children's Hospital in Los Angeles, followed by *Teresa* (MGM), an honorable failure about the problems of a young veteran and his Italian war bride. The picture introduced Pier Angeli in her first American film, John Ericson, Ralph Meeker and Rod Steiger (in a tiny role). Later that same year the director made his only Western, the classic *High Noon* (Kramer/UA). Purposely filmed with a harsh, contrast-filled style of lighting, it appeared extremely stylised for dramatic effect, which suited the tightly constructed script by Carl Foreman. Again, the performances were excellent, especially those of Grace Kelly in her first starring role, Katy Jurado, and Gary Cooper winning an Oscar for his courageous town marshal who takes on four outlaws singlehanded. It was the first Zinnemann film to be nominated for Best Picture, while he himself gained his second director's nomination.

On a smaller scale was *The Member Of*

Montgomery Clift's high-class nightclub hostess girlfriend. All five leading members of the cast were nominated, with Zinnemann winning his first for directing, along with the Best Picture award, while the film was also the biggest box-office hit of his career.

After such a success the following years proved difficult for the director. His only attempt at a musical, *Oklahoma!* (1955) did not turn out well at all. It was also his first venture into colour, using the new large format Todd AO process. Shirley Jones was adequate in her first movie role, but Zinnemann could do nothing with Gordon MacCrae in the lead role of Curley. (He had originally wished to use the then unknown, non-singing James Dean.) Early in 1956 Zinnemann was reunited with Spencer Tracy for *The Old Man And The Sea*, but withdrew from the production which was subsequently completed by director John Sturges.

Zinnemann's career only began to pick up again when he moved abroad. He filmed *The Nun's Story* (1959) in the Bel-

Above: Robert Mitchum and Deborah Kerr starred as an Irish sheepdrover and his wife, trying to make out in the Australian bush during the 20s, in *The Sundowners* (1960).

Left: Paul Scofield (left) and Nigel Davenport in *A Man For All Seasons* (1966). Adapted by Robert Bolt from his own stage play, the film dealt with the rise and fall of the ill-fated Sir Thomas More, and was one of Zinnemann's biggest successes.

Below: Hal Holbrook (left) and Jane Fonda (as Lillian Hellman) discuss a scene with the director during the filming of *Julia* (1977).

'I know I'm not terribly popular. I've come to terms with it. I'm not in pictures to promote my private personality. I'm in it for the joy of it'

The Wedding (Kramer/Columbia, 1952), sensitively adapted from the play by Carson McCullers, and providing Julie Harris and Brandon De Wilde with their first screen roles. Miss Harris was Oscar-nominated for her exceptional performance as the twelve-year-old, self-conscious ugly duckling of the title (less than half her own real age and a role she had originally created on stage). Zinnemann remained at Columbia for *From Here To Eternity*, the most ambitious project of his career thus far, adapted from the gritty bestseller by James Jones about army life in Hawaii at the time of Pearl Harbor. Here the cast was an experienced one, but Zinnemann demonstrated his individualistic approach to actors, utilising both Deborah Kerr and Frank Sinatra in roles markedly different from anything they had played before. The impact of Miss Kerr's uncharacteristically earthy scenes with Burt Lancaster proved the value of 'casting against type', while Sinatra's dramatic performance earned him an Oscar, ditto Donna Reed playing

gian Congo and Europe, then went to Australia with Robert Mitchum and Deborah Kerr to shoot the lightweight but entertaining *The Sundowners* (1960) – both for Warner Bros. and both nominated for Best Picture with Zinnemann picking up two more directing nominations. But his one last big success of the 60s was the English-based production of *A Man For All Seasons* (Columbia, 1966) adapted from the play by Robert Bolt with Paul Scofield recreating his impressive stage performance as Sir Thomas More. Once again Oscars went to the picture, to Zinnemann, and to Scofield.

Julia (20th Century-Fox, 1977) was the most memorable of his later productions, with Vanessa Redgrave winning an Oscar for her performance as a lady of courage, and friend of Lillian Hellman (well played by Jane Fonda), and bringing Zinnemann's career full circle. The director's last film, *Five Days One Summer* (Warner Bros., 1982), a romance starring Sean Connery, was, alas, a real disappointment.

CHAPTER THREE
1960-1985

Film-making went on the move in the 60s – from studios to locations, from West Coast to East, from America to Europe. Production Code restrictions virtually disappeared but audiences declined and the studios were devoured by giant multinationals. By the 70s the new pioneer directors, the so-called 'movie-brats', had arrived…

The continuing decline in audiences had serious consequences for the movie industry during the 60s. Attempting to economise in various ways, the studios cut back on their staff, sold their land for development and their old movies to TV, and diversified into recording, publishing and – especially – TV production and other media-related activities. Many of the leading companies were involved in mergers or takeovers. Thus, Warner Bros. became Warner Bros.-Seven Arts, then Warner Bros.-A Kinney Company and finally emerged as Warner Communications. United Artists became part of the Transamerica Corporation; Universal merged with MCA and Paramount was bought by Gulf & Western, aptly parodied by Mel Brooks as 'Engulf & Devour' in his *Silent Movie* (1976).

The insecurity of the film companies did, at least, encourage a wide diversity in the films being made. Many veteran directors like Ford, Hawks, Wyler and Minnelli were still active, but were reaching the end of their careers. A number of directors came unstuck on large scale and expensive 70mm productions like Lewis Milestone with the remake of MGM's *Mutiny On The Bounty*

Above: An uncharacteristic venture for comedy actor, writer and director Woody Allen was his appearance in a straight role in a serious film, *The Front* (1976). Here he is with the movie's director, Martin Ritt (left).

Left: Photographed during the filming of *Lawrence Of Arabia* (1962) are, left to right, Alec Guinness in his King Feisal costume, producer Sam Spiegel visiting the locations, actor Jack Hawkins and director David Lean.

(1962), Nicholas Ray with *55 Days At Peking* and Joseph Mankiewicz with *Cleopatra* (both released in 1963), and George Stevens with *The Greatest Story Ever Told* (UA, 1964). At the opposite extreme was the group of newest arrivals including Sidney Lumet, Martin Ritt, John Frankenheimer and Arthur Penn, all graduates from live TV drama who worked on small black-and-white pictures in the years before the changeover to com-

plete colour (around 1966-67). Most of the other movies fell somewhere in between, filmed in a variety of widescreen formats, with the new improved Panavision replacing 50s CinemaScope and the expensive VistaVision.

There was a continuing decline in the number of studio-made pictures, as most of the top producer-directors preferred to film in the appropriate locations in the US and abroad. Movie-making grew rapidly on the East Coast, for example, with New York restored as a major pro-

duction centre for the first time since the silents. Following the lead of Elia Kazan, a number of new directors such as Lumet, then Martin Scorsese, Paul Mazursky and Woody Allen in the 70s preferred New York to Los Angeles. In addition, the restrictive provisions of the Motion Picture Production Code were gradually loosened and finally abandoned, opening the way for a new explicitness in the treatment of sex and violence. Arthur Penn was quick to seize this new opportunity with *Bonnie And Clyde* (1967), followed by other leading directors like Sam Peckinpah with *The Wild Bunch* (1969), Roman Polanski in *Rosemary's Baby* (1968) and *Macbeth* (1971), and British directors Ken Russell (*Women In Love*, 1970; *The Devils*, 1971) and Nicholas Roeg (*Performance*, 1970).

A major expansion took place in international co-productions, and in filming in England where American investment contributed to a major revival in the British film industry and the emergence of a number of outstanding new directors. Thus, a number of American-financed British productions were among the top Oscar-winning pictures and box-office hits of the 60s, including *Lawrence Of Arabia* (1962), *Tom Jones* (1963), *A Man For All Seasons* (1966) and *Oliver!* (1968). But by the late 60s the bubble burst. Many British-made movies such as *Dr Dolittle* (1967), *The Battle Of Britain* (1969) and *The Private Life Of Sherlock Holmes* (1970) were among the group of expensive box office flops which had a devastating effect on the American companies who recorded losses in the tens of millions of dollars.

In 1969 the surprise success of the relatively cheaply made *Easy Rider*, co-written and directed by Dennis Hopper, followed by Paul Mazursky's smash hit first feature, *Bob & Carol & Ted & Alice*, stimulated a major investment in youth-oriented movies. Though, with a few exceptions (for example *Woodstock* in 1970), most of these flopped, a large number of young and clever directors were able to get their start in features around this time (1968-71). Indeed, with Woody Allen, Peter Bogdanovich, Francis Coppola, Brian De Palma, William Friedkin, George Lucas, Martin Scorsese and Steven Spielberg in their ranks, a veritable explosion of new directorial talent took place. In contrast to the relatively solid mature group of directors who had arrived from TV in the early 60s, these newcomers were surprisingly youthful:

Above: Japan's most eminent director, Akira Kurosawa (left), welcomes Francis Coppola (centre) and George Lucas on the beach at Hokkaido in November 1979 during the filming of *Kagemusha*. The two Americans were involved with the international presentation of the film.

Left: Fledgeling director Robert Benton (left) with the very experienced and skilful Robert Altman who produced Benton's debut film *The Late Show* (1977).

college graduates from the postwar generation who had grown up with TV and cinema. Having gained early experience making shorts, many of them had studied film at USC, UCLA or NYU, where a number of them had first met and become friends. Thus, they were in a position to help each other out, exchange ideas and maintain an interest in each others' work.

Film buffs as well as film-makers, the newcomers were aware of Hollywood successes of the past and the potential mileage which could be obtained from an imaginative revitalising of traditional genres. And this is perhaps the main thread running through a vast number of the most interesting and successful pictures of the 70s and early 80s. Already during the late 60s one can see the groundwork being laid by established directors – Stanley Kubrick's use of science fiction in *2001* (1968); Penn's interpretation of the gangster film with *Bonnie And Clyde* (1967); Polanski's exploration of the horror genre in *Rosemary's Baby* (1968), and Don Siegel's series of modern, urban thrillers extending into the 70s. Of the new directors who first made their mark, Coppola had his

initial success with a reworking of the gangster film in *The Godfather* (1972), and its sequel in 1974, while Friedkin opted for the cop thriller and horror in *The French Connection* (1971) and *The Exorcist* (1973) respectively. Peckinpah moved from Westerns (*The Wild Bunch*, 1969 and *Cable Hogue*, 1970) to thrillers (*The Getaway*, 1972, and *Alfredo Garcia*, 1974) and Bogdanovich recycled 30s comedy with *What's Up Doc?* (1972) and *Paper Moon* (1973). Scorsese made his name with a highly original treatment of the contemporary gangster film in *Mean Streets* in 1973 (at the same time that John Milius was making his feature debut with the fast-moving biopic, *Dillinger*) and followed it up with a chilling urban thriller, *Taxi Driver* (1976). He then tried his hand at other traditional Hollywood genres such as the fictional musical biopic with *New York, New York* (1977) and the tough, black-and-white boxing biopic with *Raging Bull* (1980). All four movies starred Robert De Niro in the most amazing director-star collaboration of the decade. Robert Altman moved from war comedy (*M*A*S*H*, 1970) to Western (*McCabe And Mrs Miller*, 1971) to private eye movie (*The Long Goodbye*, 1973) treating each with great originality, while Brian De Palma, and

John Carpenter both specialised in atmospheric horror-fantasy and thrillers.

But most successful of all were George Lucas and Steven Spielberg. Not only did they have eleven smash hits (and relatively few flops) between them, but they distributed them among the various major production companies as if to provide maximum benefit for the film industry as a whole. Both men were instantly characterised by their technical sophistication and expertise, and their imaginative use of special effects applied to sci fi (and action) subjects, which fuelled a sci fi boom during the late 70s. They brought with them a new professionalism and a highly developed visual sense which radically changed the look of the modern American cinema. Thus, Lucas is best known as the creator of the *Star Wars* cycle – with the term 'Star Wars' now enshrined in contemporary current political vocabulary, having been adopted by ex-movie actor President Reagan to label his plans for an elaborate nuclear defence shield for the US in outer space.

Having virtually given up directing, George Lucas has concentrated on producing (and script writing) and has developed his own elaborate special effects studio (Industrial Light and Magic). Spielberg has continued active as both director and producer, dividing his interests between sci fi (*Close Encounters Of The Third Kind*, 1977 and *E.T.*, 1982), horror-fantasy (*Poltergeist*, 1982, *The Twilight Zone*, 1983, and *Gremlins*, 1984 all of which he produced) and recycled Hollywood action-adventure with the pair of *Indiana Jones* movies. If the vulnerability of Hollywood is evident from the extent to which it has depended during recent years on the success of these two young men, it raises a fascinating question mark over the future. But the American film industry has demonstrated a remarkable resilience time and time again, and one can only wait and see.

ROBERT ALDRICH

Born Cranston, Rhode Island, 9 August 1918. **Died** 1983

A formidable talent who had completed forty years in the film industry by the time of his last feature, Robert Aldrich's movies were a mixed bunch. An outsize figure in real life and something of a Hollywood maverick, he had a special affection for larger-than-life characters, both male and female, in his movies. During the course of his career he worked with top stars from three different generations – established figures like Joan Crawford and Bette Davis, 50s stars like Burt Lancaster, Jack Palance and Lee Marvin, and more recently Burt Reynolds and Gene Wilder. He was not embarrassed by strong emotions or excessive violence, and could be crass and vulgar, particularly during the more permissive later years – dealing with the off-duty activities of a rowdy bunch of LA policemen in *The Choirboys* (1977), for example, or women's tag team wrestling in *All The Marbles ...* (1981). A strong believer in an all-American style of punchy, dramatic film entertainment, he was at his best with thrillers and action pictures like *Kiss Me Deadly* (UA, 1955), *The Dirty Dozen* (MGM, 1967) and *Ulzana's Raid* (Universal, 1972), all adapted from novels, while his sometimes equally powerful dramas, often derived from plays like Clifford Odets' *The Big Knife* (UA, 1955), could be at times slow and wordy. As he himself once pointed out in a rare flash of insight, 'I admit to having a penchant for already set up dramatic lines and conflicts, which is why most of my films have been adapted from either novels or plays.' Operating as an independent producer-director on most of his productions, Aldrich certainly had his ups and downs, but, his few big hits were evenly spaced out over three decades, thus insuring his survival as a film-maker up to the time of his death.

Aldrich, who came from a family of bankers, studied economics at university before he decided on a career in movies. He began as a production clerk, then clapper boy at RKO in 1941, and his later experience as an assistant director and production manager instilled in him a special awareness of the economic realitites of the film business which was to serve him in good stead in years to come. He also worked as an assistant director to Jean Renoir, William Wellman and Joseph Losey before he turned briefly to TV, the medium which provided him with his first opportunity to direct – on the 'China Smith' series. MGM gave him his first feature programmer, *The Big Leaguer* in 1953. But he completed a far more interesting picture soon after, *World For Ransom*, on which he served as his own co-producer and made use of a number of his technical collaborators from television (most notably cameraman Joseph Biroc), along with star Dan Duryea. A lively, entertaining and fast moving action-adventure film with a convincing feel to it which belied the tiny budget and difficult shooting conditions, it demonstrated Aldrich's qualities as a director and led on to his first masterpiece, *Kiss*

Me Deadly, one year later. Loosely based on the Mickey Spillane book and crisply photographed by Ernest Laszlo (Aldrich's other favourite cameraman), the film is rich in visual and aural textures with excellent performances from Ralph Meeker and many minor characters. As the seedy and genuinely unpleasant private eye hero, Mike Hammer, weaves his way through the unexpected twists and turns of the plot, with its moments of eroticism and violence, one sees the relatively civilised private eye genre brought into the 50s with a jolt. And more than that, the film gradually takes on a nightmarish quality as the gritty California reality is left far behind and emerges as an expression of 50s paranoia, with appro-

priate Cold War echoes and a painful allegory of the nuclear age. For the mysterious, missing box sought by foreign agents, the police and Hammer is revealed spectacularly in the final moments as no less than a lethal nuclear device.

In between *Ransom* and *Kiss Me Deadly* Aldrich had directed his first 'A' pictures, both Westerns starring Burt Lancaster and photographed in nicely toned down colour by Laszlo. *Apache* (UA, 1954) was a particularly good example of the many films made during the early 50s which treated the Indian sympathetically, with fine performances from Lancaster and Jean Peters. Aldrich disliked the happy ending, but it did not seriously alter the overall impact. It was his first hit, while *Vera Cruz* (UA, 1954) teaming Lancaster with Gary Cooper was a larger scale picture and an even bigger hit. With a cast full of heavies – Ernest Borgnine, George Macready, Charles Bronson (in an early role), Jack Elam, Jack Lambert – and a plot full of twists, double crosses, and violent action, this was the kind of mixture which would characterise Aldrich in his later action movies.

With two hits behind him, he was able to make a pair of pictures as producer-director and formed his own company, The Associates and Aldrich, as a means of keeping his favourite team of collaborators together (cameraman Joe Biroc, editor Michael Luciano, composer Frank DeVol, etc.) Unfortunately, the remarkable *Kiss Me Deadly* and *The Big Knife*, with the 'heavy', Jack Palance, totally miscast as a big Hollywood star, both flopped, and he turned to directing his first 'woman's picture' – *Autumn Leaves* starring Joan Crawford – for Columbia in 1955. *Attack!* (UA, 1956) was a hard-hitting war movie more notable for its action sequences than for its contrived human interest theme.

Aldrich had virtually completed *The Garment Jungle*, his second film for Columbia, in 1956, a tough treatment of corruption and gangsterism in the garment industry, when he was sacked. The subsequent litigation dragged on for a year-and-a-half, the beginning of a very difficult period for him, in spite of the fact that he had firmly established his reputation with his excellent group of early features and had become something of a cult figure in France. After four undistinguished films in a row, he made a comeback in 1962 with *What Ever Happened To Baby Jane?* for Warner Bros., an exercise in over-the-top American Gothic and a return to low-keyed black-and-white. The film exploited its pair of legendary stars for all they were worth as a pair of ex-showbiz sisters: Bette Davis grotesque and nasty as Baby Jane contrasted with Joan Crawford as the victimised and tortured sister. A followup, *Hush, Hush, Sweet Charlotte* (20th Century-Fox, 1964), was a better picture, but lacked the impact of its predecessor. Furthermore, Miss Crawford had to be replaced by Olivia de Havilland due to illness. A nice bonus, however, was the presence of veteran actress Mary Astor as a murderous, little old lady and Agnes Moorehead as a superbly slovenly housekeeper.

Then, in 1967 Aldrich had the biggest hit of his career with *The Dirty Dozen*, memorable for its fine collection of

heavies and its spectacular all-action climax. His profit participation meant that he was able to purchase his own studio and operate for a time as a genuine independent. But his choice of projects was unfortunate, and he was unlucky. *The Killing Of Sister George* (1968), for example, adapted from the Frank Marcus play about a lesbian relationship, with Beryl Reid recreating her stage role, suffered from the fact that it was given a newly introduced 'X' certificate in the US. Thus, the director soon found himself in another down phase of his very up and down career.

Ulzana's Raid marked a fine return to form, here reunited with Burt Lancaster in an excellent and underrated Western about a cavalry patrol tracking a renegade band of Indians. Then Aldrich had a last pair of smash hits with star Burt Reynolds, *The Longest Yard* (1974), a recycled version of *The Dirty Dozen*, with the cons on the football field rather than at war, followed by an LA cop picture, *Hustle* (1975), both for Paramount. *Twilight's Last Gleaming*, a political thriller exploiting the dangers of atomic missiles, shot in 1976 delivered less than it promised, like so many of Aldrich's later movies, and his career ended on an anticlimactic note with a last, varied group during 1977-81, including *The Frisco Kid* (1979).

Left: Bette Davis (right) as the decaying Southern belle in *Hush, Hush, Sweet Charlotte* (1964), another baroque semi-horror film in the tradition of *Whatever Happened To Baby Jane?* Aldrich's 1962 hit. With the star is Agnes Moorehead, Oscar-nominated for her splendid slut of a housekeeper.

Above: Robert Aldrich (left), on location for *The Dirty Dozen* (1967), talks to actor Robert Ryan. The film concerned a group of a dozen convicts recruited to a commando mission. One of them was John Cassavetes, Oscar-nominated for his performance.

Left: Susannah York (left) as 'Childie' and Beryl Reid as 'George', do their Laurel and Hardy routine in *The Killing Of Sister George* (1968), the somewhat tacky version of Frank Marcus' funny, sad, astringent play about a very odd lesbian relationship.

175

WOODY ALLEN

Born Brooklyn, New York, 1 December 1935

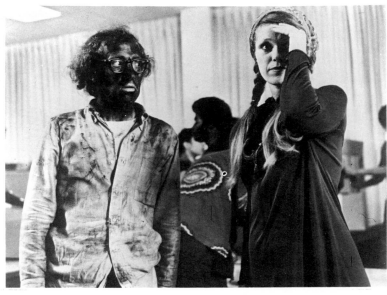

Left: A wildly anarchic, slapstick political satire on the volatility and corruption of South American politics, *Bananas* (1971), starred Woody Allen and his second wife, Louise Lasser, with him here.

While still a student, Woody Allen started out as a comedy gag writer with a gift for one-liners which he supplied to newspaper columnists and press agents. He flunked out of NYU and CCNY, but in his early twenties he was already contributing sketches to stage revues and writing regularly for television, most notably for the Sid Caesar TV show where he met established comedy writers like Larry Gelbart and Mel Brooks. Urged on by his agents, Charles Joffe and Jack Rollins (who would later produce his films), Woody took the plunge and went on stage for the first time during the early 6os. He soon began to develop the characteristic comic persona which he would refine and develop in his movies, a modern variation on the familiar theme of the lone underdog lost in a hostile world: the funny-looking little Jewish New Yorker, already beginning to lose his hair, brighter than average, but a walking catalogue of neuroses and complexes, obsessed by sex and death, has been made memorable by an individualistic and self-deprecating sense of humour. Unaffected by success and movie stardom, Allen, it has to be said, has a lot in common with his portrait gallery of comic characters.

Having moved up in the world from Greenwich Village cafés to TV talk shows and the better class of nightclub, by the mid-6os the workaholic Allen was beginning to establish himself in the New York theatre and in the movies. In 1965 he wrote, and played a supporting role in, the hit comedy *What's New Pussycat?* (UA, 1965), but was justifiably unhappy with the way his script had been cut, and altered to broaden and inflate the humour. Allen also appeared in the incredibly bad James Bond spoof, *Casino Royale* (Columbia, 1967). Far better was his own spoof movie made about the same time, for which he took a cheap Japanese Bond imitation called *Key Of Keys* (*Kagi No Kagi*, 1964) and provided an entirely new soundtrack and narration with the help of a few of his friends including his second wife, the actress Louise Lasser. The result was a delight, retitled *What's Up Tiger Lily?* (AIP, 1966), which demonstrated a wacky inventiveness in establishing a totally new and disjointed comic relationship between sound and image. With its rich selection of puns, wisecracks, and non-sequiturs, the script provided a memorably early example of Woody's verbal humour run wild.

His first full-length play, 'Don't Drink The Water', opened in November 1966 and was a big success. He continued to appear in nightclubs and on TV, began publishing comic pieces in the 'New Yorker' magazine, appeared on Broadway for the first time as the star of his own comedy, 'Play It Again, Sam' in February 1969, and found time to write, direct and star in his first feature movie, *Take The Money And Run* (1969). A comedy send-up of the semi-documentary style gangster biopic, Woody played an incompetent, would be master criminal. It was the first of a series of spoof movies. *Bananas* (1971) co-starred Louise Lasser – now his ex-wife – and began his association with United Artists which was to last throughout the 70s. It was a parody of the type of Latin American revolutionary picture set in a fictitious banana republic, with the comedy inspired by the Marx Bros. *Everything You Always Wanted To Know About Sex* (1972) was Woody's first box-office hit. It was constructed as a series of sketches of which the best were Gene Wilder as a doctor in love with a sheep named Daisy, and 'What Happens During Ejaculation' which presented an inside view of male sexual activity with Woody zanily playing a neurotic sperm.

Below: Co-writer, director and star, Woody levitates across the fields in his hilarious futuristic spoof, *Sleeper* (1973), the second of his movies with Diane Keaton.

Bottom: The first of the Allen-Keaton co-star collaborations was *Play It Again, Sam* (1972), the film version of Woody's Broadway comedy about a film critic who strikes up a relationship with the ghost of Humphrey Bogart . . .

While trying to find his film voice, Woody starred in and scripted, but did not direct, the film version of *Play It [Again,] Sam* (Paramount, 1972) which [gave] a new lease of life on the screen. [As] a movie myth it added a [touch utilising] a few clips from [Warner Bros., 1943), while [W]oody's Bogart *alter [ego was]* that much more [advant]age. Woody is a [comedia]n on stage, and the [commercia]l interest coming at [this poin]t [in hi]s career, for it helped to establish his classic image of the insecure little man with a severe inferiority complex, particularly in matters sexual, and

with a love of old movies. Here, too, he appeared on screen for the first time with two of his favourite actors, Diane Keaton and Tony Roberts, both recreating their original stage roles. In addition, the change of locale from New York to San Francisco made the hero's sexual inadequacies appear that much more comical, placed as they were within the permissive climate and freer life style of California. The location also provided the opportunity for some picturesque associations with movies past, and meant that the impact of Woody's close identification with the New York milieu could be saved to flavour his own, later films.

With *Sleeper* (1973), the best of his 'spoof movies', Woody demonstrated that he was becoming more proficient as a film-maker and was capable of controlling and integrating his gags within the picture as a whole. Here he succeeded in creating a totally convincing futuristic world on the screen, full of bizarre and imaginative touches. As the part owner of the Happy Carrot health food restaurant projected 200 years into the future, Woody gave one of his most likeable performances. *Love And Death* (1975) which followed, and which again co-starred Diane Keaton, was less good,

keeping the jokes and one-liners under control, while being most generous in his treatment of her on the screen, too. The first of his films to be photographed by the outstanding cameraman Gordon Willis who was equally at home in black-and-white or colour, *Annie Hall* marked Woody's true coming of age as a film-maker. His first really big hit, it won Oscars for Best Picture and Best Actress, with a pair going to Woody for directing, and for co-writing the script with Marshall Brickman. He was also nominated for Best Actor. *Interiors* (1978) which he wrote and directed but did not act in, was an interesting, serious-minded but unsuccessful experiment, a kind of imitation Bergman. But he had another big hit with the black-and-white *Manhattan* (1979) which stands with *Annie Hall* as one of his two best movies to date.

During the 80s Woody has struck out in new directions with the derivative *Stardust Memories* (UA, 1980) echoing Fellini, and *A Midsummer's Night Sex Comedy* (1982 – Bergman again). *Zelig* (1983), however, was a little cinematic gem, a veritable technical *tour-de-force* unmatched in the cinema since Orson Welles created his cleverly faked newsreel for the opening of *Citizen Kane*

(RKO, 1941). Allen didn't put a foot wrong, collaborating with cameraman Gordon Willis in creating a fictitious little self-effacing man who flits unobtrusively through the 20th century. Presented in the guise of a filmed documentary and commentary, the film provided Allen with the opportunity to present a witty and satirical, yet very personal view of the recent past and on the nature of fame (not unrelated to Peter Sellers' Chauncey Gardiner in *Being There*, UA, 1979). A one-joke movie perhaps, but it's a good joke. The film also started a new acting partnership with Mia Farrow, seen at her most unrecognisably dotty in *Broadway Danny Rose* (1984, Oscar-nominated for direction and original script). Finally, Allen has stepped up the pace of his filming, with two more movies already on the way – *The Purple Rose of Cairo* (1985) and *Hannah And Her Sisters* – which suggest he is still stretching himself and will entertain us for many years to come.

Above: *Annie Hall* (1977), which brilliantly captured the milieu of trendy, intellectual, middle-class Manhattan, marked a new maturity in Woody's work. An Oscar-winning performance came from Diane Keaton (right) in the title role. Her clothes set a new style in fashion, much as Faye Dunaway's had done with *Bonnie And Clyde* ten years earlier. With her and Woody here, Tony Roberts.

Left: Woody on location for *Stardust Memories* (1980) with Jessica Harper.

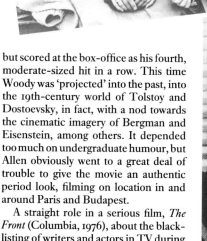

but scored at the box-office as his fourth, moderate-sized hit in a row. This time Woody was 'projected' into the past, into the 19th-century world of Tolstoy and Dostoevsky, in fact, with a nod towards the cinematic imagery of Bergman and Eisenstein, among others. It depended too much on undergraduate humour, but Allen obviously went to a great deal of trouble to give the movie an authentic period look, filming on location in and around Paris and Budapest.

A straight role in a serious film, *The Front* (Columbia, 1976), about the blacklisting of writers and actors in TV during the 50s, brought Woody back to New York and helped to point him in a new direction. Influenced, too, by his close collaboration with his ex-girlfriend and co-star, Diane Keaton, he attempted to place his own character in a more personal and true-to-life milieu than ever before in *Annie Hall* (1977), drawing on his own past relationship with her and

Left: A scene from *Zelig* (1983) featuring boxer Jack Dempsey with Allen. The film, about a man with a chameleon-like tendency to become a physical copy of whoever he is with, was a brilliant amalgam of documentary techniques in which actual and fictitious newsreel footage were blended to create a perfect illusion of reality.

'One day I think I'm going to wake up and find people have found me out, if they haven't already. I'm at the stage where I've got to be good and perhaps I'll not be able to do it.'
1982

177

ROBERT ALTMAN

Born Kansas City, Missouri, 20 February 1925

Having spent over twenty years on the fringes of the film industry, Robert Altman suddenly emerged during the early 70s as one of the most original and exciting 'new' talents working in the American cinema. No longer a young man, Altman had preserved his sense of humour and developed his creative instincts during his early years, as well as perfecting the necessary technical expertise. His eight years working in TV, for example, involved turning out two episodes of a show per week. He kept his sanity by injecting his own little jokes into the scripts – which occasionally got him into trouble, but more often than not, passed unnoticed – and by playing a private game of directing the shows as 'mimic movies'. 'The scripts would come in and I'd say, "Ok, this one is my *Foreign Correspondent* (UA, 1940), and that one will be my *Portrait Of Jennie* (Selznick, 1948)".... My attitude was to try anything which seemed remotely interesting, because if you failed it was just another bad TV show – and that's what they were getting anyway.'

First attracted to the cinema as a boy, Altman served as a pilot during the war and was stationed for a time in California. He returned to California after the war and attempted to break into films as a scriptwriter, but ended up returning to his home town of Kansas City. There he found a job making industrial films and gained excellent experience for six years as producer, director, writer and editor. A pair of cheaply made features, *The Delinquents* (UA) filmed in 1955 and *The James Dean Story* (Warner Bros., 1957) led to a new career as a TV director. But it wasn't until 1967 that he was given his first chance to direct a Hollywood feature: *Countdown* (Warner Bros.) was a fictionalised treatment of the American space programme, a kind of forerunner of *The Right Stuff* (Ladd/Warner Bros., 1983) with James Caan and Robert Duvall as a pair of astronauts. *That Cold Day In The Park* starred Sandy Dennis and was filmed cheaply in Canada in 1968 and the following year Altman finally got his big break. He was the last of a long list of directors who had been offered Ring Lardner Jr's script of *M*A*S*H* (20th Century-Fox), and the one to see how it could be turned into something quite different and interesting. Supported by producer Ingo Preminger (brother of Otto), Altman opted for a cast of new and unknown actors who could work closely together like a repertory company and planned to film on location, away from studio interference, in a manner which he was to adopt for many of his future productions. The setting and subject, with a relatively loose, episodic plot structure, lent itself to the creation of a self-contained world centred on the mobile army surgical hospital of the title, and situated not too far from the front lines. The wild, funny, disrespectful movie which emerged was entertaining and original, yet made a real, if modest, political point, too – while sup-

posedly taking place during the Korean war, the anti-war satire was clearly directed at Vietnam. Altman also made use of some audacious fast editing techniques and a complex soundtrack with overlapping dialogue to keep up the pace, while the lyrics for the picture's theme song, 'Suicide Is Painless', were provided by his fourteen-year old son Michael to supplement the witty script: 'I wonder how a degenerated person like that could have reached a position of responsibility in the army medical corps,' Sally Kellerman exclaims about Elliott Gould at a particularly fraught moment. The reply: 'He was drafted.' The movie was a tremendous, unexpected box-office hit, nominated for a Best Picture Oscar and winner of the best film award at the 1970 Cannes Film Festival. It made

Above: Burt Remsen (left) and Bud Cort in *Brewster McCloud* (1970), about a boy who hopes to fly with mechanical wings.

Left: Warren Beatty and Julie Christie were starred in *McCabe And Mrs Miller* (1971), a frontier town Western about gamblers and whorehouses which pushed naturalism through its own boundaries into the dreamlike and unreal.

Below: A pensive Robert Altman during the making of *Images* (1972), a not entirely successful, but complex and interesting psycho-drama about a woman plagued by the images of her former lovers.

the name of Altman (Oscar-nominated for directing) and its stars, Elliott Gould and Donald Sutherland, and spawned a highly successful, long-running TV series which Altman had nothing to do with (and dislikes intensely).

Suddenly the director was a 'hot property' and the studios came after him expecting more of the same, as Altman himself recalls. Thus, MGM were totally baffled by *Brewster McCloud* (1970), his bizarre fantasy satire about a boy who builds a set of mechanical wings with the aim of flying around the Houston Astrodome, and featuring a remarkable bird-man lecture from Rene Auberjonois. 'They just wanted *M*A*S*H* all over again – *M*A*S*H* with bird shit.' Similarly, Warner Bros. backed *McCabe And Mrs Miller* (1971), with Warren

Above: Elliott Gould (left) and Donald Sutherland (right) stars of the hit comedy *M*A*S*H*, which took the unlikely setting of a military hospital for its inspiration.

Right: Elliott Gould was Raymond Chandler's famous detective, Philip Marlowe, in Altman's modern treatment of *The Long Goodbye* (1973). With him, the glamorous Nina Van Pallandt, better known as half of the two-piano act of Nina and Frederick than for her sparse acting talents.

'Altman has reached the point of wearing his failures like medals. He's creating a mystique of heroism out of emptied theatres.'

Pauline Kael in 'The New Yorker', 1979

179

the private eye, casting a casual, spaced-out Elliott Gould as the most unlikely of modern-day gumshoes, ambling around LA chain smoking, mumbling to himself and looking for the right brand of pet food for his cat. It worked, so Altman signed up Gould (along with George Segal) for another picture the following year, *California Split* (Columbia, 1974) about a favourite Altman topic, gambling. In between he made a surprise choice, directing *Thieves Like Us* (UA, 1973), a straight adaptation of the Edward Anderson novel set in the 30s which had previously been filmed by Nicholas Ray in 1947 as *They Live By Night* (RKO). The central roles of the pair of young criminals on the run provided first starring parts for two of his favourite young actors, Keith Carradine and Shelley Duvall, with a key supporting role for Louise Fletcher, specially brought out of retirement to play in the film (which led to her Oscar-winning role the following year in *One Flew Over The Cuckoo's Nest*, UA).

An inveterate gambler himself, Altman recognised that an authentic picture about gambling must be loosely structured and concentrate on capturing the characters, mood and atmosphere with as little plot as possible. *California Split* met the requirements, and also included an important technical innovation in sound recording – each actor was provided with an individual radio microphone which allowed a greater freedom of movement and dialogue without having to work out an elaborate pattern of cues with the microphone boom operator. Utilised in conjunction with his wide-screen Panavision camera, ever on the move, this allowed Altman and his

Left: Shelley Duvall and Keith Carradine as the farmer's daughter and the escaped convict with whom she becomes involved in *Thieves Like Us* (1973), a remake in period – the 30s – of Nicholas Ray's *They Live By Night* (1947).

Below: Elliott Gould (left) and George Segal, somewhat the worse for wear in this scene from *California Split* (1974), a lively treatment of the adventures of a couple of gamblers.

Beatty and Julie Christie, and expecting a *M*A*S*H* Western. 'But it wasn't that at all. They didn't know what they had or how to handle it.' *McCabe* in fact marked a major step forward, following on the heels of Arthur Penn's *Little Big Man* (1970), and demonstrated Altman's talent for rethinking and redefining a familiar American movie genre – as he was to do with the 'private eye' movie two years later. Filming on location in Canada, he was aided by production designer Leon Ericksen and the superlative Panavision photography (and soft colours) of Vilmos Zsigmond, in creating an isolated little world, the frontier town at the turn of the century, where most of the action takes place. In fact, Altman carried his naturalism so far that this drab world of rain, sleet, snow and mud, reflecting the harsh realities of pioneer life (and death), with its mumbled, indistinctly heard and overlapping conversations and smoke-filled rooms, was made to appear dreamlike and distinctly *unreal*. Warren Beatty gave an introverted, mumbling, but strangely likeable performance as the small-time gambler who uses his winnings to introduce a casino and brothel into the town, in partnership with the more practical and hard-headed whore, superbly played by Julie Christie. And to cap it all Altman staged a suitably bizarre final shoot-out in the snow, a half comical, but deadly variation on the climax of *High Noon* (UA, 1952) from which there are no survivors – Altman here putting his own personal stamp on this most archetypal of Western situations.

Having beaten Hollywood at its own game Altman was steadily developing a new assurance and self-confidence. His brief honeymoon with the Hollywood establishment was already over, but he was firmly established as one of the leading independent producer-directors with a strong following in Europe and the US. By keeping his budgets low (generally under $2 million) and operating through his own company, Lion's Gate Films, he continued to average slightly over one film per year throughout the 70s.

In one of his rare ventures abroad he travelled to Ireland with Zsigmond to direct the ambitious, visually striking, but pretentious *Images* (1972), a study in psychological fantasy horror starring Susannah York. Then, continuing the zigzag pattern whereby he seemed to alternate between successes and relatively less memorable efforts, he immediately bounced back on home ground with *The Long Goodbye* (UA, 1973), updating Raymond Chandler to the 70s. Here, he deliberately set out to debunk the myth of

actors to develop a genuinely close collaboration in filming and meant that he was able to pack more visual and aural information than ever into his scenes.

He demonstrated this technique to good effect in his next film, *Nashville* (Paramount, 1975), widely regarded as his 70s masterpiece, for which he assembled a large cast (including a number of his favourite actors) and other regular associates – screen writer Joan Tewkesbury, cameraman Paul Lohmann and assistant director Alan Rudolph, among others. A long and complex work, the film presents a satirical view of a cross section of American society with particular reference to the country music scene. In addition to contributing to the script, the actors composed their own Country and Western songs, which come across with a freshness and vigour that compensates for any lack of polish. (Keith Carradine won an Oscar for his song, 'I'm Easy'.) During much of the film Altman fills the Panavision screen with so much simultaneous action and a continuously shifting counterpoint of plot and subplot, that it is impossible to take it all in in a single viewing. (Apparently there is an extant six-hour version of the film which he hoped to screen on American TV.)

company, serving as producer for a few new directors like his protege, Alan Rudolph (*Welcome To LA*, 1976), and Robert Benton (*The Late Show*, 1977). Continuing his association (as a director) with 20th Century-Fox, he returned to the *Nashville* pattern of inter-relating large numbers of characters in the black comedy, *A Wedding* (1978), then returned to Canada with Paul Newman to film a strange sci fi movie, *Quintet* (1979). After his delightful version of *Popeye* (1980) for the Disney studio failed to recoup its substantial costs, he was reduced to directing film versions of plays like *Streamers* (1983). But the latest news is that Altman is directing true features once again, and, hopefully, there will be more films to look forward to in the coming years from this substantial artist.

Above: Ronee Blakley (left), Henry Gibson and Barbara Baxley in *Nashville* (1975). The parallel stories of everyday lives were played against the backdrop of a politically sponsored pop concert in Nashville, home of Country and Western music. An enormous cast also featured Geraldine Chaplin, Karen Black, Lily Tomlin and Keenan Wynn.

Left: Robert Fortier and Sissy Spacek in *Three Women* (1976), an experimental, hypnotically effective – albeit sometimes incoherent – examination of three women's interdependence.

Below: E.C. Segar's *Popeye* (1980) was dramatised by Jules Feiffer for the screen, and the eponymous hero was given human form by Robin Williams, shown here.

On the basis of *Nashville*'s success – a box-office hit and Oscar-nominated for Best Picture and direction – Altman was offered a three-picture deal by producer Dino de Laurentiis. Given a $6 million budget, he turned *Buffalo Bill and The Indians, Or Sitting Bull's History Lesson* (UA, 1976) into an ambitious, ironic, convoluted and sometimes humorous commentary on the myth of the Western hero. But it proved a dismal flop and was not much appreciated by the critics either. His planned adaptations of a pair of novels, 'Ragtime' and 'Breakfast of Champions' were cancelled, but, resilient as ever, he immediately turned to a more intimate, personal and low-cost project without any big star names. Directed late in 1976, *Three Women* (20th Century-Fox) was one of his most original and imaginative works, demonstrating his sensitivity to the modern, femi-

nine viewpoint, a kind of softer, quieter companion piece to the more raucous, masculine vitality of *California Split*. The film is built on the inspired casting of Shelley Duvall as a walking, talking advertiser's dream with all her ideas gained from TV adverts and low-grade women's magazines, contrasted with the young newcomer, Sissy Spacek, who is overawed at first but later becomes the dominant partner, and Janice Rule as the third and older, married friend who paints strange, erotic murals. Set within the dream-like world of a California desert community, and developed from a twenty-five page outline with Altman encouraging his actressses to participate in writing their own lines, the superbly acted film emerged as his most successful 'experimental' feature.

Around the same time (in 1976), the director expanded the activities of his

HAL ASHBY

Born Ogden, Utah, 1932

An unhappy childhood, a failed marriage, some time spent as a student at Utah State University and a number of rootless years lay behind Hal Ashby when he arrived in Hollywood in the early 50s. He held down a variety of menial jobs, including operating a multilith machine, before he became interested in editing and served his apprenticeship with William Wyler's favourite editor, Robert Swink. But it was eight long years working as an assistant editor before he got his first opportunity to edit a film on his own. Once he made the breakthrough, however, with two major pictures in a row at MGM in 1964 – *The Loved One* directed by Tony Richardson and *The Cincinnati Kid* directed by Norman Jewison – his subsequent progress was rapid. Teaming up with independent producer-director Jewison (whose pictures were distributed by United Artists), he earned an Oscar nomination as co-editor of *The Russians Are Coming, The Russians Are Coming* in

Top: Director Hal Ashby (2nd left) with Charles Tyner (left) and his stars Bud Cort (centre) and Ruth Gordon, during the making of *Harold And Maude* (1971), an audacious tale of a relationship between a very young man and a very old lady.

Above: *Being There* (1979) starred Peter Sellers (right) as a bizarre creature whose only knowledge of the world outside his own four walls is gained from TV. It was the great comedian's last film before his premature death. Here, he is with Melvyn Douglas.

Left: Warren Beatty, here with Julie Christie, starred as a hairdresser-cum-sexual stud in *Shampoo* (1975).

1966 and won the Oscar for *In The Heat Of The Night* the following year.

Sympathetic to his desire to graduate to directing, Jewison suggested that Hal serve as associate producer on both *The Thomas Crown Affair* (1968) and *Gaily, Gaily* (1969), then himself took on the role of producer for Ashby's directorial debut with *The Landlord* (UA, 1970). This modestly budgeted, youth-oriented picture, filmed on location in and around New York, clearly confirmed Ashby's talent for working with actors, and his taste for subverting accepted values – which were further demonstrated in the hilarious black comedy *Harold And Maude* (Paramount, 1971). Bud Cort starred as the

death-obsessed young man who falls in love with (and marries) a sprightly, witty and eccentric little old lady who teaches him to enjoy life. This latter theme, a kind of hippy love story verges on the cloyingly whimsical but is overcome by Ruth Gordon's no-nonsense performance. However, the film is best at its blackest.

Ashby's fondness for offbeat subjects, in keeping with his own personal lifestyle (and hippy appearance), led him to team up with Jack Nicholson for *The Last Detail* (Columbia, 1973), his first box office success, and his most fully realised work thus far. As 'Bad Ass' Buddusky, the petty officer responsible for escorting a young sailor to a military prison in the

north and good-naturedly introducing him to various pleasures along the way, Nicholson was hardly ever off the screen, and gained an Oscar nomination and the New York Critics award for his performance. A collaboration with actor-producer and co-scriptwriter Warren Beatty at Columbia the following year proved even more successful at the box-office, but *Shampoo*'s weak attempt at social and political satire on the eve of Nixon's 1968 election victory worked less well than its revealing portrait of a vacuous, trendy and womanising hairdresser.

At his peak as a director, Ashby next turned his attention to the legendary hippy hero and dustbowl balladeer Woody Guthrie. Stunning, Oscar-winning photography from Haskell Wexler meant that the result was pretty to look at, but lacked the kind of gritty toughness required for its portrait of America during the Depression. Nevertheless, *Bound For Glory* (1976) earned Ashby his only directing nomination and was the first of his three UA movies in a row nominated for Best Picture. Both *Coming Home* (filmed in 1977) about American veterans wounded both physically and mentally by the Vietnam War, and *Being There* (1979) were most memorable for their outstanding performances. Jane Fonda and Jon Voight won Oscars for their sensitive performances in the former, as did veteran actor Melvyn Douglas in the latter (though best of all was Peter Sellers in his last great comedy role as the faceless Chauncey Gardiner).

Since then, Ashby has not expanded his gifts, and his subsequent work has included a pair of flops – *Second-Hand Hearts* (filmed in 1978 but not released until 1981), *Lookin' To Get Out* (1982) and a Rolling Stones concert movie, *Let's Spend The Night Together* (1982). But he is looking to make a comeback in 1985 with *The Slugger's Wife* starring Michael O'Keefe, Rebecca De Mornay, and director Martin Ritt in a rare on-screen acting appearance.

'From my being an editor, I don't camera cut; I leave everything as open as I can, because that provides more alternatives . . . It gives you choices.'
1979

RICHARD ATTENBOROUGH

Born Cambridge, 29 August 1923

Well-known for many years as a leading British movie – and stage – actor, Richard Attenborough's wish to be taken seriously as a leading director, too, can no longer be denied after the tremendous worldwide success of *Gandhi* (Goldcrest/Columbia, 1982). The picture represents the natural (and impressive) culmination of his efforts over a period of many years to help improve the quality of British filmmaking, first as an actor, then producer – having formed his own production company with writer-director Bryan Forbes in the late 50s – and finally as a producer-director.

Small in size, thickset, and with a round boyish face, Attenborough made his debut as a movie actor in the David Lean-Noel Coward war drama *In Which We Serve* (UA, 1942), and continued to play juvenile roles throughout the 40s. He graduated to adult parts in the 50s, but the pictures were generally undistinguished. His early efforts as a producer at least provided him with a pair of good roles in *The Angry Silence* (1960) and *Seance On A Wet Afternoon* (1964). He also appeared in a number of large budget British-American productions like *The Great Escape* (UA, 1963), *The Sand Pebbles* (1966) and *Dr Dolittle* (1967) – both for 20th Century-Fox – and was finally given his first opportunity to direct in 1969 with *Oh! What A Lovely War* (Paramount). Scripted by Len Deighton from the Joan Littlewood stage show, neither of their names appears on the official credits. Deighton was not happy with Attenborough's glossy, large screen, 'pop' treatment, reinforced by cameo appearances from large numbers of celebrated stars including Olivier, Gielgud, Richardson, Maggie Smith and three Redgraves, among others. (The original show was more like a gritty little black-and-white movie with a cast of young, unknown actors.) In all fairness to the director, his version did have its moments and was generally quite entertaining, especially the more naturalistic sequences away from Brighton pier, reflecting the quality of the original material and the terrific World War I songs.

Attenborough next collaborated with expatriate American writer-producer Carl Foreman on *Young Winston* (Columbia, 1972). Making use of a complex plot structure, jumping forward and back in time, the film included some exciting action, and fine performances from Simon Ward, Anne Bancroft (as Jennie) and Robert Shaw (Randolph), all of which failed to compensate for the long, dull stretches. Attenborough's attraction to ambitious productions based on real life characters and events took him to Holland in 1976 where he recreated on film a World War II operation which had gone disastrously wrong in *A Bridge Too Far* (UA). A pre-packaged international co-production – and it looked it – the film mixed British actors like Bogarde, Caine and Connery with specially imported American stars – Redford, Hackman, O'Neal and Elliott Gould. The result was

something of a mess, which failed to appeal to either critics or audiences, but Attenborough quickly moved on to an American horror thriller, *Magic* (1978), his first small scale dramatic picture, from a novel by William Goldman, which starred Anthony Hopkins and Ann-Margret and served to widen his directing experience.

All in all, his directing record prior to *Gandhi* was not an impressive one, but he excelled himself on this long cherished project which he had been trying to set up for twenty years. Filmed in India over a period of six months from November 1980 at a cost of $22 million, he was aided by the carefully constructed script of John Briley and a remarkable performance by Ben Kingsley. A solidly crafted three-hour masterpiece, he succeeded in blending the intimate, personal story with the larger scale events – the early sequences set in South Africa were particularly good. Inevitably, there were a few characteristically dull and over earnest patches, but the film was generally stunning to look at. A moderate box-office hit, *Gandhi* ended up as the most successful British Oscar winner ever with awards for Best Picture, to Attenborough, Kingsley and Briley and it swept most of the technical Oscars, too (for cinematography, art direction, editing and costume design).

At the time of writing, he is in New York directing a subject which could not be further away from his previous endeavours – the screen version of the smash-hit Broadway musical, *A Chorus Line*. The choice reflects his penchant for 'entertainment' over 'art'. Perhaps it will serve to release the lightness of touch he has hitherto lacked.

Left: Richard Attenborough directs the late, much revered, Sir Ralph Richardson in *Oh! What A Lovely War* (1969). Behind Richardson, another famous British theatrical knight, Sir John Gielgud.

Below: Robert Redford storms the Nijmegen Bridge with the pathetic remnants of his troops in *A Bridge Too Far* (1976), an international all-star cast depiction of the allied disaster at Arnhem during World War II.

Bottom: India's great and doomed prophet of peace, Mahatma Gandhi (Ben Kingsley), walks with the devoted crowds in director Attenborough's 1982 epic biopic, *Gandhi*.

ROBERT BENTON

Born Waxahachie, Texas, 29 September 1932

Robert Benton first broke into the movies in 1967 as co-scriptwriter of the spectacularly successful *Bonnie And Clyde* (Warner Bros.), directed by Arthur Penn, which earned him the Screen Writers Guild award and a first Oscar nomination. Twelve years later, and still a relatively unknown writer and director, he himself starred in the ultimate Hollywood success story, winning Oscars for directing and scripting *Kramer Vs Kramer* (Columbia, 1979), which also received the Best Picture award and was a smash hit. During the years inbetween, Benton had worked as an occasional scriptwriter on a handful of films in collaboration with David Newman, and as an even more occasional director – *Kramer* was only his third feature. A relatively late developer (as a director), Benton was in his mid-forties when he first began to work regularly as a writer-director, helped by another latecomer, Robert Altman, who produced Benton's second feature, *The Late Show* (Warner Bros.) through his own Lion's Gate company in 1977.

Benton still has vivid memories of growing up in Texas during the Depression. He left for New York in the early 50s, studied art history at Columbia University and served for a time as art editor of 'Esquire' magazine where he first began his writing partnership with David Newman. As freelance writers they had their first success with the musical comedy 'It's a Bird ... It's a Plane ... It's Superman' which opened on Broadway in 1966 and led to them being hired to write on *Superman, The Movie* (Warner Bros.) some ten years later. As budding scriptwriters and inveterate movie buffs, they were strongly influenced by the advent of the French New Wave during the early 60s, which suggested new and original ways of making feature films. (They had originally offered their *Bonnie And Clyde* script to both François Truffaut and Godard.) Their scripts were, in fact, very American, and represented a witty reworking of traditional Hollywood genres such as the gangster film, the screwball comedy (*What's Up Doc?*, Warner Bros., 1973, directed by Peter Bogdanovich), and the Western.

Perhaps veteran director Joseph Mankiewicz's failure to do justice to their script for the black comedy Western *There Was A Crooked Man ...* (Warner Bros., 1970) led them to think of directing themselves. Certainly, the two young protagonists of *Bad Company* (Paramount, 1972) appear closely related to the Kirk Douglas-Henry Fonda roles as likeable losers in *Crooked Man*, while the character of 'Big Joe' is an affectionate take-off of Mankiewicz himself. Benton's directorial debut here was remarkably assured. Aided by the gritty photography of Gordon Willis, he did an excellent job of capturing the textures and atmosphere of the vast empty prairies while bringing the rough, lawless world of the American West during the 1860s to life on the screen. The director's love of old movies was most clearly expressed in the offbeat black comedy of *The Late Show* which he then scripted and directed without Newman. An affectionate modern treatment of the private eye genre and a distant cousin to producer

Altman's *The Long Goodbye* (UA, 1973), it starred an elderly Art Carney as straight man to Lily Tomlin's irrepressible and scatty lady client.

After this pair of original works which made little impression on the box-office, Benton was suddenly discovered by the public at large which flocked to see his sensitively handled and well acted, if fairly conventional domestic drama, *Kramer Vs Kramer*, starring Dustin Hoffman and Meryl Streep (both Oscar winners) with a terrific performance from seven-and-a-half-year-old Justin Henry (Oscar nominated). Miss Streep again starred in his stylish, but disappointing homage to Hitchcock, *Still Of The Night* (MGM/UA, 1982). But Benton quickly bounced back in 1984 with his most personal and deeply felt picture, *Places In The Heart*. Based on his own memories of life in a small Texas town during the Depression and drawing on the family reminiscences of his resourceful great-grandmother, the film features a memorable performance from Sally Field, who won the Best Actress Oscar for it, and outstanding camerawork by Nestor Almendros. It garnered seven Academy nominations, including direction and script for Benton who is clearly well on the way to fulfilling his potential as one of the most interesting of the new (sic) generation of Hollywood writer-directors.

Above: Benton's second feature, *The Late Show* (1977), an affectionate comedy-drama spoof on the 'private-eye' genre, starred Art Carney (top), as the aging detective and Lily Tomlin as a scatty former actress who is his client. With them is Bill Macy who played a small-time crook.

Left: Ted Kramer (Dustin Hoffman) argues the custody of their son with his wife, Joanna (Meryl Streep), after she has walked out on them in Benton's box-office hit, *Kramer Vs Kramer* (1979).

Bottom left: Director Robert Benton photographed during the making of *Still Of The Night* (1982), a romantic thriller which co-starred Meryl Streep and Roy Scheider.

'I know that one of my great weaknesses as a director is that I try to write my way out of trouble rather than direct my way out of it.'
1980

PETER BOGDANOVICH

Born Kingston, New York, 30 July 1939

Peter Bogdanovich is best known as the film buff turned movie director who suddenly shot to prominence during the early 70s, then just as suddenly saw the dream turn sour a few years later. More recently he has been struggling to rebuild his career, returning to the kind of small-scale, low-budget pictures with which he first got started ten years earlier.

The son of a Yugoslavian painter who emigrated to the US just before the outbreak of World War II, Peter developed a serious interest in movies and theatre as a young man. He studied acting, played some bit parts on stage, directed off-Broadway and summer stock, and occasionally wrote about films. Like so many aspiring young directors during the 60s such as Coppola, Scorsese and Monte Hellman, he was given a chance to work in features by producer-director Roger Corman at AIP (American International Pictures) functioning, among other things as second unit director (uncredited) on *The Wild Angels* (1966).

Then, in 1967 Bogdanovich got his first feature to direct under a typically Corman-type arrangement: he was given the services of Boris Karloff – owed to Corman from a previous contract – for two days, had to include footage from an earlier Corman-Karloff movie (*The Terror*, 1962) and had to shoot the film in two weeks. Peter was assisted on the original scenario by his stage designer wife, Polly Platt, who also served as production designer. (She went on to work as art director on three of his first four films up to 1972 when they divorced.) The result was *Targets*, the weak subplot of which concerned Karloff and a young movie director (badly played by Bogdanovich), but the main story presented a revealing portrait of the typical middle class, American *WASP* family leading an essentially sterile life, with particular attention to 'Bobby', the clean-cut son who wears sneakers, short-sleeved shirts with button-down collars, drives a Ford Mustang, drinks Pepsi, eats Baby Ruth candy bars ... and has a lethal collection of guns. He and his father take target practice and one is reminded of the remarks of director Richard Brooks: '(In the States) every father's got a rifle: "Come on son, let's go out and shoot something"'. One

morning, for no apparent reason something snaps and Bobby becomes a killer, gunning down his family and terrorising a motorway and a drive-in cinema. These events were presented by Bogdanovich with a Hitchcockian detachment that was chillingly effective.

For his second and best-known movie, *The Last Picture Show* (BBS/Columbia, 1971), filmed in black-and-white, Bogdanovich joined forces with writer Larry McMurtry (*Hud*, 1963) to show the decline of life, symbolised by the closing of the little picture-house, in a small Texas town during the early 50s. Successfully avoiding the danger of lapsing into soap opera, he handled the variety of characters and relationships with great sensitivity, drawing fine performances from a cast which mixed young newcomers (Jeff Bridges, Cybill Shepherd, Timothy Bottoms) with established and hitherto

Above: Timothy Bottoms (left) with Cloris Leachman, the unhappy housewife with whom he has a moving affair in *The Last Picture Show* (1975), Bogdanovich's penetrating and nostalgic portrait of a small midwestern town in the 50s.

Left: Ryan O'Neal and Barbra Streisand were paired in the screwball comedy, *What's Up Doc?* (1972).

Below: Bogdanovich directing *Nickelodeon* (1976). A good cast headed by Burt Reynolds and Ryan O'Neal couldn't save this costly flop.

Bottom left: Ryan O'Neal and his precociously talented daughter, Tatum, were a hit pairing in *Paper Moon* (1973).

underrated actors like Ben Johnson and Cloris Leachman. A surprise box-office hit, the film was honoured with a large number of Oscar nominations for Bogdanovich, McMurtry and Best Picture, and for many of its cast. Now a 'hot' director able to capitalise on the early 70s vogue for encouraging new young talent (aimed at the 'youth market'), the director was given top stars Barbra Streisand and Ryan O'Neal for *What's Up Doc?*

(Warner Bros., 1972). A glossy attempt to recycle the 30s screwball comedy as epitomised by Howard Hawks' *Bringing Up Baby* (RKO, 1938), it proved tremendously popular, as did Bogdanovich's follow-up movie which teamed Ryan and his daughter, Tatum O'Neal, in *Paper Moon* (Paramount, 1973), a far better, smaller-scale bitter-sweet comedy and a throwback to the John Ford/Frank Capra-style movies of the 30s.

Late in 1973, Peter was off to Italy with the new woman in his life, Cybill Shepherd, to film *Daisy Miller* for Paramount. Quite nicely done, it failed to make any impression at the box-office, and his next two were expensive disasters: *At Long Last Love* (20th Century-Fox, 1975), a musical starring Cybill and a badly miscast Burt Reynolds, and *Nickelodeon* (Columbia, 1976). During recent years he has worked only sporadically. *Saint Jack* (1979) with Gene Hackman was filmed in Singapore. *They All Laughed* (1981) starred Audrey Hepburn and Dorothy Stratten (whose tragic murder was the subject of Bob Fosse's *Star 80*), and, most recently, he directed *Mask* (Universal, 1985) starring pop singer-turned-actress Cher.

'Bogdanovich has once again – and catastrophically – misunderstood his talent, and attempted an exercise in style instead of trusting his gift for telling popular stories with feeling.'

Pauline Kael on *Nickelodeon* in 'The New Yorker', 1977

JOHN BOORMAN

Born Shepperton, Middlesex, 18 January 1933

The most adventurously un-British of contemporary British film-makers, John Boorman has ventured forward and backward in time – to the year 2293 for *Zardoz* (20th Century-Fox, 1973) and back to Arthurian England for *Excalibur* (Orion/Warner Bros., 1981) – and has regularly travelled back and forth across the Atlantic Ocean and the Irish Sea during the course of his directing career. He is a meticulous craftsman who puts much time and effort into each of his productions, including elaborate preparation, close collaboration on (and occasionally co-writing) his scripts, and longer than average time spent on post-production (post-synching all dialogue, for example). Not surprisingly, he has completed no more than nine features in his twenty years as a director, and only three during the past ten years.

Ironically, in view of his characteristic interest in cinematic myth and fantasy, Boorman started out working on news, current affairs and documentary programmes for TV. 'Like a lot of documentary film-makers,' he recalls, 'I began to strain at the limits of what was possible.' He got his first chance to direct a feature, *Catch Us If You Can*, capitalising on the interest in 'swinging London' and the vogue for British pop groups – here represented by the Dave Clark Five – and rushed out by Warner Bros. in 1965 in the wake of UA's success with the Beatles' *A Hard Day's Night* the previous year. But the real break came two years later when he managed to interest actor Lee Marvin in playing the lead role in *Point Blank* for MGM. Marvin then backed Boorman all the way as he worked with his friend Bill Stair to develop a special look to the film. Choosing to shoot in

LA, the most bleakly modern and arid of American cities, Boorman turned out a terrifically exciting and inventive revenge thriller, using a fragmented plot structure and introducing unexpected moments of black comedy.

One of a number of British directors who achieved a fair degree of success in the US around this time (John Schlesinger and Peter Yates were among the others), Boorman immediately went on to a second, but less interesting film with Lee Marvin, casting him opposite the remarkable Japanese actor Toshiro Mifune in *Hell In The Pacific* (UA, 1968). This was a strange allegorical tale of a pair of enemy soldiers stranded on a deserted island during World War II – an intriguing idea which didn't quite come off. Far better was the director's third American movie, *Deliverance* (Warner Bros., 1972), adapted from the novel by James Dickey. A strongly dramatised, violent and visually striking adventure tale about the experiences of a group of young city men 'roughing it' on a weekend canoeing trip, it was a smash hit and Boorman's only Oscar-nominated movie, and it made Burt Reynolds' name (as well as consolidating Jon Voight's position as an actor). The film helped to restore Boorman's reputation, as his previous British film, *Leo The Last* (UA, 1970), set in a fantasy version of London, had been a dismal commercial failure in spite of winning him the Best Director award at Cannes.

During the 70s Boorman took up Irish residency and made efforts to boost film production in that country. He himself made use of the Ardmore Studios to film his pretentious futuristic allegory, *Zardoz*, starring Sean Connery and

Charlotte Rampling. Rather more successful was *Excalibur* which brought together many favourite themes – his love of the quest, of symbolism and of mixing dream with reality. After serving as producer on Neil Jordan's first feature, *Angel* (1982), Boorman's Irish production outfit ran into some problems. Undaunted, he set off into the Amazon jungle in 1984 with a production crew and cast, headed by Powers Boothe, to film *The Emerald Forest*, a true story about an American mining engineer whose son is kidnapped and raised by an Indian tribe. If the story sounds familiar, one can reasonably expect that Boorman, now only fifty-two, will turn it into something extraordinary.

Top: Lee Marvin and Sharon Acker in Boorman's tense, violent, revenge-among-criminals thriller, *Point Blank* (1967), which established the director's reputation.

Above: Lee Marvin again, with distinguished Japanese actor Toshiro Mifune in *Hell In The Pacific* (1968). Mifune, born in China of Japanese parents, became world-famous through the great director, Akira Kurosawa, who cast him first in *Rashomon* (1951).

Left: Director Boorman (right) works with Jon Voight on a scene for *Deliverance* (1972), a more than somewhat allegorical adventure of a group of men on a canoeing trip.

'People say to me that I'm not really English. I don't make restrained and ironic and underplayed films. But I tell them that there is another kind of English tradition.'
1981

JOHN CARPENTER

Born Bowling Green, Kentucky, 1948

'I have a great feeling for physical movies. I don't like intellectual films. I love suspense. I want the audience to laugh and cry – an emotional response ... I write a scene the way a composer writes a score. Then I take the baton and I conduct it as director. I'm the happiest I can ever be when I'm on the set directing.'

John Carpenter has been passionately committed to movie-making ever since, aged five, he was knocked out by the 3-D version of *It Came From Outer Space* (Universal, 1953). By the time he saw *Forbidden Planet* (MGM, 1956) three years later, he was already old enough to embark on the first of a series of 8mm epics, *Gorgon The Space Monster*, filmed with a little Eumig camera that his father gave him as a present. While a teenager he left the movies behind for a time – he played bass guitar and sang in a rock band and attended Western Kentucky University. But by his senior year the movie bug bit again and he was off to study film at USC in 1968.

A dedicated student who wished to learn about every aspect of film-making, he worked on a number of different student movies. By 1970 he had co-directed an Oscar-winning short (*The Resurrection Of Broncho Billy*) and had embarked on his first feature. Following the pattern established by former USC student George Lucas with *THX-1138*, he began the picture as a student short which he hoped to expand to feature length. As Carpenter recalls, '*Dark Star* (completed in 1973) was one of the most difficult, brutalising, devasting and satisfying experiences of my life'. An entertaining and witty send-up of the 70s sci-fi craze, parodying Kubrick's *2001: A Space Odyssey* (MGM, 1967) in particular, the action took place on board an American spaceship on a mission to seek out and destroy unstable planets. The four astronauts are accompanied by a computer with a sexy female voice, a playful pet alien who looks like a large beach ball with webbed feet, the dead ship's commander who has been frozen and wired for sound, and a talking bomb which has armed itself and engages in a metaphysical discussion with an astronaut who tries to dissuade it from exploding.

Easily the most good-natured and humorous of all his films, possibly due to the influence of co-writer Dan O'Bannon, the movie failed to do much for Carpenter's career, and he was forced to seek work as a scriptwriter, then director of TV movies. He did complete one more low budget feature, *Assault On Precinct 13* (1976), during the mid-70s. It was a suspenseful and dramatic thriller concerning a group of characters trapped and under siege in a police station. Largely ignored by the American critics and public, the film received a rather better reception in Britain.

1978 was a watershed year for Carpenter. His script, *The Eyes Of Laura Mars* (Columbia), was turned into a film by director Irvin Kershner, starring Faye Dunaway, and was a modest hit. He di-

rected a pair of successful TV movies – *Someone Is Watching Me* starring Lauren Hutton and Adrienne Barbeau (who became Mrs Carpenter), and *Elvis*, an affectionate biopic reflecting Carpenter's special interest in rock music and starring Kurt Russell who gave an excellent (Emmy-nominated) performance and was to become one of Carpenter's favourite actors. Finally, he wrote and directed the horror movie *Halloween* in collaboration with an ex-girlfriend, Debra Hill, who served as producer and co-writer. A well-made and scary film, it was a smash hit early in 1979 and could claim to be the most commercially successful independent American production ever. It spawned a couple of sequels, both produced and written by Carpenter and Miss Hill who scripted *Halloween II* (1981) with a pair of the same stars, Jamie

Lee Curtis and Donald Pleasence. Neither was directed by Carpenter, however. Now established as a leading independent writer-director specialising in thriller-adventure type subjects, he went on to *The Fog* (1980) and *Escape From New York* (1981), both produced by Hill for Avco Embassy. He suffered a temporary setback when his first large budget movie, a remake of the Howard Hawks production, *The Thing* (Universal, 1982) and offering some extraordinarily elaborate and frightening special effects, failed at the box-office. But more recently he has wisely moved in a new direction with *Starman* (1984), starring Jeff Bridges and Karen Allen, to demonstrate that he can handle a sensitive, even romantic subject and no longer need be exclusively typecast as a director of horror or violence.

'Carpenter keeps you tense in an undifferentiated way – nervous and irritated rather than pleasurably excited – and you reach the point of wanting somebody to be killed so the film's rhythms will change.'

Pauline Kael on *Halloween* in 'The New Yorker', 1979

Above: Austin Stoker (left) and Laurie Zimmer in *Assault On Precinct 13* (1971), a violent, well-made thriller about a police station held under siege by a vengeful gang.

Left: English actor Donald Pleasence, whose appearance generally betokens something sinister, in *Halloween* (1979), a blood-soaked shocker about a mad killer on the loose, and a big box-office success.

Below: Carpenter (right) rehearses with Kurt Russell (left) for *Escape From New York* (1981).

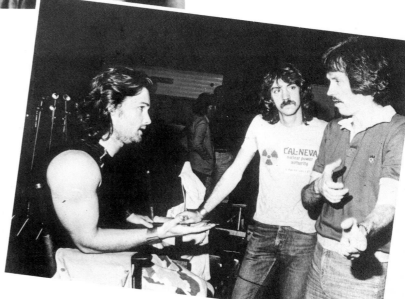

JOHN CASSAVETES

Born New York City, 9 December 1929

John Cassavetes occupies a unique position in the development of the American cinema during the past thirty years. A maverick actor who never fitted into the Hollywood system, he first turned to directing as a means of gaining more control over his career. Most important is his special creative drive and personal integrity which caused him many problems during those years when he was first establishing himself as a director. 'In being creative you just have to find out what you're trying to say and then say it. That's what I do in my films and that's why I make films.'

A wild, undisciplined youth who hated school and was a college dropout, he joined some friends in enrolling at the American Academy of Dramatic Arts for a year as a way of meeting girls. His natural talent as an actor, particularly in the role of the tough, street-wise kid at a time when Brando and Dean were first making their mark in the cinema, led to a series of TV and then film parts: The thriller, *The Night Holds Terror* (Columbia, 1955) was followed by the role of street gang leader in Don Siegel's *Crime In The Streets* (1956) and the rebellious hero of *Edge Of The City* (MGM, 1956), directed by Martin Ritt. Eager to extend himself as an actor he joined with a friend (Burt Lane) in forming a small actor's workshop in New York in 1957. His idea of turning an improvisation exercise into a little 16mm film later that year was boosted by tiny donations from hundreds of listeners to the Jean Shepherd radio show. Thus, he learned how to direct by doing it, through trial and error, working on the picture on and off over the next three years as and when he was able to raise additional cash and do some necessary reshooting. (He was only finally able to complete the film, titled *Shadows*, by signing to star in a short-lived TV series – 'Johnny Staccato' – during 1959-60.) A gritty, powerful little film dealing with the racial tensions within a close-knit black family – two brothers and a sister who can pass for white – and reflecting Cassavetes' stated wish to put 'real people' on the screen, even its flaws were an integral part of the attempt to capture an authentically downbeat view of characters and setting.

Shadows, better received in London than in the US, was seen by a Paramount executive who invited Cassavetes out to Hollywood to produce, direct and co-script *Too Late Blues* (1961). A bit daunted by the elaborate studio film-making machinery, he nevertheless got fine performances from stars Bobby Darin and Stella Stevens and succeeded in capturing the feel of the jazz world. However, he was unhappy with the result, and even more unhappy with his experience at the hands of producer Stanley Kramer who took him off *A Child Is Waiting* (UA, 1962) and, according to Cassavetes, seriously altered the tone of the movie.

Having swung from one extreme (film-making on a shoestring) to the other (Hollywood), Cassavetes finally settled down to find his own special place somewhere in between. Beginning with *Faces* (1968), which he worked on for a number of years during the mid-60s, he developed his interest in intimate, personal films, most often exploring family relationships – as in *A Woman Under The Influence* (1974) and more recently *Love Streams* (1983); or close friendships – *Husbands* (Columbia, 1970) and *Minnie And Moskowitz* (Universal, 1971), working with a small, close-knit group of friends and collaborators including actors Seymour Cassel, Peter Falk and Ben Gazzara, producer Al Ruban, and with his own relatives and family often appearing in bit parts. His leading star, however, has been his sensitive and extremely talented actress wife, Gena Rowlands, who was Oscar-nominated for her performances as a disturbed housewife (married to Peter Falk) in *A Woman Under The Influence* and as a gutsy ex-gun moll in *Gloria* (Columbia, 1980), an entertaining and uncharacteristic Cassavetes movie which provided him with his biggest hit. He has also been Oscar-nominated three times – as supporting actor for one of his two best known 60s roles, in Aldrich's *The Dirty Dozen* (MGM, 1967) (the other was *Rosemary's Baby*, Paramount, 1968), for scripting *Faces*, and as director of *A Woman Under The Influence*. His future ventures are eagerly awaited.

Left: Looking like a scene from one of the intense movies in which he acted, this picture shows John Cassavetes (right) directing Bobby Darin and Stella Stevens in *Too Late Blues* (1961), his first Hollywood directing assignment.

Below: Gena Rowlands as *Gloria* (1980), who goes on the run with a little boy (John Adames, right) to protect him from The Mob. The director's bid for commercialism, the movie was a not unentertaining blend of odd ingredients, and won Miss Rowlands an Oscar nomination.

Bottom: TV's 'Columbo', Peter Falk, has been one of the finest actors in the director's stable of regulars. Here, with Gena Rowlands, in archetypical Cassavetes, *A Woman Under The Influence* (1974).

'My characters are not violent or vile. They're everyday people. They have some money, but find themselves discontented with their own loneliness, their own mortality, the sameness of life.'

1984

MICHAEL CIMINO

Born New York City, 1940

In spite of the fact that he has directed only three features and co-scripted two others, Michael Cimino has emerged during the early 80s as one of the most controversial figures of the recent American cinema. After attending Yale University, he studied ballet and acting in New York in the 60s, then got a job with a company producing industrial and documentary films. He directed some TV commercials before moving to Hollywood in 1971, arriving at just the time when the new generation of 'movie brats', spearheaded by Spielberg, Scorsese, Lucas, and Coppola, were first establishing themselves. Cimino co-scripted the Douglas Trumbull sci-fi movie, *Silent Running* (Universal, 1971) then, along with another up-and-coming young writer, John Milius, he was taken on by producer-star Clint Eastwood. Together they fashioned a quite original sequel to *Dirty Harry* (Warner Bros., 1971), providing the hero with a black sidekick and generally making him into a more sympathetic character. But the body count was high, and some of the shoot-outs made *Magnum Force* (Warner Bros., 1973) appear more like a Western.

Recognising Cimino's obvious talent, Eastwood gave him the chance to serve as writer-director of his next picture, *Thunderbolt And Lightfoot* (UA, 1974). A fast-moving and amusing black comedy for the first hour, the pace slows down in the second half as the picture turns into a more conventionally violent thriller, but it was still fairly successful in advancing Cimino as a new writer-director. He spent some time on a couple of other projects, including an adaptation of Frederick Forsythe's 'The Dogs Of War', then embarked on a remarkable and original production in 1977 – *The Deerhunter*. A British-American co-production with financing from EMI (backed by Universal) it represented an ambitious attempt to deal with the American involvement in Vietnam, set against the background of a small steel-working town in Pennsylvania. Only a small proportion of the three-hour running time was directly concerned with the war, for the film was more about friendship and survival on a personal level, as represented most meaningfully by the central character of Michael – an amazing performance from Robert De Niro which knitted together the many diverse elements. Cimino's uncompromising attention to detail led him to use bits of eight different towns to construct the setting, and difficult location filming in Thailand escalated the original $8 million budget to $13 million.

A big hit and a success with the critics, the film won Cimino the Best Picture and directing Oscars, with well-deserved nominations for Deric Washburn's screenplay and Vilmos Zsigmond's superb atmospheric photography. On the basis of this success the director was given virtual carte blanche by United Artists to make *Heaven's Gate* (1980). Setting out to recreate the feel of the American West with great authenticity, the original $8 million budget increased to over four times that amount. When the completed three-and-half hour film opened in 1980, it was heavily attacked by the critics; and the publicity surrounding Cimino grew. He somehow came to symbolise that new generation of young producer-directors who handled multi-million dollar budgets, and became an industry scapegoat at a time when such expensive movies as Scorsese's *New York, New York* (UA, 1977), Spielberg's *1941* (Universal, 1979) and Woody Allen's *Stardust Memories* (UA, 1980) had all done poorly at the box-office. In this case, however, UA had only themselves to blame, since it should have been apparent from quite early on that Cimino was taking an extremely non-commercial,

naturalistic approach. Not only was he not using any major stars, but the film lacked any hero figures for an audience to identify with, and the underdog immigrant farmers hardly inspired audience identification either, for they were generally poor, dirty and inarticulate, speaking various (subtitled) foreign languages. Overlong, and certainly no masterpiece, *Heaven's Gate* is nonetheless excellent: well acted, beautifully photographed, and a remarkable achievement.

Unfortunately, Cimino encountered problems on all his subsequent projects, but was finally back at work in 1984 directing Mickey Rourke in *Year Of The Dragon*. In the insecure and competitive atmosphere of present-day Hollywood, however, somewhat of a question mark clearly hangs over his future.

'I do not have any regrets about the work that I do... There are no excuses, no complaints... There is an old Arab saying, "The blow that doesn't break you strengthens you."'
1983

Above left: Chuck Aspegren (left), Robert De Niro (centre) and John Cazale in the film which launched its director, *The Deer Hunter* (1977).

Above: Director Cimino photographed on location in Washington during the filming of *The Deer Hunter*.

Below: The scene at the railroad station at Casper, Wyoming, during the making of *Heaven's Gate* (1980). A mammoth undertaking, featuring a cast led by Kris Kristofferson, Isabelle Huppert and John Hurt, the film was a financial disaster. In 1984 it was re-released at selected venues in its original uncut form.

FRANCIS COPPOLA

Born Detroit, 7 April 1939

Tyro producer, director and scriptwriter, Francis Coppola is the *complete* film-maker, a larger-than-life personality who has pursued an eccentrically personal approach to mainstream feature film-making for the past twenty years. One of the first of that group of new young directing talents who began to make their mark on Hollywood during the late 60s and early 70s, he provides a classic example of the serious and committed director who has worked within the established system in order to subsidise the more personal kind of films he prefers. However, due to his proven success as a scriptwriter and/or director on commercially successful productions like *Patton* (20th Century-Fox, 1970) and the *Godfather* movies (Paramount, 1972 & 1974), he is in demand from the major companies and is often torn between commercial considerations and his wish to do his best artistically. In his best known films like *The Godfather II* and *Apocalypse Now* (Zoetrope/UA, 1979), he has been successful in blending the commercial with the artistic, but his most personal projects like *The Conversation* (Paramount, 1974) have rarely done well at the box-office.

Occasionally Coppola has been able to trade off one type of picture against the other, agreeing, for example, to direct *Godfather II* for Paramount if the studio would also back *The Conversation*. Unfortunately, Coppola has a penchant for involving himself in difficult and ambitious large-scale projects with runaway budgets and has repeatedly flirted with disaster. During more recent years this happened with *Apocalypse Now*, in production for almost three years (1976-79) – but it was a hit. Then, in 1980, the costs of the first production filmed in his own Zoetrope studio, *Hammett* (directed by Wim Wenders) escalated to $10 million, far more than the film could ever hope to recoup at the box-office. And when his own project, *One From The Heart* (Zoetrope/Columbia, 1982) ended up costing $26 million, he was in deep financial trouble. A really quite entertaining and visually stunning musical fantasy in the tradition of Vincente Minnelli, and a technical *tour de force*, it was attacked by the critics and never found its audience. Immensely talented, but rather too disorganised to succeed in the role of movie mogul, his financial difficulties led him to take on yet another much troubled project, the Robert Evans production of *The Cotton Club* which occupied him during 1983-84. Unfortunately, the first reactions suggest that he may have failed, yet again, to tread the delicate line between artistic and commercial considerations.

The son of a talented flautist and composer, Carmine Coppola, who has supplied the music for a few of his pictures, Francis was a theatre arts student at Hofstra University during the late 50s. While there he directed plays and wrote a couple of original musicals, but he was more interested in the cinema and enrolled in the film department of UCLA in

1960. He directed a pair of 'nudie' flicks during the early 60s and was hired by Roger Corman to rejig an obscure Russian sci-fi movie which emerged as *Battle Beyond The Sun* (1962). Kept busy as Corman's right-hand man, he served as dialogue director on *The Tower Of London* (UA, 1962) and travelled to Europe with the Corman unit where he doubled as sound man and second unit cameraman, shooting all the racing footage for *The Young Racers* (AIP, 1963). Clearly, Francis had earned the chance to try directing his own first low budget feature – *Dementia 13* (AIP, 1963), a horror movie which he shot at the Ardmore Studios in Ireland. After shooting some location footage with Boris Karloff for *The Terror* (AIP, 1963), Francis left Corman, accepting an offer from Seven Arts to work as a scriptwriter.

During the following few years he turned out a large number of scripts including the plodding *Is Paris Burning?*

Above: *You're A Big Boy Now* (1966) followed the adventures of a virginal young man (Peter Kastner, illustrated) who learns the facts of life in his encounters with women. One of them, with him here, was Karen Black.

Left: Tommy Steele and a by then vintage Fred Astaire in the fey and whimsical musical, *Finian's Rainbow* (1968).

(Paramount, 1965), directed by René Clément, and an adaptation of Tennessee Williams' *This Property Is Condemned* (Seven Arts/Paramount, 1966). By using his own money to buy the rights to the David Benedictus novel and writing a script, he was able to convince Seven Arts to let him direct *You're A Big Boy Now*, filmed on location in New York City in 1966. A bright, effervescent comedy about a young man (Peter Kastner) on the brink of adulthood who finds himself at odds with a legion of viragos (Julie Harris, Geraldine Page, Elizabeth Hartman and the then unknown Karen Black in her first movie role), the film was obviously influenced by the French New Wave of the early 60s. On the strength of its modest success, Coppola was invited by Warner Bros. to direct the film version of the musical *Finian's Rainbow* (1968) with Fred Astaire, Petula Clark and Tommy Steele. Unfortunately, the budget was inadequate for a big movie musical, he was forced to shoot much of it on the studio backlot, and the film

Below: Director Coppola with his star, Shirley Knight, during filming of *The Rain People* (1969), one of his earlier projects which actually conformed to his own, rather than the studios', ambitions.

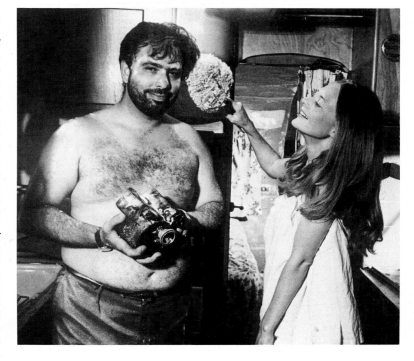

Above: The local Italian undertaker (played by Salvatore Corsitto), whose daughter has been assaulted, pleads with the all-powerful Don Vito Corleone for help in avenging the crime. The Don is, of course, Marlon Brando, *The Godfather* of Coppola's brilliant, blockbusting, 1971 success. The well-received sequel, *The Godfather II* (1974) starred Robert De Niro as the young Vito Corleone. Interestingly, the word 'Mafia' was never given utterance in either film.

Right: The still shows a moment from the main production number in *One From The Heart* (1981), a $20 million box-office catastrophe and, according to some opinion, unfairly underrated. Certainly, the money spent resulted in some extraordinarily lavish and spacious studio sets, reminiscent of the hey-day of the Hollywood musical.

production company, American Zoetrope. Its vice-president was another Young Turk of whom more would be heard, George Lucas. 'The real concept,' said Lucas, 'was that it would be an independent, free production company that would make seven or eight films a year in varying degrees of safeness. We might do a couple of films that seemed fairly safe and reasonable, and then do some really off-the-wall productions.' It did not quite work out like that. The problem was that capital was required, for which Coppola was forced to jettison some of his prized independence by applying for it at Warners. Over $3 million was pumped into the organisation, but attached were a number of escape clauses for the Hollywood major; and when Warners loathed every script they were shown, and when the first full-fledged American Zoetrope production, Lucas' austere sci-fi drama *THX-1138* (completed in 1970), flopped at the box-office, the company suffered the first of several flirtations with bankruptcy. Coppola was obliged to re-enter the rat race.

Though (despite his own ethnic background) he must have seemed a strange choice to film Mario Puzo's Mafia bestseller, *The Godfather*, Coppola achieved not merely one of the most commercially profitable films in cinema history but a gangster saga that actually improved on its source material in richness of narrative and depth of characterisation. With a uniformly brilliant cast – from Marlon Brando (who won an Oscar for his extraordinarily vivid portrayal of the aging Don Corleone) to Al Pacino, from James Caan to Robert Duvall, from Sterling Hayden to the promising young Diane Keaton – and the burnished photographic textures of Gordon Willis and production design of Dean Tavoularis, *The Godfather* has become a contempor-

'We're on the eve of something that's going to make the Industrial Revolution look like a small, out-of-town tryout ... a communications revolution that's about movies and arts and music and digital electronics and satellites, but above all, human talent.'
1979

Left: Gene Hackman in *The Conversation* (1974). He played a bugging device expert whose conscience catches up with him in a chilling performance of which the 'New Yorker' said, 'a terrifying depiction of a ransacked spirit'.

flopped badly. The whimsy in this story of leprechauns and crocks of gold seemed dated and coy and was certainly not the kind of material which the director would have chosen for himself.

Warners, however, were undaunted by its failure and, by some Byzantine yet all too characteristic logic, instantly offered him another Broadway musical, *Mame*, for a fee of $1½ million. Coppola bravely and wisely declined, asking instead for half that sum as the budget of a modest personal project, *The Rain People* (1969). Having paid his dues, he now wished to pursue the kind of career to which he felt

better adapted (and it is another of the movie industry's little ironies that he should subsequently come to be associated with just the kind of mega-budget blockbuster that he then refused). Starring Shirley Knight, James Caan and Robert Duvall, none of them conjurable names at that period, *The Rain People* was almost an 'art movie' by Hollywood's standards, an account of an alienated woman taking off across the highways of America in her motor car. It made no money; but Coppola felt at ease with his new-won independence and, in 1969, he founded his own San Francisco-based

Below: Robert De Niro in *The Godfather II* (1974) which, like its predecessor, so accurately captured the look, feel and spirit of New York's 'Little Italy' where so many ordinary lives are touched, for better or worse, by the ruling 'families' of The Mob.

ary classic and well deserved its best film Academy Award. Coppola was now, in Tinseltown parlance, 'hot'; and, as the producer of Lucas' second film, another all-time box-office triumph, *American Graffiti* (1973), he might have been described as 'scalding'. In fact, two years after adapting Puzo's novel, he topped (in artistic terms) *The Godfather* with *The Godfather II*, a multilayered, a-chronological fable of early 20th-century America and that rarest of movie phenomena, a sequel which was actually superior to the original. It, too, won the Best Picture Oscar and five others, including a pair to Coppola as director and co-scriptwriter.

Between the two *Godfathers*, however, Coppola had completed one of his most interesting films, *The Conversation* (1974), an absorbing, even haunting, thriller on the paranoia induced by technological surveillance and wire-tapping with a quite shattering performance from Gene Hackman. The film acquired unexpected extra relevance by appearing more or less concurrently with the first intimations of the Watergate scandal. 'I never meant it to be so relevant,' Coppola later claimed. 'I almost think the picture would have been better received had Watergate not happened.' The film was a greater critical than commercial success; but, in view of the staggering returns from its maker's Cosa Nostra double bill, it only enhanced his reputation.

Though he was also concerned with the day-to-day management of American Zoetrope, which he planned to run along studio system lines with a 'stable' of contract actors and technicians, as well as with the backing of a San Francisco 'alternative' publication, 'City' (which folded after one year), Coppola was now expending his energies on the most grandiose of his projects, the near-legendary *Apocalypse Now*. From the beginning, this Vietnam War epic was jinxed – by hurricanes in the Philippines (where it was mostly shot), by the reluctance of a number of Hollywood stars to involve themselves with such a long-term (and precarious) project, by the brisk firing of one actor, Harvey Keitel, and hiring of another, Martin Sheen. Its costs spiralled so rapidly that Coppola was forced to pre-sell much of his own financial interest in the film, with the result that, though a huge box-office success, it earned considerably less for him than he might have hoped. And yet, despite these travails, despite its flaws, the completed work fully justified its director's mental, psychological and financial investment, enshrining as it does a few of the most mesmerisingly powerful set-pieces in film history and capturing, as no other film has managed to do, the sheer hallucinatory obscenity of the Vietnam War.

Exhausted by the experience, and perhaps resentful of the often slightly grudging attentions which the film received from the critical Establishment, Coppola spoke of making the kind of modestly conceived romantic musical common in the 40s and 50s. It was to be rendered even more economical by capitalising on the new video technology with which he had become obsessed, like a child with an electric train set. This 'modest' musical was *One From The Heart*

(1981), a studio-bound extravaganza totally out of tune with current tastes and trends. Its commercial failure definitively ruined American Zoetrope, of which it was intended as the crown jewel. Coppola has since made two youth movies back-to-back, *The Outsiders* and *Rumble Fish* (1983), both based on novels by S.E. Hinton which have become required reading for schoolchildren in the US and Britain. The first was a sentimental melodrama patently influenced by the dynamic CinemaScope visuals of Nicholas Ray's *Rebel Without A Cause* (Warner Bros., 1955) and a modest box-office success in its country of origin; the second was more complex and ambitious, filmed in black-and-white and influenced rather by Camus (or so Coppola claimed) and Orson Welles. Most recently, he has found himself embroiled in the $50 million headache of *The Cotton Club*, a saga of the Jazz age. However, Coppola has already proved that he is a born survivor. Still only forty-six years old, no doubt he will continue to be a major force in the American cinema for many years to come.

Above: Coppola discusses a scene with his youthful cast for *The Outsiders* (1983). They are C. Thomas Howell (left), Ralph Macchio (back to camera) and the star, Matt Dillon.

Left: Diane Lane and Richard Gere recreate the fashionable children of the Jazz Age in the director's $50 million 20s saga, *The Cotton Club* (1984), another overpriced venture whose making was dogged by difficulties – including reported friction between Coppola and Gere.

'I've had no life. My whole life I've never had a vacation; I haven't been able to stay in an apartment or have fun. It's always been this absurd life.'
1984

ROGER CORMAN

Born Detroit, 5 April 1926

'The majority of my films were low budget. There was very little I could do about that at the time. My prime goal was to make movies and have a good time doing that. Once I started directing, I just kept on going . . . Gangster films. Horror films. Science fiction. Adventure. I tried to put a little bit of myself into each. I tried my best on every film no matter how low the budget or how little time there was to get it finished.' Thus, Roger Corman looks back on his prolific career as a director from 1955-1970.

He had, in fact, started out directing in the simplest way imaginable. After completing a degree in engineering at Stanford University and a brief period studying English Literature at Oxford, he began writing screenplays. He was amazed at the way in which his first script was altered by Allied Artists and the title changed to *Highway Dragnet* (1953). But at least his 'associate producer' credit and scripting fee helped finance his first film as producer, *The Monster From The Ocean Floor* (1954), followed immediately by *The Fast And The Furious* starring Dorothy Malone and John Ireland (who also co-directed). This latter he offered to a new company, American Releasing Corporation, headed by Samuel Z. Arkoff and James Nicholson, and on the basis of Corman's remarkable contribution during the following years, the company flourished and was renamed American Internation Pictures (AIP). In fact, forming a new film company in the mid-50s at a time when the industry was going through one of its periodic crises and many of the small, independent companies, like Republic, were on their last legs, should have been the height of folly. But when Corman turned to directing, having had little previous film-making experience, he found himself positively enjoying turning out a great variety of lively and entertaining pictures at an astonishing rate, learning as he went along. Beginning with the Dorothy Malone Western, *Five Guns West* (1955), and serving as his own producer, Corman di-

rected an average of five movies per year over the following six years. With budgets of only $80-100,000 per film and shooting schedules of ten days or less, he was fortunate in being able to assemble a talented and close-knit group of collaborators (headed by veteran cameraman Floyd Crosby, scriptwriter Charles Griffith and art director Daniel Haller) who helped him achieve superior results.

As Corman became more fluent and self-assured, he introduced irony and humour into his films, which often presented a subtle commentary on 50s America. In *Not Of This Earth* (1956) he mixed the theme of alien invasion with vampirism – the alien humanoid is named Paul Johnson and drives a Cadillac, but speaks with a strange accent and has blank, pupil-less eyes hidden behind dark glasses. He requires vast quantities of human blood to replace that of his own race who are suffering from diseased blood. Soon there are bodies piling up all over LA. Corman recalls the film with affection as one of the first in which he mixed horror with 'traces of humour'. The star was Beverly Garland, one of his favourite 50s actresses, while another, Susan Cabot, appeared regularly during the late 50s in *Sorority Girl*, *Viking Women* and *War Of The Satellites* (all 1957), then had her best role as *The Wasp Woman* (1959) – 'A Beautiful Woman by Day . . . A Lusting Queen Wasp by Night'. A modern morality tale reflecting the American woman's obsession with staying youthful, Cabot played the head of a cosmetics firm who uses herself as a guinea pig to test a new rejuvenating serum. Of course, she comes to a bad end. This little 73-minute black-and-white movie demonstrated Corman's ability to produce superior screen entertainment on a budget of only $50,000 and a five or six day shooting schedule. She also appeared opposite Charles Bronson in his first starring role as *Machine Gun Kelly* (1958), about a real 30s gangster. This film, which helped to make Corman's name, was conceived as an un-

usual black comedy showing Kelly as an inept and insecure crook dominated by his tough and independent-minded moll (Miss Cabot). Another star who got his start with Corman was Robert Vaughn, later famous as Napoleon Solo, who gave a likeable performance as *Teenage Caveman* later that year (1958).

Corman reached the end of his early, prolific movie-making cycle in 1960 which proved to be a turning point year for him. His mastery of black comedy and super-quick filming was demonstrated most clearly in *The Little Shop Of Horrors*. Here Jonathan Haze starred as Seymour, the clumsy, myopic little flower shop em-

Above: Peter Lorre cowers, Vincent Price looms, in *The Raven* (1963), a masterly mélange of medieval mayhem.

Below left: Vincent Price (left), as Valdemar, risen from the dead, literally frightens the life out of Basil Rathbone in 'The Case Of M. Valdemar', one of the three episodes which made up *Tales Of Terror* (1962).

Below: Jane Asher and Vincent Price in the visually striking *The Masque Of The Red Death* (1964).

ployee whose favourite exotic plant thrives on human blood and turns him into a bodysnatcher as he endeavours to keep it well-fed. The plant devours a burglar, belches, then spits out his gun, but when it eats Seymour's girlfriend he is heartbroken: 'You ate the only thing I ever loved'. Jack Nicholson made an amazing cameo appearance as an enthusiastically masochistic dental patient named Wilber Force. Corman claims that Chuck Griffith wrote the witty script in a week and that he shot it in two-and-half days. (Over twenty years later the film was turned into a smash hit Broadway musical and will no doubt be given a rather more glossy movie treatment second time round.)

In 1960 Corman embarked on the first of his series of upmarket Poe productions and related costume horror movies filmed in colour and CinemaScope (or Panavision) with Vincent Price as his favourite new star. These would occupy him for a few years and bring him greater success at the box-office, as well as a wider appreciation of his work. *The House Of Usher*, adapted from Poe by Richard Matheson, has a slowish first half but is especially memorable for the escalating drama and climax of the final reels. *The Pit And The Pendulum* (1961) was three-fourths over by the time it arrived at the Poe story, but film audiences didn't mind and it proved a bigger hit than *Usher*. *The Premature Burial* (1962) had even less to do with Poe and starred Ray Milland (in place of Price). But it led Corman to take a different tack in his next film: instead of expanding the Poe stories into a full-length feature, he put three together to form an omnibus feature, *Tales Of Terror* (1962). He assembled a stellar cast headed by Vincent Price, Basil Rathbone and Peter Lorre, and nicely counter-pointed the effective horror of 'Morella' and 'The Case of M. Valdemar' with some delightful black comedy in 'The Black Cat'. This latter, the Peter Lorre episode, naturally led on to Corman's comic masterpiece, *The Raven* (1963) in which an irrepressibly cute and cuddly Lorre stole the show. The Poe cycle ended with an impressive pair of productions – *The Masque Of The Red Death* followed by *The Tomb Of Ligeia*, both

filmed in England. *Masque* was easily the most lavish and stylish of the cycle, making use of parts of leftover sets adroitly reassembled by art director Dan Haller from Paramount's opulent historical drama, *Becket*, and with ace cinematographer (later director) Nicolas Roeg behind the camera. *Ligeia* marked a new departure as Corman decided to shoot on location, and made superb use of the authentic ruins of a 12th century abbey. Thematically the Robert Towne script brought together elements of many of the previous Poe films and represented a fitting conclusion to the cycle.

The director had also made a few movies outside the cycle during the early 60s, best of which was *X – The Man With X-Ray Eyes* (1963), starring Ray Milland as a scientist whose x-ray vision leads to unpredictable and tragic consequences. During these years Corman had expanded his activities as a producer, taking on many talented young assistants and

film school graduates at rock bottom wages, but giving them an opportunity to break into the industry. The long and impressive list of those he helped in this way included Coppola, Bogdanovich, Monte Hellman, Jack Nicholson and Stephanie Rothman during the 60s, Jonathan Demme, Scorsese, Joe Dante and many others in later years. Corman himself returned to directing during the late 60s with youth movies like *The Wild Angels* (1966) and *The Trip* (1967), both starring Peter Fonda, and an impressive pair of gangster films – *The St Valentine's Day Massacre* (1966) starring Jason Robards and George Segal for 20th Century-Fox and Shelley Winters at her most abrasive as gun-toting *Bloody Mama* (1970). He retired from directing after completing *Von Richthofen And Brown* (aka *The Red Baron*) in 1970, but that same year founded the production company New World Pictures for which he continued active as a producer up to 1983.

Above left: Peter Fonda (left) and Buck Taylor in *The Wild Angels* (1966), a youth-orientated movie about a motor-cycle gang whose members conform to Nazi-type rituals.

Above: Susan Strasberg and Peter Fonda in *The Trip* (1967), about LSD and the hallucinations it induces. Miss Strasberg is better known as the daughter of Lee Strasberg, founder of the Actors Studio and teacher of The Method, than for her largely undistinguished screen appearances.

Left: Shelley Winters, one of Hollywood's most energetic and individualistic actresses, played *Bloody Mama* (1970), about an outlaw and her four sons who conduct a reign of terror during the 30s. Here, Miss Winters chats to Roger Corman during a break in filming, while cameraman John Alonzo (standing left) ponders a problem.

'When I was making low-budget movies . . . I was working for those that let me do what I wanted. When I started to work my way up to the million-dollar budget mark . . . they wouldn't pay attention to any of my suggestions or requests.'
1982

BRIAN DE PALMA

Born Newark, New Jersey, 11 September 1940

Characterised by a bold visual style and specially attracted to bizarre, violent and sexual themes, Brian De Palma is one of the more controversial figures among the younger generation of leading American directors who has established himself on the fringes of the exploitation market. One clue to the origins of the fantastic and stylised view of the world he depicts on screen can be found in his own claim that he suffers from 'an extremely vivid visual imagination – sometimes to the point where it's disturbing. It's like something I can't turn off. Images start flowing immediately people tell me a story or I read a page of a script. You add a little emotion and that's an overload . . .'

De Palma first developed his interest in film-making while a student at Columbia University in the early 60s and gradually worked his way up from 16mm amateur shorts to a cheaply made student feature (while a postgrad at Sarah Lawrence College), and wrote, edited and financed a second feature, *Murder À La Mod* (1967), from his earnings as a documentary director. He achieved his first modest success with the feature-length *Greetings* starring Jonathan Warden and a young Robert De Niro in 1968. The title derives from the opening words of the letter from the draft board informing the hero that the army wants him for service in Vietnam. Completed at a cost of only $43,000, the film found a distributor, earned a nice profit and De Palma was soon directing a sequel, *Hi Mom!*, in 1969, again starring De Niro and again capturing the particular quality of the 60s counter-culture while dealing with young men's preoccupation with girls, sex and Vietnam.

By 1970 De Palma was in an ideal position to take advantage of the sudden Hollywood flirtation with youth-oriented movies made by new young directors, in the wake of the astonishing box-office success of *Easy Rider* (Columbia, 1969). He was signed by Warner Bros. to direct a satirical little movie, *Get To Know Your Rabbit* (1970), about a business executive dropout who becomes a tap dancing magician. But the studio was dissatisfied with the film and put it on the shelf for two years, during which time Brian had re-

turned to New York and independent production. For *Sisters* (1972) he put together a useful non-star cast including a number of actors from his earlier independent productions (Charles Durning, William Finley, Jennifer Salt) joined by Margot Kidder. He co-wrote the script about the murderous survivor of a pair of female Siamese twins, drawing on both his special interest in Hitchcock and his love of offbeat black humour, with a score from Hitchcock's favourite composer, Bernard Herrmann. Directed with great panache, the film becomes progressively more bizarre as it develops and the young lady journalist investigating the murders is sucked into a world over which she has no control until, finally, she is led away in a catatonic state. Becoming known as 'the poor man's Hitchcock' during the 70s, De Palma was to make effective use of Hitchcockian themes in later pictures like the solidly crafted *Obsession* (Columbia, 1976), obviously derived from *Vertigo* (Paramount, 1958) or the rather more nasty and violent – though undeniably stylish – *Dressed To Kill* (1980), one of many recent movies which owe a large debt to *Psycho* (Paramount, 1960). It was a big hit, in spite of voluble protests from

feminist groups who picketed certain cinemas where it was showing.

Brian made a fine job of directing the screen adaptation of Stephen King's

novel *Carrie* (UA, 1976) scripted by Larry Cohen. His most effective movie treatment of the supernatural (another was the expert but awful *The Fury*, 1979), it starred Sissy Spacek as the schoolgirl with extraordinary, telekinetic powers and Piper Laurie making a welcome comeback to the screen as her strange and fanatical mother. (Both were Oscar-nominated.) Nancy Allen also made an appearance and went on to become Mrs De Palma, starring in *Dressed To Kill* and the rather more convincing *Blow Out* (1981) co-starring John Travolta. More recently he has directed an updated remake of *Scarface* (Universal, 1983) with Al Pacino as a ruthless gangster deported from Cuba to the US, and he returned to the world of *Dressed To Kill* with *Body Double* (1984). Although clearly in danger of repeating himself, De Palma is still young (and he is certainly talented). It is to be hoped that he will find new directions to explore in the future.

Above: Carrie (Sissy Spacek, left), the schoolgirl cursed by her destructive telekinetic powers, seeks comfort from her strange mother (Piper Laurie) in *Carrie* (1976), from Stephen King's novel.

Left: Nancy Allen (Mrs De Palma in private life) and John Travolta filming *Blow Out* (1981), a murder thriller exploiting high tech surveillance devices. The director is standing behind Travolta.

Below left: The volatile, electrically talented Al Pacino in the title role in *Scarface* (1983), De Palma's violent, bloody, updated, Technicolor remake of the Howard Hawks-Paul Muni classic.

> '*When De Palma is most distinctive, his work calls up so many junky memories it's pure candied exploitation – a funny archetypal nightmare . . . No one else has ever caught the thrill that teenagers get from a dirty joke and sustained it for a whole picture.*'
>
> Pauline Kael on *Carrie* in 'The New Yorker', 1976

CLINT EASTWOOD

Born San Francisco, 31 May 1930

The story of Clint Eastwood's rise to movie stardom is well known – how he graduated from bit parts in a number of 50s movies to a successful TV Western series ('Rawhide'), then played the lead in a number of Italian 'spaghetti Westerns' directed by Sergio Leone before returning to the US to become one of the top American stars in the late 60s. Twenty years on and in his mid-fifties, he is still going strong, averaging a steady two or three new movies per year.

Less well known, however, is Eastwood's behind-the-scenes development into a shrewd producer and talented director. His own company, Malpaso, was formed in 1967, a number of years before he directed his first feature, *Play Misty For Me* (Universal, 1971). But, according to Eastwood, he had first become interested in trying his hand at directing as long ago as the 'Rawhide' days and was set to direct one of the episodes until the company reneged on the deal. His interest in the production side was stimulated by his desire to gain a greater control over his career, and was further reinforced by his work with Leone, when he helped to rewrite the *Dollar* film scripts which established his character of the tall, dark and mysterious stranger, the 'Man With No Name', as a new type of Western hero. Having regarded the films as little more than low-budget commercial assignments, he was as surprised as anyone by their success, but still had to work hard to establish himself as a star in the US.

With three new pictures in release, all produced by his own company and including his first as director, and a pair from his favourite director, Don Siegel, 1971 was a good year for Clint. *The Beguiled* (Universal) gave him an opportunity to play a stronger dramatic part than usual, while *Dirty Harry* (Warner Bros.) became his best known cop role. Encouraged by Siegel to try his hand at directing, he selected *Play Misty For Me*, a project which he had already optioned three years earlier. Nervous about his first day of shooting and wishing to have an experienced director present, he cast Siegel in a bit role as a bartender. But Siegel was even more nervous than he, and had to have lines of dialogue written on little bits of paper pasted all over the set. Unfortunately, he kept mixing them up, and Clint claims that Siegel has been more tolerant in his treatment of actors ever since. In any event, the movie turned out superbly, a gripping psychological thriller in the Hitchcock mold, in which Clint played a smooth-talking disc jockey who discovers too late that the attractive girl he has so casually slept with is really a jealous and murderous psychopath. (A convincingly scary performance here by Jessica Walter.)

During the following years, the actor-director assembled an excellent production team, headed by cameraman Bruce Surtees and editor Ferris Webster, who worked on all the films from his company, split about half and half between those he directed himself and

those he offered to young members of the team like scriptwriter Michael Cimino and assistant director James Fargo. Unfortunately, Eastwood the director has generally failed to live up to the promise of *Misty*. Now, some fifteen years and some ten directed films later, he is best known as the director of the same kind of cop films and Westerns with which he first made his name as an actor. For example, *High Plains Drifter* (Universal, 1972) presented his own variation on the lone stranger riding into town theme (echoing Leone), while in the somewhat more interesting (and violent) *The Outlaw Josey Wales* (Warner Bros., 1976) he plays a farmer turned ruthless vigilante. The two-and-a-half-hour long movie was given a much needed lift by the appearance of Chief Dan George, while Sondra Locke played her first Eastwood heroine. (When his twenty-year marriage broke up she became his regular companion and co-star.) Having left the directing of the 'Dirty Harry' movies to others, his decision to direct the fourth entry in the cycle, *Sudden Impact* (Warners Bros., 1983), reflects a new low in

Above: Clint Eastwood sees the world through the Panavision camera. The photograph was taken in 1971.

directorial imagination. At least with his latest Western, *Pale Rider* (Warner Bros., 1985), and his first for eight years, set in California during the gold rush, he has had the courage to buck the recent trend in Hollywood where Westerns are now regarded as box-office poison.

Left: Eastwood as the disc jockey under attack by a crazed fan (Jessica Walter) in *Play Misty For Me* (1971), the effective chiller with which he made his directorial debut.

Below: Director and star of *The Outlaw Josey Wales* (1976), the story of a farmer who sets out to exact vengeance for the murder of his wife by bandits.

'All you need to get into the Directors Guild is for someone to give you a job. I said to myself "Kid, you got the job".'
1981

BLAKE EDWARDS

Born Tulsa, Oklahoma, 26 July 1922

Blake Edwards has had a long love-hate relationship with Hollywood. He grew up in tinsel town, the son of a movie production manager and former stage director (Jack McEdwards), and grandson of the pioneering movie director J. Gordon Edwards who was employed by Fox (1914-25) and was the favourite director of Theda Bara during her peak years (1916-19). Blake began as a bit part actor, then turned to scriptwriting and directing during the 50s, specialising in musicals and comedy. A number of disputes with leading studios during the early 70s, however, led him to work mainly abroad for some years. Recently he has returned to make a number of hit pictures in Hollywood, and has exorcised his anger at those narrow-minded studio executives who gave him a hard time by parodying them in his unappetizing, behind-the-scenes look at the movie capital in *S.O.B.* (Paramount, 1981).

Gaining his first movie experience during the 40s by freelance work as an actor in a variety of films ranging from major studio productions to cheap programmers, Edwards soon turned to scripting. He found it relatively easy to make a breakthrough with a pair of Rod Cameron B-Westerns, *Panhandle* (1947) and *Stampede* (1949) which he co-wrote and co-produced for Monogram. He joined director Richard Quine (in whose first movie, *Leather Gloves*. Columbia, 1948, he had acted) at Columbia during the early 50s where he co-scripted half-a-dozen pictures, mainly musical comedies, and got his first opportunity to direct with a pair of Frankie Laine musicals.

A period as a comedy director (and writer) at Universal culminated in his first big box-office hit: *Operation Petticoat*

(1959) was a hilarious service comedy set aboard a submarine in the Pacific during World War II, and starring Cary Grant and Tony Curtis. Around this time Edwards made his first successful venture into TV production with the 'Peter Gunn' series, best remembered for its evocative Henry Mancini jazz score. A regular Edwards collaborator, Mancini has provided the score (and some Oscar-winning songs) for virtually every Edwards movie since 1960.

In the early 60s Edwards established himself as one of Hollywood's most interesting and successful directors. He moved easily from the sophisticated New York comedy milieu of *Breakfast At Tiffanys* (Paramount, 1961) starring Audrey Hepburn as the unforgettable Holly Golightly, to the gripping and nightmarish thriller, *Experiment In Terror* (Columbia), filmed later that same year, using effective San Francisco locations, and Lee Remick as the menaced heroine. She then gave one of her best performances, opposite Jack Lemmon, in an uncharacteristically bleak Edwards drama about alcoholism, *Days of Wine And Roses* (Warner Bros., 1962). It was a hit and won Oscar nominations for its stars, but *The Pink Panther* (UA) which followed in 1963 was a bigger hit and led to a large number of sequels, all scripted and directed by Edwards of which, arguably, the best was *A Shot In The Dark* (UA, 1964), relatively low-keyed, packed full of gags and avoiding the silliness which plagued the later entries in the 70s.

Unfortunately, the director's attempt at a large-scale, big budget comedy, *The Great Race* (Warner Bros., 1965), flopped, and marked the beginning of a difficult ten years. Worst of all was the

$22 million disaster of *Darling Lili* (Paramount) filmed in 1969, the same year that he married its star, Julie Andrews. Here, as with the offbeat Western, *The Wild Rovers* (1971), and the tough drama, *The Carey Treatment* (1972) – both for MGM – which followed, Edwards claimed that he was the victim of studio interference. He was back on top once again, however, with *Pink Panther* sequels which allowed free rein to his love of wild physical comedy and struck pay dirt at the box-office. The best of his recent pictures have been the period romp *Victor/Victoria* (MGM, 1981) giving Julie Andrews the opportunity to shine, and a pair of superior Dudley Moore comedies, *10* (Orion/Warner Bros., 1980) and *Micki And Maude* (Columbia, 1984).

Top: Ever urbane, ever attractive, Cary Grant as ship commander invites Joan O'Brien to a party on deck in *Operation Petticoat* (1959), an extremely funny comedy and Edwards' first box-office hit.

Above: Director Blake Edwards photographed in 1980 during the filming of *10*.

Left: An interesting pairing: veteran smoothie George Sanders (left) with comedian Peter Sellers in *A Shot In The Dark* (1964), one of several sequels to the immensely popular and successful *The Pink Panther* (1963), and probably the best of them.

'We got more and more away from Clouseau's character involvements and we put in more and more physical comedy so that we could use doubles for Peter [Sellers].'

1983 (about the last *Pink Panther* movies)

RICHARD FLEISCHER

Born Brooklyn, New York, 8 December 1916

One of the most consistent, reliable and prolific of the many directors who got their start during the 40s, Richard Fleischer has maintained a steady output, directing just over forty features in as many years. He has directed every type of picture, but has specialised in intimate thrillers at one extreme and large scale costumers and action movies at the other. Son of the famous animator Max Fleischer, he started out as a pre-med student at Brown University, then switched to drama studies at Yale. After directing summer stock, he was signed by RKO in the early 40s. He gained his first film experience working on newsreels and shorts like the *Flicker Flashbacks* and *This Is America* series for a number of years before he was given his first B-feature, *Child Of Divorce*, to direct in 1946. Signed to a seven-year contract, he spent much of his time on suspension for refusing many of the feeble programmers to which he was assigned.

Fleischer was happy to get away from the studio in 1952, having completed nine features, the most interesting of which was the last, *The Narrow Margin*, a tightly constructed and suspenseful *film noir* starring Charles McGraw and Marie Windsor which he had made in 1951. (He had also co-directed an Oscar-winning compilation documentary in 1947, *Design For Death*.) The Disney company had recently begun producing live action features and gave Fleischer his first opportunity to handle a big budget movie in colour and CinemaScope and with an excellent cast headed by James Mason. The result, an extremely well mounted adaptation of the Jules Verne novel, *20,000 Leagues Under The Sea* (1954) preserved a nice balance of mystery, adventure and the futuristic, with occasional comic relief provided by Kirk Douglas and Peter Lorre. In addition to the remarkable underwater photography, there was a particularly stunning action

sequence of Captain Nemo (Mason) doing battle with a giant squid.

Signed to a new contract by 20th Century-Fox, where he was to spend most of the next fifteen years, Fleischer began with a human interest thriller, *Violent Saturday* (1955), best remembered for Lee Marvin's tough gangster with a heavy cold and an inhaler. He followed it with *The Girl On The Red Velvet Swing* (1955), the first of his many crime dramas based on true case histories – this one derived from a celebrated society murder and trial set in turn-of-the-century New York, and starred Joan Collins. Far better was his version of the famous Leopold-Loeb case, *Compulsion* (1959) with Orson Welles' veteran defense lawyer

dominating the proceedings. Again for Fox, Tony Curtis transformed his appearance to play *The Boston Strangler* in 1968. The film proved to be his biggest 60s hit. Similarly, Richard Attenborough was almost unrecognisable in the role of multiple-murderer Christie in *10 Rillington Place*, directed in Britain in 1971 with John Hurt in an early role as the hapless Timothy Evans, who was erroneously hung for Christie's crimes.

Interspersed with his crime movies, Fleischer handled a number of large scale actioners. *The Vikings* (UA, 1958) reunited him with Kirk Douglas in a lively period comic strip of a movie; Anthony Quinn played *Barabbas* (De Laurentiis/ Columbia, 1961) in Fleischer's entry in the Biblical costume cycle. These were the director's only non-Fox films of the period; his career was closely linked with the fortunes of the studio, and he was in charge of three of their least successful ventures in the late 60s – the disastrous $18 million musical flop *Dr Dolittle* (1967), a misguided biopic of Guevara, *Che!* (1969) and an overblown World War II epic, *Tora! Tora! Tora!* (1970).

During the 70s he returned to smaller scale thrillers, including a pair with George Scott (*The Last Run*, MGM 1971, and *The New Centurions*, Columbia 1972) and a chillingly effective futuristic tale set in 21st-century New York which provided Edward G. Robinson with his last movie role (*Soylent Green*, MGM, 1973). Still going strong during recent years he rejoined producer Dino de Laurentiis for a series of outsize but undistinguished dramas, beginning with *Mandingo* (1975), followed a few years later by *Amityville 3-D* (1983), and a pair of comic strip adventures, *Conan The Destroyer* (1984) and *Red Sonja* (1985).

Top: In 1954 Fleischer made an excellent version of Jules Verne's classic set aboard a submarine, *20,000 Leagues Under The Sea*. James Mason (left) starred as Captain Nemo, supported by Kirk Douglas (centre), Peter Lorre (centre right) and Paul Lukas.

Above: Director Richard Fleischer (left) with his star, George C. Scott, on location in Granada, Spain, for *The Last Run* (1971).

Left: Tony Curtis proved conclusively that he was more than just a pretty face with his fine portrayal of *The Boston Strangler* (1968). The victim of his assault here is Sally Kellerman.

'A glorified mechanic, Richard Fleischer pleases movie executives because he has no particular interests and no discernible style.'

Pauline Kael in 'The New Yorker' 1976

MILOS FORMAN

Born Caslav, Czechoslovakia, 18 February 1932

Just over twenty years ago Milos Forman emerged as one of the leading figures of the new Czech cinema, gaining widespread international recognition with his first feature, *Peter And Pavla* (1963). Here, and in *A Blonde In Love* (1965), he demonstrated a special talent for working with young, semi-professional actors (often cast in tandem with non-professionals). Aiming at developing an understated and naturalistic style and a humorous yet sympathetic observation of characters and situations, Forman succeeded admirably. The pictures – filmed in black-and-white, with unknown actors and on tiny budgets – were correspondingly modest, but they revealed Forman as a major new talent.

He had previously studied in the film section of the Prague Academy of Music and Dramatic Art, then worked briefly as a scriptwriter and assistant director before making his debut as a director with a pair of medium length musical shorts, *If There Were No Bands* and *Talent Competition* (both 1963). The titles reflect his special attraction to music competitions, dances and music halls as providing a freer environment in which to observe his characters and their foibles or inhibitions. *Peter And Pavla* dealt with the experiences of a seventeen-year-old boy awkwardly coping with that most awkward of jobs – apprentice store detective in a supermarket. In *A Blonde In Love*, however, the director switched to a feminine viewpoint. In contrast to the gentle and sympathetic observation of Peter's first timid contact with his new girlfriend, Pavla, the follow-up film revolved around the heroine Andula's brief affair with a young pianist. He plays in the band at a local dance which provides one of Forman's characteristic social/musical set-pieces. When Andula turns up unexpectedly at his home one evening, it leads to an awkward and comical situation as his parents attempt to sort out the sleeping arrangements and make sense of the personal relationships. This pointed, yet perceptive and good humoured treatment of the 'generation gap' – another favourite Forman theme – was co-scripted by him. It was the first of many films photographed by his favourite cameraman, Miroslav Ondricek, who also joined him on *The Fireman's Ball* (1967), his first in colour. Here Forman's observation of human weakness had become rather more cruel and perhaps reflects the intention to satirise the ineptness of the official state bureaucracy prior to Dubcek. In any case, it proved to be Forman's last Czech film. He was in Paris in August 1968 when the Russian tanks arrived and elected to remain in the West.

The director had always wanted to shoot a film in the US, and early in 1968 had embarked on a project with the French scriptwriter (and Buñuel collaborator) Jean-Claude Carrière. Paramount expressed an interest, but declined to go ahead. By early 1970, Forman was older and wiser in the ways of Hollywood wheeling and dealing. He expressed his pent-up anger at the 'time and work spent on negotiations, contracts, money, talking with agents, producers, companies, lawyers and unions' in an article entitled *How I Came to America to Make a Film and Wound Up Owing Paramount $140,000*. But the story had a happy ending. Due to the success of *Easy Rider* (Columbia) in 1969 there was a renewed interest in all types of relatively low cost 'youth movies' and the director was finally able to begin work on *Taking Off* for Universal in 1970.

Making use of a similar formula to that which had proved so successful in his earlier features, he assembled a non-star cast (including Buck Henry and Lynn Carlin) and was aided in his extensive location filming by his Czech cameraman, Ondricek. The story was built on a relatively slender premise: A teenage girl disappears from her suburban home, her parents become worried, and her father goes to New York to look for her. A topical movie dealing with the 'generation gap' from the parents' point of view, it poked gentle fun at the father's efforts to find his daughter, and his gradual realisation of the extent of the problem of teenage runaways. When he and his wife are invited to join the S.P.F.C. (Society for Parents of Fugitive Children), their efforts to gain a better understanding of hippy culture leads them to try their first marijuana cigarette in one of the film's funniest set-pieces. By the end, the parents have been seen to let their hair down and introduce a bit of offbeat fun into their staid, middle-aged, middle-class lives. When the daughter enters a singing contest early in the film, Forman makes use of extensive cross-cutting between

the older and younger generations to make his gently satirical points.

Easily adapting his 'cinéma verité' style, Forman next turned his cameras on the Decathlon competition at the 1972 Olympics. Using a wide range of techniques, he turned the series of athletic events into a surreal cinematic ballet, and effectively stole the picture, *Visions Of Eight*, from the seven other well-known directors who also contributed, including Arthur Penn and John Schlesinger.

Taking Off didn't – in spite of a favourable response from the critics – and for Forman it meant a long gap between features. He worked on a number of abortive projects before he was offered *One Flew Over The Cuckoo's Nest* (UA, 1975). It was a smash hit and the high point of his career – the first picture to sweep all the top Oscars since *It Happened One Night*,

Above: Josef Kolb (left), Josef Sebanek (centre) and Karel Valnoha, three committee members selecting girls for the beauty contest in *The Fireman's Ball* (1967), Forman's first film in colour and his last to be made in his native Czechoslovakia.

Below: Lynn Carlin (left), the mother of a teenage daughter who has run away to New York, and her friend, Audra Lindley, learning to live it up and beat the generation gap in Forman's satirical and perceptive *Taking Off* (1970), his first American movie.

forty one years earlier. Yet the project was not initially regarded as a 'hot property' at all, rather the contrary, which is why it was offered to Forman in the first place. The rights to the Ken Kesey novel had originally been purchased by Kirk Douglas over ten years earlier. But he had grown too old to play the lead, and his son, Michael Douglas, took over as co-producer. There were casting problems, and when Jack Nicholson agreed to play the lead, Forman was faced with having to cope with a major star for the first time in his career, although he had envisaged the film as an ensemble piece. In fact, Nicholson not only gave an amazing, energetic, performance in the role of the anti-authoritarian R.P. McMurphy, but, according to Forman, 'did everything to help the atmosphere on the set' during the long and difficult shooting schedule which included eleven weeks in an Oregon mental hospital. Louise Fletcher as the inflexible Nurse Ratched provided the perfect foil to the star, preparing the audience for the change in tone of the final reels as the good-natured comedy and high jinx give way to the chillingly unpleasant final denouement. Clearly, all the cast responded well to Forman's relatively free methods of filming. The venture was a triumph for all concerned.

Moving on to direct the film version of *Hair* (UA) in 1978, Forman was helped immensely by the innovative choreography of Twyla Tharp. But he had picked the wrong time to adapt the archetypal 60s rock musical to the screen. In his own words: 'too late to be actuality and too

soon to be nostalgia.' He was then chosen by producer Dino de Laurentiis to replace Robert Altman as the director of the film version of E.L. Doctorow's *Ragtime* (1981). Forman's first period movie, budgeted at $25 million, it presented a fascinating, but not entirely convincing, panoramic view of New York society during the early years of the century. The kind of project which could have been handled equally well by any number of directors, it lacked the special insight and spontaneity which Forman had brought to his more intimate, contemporary pictures. But he got excellent performances from his cast, including James Cagney, brought out of retirement, aged eighty-

one, to play the police commissioner.

In his $18 million screen version of Peter Schaffer's hit play about Mozart and Salieri, *Amadeus* (1984), Forman opted even more audaciously for relatively unknown actors in the lead roles and demonstrated his special skill with musical subjects. The result was little more than a popularised and entertaining middle-brow view of high culture, but one which garnered eleven Oscar nominations. Having stretched himself in new and different directions and now firmly established as a leading American director, hopefully an older and wiser Forman will return to the smaller scale subjects for which he has a special gift.

Above: Jack Nicholson, brilliantly portraying the anarchic R.P. McMurphy, lets loose with the hospital equipment in the triumphant *One Flew Over The Cuckoo's Nest* (1975). The film was the first in forty-one years to run away with every top Oscar.

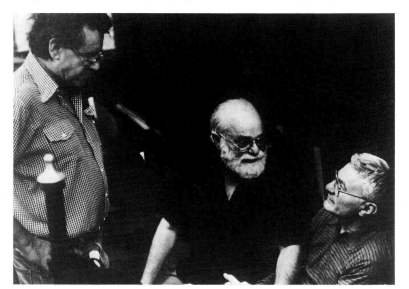

Left: The original creator of *Amadeus* (1984), Peter Schaffer (right), with director Milos Forman (left) and producer Saul Zaentz. The film was positively larded with Oscar nominations and won the coveted Award in virtually every main category, including Best Picture and director.

'In Czechoslovakia there is strong ideological pressure, but no commercial pressure whatsoever... In the West, you know you will be judged by how well your film does at the box-office.'
1982

BOB FOSSE

Born Chicago, 23 June 1927

When *All That Jazz* (20th Century-Fox, 1979) appeared – those audiences who knew little or nothing of the film's director, Bob Fosse, certainly knew rather a lot by the time they left the cinema. For this musical fantasy about the life and death of Joe Gideon (Roy Scheider), a stage musicals director addicted to overwork, women and drink was, in spite of provocative denials from Fosse, autobiographical in its inspiration – right down to the authentic open heart surgery sequence. 'I have an addictive personality and have lived most of my life to excess,' says Fosse of himself. Certainly, now in his fifties, he has chalked up three wives (Gwen Verdon lasted longest and mothered his daughter), and a generous procession of mistresses, including Jessica Lange and Ann Reinking; he has averaged near a hundred cigarettes a day, taken cocaine and other drugs, freely indulged his taste for wine – and suffered a severe heart attack. Through it all, the work record, like his fictional hero's, has been prodigious.

One of the most vibrant, pervasive and significant influences on the modern American musical, Fosse's career began in childhood in burlesque (he is the son of a vaudeville entertainer). The nightclub and theatre circuit followed, then, in the early 50s, he danced in a handful of Hollywood films, notably *Kiss Me Kate* (MGM, 1953). In 1954, he choreographed his first Broadway musical, 'The Pajama Game', a smash hit, and he won his first Tony award. A string of hits followed, including 'Damn Yankees', starring his wife, Gwen Verdon, and he developed his feel for film by choreographing the screen versions of both *The Pajama Game* (Warner Bros., 1957, starring Doris Day) and *Damn Yankees* (Warner Bros., 1958) with Gwen and Tab Hunter, in which he himself partnered his wife in a speciality dance which displayed his hard-edged *brio* to the full. A year later Fosse graduated to directing in the theatre with 'Redhead', again starring Gwen. He achieved numerous successes, among them 'Chicago' and 'Sweet Charity', all of which demonstrated his muscular imagination and a jazzy, metropolitan feel, redolent of New York's brassy nuances. It was 'Sweet Charity', a musical imaginatively based on Fellini's *Nights Of Cabiria* (1957), but with the streetwalker 'heroine' changed to a taxi-dancer in a sleazy Manhattan dance-hall, that took Fosse back to Hollywood – this time as a director.

In spite of its marvellous score, a string of memorable production numbers (including the top-hat-and-cane 'If They Could See Me Now' and the sexy, stylised 'Hey, Big Spender') and a good cast, *Sweet Charity* (Universal, 1969), shot in Panavision, was generally overblown and a disappointment. It looked tacky, and Shirley MacLaine in the central role was frenetically hoydenish. In 1972, however, Fosse got a second crack at the whip, and emerged with a major hit and the Best Director Oscar. The film was, of

course, *Cabaret*, again from a Broadway show. This time, however, the director displayed a comprehensive grasp of the medium. He drew superb performances from Liza Minnelli as Christopher Isherwood's immortal Sally Bowles, Joel Gray, and Michael York, and captured the authentically decadent flavour of 30s' Berlin in a series of dazzling set-pieces. With his status thus secured, Fosse left the world of the musical – though not of show business – behind to make *Lenny* (UA, 1974). Sombre, intimate and gritty, this biopic was filmed in effective black-and-white, and starred Dustin Hoffman who gave an amazing performance as Lenny Bruce, the scatological comedian who died of drugs, and Valerie Perrine as his wife. *Lenny*, and *All That Jazz* five years later, were well received by critics and audiences alike, and were rewarded with a large number of Academy Award nominations, including for Best Picture, director and actor.

It is surprising to realise that Fosse's output as director stands at five movies over a period of fourteen years, and there is no predicting what, if anything, he might do next. His latest venture, *Star 80* (Ladd Co./Warner Bros., 1983), cast Mariel Hemingway as Dorothy Stratten, the 'Playboy' magazine pin-up who was murdered by her estranged husband. Clearly, the director is attracted to a chemical mix of gloss and sleaze. It makes for interesting entertainment.

'All Fosse's films are condemnations and celebrations of his profession with the narrow philosophy that "There's no business, but *show business!*"'

Ronald Bergan in *A-Z Of Movie Directors*

Left: Director-choreographer Bob Fosse takes star Shirley MacLaine through the stunning dance routine for the 'If They Could See Me Now' number in *Sweet Charity* (1969). This was one of the high points of a film (the director's first) that didn't really come off.

Below: Anarchic, abrasive and brilliant, comedian Lenny Bruce was constantly in trouble with the law. Here, Dustin Hoffman in the title role of *Lenny* (1974).

Bottom: Fosse (left) in rehearsal with Eric Roberts and Mariel Hemingway for *Star 80* (1983).

JOHN FRANKENHEIMER

Born Malba, New York, 19 February 1930

Having easily made the transition from live TV drama to feature films during the early 60s, John Frankenheimer was, for a short period (1962-64), one of the most highly regarded of the new young talents of the American cinema. He first became interested in acting while attending Williams College then, having developed a special interest in film-making while serving in the Air Force, he decided that a job in television would be the best way to break into the movie industry. He worked as an assistant to Sidney Lumet in 1953 and soon established himself as a leading assistant director, before moving up to full director status a few years later. Frankenheimer estimates that he directed about one hundred-and-twenty-five live TV dramas, most notably for Playhouse 90 and including 'Days of Wine and Roses', an adaptation of Faulkner's 'The Old Man' and the Emmy-winning 'The Comedian' starring Mickey Rooney.

John was given his first chance to direct a movie feature by adapting one of his TV productions. *The Young Stranger* (RKO, 1957) starred Kim Hunter, with James MacArthur repeating his TV role as a young teenager in trouble with the police, a familiar 50s theme. The film was generally ignored and Frankenheimer returned to the small screen for another three years. He succeeded better with his second feature, *The Young Savages* (UA) in 1960, dealing with street gangs in New York. A competently directed apprentice piece, it was the first of Frankenheimer's five features with Burt Lancaster, who was well enough impressed with the young director to bring him in as replacement director on *Birdman Of Alcatraz* (UA) the following year. The latter was an extremely difficult movie to shoot: based on the true story of convicted killer Robert Stroud, most of it took place in the confines of a prison cell. Covering a period of over fifty years, during which time Stroud had developed a great love of birds and had become an authority on bird diseases, the film demonstrated that Frankenheimer had something special to offer, while Lancaster gave one of his most intense and moving performances.

The director quickly moved on to a dramatic study of a modern American family as seen through the eyes of novelist James Leo Herlihy in *All Fall Down* (MGM). The theme of a youngster (Brandon de Wilde) disillusioned with his older brother (Warren Beatty) was used to better effect in Martin Ritt's *Hud* (Paramount) a year later, but Angela Lansbury's portrayal of a domineering and possessive mother here, provided a natural link with Frankenheimer's third film in a row, *The Manchurian Candidate* (UA), which followed. Ironically, because of a delay in releasing *Birdman*, he suddenly found himself launched as a director of some substance with three rather different features all released in one year, 1962. Best of the bunch and Frankenheimer's most memorable film ever, *The Manchurian Candidate* was an extremely well plotted, well acted and

tightly directed political thriller, scripted by George Axelrod from the Richard Condon novel. John drew excellent performances from Frank Sinatra, Laurence Harvey (as a brain-washed political assassin) and, most notably, Janet Leigh as a very liberated modern lady, while Angela Lansbury was Oscar-nominated for her smoothly calculating villainess. Another gripping political thriller followed, but unfortunately *Seven Days In May* (Paramount, 1963) suffered from a weak ending. The fantasy thriller, *Seconds* (Paramount, 1966), began superbly with a middle-aged man, dissatisfied with his life, agreeing to undergo a terrifying operation. His reincarnation as Rock Hudson, however, was weak and unconvincing. On the race track, *Grand*

Prix (MGM, 1966) was exciting and dramatic. Off the track it was banal. In this respect it appears typical of the weaknesses found in so many of Frankenheimer's later films. Among the most forgettable were *The Extraordinary Seaman* starring David Niven, *The Fixer* with Alan Bates in the title role (both MGM, 1968) and *The Horsemen* (Columbia, 1970). During the 70s he became known exclusively as a director of thrillers and enjoyed his biggest successes with *French Connection II* (20th Century-Fox, 1975) and *Black Sunday* (Paramount, 1977), his biggest hit. More recently Frankenheimer has joined forces with actor Michael Caine and writer George Axelrod to film a thriller in England – *Holcroft Covenant* (1985).

Above left: Burt Lancaster (right) and Karl Malden in *The Bird Man Of Alcatraz* (1961), Frankenheimer's excellent filmic account of a murderer who became an authority on birds while in prison.

Above: Angela Lansbury was the monster at the centre of the villainy in *The Manchurian Candidate* (1962).

Below: Director John Frankenheimer (right) and cameraman James Wong Howe (centre) at work with Rock Hudson on *Seconds* (1966). They are filming in Frankenheimer's own beach house at Malibu, loaned to Paramount for the picture.

WILLIAM FRIEDKIN

Born Chicago, 29 August 1939

Of that new generation of movie whizz kids who grew up during the postwar era, coinciding with the advent of television, William Friedkin was the first to make his mark during the 50s. Almost ten years younger than John Frankenheimer, for example, he was close behind in establishing himself as a TV director in his home town of Chicago while still a teenager. Directing mainly documentaries and occasional TV specials, he worked for a time for producer David Wolper, then, with nine years of TV experience behind him, turned to directing feature films during the late 60s. An unremarkable but competently handled musical fantasy, *Good Times*, starring Sonny and Cher, which he directed for Columbia in 1966 was followed by a weak and cheaply made movie version of Harold Pinter's *The Birthday Party* (1968) filmed in Britain and scripted by Pinter with Robert Shaw starring. Finally TV (and film) producer Norman Lear gave Friedkin his first chance to direct a major feature. *The Night They Raided Minsky's* (1968) was obviously conceived as UA's answer to Columbia's *Funny Girl*, being filmed at about the same time, with Barbra Streisand's husband, Elliott Gould, here given his first starring role alongside Jason Robards, Britt Ekland, and veteran performer Bert Lahr who provided an authentic link with early American vaudeville and burlesque (but unfortunately died while the film was in production). Quite smoothly handled by Friedkin, the movie included some lively and entertaining stage acts and convincingly captured the feel of New York (and especially the Lower East Side) in the 20s.

Another birthday party play adaptation followed: 'Mart Crowley's *The Boys In The Band* . . . is not a musical' ran the adverts. 'Today is Harold's birthday. This is his present' read the caption under a photo of Cowboy, a $20 male hustler. The ad was banned by many American papers, while the film provided a first glimpse (in 1970) of Friedkin's attraction to the permissive and seamier side of the contemporary American scene. In *The French Connection* (20th Century-Fox, 1971) for example, he presented an authentic view of New York police and antinarcotics officers in action, based on real events which had taken place about eight years before. Balancing fast moving action with moments of suspense and drama, Friedkin made his name with this film, introducing such themes as electronic surveillance, but best remembered is a particularly dramatic chase through the streets of Brooklyn as cop Gene Hackman pursues a fugitive travelling on the E1 above. The movie helped establish a pattern for the new generation of 70s cop movies, and won Oscars for Friedkin, Hackman and Best Picture as well as for script and editing. It was also a big hit and led Friedkin to take on an ambitious new project dealing with the theme of a young girl's diabolical possession. Loosely based on a true case history, *The Exorcist* (Warner Bros., 1973) emerged as entertaining, scary and extremely accomplished technically, full of unexpected moments of violence coupled with black humour.

Friedkin's most controversial and widely seen movie, *The Exorcist* was by far the biggest horror film hit ever and has been much imitated but never equalled. Regarded then as Hollywood's 'golden boy', Friedkin was given carte blanche on his following projects. Paramount and Universal together co-financed his next to the tune of $20 million. Filmed under

extremely difficult conditions, *Sorcerer* (1977) was a remake of Clouzot's action-thriller *The Wages Of Fear* (1953) and failed disastrously at the box-office. (That same year, 1977, Friedkin married French actress Jeanne Moreau). Also in 1977, he had only slightly better luck with *The Brinks Job*, a relatively good-natured recreation of the famous 1950 Boston heist. Friedkin returned to controversy – and profit – with *Cruising* (UA, 1979), an exploitative treatment of the New York homosexual bars scene starring Al Pacino as an undercover cop who becomes more involved than he bargained for. *Deal Of The Century* (Warner Bros., 1983), a comedy-drama about the international market in arms failed to generate much interest. But Friedkin's new status as a family man – recently married to actress Lesley-Anne Down – may lead to a new maturity as a director. After all, he is still only in his mid-forties.

Above: Jason Robards Jr (left), Britt Ekland and English comedian Norman Wisdom performing a vaudeville routine in *The Night They Raided Minsky's* (aka *The Night They Invented Striptease*, 1968).

Below: Director William Friedkin (left) in discussion with the writer (and producer) of *The Exorcist* (1973), William Peter Blatty.

Below left: Swedish star from the Ingmar Bergman stable, Max Von Sydow (left) and Jason Miller in *The Exorcist*. This exercise in supernatural horror, about a little girl possessed by the devil, was a massive commercial success and spawned a weak sequel directed by John Boorman with Von Sydow again, and Richard Burton.

'I could have made the film into a paean of praise for the cop; or a condemnation of him and his methods . . . I saw both sides of it. So I guess the movie is capable of satisfying everybody, though that's not what I was after.'

1970 (on *The French Connection*)

GEORGE ROY HILL

Born Minneapolis, 20 December 1922

A relatively late developer, with an ability to handle actors with skill, George Roy Hill had his initial interest in acting and the theatre and, finally, in directing, interrupted by two wars. He served as a pilot in both World War II and the Korean War and only began to establish himself as a writer, then director, in TV and on Broadway during the mid-50s. He made a natural transition to directing movies in the early 60s, beginning with a pair of play adaptations. *Period Of Adjustment* (MGM, 1962) was distinctly lightweight Tennessee Williams and provided Jane Fonda with one of her early ingenue roles, while *Toys In The Attic* (UA, 1963) from Lillian Hellman was not much better. However, Hill was a little more successful with his adapted novels. A few sequences in *The World Of Henry Orient* (UA, 1964), starring Peter Sellers, suggested for the first time that he had a talent for making films, while his overblown, three-hour version of James Michener's *Hawaii* (UA, 1966) at least provided him with his first box-office hit. More recently he has made a weak attempt at filming John Irving's rambling novel, *The World According To Garp* (Warner Bros., 1982), and succeeded even less well with John Le Carré's *The Little Drummer Girl* (1984). So from where does his reputation spring?

By far the most interesting and successful period in George Roy Hill's career was the decade from 1967 to 1977. Releasing his pictures mainly through Universal, Hill directed a series of film originals written for the screen by leading young scriptwriters like William Goldman, David S. Ward and Nancy Dowd. He began in 1967 with *Thoroughly Modern Millie*, a lively and original screen musical set in the flapper era of the 20s

and meant to capitalise on the popularity of Julie Andrews. (She had starred for Hill in *Hawaii*.) At two-and-a-quarter hours Hill claims that the studio stretched the film out to road show length, putting back twenty minutes that he had cut. But when it was a hit it helped to launch him on an almost unbroken run of commercial successes. *Butch Cassidy And The Sundance Kid* (20th Century-Fox, 1969) was a smash, and Hill's inspired teaming of Paul Newman and Robert Redford initiated a whole cycle of male buddy pictures during the 70s. The most good-natured and non-violent of Westerns, based on a witty, Oscar-winning script by William Goldman, it was handled with suitable panache by Hill who received his first Oscar nomination. Undoubtedly his best picture, it worked so well that he brought the stars together again in 30s Chicago for an entertaining movie set on the fringes of the underworld, *The Sting* (1973), which proved to be the biggest success in Universal's history. For although *Jaws* surpassed it at the box-office just two years later, *The Sting* also won the studio its first Best Picture Oscar since *All Quiet On The Western Front* forty three years earlier, and won Hill his only directing Oscar. (He had been awarded the Special Jury prize at Cannes the previous year for his screen version of Kurt Vonnegut's *Slaughterhouse Five* for Universal.)

Reunited with writer Goldman and actor Redford (but sans Newman), Hill drew on his love of flying to direct *The Great Waldo Pepper* (1975), a personal tribute to the barnstorming daredevils of the 20s. The aerial stunt work was exceptional, but on the ground the film occasionally slowed to a crawl. Far more lively and energetic was *Slap Shot* (1977),

the director's solo effort for Newman which followed. Nancy Dowd's script presented a thinly disguised satirical attack on the sport – professional hockey – which encourages grown men to engage in the brutal and rowdy behaviour of schoolboys. Written from first hand experience (her brother was a hockey player), the film unfortunately fell apart in the final reel as neither Hill nor Dowd could figure out how to end it, and brought to a close Hill's most productive period. He has only directed three films in the eight years since *Slap Shot*. Semi-retired and happy to leave Hollywood, he has been teaching drama at Yale.

Top: James Fox and Julie Andrews dance 'The Tapioca' in *Thoroughly Modern Millie* (1967), a thoroughly delightful look at the Roaring Twenties, which co-starred Carol Channing, Beatrice Lillie, Mary Tyler Moore and John Gavin.

Above: Director Hill (left) with Robert Redford on location during the filming of *The Great Waldo Pepper* (1975).

Left: Paul Newman (left) and Robert Redford in *The Sting* (1973). Following the success of their pairing in *Butch Cassidy* four years earlier, the stars delivered another smash-hit for Hill – and for Universal Studios.

'You get to the point when success isolates you. It puts you right out of touch with other people's reality. It also makes you think you have to do better and better for your backers every time. . . . I don't want that anymore.'
1983

ARTHUR HILLER

Born Edmonton, Alberta, Canada, 22 November 1923

It is perhaps typical of Arthur Hiller's erratic abilities that he has made films for every one of the major American companies including Disney, and has directed many different types of movies including a weak attempt at a war picture (*Tobruk*, Universal, 1966), a feeble adaptation of the hit stage musical *Man Of La Mancha* (UA, 1972) starring Peter O'Toole and Sophia Loren, and a virtually unwatchable horror movie (*Nightwing*, Columbia, 1980). He has been most successful with human interest drama and black comedy but generally appears to be at the mercy of his cast and scriptwriters. Thus, he was fortunate in his collaborations with Paddy Chayefsky and Neil Simon, but is best known as the director of the surprise smash hit film version of Erich Segal's *Love Story* (Paramount, 1970), earning a percentage interest from it which turned him into a millionaire many times over.

Educated at the Universities of Alberta and Toronto, Hiller worked for a time for CBC radio, then gained his first directing experience at CBC TV before moving on to the US. There he established himself as a leading TV director during the mid-50s with such programmes as 'Playhouse 90' and 'Alfred Hitchcock Presents', and 'Route 66' and 'Naked City' in the early 60s. He directed one modest seventy-minute feature, *The Careless Years* (UA) starring Dean Stockwell in 1957, but didn't break into the film industry proper until 1963.

The best of his early movies was *The Americanization Of Emily* (MGM, 1964), an offbeat but distinctly 60s view of World War II as seen through the eyes of Paddy Chayefsky who provided his characters with lots of suitably cynical dialogue. The cast was headed by Jameses Garner and Coburn, perfectly cast as a pair of American anti-hero types, while Julie Andrews made an early 'anti-Mary Poppins' appearance as an English war widow in love with and bedded by Garner. Hiller made more of a contribution to a number of his later films and achieved his greatest success during the years 1970-71. A pair of Neil Simon comedy vehicles – one each for Jack Lemmon and Walter Matthau – served as an appropriate follow-up to their highly successful appearance together as *The Odd Couple* (1968) – all for Paramount. In *The Out-Of-Towners* (1970) Jack Lemmon and Sandy Dennis played a couple visiting New York for one day and experiencing one mishap after another. In contrast to his effectively staged location filming here, Hiller was equally at home concentrating on the actors alone, confined within New York's Plaza Hotel in *Plaza Suite* (1971). Adapted from three Neil Simon one-act plays, the movie gave Walter Matthau the opportunity to show his range in three contrasting roles.

In between the Simon films Hiller directed *Love Story*, a slickly packaged appeal to old fashioned romantic values, a kind of updated *Camille*, which at least

provided the director with the opportunity to demonstrate his qualities in handling young and relatively inexperienced actors. Ryan O'Neal gave one of his better performances, Ray Milland (sans toupee) made an effective appearance as his father, and Ali McGraw attempted to humanise her role with the help of some un-ladylike language. She also died nicely – which led Hiller on to *The Hospital* (UA, 1971), reuniting him with writer Paddy Chayefsky in one of his craziest moods, taking aim at one of the most disaster-prone of modern institutions. His Oscar-winning script provided George C. Scott with a suitably larger-than-life role as the medical chief who tries to carry on running his hospital while everything is falling apart around him. He was ably supported by the fine British actress Diana Rigg.

Hiller's talent for directing black comedy was also in evidence in his biggest success of the mid-70s – *Silver Streak* (20th Century-Fox, 1976), filmed back in his native Canada. A take-off on the classic thriller-set-aboard-a-train genre, it starred Gene Wilder, Richard Pryor and Jill Clayburgh. More recently, he filmed *Making Love* (20th Century-Fox 1982), a weak attempt to demonstrate the liberal attitude of modern-day Hollywood to homosexuality. Similarly, Hiller demonstrated yet again, in his high school black comedy *Teachers* (UA, 1984), that his skills are insufficient to overcome a weak script.

'I don't think – contrary to popular opinion these days – that film is a director's medium. At any rate, if it is, it's his by default.'

1970

NORMAN JEWISON

Born Toronto, 21 July 1926

Norman Jewison is the best known and most successful of that group of Canadian-born directors who moved on from TV to the movies during the early 60s. After graduating from the University of Toronto, he got his start directing for the BBC in England, then returned to work for CBC TV in Canada before going on to CBS in New York. He arrived in Hollywood to begin directing movies for Universal in 1962, and, aside from a few ventures abroad in the early 70s, he has been happily making films in the US ever since. His *oeuvre* in sum presents a panoramic view of 20th-century America. One of Jewison's strengths is his ability to bring a setting alive on the screen, making special use of a variety of locations spread geographically around the US (and occasionally abroad) – his pictures have ranged from 1910 Chicago to Cleveland during the late 30s, from 50s Washington to the South in the 40s; while his portrait of America has been kept up-to-date by various productions set in contemporary LA, Boston, Baltimore, etc. He ventured abroad (with mainly American stars) to film *Jesus Christ Superstar* (Universal, 1973) in Israel, *Rollerball* (UA, 1975), in Munich, and *Fiddler On The Roof* (Mirisch/UA, 1971) in Yugoslavia and at Shepperton Studios, England.

Jewison's first at Universal was a Tony Curtis comedy, *40 Pounds Of Trouble* (1962), set in Nevada and California and only memorable for a wild and climactic chase through Disneyland. His stay at the studio also included a pair of Doris Day comedies, and Jewison recalls, 'I didn't feel free creatively throughout that period. But I must say that I enjoyed working with Doris Day. Some critics branded her as a kind of artificial girl-next-door, but I found Doris an extremely exciting actress to work with'.

He welcomed the opportunity to direct *The Cincinnati Kid* (MGM, 1965, replacing Sam Peckinpah), which gave him a measure of creative control over a picture for the first time. He made good use of the New Orleans settings, and veteran Edward G. Robinson walked off with the acting honours. But the picture was really an inferior imitation of Robert Rossen's *The Hustler* (20th Century-Fox, 1961) with young Steve McQueen pitted against Edward G. at stud poker. The script was too packed full of incident, lacking depth in its treatment of the characters, and the period feel of the 30s was weak. Only a moderate success for Jewison, he was more fortunate with *The Russians Are Coming, The Russians Are Coming* the following year. He had teamed up with scriptwriter William Rose on a loose adaptation of a Nathaniel Benchley novel, 'The Off-Islanders', but they had great difficulty in finding a Hollywood company to back them. This Cold War comedy-satire about an isolated New England community 'menaced' by a Russian sub was like a comic version of *Jaws* (written by Nathaniel's son, Peter, a decade later) in which the locals are at-

tacked by a shark, with police chief Brian Keith as a comic version of Roy Scheider in the later film. Jewison was able to serve as producer-director for the first time when the Mirisch company agreed to back the film for UA release. A crazy Oscar-nominated performance from Alan Arkin, starring in his first film, as a Russian lieutenant, helped turn the venture into a surprise hit and launched Jewison on an amicable and highly successful six-year period as an independent working for Mirisch/UA.

He next made the highly successful *In The Heat Of The Night* (1967) which immediately established him as one of the 'hottest' producer-directors in Hollywood. For this Oscar-winning movie he assembled a top production team, including scriptwriter Stirling Silliphant and editor Hal Ashby, both of whom won Oscars, while Jewison was nominated for the first time. The fascinating core of the film pitted Rod Steiger's Southern redneck police chief (an Oscar-winning performance) against Sidney Poitier's black police detective from Philadelphia who happens to be passing through the town of Sparta, Mississippi on the night that a mysterious murder is committed. As Steiger grows to respect the superior intelligence of his black 'colleague', the picture's modest but effective anti-racist theme gradually and tellingly emerges. *The Thomas Crown Affair* (1968) was a slickly made, sophisticated and good-natured, but superficial variation on the heist movie theme, given added glamour by the presence of Steve McQueen and Faye Dunaway on opposing sides of the

law. Their sexual repartee during a game of chess has become a famous set-piece. Again Jewison made effective use of locations in and around Boston, then moved back in time to 1910 Chicago for *Gaily, Gaily* (1969), a disappointingly superficial treatment of a potentially fascinating subject (supposedly adapted from the autobiography of writer Ben Hecht) about a young, future news reporter's sojourn in a Chicago brothel, but given terrific settings and authentic period flavour. Having gained his early reputation as a TV director in part for his musical specials with Harry Belafonte, Judy Garland and others, it was inevitable that Jewison would turn to the movie musical at some point. He directed two in a row in the early 70s beginning with the

Above: The Cincinnati Kid (1965) concerned the world of stud-poker. Here, Jay Ose (centre), a card master, advises Karl Malden (left) and Edward G. Robinson who played veteran gamblers, on the niceties of a complicated hand. Looking on is John Hart, cast as a loser at the game.

Below: Script supervisor Meta Rebner and a remarkably youthful-looking Norman Jewison discuss the script for *In The Heat Of The Night* (1967) with the stars of the Oscar-winning movie, Rod Steiger and Sidney Poitier (right).

screen version of the Broadway smash, *Fiddler On The Roof*, about a simple little Jewish farming community driven out of Russia by the pogroms. It was the biggest hit of his career and earned him a second Oscar nomination. Approaching the film more as a 'folk opera' than stage musical, he spent many months searching for a location which would convey the mood of turn-of-the century Russia and finally found what he was looking for in a tiny, isolated village in Yugoslavia. Filmed with great verve and vitality, the movie starts on a generally happy note, but becomes progressively more downbeat when the artificiality of the musical conventions are less easy to accept. The last of his Mirisch productions, it was followed by a far less successful adaptation of the 60s rock musical *Jesus Christ Superstar*. It appeared trendy and vacuous when it wasn't being pretentious, and an inadequate cast (especially Ted Neeley in the title role) did not help.

Jewison then moved on to Munich to

Valerie Curtin and Barry Levinson who remained with Jewison to write.... a movie about a Hollywood scriptwriting couple(!) The most blatantly commercial of Jewison's projects, and starring Burt Reynolds and Goldie Hawn, *Best Friends* (Warner Bros., 1982) had a few entertaining moments and was a hit. Barry Levinson has since developed into a writer-director of note, while Jewison made his first major attempt in many years to break out of the commercial rut with *A Soldier's Story* (Columbia, 1984). Scripted by Charles Fuller from his Pulitzer prize-winning play, the film earned a number of Oscar nominations and suggests that it is still possible to find an audience for a serious picture with a mainly black cast – the dramatic story deals with a murder investigation in a black US Army base in the South, towards the end of World War II. It perhaps also represents a new departure for Jewison, now in his late fifties, and less concerned with commercial success. His latest project is an adaptation of a serious Broadway play, *Agnes Of God*, set in a convent and starring Jane Fonda, Meg Tilly and Anne Bancroft.

> '*I'm more concerned with people than with action for its own sake. Whatever happens in any of my films grows out of who and what its characters are and what motivates them.*'
>
> 1983

Above: Israeli star Topol as Tevye the Milkman and Norma Crane as his wife, Golda, in the screen version of *Fiddler On The Roof* (1971). The stories of Sholom Aleichem were the basis of the show and, in the film, the fiddle was played by no less than Isaac Stern.

Left: Faye Dunaway and Steve McQueen starred in *The Thomas Crown Affair* (1968).

Below: Jewison (right) and Howard E. Rollins Jr during filming of *A Soldier's Story* (1984). The film received three Academy nominations but was criticised for being a throwback to *In The Heat Of The Night*.

direct *Rollerball* (UA, 1975), a nasty, violent, futuristic tale set in the 21st century and starring James Caan as a rebellious superstar who refuses to be crushed by the 'system'. *F.I.S.T.* (UA, 1978) started out in 1976 as a serious attempt by scriptwriter Joe Eszterhas to deal with the struggle of the labour unions (and particularly the teamsters) to gain recognition during the late 30s. But his script was far too long and by the time it was rewritten and cut by Sylvester Stallone for star Stallone and brought to the screen by Jewison, it appeared like just another Stallone vehicle.... *And Justice For All* (Columbia, 1979) worked somewhat better as a quirky exposé and black comedy directed at the American legal system, firing in all directions and hitting a few targets. Jack Warden's eccentric judge was balanced by Al Pacino's much troubled young Baltimore lawyer – one of his most hyper-active performances. He was Oscar-nominated along with the husband-and-wife scriptwriting team of

STANLEY KRAMER

Born New York City, 23 September 1913

The most frequently employed, and also perhaps most generous, adjective to describe Stanley Kramer's work in the cinema is 'sincere'; and it is true to say that, without his fabled sincerity, Kramer would not have received, in 1961, the Irving Thalberg Award, for 'consistently high quality in film-making'. Yet, no matter how well-intentioned, his films are on the whole weak and unconvincing, pummelling the spectator with dubiously loaded arguments and special pleading, elephantine in conception and flat in execution. If ever subject matter rode roughshod over more strictly aesthetic considerations, it is in Kramer's generally heavy-handed dramas, a fact of which he seems to have been vaguely aware himself: 'The theme has dominated to too great an extent everything in which I have been involved. . .'

Kramer began in the cinema as an editor, writer and producer, and it would be fair to claim that, in this latter capacity, he enjoyed a not undistinguished career. Working at first as an independent (in fact, as a pioneer of independent film-making in Hollywood) with his own company, Screen Plays Inc., he produced such memorable films as *The Moon And Sixpence* (1942), *Champion* and *Home Of The Brave* (1949), *The Men* (1950: Marlon Brando's screen debut), *Death Of A Salesman* (1951) and *High Noon* (1952). A period as associate producer at Columbia was less happy, with only *The Caine Mutiny* (1954) showing any profit, and only the delirious fantasy musical, *The 5,000 Fingers of Dr T* (1953), and the first of the 'bike movies', *The Wild One* (1954), of any artistic interest.

It was when the Columbia contract was terminated, that Kramer launched himself as a producer-director through United Artists. After a couple of false starts – a soapy but starry operating-room melodrama, *Not As A Stranger* (1955), with Robert Mitchum, Frank Sinatra, Olivia de Havilland and Gloria Grahame; a ludicrous C.S. Forester period piece, *The Pride And The Passion* (1957), with the unlikely casting of Cary Grant, Sophia Loren and Sinatra again – he switched gears into the kind of solemn 'message' movie in which he was subsequently to specialise. *The Defiant Ones* (1958), with Tony Curtis and Sidney Poitier, might stand as a model for all those to follow: A burning issue (racism); a meretriciously 'symbolic' treatment (two convicts, a black and a white man, are chained together); and a sledgehammer visual style. It gained six nominations, including Best Picture and direction. In 1959, with a bloated adaptation of Nevil Shute's bestseller *On The Beach* (UA), the theme was no less than the end of the world by atomic annihilation; and, since the film's cast included Gregory Peck, Ava Gardner, Fred Astaire and Anthony Perkins, it would appear that stars have a better chance of survival than ordinary mortals. In the same vein were *Inherit The Wind* (1960), whose subject was a famous Darwinism vs fundamentalism trial in the Deep South of America, and *Judgment At Nuremberg* (1961), about the Nuremberg Trials (Oscar-nominated for Best Picture and direction); both were more moving and lively, thanks to some snappy performances and the basic courtroom drama format. But the melodrama, *Ship Of Fools* (Columbia, 1965), and the little-seen *R.P.M.* (1970), a hopelessly misguided study of the college campus revolts of the 60s, were disasters, both critically and commercially; and if *Guess Who's Coming To Dinner* (1967) lives on in the memory, it is less for its anti-racist message, which was both naive and speciously argued, than as the last appearance together of Spencer Tracy and Katharine Hepburn. (An Oscar for Kate, another nomination for Stanley.)

Unfortunately, the films with which Kramer endeavoured to vary this staple diet of 'messages' were no more convincing. *It's A Mad, Mad, Mad, Mad World* (UA, 1963) was a monstrosity, a gigantic slapstick farce starring a lengthy roster of American comics, but a big hit. And most of his later work, from *Bless The Beasts And The Children* (1971) to *Oklahoma Crude* (1973), from the weird political thriller *The Domino Principle* (1977) to *The Runner Stumbles* (1979), in which Dick Van Dyke was preposterously cast against type as a priest, has vanished without leaving a trace. If Kramer deserves to be remembered as a director, it is as the subject of a cautionary tale about the very relative importance of a 'message' in any work of art.

Above: Feelings run high between two convicts on the run from a chain gang and manacled to each other. Tony Curtis and Sidney Poitier were *The Defiant Ones* (1958) in this archetypical Kramer movie that gained six Oscar nominations.

Below left: Spencer Tracy and Katharine Hepburn in their last joint appearance (and Tracy's last film before his death) were the classy parents of a daughter who announces she is going to marry a negro doctor in *Guess Who's Coming To Dinner* (1967).

Below: Kramer (left) at work with Hardy Kruger on location in Italy for *The Secret Of Santa Vittoria* (1969).

'Certain things are private and I prefer not to show them. But we've become a nation of watchers. We don't want to do any more; we want to watch other people do things for us.'
1979

STANLEY KUBRICK

Born Bronx, New York, 26 July 1928

A fascinating and enigmatic figure, Stanley Kubrick is unique among modern movie directors. Most valued for his technical brilliance and his qualities as a visual stylist, he has worked successfully in a variety of genres and formats, in both black-and-white and colour, but has rightly been criticised as a cold and calculating director who can be self-indulgent and pretentious at times. Kubrick's career divides easily into two parts: During the years up to and culminating in the exceptionally witty and imaginative black comedy of *Dr Strangelove* (Columbia, 1963), he completed seven features, mostly thrillers and war drama, working mainly in black-and-white. In the twenty-plus years since then, based in Britain and beginning with his outstanding contribution to 60s sci fi, *2001: A Space Odyssey* (MGM, 1968), he has only completed four features but has demanded – and achieved – complete creative control over every aspect of his pictures. In this respect, and in his preferred pattern of producing one new film every five years, he is following the example set by only one other director – Chaplin.

Kubrick meticulously plans out and supervises the design, photography and editing of his movies, serving as his own producer and scriptwriter and occasionally taking a camera in hand to film a sequence himself. And when the picture is completed, he thinks nothing of personally controlling the release patterns, advertising and publicity campaigns, aided by the latest in computer and video technology, and even checking out the colour grading of release prints. As one who has always been specially interested in movie techniques and technology, he was in the forefront of those making use of personal computer/video equipment in the 60s and 70s – one of the first to use video monitors when filming, for example. Having grown progressively more private and reclusive over the years, he gives few interviews and has turned his home into an extension of his technological and cinematic obsessions, with the installation of all the latest video equipment and editing facilities and a 35mm projection room. For his latest project, a film about the American marines in Vietnam, *Full Metal Jacket* adapted for Warner Bros. from the Gustave Hasford novel 'The Short Timers', Kubrick has dispensed with the services of a casting director in his search for eighteen-year old acting unknowns. Instead, all the potential actors are requested to send him an audition recorded on videotape. Kubrick lives with his wife and daughters in the London suburb of Borehamwood, only a few minutes from his own executive offices and the EMI studio with its sound stages and dubbing theatres. His control over his environment is virtually complete and he can thus do much of his work without venturing out of his home territory. The appearance of each new Kubrick picture has become an eagerly awaited media event with all the advantages and disadvantages which that en-

tails. The pressures on Kubrick himself must be enormous. Unfortunately, his two most recent productions, *Barry Lyndon* (1975) and *The Shining* (1980) were less than his best, but did just well enough at the box-office to sustain his amicable, necessary and exceptional fifteen-year long relationship with Warner Bros. which finances and distributes his movies. It is difficult to imagine a now sixty-year old Kubrick ever forced to return to making his films in the way that ordinary mortals must.

Born and raised in the Bronx, young Stanley attended Taft High School. He was an average student but, encouraged by his doctor father, developed a special interest in chess and photography. Having served as the official photographer of his school paper, instead of continuing his studies he took a job as an apprentice staff photographer with 'Look' magazine at the age of seventeen. He soon developed into one of the leading young magazine photographers in the US, travelling widely during his four-and-a-half years with 'Look'. But at the same time he was becoming increasingly interested in the cinema. Hiring the necessary equipment, including a spring-wound 35mm Eyemo camera, he easily made the leap to film-maker, turning out a pair of documentary shorts which were the movie counterpart to the kind of photo-journalism in which he had previously specialised.

With the money he managed to raise from a few friends and relatives, Stanley had soon moved on to attempt his first short feature, *Fear And Desire*. The tiny cast of this war drama included future movie director Paul Mazursky in his first small acting role, while the star, Frank Silvera, also appeared in *Killer's Kiss* (1955) which followed. A more accomplished work, the latter was the first of three Kubrick features distributed by UA

in the 50s. Remarkably enterprising and ahead of their time, these apprentice works demonstrated Kubrick's ability to master the mechanics of movie making, while working virtually on his own and at a relatively early stage in his career. But unfortunately the acting in both films is weak and not helped by poor post-synching of dialogue.

Filmed, of necessity, on the streets of New York by night in an appropriately low-keyed, gritty style, *Killer's Kiss* was a thriller about a young boxer who falls in love with a girl he meets by chance, then heroically rescues from the clutches of her boss, a sadistic dance hall owner who

Above: *The Killing* (1955) was Kubrick's first fully-fledged feature. Here, planning the race-track robbery are, left to right, Ted de Corsia, Joe Sawyer, Elisha Cook Jr, Sterling Hayden and Jay C. Flippen.

Below: Suzanne Christiane (the future Mrs Stanley Kubrick), director Kubrick (centre) and Kirk Douglas take a coffee break on location in Germany while filming the controversial *Paths Of Glory* (1957).

rights to Nabokov's *Lolita*, not the sort of subject one would normally associate with him, and, in fact, the film was a major disappointment. Sue Lyon was too sexually mature – not a 'nymphet' at all. James Mason tried hard but was too serious and pathetic in the role, lacking the marvellous, humorous sense of the absurd that characterised Humbert Humbert in the novel, while his relationship with Lolita was never very convincing. Filmed mainly in England (in 1961) the movie failed to capture the wicked Nabokovian satire of middle-America, although Shelley Winters was fun as the frustrated wife, and Peter Sellers injected some appropriately lively and improvised comedy into the role of Quilty. Kubrick, however, made better us of Sellers' talents in his following picture, and his masterpiece, *Dr Strangelove*. (It's full title, seldom used for reference, is *Dr Strangelove, Or How I*

'People can misinterpret almost anything so that it coincides with views they already hold. They take from art what they already believe, and I wonder how many people have ever had their views about anything important changed by a work of art?'
1980

has kidnapped her. The picture's modest success made it possible for Kubrick to direct his first fully professional feature in Hollywood later that same year (1955). He assembled an interesting cast headed by Sterling Hayden and Elisha Cook Jr and shot the film in only twenty days on a budget of about $330,000, almost half of it supplied by his friend and the film's producer, James B. Harris. Still modest by Hollywood standards, it was well up on the cost of his previous features. *The Killing* is best remembered for its complex plot structure, flashing forward and backward in time leading up to the ingeniously planned-out race-track robbery carried out by Hayden with split second timing. Generally well received by critics at the time, in retrospect the film, although gripping, appears as little more than a quite well crafted, reasonably acted work from a young director who makes the familiar mistake of attempting to cram too much material into the brief running time.

The Killing is revealing of a weakness which would recur in later, more mature works – Kubrick's generally cold and impersonal approach which makes it difficult for him to develop a meaningful and sympathetic involvement with his characters. In *Paths Of Glory*, for example, the most appealing and fully realised character is the sly, cynical and corrupt General Broulard superbly played by Adolphe Menjou. In contrast, the ambitious general (George Macready) provides a rather too obvious target to attack as the villain who orders his troops to attack knowing that there is no hope of success. Kirk Douglas, as the major caught between the impossible orders from above and genuine concern for his men, comes across as a typically suffering hero, but lacking in depth. Where the film succeeds best, however, is as a hard hitting statement about the nature of war, given added impact by a typically Kubrick fascination with the behind-the-scenes machinery of war and decision making among the generals. *Paths Of Glory* was adapted from the novel by Humphrey Cobb, which was itself based on true events which had occurred during World War I when French troops had mutinied and a few men were chosen by lot to be executed as an example to others. It was a project which Kubrick and his producer

Harris had tried to set up after wasting six months at MGM in 1956. Regarded as too downbeat and uncommerical by all the Hollywood studios, it was only backed by UA when Douglas agreed to star. Filmed in Germany in 1957, it was the director's first opportunity to direct a major production with a budget at slightly under $1 million (about one third going to pay Douglas). The completed film stirred up much controversy when it was first released, though favourably received by the critics and breaking even at the box-office. It was slightly cut by the British censor and banned in France for almost twenty years. Then, in 1959, after a period out of work, Kubrick was summoned by producer-star Kirk Douglas to replace Anthony Mann on the $12 million Universal production of *Spartacus*. Thus, he became the youngest director up to that time to handle such a multi-million dollar production, filming in the new Super Technirama (70mm) and his first in colour, too. Kubrick himself did not enjoy making the film – it was the only time he worked on a picture without being given full creative control, and he was prevented from making desired script changes. Written by Dalton Trumbo from the novel by Howard Fast about the slave uprising in ancient Rome, the film emerged as one of the most intelligent and interesting of the cycle of Hollywood costume epics of that period.

In 1959 Kubrick had joined with James Harris to purchase the screen

Above left: Kirk Douglas, a Roman slave, about to be sent off by Peter Ustinov (right) to train as a gladiator in *Spartacus* (1960), Kubrick's bloody epic about the slave uprising in Ancient Rome.

Left: Sue Lyon as the nymphet *Lolita* with James Mason as Humbert Humbert in Kubrick's ill-received 1961 screen version of the Nabokov novel.

Below: George C. Scott (left) and Peter Sellers in *Dr Strangelove* (1963), the director's famous black comedy about the dangers of nuclear weapons.

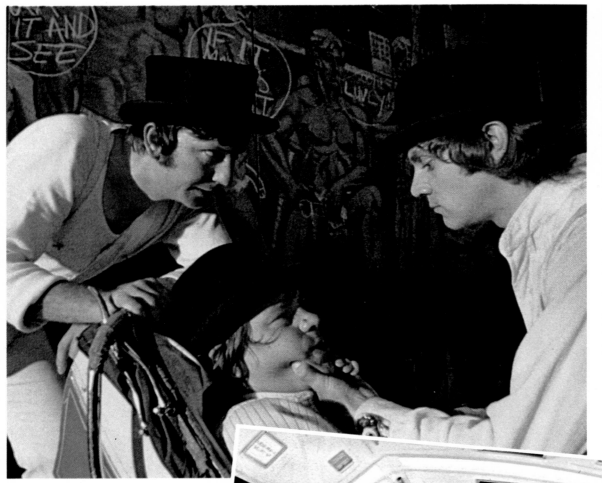

Left: Malcolm McDowell was Alex, dedicated to laid-back violence – kicking a woman to death to the tune of 'Singin' In The Rain', for example – in the violent, futuristic A Clockwork Orange (1971). Here he is (right) with a couple of his henchmen.

Above: Jack Nicholson at full throttle as a hotel caretaker who goes completely berserk and terrorizes his family with, among other things, an axe, in The Shining (1980), adapted from the novel by Stephen King.

Learned To Stop Worrying And Love The Bomb.) Drawing on the experience of his previous black-and-white movies, combining thriller elements with black comedy and war drama, Kubrick made use of an effective cross-cutting pattern which neatly fitted all the pieces together. His frightening vision of the ultimate nuclear slip-up – an American plane heading to Russia to deliver its nuclear payload and impossible to recall – reflects a very real social concern. Yet it also reflects Kubrick's personal fascination with military hardware, with the workings of the Presidential hot-line and all the mechanics and gadgetry of the nuclear age. With the help of an outstanding British production team and a notable contribution from production designer Ken Adam, in particular, Kubrick brought an extraordinary yet plausible world to life, including a US Air Force base under siege and the giant Pentagon War Room. Best of all, he presents us with a remarkable group of larger than life characters to match. Peter Sellers excelled himself in a multiple role which earned him his first Oscar nomination, ditto Kubrick as director and co-scripter along with a Best Picture nomination.

Unfortunately, Kubrick never again came up with the kind of balanced blend between characters and settings which he accomplished here. Spending three years on 2001, he created a remarkable and convincing vision of the future, technically far in advance of anything that had ever been done on film before, and posed the profoundest of questions regarding man's relationship to the universe (in collaboration with writer Arthur C. Clarke). But the characters were dwarfed by the technology. In A Clockwork Orange

(1971), from the novel by Anthony Burgess, which marked the beginning of his association with Warner Bros., he succeeded in bringing a Pop Art, futuristic and astonishingly violent and heartless world alive on the screen, clearly anticipating (and influencing?) the Punk phenomenon of the 70s. The central character of Alex (Malcolm McDowell) is one of Kubrick's most remarkable realisations but was supported by a strange (and often unconvincing) assortment of minor characters. Then, in a remarkable and unexpected change of direction, Kubrick made his first costume picture, Thackeray's Barry Lyndon (1975), and re-created a world on screen every bit as exceptional and original in its way as his

futuristic films before. But he was badly let down by a weak script and the miscasting of Ryan O'Neal in the lead role. Both A Clockwork Orange and Barry Lyndon earned Kubrick an identical set of Oscar nominations – Best Picture, director and adapted script. He had also been nominated for directing and co-scripting 2001, but has only won one Oscar – for designing the 2001 special effects.

The Shining (1980) featuring a terrific manic performance from Jack Nicholson was also disappointing and the first Kubrick film in twenty years which was not in some respect exceptional. Hopefully, this unique director will be back on form with his forthcoming movie on the military madness that was Vietnam.

Above: The interior of the ship in 2001: A Space Odyssey (1968), Kubrick's visually and technically brilliant exploration of Man's evolution from ape to scientist. Atmospheric and mysterious, it was heavy with not always successful symbolism. The astronaut (though you'd never know it!) is Gary Lockwood.

'Define Kubrick? Umm . . . gives a new meaning to the word meticulous.'

Jack Nicholson, 1980

RICHARD LESTER

Born Philadelphia, 19 January 1932

In the 60s Richard Lester was one of the best known movie directors linked with the image of 'Swinging London' – indeed, he was jokingly referred to as the 'American Goon' and the fifth Beatle. In the 70s he went in for making action epics, including the Superman movies. But where will he go from here? Is there a new style Dick Lester for the 80s?

Lester's early movie success was due in part to the fact that he was in the right place at exactly the right time. While a psychology student at the University of Pennsylvania, he began writing music and formed his own vocal group which appeared briefly on TV. When the group was sacked he stayed behind to work as a floor manager and soon graduated to directing. He took a year off to travel in the mid-50s, arriving in England just as the new commercial (ITV) network was being launched and found himself much in demand to direct comedy, music shows, and commercials.

Teaming up with Peter Sellers to do 'A Show Called Fred' on TV and the Goon Shows, Lester got a chance to direct his first short film, a typically manic and surreal Goon-style effort with Sellers and Spike Milligan called *The Running, Jumping And Standing Still Film* in 1959. With his TV and musical background and a sympathetic attitude to the younger generation, Lester was the obvious choice for a pop music feature, *It's Trad Dad* (Columbia, 1962), which properly launched his movie career. He packed an incredible amount of music and fast filming techniques into the seventy-five-minute running time and was then signed by producer Walter Shenson to direct *The Mouse On The Moon* (UA, 1963) making use of leftover castle sets from Cornel Wilde's *Lancelot And Guinevere* (1962). When UA asked Shenson to set up a film to promote a new pop group called The Beatles, he immediately turned to Lester. The latter got on well with the foursome and joined with writer Cliff Owen to devise *A Hard Day's Night*, with a relatively simple format that allowed room for comic improvisation and

off-the-cuff Beatle wit. Semi-documentary in style, the movie followed them from their arrival in London by train through a period of thirty-six hours leading up to a live TV performance. 'The shooting of the concert sequence was astonishing,' Lester recalled. 'We used six film and three TV cameras to shoot the final seventeen minutes of film in a single day.' They then had to defend themselves with camera tripods from the onslaught of hysterical young fans.

A second Beatles movie, *Help!* (1965), was more polished, but less original, but Lester's adaptation of *The Knack* that same year further developed the characteristic Lester style of fast-paced visual and verbal humour. The picture unexpectedly won the best film award at the Cannes Festival, but an elaborate movie version of the hit stage musical starring Zero Mostel, *A Funny Thing Happened On The Way To The Forum* (1966), failed to take off (and wasted Buster Keaton in his last screen role). Similarly, the anti-war satire *How I Won The War* (1967) fell flat, but Lester found the ultimate expression of 60s surrealism and Goonery in his witty and visually inventive treatment of

the 'After-the-Bomb' movie, *The Bed Sitting Room* (1969). Adapted from the Spike Milligan-John Antrobus play, it was a kind of extended black comedy sequel to Kubrick's *Dr Strangelove* (1963), and a sadly underrated movie which never found its audience and was never promoted properly. It ended the director's seven-year association with UA, and for a time he was forced to return to making TV commercials.

Lester bounced back in 1973 with *The Three Musketeers* (1973) for Salkind-Spengler, treating the classic story with panache and good humour. Having recognised its many filmic possibilities, he was similarly attracted to an unusual and nostalgic treatment of the story of Robin Hood, many years past his prime in *Robin And Marian* (Columbia, 1976), with Sean Connery and Audrey Hepburn as an extremely likeable screen couple. Currently, Lester is best known as the producer of *Superman* (Warner Bros., 1977), and director of its two sequels. Thus, his suitably comic strip style of humour has reached a larger world wide audience than all of his previous films put together.

Left: The Beatles were a seminal influence on pop music the world over, and a key icon of the famous London 'Swinging Sixties'. Their first film, *A Hard Day's Night* (1964) – madcap clowning and lots of music – was filmed with adroit and adventurous technical expertise by Richard Lester (centre). The boys, still relatively short-haired, are George Harrison (left foreground), Ringo Starr (the film's producer, Walter Shenson, behind him), John Lennon (right of Lester) and Paul McCartney.

Above: Michael Hordern in *The Bed Sitting Room* (1969), Spike Milligan's surreal fantasy about a mad post-nuclear wasteland. The film, which co-starred such quality actors as Ralph Richardson and Dudley Moore, was a huge flop which sent Lester into the wilderness for four years.

Left: Michael York (left), Spike Milligan (centre) and Roy Kinnear in *The Three Musketeers* (1973).

'I used to make films in a kind of smash and grab manner, working on my nerves . . . but I'm over 50 now and I don't know how long I would be able to keep that up.'
1983

213

JOSEPH LOSEY

Born La Crosse, Wisconsin, 14 January 1909. **Died** 1984

Best known of all the American expatriate directors exiled abroad by the 50s blacklist, Joseph Losey settled in Britain and became thoroughly anglicised while preserving a welcome perceptiveness as well as a useful detachment in his often stylised treatment of British subjects. A dedicated and serious director who was attracted to subjects with a strong social content, and who aspired to profound insight into characters and relationships – resulting, at times, in pretentiousness – most of his films were distinctly non-commercial. Thus, throughout most of his life he had great difficulty in setting up projects and worked far less often than he would have liked. He had always hoped to return to direct again in the US, but never managed to do so.

Losey was born into a cultivated American family of Dutch extraction: his father was a lawyer and he himself initially decided to study medicine at Dartmouth College. The restlessly lively period of the early 30s, however, was crucial to his subsequent development: abandoning his studies, he found work as an extra and bit-part player on the Broadway stage, concurrently contributing play and book reviews for various national publications. He worked as a stage manager and director for the first time during 1932-33. When he returned to America after travelling in Europe in 1935, he established his theatrical reputation with the creation of 'The Living Newspaper', a WPA-subsidised and Brecht-influenced 'happening', whose personnel included writers, researchers, dancers, actors and musicians. This, and many of his other stage productions of the period, were already clearly marked by a left-wing political orientation, a concern for social issues and an evident flair for audacious and near-experimental stagecraft, which reached its culmination in a celebrated production of Brecht's 'Galileo Galilei' in 1947 starring Charles Laughton (and filmed – rather stiffly – by Losey in 1974). He spent the immediate pre-war years supervising documentary shorts for the Rockefeller Foundation; and the war years themselves, when not on active service, producing radio dramas for NBC and under contract to MGM, where he directed an Oscar-nominated short in the 'Crime Does Not Pay' series, *A Gun In His Hand* (1945).

Soon after 'Galileo', RKO's Dore Schary offered Losey an opportunity to direct his first feature film. This was *The Boy With Green Hair* (1948), a naive, over-explicit but not unaffecting Technicolor drama on the theme of non-conformism, which reflected Losey's (and Schary's) unease at the jingoist isolationism of the Cold War period. Losey was able, in all, to complete four additional features in the US, with extremely modest budgets and shooting periods of a few weeks only. Yet, in a less superficial sense, they cannot be called B-pictures: the director's concern with social issues, his beady, almost clinical scrutiny of human psychology, and the visible in-

Left: Hardy Kruger, the lover of a beautiful French actress (Micheline Presle), is the chief suspect when she is murdered. Here, Stanley Baker's police inspector (standing) questions him in *Blind Date* (1959).

Below: The distorting mirror is appropriate to the distorted master-servant relationship it is reflecting in *The Servant* (1963), starring Dirk Bogarde (left) and James Fox.

fluence of the then predominant *film noir*, lent an unexpected depth and ambition to such apparent programmers as *The Lawless* (1950), *M*, a remake of Fritz Lang's famous German classic, and *The Big Night* (both 1951). Best of the lot, however, was *The Prowler* (1951), an atmospheric and gripping thriller starring Van Heflin and Evelyn Keyes.

It was while he was based in Italy for the shooting of *Stranger On The Prowl* (a 1952 Italian-American co-production) that Losey received a summons to testify before the House Un-American Activities Committee after being identified by a 'friendly' witness as a former Communist. When he finally returned to Hollywood, he discovered that in his absence he had been blacklisted by the industry and thus, in 1953 he settled in England.

Taking work where he could find it, Losey's first British efforts tended to be rather weak and confused, psychological thrillers and melodramas characterised by empty, pyrotechnical camerawork:

est stylists of his generation, as well as establishing a collaboration with the dramatist Harold Pinter which, beside that with Brecht, was to be the most fruitful of his career. *The Servant* (1963), starring Dirk Bogarde and the young James Fox, was a superb adaptation of Robin Maugham's novel of the malevolent ascendancy which a manservant gains over his upper-class, weak-willed employer, It also constituted an interesting example of what Losey called 'pre-design' (on which he worked in tandem with his habitual set designer, Richard Mac-Donald). 'It isn't necessarily pre-design,' he once explained, 'because very often on a film there are no sketches at all, it is all simply worked out in talk; and on the drawing-board with practical building plans; on the stage with props; and then on the set where we decide what colours and other things we want.' However it was articulated, Losey's concern with the

The Sleeping Tiger and *The Intimate Stranger* (1954 and 1956: both pseudonymously credited to him); *Time Without Pity* (1957) and *The Gypsy And The Gentleman* (1958), an over-the-top costume drama starring Melina Mercouri and Keith Michell. *Blind Date* in 1959 was another matter altogether, and announced his most productive 'British' period. Starring Stanley Baker, Hardy Kruger and Micheline Presle, it was a taut little thriller which brilliantly deployed its exterior settings in London. Even stronger were *The Criminal* (1960), a tough prison melodrama which again starred Baker, *The Damned* (1962), a strange futurist fable eerily set in the seaside resort of Weymouth, and the gorgeously baroque *Eva* (also 1962), with Baker and Jeanne Moreau draped elegantly, if on occasion over-symbolically, around the churches and piazzas of a wintry Venice. Losey's confidence at that period could only have been boosted by the fact that he found himself at the centre of a growing cult based in France. Certainly, his next film earned him a worldwide reputation as one of the great-

'look' of his work, through sets, camera movement and such 'significant' props as the ubiquitous mirror, was increasingly manifest in such ambitious works as *King And Country* (1964), a muted World War I drama with Bogarde again and Tom Courtenay, *Modesty Blaise* (1966), an uncharacteristically lightweight psychedelic comic-strip spy spoof with a resplendent Monica Vitti in the title role, and, less effectively, three weird symbol-conscious melodramas, *Secret Ceremony*, with Elizabeth Taylor, Robert Mitchum and Mia Farrow, *Boom!*, with Taylor and her current husband Richard Burton (both 1968) and *Figures In A Landscape* (1970), with Robert Shaw and Malcolm McDowell. Meanwhile, however, there were the second and third of his Pinter-scripted films: *Accident* (1967), based on a Nicholas Mosley novel set in Oxford, and *The Go-Between* (1971), which won the Palme d'Or at the Cannes Film Festival for its exquisitely subtle delineation of a doomed love affair in a lush, complacent England just prior to World War I, and how it forever marked a child who unwittingly became involved.

The Go-Between represented perhaps

the last highlight of Losey's uneven career. The films which followed (often made in France, where he settled in the 70s) were more ambitious than fully achieved. By far the weakest of this later group was *The Assassination Of Trotsky* (1972) with Richard Burton quite unconvincing in the title role. *A Doll's House* (1973), a solidly crafted, attractive version of Ibsen's play starring Jane Fonda, never managed to overcome its theatrical origins. *The Romantic Englishwoman* (1975) was an over-literary and unconvincing drama scripted by Tom Stoppard, while *Don Giovanni* (1979) presented a beautifully photographed but otherwise heavy-handed screen adaptation of Mozart's masterpiece. Best of Losey's three French-language movies was *Mr Klein* (1976), a disquieting study of an identity crisis during the Occupation of Paris. Losey died quite suddenly in 1984 after completing a film adaptation of Nell Dunn's vaguely feminist play, *Steaming*, with Vanessa Redgrave.

Above: The director observes his stars at work. Mia Farrow (left) and Elizabeth Taylor in *Secret Ceremony* (1968), an overheated and incredible melodrama in which Miss Taylor played a prostitute who takes Miss Farrow, a girl with a very odd past, under her wing.

Left: Tom Courtenay (centre) as the young World War I private who is court-martialled and shot in *King And Country* (1964). Dirk Bogarde is seated centre.

Below: Alan Bates (left), the tenant farmer, and Edward Fox, the upper-class gentleman, in Losey's superb evocation of Edwardian England and a tragic love affair which defies class barriers. Julie Christie and Margaret Leighton co-starred, Dominic Guard was *The Go-Between* (1970), and Pinter scripted L.P. Hartley's fine novel.

GEORGE LUCAS

Born Modesto, California, 14 May 1944

'I came up from the film-makers' school of doing movies, which means I did everything myself. If you are a writer-director, you *must* get involved with everything. It's very hard for me to get into another system where everybody does things for me.' Surprising words indeed from George Lucas, the most successful Hollywood producer of recent years who has virtually given up directing. His three feature films as director, however, include a pair of the most profitable ever made – *American Graffiti* (Universal, 1973) and *Star Wars* (20th Century-Fox, 1977). Still only in his early forties, and with virtually unlimited film-making options open to him, it is hard to believe that he will not once gain try his hand at directing some time in the future.

Small in size, thin and shy, young George was an indifferent student at school, obsessed – in his teens – with cars and racing. A horrific auto accident which almost killed him in 1962 had the effect of making him take his studies more seriously, and two years later he enrolled in the film department of USC. Determined to master every aspect of film-making, he soon developed self-confidence and demonstrated a remarkable, instinctive grasp of the medium. He quickly became recognised as one of the most promising and brilliant of American film students from the range and sheer inventiveness of his student shorts. At the Third National Student Film Festival in 1967 he won the top dramatic award with *THX 1138: 4EB* and came close to winning the documentary and experimental awards for two other films.

Lucas was, in fact, to develop into one of the leaders of a new generation of film-makers who were emerging from the film schools in the mid-60s. Arriving as an 'apprentice' at Warner Bros. in 1967 Lucas immediately became friends with Coppola who was just then shooting *Finian's Rainbow*. He joined him on the road during *The Rain People* in 1968 and made an excellent short documentary about the production titled *Filmmaker*. Finally, the setting up of Coppola's

American Zoetrope studio gave Lucas the facilities to direct his first feature, an improved and expanded version of *THX 1138* (the *4EB* was dropped). The budget was modest, the crew made up of young and relatively inexperienced technicians, and the story the relatively familiar tale of one man's rebellion against a mindless society of the future. But the film, as conceived by Lucas, had a distinctive visual quality, displaying an imaginative use of a variety of graphic images and of the wide screen Techniscope format, while the well disguised settings (all found in the San Francisco area) included the Bay Area Rapid Transit tunnels and control centre which were not yet in use. Filmed in 1969, completed in 1970 and released by Warner Bros. early in 1971, the movie didn't make enough to cover its costs and Lucas spent the next year and a half trying to set up a new project, namely *American Graffiti*. Set in 1962, the year of his near-fatal accident, the movie was directly based on his own teenage experience of 'cruising' in his car night after night, chasing girls, drag racing and listening to rock music (which provided a memorable 60s sound-track) – a world which had a

strong nostalgic appeal to 70s audiences. The film, when finally completed, was a big hit and a great personal success for Lucas, gaining a number of Oscar nominations including Best Picture, director and script. As a suddenly 'hot' property Lucas was soon able to make a deal with Fox over his planned sci fi adventure movie in the Flash Gordon mold. But he was never very good at scriptwriting and it took him about two years to knock the screenplay into shape. He then took a tremendous personal risk, spending over $1 million of his own money in pre-production before getting final approval from Fox to start filming early in 1976. The movie was *Star Wars*. The rest is history. Using a largely unknown cast (aside from Alec Guinness), an assortment of strange creatures including a likeable pair of robots and stunning special effects, Lucas fashioned *the* smash hit movie of the 70s. More recently he was the executive producer and writer on the two almost equally successful sequels and has served as producer for his director-friend, Steven Spielberg on his pair of phenomenally successful *Indiana Jones* movies starring Harrison Ford.

Above: Paul Le Mat drives a 1932 Ford coupe (right) in *American Graffiti* (1973). Note the registration number, THX 138. Is this merely coincidence. . . ?

Above: Carrie Fisher, daughter of Debbie Reynolds and Eddie Fisher, and Mark Hamill in *Return Of The Jedi* (1983), produced and scripted by Lucas, directed by Richard Marquand, and yet another success in the *Star Wars* series.

Left: Alec Guinness (left) lent a special distinction to *Star Wars* (1977). Here, he discusses a scene during filming with director George Lucas.

'Sometimes I get the feeling that if I have any more success, it's going to be obscene. I'm embarrassed by it. I'm beginning to impress even myself. I don't like that.'
1983

SIDNEY LUMET

Born Philadelphia, 25 June 1924

Uniquely, there is, to Sidney Lumet, both more and less than meets the eye. Less, in that despite his currently high reputation, he has worked in a bewildering catalogue of styles, adapting from writers Mary McCarthy and Agatha Christie, Chekhov and Ira Levin, so that it has become virtually impossible to predict, when a new title is announced, whether it will be major Lumet or a mere potboiler. More, in that, despite the casual eclecticism of which he has justly been accused, the best of his output has somehow contrived to be personal and worthy of attention, rooted in his East Coast, essentially New York persona – he has never made a film in California or Hollywood. Then there is his special gift, which even his detractors are forced to concede, for the direction of actors. Listen to some of the performers who have appeared in his films. Sean Connery: '. . . one of my favourite directors'; Simone Signoret: 'He has fantastic energy, he's optimistic, he's nice, he loves actors'; James Coburn: 'Sidney is the only director I've ever worked with who makes me feel I'm working towards a totality instead of a piece of nothing.' What is most disheartening about any survey of his work is the absence of continuity, of development; the movies he is making now he might have made in the 60s, and vice-versa.

Lumet's father was an actor, a celebrated player of the American Yiddish theatre, which makes it not too surprising that he himself made his public debut at the age of four on radio, and later performed in numerous Broadway plays. In his mid-teens, he even made his sole appearance (to date) in front of a movie camera, in *One Third Of A Nation* (1939). Drafted in 1942, he did not return to the US until four years later, at which time he began directing plays for an off-Broadway theatre company and in summer stock. In the early 50s, however, it was television which seemed to hold the brightest future for Lumet's gifts and temperament, and he was soon associated with the best of TV live drama. A move into feature film-making in those years was the next step and, on the insistence of its star, Henry Fonda, Lumet was given his first, and auspicious, opportunity with *Twelve Angry Men*, Reginald Rose's courtroom drama. *Twelve Angry Men* was facile and glib; but though it may have aged badly, it won instant acclaim for its tyro director and, in his ability to distinguish clearly between the twelve jurymen who make up its *dramatis personae*, he already displayed his sympathy with actors. *Stage Struck* and *That Kind Of Woman* (1958 and 1959), which followed his debut, were more conventional, more 'Hollywoodian' melodramas which attracted little attention from either critics or paying customers. But Lumet immediately returned to the province with which he was familiar by filming, in succession, three plays by the most admired of American dramatists: Tennessee Williams' *The Fugitive Kind* (1960), Arthur

Miller's *A View From The Bridge* and Eugene O'Neill's *Long Day's Journey Into Night* (both 1962). These were very variable in quality, none was a commercial success (not ever likely to be), but all are distinguished by fiercely intense, almost hypnotic performances from their casts: respectively, Marlon Brando, Anna Magnani, Joanne Woodward, Victor Jory; Raf Vallone, Maureen Stapleton, Carol Lawrence and Jean Sorel; and, supremely, Katharine Hepburn, Ralph Richardson, Jason Robards Jr and Dean Stockwell in what was little more than a filmed transcription of O'Neill's marathon autobiographical drama (and none the worse for that).

Again Lumet changed tack, on occasion from film to film. *Fail Safe* (1964), for example, was a suspenseful 'what-if . . .' thriller, unfairly overshadowed by its proximity to Kubrick's similar *Dr Strangelove*; *The Pawnbroker* (1965), a sweatily overdirected study of a traumatised concentration camp survivor (Rod Steiger), which got entangled in its own complex flashback structure; and *The Hill* (also 1965), a chilling if heavy-handed war drama filmed in Britain which displayed Lumet's regrettable weakness for insistent close-ups. By complete contrast, *The Group* (1966), a feeble adaptation of Mary McCarthy's best-selling account of a generation of

Above: The exciting, uninhibited and powerful Italian actress, Anna Magnani, was paired with the intense, sexually magnetic Marlon Brando in *The Fugitive Kind* (1960) by Tennessee Williams. The acting in this heavily doom-laden melodrama was memorable, but the film was a much criticised failure.

Left: Director Lumet on the ground in New York's Washington Square, making *The Group* (1966). With him is cameraman Boris Kaufman. The woman is Joan Hackett, one of a bevy of very fine actresses in the movie. Others included Shirley Knight, Jessica Walter, Candice Bergen and Joanna Pettet.

'I cannot take myself that seriously . . . and if I get fired, I've got 12 New York Jewish ways to survive. I can lecture, I can teach. I can become a festival bum. Believe me, directors think of these things.'
1983

Vassar girls, was a much more relaxed affair, greatly aided by Boris Kaufman's graceful location shooting.

From this point on, however, it becomes increasingly tricky to make sense of Lumet's career as it appears that he is most concerned to keep working, irrespective of the critical reaction to his pictures. As he has noted, 'I've never analysed why I say yes to a movie. I don't hold much with this cult of the director ... We're just humble toilers in the vineyard. We've simply got to do the best we can.' Unfortunately, this means that the weak and all but forgotten movies have far outnumbered the successful ones. He experienced a particularly bad run during the late 60s and early 70s, for example, and was unfortunate in his choice of three projects starring James Mason: *The Deadly Affair* (Columbia, 1966) was but a pale imitation of its source material, John Le Carré's convoluted espionage novel 'Call for the Dead', and clearly unsuited to Lumet's talents; *The Sea Gull* (Warner Bros.-Seven Arts, 1968) was a static and sometimes stilted reading of Chekhov's stage masterpiece co-starring Vanessa Redgrave, Simone Signoret and David Warner; and *Child's Play* (Paramount, 1972), a diabolic and overheated schoolboy drama, failed to convince, although Mason was excellent as the unpopular and victimised Latin master.

Lumet had no luck either with such efforts as his New York Jewish comedy, *Bye, Bye Braverman* filmed for Warner Bros.-Seven Arts in 1967, or the derivative suspense drama, *The Appointment* (MGM, 1968) – a pale imitation of a number of popular 60s French movies (*Lola, A Man And A Woman, Belle de Jour*) – or an attempt to adapt one of Tennessee Williams' poorer plays to the screen, *Last Of The Mobile Hot-Shots* (Warner Bros., 1969) starring James Coburn. But there were signs that things were starting to pick up early in 1971 when Lumet completed an effective contemporary thriller, *The Anderson Tapes* (Columbia), and began to focus his interest on his favourite town, New York City.

Serpico (Paramount) in 1973 marked a major step forward, the first of a series of

films which were the closest to personal works of any in his career. These were sleek, even hyper-realist, urban thrillers, full of the nervous energy and crisp intelligence which are, according to his acquaintances and collaborators, the most striking of Lumet's own personal qualities. Based on the true story of an honest New York undercover cop and his obsessive efforts to rid the force of corruption, *Serpico* was a modest hit and earned well-deserved Oscar nominations for star Al Pacino and for a fine script. It led on to a similarly offbeat New York subject two years later, the smash hit *Dog Day Afternoon* (Warner Bros., 1975). Again Pacino starred in a true story – of a disturbed homosexual who tried to rob a bank to pay for his lover's sex change operation. Clearly Lumet was back in favour. For the first time since *Twelve Angry Men*, both the picture and its director were nominated for Oscars. And he repeated the following year with *Network* (MGM) from an Oscar-winning Paddy Chayefsky script – a wonderfully funny and sharp satire of TV with gloriously

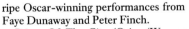

ripe Oscar-winning performances from Faye Dunaway and Peter Finch.

Prince Of The City (Orion/Warner Bros., 1981), *The Verdict* (20th Century-Fox, 1982) and *Daniel* (Paramount, 1983) also fruitfully explored grey areas of power and justice. These are among Lumet's richest and most individual films, and one looks forward to more in the same vein. *The Verdict* was in fact his third big hit of recent years – following *Murder On The Orient Express* (Paramount, 1974) and *Dog Day Afternoon* – and earned him a fourth nomination for directing, while adding to the impressive roster of outstanding performances in his pictures. Here Paul Newman played the lead as a down-on-his-luck Boston lawyer trying to make a comeback, with James Mason as his wiley opponent (both Oscar-nominated, too). Lumet's most recent work is *Garbo Talks* (1984), a black comedy set in New York with Anne Bancroft giving a memorable performance as an oddball lady obsessed with meeting the title's reclusive movie goddess ...

Top: The Hungarian diplomat Count Andrenyi (Michael York, left) is questioned in the course of a murder investigation by Agatha Christie's immortal detective, Hercule Poirot (Albert Finney). *Murder On The Orient Express* (1974) was a big, popular hit.

Above: Al Pacino, dressed to go undercover, was the dedicated cop in *Serpico* (1973).

Above left: Based, like *Serpico*, on a true story, *Dog Day Afternoon* (1975), starred Pacino (right) again, this time on the other side of the law, and John Cazale as his partner-in-crime.

Left: Sidney Lumet discusses a scene in *The Verdict* (1982) with star Paul Newman (left), who won his fifth Oscar nomination for his performance as a Boston attorney on the skids who bids for a dramatic comeback.

PAUL MAZURSKY

Born Brooklyn, New York, 25 April 1930

A sort of cross between his fellow New Yorkers Woody Allen and John Cassavetes, writer-director Paul Mazursky balances the New York Jewish humour of the former with the latter's sensitivity to contemporary characters and relationships; Mazursky is notable for his sympathetic treatment of his actors who are allowed a large measure of freedom within his relatively loose plot structures. (It is more than coincidence that all three directors are also actors.) Blessed with the good fortune to enjoy a big hit with his first film as director (and co-scripter), *Bob & Carol & Ted & Alice* (Columbia, 1969), Mazursky has been able to preserve his creative independence ever since, especially by keeping his budgets low and balancing the occasional flops against the modest box-office success of most of the others. One of the most likeable of the new generation of American writer-directors, one feels that he rarely stretches himself, being content to stick to those white middle-class characters and subjects he knows and which appeal to him personally.

Educated at Brooklyn College where he first developed an interest in acting, Mazursky landed a small role in Stanley Kubrick's first, cheaply made feature, *Fear And Desire*, in 1951, and began hanging around in Greenwich Village during the 50s. He landed a small part in Richard Brooks' *The Blackboard Jungle* (MGM, 1955), found occasional work in live TV, developed his own night club act and tried his hand at writing TV scripts. Moving to California in the 60s with his wife and kids, he first began to establish himself as a writer working on the Danny Kaye Show for four years (1963-67), all the while moving closer to the movies. After having a number of scripts rejected, he and his co-writer at the time, Larry Tucker, finally managed to sell the script of *I Love You, Alice B. Toklas* to Warner Bros. in 1968. Its satirical view of the middle-aged California hippy (here represented by Peter Sellers) turning on and dropping out represented a natural extension of Mazursky and Tucker's work with the satirical theatre company, Second City.

Continuing in the same vein, but determined to keep a firmer grip on their next project, Mazursky directed and Tucker produced *Bob & Carol & Ted & Alice*. Typically of Mazursky's approach, he remains a sympathetic observer of the marital problems experienced by his well meaning but not too bright characters, and their unsuccessful attempts to solve them in the accepted modern California fashion: extra-marital affairs, wife swapping, group therapy. Straight scenes alternate with moments of light relief, and the appeal of the movie is strengthened by its four central performances and a perceptive, Oscar-nominated, script.

Mazursky's movie about contemporary Hollywood, *Alex In Wonderland* (MGM, 1970), was never given a proper release and flopped, while George Segal's self-indulgent title character in

Blume In Love (Warners Bros., 1973) failed to engage one's sympathy. But the director was back on more solid ground with *Harry And Tonto* the following year. Based on a slender script about an elderly man's travels with his cat and filmed on a tiny $1 million budget, it showed Mazursky at his best, relaxed and unpretentious. It earned him a second co-scripting nomination, while Art Carney won a surprise Oscar for his suitably laid-back performance. The first of four movies for 20th Century-Fox, it marked Mazursky's return to his New York roots, as did the semi-autobiographical *Next Stop, Greenwich Village* (20th Century-Fox, 1975) featuring Shelley Winters as a larger than life Jewish momma. Two

years later – his favourite pattern appears to be one new film every other year – Jill Clayburgh starred as *An Unmarried Woman*, opposite Alan Bates. In the first hour and a half, showing the heroine as she attempts to lead an independent life, Mazursky (and Clayburgh) are in peak form, but the film deteriorates badly in the last half hour. However, it proved to be his biggest critical and commercial success of the 70s and his only movie to be nominated for the top Oscar, with further nominations to Clayburgh and his script. Most recently he has teamed up with actor Robin Williams in a charming comedy about a Russian defector coping with New York in *Moscow On The Hudson* (Columbia, 1984).

'True, I work on what I know and I reckon to have a reasonable knowledge of what makes town life revolve, wherever it may be. I'd be far happier doing a film about London than one set in Kansas.'
1984

Above left: Art Carney won an Oscar for his sympathetic portrayal of the septuagenarian Harry, whose best friend is his cat, in *Harry And Tonto* (1973).

Above: Robert Culp and Natalie Wood in *Bob & Carol & Ted & Alice* (1969), skilfully scripted and directed by Mazursky to reflect his sense of the contemporary. The film was about marital encounter group therapy, and co-starred Elliott Gould and Dyan Cannon.

Below: Director Mazursky on location in New York City with Jill Clayburgh for *An Unmarried Woman* (1977).

JOHN MILIUS

Born St Louis, Missouri 1944

Over the past fifteen years or so John Milius has developed a reputation as one of the most elusive and fiercely individualistic of that new generation of young writer-directors who took Hollywood by storm during the 70s. Characterised by his outspokenly right-wing political views, his love of guns and weaponry and an attraction to violence and old fashioned heroism, he describes himself as a 'Zen anarchist'. He obviously made an impression on John Huston, whom he worked with as a writer, and later directed as an actor, and who commented: 'John Milius is not of our time. He is a throwback to a different age, a Viking or a samurai, an extraordinary individual.' Milius in fact demonstrated a remarkable talent for translating his eccentric personal viewpoint into some of the most forceful and dynamic scripting of the early 70s. The least well known of the group of friends with whom he worked, including Spielberg, he has only become better known during recent years as the writer-director of popular action movies like *Red Dawn* (UA, 1984).

Tall, dark and heavily built, Milius was a surfing freak who led a wild and sometimes violent life as a teenager. He attended L.A. City College and was first attracted to the cinema by the action pictures of such directors as Kurosawa and John Ford. He was a friend and classmate of George Lucas at USC and, with Lucas, joined Francis Coppola in setting up the latter's American Zoetrope studio in the late 60s. (They developed a story idea about Vietnam which emerged years later as *Apocalypse Now*, UA, 1979, directed by Coppola and earning Milius his only Oscar nomination, for co-scripting).

Milius gained his first screen credit for scripting the AIP exploitation movie *The Devil's Eight* (1968), a scaled-down variation on *The Dirty Dozen* about a group of tough convicts who are used to smash a moonshine ring. He established himself as a leading scripter with his work on a number of popular Warner Bros. pictures in the early 70s – he made important (uncredited) contributions to the script of *Dirty Harry* (1971), co-wrote the first sequel, *Magnum Force* (1973) with Michael Cimino, and co-scripted the Robert Redford film about a man of the wilderness, *Jeremiah Johnson* (1972). About the same time he hoped to launch his career as a writer-director with a script about a famous individualist of the West, *The Life And Times Of Judge Roy Bean* (1972). Preferring John Huston to direct, the production company upped Milius' writing fee from $150,000 to $300,000 in compensation. Milius watched Huston in action and was particularly interested in seeing how the veteran director handled his actors. He was finally given his own chance on a relatively small budget AIP gangster movie, *Dillinger* (1973) – one of many made in the wake of *Bonnie And Clyde*'s success and generally dismissed by the critics for that reason. *Dillinger*, however, *was* different. It was scripted and directed with a

tremendous vitality, sense of pace and black humour: 'I rob banks for a living,' states Warren Oates picking up a girl in a bar, 'What do you do?'. The spurts of comic strip violence were handled by Milius like a veteran, and the film immediately made it clear that this was no ordinary young director.

He was able to follow it with his first major production, a rather different and unusual comment on the nature of power and heroism – favourite Milius themes. *The Wind And The Lion* (Columbia/ MGM, 1975) starred Sean Connery as a Berber chieftain who kidnaps an American lady and her children. Very loosely based on a true incident, Milius made use of some adroit cross-cutting to balance the morality and code of honour of the Berber with the respected American president of the time, Theodore Roosevelt. *Big Wednesday* (Warner Bros., 1978) was Milius' most intensely personal and nostalgic tribute to the cult of the surfer. It flopped badly, but the direc-

tor has emerged during the 80s as a more commercial film-maker who enjoys handling popular adventure stories, and has had hits with both *Conan The Barbarian* in 1982 and the controversial war 'fantasy' *Red Dawn* about a Russian (and Cuban) invasion of the US opposed by a heroic band of teenage guerrillas.

Left: John Milius (left) made an impressive feature debut with *Dillinger* (1973), an account of the famous criminal, scripted as well as directed by Milius, and with Warren Oates (right) cast in the title role.

Above: Milius (left) with co-writer Dennis Aaberg during the filming of *Big Wednesday* (1978). Jan-Michael Vincent, William Katt and Gary Busey played three friends who get together to surf after the Vietnam War, in an interesting movie which flopped.

Left: Bodybuilder Arnold Schwarzenegger is hardly likely to be remembered for his acting. However, his gigantic torso came into its own and brought him a measure of fame as *Conan The Barbarian* (1982), a Dark Ages saga which was hardly a credit to Milius.

ROBERT MULLIGAN

Born Bronx, New York, 23 August 1925

One of several leading directors who turned to films in the early 60s after distinguishing themselves for their handling of live TV drama, Robert Mulligan quickly developed a reputation as an 'actor's director'. He is apparently most comfortable dealing with intimate, family drama and relationships within contemporary settings, and has not been successful at widening his range.

The son of a New York policeman, Robert had his education interrupted by the war, but he eventually got his degree at Fordham University, then landed a lowly job at CBS-TV in the early 50s. After a few years he had advanced to full director status and worked on such leading TV drama programmes as 'Playhouse 90' and 'Hallmark Hall of Fame'. In 1956 he was selected by Paramount and producer Alan Pakula to direct his first feature, *Fear Strikes Out*. A solid but predictable family drama based on the true story of baseball star Jimmy Piersall, it pitted the neurotic young man (played by Tony Perkins in his first starring role) against his domineering father (Karl Malden). A modest critical success, it at least broke the ice for Mulligan, though he was forced to return to TV to complete his contract. Four years later he was back in Hollywood directing a mixture of comedies and drama for Universal, mainly Tony Curtis and Rock Hudson vehicles.

For his last Universal movie, *To Kill A Mockingbird* in 1962, Mulligan was reunited with his favourite producer, Alan Pakula. The film, adapted from the bestselling novel by Harper Lee, was Mulligan's first prestige production and starred Gregory Peck as a liberal Southern lawyer – a more or less archetypal Mulligan hero – who defends a black man accused of murder. In spite of the weaknesses of the long courtroom sequences, Mulligan's sensitive handling of the world of the children, who are the principal observers of the drama, was impeccable. The movie proved to be the director's first big critical and commercial success, earning Oscar nominations for Best Picture and director and with Awards actually going to Peck, the screenplay and the art direction.

Firmly launched into his most productive period, Mulligan continued his partnership with Pakula, and returned to New York to shoot the first of two films starring Steve McQueen. The naturalistically observed and charming combination of characters found in *Love With The Proper Stranger* (Paramount, 1963) reflected Mulligan's strengths as a director. Natalie Wood was appealing in one of her first young adult roles. McQueen carried the movie with his characteristically cool, laid-back style, while Edie Adams gave her best ever performance in the small role of his ex-girlfriend. *Baby The Rain Must Fall* (Columbia, 1964), this time pairing Steve with Lee Remick, was less successful, while *Inside Daisy Clover* (Warner Bros., 1965) made very effective use of twenty-seven-year-old Natalie Wood's talent to appear half her

true age in a made-to-order role as a Hollywood juvenile star. But in other respects the movie's behind-the-scenes look at 30s Hollywood was merely another interesting failure. Somewhat better were *Up The Down Staircase* (Warner Bros., 1967) in which Sandy Dennis gave a convincing performance as a New York schoolteacher trying to cope, and *The Stalking Moon* (1968), a solidly crafted Western starring Gregory Peck and Eva Marie Saint.

Finding himself once more on his own after the departure of Pakula (to begin a directing career of his own), Mulligan came up with a quite likeable and underrated entry in the 'youth movie' cycle, *The Pursuit Of Happiness* (Columbia, 1970), then had the surprise smash hit of his career with the romantically nostalgic *Summer Of '42* (Warner Bros., 1971). Here, and in *The Other* (20th Century-Fox, 1972) which followed, Mulligan confirmed his special talent for coaxing fine performances from relatively inexperienced, young actors. Disappointed by the box office failure of *The Other*, he has made less than a handful of movies since then, including the play adaptation *Same Time, Next Year* (Universal, 1978) and, most recently, *Kiss Me Again* (20th Century-Fox, 1982) starring James Caan and the very talented Sally Field.

Left: Mulligan's first big success was *To Kill A Mockingbird* (1962), which starred Gregory Peck (illustrated). This actor, in the words of Ephraim Katz, '. . . has projected for three decades of filmgoers moral and physical strength, intelligence, virtue and sincerity'. Peck was also handsome, and won an Oscar for his performance.

Below: Robert Mulligan, looking more like a bank manager than a movie director, discusses a take with Natalie Wood during filming of *Love With The Proper Stranger* (1963). The unit is on location on 34th Street in mid-town Manhattan.

Left: Ruth Gordon (foreground) and Natalie Wood were mother and daughter in *Inside Daisy Clover* (1965). The formidable Miss Gordon – writer, actress, and Mrs Garson Kanin in private life – was celebrating fifty years in show biz at the time of filming.

'As far as my films are concerned, if the story isn't about someone who moves me in some way, I turn it down. Because if the making of the film is not a personal experience for you how can it be for the audience.'
1972

MIKE NICHOLS

Born Berlin, 6 November 1931

Hollywood's golden boy for a brief period during the mid-60s, successful stage director-turned-movie director Mike Nichols started at the top, with two big hit pictures in a row, then gradually worked his way down over a period of eight years or so. He had apparently reached the end of his movie career in 1975 after a number of costly flops, but recently made something of a comeback with the Meryl Streep picture *Silkwood* in 1983.

Having fled from Nazi Germany to the US as a young boy, Mike grew up in New York and studied at the University of Chicago. When he became interested in acting he joined the Compass Players, a small improvisational acting group which led in turn to his extremely successful stage partnership with Elaine May. Their 1961 satirical show, 'An Evening with Mike Nichols and Elaine May', was a smash on Broadway, and two years later Mike turned his gifted hand to directing for the first time. After a series of big stage hits, mainly comedies, which won him wide recognition as one of the hottest new young talents, it was only a matter of time before he received his first movie offer. Not surprisingly, he was hired by Warner Bros. in 1965 to direct the film version of the well known play, *Who's Afraid Of Virginia Woolf?* by Edward Albee. He immediately insisted on and, unusually, received permission to rehearse the tiny cast of four for three weeks before filming began and was fully vindicated by the results. From Elizabeth Taylor he got the best performance of her career as the frumpy, vulgar Martha, while Richard Burton gave one of his last really memorable portrayals as her cruelly bitter husband. (She won her second Oscar, while he was nominated for the umpteenth time.) One of the last major Hollywood productions shot in black-and-white, the film was a big hit and swept the last black-and-white Oscars – for cinematography, art direction and costumes, with nominations for Best Picture and for director Nichols. He won the following year for directing *The Graduate*. Here, working in colour and Panavision,

Nichols enjoyed the freedom to indulge himself cinematically after having been confined within the claustrophobic setting of George and Martha's house for most of *Virginia Woolf*. *The Graduate* was a superficial but nonetheless entertaining and enjoyable attempt to capture the topical 60s theme of youthful rebellion on the screen. The director's work was enhanced by a fine performance from Dustin Hoffman who made a terrific impact in his first starring role – Nichols had taken a chance on him, having first spotted him on the New York stage. Another Broadway talent, the formidable Anne Bancroft, was cast opposite Hoffman in a role that did not allow real scope for her special qualities. Even though the characters lacked depth and, indeed, credibility, the picture was a lot of fun and held tremendous appeal for contemporary audiences, ranking second to *The Sound Of Music* (20th Century-Fox, 1965) as the top hit of the decade.

With two such big successes behind him, Nichols was given *carte blanche* on his next project – an elaborate attempt to film Joseph Heller's satirical novel of World War II, *Catch-22* (for Paramount).

Starting out with an $11 million budget, a reconditioned squadron of old B-25 bombers and a stellar cast headed by Alan Arkin and Orson Welles, Nichols spent six months filming in Mexico in 1969 while the costs continued to escalate. Attempting the impossible, a literal translation of the book to the screen, the result was generally heavy handed and only came to life sporadically, helped by Arkin's perfect incarnation of the otherwise sane Captain Yossarian who endeavours to be certified mad. The movie was a box-office flop, but Nichols was more commercially successful with *Carnal Knowledge* (1971). This was originally conceived as a play by humorist Jules Feiffer – and looked like it – and Nichols still appeared unable to develop a recognisable cinematic style. After two more flops in a row and one picture abandoned in mid-production, he returned to the New York theatre. A more mature Nichols returned eight years later with the well acted but otherwise undistinguished *Silkwood*. However, it is not clear what the future may hold for Mike Nichols, aspiring movie director.

'I think the role of the director satisfies me partly because I am creating a father that I miss. The great thing about playing an adult role, is that it reassures you as well.'
1982

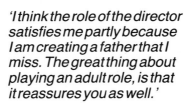

ALAN PAKULA

Born New York City, 7 April 1928

Alan Pakula is one of the few directors who successfully made the transition from producer to director. Here, Joseph Mankiewicz's name immediately springs to mind and, like Mankiewicz, Pakula insists that he always wanted to direct although it took him almost twenty years to make the breakthrough, from the time he first entered the film industry. A liberal arts student at Yale University with a special interest in the theatre, Alan directed a few student productions and, after graduating, landed a job in Hollywood as assistant to a producer. He spent much of the 50s in the Paramount front office, then began a close working partnership with tyro movie director Robert Mulligan with *Fear Strikes Out* in 1956 which he produced. Pakula continued to direct occasionally in the theatre while his partnership with Mulligan on half a dozen pictures flourished during the 60s. A creative producer who undoubtedly made a major contribution to the success of these films, he finally decided it was time for him to start directing himself and chose, for his debut film, *The Sterile Cuckoo* (Paramount, 1969).

The new fledgeling director was fortunate in teaming up with Liza Minnelli who had never starred in a movie before. The impact of her personality, playing a neurotic oddball college girl named Pookie, undoubtedly helped at the box-office. She was nominated for an Oscar, the picture was a hit, and Pakula was able to move on to a very different subject for his second. Whereas the bitter-sweet comedy-drama of *Sterile Cuckoo* was similar to the kind of movies he had previously produced for Mulligan, like *Love With The Proper Stranger* (Paramount, 1963), for example, *Klute* (Warner Bros., 1971) was markedly different and reflected his desire, and his ability, to stretch himself as a director. A chillingly effective and suspenseful thriller set in New York City, *Klute* was notable for its intelligent treatment of the characters played by Jane Fonda (a high-priced hooker) and Donald Sutherland (a private detective) and the relationship which develops between them. In retrospect, Pakula himself recognised what he had accomplished: 'There were certain things about *Klute* that were enormous advances for me in terms of visual storytelling and use of the camera, in terms of creating a mood visually.'

As a further indication of Pakula's qualities as a director, late in 1973 he began work on *The Parallax View* (for Paramount), even more original in its way than *Klute*. The ultimate expression of 70s political paranoia at the time of Watergate, it starred Warren Beatty as a reporter investigating a series of assassinations and was the first entry in a new cycle of political thrillers. It flopped at the box-office, however, for it was perhaps too pessimistic, downbeat, even fatalistic in tone, in spite of a witty undercurrent of black humour. The director succeeded in giving the film an appropriately futuristic feel aided by his regular

cameraman, Gordon Willis, and art director George Jenkins, who had both worked on *Klute* and who joined him again on his best known and most successful picture which followed, *All The President's Men* (Warner Bros., 1976). Combining the urban thriller qualities of *Klute* with the political paranoia and investigative journalism of *Parallax*, the true story of Watergate is so remarkable, that with Redford and Hoffman in the roles of 'Washington Post' reporters Bob Woodward and Carl Bernstein, and Jason Robards as editor Ben Bradlee, the film could hardly fail. (Oscars went to Robards and screenwriter William Goldman along with nominations for

the picture and director – Pakula's first.)

During more recent years Pakula's work has generally failed to live up to its early promise. He has been best known for his direction of female stars like Jill Clayburgh and Candice Bergen, teamed with Burt Reynolds, in *Starting Over* (Paramount, 1979), of Jane Fonda in *Comes A Horseman* (UA, 1978) and *Rollover* (Warner Bros., 1981), and Meryl Streep, who gave a remarkable, Oscar-winning performance as a Polish-Jewish refugee in the title role of *Sophie's Choice* (Universal, 1982). Most recently he directed Kristy McNichol as the girl traumatised by violent nightmares in *Dream Lover* (MGM, 1985).

Top: Dustin Hoffman (left) as Carl Bernstein, Robert Redford as Bob Woodward, and Alan Pakula on location for *All The President's Men* (1976), the director's successful account of the Watergate investigations.

Above: As the call girl involved in a missing person investigation in *Klute*, Jane Fonda won an Oscar, and confirmed the growing suspicion that she was becoming one of Hollywood's finest actresses.

Left: Superstar Meryl Streep won an Oscar for *Sophie's Choice* (1982), Pakula's screen treatment of William Styron's bestseller. Here, she is with one of her two co-stars, Kevin Kline. The other was Peter MacNicol.

'Usually on a film, I spend a great deal of time on research and preparation. I didn't have much time before we had to start filming this one, but as someone said, I don't have to research, I lived it.'

1980 (on *Starting Over*)

SAM PECKINPAH

Born Fresno, California, 21 February 1925. **Died** 1984

Best known for the powerful, often violent qualities of his personal cinematic vision, Sam Peckinpah was attracted to both the myth and the reality of the American West. His pictures celebrate the old fashioned virtues of friendship, honour, independence, courage and other manly attributes. 'I love outsiders,' he insists. 'Look, unless you conform you're going to be alone in this world. But by giving in you lose your independence as a human being. So I go for the loners. I'm nothing if not a romantic, and I've got this weakness for losers on a grand scale...' More than any other American director, he was involved in the reshaping of the screen Western during the 60s.

Not a commercial director at all, Peckinpah's career was dogged by disputes with producers and studios, and a number of his movies were taken away from him, then badly cut or re-edited behind his back. The difficult situations which occasionally developed were not helped by his volatile temperament and his reputation as a hard living, hard drinking, outspoken and rebellious personality. His refusal to compromise meant that he only directed fourteen features in twenty-two years and was only offered one Western after 1969. With the decline of interest in the Western he was forced to turn to other closely related action genres, mainly dramatic thrillers, and achieved a moderate commercial success during the 70s.

Peckinpah's involvement in the history of the West began when he was a young boy. He grew up on a ranch, the grandson of pioneers who had settled in California in the 1870s, and was fascinated by the stories he heard about his family. After serving in the Marines in World War II he studied drama at USC, began acting and directing in the theatre, then landed a job at a local TV station. His first professional work in the cinema came when he was employed by Allied Artists and served as an assistant to director Don Siegel in the mid-50s. He played occasional bit parts, too, as in *The Invasion Of The Body Snatchers* in 1955, but soon turned to writing Western scripts for TV shows like 'Gunsmoke'. By 1958 he had begun directing as well, and initiated a pair of Western series himself: 'The Rifleman' (1958), and 'The Westerner' (1960-61) which is generally regarded as one of the best ever TV Western series.

Peckinpah's excellent working relationship with the star of 'The Westerner', Brian Keith, led to him being offered his first feature, *The Deadly Companions* (1961), starring Keith and Maureen O'Hara. Little more than an above-average apprentice work, Peckinpah suffered from the fact that he had to shoot the weak and confusing script as written, although he did his best to liven it up and make the movie visually interesting. Far better was *Ride The High Country* (MGM, 1962) which followed and immediately established him as a remarkable new directing talent. The film provided him with his first opportunity to draw on his own knowledge and love of the West.

Old-timers Joel McCrea and Randolph Scott were cast as an unlikely pair of creaky heroes in roles which represented an appealing summary of their long and distinguished Western careers. The film included its share of traditional Western themes – the rough and tumble brawl which destroys a Chinese restaurant, a classic final showdown between the two elderly gunmen and three nasty brothers. But it is notable for a sophisticated, anti-heroic, naturalistic and sometimes humorous treatment of characters and settings. The authentic look and feel of the mining camp and brothel sequences, for example, anticipate Altman's *McCabe And Mrs Miller* (Warner Bros.) by ten

Above: Jason Robards starred in *The Ballad Of Cable Hogue* (1969), an uncharacteristically non-violent offering from Peckinpah. With him here is Stella Stevens playing the part of a supportive prostitute.

Below: *The Wild Bunch* (1969) focused attention on Peckinpah as a purveyor of violence – an image which stuck and which brought him due recognition. The scene shows the desolation of a characteristic shoot-out, and its inevitable blood-letting.

years. Visually, too, the movie is exceptional, exhibiting fluid camerawork and effective use of the wide CinemaScope image – the first of many Peckinpah pictures photographed by his favourite cameraman, the veteran Lucien Ballard.

The director then returned briefly to TV, directing and co-writing a pair of hour-long episodes for the Dick Powell Theatre – he especially enjoyed doing 'The Losers', a rowdy comedy with Lee Marvin and Keenan Wynn as a couple of con men on the run. A new movie offer to direct Charlton Heston in *Major Dundee* for Columbia in 1964 meant a first opportunity to handle a large-scale Western, but once again he had to work hard to patch up a weak script. Representing a variation on the familiar Peckinpah travelling theme, Dundee leads a diverse company of Yankees, rebels, blacks, and various oddball types in an expedition against the Apaches. There is

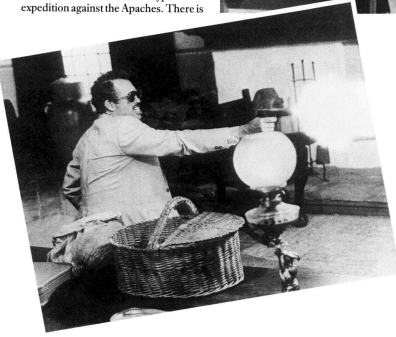

a marvellous feel to the picture initially, but it deteriorates badly later on, for the film was taken away from Peckinpah and later disowned by him. It was his first major row with a Hollywood studio and led to a gap of four years between films. (MGM had hated *Ride The High Country* but had been forced to give it a proper release due to unexpectedly good reactions from the critics – especially in Europe – and from audiences.) He was sacked from MGM's *Cincinnati Kid* in 1965 (replaced by Norman Jewison), directed an outstanding TV adaptation of Katherine Anne Porter's novella 'Noon Wine' in 1966, and was finally given a good break by Kenneth Hyman, the new head of Warner-Seven Arts. It was the only time in his career that he was hired to direct two pictures back-to-back.

The Wild Bunch (1969) was Peckinpah's first moderate box-office success and the film with which his name is most closely identified. The succession of violent and bloody deaths, filmed in slow motion in the final shoot-out, caused such controversy at the time that the director gained instant notoriety and has been identified with excessive screen violence ever since. Shot in Mexico where he had filmed much of *Major Dundee*, the film presented his most pessimistic view

of the old West, depicting the last days of an outlaw gang pursued by bounty hunters and antagonised by a Mexican general. Extremely original, exciting, and of course violent, the film has been much imitated and earned Peckinpah his only Oscar nomination (as co-scriptwriter).

In marked contrast *The Ballad Of Cable Hogue*, which followed later that same year (1969), was Peckinpah's most personal and lyrical tribute to the West. The movie starred Jason Robards as the lone-wolf prospector who discovers water in the desert. But he outlives his time and ends up dying in a bizarre accident with a driverless, new-fangled motorcar. It flopped badly, bringing Peckinpah's personal Western cycle to an abrupt end. He then accepted an offer to direct *Straw Dogs* (1970) in England – the extreme violence of the West was transferred to a farmhouse siege in Cornwall where a quiet American academic (Dustin Hoffman) makes bloody use of a shotgun in defence of his home. *Junior Bonner* (1971) found Peckinpah at his most genial in his depiction of one eventful day in the life of an Arizona rodeoing family. Steve McQueen was the star, but veteran performers Ida Lupino and Robert Preston stole the acting honours. Yet another box-office flop, this was fol-

lowed by the biggest hit of Peckinpah's career, the conventional but entertaining thriller, *The Getaway* (1972), again starring McQueen. Far more original, however, was *Bring Me The Head Of Alfredo Garcia* (UA, 1974), Peckinpah's most underrated film. In the course of its development from lyrical opening to naturalistic observation of low-life Mexico, the down-and-out piano player hero (Warren Oates) is transformed from a 'loser' into a kind of 'avenging angel' who turns the tables on a large number of nasty characters. *Alfredo Garcia* is characterised by its underplayed, offbeat humour, by a truly existential view of the world, and by the pure (but not gratuitous) comic-strip violence depicted in the final reels.

Sam Peckinpah's last movies were generally disappointing: a final Western, the atmospheric but downbeat *Pat Garrett And Billy The Kid* (1973), badly cut by his old nemesis MGM; a violent war movie, *Cross Of Iron* (1977); and a gung-ho trucker's movie, *Convoy* (UA, 1977), which was his last hit. After a six-year gap he resurfaced with the disappointing *The Osterman Weekend* (20th Century-Fox, 1983). It too was taken away from him and recut, and, in the event, marked the sad end to Peckinpah's much troubled movie career.

Above: Ali McGraw, rather better known as the stricken heroine of *Love Story*, and Steve McQueen in *The Getaway* (1972). Ironically it was Peckinpah's biggest hit.

Left: Warren Oates in *Bring Me The Head Of Alfredo Garcia* (1974). The film, about a wealthy Mexican who offers $1 million for the head of the man who seduced his daughter, is memorably violent.

Below: Peckinpah, looking much like one of his revered and grizzled heroes, photographed during the making of *Cross Of Iron* (1977), one of the last, and least, of his movies.

'You can't make violence real to audiences today without rubbing their noses in it. We've all been anaesthetized by the media.'
1973

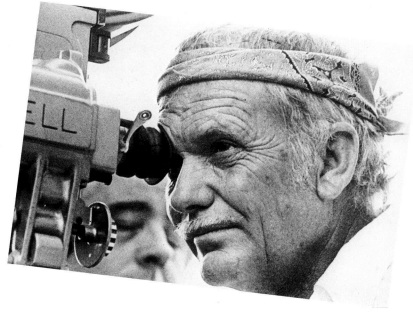

ARTHUR PENN

Born Philadelphia, 27 September 1922

Arthur Penn is one of the most intelligent and eclectic of that group of movie directors who first emerged from work in live TV drama and the theatre during the 60s. For Penn this decade was his most productive and successful, the time when he played a major role in helping to bring a new maturity to Hollywood in dealing with traditional subjects. He collaborated with leading writers like William Gibson, Lillian Hellman, Robert Benton and Calder Willingham, and quickly developed a reputation as a fine director of actors, particularly noted for his work with the new, younger generation of stars – Warren Beatty, Jane Fonda, Robert Redford, Faye Dunaway, Gene Hackman and Dustin Hoffman. Yet, ironically, Penn succeeded better with his powerful and imaginative reworking of familiar genres like the Western, gangster film or thriller, than with contemporary drama and contemporary settings. His first feature, for example, was a Western, *The Left Handed Gun* (Warner Bros., 1957) which had its source in a play by Gore Vidal, while he had the biggest success of his career with that notorious gangster couple of the 30s, *Bonnie And Clyde* (Warner Bros., 1967).

Penn had grown up in Philadelphia and New York and first developed an interest in the theatre while serving in the army during World War II. He resumed his studies after the war, then got himself a job in TV in 1951. By the mid-50s he had established himself as a leading director with 'Philco Playhouse', then 'Playhouse 90', working with many top actors and writers. From 1957 on he was active in the theatre and became one of the leading directors on Broadway with such celebrated productions as 'Two For the Seesaw' starring Anne Bancroft and Henry Fonda, 'The Miracle Worker', 'Toys in the Attic' and also 'An Evening with Nichols and May'. Although his film career did not get properly under way until the 60s with *The Miracle Worker* (UA, 1962), which he had previously done on TV and on the stage, Penn had directed *The Left Handed Gun* five years earlier. The two pictures have much in common. Both were filmed on a relatively small scale in black-and-white at a time when most major productions were in colour and used the wide screen. Both were based on the story of real, larger-than-life Americans of the past, and dealt with the relationship between an older, parent figure – Pat Garrett, Annie Sullivan – and a young, disturbed person – William Bonney (Billy the Kid) and Helen Keller. Both were powerful and physically intense dramas reflecting Penn's willing involvement with strong emotions, unconventional behaviour, and violence when it is integral to the stories. Relatively sparing in his use of dialogue, though both films were based on plays, Penn further demonstrated a strong and confident visual sense at this early stage in his career. Both Billy and Helen are inarticulate characters forced to fall back

on primitive emotions to express their feelings in an extremely physical manner. Deaf, dumb and blind, Helen's main contact with the world comes through her sense of touch. Similarly, the uneducated and mentally unstable young Billy sees his one good friend killed and becomes obsessed with revenge. His subsequent experiences reflect the picture's intensely *tactile* qualities. The killings themselves were staged with unexpected ferocity – a man blown off his horse and another hurled backwards through a door by the force of the gunfire. Most chilling of all, a later victim blasted with such force that he hurtles backward leav-

ing a lone boot standing in the spot where he had been a moment before. The latent violence of Billy's character and his readiness to explode at any provocation, superbly conveyed by the raw energy of Paul Newman's performance, gave a special tension to innocent sequences, too, like the wild game with sacks of flour which escalates into a crazy battle and threatens to get out of hand.

Similarly, the development of Helen Keller is observed through a series of physical encounters – with her family and, especially, with her teacher, Miss Sullivan. Both Patty Duke and Anne Bancroft had played these roles for Penn

'The people who aren't outcasts – either psychologically, emotionally or physically – seem to me good material for selling breakfast food, but they're not material for films.'

1970

Left: James Best (left), Paul Newman and Lita Milan in *The Left Handed Gun* (1957), a Western about Pat Garrett and Billy the Kid, and Arthur Penn's first feature film.

Below: Anne Bancroft (left) and Patty Duke in one of the emotionally harrowing moments from *The Miracle Worker* (1962). Adapted for the screen by William Gibson from his own hit play, the film dealt with the relationship between the world's most famous blind deaf mute, Helen Keller, and her dedicated and inspired teacher, Annie Sullivan, whose will and patience gave the child Helen the means to make a life in the normal world.

on Broadway, and he found it difficult to rework the material in a manner which was fresh and cinematic. But the strength of the basic material and the performances carried one easily over the few weak patches. Both actresses won Oscars (Patty in the supporting role), while Penn was nominated for directing.

After he was replaced by John Frankenheimer as director of UA's *The Train* in 1963, Penn returned briefly to the theatre, directing a number of shows including a musical version of 'Golden Boy' starring Sammy Davis Jr. Columbia then offered to back him on a relatively small budget black-and-white movie original (from an Alan Surgal script) in 1964. Warren Beatty starred as *Mickey One*, a nightclub comic on the run from 'the mob' for committing some nameless offence. The film is a pretentious, Kafkaesque fable, but Penn regards it as his personal comment on the McCarthyite menace and blacklisting which still lingered on into the 60s. He indulged himself with a range of arty compositions, jump cutting, overlapping dialogue, low angle shots and fast editing techniques, assisted by ace French cameraman Ghislan Cloquet. A fascinating but misconceived attempt to make a European-style 'art' film in the US (the heroine was played by French-Canadian actress Alexandra Stewart most often seen in French movies), Penn immediately swung to the opposite extreme (in spite of the fact that it was the only time in his career when he made two movies back to back). *The Chase* which he directed in 1965 was a Sam Spiegel production scripted by Lillian Hellman with a dozen top stars headed by Marlon Brando, Jane Fonda and Robert Redford, by far the largest and most expensive of Penn's films thus far and his first in colour and Panavision. Advertised as 'a breathless explosive story of today', the movie, adapted from Horton Foote's novel and play, suffered from an overly literary format, and attempted to pack too many characters and too much strong dramatic incident into the two-hour running time. Most of the movie concerned the events of a particular evening as the residents of a small Texas town are shuttled about like so many pieces on a chess board. In spite of some interesting performances, most of the characters were mere caricatures, mouthpieces for a worthy comment on the dangers of a society in which everyone is running around with guns. The parallels with the assassination of President Kennedy in Texas a year earlier were rather obvious, and were used to drive the point home with relentless overkill.

Mickey One and *The Chase* were both failures. But they had served to broaden Penn's film experience. If his career had ended at this point (1966) he would have merited only a footnote in the history of the American cinema, for the best was still to come. The director finally hit his stride in the late 60s with three quite different pictures, all of them memorable and successful works, which fulfilled the early promise that had been evident from his first film venture ten years before. The three were *Alice's Restaurant* (UA, 1969), *Little Big Man* also filmed in 1969 and *Bonnie And Clyde* (Warner Bros., 1967) the first of the group. This was so

obviously ideally suited to his talents that it is difficult to believe that the script, by Robert Benton and David Newman, had been offered to many other directors before Warren Beatty bought the rights with a view to producing and starring, and showed it to Penn. The subject obviously had much in common with the director's first two features, dealing with a gangster couple who had attained the status of folk heroes for a brief period during the early 30s. He made a fine job of developing the script's various interlocking themes, mixing drama with black comedy, introducing some relevant social comment appropriate to the Depression background, and exploring characters and relationships – all this punctuated by occasional well-placed bursts of violence. The film clearly benefitted from the impact of colour which had begun to be used for every type of movie around this time. With the leads played by Beatty and Faye Dunaway, the sordid subject matter was noticeably glamourised, and Theadora van Runkle's stylish costume designs actually started a new vogue for the clothes worn by the attractive stars. The role of the neurasthenic but good-natured yokel Clyde Barrow, who suffered from sexual impotence, provided Beatty with the best opportunity of his career and suited his clumsy, slightly mannered style of acting. But in fact the movie made the names of all five members of the gang (including Gene Hackman, Estelle Parsons and Michael Pollard), all of whom were nominated for Oscars. The picture came along at just the right time to capitalise on a new wave of 30s nostalgia, while the stars were just young (and re-

bellious) enough to appeal to younger filmgoers and helped spark off the youth movie cycle of the late 60s. The film also gained its share of notoriety due to the graphic violence (in colour) effectively staged by Penn, especially the balletic slow motion death of the couple at the end – a successful technique which was much imitated in later years.

A tremendous hit and the only Penn production to be nominated for a Best Picture Oscar, it earned him his second directing nomination, while he gained his third for the markedly different movie which followed two years later – *Alice's*

Top: Dustin Hoffman as Jack Crabb in his young manhood (he lived to be 121 years old!) in *Little Big Man* (1970), Penn's ambitious recreation of Thomas Berger's novel about the American West.

Above: Producer and star of *Bonnie And Clyde*, Warren Beatty (left), in his Clyde Barrow clothes, confers with co-star Faye Dunaway and director Arthur Penn while filming on location in Texas.

the Cheyenne and leads a strange double life as both Indian and white man. The film was notable for its authentic depiction of a small frontier town and of life among the Indians, who are seen at their most honorable and dignified in contrast to the petty, bloodthirsty whites. Dustin Hoffman delivered a remarkable multi-faceted character performance as Crabb, but Chief Dan George virtually stole the picture as Old Lodge Skins, the noblest Indian of them all.

In the sixteen years since *Little Big Man* Penn has only completed four features, along with the pole vault episode in *Visions Of Eight*, the film record of the 1972 Olympics. In *Night Moves* (Warner Bros., 1975) he demonstrated a special originality in his reworking of the classic private eye *film noir* formula aided by the low-keyed lighting of Bruce Surtees and a convincing performance from Gene Hackman. He returned to the Western with *The Missouri Breaks* (UA, 1976) as part of a high-priced package assembled by producer Elliott Kastner, but he failed to control the bizarre antics of Marlon Brando who tried to act Jack Nicholson and everyone else off the screen. After a five-year gap, *Four Friends* (1981) came as a sad disappointment but, hopefully, his newest adventure thriller, *Target* (1985), his first picture to be filmed in Europe and reuniting him once again with Gene Hackman, will mark a return to form.

'I really don't know how to eliminate violence from a graphic art form like film. It would be like eliminating one of the primary colours from the palette of a painter.'
1970

Left: *Four Friends* (1981) was about the growing pains of a group of adolescents, particularly Danilo (Craig Wasson), a young Yugoslavian boy. Here, Georgia (Jody Thelen) tries to get into Danilo's room, having chosen him as her first lover.

Below: Jack Nicholson (left) and Marlon Brando in *The Missouri Breaks* (1976), the director's return to the Western. The 'Los Angeles Times' critic, Charles Champlin, said of the venture and its two superstars, 'A pair of million dollar babies in a five and ten cent flick'!

Bottom: Melanie Griffith (centre) as a wayward teenager tracked down by private eye Gene Hackman (left) in *Night Moves* (1975). Jennifer Warren is on the right.

Restaurant. Here, he made a special attempt to capture the feel of the late 60s youth revolution. His script was loosely based on the events which took place in a real commune in Stockbridge, Massachusetts a few years before as described, in part, in the well known talking blues ballad by Arlo Guthrie, 'The Alice's Restaurant Massacree'. A strangely episodic, naturalistic and deglamourised picture, it mixed offbeat humour with a generally down-beat viewpoint. Arlo himself starred, along with a cast of virtual unknowns and semi-professional actors. It is the only film on which Penn is credited as co-scriptwriter, though he works closely with the writers on all his scripts.

Finally, to round out the 60s and conclude his most active period as a filmmaker, Penn embarked on the most ambitious movie of his career, returning to the Western for the first time since his debut picture, and emerging with *Little Big Man* (UA). Broad in scope, mixing comedy, drama, and satire, characterised by its sympathetic treatment of the Indians and its attack on the old myths of the West as misrepresented by the white man, the film was a remarkable achievement in every respect. It represented the final realisation of a project which was of special interest to him and had taken almost six years to set up. Based on the novel by Thomas Berger, the film made use of an audacious framing device of a narration provided by the 121-year-old

Jack Crabb (Dustin Hoffman), a fictitious Everyman figure. But the events he witnesses are true, like the notorious Washita River massacre of the Indians by General Sherman, the final stand of a deranged Custer at the Little Big Horn, and the death of Wild Bill Hickok. Orphaned as a young boy, Crabb is raised by

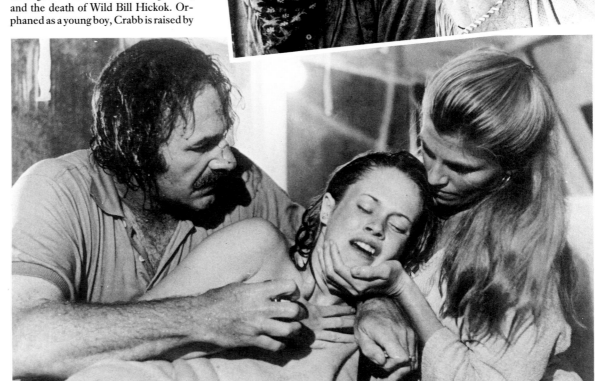

ROMAN POLANSKI

Born Paris, 18 August 1933

When the resilient Roman Polanski, the most controversial of contemporary directors, began shooting on his multi-million dollar production of *Pirates* late in 1984, he proved yet again that he is a born survivor. Having passed the age of fifty, he is apparently not yet ready to retire, in spite of his own joking references to himself as a 'former' director and the fact that he has not made a picture for five years – the longest break since he first started directing – and that he still has some problems with the financing of his projects since, technically, he is a fugitive from American justice.

A favourite project which he had been trying unsuccessfully to set up over a ten-year-period, *Pirates* stars Walter Matthau in the unlikely role of a 17th century pirate captain. (The original version of this swashbuckling spoof had been written by Polanski and his regular writer collaborator, Gerard Brach, with Jack Nicholson in mind.) With principal filming in Malta and Tunisia, this movie further reflects Polanski's reputation as the most international of directors, having made films in France, Holland, Britain, Italy and the US as well as in his native Poland where it all began.

Born in Paris of Polish-Jewish parents who returned to Poland in 1937, young Roman had not yet reached his seventh birthday when he was confronted with all the horrors of the Nazi occupation. Along with the other Jewish residents of Cracow, he and his family were imprisoned in the ghetto set up by the Germans. When his parents were taken away to concentration camps, he managed to escape and spent the entire war period evading the Nazis. As the only form of entertainment available he used to sneak into the movies – mainly German propaganda features – and thus fell in love with the cinema at an early age.

Reunited with his father after the war – his mother and other members of his family had been killed – Roman endeavoured to catch up on his missed studies and soon developed a new part time career as an actor, first in radio and then on the stage. By chance in 1953 he managed to land a small role as a young, rebellious resistance fighter in *A Generation*, the first feature directed by Andrzej Wajda. He impressed the director with his enthusiasm, intelligence and determination and, with Wajda's support, he was admitted to the excellent Polish film school at Lodz where he spent the next five years studying, while working part-time as assistant to director Andrzej Munk and acting in a few pictures, including Wajda's *Kanal* (1955).

Polanski soon emerged as one of the most promising students at the school. By 1958 he directed a student film of such quality that it would bring him his first worldwide recognition a year or two later. The film was *Two Men And A Wardrobe*, a thirteen-minute short which he scripted from an idea by fellow student Jakob Goldberg. Two men emerge from the sea carrying a wardrobe. Regarded by the in-

habitants of the town as outcasts, they are by turns shunned, ignored and mistreated until, defeated, they disappear back into the sea. Full of unexpected twists, and imaginatively conceived, the film was inspired by the surrealist experimental tradition in the cinema and by the Absurdist theatre of Beckett and Ionesco. *When Angels Fall* (1959) provided Polanski with his first opportunity to experiment with colour, using a flashback form to show the dreams/memories/fantasies of an old lady toilet attendant. (It was the only one of his shorts in which his first wife, actress Barbara Kwiatkowska, appeared.) He played a small role himself, then took a larger part in the amusing short he made on a brief visit to Paris in 1960, *The Fat And The Lean*. He, of course, played the thin, servant-slave character, continually mistreated by his fat master, leaping and bouncing about and dancing like a puppet on a string. Another simple but effective cinematic parable recalling *Wardrobe*, this was soon followed by a third short of the same ilk, *Mammals*, in which two men are observed travelling through a snowbound landscape with a sled. They take turns riding, then fake injuries in order to spend more time riding than pulling, but while they are fighting the sled is stolen. They are forced to walk, but soon the old competitiveness begins again as one appears to sprain his ankle and leaps on the other's back . . .

Polanski completed this short quickly early in 1961 anticipating the opportunity to direct his first feature, *Knife In The Water*, later that year. Based on a script he had been working on with Goldberg, and completed with the help of future director Jerzy Skolimowski, it was conceived as a relatively simple three-

character film not too different from his shorts. On their way to spend a weekend on their yacht, a sportswriter and his younger wife encounter a hitchhiker who joins them. The film then explores the various conflicts which develop between these three characters, thrown together for a brief period of time. The various shifts and balances, rivalries and games playing are explored with great wit and visual inventiveness, while the lively jazz score was provided by Polanski's friend Krzysztof Komeda, who composed the music for virtually every one of his films from the early shorts up to and including *Rosemary's Baby* (Paramount, 1968).

For Polanski the film was a major breakthrough and a tremendous international success, nominated for a best foreign picture Oscar. But ironically, by the time that he was being hailed as one of the most promising figures in the new younger generation of Polish directors,

scale, his observation of the interaction, conflict and violence which develops between a small, isolated group of characters (echoes of Beckett and Pinter) within an appropriately surreal setting – the lone castle on Holy Island, Northumberland. *Cul-De-Sac* appears as the natural culmination of Polanski's early career, his last relatively cheap and personal black-and-white picture before he was taken up by the big American companies like MGM who backed him in his entertaining horror movie spoof, *Dance Of The Vampires* (aka *The Fearless Vampire Killers*, or *Pardon Me, But Your Teeth Are In My Neck*), filmed in Panavision and Metrocolor in 1967. A professor and his assistant travel into the heart of Transylvania on a mission to search out and destroy the dreaded vampires. Polanski himself played the comical assistant, the first time he had taken a role in one of his features, acting opposite an attractive young American actress, Sharon Tate,

'Nothing is too shocking for me. When you tell the story of a man who loses his head, you have to show the head being cut off. Otherwise it's just a dirty joke without a punch line.'
1971 (on *Macbeth*)

Above left: Catherine Deneuve wanders through her desolate apartment in the grip of hallucinatory madness. *Repulsion* (1964), made in Britain, was Polanski's first film in the English language, and indicated the director's gift for drawing superb performances from actresses. Miss Deneuve was not previously noted for her acting ability.

he had already decided to settle in the West. The first offer he received was to contribute the Dutch episode, 'The Diamond Necklace', to a French omnibus movie, *The Best Swindles In The World*. Another of his short fables, this one was more advanced technically, filmed in Amsterdam in 1963 from a script by the director and his French collaborator, Gerard Brach. It revolved around an attractive French girl, who lives only for the moment. She appears to have no deeper feelings other than reacting spontaneously to whatever is happening around her – stealing a sports car and just as suddenly abandoning it, making a fool of a middle-aged businessman, swindling a jewellery shop out of an expensive necklace, which she impulsively exchanges for a parrot, and is last seen strolling happily off with the parrot perched on her shoulder.

This existential heroine with no past and no future provides an interesting link between the wife in *Knife In The Water*, and the rather more deadly character played by Catherine Deneuve in *Repulsion*. Filmed in England in 1964, again from a Polanski-Brach script, there is an awkwardness to the dialogue and to some of the acting in the opening reels which betrays Roman's lack of familiarity with the language. But the movie takes on a new life in the second half when the disturbed heroine is left alone in her apartment. As she lapses further into insanity, with occasional violent outbursts which leave two male visitors dead, Polanski succeeds superbly in making the horror seem totally real and convincing, aided by a remarkable performance from Miss Deneuve. His use of the apartment setting is particularly effective, conveying the claustrophobic, even threatening, feeling of the rooms and corridors, mixing naturalistic details of neglect – the decomposing rabbit's head, the spilled sugar, and so on – with her fantasies of giant cracks opening in the walls, then

of the walls growing hands which clutch at her as a kind of extension of her own violent and bloody nightmares.

Attracted to the quality of the American cinema as a film student, Polanski the fully-fledged film-maker enjoyed giving a modern and original treatment to such traditional American genres as the psychological horror movie – *Repulsion* owes an obvious debt to Hitchcock's *Psycho* (Paramount, 1960), for example – or the psychological thriller. In his second British-made feature, *Cul-De-Sac*, filmed in 1965, Polanski and Brach reworked the familiar theme of the gangster on the run – here played by veteran American character actor Lionel Stander – and taking refuge at an isolated house. Here Polanski demonstrated a new visual and technical assurance blended with qualities found in earlier films, his black and offbeat sense of humour, his ability to work on a small

Left: Lionel Stander (left) and Irish actor Jack MacGowran in *Cul-De-Sac* (1965), a bizarre black comedy in which Catherine Deneuve's sister, Françoise Dorleac, was the female lead opposite Donald Pleasance. Future star Jacqueline Bissett (billed as Jackie) also had a small part in this film.

Below: John Cassavetes and Mia Farrow in *Rosemary's Baby* (1968), the director's highly successful screen version of Ira Levin's terrifying novel. Polanski drew a marvellous performance from Miss Farrow, but it was the veteran Ruth Gordon (as the kindly seeming neighbour who is really chief witch) who picked up an Oscar for the movie.

who became his regular girlfriend, then his second wife the following year.

The movie enjoyed only a limited cult following, and Polanski was angry over the fact that it had been taken away from him and cut by twenty minutes. But he was soon back at work on his first Hollywood movie, *Rosemary's Baby*, which was to prove the biggest commercial success of his career. He was Oscar-nominated for his script adaptation of Ira Levin's novel about a pregnant young wife (Mia Farrow) who fears that she is the victim of devil-worshippers in modern day New York. Though Polanski's atmospheric use of the main apartment setting recalled his work on *Repulsion*, the film appeared less a personal expression than the product of a strong team effort from a fine cast and crew. Having always been bothered by the problem of getting onto film exactly what he saw through his viewfinder, the diminutive Polanski made a great discovery: 'Besides this cameraman's willingness to understand me and follow my ideas, he was hardly any taller than I am. And then I understood... On *Macbeth* (1971) I have a camera operator exactly my size, and that works wonders, because it means he sees the world the way I see the world.'

In 1969 Polanski was shattered by the horrific and brutal murder of his pregnant wife and three of his friends by the Manson gang in LA while he was in London working on a script. Because of the violence depicted in some of his films, his unconventional life style and his past reputation as a playboy, he was viciously and unjustly attacked in the press. And the attacks continued when he returned to work and created a characteristically bloody movie version of *Macbeth*. An expensively mounted and well-crafted production (financed by 'Playboy' magazine), it suffered from the lightweight casting of the two leads, Jon Finch and Francesca Annis, though the conception of the Macbeths as so youthful was refreshingly original. An ephemeral Italian comedy *What?* (1973) appeared like a

movie version of the 'Playboy' comic strip 'Little Annie Fanny' about the sexual adventures of a busty young American girl who keeps losing her clothes. It was Polanski at less than his best, but he bounced back in 1974 with his most impressive and memorable picture of the 70s, *Chinatown*. Again backed by producer Bob Evans and Paramount (who had financed *Rosemary's Baby*) he proved that his reputation as a talented perfectionist who pays scrupulous attention to every detail in his movies was well earned, and that he could still produce impressive results. Here he succeeded in bringing the world of the 30s private eye stunningly to life on the screen, enhanced by Oscar-nominated performances from Jack Nicholson and Faye Dunaway and an Oscar-winning original script from Robert Towne. The film was nominated for eleven awards in all, including Best Picture and director.

Finding himself between major productions, Polanski put together a bizarre little horror thriller, *The Tenant*, which he made in France in 1976, and in which he starred. Then disaster struck once again. In 1977 he was convicted in California of

having sex with an underage girl. Fleeing to France he managed to find backing for a multi-million dollar version of Thomas Hardy's 'Tess of the D'Urbervilles'. *Tess* (1978) was a starring vehicle for his teenage girlfriend, Nastassia Kinski, and a visually impressive production which helped to restore him to favour and earned further Oscar nominations for Best Picture and director. Miss Kinski went on to stardom, and the film demonstrated conclusively that Polanski's talent as a film-maker was unaffected by the problems of his private life.

Left: The diminutive Polanski at work with Jon Finch for a scene in *Macbeth* (1971). Visually breathtaking and extremely violent and bloody, this screen Shakespeare was indisputably entertaining.

Below: Jack Nicholson as a private investigator in *Chinatown* (1974), gets his nostril slit for poking his nose in where it is unwelcome. Wielding the blade is Polanski, who played a small role in, as well as directing, this much acclaimed but really rather pretentious drama thriller.

Left: The young German actress, Nastassia Kinski, played the quintessentially English *Tess* (1978), against breathtaking French locations which served as Thomas Hardy's Wessex. Here, the tragic heroine nurses her illegitimate baby.

SYDNEY POLLACK

Born South Bend, Indiana, 1 July 1934

One of the most consistent and commercially successful of American directors throughout the 70s and early 80s, Sydney Pollack is best known for his ability to give a popular appeal to serious subjects. His pictures have attacked the commercialism of advertising and the exploitative qualities of so-called investigative journalism, and have recalled the plight of ordinary people crushed by the 30s Depression. But, unfortunately, his movies are generally more form than substance and he rarely succeeds in penetrating beneath the surface of characters or situations. In *The Way We Were* (Columbia, 1973), for example, he attempted to present a radical view of American society and politics from the late 30s through the early, McCarthyite, 50s, but the movie is best remembered for its Oscar-winning score and its theme song as sung by Barbra Streisand who played the left-wing heroine. On the other hand, when not trying too hard to appear significant, Pollack has often been at his best with genre pictures – Westerns, thrillers and, most recently, comedy. *Tootsie* (Columbia, 1982) was undoubtedly the highlight of his career and a tremendous hit with critics and audiences alike.

Sydney first trained as an actor at New York's Neighborhood Playhouse under Sanford Meisner, then served for a time as Meisner's assistant and achieved a moderate success acting on stage and on TV during the 50s. He appeared on 'Playhouse 90', 'Alfred Hitchcock Presents' and 'Ben Casey' and, by the early 60s, had begun directing for TV as well. He played opposite Robert Redford in the latter's first movie, *War Hunt* (UA, 1962), then began directing features himself, beginning with the human interest drama *The Slender Thread* (Paramount, 1965), followed by a Tennessee Williams adaptation, *This Property Is Condemned* (Paramount, 1966) starring Redford and Natalie Wood. These were competent but unmemorable works, and Pollack did rather better with a pair starring Burt Lancaster: *The Scalphunters* filmed for UA in 1967 was an entertaining, offbeat Western co-starring Shelley Winters, and Ossie Davis as an educated ex-slave heading for Mexico, while *Castle Keep* (Columbia, 1969) was a strangely surreal World War II battle picture blending action with fantasy in such a way that one was never quite sure where one ended and the other began. Pollack then achieved his first major success later that same year with *They Shoot Horses, Don't They?* starring Jane Fonda. Justly famous for its recreation of a gruelling 30s dance marathon, the film owed a lot to the original novel by Horace McCoy and, in spite of his generally heavy handed direction, it earned for Sydney his first Oscar nomination.

Newly established as a 'prestige' director, Pollack rejoined superstar Robert Redford in 1971 for *Jeremiah Johnson* (Warner Bros.), their first film together in five years, re-establishing their close working relationship which has lasted ever since. They have made six pictures together in all, most recently *Out Of Africa* (Universal, 1985) co-starring Meryl Streep, about the life of writer Karen Blixen (Isak Dinesen). Pollack clearly depends on good subjects and strong scripts to produce memorable results. Thus, *Jeremiah Johnson* – shot in stunning mountain locations in Utah – bears the imprint of John Milius, who based his script on two books about a true mythic character of the old West, a lone fur trapper and 'mountain man' of the early 1800s who married an Indian squaw. *Three Days Of The Condor* (Paramount, 1975), scripted by Lorenzo Semple Jr, was a useful entry in the mid-70s cycle of political conspiracy thrillers, but it was Robert Mitchum whose characteristically craggy features and low-keyed style perfectly suited *The Yakuza* (Warner Bros., 1974). Pollack's most effective thriller, set in Japan, it was scripted by Paul Schrader and Robert Towne. Pollack and Redford had a hit with *The Electric Horseman* (Columbia, 1979), bland and pre-packaged though it was, but Sydney finally got it all together with *Tootsie* in 1982, aided by a witty script from Larry Gelbart and Murray Schisgal, an amazing performance from Dustin Hoffman as the unemployed actor whose life is transformed and complicated when he makes it as an actress; and with fine support from Jessica Lange, and from Pollack himself in an amusing cameo role as Tootsie's agent.

'People often ask me, "Don't you ever want to do a picture with unknowns?" I would like to try it some time, but I don't feel it's a hardship working with stars. Stars are like thoroughbreds. Yes, it's a little more dangerous with them.'
1983

Left: Michael Sarrazin and Jane Fonda may look a little tired, but it's early days yet in the dance marathon contest. *They Shoot Horses, Don't They?* (1969) earned Pollack his first Oscar nomination and Jane Fonda hers.

Below: The director rehearses a scene for *The Way We Were* (1973) with Barbra Streisand.

Bottom: The lady, Dorothy, is actually Dustin Hoffman in Pollack's hilarious and penetrating study of New York show biz, *Tootsie* (1982), in which a talented but struggling actor is forced into drag in order to get a job.

BOB RAFELSON

Born New York City, 1934 (or 1935)

With his extremely personal style of directing, his preference for working in intimate conditions on a small scale and developing a close working relationship with his cast and crew in a manner more usually associated with European rather than American film-making, Bob Rafelson occupies a special place among the younger generation of American directors who first emerged during the 60s. As he has pointed out, 'I shoot in continuity, and I pay very close attention to what the characters in the movie are telling me. . . I place a great deal of faith in the collaboration of the entire company and in the atmosphere in which I am shooting.' Thus, he prefers working with a regular group of collaborators – three of his five features were made for the same company,

completing his degree, then found work in TV where he began to make a name for himself as a writer on the highly regarded 'Play of the Week' series during the early 60s. The big turning point in his career came when he joined with producer Bert Schneider in originating The Monkees TV series. He served as co-producer and writer, and got his first opportunity to direct, then made his feature debut as writer-director of the Monkees movie *Head* (1968) with Jack Nicholson as his co-writer. A lively and fast moving spoof, following the pattern set by Richard Lester with the Beatles, it included in-joke references to a variety of movie genres including war and harem films and a tribute to the Minnelli musical.

Sensitive to Nicholson's thus far un-

for best picture, director and actress, *Five Easy Pieces* was nominated by the Academy for Best Picture, actor, supporting actress and screenplay Oscars.)

Unfortunately, Bob and Jack were less successful with *The King Of Marvin Gardens* (1972) which followed. Conceived by Rafelson as a 'comic nightmare' set, appropriately, in the glitzy wasteland of Atlantic City, the film was far too offbeat for the American public, mixing drama, comedy and violence in a distinctly non-naturalistic manner. Virtually the same comments could be applied to *Stay Hungry* (UA, 1976), which provided Jeff Bridges with one of his best roles as the confused hero who becomes involved with some shady property speculators and a strange group of characters who run a local health club. Rafelson's quite original approach to the filming of the

Above: Scatman Crothers (left) and Jack Nicholson in *The King Of Marvin Gardens* (1972), a dense fable which did not attract a favourable reception.

Left: Director Rafelson (foreground) with star Jack Nicholson on location making *Five Easy Pieces* (1970), the movie which held so much promise for the director who, in the event, has made only three films since.

BBS Productions, and he worked with Jack Nicholson on four of them. In fact, Rafelson was the most important producer-director connected with the short-lived BBS company which he helped to found in 1968 with Bert Schneider and Steve Blauner. BBS also produced movies directed by Peter Bogdanovich, Jack Nicholson and Henry Jaglom during 1971-72 (all distributed through Columbia). The phenomenal sucess of *Easy Rider* (1969) sustained BBS for a time, and the company achieved its most prestigious critical success with Rafelson's *Five Easy Pieces* (1970), which was also a modest box-office hit. But Bob has only directed two features since the company folded.

A much travelled young man, Bob saw a lot of the US and Europe and tried a number of jobs before he attended Dartmouth College. He dropped out before

tapped potential as an actor, Rafelson recommended him to Dennis Hopper for *Easy Rider*, then cast him as the lead in *Five Easy Pieces* the following year opposite Karen Black. Her dumb but likeable waitress proved the perfect foil to bring out Jack's cynical, world-weary qualities, and the film marked a major breakthrough for both of them, as for Rafelson, whose intensely personal concentration on the characters and their troubled relationships, to the exclusion of all else – there is hardly any plot – served his actors well. A landmark in its expression of late 60s disillusionment with American society, Nicholson's role as Bobby Dupea, drifter, loner and ex-classical pianist who has rejected his middle class background, demonstrated for the first time that he was a star of the first magnitude who could carry a film on his own. (In addition to the New York Critics' awards

prison movie *Brubaker* in 1979 was so disliked by the studio (20th Century-Fox) that he was sacked. He has only made one film since, a characteristically intense and very powerful version of James M. Cain's steamy tale of passion and violence, *The Postman Always Rings Twice* (Lorimar/Paramount, 1980) starring Jack Nicholson and Jessica Lange.

Above: Sally Field and Jeff Bridges in *Stay Hungry* (1976). Miss Field went on to win two Best Actress Oscars – for *Norma Rae* (1979) and *Places In The Heart* (1984), proving Rafelson's nose for spotting talent.

KAREL REISZ

Born Ostrava, Czechoslovakia, 21 July 1926

One of the sadly wasted talents of the British cinema, Karel Reisz has only had the opportunity to direct eight feature films in twenty-six years. Like so many British directors he has had to depend on American financing for most of his pictures and has never had the kind of smash hit – like his friend Tony Richardson with *Tom Jones* – which would have helped him to appear more 'bankable' in the eyes of the big American companies. A thoughtful, intelligent director, he has frequently been faced with the choice of directing flawed or otherwise unsuitable projects, like MGM's misconceived remake of *Night Must Fall* (1964), or not filming at all. However, during recent years he has made a mild comeback. Although his excellent post-Vietnam thriller, *Who'll Stop The Rain* (UA, aka *Dog Soldiers*, 1978), filmed in the US and based on Robert Stone's novel 'Dog Soldiers' was sadly neglected, he had the most favourable critical and commercial response to his film version of John Fowles' *The French Lieutenant's Woman* (UA, 1981) since his first feature over twenty years earlier.

That first feature was *Saturday Night And Sunday Morning* (1960). It grew directly out of Reisz's involvement with the Free Cinema documentary movement during the 50s and made his name, along with that of its star, Albert Finney, on both sides of the Atlantic. A Czech-born Jew, Karel had arrived in England at the age of twelve, shortly before the outbreak of World War II. He studied at Cambridge after the war and worked briefly as a school-teacher before turning to journalism and film criticism during the early 50s. He completed a notable book, 'The Technique of Film Editing', and became increasingly interested in film-making while working as programmes officer for the National Film Theatre. *Momma Don't Allow* was his first documentary short, made in collaboration with Tony Richardson in 1955 about the young people at a North London jazz club. It was one of a group of shorts directed by Reisz, Richardson, Lindsay Anderson, and other young directors in what came to be known as the Free Cinema movement. It represented a modest attempt at independent, creative film-making, presenting an authentic and unglamourised treatment of British working class life in a manner which the directors were all to develop in their later features.

Thus, two years after completing a second short, *We Are The Lambeth Boys* (1958), about a group of working class boys in a London youth club, Reisz travelled to Nottingham to shoot *Saturday Night And Sunday Morning*. Adapted from the novel by Alan Sillitoe, it made a tremendous impact at the time of its initial release for its accuracy in bringing a particular slice of contemporary working class reality to the screen. The director was less successful with the rebellious, anarchist hero of *Morgan, A Suitable Case For Treatment* (1966), based on David

Mercer's TV play. Though superbly incarnated on the screen by the gaunt and lanky David Warner, the picture's social comment appeared too glib, and its fantasy techniques derivative. Two years later, in 1968, Morgan's ex-wife, Vanessa Redgrave, was transformed into Reisz's screen *Isadora* (Universal), marking a new departure for the director, here given a big budget, colour and an international star cast for the first time. Unfortunately, the film was neither satisfactory as a serious character study of Isadora Duncan, the innovative dancer with the scandalous life style, nor as a popular, glossy entertainment set against a colourful 20s background, and it was so horribly cut down by the American distributors that it never had a chance in the US.

Almost ten years later Reisz made a comeback with *Who'll Stop The Rain* starring Nick Nolte and Tuesday Weld, followed by *The French Lieutenant's Woman* scripted by Harold Pinter and starring Meryl Streep with Jeremy Irons. A tasteful, atmospheric and well acted costumer which clearly betrayed its literary origins, it at least served to restore Karel Reisz to favour, and he has recently been back to the US to direct Jessica Lange in *Sweet Dreams* (1985), the true story of 50s country singer Patsy Cline.

Top: The gutsy, exciting Rachel Roberts starred opposite then newcomer, Albert Finney, in *Saturday Night And Sunday Morning* (1960), as a married woman with whom he, a young factory worker, has an affair. The film was a watershed in the British cinema's change of attitude to sex, which had begun with *Room At The Top* (1958).

Above: Director Reisz (centre) with David Warner (right), shooting a scene at London Zoo for *Morgan, A Suitable Case For Treatment* (1966).

Left: The star waits patiently while the director lines up a shot. Meryl Streep, Karel Reisz – *The French Lieutenant's Woman* (1981).

'I used to think the promotion of a film didn't matter. But the first thing the audience sees are your advertisements and it conditions them.'
1981

TONY RICHARDSON

Real Name Cecil Antonio Richardson **Born** Shipley, England, 5 June 1928

Tony Richardson's career is one of the most curious in contemporary film history. Following a distinguished series of successes in the English theatre – at the very moment in the late 50s when it shifted gears from amiable drawing-room comedies to a concern with what came to be known as 'kitchen sink realism' – he effected a relatively smooth transition to the screen and reached his peak with a film that travelled around the world, *Tom Jones* (UA, 1963). Thereafter, with very few exceptions, his work has ranged from the mediocre to the frankly dreadful; and he has steadily regressed from being one of the industry's 'hottest' properties to being a director from whom little is expected.

Richardson studied at Oxford, where he was a memorable Dramatic Society president. On graduating, he was offered a producer's job at the BBC, but, concurrently, he had already become involved with both the theatre and the cinema, writing reviews for the magazine 'Sight And Sound' and, in 1955, co-directing (with Karel Reisz) the short *Momma Don't Allow*, a key film in the burgeoning Free Cinema movement. The following year he achieved fame with his staging, at the Royal Court Theatre, of John Osborne's epoch-making drama 'Look Back In Anger', which established a productive collaboration with the dramatist and helped to identify Richardson with the so-called 'Angry Young Men' of the period. It was with the intention of filming the play that he and Osborne founded their own production company, Woodfall, in 1958. His adaptation of *Look Back In Anger* (1959), with Richard Burton and Mary Ure, though somewhat stagey, heralded a promising cinematic talent. This was confirmed a year later with another Osborne adaptation, *The Entertainer*, in which Laurence Olivier reprised his brilliant, award-winning portrayal of the tired, down-at-heel music hall comedian Archie Rice. The film's cultural prestige was such that Richardson was invited to Hollywood by Fox and offered the chance to direct *Sanctuary* (1961), with Lee Remick, Yves Montand and Bradford Dillman. The result was widely acknowledged as a disaster: the director was totally out of his depth with Faulkner's steamy Deep South melodrama, and the film was bereft of rhythm and of conviction. Richardson hurried back to his native patch to direct *A Taste Of Honey* in the same year, from Shelagh Delaney's drama of an unprepossessing young girl from the North of England (Rita Tushingham) and her painful evolution into womanhood. By now influenced by France's New Wave, and Truffaut in particular, the director's visual style had considerably loosened up: the location shooting impressed as novel and invigorating, the performers were uniformly excellent and the film, despite a vein of meretricious modishness, was Richardson's first to remain watchable today. *The Loneliness Of The Long Distance*

Runner, from Alan Sillitoe's novel, which followed in 1962, possessed the same faults and the same virtues, but also introduced the haunted, emaciated Tom Courtenay to the screen in the title role and demonstrated that Richardson had the capacity to transform a literary work into a genuinely filmic artefact.

Yet its success was as nothing compared to that enjoyed by *Tom Jones*, cunningly adapted from Fielding's classic novel by John Osborne, and starring Albert Finney, Susannah York, Edith Evans, and a host of gloriously eccentric English character actors. Though it could be criticised for its complacent deployment of a battery of fashionable cinematic tricks, and though it was beyond question a jocular travesty of a great novel, *Tom Jones* appeared such a joyous anomaly in the prevailing drabness of the English cinema that it would be churlish to take issue with it. On the wave of its

phenomenal box-office returns and Oscars for Best Picture, director and script, Richardson once more succumbed to Hollywood's lure and once more took a tumble: despite an amazing cast (including Rod Steiger, John Gielgud, Dana Andrews and Liberace), his version of Evelyn Waugh's witty satire of the funeral industry, *The Loved One* (1956) was as limp as a sodden rag. The débâcle had begun with a vengeance: two risibly pretentious adaptations of Genet and Duras, *Mademoiselle* (1966) and *The Sailor From Gibraltar* (1967), an Australian folk-epic with Mick Jagger, *Ned Kelly* (1970), a lame adaptation of a Dick Francis thriller, *Dead Cert* (1973) and, most embarrassingly, a stillborn endeavour to recapture his former triumph with a leadenly larky version of another Fielding novel, *Joseph Andrews* (1977). Only his quite poignant recounting of *The Charge Of The Light Brigade* (1968), with Trevor Howard and the director's former wife, Vanessa Redgrave, and an appealing attempt to make cinematic sense of John Irving's whimsical bestseller, *The Hotel New Hampshire* (1984) starring Jody Foster, could possibly be said to even hint at his early promise.

Above: Rita Tushingham (left) and Dora Bryan, mother and daughter in *A Taste Of Honey* (1961), one of Richardson's several contributions to the 'kitchen sink' realism which was popular at that time.

Left: Borstal boy Tom Courtenay allows public school opponent James Fox to pass him in *The Loneliness Of The Long Distance Runner* (1962), one of Richardson's early successes.

Below: Director Richardson (left) dressed for a bit part in *Tom Jones* (1963) talks to Albert Finney during a break.

MARTIN RITT

Born New York City, 2 March 1920

A solid, serious, well-meaning director of 'quality' pictures, Martin Ritt has occupied the position of Hollywood's favourite 'committed' liberal director for almost thirty years. More concerned with characters and themes than with filmic style or visuals, his films reflect his strong social conscience, dealing with racial and political intolerance, with the rights of workers and the underprivileged, both black and white. If his mildly leftish solutions often appear naive and simplistic, yet the pictures remain interesting for their strong dramatic qualities and frequently outstanding performances. He has developed good working relationships with such stars as Paul Newman, Sidney Poitier and Joanne Woodward early in his career and, more recently, Sally Field. For his scripts he has depended on favourite writers like Walter Bernstein, and the husband and wife team of Irving Ravetch and Harriet Frank, each of whom has worked on a number of his movies, while he has been fortunate to have James Wong Howe as his cameraman during the 60s, and John Alonzo from 1972 on to lend his films some visual distinction.

Educated at Elon College and St John's University, Marty joined the left-wing Group Theatre in New York as an actor and first appeared on the stage in Clifford Odets' 'Golden Boy' in 1937. After a break for war service, he established himself as a stage director during the late 40s, then worked as a director-producer and sometimes actor on TV during 1948-51, mainly associated with the 'Danger' series. In 1951 he was blacklisted due to his previous leftwing activities – he had briefly been a member of the Communist Party as a teenager – and was thus unable to find work on TV. This was a difficult period for him. He returned to the theatre and occasionally lectured at the Actors' Studio where he worked with Paul Newman and Joanne Woodward, among others.

Finally, in 1956, after Ritt had directed a play by Robert Alan Aurthur, they began collaborating on a number of other projects which led to Ritt being offered his first feature film, *Edge Of The City* (aka *A Man Is Ten Feet Tall*) scripted by Aurthur for MGM later that same year. A generally weak imitation of the Kazan-Schulberg *On The Waterfront* (Columbia, 1954), it starred John Cassavetes who gave one of his most mannered Method performances opposite Sidney Poitier, who was rather better as the sympathetic black dockyard foreman. Hired by Fox in 1957-58 where he directed three movies starring Joanne Woodward, Ritt had his first modest success with *The Long Hot Summer* scripted by Ravetch and Frank from stories by William Faulkner. A superior example of the kind of larger-than-life hokum being dished up by Fox in CinemaScope and glossy colour during those years, it was quite enjoyable if one didn't take it too seriously. Orson Welles gave an extraordinary, over-the-top performance, but it was the more

conventionally solid acting of Paul Newman and Joanne Woodward which reflected Ritt's qualities as a director, both here and in *Paris Blues* (UA, 1961).

Having already directed eight features of variable quality, Ritt finally had his first big success with *Hud* (Paramount), more serious (and somewhat pretentious) and less fun than *The Long Hot Summer*, but benefitting immensely from the stylish, Oscar-winning camerawork of James Wong Howe (in black-and-white Panavision). A modern Western filmed on location in Texas in 1962, the literary conventions of a rather too neatly structured plot and balancing of characters and relationships reflected its origins in a novel by Larry McMurtry, author of 'The Last Picture Show'. The most original quality of the movie, however, was the casting of Paul Newman as the charming but nasty and selfish anti-hero, Hud. He was in peak form and more than ably supported by Patricia Neal and Melvyn Douglas, both of whom won supporting Oscars, while Ritt received the only directing nomination of his career.

Above: Joanne Woodward and Paul Newman in *The Long Hot Summer* (1958). The stars married in real life that same year and have remained so since.

Left: Paul Newman with Patricia Neal in *Hud* (1963). Miss Neal, an actress of superior quality, is also known for her courage in overcoming severe illness – strokes, semi-paralysis and impaired speech – to make a triumphant Oscar-nominated comeback in *The Subject Was Roses* (1968).

Above: Richard Burton was *The Spy Who Came In From The Cold* (1965). The actor was Oscar-nominated for his excellent performance, as he was for six other films. Amazingly, he never won the coveted statuette before his tragically premature death in 1984.

In a rare venture abroad Ritt went to London in 1965 to direct his last black-and-white film, a suitably low-keyed example of the then fashionable spy thriller genre. Based on the John Le Carré best-seller and starring Richard Burton in one of his grimmest and most impressive roles, *The Spy Who Came In From The Cold* (Paramount) added further to Ritt's reputation as a serious director who was capable of extending himself into traditional genres. This was confirmed by his first venture into the old West the fol-

lowing year (1966). 'Paul Newman is *Hombre*' read the posters, forcing audiences to make the connection with *Hud* four years earlier. This time Diane Cilento played the role of the earthy, mature woman attracted to Newman, who gave a cool and convincing performance as a young loner who had been carried off as a child and raised by Apaches, and still prefers to dress and behave like an Indian. Going one step beyond the innovation of 50s Westerns whereby the Indian was treated with some respect on

'I don't think I'm a great artist, come to that, I'm not wholly sure whether film is an art-form at all . . . I'd like to be valued as a professional who knows his job and to hell with pretentions.'
1977

Left: Director Martin Ritt (centre ground level) on location with cast and crew of *Hombre* (1966). James Wong Howe, who photographed the picture, is kneeling centre foreground of the platform.

Above: Paul Winfield (left) and Kevin Hooks, father and son with their faithful hound *Sounder* (1972).

Below: Sally Field (left) and director Ritt at work on a scene for *Norma Rae* (1979), an impassioned socially conscious film about the rights of female factory workers.

the screen, here Ritt presented his 'white Indian' character as more intelligent, resourceful, sensitive and moral, in fact superior to the whites in every way. (The racial theme is not unlike that developed with Sidney Poitier as the highly intelligent black detective in Norman Jewison's *In The Heat Of The Night* (UA), released a few months after *Hombre* in 1967.)

With a pair of modest hits behind him – *Hud* and *Hombre* – Ritt was given the biggest budget of his career for *The Molly Maguires* (Paramount, 1969). A stickler for authenticity, he took his cast and crew to the coal mining region of Pennsylvania where the original events of the story had taken place. A strong, dramatic and sometimes violent movie about the true hardships experienced by immigrant coalminers in the 1870s, and the terrorist tactics employed by a small, secret group to improve their conditions, it had all the ingredients for success, including exceptional camerawork from James Wong Howe, and the popular Sean Connery as the star. But it turned out surprisingly dull and unappealing and was Ritt's biggest box-office flop.

Since his survival in Hollywood depended on his proven ability to make his films on relatively modest budgets and thus ensure that most of them earned a small profit, this failure represented a major setback. Fortunately Ritt was able to bounce back immediately with a boxing drama, *The Great White Hope* (20th Century-Fox, 1970). Based on a play version of the true story of black heavyweight champ Jack Johnson, it dealt with the kind of racial theme which appealed to the director, and benefitted from a pair of Oscar-nominated performances from James Earl Jones and Jane Alexander. Then, in 1972, he enjoyed the most commercially successful year of his career with his two biggest hits released back to back. *Sounder* (for 20th Century-Fox) was a typical example of a well meaning Ritt movie, made with the

intention of showing the plight of a black sharecropper family in the South during the 30s Depression. Here, as in *White Hope*, Ritt was able to take advantage of Hollywood's brief interest in movies about blacks in the early 70s. But although the film captured the authentic flavour of the period, filmed on location in Louisiana, the story was overly-sentimentalised with only the performances of Cicely Tyson and Paul Winfield to recommend it. *Pete 'N Tillie* (for Universal) started out as a slightly offbeat and witty comedy, became progressively more serious, then turned sour with the death of the couple's son and fizzled out weakly in the final reels. (Walter Matthau and Carol Burnett were the stars.)

In *Conrack* (20th Century-Fox, 1974) the likeable Jon Voight proved that he was

not a strong enough actor to carry a picture on his own. It was another typical Ritt subject about the efforts of an idealistic young teacher to make contact with a group of underprivileged school kids in the South. But surely the biggest disappointment of the 70s was Ritt and writer Walter Bernstein's slack handling of the theme of 50s blacklisting in *The Front* (Columbia, 1976). Both of them, as well as actor Zero Mostel had experienced the blacklist at first hand. A moderately entertaining film, with Woody Allen in a rare serious role, it failed to do justice to the subject. Ritt had his last big success with *Norma Rae* (20th Century-Fox, 1979), for which Sally Field won an Oscar for her performance as a gutsy union organiser in the South, based, like *Conrack*, on a true story.

NICOLAS ROEG

Born London, 15 August 1928

If one were to see Nicolas Roeg's controversial and imaginative films without knowing anything about the man who had directed them, one would probably be quite surprised to learn that he is in his late fifties, is the product of an extremely conventional and orthodox film background, and spent over twenty years in the film industry before he was given his first opportunity to direct. Somehow he managed to maintain his enthusiasm, integrity and originality in spite of a system which encourages conformity, and he emerged during the early 70s as one of the most individualistic and highly regarded of British directors.

Nic in fact got his first film job after army service during the war, working briefly in the MGM (British) dubbing rooms, then as a clapper boy. He eventually graduated to camera operator and was employed for a short time as a lighting cameraman in TV before he established himself as a leading film cameraman in the 60s on such pictures as Corman's *The Masque Of The Red Death* (1964), Truffaut's *Fahrenheit 451* (Universal, 1966) and John Schlesinger's *Far From The Madding Crowd* (MGM, 1967). He also had some experience as a second unit director and scriptwriter behind him by the time he began his first feature as co-director and cameraman – *Performance*, for Warner Bros. (1970).

Working within a relatively modest $1 million budget and shooting much of the film in sequence, Roeg and his co-director and writer, Donald Cammell, succeeded in injecting an imaginatively conceived contemporary relevance into the familiar theme of the gangster on the run. The first half of the picture was astonishing for its authentic and violent depiction of London's gangster underworld (provoking a number of censor cuts), while the later scenes were set in the house of ex-pop star Turner (Mick Jagger) and his two bisexual girlfriends. When Chas (James Fox) turns up unexpectedly, he enters into an extraordinary, enclosed world of eroticism, pop culture and drug culture. And when encouraged to become involved in the bizarre games

played by the threesome, he finds that he is losing his identity under the influence of drugs, and undergoing a strange exchange of roles with Turner. A remarkable and original work which gave rise to much controversy at the time of its release, it was followed by a rather more conventional, but equally effective, movie set in the Australian outback. Here an English girl (Jenny Agutter) and her younger brother (played by Roeg's son) are stranded in the bush by the sudden death of their father and are forced to undergo a variety of hardships in their efforts to find their way back to civilisation. A strange and at times almost surreal work, it was given a special poignancy by the appearance of a young aborigine boy on *Walkabout* (1970) whose primitive

Above: Bewigged and befuddled – doubtless by drugs – James Fox (centre) is confronted by a pair of 'nasties' in Roeg's psychedelic first feature, *Performance* (1970).

Left: Tormented with grief, Donald Sutherland carries his drowned daughter back to the house in *Don't Look Now* (1973).

efforts to develop a relationship with the girl are doomed to failure.

From the bleak and arid Australian desert Roeg next turned to a canal-lined, watery Venice for *Don't Look Now* (Paramount, 1973), a powerful suspense

'One thing about Nic is that he has never replaced a writer on a screenplay. That comes from loyalty and real conviction about the film he wants to make. In Eureka many of the images were suggested by me. And many of the lines of dialogue were suggested by him.'

Paul Mayersburg (scriptwriter) in 'Sight And Sound' (1982)

drama with supernatural overtones, based on the story by Daphne du Maurier. The film is best remembered for its powerful visual qualities and a fine performance by Donald Sutherland. A sub-plot concerning his wife (Julie Christie) and a pair of psychic old ladies was more cloying than convincing. But Roeg was at his most visually inventive with the sci-fi drama, *The Man Who Fell To Earth* (1976), which starred David Bowie as the strange and sensitive alien of the title. His performance provided one further example of Roeg's special ability for working with non-professional actors and his preference for pop stars in particular, like Mick Jagger, and Art Garfunkel who starred in *Bad Timing* in 1979. Unfortunately, this film and *Eureka* (UA, 1983), demonstrated a tendency to concentrate on the visuals while neglecting serious weaknesses in plot and characterisation. Both these and his most recent production, *Insignificance* (1985), co-starred his American actress girlfriend, Theresa Russell, who can be seen to embody the important erotic themes which run through all his works.

Above: Director Roeg (foreground) and actor Buck Henry during the making of the technically skilful, somewhat bizarre sci-fi movie, *The Man Who Fell To Earth* (1976).

Left: David Bowie (right), here with Cindy Clark, was *The Man Who Fell To Earth*.

KEN RUSSELL

Born Southampton, England, 3 July 1927

A colourful, flamboyant and controversial figure, Ken Russell and his always imaginative, sometimes outrageous, movies have generally received a bad press. The reaction of critics and reviewers has ranged from merely nasty to the excessively vindictive, while there is also an intellectually snobbish approach which considers Russell's works vulgar, degrading to their subjects and unworthy of serious comment. These charges are not untrue when he indulges in his worst excesses but, at his best, this *enfant terrible* is a uniquely imaginative and stimulating interpreter of the artist's neurosis. Although his pictures have been noticeably variable in quality, one would hardly realise it from the way they have tended to be somewhat arbitrarily lumped together as 'Ken Russell movies'. He was in top form relatively early in his feature film-making career, and was most prolific during the early 70s when he was given a fairly free hand in turning out much of his best work, including *The Music Lovers* (UA) and *The Devils* (Warner Bros.), both released in 1971.

In spite of the fact that he is an instinctive and intuitive film-maker, it took Russell a long time to discover the cinema. He was in his thirties when he first began working in TV and fortyish by the time he had begun directing feature movies. After attending nautical school, he served – still a teenager – in the merchant navy, briefly tried the RAF, then studied dancing and did brief stints as a dancer and actor before taking up photography. He attended Southampton Technical College where he met his first wife, Shirley Kingdon, who would later serve as costume designer on all his films up to the late 70s when they separated. Establishing himself as a successful freelance photographer in the late 50s, Ken also developed a new interest in the cinema and completed three short films. Huw Wheldon at the BBC was sufficiently impressed by them to offer him a job turning out shorts, mainly on a range of arts subjects, for the 'Monitor' programme. He completed twenty-two of these little films averaging about fifteen minutes each, of which the best known was a slightly longer biographical documentary on Elgar in 1962. A cheaply made but imaginative visual treatment of the composer's life, it paid particular attention to how he was inspired by nature, a theme which appealed to Russell and allowed him to make use of some striking locations.

After a break to make his first feature, a conventional seaside comedy entitled *French Dressing* in 1963, Ken returned to the BBC to direct a new series of programmes, all concerning the lives of artists. Highly regarded at the time, they reflect Russell's major areas of interest and a control of subject matter which would desert him in certain later feature films. All but one were made in black-and-white, earned him his reputation and, together, form his most consistently impressive body of work. These included 'Dante's Inferno' (1967) starring Oliver

Reed as the poet Rossetti, filmed on location in the Lake District; 'Song Of Summer' (1968), a moving evocation of the life of Delius, with former ballet star, Christopher Gable, turned actor for the first time as the composer's amanuensis. Best of all, perhaps, was his film on the life and work of Isadora Duncan – a subject which, ironically, would be turned over to Karel Reisz for cinema treatment, without much success. The concluding TV work, in 1969, was also the most controversial, foreshadowing what was to come on the large screen: 'The Dance Of The Seven Veils: A Comic Strip In Seven Episodes On the Life of Richard Strauss' was Russell's only 60s TV film in colour, and was by turns outrageous and extravagant, making no attempt to nod in the direction of any documentary facts. It caused a furore on transmission and has never been shown again.

During these years Ken Russell had put together a more impressive body of TV work in his field than any other leading British director before or since, and used this extended apprenticeship as a launching pad for his subsequent career in the cinema. In 1967 he had directed his second – and undistinguished – feature, *Billion Dollar Brain*, adapted from Len Deighton with Michael Caine as Harry Palmer. Then, near the end of his TV career in 1968 he had an offer from the same company, United Artists, to make his first important feature, *Women In Love*, based on the D.H. Lawrence novel. It was a fairly successful, reasonably straightforward, colourfully photographed adaptation, and Russell enjoyed bringing the period to life on the screen,

Above: Oliver Reed and Glenda Jackson were Gerald and Gudrun, lovers in Russell's screen translation of D.H. Lawrence's *Women In Love* (1968). The film co-starred Alan Bates, Jennie Linden and Eleanor Bron.

helped by a variety of picturesque locations in Sheffield, Newcastle, Derbyshire and Switzerland. If his insight into the characters left something to be desired, this was offset by fine performances from Oliver Reed (one of his favourite actors) and Alan Bates who appeared together in a famous nude wrestling sequence, and Glenda Jackson who won her first Oscar. (The picture was also nominated for script and photography and Russell received his only nomination to date for directing.)

The success of *Women In Love* in 1969 made it possible for Russell to proceed with one of his own longstanding projects, a highly personalised film interpretation of the life of Tchaikovsky starring Richard Chamberlain as the homosexual

Below: Ken Russell (left) discusses a scene for *The Music Lovers* (1971) with his star, Richard Chamberlain, as Tchaikovsky. On the right is Kenneth Colley, who was featured as the famous composer's brother.

composer. He immediately launched himself into creating a vivid and entertaining Panavision fantasy, aided by an extraordinary performance from Glenda Jackson as Tchaikovsky's depraved and unbalanced wife, who ends up in an insane asylum – which called forth some intense and powerful imagery. Unfortunately, *The Music Lovers* was totally misunderstood by many of the critics, who seemed – particularly in America – to be incapable of appreciating the special vitality of Ken's direct and uncomplicated approach, and were perhaps offended by his rejection of the traditional clichéd image of the composer as an elevated and romantic figure. And they fared no better with *The Devils*, Russell's next film and his most brilliant cinematic achievement, but widely regarded as his most distasteful and offensive work. He found his ideal subject in the extraordinary true events which took place in 17th-century France as dramatised by John Whiting and in Aldous Huxley's 'The Devils Of Loudun'. It had all the ingredients for a modern exercise in Grand Guignol, including horrible deaths by plague, execution by fire, nuns who are 'possessed' with powerful sexual fantasies and the appalling tortures used to extract the devils. With its blend of violence, nudity, religious symbolism and sexual activity, and with fascinating political overtones relating to the policies of Cardinal Richelieu, here Russell was able to achieve a coherent blend of style and content. Art director Derek Jarman created an impressive stylised representation of the walled town of Loudun, and the film, with its effective use of monochromatic imagery, was visually very striking. The performances from a large cast, headed by Oliver Reed again, and Vanessa Redgrave, were remarkable.

Russell's third movie released in 1971, thus making it the peak year of his career, was *The Boy Friend* (MGM) from Sandy Wilson's hit stage musical made on a tiny budget and starring Twiggy and Christopher Gable. Originally a charming 20s pastiche, the director chose to extend the pastiche elements to include an ill-judged and sub-standard homage to Busby Berkeley. Then, taking a welcome break from the problems associated with large-scale and elaborate productions, Ken returned to the type of intimate biopic which recalled his early TV work with *Savage Messiah* (MGM, 1972), a modest, but lively and enjoyable portrait of the early life of the sculptor Henri Gaudier and his writer companion Sophie Brzeska. Returning to the world of extravagant musical biopics with *Mahler* in 1973 and *Lisztomania* (1975), Russell was unable to add anything new to the genre. Both were uneven works with the familiar mixture of symbolism, fantasy and eroticism, and missed their targets as often as not, suggesting that the director was beginning to repeat himself. This was confirmed by the embarrassing weaknesses of *Valentino* two years later. He did have one big success with his version of the rock opera *Tommy* (Stigwood/Columbia, 1975). Here his vivid imagery – a series of loosely linked set-pieces in comic strip style matched to the rock numbers of The Who – was regarded as more acceptable by the critics and did well at the box-office, too.

During more recent years Russell has had few offers in Britain and has attempted to revive his flagging career in the US with *Altered States* (Warner Bros., 1980) scripted by Paddy Chayefsky from his own novel, and the violent and erotic *Crimes Of Passion* (1984).

FRANKLIN SCHAFFNER

Born Tokyo, 30 May 1920

Franklin Schaffner is a director who, if judged by his best work alone, could fairly be considered as a solid, dependable craftsman of a type that has occupied the middle ground of Hollywood's artistry since the 30s. If judged by his less distinguished contributions to the medium, however, he must be considered little more than a journeyman, lacking in originality and thematic preoccupations.

The son of American missionaries based in Japan, he lived there until his father's death in 1936. Returning to the US with his widowed mother, he enrolled at Franklin and Marshall College, studied law at Columbia University, and saw service in the US Navy during World War II. After working briefly for 'March Of Time', Schaffner was hired to direct public affairs shows for CBS TV, then moved on to Studio One (live drama) and Ed Murrow's prestigious 'Person To Person' interview programme. Having made his name as a leading director of TV drama with such productions as 'Twelve Angry Men' and 'The Caine Mutiny Court Martial', he accepted an offer from Fox to direct Joanne Woodward in his competent but unremarkable first movie, *The Stripper*, in 1962. He fared better with *The Best Man* (UA,

1964), from Gore Vidal's witty, cynical and sometimes glib satire on the manners and *moeurs* of American politics. Working again in black-and-white, Schaffner brought a useful hint of TV news-reporting immediacy to the scenes of convention razzmatazz and handled well a superlative cast which included Henry Fonda, a malignant Cliff Robertson in one of his very best performances, and Lee Tracy, who was outstanding as a homespun ex-President dying of cancer. *The Best Man* won the top award at the 1964 Karlovy Vary Festival, no doubt in part because the East Europeans were gratified by its muckraking aspect.

Schaffner's following effort represented a total change of pace. *The War Lord*, made for Universal in 1965, and starring Charlton Heston, Richard Boone and the stage actor Maurice Evans, was a visually handsome and stiffly intelligent costume drama set in 11th-century England. Though it consolidated his reputation among critics, it did poor box-office business, which is probably why he felt compelled to accept the assignment of *The Double Man* (1967), a pallid espionage thriller with Yul Brynner. In 1968, however, he made his best film to date, an adaptation (like

almost all of his work) of Pierre Boulle's bestselling novel, *Planet Of The Apes*, which enjoyed such commercial success that it spawned a whole cycle of inferior sequels (none of which, to his credit, was directed by Schaffner). And when that was succeeded by *Patton* in 1970, also for 20th Century-Fox – notorious as Richard Nixon's favourite film but deserving rather to be remembered as a wholly engrossing and brilliantly staged biopic of the problematical war hero, with a gargantuan performance from George C. Scott – it seemed that Schaffner's stock was as high as that of virtually any Hollywood director. The top Oscar winner of the year, *Patton* received awards for Best Picture, director, actor (Scott) and screenplay (among others).

It was at that point, unfortunately, that a decline set in which has not, to date, been reversed. Part of the problem was *Patton's* own larger-than-life quality, as Schaffner now found himself saddled with mega-budgeted spectacles for which he was really, by temperament, unsuited: *Nicholas And Alexandra* (1971), a redundant and ponderous re-telling of the downfall of Tsarist Russia; *Papillon* (1973), with Steve McQueen and Dustin Hoffman laboriously vying for the Oscar which neither in the end received; *Islands In The Stream* (Paramount, 1977), a bloated version of Hemingway's autobiographical but uncompleted last novel; and *The Boys From Brazil* (1978), a weak adaptation of Ira Levin's fantasy about Hitler clones, with Gregory Peck and Laurence Olivier tiresomely out-hamming each other. The signs for Schaffner are not propitious; and the most generous comment which can be made is that, after a disaster of the magnitude of *Yes, Giorgio* (MGM, 1982), opera star Luciano Pavarotti's farewell debut to the cinema, the outlook can only improve.

Top: Charlton Heston as the astronaut hero, and Linda Harrison in the sci-fi fantasy adventure *Planet Of The Apes* (1968).

Above: The one with marginally more hair is director Schaffner! The star, of course, the inimitable Yul Brynner. The scene on which they are working was, alas, for a very mediocre film, *The Double Man* (1967).

Left: George C. Scott – who refused to accept the Oscar he won for his portrayal – was *Patton* (1970), the legendary World War II general.

'Schaffner is so honest and above board that he shows you the thumbscrews instead of applying them . . . By the time he gets a suspense story started, the audience is snoring.'

Pauline Kael on *The Boys From Brazil* 'The New Yorker', 1978

241

JOHN SCHLESINGER

Born London, 6 February 1926

A man of fine intellect who makes periodic directorial forays into the theatre (often Shakespearean) and the opera house, John Schlesinger's contribution to the cinema is defined by the 60s, the decade in which he first emerged as one of a group of new and respected British film directors. He became the most successful of his peers, producing work which was distinguished by downbeat themes dealing with the complexity of sexual and social relationships. His acknowledged gift for drawing splendid performances from actors helped to turn several into stars (Alan Bates, Tom Courtenay, Julie Christie, Jon Voight), and his films have been executed with style and skill. To his admirers, the expertise and pungent contemporary flavour of such successes as *Darling* (1965), *Midnight Cowboy* (1969) and *Sunday, Bloody Sunday* (1971) mark Schlesinger as a merciless chronicler of his times; to his detractors (who include a handful of serious critics), the easy gloss reflects a superficial talent exploiting a hollow view of metropolitan society. Certainly, his later works have largely failed to capture the public imagination. A thoughtful director who selects his projects with care, Schlesinger prefers making commercials to pay the rent, rather than accept feature assignments which do not please him. His films have appealed to selective audiences, but he has had the occasional big hit, sufficient to keep himself 'bankable'.

The director, who readily admits that he was a slow starter, an 'underachiever' as a boy, and a major disappointment to his successful doctor father, had his first taste of show biz while serving in the armed forces in World War II. He managed to transfer into a services entertainment unit where he performed in revue sketches and, as a student at Oxford after the war, he acted in a number of undergraduate productions. He found occasional work as an actor during the 50s in films, TV and on the stage, but was not very successful. Having made a few short films, he was employed by the BBC in 1957 as a freelance director to make programmes for 'Tonight' and, later, for 'Monitor'. In 1961, John had a terrific, unexpected success with his first independent documentary short, *Terminus*, which carried off a prize at Venice that year. Presenting a *cinéma vérité* slice of life as observed in a busy London railroad station (Waterloo), it immediately opened doors to a new career in feature films. He was approached by producer Joseph Janni to direct *A Kind Of Loving* (1962), adapted from Stan Barstow's novel by Keith Waterhouse and Willis Hall. Schlesinger filmed on location in Lancashire and demonstrated a remarkable maturity in his treatment of characters and relationships – in this case between Vic Brown (Alan Bates) a white collar worker and Ingrid (June Ritchie) whose romance leads, with sad inevitability, to her pregnancy and their forced marriage. Their subsequent difficulties

as they move in with her family, were handled with sensitivity and insight – a depressing view of a dreary world and an accurate depiction of early 60s life in northern England.

A Kind Of Loving served to launch its new young stars, and Schlesinger repeated the feat with his next film, *Billy Liar* (1963) starring Tom Courtenay and new discovery Julie Christie. Based on the novel (and hit play) by Waterhouse and Hall, the movie dealt with a weak young man who attempts to rebel against the drabness of life in his provincial town in the North of England by retreating into a world of fantasy – a behaviour pattern reminiscent of James Thurber's Walter Mitty in which fantasy melded with farce and real-life comedy, at the same time capturing a very 60s milieu on film. Producer Janni, and Schlesinger immediately moved on to make their third movie together with their find, Julie Christie, in the title role, and this time broadening their horizons and working with a more substantial budget. *Darling* (1965) attempted an ironic depiction of life as lived by the 'beautiful people' in the swinging London of the 60s, exemplified by the rise to empty wealth and fame of the attractive model girl of the title. In spite of the efforts of the director, and a cast that included Dirk Bogarde and Laurence Harvey, the result was hollow and superficial. It was reasonably successful in the US, however, reflecting a then current vogue for all things British, and earned Oscar nominations for Best Picture and director (Schlesinger's first), with Julie Christie and writer Frederic Raphael as surprise winners.

The same team (Schlesinger, Janni, Raphael and Christie) were prompted to capitalise on their success with a larger, more expensive ($3 million) production, *Far From The Madding Crowd* (MGM, 1967), which marked a number of firsts for the director – colour, Panavision and a period setting. As in *Darling*, Miss Christie played the ambitious heroine torn between three different men, but the quality which had made her so suitable for the previous film – her very modern, typically 60s look – added to her short-

Left: Schlesinger's first feature was the well-made, well-acted *A Kind Of Loving* (1962). Here Vic Brown (Alan Bates, centre) is at tea with his north country, working-class family – Dad (Bert Palmer, left), Mum (Gwen Nelson) and brother (Malcolm Patton).

Below: The many faces of *Billy Liar*, the inventive, pathological dreamer and liar, played by Tom Courtenay in the 1963 film.

Bottom: Julie Christie with Dirk Bogarde in *Darling* (1965), the director's stylish view of fashionable mid-60s amorality, but ultimately as empty as its characters and milieu.

comings as an actress, made it difficult to accept her as Thomas Hardy's 19th-century Wessex heroine. Alan Bates and Peter Finch provided solid support, and there was stunning camerawork from Nicolas Roeg, but the film was not a success. It was only a slight setback, however, as Schlesinger soon received an offer to direct his first American movie, *Midnight Cowboy*, in New York in 1968. As a Londoner who had succeeded so well in capturing the North of England on the screen in his first features, the director now demonstrated a similar ability to look at the sleazy side of Manhattan with a fresh eye and with a sympathetic understanding of the situation faced by his

naive Texan hero (Jon Voight) arriving in New York for the first time. An intimate character study of a would-be male hustler and a seedy tubercular con man, the film provided a welcome opportunity to work closely with two leading American actors, Voight and a virtually unrecognisable Dustin Hoffman. Both responded well to Schlesinger's direction and gave splendid (Oscar-nominated) performances. The director won his only Oscar, and the movie was voted Best Picture.

Given *carte blanche* for his next project, it was typical of Schlesinger that he selected an extremely personal and non-commercial subject. *Sunday, Bloody Sunday* (UA, 1971) presented a sexual triangle in which a fashionable young male designer engages in simultaneous affairs with a high-powered lady executive (Glenda Jackson) and a Jewish doctor (Peter Finch). Something of a landmark in the screen treatment of homosexuality, it is also a piercingly accurate treatment of trendy, 60s middle-class London lifestyles, but too cold and calculatingly 'tasteful' to be fully convincing. It earned Academy Award nominations for Jackson, Finch, Schlesinger and scriptwriter Penelope Gilliatt.

After contributing an episode to the 1972 Olympic film, intercutting footage of the tragic Israeli massacre with an appropriately subdued treatment of the marathon, Schlesinger found himself back in the US, on the West Coast, to film Nathanael West's 30s Hollywood novel *Day Of The Locust* in 1974. With its strange assortment of characters and melodramatic climax it failed to arouse much enthusiasm in critics or public. *Marathon Man* (Paramount) two years later, fared even less well with the critics. Reunited with Dustin Hoffman, this was the most commercial of Schlesinger's projects, a violent and dramatic thriller with a Nazi theme. Scripted by William Goldman from his own novel, with Laur-

ence Olivier and Roy Scheider in supporting roles, a lot of talent combined to produce a really unpleasant movie which nevertheless did well at the box-office.

Having failed in various attempts to film in Britain during the 70s, John persuaded UA to back *Yanks* in 1978, a perceptive and nostalgic look at 40s wartime Britain when the arrival of large numbers of American troops led to the inevitable culture clashes, romances, heartbreaks. Richard Gere and Vanessa Redgrave starred, but it flopped at the box-office as did his underrated comedy *Honky Tonk Freeway* (1981). More recently he has made a major comeback with a superb TV film, *An Englishman Abroad* (1983), starring Alan Bates as spy Guy Burgess, and another true life story about a pair of young American spy-traitors, *The Falcon And The Snowman* (1984).

Top: Cowboy Joe Buck (Jon Voight) and down-and-outer Ratso (Dustin Hoffman) argue in a scruffy eaterie in *Midnight Cowboy* (1968), Schlesinger's first—and highly successful—American film.

Above: Director John Schlesinger in discussion on set with his leading lady Glenda Jackson during *Sunday, Bloody Sunday*, now a monument to the trendy middle-class lifestyle of 60s London.

Left: American serviceman Richard Gere, dances with a local girl in Lancashire where he and his fellow GIs are billeted during World War II. *Yanks* (1979) was a nostalgic look at wartime romance and relationships between the English and the Americans.

'Making a film is like going down a mine. Once you've started you bid a metaphorical goodbye to the daylight and the outside world for the duration.'
1973

MARTIN SCORSESE

Born Flushing, New York, 17 November 1942

A dedicated and obsessive film-maker, Martin Scorsese is widely regarded as one of the most brilliant, but also the most unpredictable of the generation of young directors who first emerged during the 70s. Small, dark and bearded, he is as intense and neurotic as he looks, a hyperactive workaholic with religious and sexual hangups and a fascination with violence – all of which tends to surface in his most personal movies. But he is also a tough and courageous person who spent a dozen hard years overcoming illness to work his way up from film school graduate to one of America's leading directors.

A sickly child, Martin was hooked on movies from an early age. When he was three, for example, he saw his first Roy Rogers trailer and has loved trailers ever since. As he jokingly recalls, 'I saw *Hamlet* and *Duel In The Sun* when I was six. I guess I'm inbetween the two someplace'. His family acquired their first television set in the late 40s, and from then on he could watch old movies on TV, but was a teenager by the time he first saw a film which he felt related to his own experience – *On The Waterfront* (Columbia, 1954). Planning initially to study for the priesthood, Martin's poor school record meant that he was rejected by Fordham University and ended up at NYU instead. There he soon discovered the film department and, when he attended his first lecture, he immediately realised where his vocation really lay. While still a student, he made his first short films, including the excellent *It's Not Just You, Murray* (1964). Strongly influenced by the French New Wave and a few independent American films like Cassavetes' *Shadows* (1959), he set out to direct his own first feature on a shoestring budget. Originally titled *Bring On The Dancing Girls* in 1965, then retitled *I Call First* (1967) when additional footage was included, it finally emerged in 1968 as *Who's That Knocking At My Door?* The script grew out of Scorsese's own youthful experiences in New York's Little Italy, bumming around with friends and chasing girls. Filmed mainly during two different periods, the completed feature awkwardly intercut two parallel stories linked by the hero character who appears in almost every sequence. A useful apprentice work, it appears extremely interesting in retrospect as a step toward his first outstanding feature, *Mean Streets* (Warner Bros., 1973) in which the same leading actor, Harvey Keitel, played a very similar character, albeit a few years older and wiser.

Scorsese was involved in a large number of different movie projects during the late 60s. He directed a black comedy short, *The Big Shave* (1967), did a week's work on *The Honeymoon Killers* in 1968 before being replaced by another director, shot some publicity films in Europe, then made a major contribution to the success of the well-known rock movie, *Woodstock*, in 1969 as a supervising editor, helping to knock 120 hours of rough footage into its final three-hour

running time and making effective use of split screen and multiple image techniques. He also helped edit another rock documentary, *Medicine Ball Caravan*, for the same company, Warner Bros., in 1970, and spent some time teaching at NYU where he contributed to a militant student documentary, *Street Scenes*. Finally, in 1971, he was given his long overdue chance to direct a feature by Roger Corman who had seen *Who's That Knocking At My Door?* Set during the 30s Depression and made on location in Arkansas, the film was based on 'Sister Of The Road', the fascinating true story of *Boxcar Bertha* (Thompson) and starred Barbara Hershey with her real-life boyfriend, David Carradine. It was originally conceived as a kind of follow-up to Corman's own *Bloody Mama* (1970) and, although presenting a familiar exploitation movie blend of action, sex and violence, the theme of sticking up trains was in fact subordinated to the bitter struggle between labour organisers and the railroad company bosses, notorious for mistreating their employees.

Not recognisably a Scorsese film, *Boxcar Bertha* at least served to demonstrate his abilities. And the experience was essential for *Mean Streets* which followed, using many members of the same crew on a similarly tight budget and shooting schedule. But here, for the first time, the *real* Scorsese made a remarkable breakthrough, capturing the raw edged macho world of Little Italy on film – the bars, the pool rooms, the street life – and drawing on a full range of techniques such as hand-held filming, long takes with a mobile camera, semi-improvised acting and jump cutting, all perfectly matched to a selection of 60s rock numbers. Using a low-keyed style, with much of the episodic narrative taking place at night, the young director did an incredible job of matching New York settings with LA streets and studio interiors. (The tight budget meant that he was only allowed

Above: David Carradine in the throes of the violent end he met as the consort to *Boxcar Bertha* (1971), Scorsese's first major feature, set in the mid-west of the 30s.

one week of location shooting in New York.) Most remarkable of all was the way in which he succeeded in balancing the intense, insecure, respectable looking hood, Charlie (Harvey Keitel) with his small-time Mafia connections, but troubled by religious and sexual guilt, with the more flashy, extrovert and mentally unstable figure of his friend Johnny Boy as played by Robert De Niro.

The result was an exceptionally powerful and original contribution to bringing the crime movie into the 70s at a contemporary gut level. The achieve-

Left: Martin Scorsese (centre), at work with Harvey Keitel (right) and Robert De Niro on *Mean Streets* (1973), the impressive film which set the tone for the director's future work and started one of the outstanding director-star collaborations in movie history between Scorsese and De Niro.

'I like neuroses, and I find so-called neurotic people much more interesting than so-called well-adjusted persons. As a director, the fact that either my characters or actors are neurotic gives them an added dimension.'
1976

ment was confirmed by *Taxi Driver* two years later, when Scorsese and De Niro resumed a collaboration which was to develop into the most outstanding actor-director partnership of recent years. They made five films together in all during 1973-82, all of them different and each exceptional in its own way. (Scorsese's only non-De Niro films during these years were the occasional documentaries, of which the most memorable was the feature-length rock concert recording, *The Last Waltz*, UA, 1977, and the well-made but not particularly original story of a newly 'liberated' housewife and her precocious son, their travels and experiences, in *Alice Doesn't Live Here Anymore*, Warner Bros., 1974), which won an Oscar for Ellen Burstyn.

On *Taxi Driver* the intense and obsessive director-star combination were joined by the equally offbeat writer (and future director) Paul Schrader. His script presented a powerfully violent and paranoid view of the sleazy underside of New York, a real *film noir* for the 70s, reflecting the attitudes of a post-Vietnam, post-permissive society, technically more polished than *Mean Streets*, though made on a relatively economical budget of under $2 million. Here De Niro as the restless, psychotic title character clearly proved that he was capable of carrying an entire film. Harvey Keitel was present again as a pimp, while Jodie Foster gave an amazing performance which earned a bizarre notoriety a number of years later. For her child-whore image on the screen came to obsess the mentally unbalanced John Hinckley in real life, and his assassination attempt on the life of President Reagan to prove his love for her echoed the murderous behaviour of the fictional taxi driver character which led to the film's apocalyptic final bloodbath. (Winner of the top award at Cannes, *Taxi Driver* was the first Scorsese movie to be nominated for Best Picture Oscar, with additional nominations for De Niro and the thirteen-year-old Miss Foster.)

Given the largest budget of his career Scorsese then turned out a loving, studio-created homage to the old Hollywood musical biopics of the 40s and 50s with De Niro's sax player paired with Liza Minnelli's jazz singer. Sadly *New*

York, New York (UA, 1977) was badly cut and flopped at the box-office, but Scorsese and a totally physically transformed De Niro bounced back in 1980 with a tremendously effective and convincingly updated version of another Hollywood genre, the boxing biopic, in *Raging Bull* (UA). De Niro's Jake La Motta won the Oscar, while Scorsese received his first (and only) directing nomination. Unfortunately, the quirky humour of *King Of Comedy* (1983), starring De Niro and and Jerry Lewis failed to find its audience, continuing the director's recent (unplanned) pattern of alternating flops with hits – which means his latest, *After Hours* (1985), should be a success, but in any case is bound to provide a few characteristic surprises.

DON SIEGEL

Born Chicago, 26 October 1912

Don Siegel is best known as an exceptional and stylish director of thrillers, who has also handled a wide range of other subjects, including Westerns and sci fi, during the course of his long career. As the most youthful of Hollywood's veterans (and the very last survivor of the old Hollywood studio system) it seems appropriate that he should have found himself keeping company with such relative newcomers as Scorsese and Spielberg. In fact, Siegel only began to gain his own wide and well-earned recognition during the late 60s, after virtually thirty-five years in the film industry.

Educated at Jesus College, Cambridge, the twenty-year-old Donald had arrived back in the States in 1933 to look for his first job. Fortuitously, he had an uncle with contacts in the movie industry and he soon found himself working as a lowly assistant in the Warner Bros. film library. He quickly moved on to a spell as an assistant editor, but found the work boring. Far better was the Insert Department and then montages where he remained for many years. He found it exciting to have control over his own camera unit, albeit a tiny one, with a certain degree of independence in shooting non-dialogue insert shots and time lapse sequences. As head of the Montage Department, a kind of unofficial title, he was given a free hand to write his own, sometimes extremely complicated scripts for his short sequences. Tremendously busy every day, Siegel estimates that he was shooting far more film during these years than even the busiest of Warner Bros.' feature directors. Some of his best montage work can be found in *Confessions Of A Nazi Spy*, filmed in 1938, *The Roaring Twenties* (1939) and *Casablanca* (1943), while he also served as second-unit director on *Sergeant York* (1941) and *Passage To Marseilles* (1944) among others. Relatively overworked and underpaid in comparison with the feature directors and stars, Siegel was obviously a great asset to the studio, but Jack Warner's treatment of him was despicable and an example of how badly a director could suffer at the hands of the old studio bosses. For Warner was not eager for Don to graduate to full director status and placed him on suspension for a time, before allowing him to direct a pair of shorts – *Star In The Night*, a dramatised modern parable of the birth of Christ, and *Hitler Lives?*, a compilation documentary warning of the continuing dangers of fascism after the war.

Both won Oscars and finally, as Don expressed it, 'through unending persistence, through tenacity... the millenium came and I got my first feature, *The Verdict* (1946).' A cheaply made but effective Victorian thriller, set in a fog-bound studio London, it starred Peter Lorre and Sidney Greenstreet, the latter as an embittered ex-Scotland Yard police inspector who plans a bizarre revenge, staging a murder which his successor will be unable to solve. Then, in 1948, Siegel's long association with Warner

Bros. ended after he completed a second feature, *Night Unto Night*, mainly memorable for the fact that all the leads were miscast, including the robustly healthy Ronald Reagan as a scientist dying from a mysterious illness and the Swedish actress Viveca Lindfors as a troubled American widow with whom he falls in love. (Don, too, fell for his leading lady and they were married that same year, but divorced five years later.)

The Big Steal (1949) was the first and best of three which Don directed for RKO during 1949-52. An extended chase movie, filmed on location in Mexico and starring Robert Mitchum with William Bendix and Jane Greer, it gave Siegel his first opportunity to demonstrate his qualities as one of Hollywood's best action directors. On loanout to Universal, the studio where he would find a relatively congenial home during the 60s, he made *Duel At Silver Creek* (1952), a fast, action packed comic strip Western (his first, and his first in colour). Presented with a feeble script and Audie Murphy as star, Siegel did a surprisingly good job, injecting some tongue-in-cheek humour into the proceedings and giving Lee Marvin one of his earliest villain roles. With directing assignments relatively few and far between, Siegel did a first stint as a TV writer and director during 1953-54 around the same time that he arrived at the Allied Artists studio where he was to spend the better part of three ears. or his first AA movie, *Riot In Cell Block II* in 1953, Siegel had the rare benefit of a reasonably good script

and a reasonably intelligent producer, Walter Wanger. Having himself served a brief stretch for shooting at his wife's agent, Wanger was a champion of prison reform. Taking advantage of the opportunity thus offered to him, Siegel did a terrific job of mixing occasional violent action sequences with a gritty, semi-documentary visual style, social comment – illustrating the legitimate grievances of prisoners – and intelligent characterisation of prisoners and warders who were *both* seen as victims of a bad system. The film, shot at California's Folsom prison using some actual guards

Above: William Bendix (left) and former romantic matinée idol of the 20s Ramon Novarro (right) in *The Big Steal* (1949), the first of a trio that Siegel made for RKO.

Below: John Cassavetes (left) and Mark Rydell in *Crime In The Streets* (1956). Rydell, too, became a director, making his debut with a steamy version of D.H. Lawrence's *The Fox* (1968). He also directed *The Rose* (1978) with Bette Midler and the cloying but successful nostalgia trip with Henry Fonda and Katharine Hepburn, *On Golden Pond* (1981).

and prisoners as extras, drew conclusions that are just as relevant today as they were thirty years ago.

If Siegel's other AA pictures failed to match this high standard, at least *Crime In The Streets* (1956) was a reasonably interesting, solidly scripted and directed entry in the mid-50s cycle of juvenile delinquent movies. And then there was *Invasion Of The Bodysnatchers* (1956) which reunited Siegel with Wanger on one of the classic 50s sci fi productions, a downbeat reflection of the decade's small town paranoia in the members of a California community who find themselves gradually being replaced by alien 'pods' from outer space. Combining stringent social comment with plenty of action and drama, it was Siegel's first in SuperScope and he made effective use of the wide shape, placing his characters in isolation, and using contrasty black-and-white lighting to convey an unsettling, vaguely threatening landscape. The film also provided a bit role for Siegel's assistant during these years – Sam Peckinpah played Charlie, the gas meter reader who later leads the vengeful crowd in pursuit of Kevin McCarthy, the doctor hero. (Unfortunately, the studio made a number of changes, eliminating some of the director's characteristic black humour, and tacking on an optimistic prologue and epilogue which seriously altered the film's impact.) Siegel's failure to gain wider recognition for the quality of his work meant that he constantly had to struggle with inferior scripts and stars. He had a lean period during the late 50s

and early 60s, but 1957 was a good year. Forced to work within a tiny budget on *Baby Face Nelson* (UA), he put his own personal stamp on the traditional black-and-white gangster biopic, directing with terrific pace and vitality. Neither the efficient script (by Dan Mainwaring who had written *Body Snatchers*) nor the direction made any effort to explain or justify Nelson's psychotic and violent behaviour, they merely presented it. Mickey Rooney perfectly conveyed the manic intensity of the title character, and Carolyn Jones was excellent as his faithful moll. Also in 1957, Siegel directed *The Lineup* for Columbia, an effective *film noir* which took its lead characters from the CBS TV series of the same name, the pilot episode of which Don had directed three years earlier.

Working in colour and CinemaScope at 20th Century-Fox, the director turned *Hound Dog Man* (1959) into a likeable vehicle for Fabian, and got a surprisingly good performance out of Elvis Presley, playing an Indian in *Flaming Star* (1960). Brought in late on a Paramount war movie project which was in trouble, he managed to do an incredible salvage job on *Hell Is For Heroes* (1962), working closely with star Steve McQueen and the other members of the all-male cast. Making use of the familiar approach of concentrating on the experiences of a particular squad (fighting on the Siegfried Line in World War II), the film is especially memorable for the tough and gritty black-and-white action sequences. Forced to seek work in TV (which he dis-

liked) in order to supplement the all too few movie offers, Siegel landed at Universal, the studio which was heavily committed to both TV and cinema filming. This was to develop into the most fruitful relationship of his career as he moved from TV work to feature films and established himself for the first time as a producer-director, remaining with the company through 1973. He worked on such Universal TV series as 'Twilight Zone' and directed the pilots for 'Destroy' (1965) and 'Convoy' (1966), and when the studio initiated the TV movie format during 1964-65, Siegel directed three of the very first examples. Best known is *The Killers* (1964), a remake of Siodmak's 1946 movie adapted from Hemingway. It

Top: Siegel secured his reputation with one of the best-known, best-remembered sci-fi classics of the 50s, *Invasion Of The Body Snatchers* (1956). Here, leading man Kevin McCarthy (right), King Donovan (foreground). Dana Wynter (left) and Carolyn Jones attempt to conquer the alien 'pods' which are taking over the minds of people.

Above: Once a child star, and an adept song and dance man, the versatile Mickey Rooney was an excellent *Baby Face Nelson* (1957), the legendary psychopathic criminal.

'I loathe gratuitous violence. I fight very hard against it. My violence is very sharp and abrupt. I infer violence, it's lying there, waiting for you, but I don't really have that much violence in my pictures and certainly not in Dirty Harry there wasn't.'

1981

Left: *The Killers* (1964) was Ronald Reagan's swan song as a movie star before moving on to higher things. The villain of this particular piece, here he is with co-star Angie Dickinson.

starred Ronald Reagan in his last movie role (as a villain), along with Lee Marvin, John Cassavetes and Angie Dickinson. The director made few allowances for the fact that it was meant for TV, using perhaps a few more close-ups than usual, but generally presenting a familiar mix of fast paced action, offbeat black humour, and occasional violence which was considered too strong for TV. Thus the film was released to cinemas instead.

Three years later, in 1967, Don was given the opportunity to start directing features again with *Madigan*, a New York cop movie which balanced the story of the tough detective of the title (Richard Widmark) with that of the liberal police commissioner (Henry Fonda). In retrospect it is of special interest in foreshadowing the two Clint Eastwood cop pictures which followed, and in reflecting Siegel's successful first step toward earning a wider appreciation of his talents. Thus, on his first with Eastwood, *Coogan's Bluff* (1968), he was upgraded to producer-director for the first time, allowing him a greater freedom and control then ever before. He himself thought he recognised a 'kind of new spirit' at Universal at the time, remarking that 'I really feel that they want to do better things...'. Appropriately for an Eastwood movie, *Coogan* blended Western and cop themes – the tough, honest, upright Westerner adrift in the evil city, but determined to get his man: 'A man's gotta do what a man's gotta do, that it Wyatt? This isn't the OK Corral' insists Detective Lieutenant Lee

J. Cobb early in the film. The odds are strongly loaded in Clint's favour, however, and the NY cops are made to look foolish, but such a bias was corrected in *Dirty Harry* which followed in 1971 (filmed by Siegel on loan-out to Warner Bros.) Here Eastwood was no longer the moral cop in an immoral city, but rather an avenger figure operating ruthlessly outside the law. Siegel directed with great panache, economy and skill, assured and precise in his handling of the Panavision frame and introducing characteristic touches of black humour. Originally meant to be filmed in New York, the movie benefits from a change of locale to San Francisco, used to excellent

Above: Richard Widmark (right) shoots it out with suspected killer Steve Ihnat in *Madigan* (1967), a tough police drama from Richard Dougherty's novel 'The Commissioner'. The part of the commissioner himself was in fact played by Henry Fonda.

Left: Young stage actor Andy Robinson made his movie debut as a sadistic kidnapper and sniper in *Dirty Harry* (1971). Here, Robinson (left) discusses a scene with producer-director Don Siegel.

entertaining, offbeat heist movie with Walter Matthau cast against type as the shrewd, resourceful and independent crook of the title. Don came to England to direct Michael Caine in *The Black Windmill* in 1973, the last of his Universal pictures, then directed John Wayne's final movie, *The Shootist* in 1975 (for Paramount). His last of note (also for Paramount) was *Escape From Alcatraz* (1979) reuniting him with Eastwood one last time. A meticulously crafted, downbeat film reflecting Clint's willingness to get away from his usual action vehicles, it was a big hit.

Unfortunately, Siegel's career appears to have ended on a sour note with the much troubled, appropriately titled Bette Midler vehicle, *Jinxed* (UA, 1982) just short of his 50th anniversary in films.

'Don Siegel has managed, often against stifling odds, to bring a disquieting ambiguity as well as a unified viewpoint to assignments which, in other hands, could easily have been routine.'

Peter Bogdanovich in 'Picture Shows'

effect throughout. Striking a topical chord in the film-going public, *Dirty Harry* was the first really big hit for both Siegel and Eastwood, confirming the actor's 'superstar' status.

Between *Coogan* and *Harry*, Siegel had directed Clint in two other movies: *Two Mules For Sister Sara* (1969) drew on Clint's familiar Western persona, but here attempting to cope with a tough and resourceful woman (played by Shirley MacLaine) with amusing and unexpected consequences; and in *The Beguiled* (1970) director and star fashioned an exceptional and uncharacteristic drama set during the Civil War which sadly failed to find its audience. The best of Siegel's post-Eastwood thrillers during the 70s was *Charley Varrick* (1973), a superbly

Above left: Much loved comedian Walter Matthau starred as bank robber *Charley Varrick* (1973), in Siegel's clever, well-made and immensely entertaining thriller. The back to camera belongs to Andy Robinson.

Left: After half-a-century in the movies, superstar John Wayne (right) bowed out with *The Shootist* (1976). Siegel's thoughtful treatment of the tale of a dying ex-gunfighter, was lent additional poignancy by Wayne's own failing health, with which he coped so courageously.

Below: On location for *Escape From Alcatraz* (1979), Clint Eastwood (left) and Don Siegel.

STEVEN SPIELBERG

Born Cincinnati, 18 December 1947

Variously known as the cinema's boy wonder, the most successful of the movie brats, the Hollywood wunderkind or the Peter Pan of the picturedrome, Steven Spielberg has compiled an amazing record in less than a dozen years as a feature film director. Along with his friend and occasional producing partner George Lucas, he is credited with bringing audiences back into the cinemas once again with his imaginative and exciting pictures beginning with *Jaws* (Universal, 1975) and extending up to his most recent blockbuster successes, as a director – with *Indiana Jones And The Temple Of Doom* (Paramount) – and as producer – *Gremlins* (Warner Bros.) both in 1984. Together he and Lucas have directed or produced almost a dozen of the most popular movies ever made.

A master technician whose films are known for their sense of pace, action, humour, fantasy, occasional comic strip violence and stylish visual qualities, Spielberg has remained relatively modest and unspoilt by success, preserving his boyish enthusiasm for the cinema and a nicely ironic, unpretentious quality which comes across in the movies themselves. His most personally felt pictures have been those that he has also written or co-written, like *Close Encounters Of The Third Kind* (Columbia, 1977) and *E.T. – The Extra-Terrestrial* (Universal, 1982), and including *Poltergeist* (MGM, 1982) which he co-scripted and co-produced, but did not direct. All of them were centred on middle class suburban families, recalling Steven's own upbringing, and derived from his own childhood fantasies. In fact, children play an important role in many of his films and he appears to have a special pleasure in, and talent for, working with them. He is a sensitive and competent director of adults, too, and in spite of his great technical expertise, he never lets technical wizardry or special effects overwhelm his characters. He has succeeded in bringing back to the cinema the kind of action and adventure pictures and fantasies of a kind he used to love to see, and which he realised were missing from the modern cinema. As one of the generation of directors who grew up on films and TV during the postwar years, he himself draws on a variety of movie references and popular movie styles and genres of the past. His incredible success as a director has made it possible for him to branch out into producing, having more projects of interest on hand than he has either the time or inclination to direct himself, and he sees this as a way of helping other young directors. He has, in fact, been more active as producer than director for a while, with his most recent project, *Young Sherlock Holmes* shooting in England from early 1985, directed by Barry Levinson. Whether this reflects a serious falling off in his creative drive similar to the pattern of his friend George Lucas who gave up directing a number of years ago, only time will tell. But the fact remains that ever since 1981 when he di-

rected *E.T.*, Spielberg has only directed one feature (the *Indiana Jones* sequel) and an undistinguished segment of *The Twilight Zone* (Warner Bros., 1983). Spielberg is now in his late thirties, an age when most directors are just getting started, yet there is no sign of him maturing, or his being ready or able or interested to deal with a large area of adult experience, of the darker side of human nature which he has generally avoided in his pictures, aside from his first, oft forgotten, and least commercial feature, *The Sugarland Express* (Universal, 1974). He appears like a lightweight suburban country cousin to, for example, Martin Scorsese, when compared with that young director's complex, black and violent preoccupations of a tough city kid, and it is hard to imagine what pictures a sixty-year-old Spielberg will be making.

The young Steven grew up in a variety of bland American suburbs and small towns including Haddonfield, New Jersey and Scottsdale, Arizona, and finally arrived in California with his mother when his parents divorced. A skinny, unathletic and not very popular kid at school, Steven had a vivid imagination, loved going to the movies and enjoyed playing scary tricks on his three younger sisters. When his father bought an 8mm camera to make home movies the results were so appalling that Steve took over and, by the age of thirteen, was making his own 8mm genre movies – Westerns, war pictures – using his family and friends as actors and gaining a new status with the other kids. He was sixteen

when he put together his first feature length effort in 16mm, a sci-fi epic called *Firelight* (1964). It took a year to complete at a cost of $500, then was screened at a local cinema which his father hired for the occasion. Steven's school record was too poor for him to get into the film department at USC, so he ended up studying English and humanities at the California State College, Long Beach, where he carried on making 16mm movies. Eager to break into the film industry and finding it difficult to get anyone to look at his work in 16mm, he managed to find a backer to finance his first 35mm short about hitchhikers, *Amblin'* (1969). The movie was specially designed to demonstrate Spielberg's expertise as a film-maker, and it worked.

Above: Dennis Weaver in *Duel* (1971), Spielberg's highly original and very suspenseful made-for-TV movie about a man menaced by a gigantic and apparently driverless truck.

Below: *The Sugarland Express* (1974) starred William Atherton (left) and Goldie Hawn as the convict and his wife who kidnap a cop (Michael Sacks, right).

Sidney Sheinberg of Universal was impressed by the film and signed Steven to a seven-year directing contract at the age of twenty-one. Thrown in at the deep end, his first assignment was to direct Joan Crawford (!) in a thirty-minute segment of a three-part TV movie, the pilot for *Night Gallery* (1969). He graduated from TV episodes – 'Marcus Welby', 'Owen Marshall', a feature-length 'Columbo' – to TV movies, then features. He had his first substantial success when his TV movie, *Duel* (1971), was shown in cinemas in Europe and Britain. Scripted by the noted fantasy writer Richard Matheson from his own story, the film depicts a battle for survival on the highway between a neurotic and insecure businessman (Dennis Weaver) driving to an appointment in his car, and a giant, ferocious and seemingly driverless truck. This situation was exploited to the full by the inventive script and direction which combined menace and black humour.

After two more TV movies, one of them the scary *Something Evil*, filmed later in 1971 and starring Sandy Dennis, Spielberg was given his first chance to direct a feature in 1973. *The Sugarland Express* was based on a true event which took place in 1969 when a convict and his wife kidnapped a state trooper as part of an escape attempt, were followed across Texas by a convoy of cop cars, and later joined by TV, the press and curiosity seekers. Having demonstrated a special talent for handling an action movie on the road in *Duel*, here the young director was more ambitious, with a feature budget at his disposal, the use of almost fifty different Texas locations, a full contingent of stunt men and one of Hollywood's top cameramen, Vilmos Zsigmond. The film was an unusual blend of black comedy, action and a strong human interest story. One came to sympathise with the plight of the young couple – especially the scatty young wife and mother (Goldie Hawn) obsessed with getting her baby back – and

to identify with the friendly but helpless cop-hostage (Michael Sacks) who can foresee the tragic end to the events. It was a difficult movie to sell and Universal never really tried, but by the time it was released in 1974, Steven was already hard at work on a little shark movie called *Jaws*. Originally budgeted at $3.5 million with a fifty-two day schedule, it ended up costing more than twice that, while the filming took almost six tortuous months. Here for the first time Steven was forced to draw on his technical expertise as well as his ability to cope with the unexpected, and he required all his physical stamina to see the movie through to a successful conclusion. Filming began without adequate preparation or a satisfactory

script, and he worked closely with the writers (making a major improvement on the tacky bestseller on which it was based), with the various special effects and mechanical experts (whose major difficulties related to a giant mechanical shark nicknamed 'Bruce'), and had to cope with all the logistical problems of filming on the open ocean off the coast of Martha's Vineyard. The opening reels effectively set the situation, of a New England resort town threatened by a giant Great White Shark. Though the characters were somewhat stereotyped, he developed a successful blend of suspense, cinematic shock effects and black humour. But the film only really came to life in the final hour when the three male

Above left: Roy Scheider (left) as the chief of police and Robert Shaw as the tough skipper of the boat that sets off to catch the shark, in *Jaws* (1975). The attractive Shaw, novelist as well as actor, died of a heart attack in 1978, aged only fifty-one.

Above: Steven Spielberg (right) with the great French director François Truffaut who acted, as a French scientist, in *Close Encounters Of The Third Kind* (1977). Truffaut died tragically of cancer in 1984 at the age of fifty-two.

Below: The little boy (Cary Guffey) who is 'chosen' by the aliens to go with them in *Close Encounters Of The Third Kind* (1977), here with his mother (Melinda Dillon).

had a tremendous box-office appeal and earned the equal largest number of Oscars and nominations as his following movie, *E.T.* (Both were nominated for Best Picture and director, but won only in the technical categories such as sound and visual effects.)

A kind of follow-up to *Close Encounters*, but concentrating on the story of a little boy who makes contact with an alien, *E.T.* clearly bore the Spielberg stamp – warmth, humour, humanity and some marvellously imaginative visual sequences. The most universally appealing and touching of all his films, with children as the leading characters, the family home as the main setting and the special effects generally relegated to the background, *E.T.* gave Steven a box-office success to match that of *Star Wars*. Where does the most commercially successful director in the history of the cinema go from here? All Hollywood is watching with eager anticipation.

'I've been waiting for Hollywood to leave me alone and stop forcing me to make these $30 million movies, so I can get around to something I really want to make'
1982

Left: Harrison Ford (right) as Indiana Jones, the tough archaeologist hero of *Raiders Of The Lost Ark* (1980) – illustrated – and its sequel, *Indiana Jones And The Temple Of Doom* (1984), both of them blockbustingly successful tales of escapist adventure.

leads put to sea in a fool-hardy venture which culminated in a stunning and climactic final reel. Aspiring to a 'mythic' quality, with obvious echoes of 'Moby Dick', the completed movie obviously hit a subconscious chord in the film-going public, for it emerged as the box-office phenomenon of the mid 70s. (Nominated for a Best Picture Oscar, the only winners were editor Verna Fields and John Williams for his music score; Spielberg was not even nominated.)

No longer a young unknown, but recognised as the newest Hollywood *wunderkind*, Spielberg was able to choose his next film with complete freedom. He immediately embarked on the most expensive, risky and personal project of his career thus far, a sci fi story about alien visitors to earth (otherwise known as UFO's) on which he had previously been working. Here, the technical problems proved to be just as daunting as those of *Jaws*, but mostly took place within a controlled studio environment, the studio in question being a giant converted blimp hangar in Mobile, Alabama, many times larger than the largest Hollywood sound stage. Writing his own script with the help of a few friends, film buff Steven drew on his affectionate memories of 50s sci fi movies like *The Day The Earth Stood Still* (20th Century-Fox, 1951), *War Of The Worlds* (Paramount) and *Invaders From Mars* (both 1953), but planned to make the special effects appear utterly convincing with the help of modern film technology. Thus, one is stunned by the speed and power of the alien spacecraft, first seen shooting through the sky, and the impressive appearance of the giant mother ship created with astonishing light effects. But the film also includes many equally effective intimate touches: like the little boy's mechanical toys which are suddenly activated, or the way every-

thing goes haywire in Richard Dreyfuss' car, dials madly spinning; and a warm, sympathetic treatment of the characters. Making use of a classic cross-cutting pattern, Spielberg gradually wove all the strands of his story to bring all the protagonists together for the climactic final rendezvous with the giant space ship at Devil's Tower, Wyoming. A far better, more original (and expensive) movie than *Star Wars* which had opened earlier that same year, *Close Encounters Of The Third Kind* (for Columbia – Steven's first venture away from Universal) did tremendously well at the box-office and earned Steven the first of three Oscar nominations. (He has so far never won.)

Spielberg finally came unstuck with the vastly expensive *1941* (Universal, 1979). Billed as a comedy spectacle, it was more spectacular than amusing, with some stunning special effects, but all treated in an uncharacteristically heavy handed manner. He immediately bounced back the following year, however, with *Raiders Of The Lost Ark* (for Paramount) which he filmed in partnership with his producer friend George Lucas. The film drew its inspiration from the old Hollywood adventure flicks and serials, and starred Harrison Ford. Less original than *Close Encounters*, it was wonderfully entertaining escapist fare, which

Left: Spielberg and his camera photographed during the making of *E.T. – The Extra-Terrestrial* (1982).

Below: The boy wonder grown venerable by the age of thirty-seven! Spielberg (left), the executive producer of another sensational box-office hit, *Gremlins* (1984), confers on set with the film's director, Joe Dante.

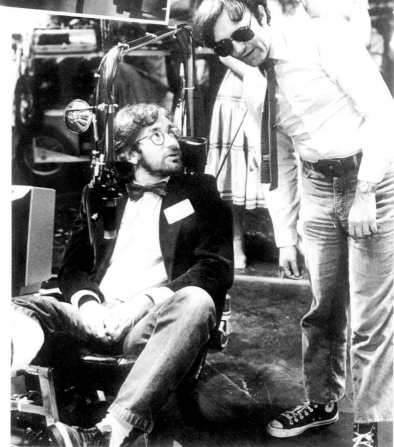

Above: Harrison Ford and Kate Capshaw in *Indiana Jones And The Temple Of Doom* (1984), find themselves struggling through the native crowds in one of the many far-flung, exotic locales for their wild adventures.

Right: The magical stranded alien, *E.T.*, created by Carlo Rimbaldi, and Henry Thomas as the little boy who gives him refuge and helps him to get home, in Spielberg's immensely successful fairy tale for children of all ages – and morality tale for adults who care to see it that way . . .

'For me, E.T. is the greatest political film of all time. I think Spielberg should be given the Nobel Peace Prize for that film.'

Claude Lelouch, 1982

SYLVESTER STALLONE

Born New York City, 6 July 1946

A tough, well-built, ex-street kid with droopy eyes and a slightly punch-drunk look, Sylvester Stallone has managed to carve a special niche for himself in the American cinema over the past decade or so. Starting out as an actor playing hoodlums, gangsters and street kids, he later graduated to the more 'respectable' roles of Vietnam veteran, truck driver and, of course, boxer, at the same time managing to establish himself as a scriptwriter and, later, as a writer-director-star. The product of a broken home, the young Sylvester was a difficult, delinquent youth who grew up in New York, Philadelphia and Maryland, and only began to adjust to life in his early twenties when he became interested in acting. As an aspiring but out of work actor, he was forced to take a number of menial jobs, but also, wisely, spent his spare time struggling to develop as a writer, drawing on his own street experience for inspiration. He rightly re-

completing the screenplay, he decided he should star in it himself, and so refused the most lucrative offers (of about $300,000) for the script alone – in spite of the fact that he was virtually broke at the time. The gamble paid off when United Artists finally agreed to take a chance on the relatively small budget movie, titled *Rocky*, with John G. Avildsen as director. In fact, Sylvester was perfect casting for the relatively undemanding lead: as an amateur body builder he was in excellent shape, with a physique and talent as a boxer which contrasted with the usual movie star types. Thus, he had the natural appearance of a heavyweight and was able to look convincing in the ring – an important plus factor, considering that this was where the dramatic climax of *Rocky* (and its sequels) took place. When the film emerged as an unexpected but tremendous hit, it was a case of life imitating art, for Stallone's sudden leap

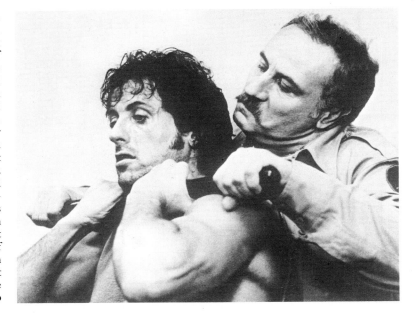

Above: Galt (Jack Starrett, right), the cop, brutally restrains Rambo (Stallone) in *First Blood* (1982), written by Stallone but directed by Ted Kotcheff.

Left: Rocky releases a powerful left in the direction of clubber Lang (Mr T) during their title fight in *Rocky II* (1982).

Below: Producer, director and co-writer of *Staying Alive* (1983), Sylvester Stallone (left) with his star, John Travolta.

tern whereby sequels are generally inferior and do less well at the box-office. Perhaps the biggest surprise of all was the success of *Rocky II* (UA, 1979) which was less of a sequel than a 'remake'. The jack-of-all-trades, however, fared substantially better with *Rocky III* in 1982. In spite of playing many other roles, Stallone is, and will forever be, closely identified with Rocky it seems – no writer-director-star since Charlie Chaplin and his baggy-trousered tramp has squeezed so much mileage out of a single character.

Stallone has recently enjoyed a big popular success with his first movie as producer, director and co-writer (but not star): *Staying Alive* (Paramount, 1983) was a reasonably competent and entertaining musical with John Travolta as the dancer who suddenly gets his big break, a kind of 'Rocky on Broadway'. Stallone has also scripted and starred in *First Blood* (1982), *Rhinestone* (1984) opposite Dolly Parton, and *Rambo: First Blood Part II* (1985). Now, *Rocky IV* seems a likely future prospect. . . . .

'Rocky is my symbiotic twin. We're connected at the soul. My life is a reflection of his and his mine. There's so much of me in there.'

1983

alised that these endeavours could become his passport to acting work.

By the early 70s Stallone was beginning to land his first small roles and had his best part in *The Lords Of Flatbush* (Columbia) in 1973, a cheaply made, independent New York movie in which he played a tough member of the street gang of the title and contributed some 'additional dialogue' to the script. Later that year he headed west to California (with his wife, Sasha) where he continued to write and to play bit roles. The Wepner-Ali fight early in 1975 (and Chuck Wepner's unexpectedly good showing) immediately inspired him to write a new script about a no-hope amateur boxer who is given a crack at the title. After

to fame was very similar to that of the character he had created.

Oscar-nominated for both writing and starring in *Rocky* – it won for Best Picture and director Avildsen – Stallone then took over the direction of the sequels as well. In the meantime he had established his competence as a writer-director-star with *Paradise Alley* (Universal, 1978) which recalled his own early life, set in the Hell's Kitchen section of New York where he was born, and telling of the attempts of three brothers to break away from their environment and make it on their own. (The film owed an obvious debt to Scorsese's *Mean Streets*.)

All three Rocky pictures have been enormous hits and have defied the pat-

JOHN STURGES

Born Oak Park, Illinois, 3 January 1911

A relatively late developer as a director, John Sturges spent the 30s at RKO serving a lengthy apprenticeship in the art department and the cutting rooms. During World War II he joined the air force where he got his first opportunity to direct, turning out a number of short documentaries and training films, then collaborating with William Wyler on a forty-five minute colour documentary, *Thunderbolt* (1945), about US fighter bombers in Italy. Signed to a contract by Columbia after the war, Sturges directed a large number of programmers, averaging two pictures per year, and continued more or less in the same vein at MGM from 1949 on, though with slightly larger budgets, bigger stars and better material. Concentrating on action movies and Westerns, he first began to make his name during the mid-50s and had an outstanding personal success with one film in particular, *Bad Day At Black Rock*, filmed in 1954 for MGM. A tense and exciting thriller with a modern Western setting and a strong social theme, the picture was a pet project of MGM's socially conscious production chief Dore Schary who served as producer. Spencer Tracy starred as the lone stranger who arrives at the isolated town of the title and gradually uncovers, then avenges, the injustice done to a Japanese-American during the war. With a well-written allegorical script in the *High Noon* mold and a first rate cast, Sturges was merely required to do his usual craftsman-like job. He did demonstrate a good eye for placing the camera, however, and made effective use of the wide, CinemaScope image – his first in this process – in order to convey a sense of the space and settings which played an important role in the story. The director thus earned the only Oscar nomination of his career, along with old-hand Spencer Tracy (who delivered a superbly judged, lowkeyed performance) and scriptwriter Millard Kaufman.

After leaving MGM, Sturges directed a number of quality Westerns, the best of which was *Gunfight At The OK Corral* (Paramount, 1957) in which he nicely balanced the serious upright professionalism of Burt Lancaster's Sheriff Wyatt Earp against the slightly crazy, colourful and nihilistic qualities of Kirk Douglas' Doc Holliday. The following year Sturges was reunited with Tracy (and replaced Fred Zinnemann) on the extremely difficult and fascinating, but not entirely successful film version of Hemingway's *The Old Man And The Sea* (Warner Bros., 1958). With such successful movies as *The Magnificent Seven* (1960) and *The Great Escape* (1963) – with their virtually all-male casts – Sturges established himself as one of the leading men's directors of the 60s. His cast lists read like a virtual Who's Who of leading Hollywood male stars. At the same time he began to function as an independent producer-director, releasing his pictures through United Artists.

During the following years Sturges continued to add to his reputation as one

of Hollywood's most efficient and successful action directors, broadening his range to include a dramatic East-West confrontation at the polar icecap in *Ice Station Zebra* (MGM, 1968), and venturing into outer space for the first time in *Marooned* (Columbia, 1969). But he continued to return to the Western, as in *Hour Of The Gun* (UA, 1967) which – in contrast to *Gunfight At The OK Corral* – was notable for its more original and subtle emphasis on characterisation rather than action in this second crack at the Earp and Holliday story. Following the pattern of other better known action directors like Raoul Walsh and Henry Hathaway, Sturges, too, liked to film on location and shoot fairly quickly, hoping to catch the scene on the first or second take. His pictures are known for their crisp pace, reflecting his early training as an editor. During the 70s he enjoyed working with a new generation of stars like Clint Eastwood, doing his standard Western number as the tough bounty hunter *Joe Kidd* (Universal, 1972), or Michael Caine and Donald Sutherland, the stars of Sturges' last feature, the World War II action-drama *The Eagle Has Landed* (Columbia, 1976).

Left: On location in the desert for *Bad Day At Black Rock* (1954), stars Spencer Tracy (left) and Robert Ryan (2nd left), chat with producer Dore Schary, who appears to be in high good humour, and director John Sturges.

Below: Jo Van Fleet and Kirk Douglas in *Gunfight At The OK Corral* (1957). Miss Van Fleet, a fine theatre actress, has appeared only sporadically, but always effectively, in films. She won a Best Supporting Oscar for her first screen role as James Dean's brothel-madam mother in *East Of Eden* (1955), and was Susan Hayward's mother the same year in the Lillian Roth biopic, *I'll Cry Tomorrow*.

Left: Jason Robards as Doc Holliday in *Hour Of The Gun* (1967). With him is William Windom, sitting in the buggy.

'I've no objection to being called an action director . . . but I don't think people realize how much they're laughing, how many lumps in the throat there are in my films.'

1976

PETER WEIR

Born Sydney, 21 August 1944

Peter Weir is the most important of that group of young film-makers who put the Australian cinema on the international movie map for the first time in the mid-70s. A talented and imaginative director who writes (or co-writes) most of his own scripts, he has gone from strength to strength in the years since he directed his first feature, *The Cars That Ate Paris*, in 1973. Weir likes to work on a broad canvas and is attracted to the extraordinary and the cataclysmic. As he himself noted with reference to *The Last Wave* (1977): 'I'm probably just more interested in events, in catastrophic events, like death or revolution. I'm not really interested in the day to day life. . .'. Not surprisingly, his pictures have tended to grow larger and more expensive as he has become more successful and been able to tap the resources of the big American companies. But he demonstrates a welcome versatility and flexibility, too, as reflected in his most recent (and first American) film *Witness* (Paramount), a straight genre piece which he took over at short notice early in 1984 and developed into a quite superior thriller.

Having studied arts and law at Sydney University, Weir landed a job with Australian TV (ATN 7, Sydney) in 1967 and began directing the first of his early shorts around the same time. In 1969 he joined the government sponsored film unit (Film Australia) as an assistant cameraman and production assistant, and went on to make a number of award-winning documentaries before making a spectacular feature debut: In *The Cars That Ate Paris* he created a strange, nightmarish world revolving around an isolated Australian community of ghoulish, zombie-like, though very ordinary looking people who prey on passing motorists, but are in turn terrorized by a gang of young thugs who roam the streets in grotesquely decorated and lethal, spiked vehicles. The climax is suitably apocalyptic. Weir then achieved a remarkable international breakthrough with *Picnic At Hanging Rock* (1975), a totally different venture into movie fantasy. A beautifully photographed, sensitively directed and atmospheric period piece, it was based on the novella by Joan Lindsay about a group of schoolgirls and their teacher who disappear while out on a holiday excursion. This baffling but evocative psychological mystery story demonstrated for the first time that the young Australian directors were capable of making pictures of the highest quality.

Weir followed it with a mystical piece of a different sort – *The Last Wave* effectively blended aboriginal magic and superstitions with an apocalyptic vision of the destruction of the city of Sydney as seen through the eyes of a young and sensitive lawyer played by Richard Chamberlain. After completing this powerful (if slightly pretentious) work, he scripted and directed a more modest TV movie, *The Plumber*, in 1978, which reflected his characteristically black, and occasionally chilling, sense of humour.

He then devoted much time and effort to setting up his next feature, a favourite project which finally emerged as *Gallipoli* (1981) backed by producer Robert Stigwood and Paramount, the most expensive movie filmed in Australia up to that date. Following the experiences of two young men played by Mel Gibson and Mark Lee, Weir took his time building up to the famous (and disastrous) World War I battle of the title in which so many young Aussies so tragically and unnecessarily met their deaths. If the result was slightly disappointing, Weir was on better form with the American-financed $6 million production of *The Year Of Living Dangerously* (MGM, 1982). Here the director's fascination with extraordinary historical events led him to turn his attention to 1965 Indonesia, making better use of the same star, Mel Gibson, as his naive reporter hero. He succeeded superbly in balancing the personal story against the political turmoil, aided by fine supporting performances from Sigourney Weaver, and little Linda Hunt who won an Oscar. Weir has doubtless joined the Hollywood ranks and his future projects are awaited with interest.

Left: Anne Lambert leads a small party of schoolgirls through the awesome caverns of Hanging Rock, a beauty spot outside Melbourne, Australia, in *Picnic At Hanging Rock* (1975).

Below: Mel Gibson, army runner, in *Gallipoli* (1981), Weir's moving account of the appalling battle in which so many young Australian soldiers needlessly died.

Left: Director Peter Weir (in hat) discusses a scene with Mel Gibson during the filming of *The Year Of Living Dangerously* (1982). The movie was set against the background of the 1965 Indonesian civil war.

'With the decline of Christianity, I feel the need to bring back some kind of spirituality in the widest sense of the word.'
1978

PETER YATES

Born Aldershot, England, 24 July 1929

A versatile and intelligent director who has handled a wide variety of subjects during the past twenty years, Peter Yates has endeavoured to strike a healthy balance between popular, action movies and more personal ones, and between commercial and critical successes, mixing action movies and thrillers with comedy and drama. Generally working within relatively modest budgets, he has directed some elaborate and large scale productions, too, like *The Deep* (1977), his biggest box office hit, and *Krull* – both for Columbia. In fact, when Yates returned to Pinewood Studios in 1982 to direct this latter fantasy of sword and sorcery, he was working in Britain for the first time in fifteen years. For, of all the British movie directors who headed west to work in the late 60s, he was the only one who stayed on and subsequently directed a wide range of American pictures and stars, and in fact established himself as a leading 'American' director.

Yates had originally studied at RADA, then spent a number of years in rep, mixing a bit of acting with work as a stage manager and occasional theatre director. After a brief involvement with the world of motor racing, he broke into films in the mid-50s as a dubbing assistant and gained some experience as an assistant director. This was followed by a short stint as a theatre director (at the Royal Court) and TV director ('Danger Man' and 'The Saint') at about the same time that he directed his first feature – the lightweight Cliff Richard musical *Summer Holiday* (1962).

Drawing on his experience as a racing driver, Yates staged a dramatic chase in the opening reel of an otherwise undistinguished thriller titled *Robbery* (1967). It caught the eye of Steve McQueen who invited him to California, then hired him to direct *Bullitt* (Warner Bros., 1968). This was the break which Yates needed to properly launch him in features. The film was a superior thriller, and the director made effective use of the San Francisco settings, mixing quiet moments with fast moving action including a memorable chase up and down the hilly streets. With a smash hit now under his belt, it seemed like an opportune moment for Yates to break away from being type cast as an action director, but his choice of an intimate two-character movie, starring Dustin Hoffman and Mia Farrow as *John And Mary* (20th Century-Fox, 1969), proved such a disaster that he was soon back directing actioners again, like *Murphy's War* (Paramount, 1971) starring Peter O'Toole. *The Friends Of Eddie Coyle* which he made in 1972 (again for Paramount) was an outstanding psychological thriller with Robert Mitchum giving a characteristically laid back performance in the title role. Around the same time Yates demonstrated his talent for handling offbeat, black comedy in such movies as *The Hot Rock* (1971) a suspenseful and comical heist movie with Robert Redford, *For Pete's Sake* (Columbia, 1974) starring Barbra Streisand, and

Mother, Jugs and Speed (1975) about the crazy and bloody experiences of an LA ambulance crew – a kind of cross between *M*A*S*H* and 'Hill St. Blues'.

The not too surprising box-office success of *The Deep*, with its commercial blend of underwater drama, fast moving action and Jacqueline Bisset in a provocatively clinging wet tee-shirt, once again gave a boost to Yates' career. Thus, during the years since 1977 he has been better able to achieve his preferred balance between personal projects and more commercial ones. He had a surprise success with *Breaking Away* (20th Century-Fox, 1979), his comedy about a group of teenagers in Bloomington, Indiana led by the tall, gangling Dave (Dennis Christopher) who aspires to be an Italian-style bicycle racing champion. Back in England, *Krull* was followed by the film of Ronald Harwood's play, *The Dresser* (Columbia, 1983), a tribute to the traditions of the British theatre with Oscar-nominated performances from Albert Finney and Tom Courtenay. (Both *Breaking Away* and *The Dresser* were

nominated for Academy Awards as Best Picture, with Yates, too, twice nominated as director.) Most recently he has completed another personal venture, the film versions of Nicholas Gage's bestseller *Eleni* (1985), set during the Greek civil war and starring John Malkovich.

Left: Steve McQueen (right) in *Bullitt*, Yates' first American film which the star invited him to direct, thus opening up a Hollywood career for the Briton.

Above: Director Peter Yates (right) with star Robert Mitchum during the filming of *The Friends Of Eddie Coyle* (1972), a slick thriller which drew a splendid central performance from Mitchum.

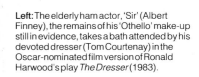

Left: The elderly ham actor, 'Sir' (Albert Finney), the remains of his 'Othello' make-up still in evidence, takes a bath attended by his devoted dresser (Tom Courtenay) in the Oscar-nominated film version of Ronald Harwood's play *The Dresser* (1983).

ACADEMY NOMINATIONS AND AWARDS

The Academy of Motion Picture Arts and Sciences has honoured members of the movie profession every year since it was inaugurated in 1927. Over the years the coveted Oscar, as the golden statuette awarded to the winners is nicknamed, has come to represent the highest accolade to which a film, or those associated with its production, can aspire. The annual ceremonial presents contenders under various category headings which cover most of the creative elements and roles that go into the making of a motion picture – ranging from Best Picture itself to Best Sound Recording and other less glamorous but no less deserving categories. Short subjects, documentaries etc., are also honoured and, in addition, the Academy make special or honorary awards to particularly deserving individuals. One or two commemorative awards, inaugurated to the memory of much respected individuals within the business, have been introduced from time to time.

Direction has its own category and the complete listing of all its nominations is given below. For interest, those directors who are featured in this book are distinguished in **bold** type, and it can be seen that they make up three-quarters of all nominations and over 85% of all the winners.

Directors are versatile people, however, and their names are often found under several other category headings, most notably Best Writing and, latterly, Best Actor; but they also turn up in areas as remote from direction as Interior Decoration, for example. On pages 260/261 are listed all these 'other categories' nominations, but here they are restricted to those involving the directors featured in this book. Special, honorary and memorial awards are also listed here, again restricted to featured directors. Short Subjects and Documentary nominations do not usually name individuals but here we have credited the director.

BEST DIRECTOR

1927/1928
★ **Frank Borzage** *Seventh Heaven*
 Herbert Brenon *Sorrell And Son*
 King Vidor *The Crowd*

 (comedy direction)
 Charles Chaplin *The Circus*
★ **Lewis Milestone** *Two Arabian Knights*
 Ted Wilde *Speedy*

1928/1929
 Lionel Barrymore *Madame X*
 Harry Beaumont *Broadway Melody*
 Irving Cummings *In Old Arizona*
★ Frank Lloyd *The Divine Lady*
 Frank Lloyd *Weary River*
 Frank Lloyd *Drag*
 Ernst Lubitsch *The Patriot*

1929/1930
 Clarence Brown *Anna Christie*
 Clarence Brown *Romance*
 Robert Leonard *The Divorcee*
 Ernst Lubitsch *The Love Parade*
★ **Lewis Milestone** *All Quiet On The Western Front*
 King Vidor *Hallelujah*

1930/1931
 Clarence Brown *A Free Soul*
 Lewis Milestone *The Front Page*
 Wesley Ruggles *Cimmarron*
★ Norman Taurog *Skippy*
 Josef von Sternberg *Morocco*

1931/1932
★ **Frank Borzage** *Bad Girl*
 King Vidor *The Champ*
 Josef von Sternberg *Shanghai Express*

1932/1933
 Frank Capra *Lady For A Day*
 George Cukor *Little Women*
★ Frank Lloyd *Cavalcade*

1934
★ **Frank Capra** *It Happened One Night*
 Victor Schertzinger *One Night Of Love*
 W.S. Van Dyke *The Thin Man*

1935
★ **John Ford** *The Informer*
 Henry Hathaway *Lives Of A Bengal Lancer*
 Frank Lloyd *Mutiny On The Bounty*

1936
★ **Frank Capra** *Mr Deeds Goes To Town*
 Gregory La Cava *My Man Godfrey*
 Robert Z. Leonard *The Great Ziegfeld*
 W.S. Van Dyke *San Francisco*
 William Wyler *Dodsworth*

1937
 William Dieterle *The Life of Emile Zola*
 Sidney Franklin *The Good Earth*
 Gregory La Cava *Stage Door*
★ **Leo McCarey** *The Awful Truth*
 William A. Wellman *A Star Is Born*

1938
★ **Frank Capra** *You Can't Take It With You*
 Michael Curtiz *Angels With Dirty Faces*
 Michael Curtiz *Four Daughters*
 Norman Taurog *Boys Town*
 King Vidor *The Citadel*

1939
 Frank Capra *Mr. Smith Goes To Washington*
★ **Victor Fleming** *Gone With The Wind*
 John Ford *Stagecoach*
 Sam Wood *Goodbye, Mr. Chips*
 William Wyler *Wuthering Heights*

1940
 George Cukor *The Philadelphia Story*
★ **John Ford** *The Grapes Of Wrath*
 Alfred Hitchcock *Rebecca*
 Sam Wood *Kitty Foyle*
 William Wyler *The Letter*

1941
★ **John Ford** *How Green Was My Valley*
 Alexander Hall *Here Comes Mr. Jordan*
 Howard Hawks *Sergeant York*
 Orson Welles *Citizen Kane*
 William Wyler *The Little Foxes*

1942
 Michael Curtiz *Yankee Doodle Dandy*
 John Farrow *Wake Island*
 Mervyn LeRoy *Random Harvest*
 Sam Wood *Kings Row*
★ **William Wyler** *Mrs. Miniver*

1943
 Clarence Brown *The Human Comedy*
★ **Michael Curtiz** *Casablanca*
 Henry King *The Song Of Bernadette*
 Ernst Lubitsch *Heaven Can Wait*
 George Stevens *The More The Merrier*

1944
 Alfred Hitchcock *Lifeboat*
 Henry King *Wilson*
★ **Leo McCarey** *Going My Way*
 Otto Preminger *Laura*
 Billy Wilder *Double Indemnity*

1945
 Clarence Brown *National Velvet*
 Alfred Hitchcock *Spellbound*
 Leo McCarey *The Bells Of St Mary's*
 Jean Renoir *The Southerner*
★ **Billy Wilder** *The Lost Weekend*

1946
 Clarence Brown *The Yearling*
 Frank Capra *It's A Wonderful Life*
 David Lean *Brief Encounter*
 Robert Siodmak *The Killers*
★ **William Wyler** *The Best Years Of Our Lives*

1947
 George Cukor *A Double Life*
 Edward Dmytryk *Crossfire*
★ **Elia Kazan** *Gentleman's Agreement*
 Henry Koster *The Bishop's Wife*
 David Lean *Great Expectations*

1948
★ **John Huston** *Treasure Of Sierra Madre*
 Anatole Litvak *The Snake Pit*
 Jean Negulesco *Johnny Belinda*
 Laurence Olivier *Hamlet*
 Fred Zinnemann *The Search*

1949
★ **Joseph L. Mankiewicz** *A Letter To Three Wives*
 Carol Reed *The Fallen Idol*
 Robert Rossen *All The King's Men*
 William A. Wellman *Battleground*
 William Wyler *The Heiress*

1950
 George Cukor *Born Yesterday*
 John Huston *The Asphalt Jungle*
★ **Joseph L. Mankiewicz** *All About Eve*
 Carol Reed *The Third Man*
 Billy Wilder *Sunset Boulevard*

1951
 John Huston *The African Queen*
 Elia Kazan *A Streetcar Named Desire*
 Vincente Minnelli *An American In Paris*
★ **George Stevens** *A Place In The Sun*
 William Wyler *Detective Story*

1952

Cecil B. DeMille *The Greatest Show On Earth*
★ John Ford *The Quiet Man*
John Huston *Moulin Rouge*
Joseph L. Mankiewicz *Five Fingers*
Fred Zinnemann *High Noon*

1953

George Stevens *Shane*
Charles Walters *Lili*
Billy Wilder *Stalag 17*
William Wyler *Roman Holiday*
★ Fred Zinnemann *From Here To Eternity*

1954

Alfred Hitchcock *Rear Window*
★ Elia Kazan *On The Waterfront*
George Seaton *The Country Girl*
William A. Wellman *The High And The Mighty*
Billy Wilder *Sabrina*

1955

Elia Kazan *East Of Eden*
David Lean *Summertime*
Joshua Logan *Picnic*
★ Delbert Mann *Marty*
John Sturges *Bad Day At Black Rock*

1956

Michael Anderson *Around The World In 80 Days*
Walter Lang *The King And I*
★ George Stevens *Giant*
King Vidor *War And Peace*
William Wyler *Friendly Persuasion*

1957

★ David Lean *The Bridge On The River Kwai*
Joshua Logan *Sayonara*
Sidney Lumet *12 Angry Men*
Mark Robson *Peyton Place*
Billy Wilder *Witness For The Prosecution*

1958

Richard Brooks *Cat On A Hot Tin Roof*
Stanley Kramer *The Defiant Ones*
★ Vincente Minnelli *Gigi*
Mark Robson *The Inn Of The Sixth Happiness*
Robert Wise *I Want To Live!*

1959

Jack Clayton *Room At The Top*
George Stevens *The Diary Of Anne Frank*
Billy Wilder *Some Like It Hot*
★ William Wyler *Ben-Hur*
Fred Zinnemann *The Nun's Story*

1960

Jack Cardiff *Sons And Lovers*
Jules Dassin *Never On Sunday*
Alfred Hitchcock *Psycho*
★ Billy Wilder *The Apartment*
Fred Zinnemann *The Sundowners*

1961

Federico Fellini *La Dolce Vita*
Stanley Kramer *Judgement At Nuremberg*
Robert Rossen *The Hustler*
J. Lee Thompson *The Guns Of Navarone*
★ Robert Wise and Jerome Robbins *West Side Story*

1962

Pietro Germi *Divorce – Italian Style*
★ David Lean *Lawrence Of Arabia*
Robert Mulligan *To Kill A Mockingbird*
Arthur Penn *The Miracle Worker*
Frank Perry *David And Lisa*

1963

Federico Fellini *8½*
Elia Kazan *America America*
Otto Preminger *The Cardinal*
★ Tony Richardson *Tom Jones*
Martin Ritt *Hud*

1964

Michael Cacoyannis *Zorba The Greek*
★ George Cukor *My Fair Lady*
Peter Glenville *Becket*
Stanley Kubrick *Dr. Strangelove Or: How I Learned To Stop Worrying And Love The Bomb*
Robert Stevenson *Mary Poppins*

1965

David Lean *Doctor Zhivago*
John Schlesinger *Darling*
Hiroshi Teshigahara *Woman In The Dunes*
★ Robert Wise *The Sound Of Music*
William Wyler *The Collector*

1966

Michelangelo Antonioni *Blow-Up*
Richard Brooks *The Professionals*
Claude Lelouch *A Man And A Woman*
Mike Nichols *Who's Afraid Of Virginia Woolf?*
★ Fred Zinnemann *A Man For All Seasons*

1967

Richard Brooks *In Cold Blood*
Norman Jewison *In The Heat Of The Night*
Stanley Kramer *Guess Who's Coming To Dinner*
★ Mike Nichols *The Graduate*
Arthur Penn *Bonnie And Clyde*

1968

Anthony Harvey *The Lion In Winter*
Stanley Kubrick *2001: A Space Odyssey*
Gillo Pontecorvo *The Battle Of Algiers*
★ Carol Reed *Oliver!*
Franco Zeffirelli *Romeo And Juliet*

1969

Costa-Gavras *Z*
George Roy Hill *Butch Cassidy And The Sundance Kid*
Arthur Penn *Alice's Restaurant*
Sydney Pollack *They Shoot Horses, Don't They?*
★ John Schlesinger *Midnight Cowboy*

1970

Robert Altman *M*A*S*H*
Federico Fellini *Fellini Satyricon*
Arthur Hiller *Love Story*
Ken Russell *Women In Love*
★ Franklin J. Schaffner *Patton*

1971

Peter Bogdanovich *The Last Picture Show*
★ William Friedkin *The French Connection*
Norman Jewison *Fiddler On The Roof*
Stanley Kubrick *A Clockwork Orange*
John Schlesinger *Sunday Bloody Sunday*

1972

John Boorman *Deliverance*
Francis Ford Coppola *The Godfather*
★ Bob Fosse *Cabaret*
Joseph L. Mankiewicz *Sleuth*
Jan Troell *The Emigrants*

1973

Ingmar Bergman *Cries And Whispers*
Bernardo Bertolucci *Last Tango In Paris*
William Friedkin *The Exorcist*
★ George Roy Hill *The Sting*
George Lucas *American Graffiti*

1974

John Cassavetes *A Woman Under The Influence*
★ Francis Ford Coppola *The Godfather Part II*
Bob Fosse *Lenny*
Roman Polanski *Chinatown*
François Truffaut *Day For Night*

1975

Robert Altman *Nashville*
Federico Fellini *Amarcord*
★ Milos Forman *One Flew Over The Cuckoo's Nest*
Stanley Kubrick *Barry Lyndon*
Sidney Lumet *Dog Day Afternoon*

1976

★ John G. Avildsen *Rocky*
Ingmar Bergman *Face To Face*
Sidney Lumet *Network*
Alan J. Pakula *All The President's Men*
Lina Wertmuller *Seven Beauties*

1977

★ Woody Allen *Annie Hall*
George Lucas *Star Wars*
Herbert Ross *The Turning Point*
Steven Spielberg *Close Encounters Of The Third Kind*
Fred Zinnemann *Julia*

1978

Woody Allen *Interiors*
Hal Ashby *Coming Home*
Warren Beatty and Buck Henry *Heaven Can Wait*
★ Michael Cimino *The Deer Hunter*
Alan Parker *Midnight Express*

1979

★ Robert Benton *Kramer Vs. Kramer*
Francis Coppola *Apocalypse Now*
Bob Fosse *All That Jazz*
Edouard Molinaro *La Cage Aux Folles*
Peter Yates *Breaking Away*

1980

David Lynch *The Elephant Man*
Roman Polanski *Tess*
★ Robert Redford *Ordinary People*
Richard Rush *The Stunt Man*
Martin Scorsese *Raging Bull*

1981

★ Warren Beatty *Reds*
Hugh Hudson *Chariots Of Fire*
Louis Malle *Atlantic City*
Mark Rydell *On Golden Pond*
Steven Spielberg *Raiders Of The Lost Ark*

1982

★ Richard Attenborough *Gandhi*
Sidney Lumet *The Verdict*
Wolfgang Petersen *Das Boot*
Sydney Pollack *Tootsie*
Steven Spielberg *E.T. The Extra-Terrestrial*

1983

Bruce Beresford *Tender Mercies*
Ingmar Bergman *Fanny and Alexander*
★ James L. Brooks *Terms Of Endearment*
Mike Nichols *Silkwood*
Peter Yates *The Dresser*

1984

Woody Allen *Broadway Danny Rose*
Robert Benton *Places In The Heart*
★ Milos Forman *Amadeus*
Roland Joffe *The Killing Fields*
David Lean *A Passage To India*

★ Denotes the winner.

OTHER CATEGORIES

1927/1928

Actor
Charles Chaplin *The Circus*

Special Award
● Charles Chaplin, for versatility and genius in writing, acting, directing and producing *The Circus*

1928/1929

Interior Decoration
Mitchell Leisen *Dynamite*

1930/1931

Writing (adaptation)
Joseph Mankiewicz (co-writer) *Skippy*

1935

Dance Direction
Busby Berkeley 'Lullaby Of Broadway' number and 'The Words Are In My Heart' number from *Gold Diggers Of 1935*

Special Award
● David Wark Griffith, for his distinguished creative achievements as director and producer and his invaluable initiative and lasting contributions to the progress of the motion picture arts.

1936

Dance Direction
Busby Berkeley 'Love And War' number from *Gold Diggers of 1937*.

1937

Writing (original story)
● William Wellman (co-writer) *A Star Is Born*

1938

Short Subjects (one-reel)
Fred Zinneman (director) *That Mothers Might Live*

1939

Writing (original story)
Leo McCarey (co-writer) *Love Affair*
(screenplay)
Billy Wilder (co-writer) *Ninotchka*

Short Subjects (two-reel)
★ Michael Curtiz *Sons Of Liberty*

1940

Actor
Charles Chaplin *The Great Dictator*

Writing
(original story)
Leo McCarey (co-writer) *My Favorite Wife*
(original screenplay)
Charles Chaplin *The Great Dictator*
John Huston (co-writer) *Dr. Ehrlich's Magic Bullet*
● Preston Sturges *The Great McGinty*

Short Subjects (one-reel)
★ George Sidney (director) *Quicker 'N A Wink*

1941

Actor
Orson Welles *Citizen Kane*

Writing
(original story)
Billy Wilder (co-writer) *Ball Of Fire*
(original screenplay)
★ Orson Welles (co-writer) *Citizen Kane*
John Huston (co-writer) *Sergeant York*
(screenplay)
Billy Wilder (co-writer) *Hold Back The Dawn*
John Huston *The Maltese Falcon*

Film Editing
Robert Wise *Citizen Kane*

Short Subjects
(one-reel)
★ George Sidney (director) *Of Pups And Puzzles*
(two-reel)
Jean Negulesco (director) *The Gay Parisian*

Documentary
Carol Reed (director) *Letter From Home*

1942

Writing (original screenplay)
Michael Powell (co-writer) *One Of Our Aircraft Is Missing*

Short Subjects (one-reel)
Jean Negulesco (director) *United States Marine Band*

Documentary
★ Frank Capra (director) *Prelude To War*
★ John Ford (director) *Battle Of Midway*
Jean Negulesco (director) *A Ship Is Born*

Irving G. Thalberg Memorial Award†
● Sidney Franklin

1943

Short Subjects
(one-reel)
Jean Negulesco (director) *Cavalcade Of The Dance With Veloz And Yolanda*
(two-reel)
Jean Negulesco (director) *Women At War*

Documentary
(short subjects)
★ John Ford (director) *December 7th*
(features)
John Huston (director) *Report From The Aleutians*
Anatole Litvak (director) *Battle Of Russia*

1944

Writing
(original story)
★ Leo McCarey *Going My Way*
(original screeplay)
Preston Sturges *Hail The Conquering Hero*
Preston Sturges *The Miracle Of Morgan's Creek*
(screenplay)
Billy Wilder (co-writer) *Double Indemnity*

Short Subjects (cartoons)
Frank Tashlin (director) *Swooner Crooner*

Documentary (features)
★ William Wyler (director) *The Fighting Lady*

1945

Actor
Gene Kelly *Anchors Aweigh*

Writing (screenplay)
★ Billy Wilder (co-writer) *The Lost Weekend*

Short Subjects (two-reel)
Joseph Losey (director) *A Gun In His Hand*
★ Don Siegel (director) *Star In The Night*

Documentary
(short subjects)
★ Don Siegel (director) *Hitler Lives?*
(features)
★ Carol Reed (co-director) *The True Glory*

Special Award
● Mervyn LeRoy (co-producer & director) *The House I Live In*

1946

Writing (screenplay)
John Huston (uncredited co-writer) *The Killers*
David Lean (co-writer) *Brief Encounter*

Special Award
● Ernst Lubitsch, for his distinguished contributions to the art of the motion picture.

1947

Writing
(original screenplay)
Charles Chaplin *Monsieur Verdoux*
(screenplay)
David Lean (co-writer) *Great Expectations*

1948

Writing
(original story)
Robert Flaherty (co-writer) *The Louisiana Story*
(adapted screenplay)
★ John Huston *The Treasure Of The Sierra Madre*
Billy Wilder (co-writer) *A Foreign Affair*

1949

Writing (adapted screenplay)
★ Joseph L. Mankiewicz *A Letter To Three Wives*
Robert Rossen *All The King's Men*

Special Award
● Cecil B. DeMille, distinguished motion picture pioneer, for 37 years of brilliant showmanship.

1950

Supporting Actor
Erich von Stroheim *Sunset Boulevard*

Writing
(original screenplay)
Joseph L. Mankiewicz (co-writer) *No Way Out*
★ Billy Wilder (co-writer) *Sunset Boulevard*
(adapted screenplay)
John Huston (co-writer) *The Asphalt Jungle*
★ Joseph L. Mankiewicz *All About Eve*

1951

Writing
(original story)
Budd Boetticher (co-writer) *The Bullfighter And The Lady*
(original screenplay)
Billy Wilder (co-writer) *The Big Carnival* (aka *Ace In The Hole*)
(adapted screenplay)
John Huston (co-writer) *The African Queen*

Documentary (short subjects)
● Fred Zinnemann (director) *Benjy*

Honorary Award
● Gene Kelly, in appreciation of his versatility as an actor, singer, director and dancer, and specifically for his brilliant achievements in the art of choreography on film.

1952

Writing
(original story)
Leo McCarey *My Son John*
(adapted screenplay)
Alexander Mackendrick (co-writer) *The Man In The White Suit*

Irving G. Thalberg Memorial Award
● Cecil B. DeMille

1953

Irving G. Thalberg Memorial Award
● George Stevens

1954

Writing
(original screenplay)
Joseph L. Mankiewicz *The Barefoot Contessa*
(adapted screenplay)
Billy Wilder (co-writer) *Sabrina*

1955

Writing
(original story)
Nicholas Ray *Rebel Without A Cause*
(adapted screenplay)
Richard Brooks *Blackboard Jungle*

1956

Short Subjects (two-reel)
Jean Negulesco (director) *The Dark Wave*

1957

Writing (adapted screenplay)
John Huston (co-writer) *Heaven Knows, Mr Allison*

Music (song)
Leo McCarey (co-writer of lyrics) theme song from *An Affair To Remember*

1958

Writing (adapted screenplay)
Richard Brooks (co-writer) *Cat On A Hot Tin Roof*

1959

Writing (adapted screenplay)
Billy Wilder (co-writer) *Some Like It Hot*

Short Subjects (live action)
Dick Lester (director) *The Running, Jumping and Standing Still Film*

Honorary Award
● Buster Keaton, for his unique talents which brought immortal comedies to the screen.

1960

Writing (original screenplay)
Jules Dassin *Never On Sunday*
★ Billy Wilder (co-writer) *The Apartment*
(adapted screenplay)
★ Richard Brooks *Elmer Gantry*

1961

Writing (adapted screenplay)
Robert Rossen (co-writer) *The Hustler*

Irving G. Thalberg Memorial Award
● Stanley Kramer

1963

Supporting Actor
John Huston *The Cardinal*

Writing (original screenplay)
Elia Kazan *America, America*

Foreign Language Film
Roman Polanski (director) *Knife In The Water*

1964

Writing (adapted screenplay)
Stanley Kubrick (co-writer) *Dr. Strangelove Or: How I Learned To Stop Worrying And Love The Bomb*

1965

Irving G. Thalberg Memorial Award
● William Wyler

1966

Writing (original screenplay)
Billy Wilder (co-writer) *The Fortune Cookie*
(adapted screenplay)
Richard Brooks *The Professionals*

Film Editing
Hal Ashby (co-editor) *The Russians Are Coming, The Russians Are Coming*

Irving G. Thalberg Memorial Award
● Robert Wise

1967

Supporting Actor
John Cassavetes *The Dirty Dozen*

Writing (original screenplay)
Robert Benton (co-writer) *Bonnie And Clyde*
(adapted screenplay)
Richard Brooks *In Cold Blood*

Film Editing
★ Hal Ashby *In The Heat Of The Night*

Irving G. Thalberg Memorial Award
● Alfred Hitchcock

1968

Writing (original screenplay)
John Cassavetes *Faces*
Stanley Kubrick (co-writer) *2001: A Space Odyssey*
(adapted screenplay)
Roman Polanski *Rosemary's Baby*

Special Visual Effects
★ Stanley Kubrick *2001: A Space Odyssey*

Foreign Language Film
Milos Forman (director) *The Firemen's Ball*

1969

Writing (original screenplay)
Paul Mazursky (co-writer) *Bob & Carol & Ted & Alice*
Sam Peckinpah (co-writer) *The Wild Bunch*

1970

Writing (original screenplay)
★ Francis Ford Coppola (co-writer) *Patton*
Bob Rafelson (co-writer) *Five Easy Pieces*

Short Subjects (live action)
● John Carpenter (co-director) *The Resurrection Of Bronco Billy*

Documentary (features)
Sidney Lumet (co-director) *King: A Filmed Record . . . Montgomery To Memphis*

Honorary Award
● Orson Welles, for superlative artistry and versatility in the creation of motion pictures.

1971

Writing (adapted screenplay)
Peter Bogdanovich (co-writer) *The Last Picture Show*
Stanley Kubrick *A Clockwork Orange*

Honorary Award
● Charles Chaplin, for the incalculable effect he has had in making motion pictures the art form of this century.

1972

Writing (adapted screenplay)
★ Francis Ford Coppola (co-writer) *The Godfather*

Music (original dramatic score)
★ Charles Chaplin (co-writer) *Limelight* (1952)

1973

Writing (original screenplay)
George Lucas *American Graffiti*

1974

Writing (original screenplay)
Francis Ford Coppola *The Conversation*
Paul Mazursky (co-writer) *Harry And Tonto*
(adapted screenplay)
★ Francis Ford Coppola (co-writer) *The Godfather Part II*

Honorary Award
● Howard Hawks, a master American film maker whose creative efforts hold a distinguished place in world cinema.
● Jean Renoir, a genius who, with grace, responsibility and enviable devotion through silent film, feature, documentary and television, has won the world's admiration.

1975

Writing (adapted screenplay)
John Huston (co-writer) *The Man Who Would Be King*
Stanley Kubrick *Barry Lyndon*

Irving G. Thalberg Memorial Award
● Mervyn LeRoy

1976

Actor
Sylvestor Stallone *Rocky*

Writing (original screenplay)
Sylvester Stallone *Rocky*

1977

Actor
Woody Allen *Annie Hall*

Writing (original screenplay)
★ Woody Allen (co-writer) *Annie Hall*
Robert Benton *The Late Show*
George Lucas *Star Wars*

1978

Writing (original screenplay)
Woody Allen *Interiors*
Michael Cimino (co-writer) *The Deerhunter*
Paul Mazursky *An Unmarried Woman*

Honorary Award
● King Vidor, for his incomparable achievements as a cinematic creator and innovator.

1979

Writing (original screenplay)
Woody Allen (co-writer) *Manhattan*
Bob Fosse (co-writer) *All That Jazz*
(adapted screenplay)
★ Robert Benton *Kramer Vs Kramer*
Francis Coppola (co-writer) *Apocalypse Now*
John Milius (co-writer) *Apocalypse Now*

1981

Writing (adapted screenplay)
Sidney Lumet (co-writer) *Prince Of The City*

1982

Writing (adapted screenplay)
Blake Edwards *Victor/Victoria*

1984

Writing (original screenplay)
● Robert Benton *Places In The Heart*
Woody Allen *Broadway Danny Rose*
(adapted screenplay)
David Lean *A Passage To India*

Film Editing
David Lean *A Passage To India*

---

† This award was inaugurated in 1937 in memory of Irving G. Thalberg, whose career as a producer was perhaps the most spectacular Hollywood has ever seen. General manager of Universal Studios when he was only 21 and then head of production at MGM, he died tragically in 1936 at the age of 37. The award is given at the discretion of the Academy Board of Governors 'to creative producers whose body of work reflects a consistently high quality of motion picture production'.

★ Denotes the winner in an 'open category', that is one in which there are other nominations.

● Denotes the recipient of a special award which is not competitive, in the sense that other contenders, if indeed there are any, are not publicly nominated.

INDEX OF DIRECTORS

This index lists the names of all movie directors mentioned in text or captions on pages 8 to 257 (appendix material beginning on page 258 is not indexed). The 140 directors featured in the book are denoted by a page number in bold type; this is the first page of their main entry. Passing mentions of featured directors outside their own entry are denoted by page numbers in normal type, as are all mentions of non-featured directors. Page numbers in italic type refer to illustrations in which the director is depicted. Multiple mentions of the same director in different contexts on the same page, or more than one illustration of the director on the same page, are denoted by the appropriate number in brackets after the page number. Directors with surnames preceded by De, Del, Van or Von (as separate words) are indexed under 'D' or 'V', as appropriate.

INDEX OF OTHER PERSONNEL

This index lists the names of all non-director personnel mentioned in text or captions on pages 8 to 257 (appendix material beginning on page 258 is not indexed). Numbers in italic type refer to pages on which an illustration of the person will be found. Multiple mentions of the same person in different contexts on the same page, or more than one illustration of the person on the same page, are denoted by the appropriate number in brackets after the page number. People with surnames preceded by De, Del, La, St, Van or Von are indexed under 'D', 'L', 'S' or 'V', as appropriate. Surnames beginning with Mc- are separated from those beginning with Mac- by all names beginning Mad- to Maz-.

INDEX OF FILMS

This index lists the titles of all films mentioned in text or captions on pages 8 to 257 (appendix material beginning on page 258 is not indexed). Where a title begins with an arabic numeral it is indexed as though the number were spelt out: *10 Rillington Place*, for example, will be found under 'T', as if it were *Ten Rillington Place*. Multiple mentions of the same film in different contexts on the same page are denoted by the appropriate number in brackets after the page number.

V

W

X

Y

Z